THE

HISTORY

OF

THE DECLINE AND FALL

OF THE

ROMAN EMPIRE.

By EDWARD GIBBON, Esq.

WITH NOTES,

By the Rev. H. H. MILMAN,

PREBENDARY OF ST. PETER'S, AND RECTOR OF ST. MARGARET'S, WESTMINSTER.

A New Edition,

TO WHICH IS ADDED

A COMPLETE INDEX OF THE WHOLE WORK.

IN SIX VOLUMES.

VOL. II.

PHILADELPHIA:
CLAXTON, REMSEN & HAFFELFINGER,
624, 626 & 628 Market Street.
1880.

CONTENTS

OF THE SECOND VOLUME.

CHAPTER XVI.

THE CONDUCT OF THE ROMAN GOVERNMENT TOWARDS THE CHRISTIANS, FROM THE REIGN OF NERO TO THAT OF CONSTANTINE.

iv

CHAPTER XVII

FOUNDATION OF CONSTANTINOPLE. — POLITICAL SYSTEM OF CONSTANTINE, AND HIS SUCCESSES. — MILITARY DISCIPLINE. — THE PALACE. — THE FINANCES.

CHAPTER XVIII.

CHARACTER OF CONSTANTINE. — GOTHIC WAR. — DEATH OF CONSTANTINE. — DIVISION OF THE EMPIRE AMONG HIS THREE SONS. — PERSIAN WAR. — TRAGIC DEATHS OF CONSTANTINE THE YOUNGER, AND CONSTANS. — USURPATION OF MAGNENTIUS. — CIVIL WAR. — VICTORY OF CONSTANTIUS.

CHAPTER XX.

THE MOTIVES, PROGRESS, AND EFFECTS OF THE CONVERSION OF CONSTANTINE. — LEGAL ESTABLISHMENT AND CONSTITUTION OF THE CHRISTIAN, OR CATHOLIC, CHURCH.

CHAPTER XXI.

PERSECUTION OF HERESY. — THE SCHISM OF THE DONATISTS. — THE ARIAN CONTROVERSY. — ATHANASIUS. — DISTRACTED STATE OF THE CHURCH AND EMPIRE UNDER CONSTANTINE AND HIS SONS. — TOLERATION OF PAGANISM.

28 *

CHAPTER XXII.

JULIAN IS DECLARED EMPEROR BY THE LEGIONS OF GAUL. — HIS MARCH AND SUCCESS. — THE DEATH OF CONSTANTIUS. — CIVIL ADMINISTRATION OF JULIAN.

CHAPTER XXIII.

THE RELIGION OF JULIAN. — UNIVERSAL TOLERATION. — HE ATTEMPTS TO RESTORE AND REFORM THE PAGAN WORSHIP — TO REBUILD THE TEMPLE OF JERUSALEM. — HIS ARTFUL PERSECUTION OF THE CHRIS TIANS. — MUTUAL ZEAL AND INJUSTICE.

CHAPTER XXIV.

RESIDENCE OF JULIAN AT ANTIOCH. — HIS SUCCESSFUL EXPEDITION
AGAINST THE PERSIANS. — PASSAGE OF THE TIGRIS. — THE RETREAT
AND DEATH OF JULIAN. — ELECTION OF JOVIAN. — HE SAVES THE
ROMAN ARMY BY A DISGRACEFUL TREATY.

CHAPTER XXV.

THE HISTORY

OF

THE DECLINE AND FALL

OF THE

ROMAN EMPIRE.

CHAPTER XVI.*

THE CONDUCT OF THE ROMAN GOVERNMENT TOWARDS THE CHRISTIANS, FROM THE REIGN OF NERO TO THAT OF CONSTANTINE.

IF we seriously consider the purity of the Christian religion, the sanctity of its moral precepts, and the innocent as well as austere lives of the greater number of those who during the first ages embraced the faith of the gospel, we should naturally suppose, that so benevolent a doctrine would have been received with due reverence, even by the unbeliev-

---

* The sixteenth chapter I cannot help considering as a very ingenious and specious, but very disgraceful extenuation of the cruelties perpetrated by the Roman magistrates against the Christians. It is written in the most contemptibly factious spirit of prejudice against the sufferers; it is unworthy of a philosopher and of a man of humanity. Let the narrative of Cyprian's death be examined. He had to relate the murder of an innocent man of advanced age, and in a station deemed venerable by a considerable body of the provincials of Africa, put to death because he refused to sacrifice to Jupiter. Instead of pointing the indignation of posterity against such an atrocious act of tyranny, he dwells, with visible art, on the small circumstances of decorum and politeness which attended this murder, and which he relates with as much parade as if they were the most important particulars of the event.

Dr. Robertson has been the subject of much blame for his real or supposed lenity towards the Spanish murderers and tyrants in America. That

ing world ; that the learned and the polite, however they may deride the miracles, would have esteemed the virtues, of the new sect ; and that the magistrates, instead of persecuting. would have protected an order of men who yielded the most passive obedience to the laws, though they declined the active cares of war and government. If, on the other hand, we recollect the universal toleration of Polytheism, as it was invariably maintained by the faith of the people, the incredulity of philosophers, and the policy of the Roman senate and emperors, we are at a loss to discover what new offence the Christians had committed, what new provocation could exasperate the mild indifference of antiquity, and what new motives could urge the Roman princes, who beheld without concern a thousand forms of religion subsisting in peace under their gentle sway, to inflict a severe punishment on any part of their subjects, who had chosen for themselves a singular but an inoffensive mode of faith and worship.

The religious policy of the ancient world seems to have assumed a more stern and intolerant character, to oppose the progress of Christianity. About fourscore years after the death of Christ, his innocent disciples were punished with death by the sentence of a proconsul of the most amiable and philosophic character, and according to the laws of an emperor distinguished by the wisdom and justice of his general administration. The apologies which were repeatedly addressed to the successors of Trajan are filled with the most pathetic complaints, that the Christians, who obeyed the dictates, and solicited the liberty, of conscience, were alone, among all the subjects of the Roman empire, excluded from the common benefits of their auspicious government. The deaths of a few eminent martyrs have been recorded with care ; and from the time that Christianity was invested with the supreme power, the governors of the church have been no less diligently employed in displaying the cruelty, than in imitating the conduct, of their Pagan adversaries. To separate (if it be possible) a few authentic as well as interesting facts from an undigested mass of fiction and error, and to relate, in a clear and rational manner, the causes, the extent, the duration, and the most important circumstances of the persecutions

---

the sixteenth chapter of Mr. G. did not excite the same or greater disapprobation, is a proof of the unphilosophical and indeed fanatical animosity against Christianity, which was so prevalent during the latter part of the eighteenth century. — *Mackintosh :* see Life, i. p. 244, 245.

to which the first Christians were exposed, is the design of the present chapter.[*]

The sectaries of a persecuted religion, depressed by fear, animated with resentment, and perhaps heated by enthusiasm, are seldom in a proper temper of mind calmly to investigate, or candidly to appreciate, the motives of their enemies, which often escape the impartial and discerning view even of those who are placed at a secure distance from the flames of persecution. A reason has been assigned for the conduct of the emperors towards the primitive Christians, which may appear the more specious and probable as it is drawn from the acknowledged genius of Polytheism. It has already been observed, that the religious concord of the world was principally supported by the implicit assent and reverence which the nations of antiquity expressed for their respective traditions and ceremonies. It might therefore be expected, that they would unite with indignation against any sect or people which should separate itself from the communion of mankind, and claiming the exclusive possession of divine knowledge, should disdain every form of worship, except its own, as impious and idolatrous. The rights of toleration were held by mutual indulgence : they were justly forfeited by a refusal of the accustomed tribute. As the payment of this tribute was inflexibly refused by the Jews, and by them alone, the consideration of the treatment which they experienced from the Roman magistrates, will serve to explain how far these speculations are justified by facts, and will lead us to discover the true causes of the persecution of Christianity.

Without repeating what has been already mentioned of the reverence of the Roman princes and governors for the temple of Jerusalem, we shall only observe, that the destruction of the temple and city was accompanied and followed by every

---

[*] The history of the first age of Christianity is only found in the Acts of the Apostles, and in order to speak of the first persecutions experienced by the Christians, that book should naturally have been consulted ; those persecutions, then limited to individuals and to a narrow sphere, interested only the persecuted, and have been related by them alone. Gibbon, making the persecutions ascend no higher than Nero, has entirely omitted those which preceded this epoch, and of which St. Luke has preserved the memory. The only way to justify this omission was, to attack the authenticity of the Acts of the Apostles ; for, if authentic, they must necessarily be consulted and quoted. Now, antiquity has left very few works of which the authenticity is so well established as that of the Acts of the Apostles. (See Lardner's Cred. of Gospel Hist. part ii.) It is, therefore, without sufficient reason, that Gibbon has maintained silence concerning the narrative of St. Luke, and this omission is not without importance. — G.

circumstance that could exasperate the minds of the conquerors, and authorize religious persecution by the most specious
arguments of political justice and the public safety. From
the reign of Nero to that of Antoninus Pius, the Jews discovered a fierce impatience of the dominion of Rome, which
repeatedly broke out in the most furious massacres and insur-
rections. Humanity is shocked at the recital of the horrid
cruelties which they committed in the cities of Egypt, of
Cyprus, and of Cyrene, where they dwelt in treacherous
friendship with the unsuspecting natives;[1] and we are tempted
to applaud the severe retaliation which was exercised by the
arms of the legions against a race of fanatics, whose dire and
credulous superstition seemed to render them the implacable
enemies not only of the Roman government, but of human
kind.[2] The enthusiasm of the Jews was supported by the
opinion, that it was unlawful for them to pay taxes to an idolatrous master ; and by the flattering promise which they de
rived from their ancient oracles, that a conquering Messiah
would soon arise, destined to break their fetters, and to invest
the favorites of heaven with the empire of the earth. It was
by announcing himself as their long-expected deliverer, and
by calling on all the descendants of Abraham to assert the
hope of Israel, that the famous Barchochebas collected a
formidable army, with which he resisted during two years the
power of the emperor Hadrian.[3]

Notwithstanding these repeated provocations, the resentment of the Roman princes expired after the victory; nor

---

[1] In Cyrene, they massacred 220,000 Greeks; in Cyprus, 240,000 ;
in Egypt, a very great multitude. Many of these unhappy victims
were sawn asunder, according to a precedent to which David had
given the sanction of his example. The victorious Jews devoured
the flesh, licked up the blood, and twisted the entrails like a girdle
round their bodies. See Dion Cassius, l. lxviii. p. 1145.*

[2] Without repeating the well-known narratives of Josephus, we
may learn from Dion, (l. lxix. p. 1162,) that in Hadrian's war 580,000
Jews were cut off by the sword, besides an infinite number which
perished by famine, by disease, and by fire.

[3] For the sect of the Zealots, see Basnage, Histoire des Juifs, l. i.
c. 17 ; for the characters of the Messiah, according to the Rabbis,
l. v. c. 11, 12, 13 ; for the actions of Barchochebas, l. vii. c. 12. (Hist
of Jews, iii. 115, &c.) — M.

---

* Some commentators, among them Reimar, in his notes on Dion Cassius, think that the hatred of the Romans against the Jews has led the
historian to exaggerate the cruelties committed by the latter. Dion Cass
lxviii. p. 1148. — G.

were their apprehensions continued beyond the period of war and danger. By the general indulgence of polytheism, and by the mild temper of Antoninus Pius, the Jews were restored to their ancient privileges, and once more obtained the permission of circumcising their children, with the easy restraint that they should never confer on any foreign proselyte that distinguishing mark of the Hebrew race.[4] The numerous remains of that people, though they were still excluded from the precincts of Jerusalem, were permitted to form and to maintain considerable establishments both in Italy and in the provinces, to acquire the freedom of Rome, to enjoy municipal honors, and to obtain at the same time an exemption from the burdensome and expensive offices of society. The moderation or the contempt of the Romans gave a legal sanction to the form of ecclesiastical police which was instituted by the vanquished sect. The patriarch, who had fixed his residence at Tiberias, was empowered to appoint his subordinate ministers and apostles, to exercise a domestic jurisdiction, and to receive from his dispersed brethren an annual contribution.[5] New synagogues were frequently erected in the principal cities of the empire; and the sabbaths, the fasts, and the festivals, which were either commanded by the Mosaic law, or enjoined by the traditions of the Rabbis, were celebrated in the most solemn and public manner.[6] Such gentle treatment insensibly assuaged the stern temper of the Jews. Awakened from their dream of prophecy and conquest, they assumed the behavior of peaceable and industrious subjects. Their irreconcilable hatred of mankind, instead of flaming out in acts of blood and violence, evaporated in less dangerous gratifications. They embraced every opportunity of overreaching the idolaters in trade; and they pronounced secret and ambiguous imprecations against the haughty kingdom of Edom.[7]

---

[4] It is to Modestinus, a Roman lawyer (l. vi. regular.) that we are indebted for a distinct knowledge of the Edict of Antoninus. See Casaubon ad Hist. August. p. 27.

[5] See Basnage, Histoire des Juifs, l. iii. c. 2, 3. The office of Patriarch was suppressed by Theodosius the younger.

[6] We need only mention the Purim, or deliverance of the Jews from the rage of Haman, which, till the reign of Theodosius, was celebrated with insolent triumph and riotous intemperance. Basnage, Hist. des Juifs, l. vi. c. 17, l. viii. c. 6.

[7] According to the false Josephus, Tsepho, the grandson of Esau, conducted into Italy the army of Eneas, king of Carthage. Another colony of Idumæans, flying from the sword of David, took refuge in

Since the Jews, who rejected with abhorrence the deities adored by their sovereign and by their fellow-subjects, enjoyed, however, the free exercise of their unsocial religion, there must have existed some other cause, which exposed the disciples of Christ to those severities from which the posterity of Abraham was exempt. The difference between them is simple and obvious ; but, according to the sentiments of antiquity it was of the highest importance. The Jews were a *nation ,* the Christians were a *sect :* and if it was natural for every community to respect the sacred institutions of their neighbors, it was incumbent on them to persevere in those of their ancestors. The voice of oracles, the precepts of philosophers, and the authority of the laws, unanimously enforced this national obligation. By their lofty claim of superior sanctity the Jews might provoke the Polytheists to consider them as an odious and impure race. By disdaining the intercourse of other nations, they might deserve their contempt. The laws of Moses might be for the most part frivolous or absurd ; yet, since they had been received during many ages by a large society, his followers were justified by the example of mankind ; and it was universally acknowledged, that they had a right to practise what it would have been criminal in them to neglect. But this principle, which protected the Jewish synagogue, afforded not any favor or security to the primitive church. By embracing the faith of the gospel, the Christians incurred the supposed guilt of an unnatural and unpardonable offence. They dissolved the sacred ties of custom and education, violated the religious institutions of their country, and presumptuously despised whatever their fathers had believed as true, or had reverenced as sacred. Nor was this apostasy (if we may use the expression) merely of a partial or local

---

the dominions of Romulus. For these, or for other reasons of equal weight, the name of Edom was applied by the Jews to the Roman empire.*

---

* The false Josephus is a romancer of very modern date, though some of these legends are probably more ancient. It may be worth considering whether many of the stories in the Talmud are not history in a figurative disguise, adopted from prudence. The Jews might dare to say many things of Rome, under the significant appellation of Edom, which they feared to utter publicly. Later and more ignorant ages took literally, and perhaps embellished, what was intelligible among the generation to which it was addressed. Hist. of Jews, iii. 131.

The false Josephus has the inauguration of the emperor, with the seven electors and apparently the pope assisting at the coronation ! Pref. page xxvi. — M.

kind ; since the pious deserter who withdrew himself from the temples of Egypt or Syria, would equally disdain to seek an asylum in those of Athens or Carthage. Every Christian rejected with contempt the superstitions of his family, his city, and his province. The whole body of Christians unanimously refused to hold any communion with the gods of Rome, of the empire, and of mankind. It was in vain that the oppressed believer asserted the inalienable rights of conscience and private judgment. Though his situation might excite the pity, his arguments could never reach the understanding, either of the philosophic or of the believing part of the Pagan world. To their apprehensions, it was no less a matter of surprise, that any individuals should entertain scruples against complying with the established mode of worship, than if they had conceived a sudden abhorrence to the manners, the dress, or the language of their native country.[8] *

The surprise of the Pagans was soon succeeded by resentment ; and the most pious of men were exposed to the unjust but dangerous imputation of impiety. Malice and prejudice concurred in representing the Christians as a society of atheists, who, by the most daring attack on the religious constitution of the empire, had merited the severest animadversion of the civil magistrate. They had separated themselves (they gloried in the confession) from every mode of superstition which was received in any part of the globe by the various temper of polytheism : but it was not altogether so evident what deity, or what form of worship, they had substituted to the gods and temples of antiquity. The pure and sublime idea which they entertained of the Supreme Being escaped the gross conception of the Pagan multitude, who were at a loss to discover a spiritual and solitary God, that was neither represented under any corporeal figure or visible symbol, nor was adored with the accustomed pomp of libations and festivals, of

---

[8] From the arguments of Celsus, as they are represented and refuted by Origen, (l. v. p. 247—259,) we may clearly discover the distinction that was made between the Jewish *people* and the Christian *sect*. See, in the Dialogue of Minucius Felix, (c. 5, 6,) a fair and not inelegant description of the popular sentiments, with regard to the desertion of the established worship.

---

* In all this there is doubtless much truth; yet does not the more important difference lie on the surface? The Christians made many converts, the Jews but few. Had the Jewish been equally a proselytizing religion, would it not have encountered as violent persecution? — M.

altars and sacrifices.[9] The sages of Greece and Rome, who
had elevated their minds to the contemplation of the existence
and attributes of the First Cause, were induced by reason or
by vanity to reserve for themselves and their chosen disciples
the privilege of this philosophical devotion.[10] They were far
from admitting the prejudices of mankind as the standard of
truth, but they considered them as flowing from the original
disposition of human nature ; and they supposed that any popular mode of faith and worship which presumed to disclaim
the assistance of the senses, would, in proportion as it receded
from superstition, find itself incapable of restraining the wanderings of the fancy, and the visions of fanaticism.   The
careless glance which men of wit and learning condescended to
cast on the Christian revelation, served only to confirm their
hasty opinion, and to persuade them that the principle, which
they might have revered, of the Divine Unity, was defaced by
the wild enthusiasm, and annihilated by the airy speculations,
of the new sectaries. The author of a celebrated dialogue
which has been attributed to Lucian, whilst he affects to treat
the mysterious subject of the Trinity in a style of ridicule
and contempt, betrays his own ignorance of the weakness of
human reason, and of the inscrutable nature of the divine
perfections.[11]

It might appear less surprising, that the founder of Christianity should not only be revered by his disciples as a sage and

---

[9] Cur nullas aras habent? templa nulla? nulla nota simulacra?
- - - - Unde autem, vel quis ille, aut ubi, Deus unicus, solitarius, desti-
tutus? Minucius Felix, c. 10. The Pagan interlocutor goes on to
make a distinction in favor of the Jews, who had once a temple, altars,
victims, &c.

[10] It is difficult (says Plato) to attain, and dangerous to publish,
the knowledge of the true God. See the Theologie des Philosophes,
in the Abbé d'Olivet's French translation of Tully de Naturâ Deorum, tom. i. p. 275.

[11] The author of the Philopatris perpetually treats the Christians
as a company of dreaming enthusiasts, δαιμόνιοι ἀιθέριοι ἀιθεροβα-
τοῦντες ἀεροβατοῦντες, &c. ; and in one place manifestly alludes to the
vision in which St. Paul was transported to the third heaven. In
another place, Triephon, who personates a Christian, after deriding
the gods of Paganism, proposes a mysterious oath.

Ὑψιμέδοντα θεὸν, μέγαν, ἄμβροτον, οὐρανίωνα,
Υἱὸν πατρός, πνεῦμα ἐκ πατρὸς ἐκπορευόμενον,
Ἕν ἐκ τριῶν, καὶ ἐξ ἑνὸς τρία.

Ἀριθμέειν με διδάσκεις, (is the profane answer of Critias,) ὶ ἔοχε ἡ
ἀριθμητιλη· οὐκ οἶδα γάρ τι λέγεις· ἓν τρία, τρία ἕν.

a prophet but that he should be adored as a God. The Polytheists were disposed to adopt every article of faith, which seemed to offer any resemblance, however distant or imperfect, with the popular mythology ; and the legends of Bacchus, of Hercules, and of Æsculapius, had, in some measure, prepared their imagination for the appearance of the Son of God under a human form.[12] But they were astonished that the Christians should abandon the temples of those ancient heroes, who, in the infancy of the world, had invented arts, instituted laws, and vanquished the tyrants or monsters who infested the earth ; in order to choose for the exclusive object of their religious worship, an obscure teacher, who, in a recent age, and among a barbarous people, had fallen a sacrifice either to the malice of his own countrymen, or to the jealousy of the Roman government. The Pagan multitude, reserving their gratitude for temporal benefits alone, rejected the inestimable present of life and immortality, which was offered to mankind by Jesus of Nazareth. His mild constancy in the midst of cruel and voluntary sufferings, his universal benevolence, and the sublime simplicity of his actions and character, were insufficient, in the opinion of those carnal men, to compensate for the want of fame, of empire, and of success ; and whilst they refused to acknowledge his stupendous triumph over the powers of darkness and of the grave, they misrepresented, or they insulted, the equivocal birth, wandering life, and ignominious death, of the divine Author of Christianity.[13]

The personal guilt which every Christian had contracted, in thus preferring his private sentiment to the national religion, was aggravated in a very high degree by the number and union of the criminals. It is well known, and has been already observed, that Roman policy viewed with the utmost jealousy and distrust any association among its subjects ; and that the privileges of private corporations, though formed for the most harmless or beneficial purposes, were bestowed with a very

---

[12] According to Justin Martyr, (Apolog. Major, c. 70—85,) the dæmon who had gained some imperfect knowledge of the prophecies, purposely contrived this resemblance, which might deter, though by different means, both the people and the philosophers from embracing the faith of Christ.

[13] In the first and second books of Origen, Celsus treats the birth and character of our Savior with the most impious contempt. The orator Libanius praises Porphyry and Julian for confuting the folly of a sect, which style a dead man of Palestine, God, and the Son of God. Socrates, Hist. Ecclesiast. iii. 23.

sparing nand.[14]   The religious assemblies of the Christians, who had separated themselves from the public worship, appeared of a much less innocent nature : they were illegal in their principle, and in their consequences might become dangerous ; nor were the emperors conscious that they violated the laws of justice, when, for the peace of society, they prohibited those secret and sometimes nocturnal meetings.[15]   The pious disobedience of the Christians made their conduct, or perhaps their designs, appear in a much more serious and criminal light ; and the Roman princes, who might perhaps have suffered themselves to be disarmed by a ready submission, deeming their honor concerned in the execution of their commands, sometimes attempted, by rigorous punishments, to subdue this independent spirit, which boldly acknowledged an authority superior to that of the magistrate.   The extent and duration of this spiritual conspiracy seemed to render it every day more deserving of his animadversion.   We have already seen that the active and successful zeal of the Christians had insensibly diffused them through every province and almost every city of the empire.   The new converts seemed to renounce their family and country, that they might connect themselves in an indissoluble band of union with a peculiar society, which every where assumed a different character from the rest of mankind.   Their gloomy and austere aspect, their abhorrence of the common business and pleasures of life, and their frequent predictions of impending calamities,[16] inspired the Pagans with the apprehension of some danger, which would arise from the new sect, the more alarming as it was the more obscure.   " Whatever," says Pliny, " may be the principle of their conduct, their inflexible obstinacy appeared deserving of punishment." [17]

---

[14] The emperor Trajan refused to incorporate a company of 150 firemen, for the use of the city of Nicomedia.   He disliked all associations.   See Plin. Epist. x. 42, 43.

[15] The proconsul Pliny had published a general edict against unlawful meetings.   The prudence of the Christians suspended their Agapæ ; but it was impossible for them to omit the exercise of public worship.

[16] As the prophecies of the Antichrist, approaching conflagration, &c., provoked those Pagans whom they did not convert, they were mentioned with caution and reserve ; and the Montanists were censured for disclosing too freely the dangerous secret.   See Mosheim, p 413.

[17] Neque enim dubitabam, quodcunque esset quod faterentur, (such are the words of Pliny,) pervicaciam certe et inflexibilem obstinationem debere puniri.

The precautions with which the disciples of Christ performed the offices of religion were at first dictated by fear and necessity; but they were continued from choice. By imitating the awful secrecy which reigned in the Eleusinian mysteries, the Christians had flattered themselves that they should render their sacred institutions more respectable in the eyes of the Pagan world.[18] But the event, as it often happens to the operations of subtile policy, deceived their wishes and their expectations. It was concluded, that they only concealed what they would have blushed to disclose. Their mistaken prudence afforded an opportunity for malice to invent, and for suspicious credulity to believe, the horrid tales which described the Christians as the most wicked of human kind, who practised in their dark recesses every abomination that a depraved fancy could suggest, and who solicited the favor of their unknown God by the sacrifice of every moral virtue. There were many who pretended to confess or to relate the ceremonies of this abhorred society. It was asserted, "that a new-born infant, entirely covered over with flour, was presented, like some mystic symbol of initiation, to the knife of the proselyte, who unknowingly inflicted many a secret and mortal wound on the innocent victim of his error; that as soon as the cruel deed was perpetrated, the sectaries drank up the blood, greedily tore asunder the quivering members, and pledged themselves to eternal secrecy, by a mutual consciousness of guilt. It was as confidently affirmed, that this inhuman sacrifice was succeeded by a suitable entertainment, in which intemperance served as a provocative to brutal lust; till, at the appointed moment, the lights were suddenly extinguished, shame was banished, nature was forgotten; and, as accident might direct, the darkness of the night was polluted by the incestuous commerce of sisters and brothers, of sons and of mothers." [19]

But the perusal of the ancient apologies was sufficient to remove even the slightest suspicion from the mind of a candid adversary. The Christians, with the intrepid security of innocence, appeal from the voice of rumor to the equity of the

---

[18] See Mosheim's Ecclesiastical History, vol. i. p. 101, and Spanheim, Remarques sur les Cæsars de Julien, p. 468, &c.

[19] See Justin Martyr, Apolog. i. 35, ii. 14. Athenagoras, in Legation. c. 27. Tertullian, Apolog. c. 7, 8 9. Minucius Felix, c. 9, 10. 30, 31. The last of these writers relates the accusation in the most elegant and circumstantial manner. The answer of Tertullian is the boldest and most vigorous.

magistrates. They acknowledge, that if any proof can be produced of the crimes which calumny has imputed to them, they are worthy of the most severe punishment. They provoke the punishment, and they challenge the proof. At the same time they urge, with equal truth and propriety, that the charge is not less devoid of probability, than it is destitute of evidence; they ask, whether any one can seriously believe that the pure and holy precepts of the gospel, which so frequently restrain the use of the most lawful enjoyments, should inculcate the practice of the most abominable crimes; that a large society should resolve to dishonor itself in the eyes of its own members; and that a great number of persons of either sex, and every age and character, insensible to the fear of death or infamy, should consent to violate those principles which nature and education had imprinted most deeply in their minds.[20] Nothing, it should seem, could weaken the force or destroy the effect of so unanswerable a justification, unless it were the injudicious conduct of the apologists themselves, who betrayed the common cause of religion, to gratify their devout hatred to the domestic enemies of the church. It was sometimes faintly insinuated, and sometimes boldly asserted, that the same bloody sacrifices, and the same incestuous festivals, which were so falsely ascribed to the orthodox believers, were in reality celebrated by the Marcionites, by the Carpocratians, and by several other sects of the Gnostics, who, notwithstanding they might deviate into the paths of heresy, were still actuated by the sentiments of men, and still governed by the precepts of Christianity.[21] Accusations of a similar kind were retorted upon the church by the schismatics who had departed from its communion,[22] and it was confessed on all sides, that

---

[20] In the persecution of Lyons, some Gentile slaves were compelled, by the fear of tortures, to accuse their Christian master. The church of Lyons, writing to their brethren of Asia, treat the horrid charge with proper indignation and contempt. Euseb. Hist. Eccles. v. i.

[21] See Justin Martyr, Apolog. i. 35. Irenæus adv. Hæres. i. 24. Clemens Alexandrin. Stromat. l. iii. p. 438. Euseb. iv. 8. It would be tedious and disgusting to relate all that the succeeding writers have imagined, all that Epiphanius has received, and all that Tillemont has copied. M. de Beausobre (Hist. du Manicheisme, l. ix. c. 8, 9) has exposed, with great spirit, the disingenuous arts of Augustin and Pope Leo I.

[22] When Tertullian became a Montanist, he aspersed the morals of the church which he had so resolutely defended. " Sed majoris est Agape, quia per hanc adolescentes tui cum sororibus dormiunt appendices scilicet gulæ lascivia et luxuria ' De Jejuniis, c. 17 The

the most scandalous licentiousness of manners prevailed among great numbers of those who affected the name of Christians. A Pagan magistrate, who possessed neither leisure nor abilities to discern the almost imperceptible line which divides the orthodox faith from heretical pravity, might easily have imagined that their mutual animosity had extorted the discovery of their common guilt. It was fortunate for the repose, or at least for the reputation, of the first Christians, that the magistrates sometimes proceeded with more temper and moderation than is usually consistent with religious zeal, and that they reported, as the impartial result of their judicial inquiry, that the sectaries, who had deserted the established worship, appeared to them sincere in their professions, and blameless in their manners; however they might incur, by their absurd and excessive superstition, the censure of the laws.[23]

History, which undertakes to record the transactions of the past, for the instruction of future ages, would ill deserve that honorable office, if she condescended to plead the cause of tyrants, or to justify the maxims of persecution. It must, however, be acknowledged, that the conduct of the emperors who appeared the least favorable to the primitive church, is by no means so criminal as that of modern sovereigns, who hav employed the arm of violence and terror against the religious opinions of any part of their subjects. From their reflections, or even from their own feelings, a Charles V. or a Lewis XIV. might have acquired a just knowledge of the rights of conscience, of the obligation of faith, and of the innocence of error. But the princes and magistrates of ancient Rome were strangers to those principles which inspired and authorized the inflexible obstinacy of the Christians in the cause of truth, nor could they themselves discover in their own breasts any motive which would have prompted them to refuse a legal, and as it were a natural, submission to the sacred institutions of their country. The same reason which contributes to alleviate the guilt, must have tended to abate the rigor, of their persecutions. As they were actuated, not by the furious zeal of bigots, but by the temperate policy of legis-

35th canon of the council of Illiberis provides against the scandals which too often polluted the vigils of the church, and disgraced the Christian name in the eyes of unbelievers.

[23] Tertullian (Apolog. c. 2) expatiates on the fair and honorable testimony of Pliny with much reason, and some declamation.

lators, contempt must often have relaxed, and humanity must frequently have suspended, the execution of those laws which they enacted against the humble and obscure followers of Christ. From the general view of their character and motives we might naturally conclude : I. That a considerable time elapsed before they considered the new sectaries as an object deserving of the attention of government. II. That in the conviction of any of their subjects who were accused of so very singular a crime they proceeded with caution and reluctance. III. That they were moderate in the use of punishments ; and, IV. That the afflicted church enjoyed many intervals of peace and tranquillity. Notwithstanding the careless indifference which the most copious and the most minute of the Pagan writers have shown to the affairs of the Christians,[24] it may still be in our power to confirm each of these probable suppositions, by the evidence of authentic facts.

1. By the wise dispensation of Providence, a mysterious veil was cast over the infancy of the church, which, till the faith of the Christians was matured, and their numbers were multiplied, served to protect them not only from the malice but even from the knowledge of the Pagan world. The slow and gradual abolition of the Mosaic ceremonies afforded a safe and innocent disguise to the more early proselytes of the gospel. As they were, far the greater part, of the race of Abraham, they were distinguished by the peculiar mark of circumcision, offered up their devotions in the Temple of Jerusalem till its final destruction, and received both the Law and the Prophets as the genuine inspirations of the Deity. The Gentile converts, who by a spiritual adoption had been associated to the hope of Israel, were likewise confounded under the garb and appearance of Jews,[25] and as the Polythe-

---

[24] In the various compilation of the Augustan History, (a part of which was composed under the reign of Constantine,) there are not six lines which relate to the Christians ; nor has the diligence of Xiphilin discovered their name in the large history of Dion Cassius.●

[25] An obscure passage of Suetonius (in Claud. c. 25) may seem to offer a proof how strangely the Jews and Christians of Rome were confounded with each other.

● The greater part of the Augustan History is dedicated to Diocletian. This may account for the silence of its authors concerning Christianity. The notices that occur are almost all in the lives composed under the reign of Constantine. It may fairly be concluded, from the language which he puts into the mouth of Mæcenas, that Dion was an enemy to all innova

ists paid less regard to articles of faith than to the external worship, the new sect, which carefully concealed, or faintly announced, its future greatness and ambition, was permitted to shelter itself under the general toleration which was granted to an ancient and celebrated people in the Roman empire It was not long, perhaps, before the Jews themselves, animated with a fiercer zeal and a more jealous faith, perceived the gradual separation of their Nazarene brethren from the doctrine of the synagogue ; and they would gladly have extinguished the dangerous heresy in the blood of its adherents. But the decrees of Heaven had already disarmed their malice ; and though they might sometimes exert the licentious privilege of sedition, they no longer possessed the administration of criminal justice ; nor did they find it easy to infuse into the calm breast of a Roman magistrate the rancor of their own zeal and prejudice. The provincial governors declared themselves ready to listen to any accusation that might affect the public safety ; but as soon as they were informed that it was a question not of facts but of words, a dispute relating only to the interpretation of the Jewish laws and prophecies, they deemed it unworthy of the majesty of Rome seriously to discuss the obscure differences which might arise among a barbarous and superstitious people. The innocence of the first Christians was protected by ignorance and contempt ; and the tribunal of the Pagan magistrate often proved their most assured refuge against the fury of the synagogue.[26] If indeed we were disposed to adopt the traditions of a too credulous antiquity, we might relate the distant peregrinations, the wonderful achievements, and the various deaths of the twelve apostles : but a more accurate inquiry will induce us to doubt, whether any of those persons who had been witnesses to the miracles of Christ were permitted, beyond the limits of Palestine, to seal with their blood the truth of their testimony.[27]

---

[26] See, in the xviiith and xxvth chapters of the Acts of the Apostles, the behavior of Gallio, proconsul of Achaia, and of Festus, procurator of Judea.

[27] In the time of Tertullian and Clemens of Alexandria, the glory of martyrdom was confined to St. Peter, St. Paul, and St. James. It was gradually bestowed on the rest of the apostles, by the more recent Greeks, who prudently selected for the theatre of

---

tions in religion. (See Gibbon, *infra*, note 105.) In fact, when the silence of Pagan historians is noticed, it should be remembered how meagre and mutilated are all the extant histories of the period. — M.

From the ordinary term of human life, it may very naturally
be presumed that most of them were deceased before the discontent of the Jews broke out into that furious war, which
was terminated only by the ruin of Jerusalem. During a
long period, from the death of Christ to that memorable
rebellion, we cannot discover any traces of Roman intolerance,
unless they are to be found in the sudden, the transient, but
the cruel persecution, which was exercised by Nero against
the Christians of the capital, thirty-five years after the former,
and only two years before the latter, of those great events.
The character of the philosophic historian, to whom we are
principally indebted for the knowledge of this singular transaction, would alone be sufficient to recommend it to our
most attentive consideration.

In the tenth year of the reign of Nero, the capital of the
empire was afflicted by a fire which raged beyond the memory or example of former ages.[28] The monuments of Grecian
art and of Roman virtue, the trophies of the Punic and Gallic
wars, the most holy temples, and the most splendid palaces,
were involved in one common destruction. Of the fourteen
regions or quarters into which Rome was divided, four only
subsisted entire, three were levelled with the ground, and the
remaining seven, which had experienced the fury of the
flames, displayed a melancholy prospect of ruin and desolation. The vigilance of government appears not to have
neglected any of the precautions which might alleviate the
sense of so dreadful a calamity. The Imperial gardens were
thrown open to the distressed multitude, temporary buildings
were erected for their accommodation, and a plentiful supply
of corn and provisions was distributed at a very moderate
price.[29] The most generous policy seemed to have dictated
the edicts which regulated the disposition of the streets and
the construction of private houses; and as it usually happens
in an age of prosperity, the conflagration of Rome, in the
course of a few years, produced a new city, more regular and
more beautiful than the former. But all the prudence and

their preaching and sufferings some remote country beyond the limits
of the Roman empire. See Mosheim, p. 81; and Tillemont, Mémoires
Ecclesiastiques, tom. i. part iii.

[28] Tacit. Anal. xv. 38—44. Sueton. in Neron. c. 38. Dion Cassius,
l. lxii. p. 1014. Orosius, vii. 7.

[29] The price of wheat (probably of the *modius*) was reduced as low
as *terni Nummi;* which would be equivalent to about fifteen shillings
the English quarter.

humanity affected by Nero on this occasion were insufficient to preserve him from the popular suspicion. Every crime might be imputed to the assassin of his wife and mother, nor could the prince who prostituted his person and dignity on the theatre be deemed incapable of the most extravagant folly. The voice of rumor accused the emperor as the incendiary of his own capital; and as the most incredible stories are the best adapted to the genius of an enraged people, it was gravely reported, and firmly believed, that Nero, enjoying the calamity which he had occasioned, amused himself with sing-ing to his lyre the destruction of ancient Troy.[30] To divert a suspicion, which the power of despotism was unable to sup-press, the emperor resolved to substitute in his own place some fictitious criminals. " With this view," continues Tacitus, " he inflicted the most exquisite tortures on those men, who, under the vulgar appellation of Christians, were already branded with deserved infamy. They derived their name and origin from Christ, who in the reign of Tiberius had suffered death by the sentence of the procurator Pontius Pilate.[31] For a while this dire superstition was checked; but it again burst forth ; * and not only spread itself over Judæa, the first seat of this mischievous sect, but was even introduced into Rome, the common asylum which receives and protects whatever is

---

[30] We may observe, that the rumor is mentioned by Tacitus with a very becoming distrust and hesitation, whilst it is greedily tran-scribed by Suetonius, and solemnly confirmed by Dion.

[31] This testimony is alone sufficient to expose the anachronism of the Jews, who place the birth of Christ near a century sooner. (Bas-nage, Histoire des Juifs, l. v. c. 14, 15.) We may learn from Josephus. (Antiquitat. xviii. 3.,) that the procuratorship of Pilate corresponded with the last ten years of Tiberius, A. D. 27—37. As to the particu-lar time of the death of Christ, a very early tradition fixed it to the 25th of March, A. D. 29, under the consulship of the two Gemini. (Tertullian adv. Judæos, c. 8.) This date, which is adopted by Pagi, Cardinal Norris, and Le Clerc, seems at least as probable as the vulgar æra, which is placed (I know not from what conjectures) four years later.

---

* This single phrase, Repressa in præsens exitiabilis superstitio rursus erumpebat, proves that the Christians had already attracted the attention of the government; and that Nero was not the first to persecute them. I am surprised that more stress has not been laid on the confirmation which the Acts of the Apostles derive from these words of Tacitus Repressa in præsens, and rursus erumpebat. — G.

I have been unwilling to suppress this note, but surely the expression of Tacitus refers to the expected extirpation of the religion by the death of its founder, Christ. — M.

impure, whatever is atrocious. The confessions of those who were seized discovered a great multitude of their accomplices and they were all convicted, not so much for the crime of setting fire to the city, as for their hatred of human kind.[32] They died in torments, and their torments were imbittered by insult and derision. Some were nailed on crosses; others sewn up in the skins of wild beasts, and exposed to the fury of dogs; others again, smeared over with combustible materials, were used as torches to illuminate the darkness of the night. The gardens of Nero were destined for the melancholy spectacle, which was accompanied with a horse-race, and honored with the presence of the emperor, who mingled with the populace in the dress and attitude of a charioteer. The guilt of the Christians deserved indeed the most exemplary punishment, but the public abhorrence was changed into commiseration, from the opinion that those unhappy wretches were sacrificed, not so much to the public welfare, as to the cruelty of a jealous tyrant."[33] Those who survey with a curious eye the revolutions of mankind, may observe, that the gardens and circus of Nero on the Vatican, which were polluted with the blood of the first Christians, have been rendered still more famous by the triumph and by the abuse of the persecuted religion. On the same spot,[34] a temple, which far surpasses the ancient glories of the Capitol, has been since erected by the Christian Pontiffs, who, deriving their claim of universal dominion from an humble fisherman of Galilee, have succeeded to the throne of the Cæsars, given laws to the barbarian conquerors of Rome, and extended their spiritual jurisdiction from the coast of the Baltic to the shores of the Pacific Ocean.

---

[32] *Odio humani generis convicti.* These words may either signify the hatred of mankind towards the Christians, or the hatred of the Christians towards mankind. I have preferred the latter sense, as the most agreeable to the style of Tacitus, and to the popular error, of which a precept of the gospel (see Luke xiv. 26) had been, perhaps, the innocent occasion. My interpretation is justified by the authority of Lipsius; of the Italian, the French, and the English translators of Tacitus; of Mosheim, (p. 102,) of Le Clerc, (Historia Ecclesiast. p 427,) of Dr. Lardner, (Testimonies, vol. i. p. 345,) and of the Bishop of Gloucester, (Divine Legation, vol. iii. p. 38.) But as the word *convicti* does not unite very happily with the rest of the sentence, James Gronovius has preferred the reading of *conjuncti*, which is authorized by the valuable MS. of Florence.

[33] Tacit. Anal. xv. 44.

[34] Nardini Roma Antica, p. 487. Donatus de Româ Antiquâ, L. iii p. 449.

But it would be improper to dismiss this account of Nero's persecution, till we have made some observations that may serve to remove the difficulties with which it is perplexed, and to throw some light on the subsequent history of the church.

1. The most sceptical criticism is obliged to respect the truth of this extraordinary fact, and the integrity of this celebrated passage of Tacitus. The former is confirmed by the diligent and accurate Suetonius, who mentions the punishment which Nero inflicted on the Christians, a sect of men who had embraced a new and criminal superstition.[35] The latter may be proved by the consent of the most ancient manuscripts; by the inimitable character of the style of Tacitus; by his reputation, which guarded his text from the interpolations of pious fraud; and by the purport of his narration, which accused the first Christians of the most atrocious crimes, without insinuating that they possessed any miraculous or even magical powers above the rest of mankind.[36]

2. Notwithstanding it is probable that Tacitus was born some years before the fire of Rome,[37] he could derive only from reading and conversation the knowledge of an event which happened during his infancy. Before he gave himself to the public, he calmly waited till his genius had attained its full

---

[35] Sueton. in Nerone, c. 16. The epithet of *malefica*, which some sagacious commentators have translated *magical*, is considered by the more rational Mosheim as only synonymous to the *exitiabilis* of Tacitus.

[36] The passage concerning Jesus Christ, which was inserted into the text of Josephus, between the time of Origen and that of Eusebius, may furnish an example of no vulgar forgery. The accomplishment of the prophecies, the virtues, miracles, and resurrection of Jesus, are distinctly related. Josephus acknowledges that he was the Messiah, and hesitates whether he should call him a man. If any doubt can still remain concerning this celebrated passage, the reader may examine the pointed objections of Le Fevre, (Havercamp. Joseph. tom. ii. p. 267—273,) the labored answers of Daubuz, (p. 187—232,) and the masterly reply (Bibliothèque Ancienne et Moderne, tom. vii. p. 237—288) of an anonymous critic, whom I believe to have been the learned Abbé de Longuerue.*

[37] See the lives of Tacitus by Lipsius and the Abbé de la Bleterie, Dictionnaire de Bayle à l'article Tacite, and Fabricius, Biblioth. Latin. tom. ii. p. 386, edit. Ernest.

---

* The modern editor of Eusebius, Heinichen, has adopted, and ably supported, a notion, which had before suggested itself to the editor, that this passage is not altogether a forgery, but interpolated with many additional clauses. Heinichen has endeavored to disengage the original text from the foreign and more recent matter. — M.

maturity, and he was more than forty years of age, when a grateful regard for the memory of the virtuous Agricola extorted from him the most early of those historical compositions which will delight and instruct the most distant posterity. After making a trial of his strength in the life of Agricola and the description of Germany, he conceived, and at length executed, a more arduous work ; the history of Rome, in thirty books, from the fall of Nero to the accession of Nerva. The administration of Nerva introduced an age of justice and prosperity, which Tacitus had destined for the occupation of his old age ;[38] but when he took a nearer view of his subject, judging, perhaps, that it was a more honorable or a less invidious office to record the vices of past tyrants, than to celebrate the virtues of a reigning monarch, he chose rather to relate, under the form of annals, the actions of the four immediate successors of Augustus. To collect, to dispose, and to adorn a series of fourscore years, in an immortal work, every sentence of which is pregnant with the deepest observations and the most lively images, was an undertaking sufficient to exercise the genius of Tacitus himself during the greatest part of his life. In the last years of the reign of Trajan, whilst the victorious monarch extended the power of Rome beyond its ancient limits, the historian was describing in the second and fourth books of his annals, the tyranny of Tiberius ;[39] and the emperor Hadrian must have succeeded to the throne, before Tacitus, in the regular prosecution of his work, could relate the fire of the capital, and the cruelty of Nero towards the unfortunate Christians. At the distance of sixty years, it was the duty of the annalist to adopt the narratives of contemporaries ; but it was natural for the philosopher to indulge himself in the description of the origin, the progress, and the character of the new sect, not so much according to the knowledge or prejudices of the age of Nero, as according to those of the time of Hadrian. 3. Tacitus very frequently trusts to the curiosity or reflection of his readers to

---

[38] Principatum Divi Nervæ, et imperium Trajani, uberiorem senectuti materiam senectuti seposui. Tacit. Hist. i.
[39] See Tacit. Annal. ii. 61, iv. 4.*

---

* The perusal of this passage of Tacitus alone is sufficient, as I have already said, to show that the Christian sect was not so obscure as not already to have been repressed, (repressa,) and that it did not pass for innocent in the eyes of the Romans. —G.

supply those intermediate circumstances and ideas, which, in his extreme conciseness, he has thought proper to suppress We may therefore presume to imagine some probable cause which could direct the cruelty of Nero against the Christians of Rome, whose obscurity, as well as innocence, should have shielded them from his indignation, and even from his notice. The Jews, who were numerous in the capital, and oppressed in their own country, were a much fitter object for the suspicions of the emperor and of the people : nor did it seem unlikely that a vanquished nation, who already discovered their abhorrence of the Roman yoke, might have recourse to the most atrocious means of gratifying their implacable revenge. But the Jews possessed very powerful advocates in the palace, and even in the heart of the tyrant ; his wife and mistress, the beautiful Poppæa, and a favorite player of the race of Abraham, who had already employed their intercession in behalf of the obnoxious people.[40] In their room it was necessary to offer some other victims, and it might easily be suggested that, although the genuine followers of Moses were innocent of the fire of Rome, there had arisen among them a new and pernicious sect of GALILÆANS, which was capable of the most horrid crimes. Under the appellation of GALILÆANS, two distinctions of men were confounded, the most opposite to each other in their manners and principles ; the disciples who had embraced the faith of Jesus of Nazareth,[41] and the zealots who had followed the standard of Judas the Gaulonite.[42] The former were the friends, the latter were the enemies, of human kind ; and the only resemblance between them consisted in the same inflexible constancy, which, in the defence of their cause, rendered them insensible of death and tortures. The

[40] The player's name was Aliturus. Through the same channel, Josephus, (de vitâ suâ, c. 2,) about two years before, had obtained the pardon and release of some Jewish priests, who were prisoners at Rome.

[41] The learned Dr. Lardner (Jewish and Heathen Testimonies, vol. ii p. 102, 103) has proved that the name of Galilæans was a very ancient, and perhaps the primitive appellation of the Christians.

[42] Joseph. Antiquitat. xviii. 1, 2. Tillemont, Ruine des Juifs, p. 742. The sons of Judas were crucified in the time of Claudius. His grandson Eleazar, after Jerusalem was taken, defended a strong fortress with 960 of his most desperate followers. When the battering-ram had made a breach, they turned their swords against their wives, their children, and at length against their own breasts. They died to the last man.

followers of Judas, who impelled their countrymen into rebellion, were soon buried under the ruins of Jerusalem; whilst those of Jesus, known by the more celebrated name of Christians, diffused themselves over the Roman empire. How natural was it for Tacitus, in the time of Hadrian, to appropriate to the Christians the guilt and the sufferings,* which he might, with far greater truth and justice, have attributed to a sect whose odious memory was almost extinguished! 4. Whatever opinion may be entertained of this conjecture, (for it is no more than a conjecture,) it is evident that the effect, as well as the cause, of Nero's persecution, were confined to the walls of Rome,[43] † that the religious tenets of the Galilæans, or Christians, were never made a subject of punishment, or even of inquiry; and that, as the idea of their sufferings was for a long time connected with the idea of cruelty and injustice, the moderation of succeeding princes inclined them to spare a sect, oppressed by a tyrant, whose rage had been usually directed against virtue and innocence.

It is somewhat remarkable that the flames of war consumed, almost at the same time, the temple of Jerusalem and the

---

[43] See Dodwell. Paucitat. Mart. l. xiii. The Spanish Inscription in Gruter, p. 238, No. 9, is a manifest and acknowledged forgery, contrived by that noted impostor, Cyriacus of Ancona, to flatter the pride and prejudices of the Spaniards. See Ferreras, Histoire D'Espagne, tom. i. p. 192.

---

* This conjecture is entirely devoid, not merely of verisimilitude, but even of possibility. Tacitus could not be deceived in appropriating to the Christians of Rome the guilt and the sufferings which he might have attributed with far greater truth to the followers of Judas the Gaulonite; for the latter never went to Rome. Their revolt, their attempts, their opinions, their wars, their punishment, had no other theatre but Judæa. (Basn. Hist. des Juifs, t. i. p. 491.) Moreover, the name of Christians had long been given in Rome to the disciples of Jesus; and Tacitus affirms too positively, refers too distinctly to its etymology, to allow us to suspect any mistake on his part.—G.

M. Guizot's expressions are not in the least too strong against this strange imagination of Gibbon; it may be doubted whether the followers of Judas were known as a sect under the name of Galilæans. — M.

† M. Guizot, on the authority of Sulpicius Severus, ii. 37, and of Orosius, viii. 5, inclines to the opinion of those who extend the persecution to the provinces. Mosheim rather leans to that side on this much disputed question. (c. xxxv.) Neander takes the view of Gibbon, which is in general that of the most learned writers. There is indeed no evidence, which I can discover, of its reaching the provinces; and the apparent security, at least as regards his life, with which St. Paul pursued his travels during this period, affords at least a strong inference against a rigid and general inquisition against the Christians in other parts of the empire. — M

Capitol of Rome;[44] and it appears no less singular, that the tribute which devotion had destined to the former, should have been converted by the power of an assaulting victor to restore and adorn the splendor of the latter.[45] The emperors levied a general capitation tax on the Jewish people; and although the sum assessed on the head of each individual was inconsiderable, the use for which it was designed, and the severity with which it was exacted, were considered as an intolerable grievance.[46] Since the officers of the revenue extended their unjust claim to many persons who were strangers to the blood or religion of the Jews, it was impossible that the Christians who had so often sheltered themselves under the shade of the synagogue, should now escape this rapacious persecution. Anxious as they were to avoid the slightest infection of idolatry, their conscience forbade them to contribute to the honor of that dæmon who had assumed the character of the Capitoline Jupiter. As a very numerous though declining party among the Christians still adhered to the law of Moses, their efforts to dissemble their Jewish origin were detected by the decisive test of circumcision;[47] nor were the Roman magistrates at leisure to inquire into the difference of their religious tenets. Among the Christians who were brought before the tribunal of the emperor, or, as it seems more probable, before that of the procurator of Judæa, two persons are said to have appeared, distinguished by their extraction, which was more truly noble than that of the greatest monarchs. These were the grandsons of St. Jude the apostle, who him-

---

[44] The Capitol was burnt during the civil war between Vitellius and Vespasian, the 19th of December, A. D. 69. On the 10th of August, A. D. 70, the temple of Jerusalem was destroyed by the hands of the Jews themselves, rather than by those of the Romans.

[45] The new Capitol was dedicated by Domitian. Sueton. in Domitian. c. 5. Plutarch in Poplicola, tom. i. p. 230, edit. Bryant. The gilding alone cost 12,000 talents, (above two millions and a half.) It was the opinion of Martial, (l. ix. Epigram 3,) that if the emperor had called in his debts, Jupiter himself, even though he had made a general auction of Olympus, would have been unable to pay two shillings in the pound.

[46] With regard to the tribute, see Dion Cassius, l. lxvi. p. 1082, with Reimarus's notes. Spanheim, de Usu Numismatum, tom. ii. p. 571; and Basnage, Histoire des Juifs, l. vii. c. 2

[47] Suetonius (in Domitian. c. 12) had seen an old man of ninety publicly examined before the procurator's tribunal. This is what Martial calls, Mentula tributis damnata.

self was the brother of Jesus Christ.[48] Their natural pretensions to the throne of David might perhaps attract the respect of the people, and excite the jealousy of the governor; but the meanness of their garb, and the simplicity of their answers, soon convinced him that they were neither desirous nor capable of disturbing the peace of the Roman empire. They frankly confessed their royal origin, and their near relation to the Messiah; but they disclaimed any temporal views, and professed that his kingdom, which they devoutly expected, was purely of a spiritual and angelic nature. When they were examined concerning their fortune and occupation, they showed their hands, hardened with daily labor, and declared that they derived their whole subsistence from the cultivation of a farm near the village of Cocaba, of the extent of about twenty-four English acres,[49] and of the value of nine thousand drachms, or three hundred pounds sterling. The grandsons of St. Jude were dismissed with compassion and contempt.[50]

But although the obscurity of the house of David might protect them from the suspicions of a tyrant, the present greatness of his own family alarmed the pusillanimous temper of Domitian, which could only be appeased by the blood of those Romans whom he either feared, or hated, or esteemed. Of the two sons of his uncle Flavius Sabinus,[51] the elder was soon convicted of treasonable intentions, and the younger, who

---

[48] This appellation was at first understood in the most obvious sense, and it was supposed, that the brothers of Jesus were the lawful issue of Joseph and Mary. A devout respect for the virginity of the mother of God suggested to the Gnostics, and afterwards to the orthodox Greeks, the expedient of bestowing a second wife on Joseph. The Latins (from the time of Jerome) improved on that hint, asserted the perpetual celibacy of Joseph, and justified by many similar examples the new interpretation that Jude, as well as Simon and James, who were styled the brothers of Jesus Christ, were only his first cousins. See Tillemont, Mem. Ecclesiast. tom. i. part iii.; and Beausobre, Hist Critique du Manicheisme, l. ii. c. 2.

[49] Thirty-nine $\pi\lambda\epsilon\vartheta\rho\alpha$, squares of a hundred feet each, which, if strictly computed, would scarcely amount to nine acres. But the probability of circumstances, the practice of other Greek writers, and the authority of M. de Valois, incline me to believe that the $\pi\lambda\epsilon\vartheta\rho\upsilon\nu$ is used to express the Roman jugerum.

[50] Eusebius, iii. 20. The story is taken from Hegesippus.

[51] See the death and character of Sabinus in Tacitus. (Hist. iii. 74, 75.) Sabinus was the elder brother, and, till the accession of Vespasian, had been considered as the principal support of the Flavian family.

bore the name of Flavius Clemens, was indebted for his safety to his want of courage and ability.[52]   The emperor, for a long time, distinguished so harmless a kinsman by his favor and protection, bestowed on him his own niece Domitilla, adopted the children of that marriage to the hope of the succession, and invested their father with the honors of the consulship.

But he had scarcely finished the term of his annual magistracy, when, on a slight pretence, he was condemned and executed; Domitilla was banished to a desolate island on the coast of Campania;[53] and sentences either of death or of confiscation were pronounced against a great number of persons who were involved in the same accusation.   The guilt imputed to their charge was that of *Atheism* and *Jewish manners*;[54] a singular association of ideas, which cannot with any propriety be applied except to the Christians, as they were obscurely and imperfectly viewed by the magistrates and by the writers of that period.   On the strength of so probable an interpretation, and too eagerly admitting the suspicions of a tyrant as an evidence of their honorable crime, the church has placed both Clemens and Domitilla among its first martyrs, and has branded the cruelty of Domitian with the name of the second persecution.   But this persecution (if it deserves that epithet) was of no long duration.   A few months after the death of Clemens, and the banishment of Domitilla, Stephen, a freedman belonging to the latter, who had enjoyed the favor, but who had not surely embraced the faith, of his mistress,* assassinated the emperor in his palace.[55]   The memory of Domitian was condemned by the

---

[52] Flavium Clementem patruelem suum *contemptissimæ inertiæ* . . ex tenuissimâ suspicione interemit.   Sueton. in Domitian. c. 15.

[53] The Isle of Pandataria, according to Dion.   Bruttius Præsens (apud Euseb. iii. 18) banishes her to that of Pontia, which was not far distant from the other.   That difference, and a mistake, either of Eusebius or of his transcribers, have given occasion to suppose two Domitillas, the wife and the niece of Clemens.   See Tillemont, Mémoires Ecclesiastiques, tom. ii. p. 224.

[54] Dion. l. lxvii. p. 1112.   If the Bruttius Præsens, from whom it is probable that he collected this account, was the correspondent of Pliny, (Epistol. vii. 3,) we may consider him as a contemporary writer.

[55] Suet. in Domit c. 17.   Philostratus in Vit. Apollon. l. viii.

---

* This is an uncandid sarcasm.   There is nothing to connect Stephen with the religion of Domitilla.   He was a knave detected in the malversation of money—interceptarum pecuniarum reus.—M.

senate; his acts were rescinded; his exiles recalled; and under the gentle administration of Nerva, while the innocent were restored to their rank and fortunes, even the most guilty either obtained pardon or escaped punishment.[56]

II. About ten years afterwards, under the reign of Trajan, the younger Pliny was intrusted by his friend and master with the government of Bithynia and Pontus, He soon found himself at a loss to determine by what rule of justice or of law he should direct his conduct in the execution of an office the most repugnant to his humanity. Pliny had never assisted at any judicial proceedings against the Christians, with whose name alone he seems to be acquainted ; and he was totally uninformed with regard to the nature of their guilt, the method of their conviction, and the degree of their punishment. In this perplexity he had recourse to his usual expedient, of submitting to the wisdom of Trajan an impartial, and, in some respects, a favorable account of the new superstition, requesting the emperor, that he would condescend to resolve his doubts, and to instruct his ignorance.[57] The life of Pliny had been employed in the acquisition of learning, and in the business of the world. Since the age of nineteen he had pleaded with distinction in the tribunals of Rome,[58] filled a place in the senate, had been invested with the honors of the consulship, and had formed very numerous connections with every order of men, both in Italy and in the provinces. From *his* ignorance therefore we may derive some useful information. We may assure ourselves, that when he accepted the government of Bithynia, there were no general laws or decrees of the senate in force against the Christians ; that neither Trajan nor any of his virtuous predecessors, whose edicts

---

[56] Dion. l. lxviii. p. 1118. Plin. Epistol. iv. 22.

[57] Plin. Epistol. x. 97. The learned Mosheim expresses himself (p. 147, 232) with the highest approbation of Pliny's moderate and candid temper. Notwithstanding Dr. Lardner's suspicions (see Jewish and Heathen Testimonies, vol. ii. p. 46,) I am unable to discover any bigotry in his language or proceedings.*

[58] Plin. Epist. v. 8. He pleaded his first cause A. D. 81 ; the year after the famous eruptions of Mount Vesuvius, in which his uncle lost his life.

---

* Yet the humane Pliny put two female attendants, probably deaconesses, to the torture, in order to ascertain the real nature of these suspicious meetings: necessarium credidi, ex duabus ancillis, quæ ministræ dicebantur, quid esset veri et *per tormenta* quærere —M

were received into the civil and criminal jurisprudence, had publicly declared their intentions concerning the new sect and that whatever proceedings had been carried on against the Christians, there were none of sufficient weight and authority to establish a precedent for the conduct of a Roman magistrate.

The answer of Trajan, to which the Christians of the succeeding age have frequently appealed, discovers as much regard for justice and humanity as could be reconciled with his mistaken notions of religious po icy.[59] Instead of displaying the implacable zeal of an Inquisitor, anxious to discover the most minute particles of heresy, and exulting in the number of his victims, the emperor expresses much more solicitude to protect the security of the innocent, than to prevent the escape of the guilty. He acknowledges the difficulty of fixing any general plan ; but he lays down two salutary rules, which often afforded relief and support to the distressed Christians. Though he directs the magistrates to punish such persons as are legally convicted, he prohibits them, with a very humane inconsistency, from making any inquiries concerning the supposed criminals. Nor was the magistrate allowed to proceed on every kind of information. Anonymous charges the emperor rejects, as too repugnant to the equity of his government ; and he strictly requires, for the conviction of those to whom the guilt of Christianity is imputed, the positive evidence of a fair and open accuser. It is likewise probable, that the persons who assumed so invidious an office, were obliged to declare the grounds of their suspicions, to specify (both in respect to time and place) the secret assemblies, which their Christian adversary had frequented, and to disclose a great number of circumstances, which were concealed with the most vigilant jealousy from the eye of the profane. If they succeeded in their prosecution, they were exposed to the resentment of a considerable and active party, to the censure of the more liberal portion of mankind, and to the ignominy which, in every age and country, has attended the character of an informer. If, on the contrary, they failed in their proofs, they incurred the severe and perhaps capital

---

[59] Plin. Epist. x. 98. Tertullian (Apolog. c. 5) considers this rescript as a relaxation of the ancient penal laws, " quas Trajanus ex parte frustratus est : " and yet Tertullian, in another part of his Apology, exposes the inconsistency of prohibiting inquiries, and enjoining punishments.

penalty, which, according to a law published by the emperor
Hadrian, was inflicted on those who falsely attributed to their
fellow-citizens the crime of Christianity. The violence of
personal or superstitious animosity might sometimes prevail
over the most natural apprehensions of disgrace and danger;
but it cannot surely be imagined, that accusations of so un-
promising an appearance were either lightly or frequently
undertaken by the Pagan subjects of the Roman empire.[60] *

The expedient which was employed to elude the prudence
of the laws, affords a sufficient proof how effectually they disappointed the mischievous designs of private malice or superstitious zeal. In a large and tumultuous assembly, the restraints
of fear and shame, so forcible on the minds of individuals, are
deprived of the greatest part of their influence. The pious
Christian, as he was desirous to obtain, or to escape, the glory
of martyrdom, expected, either with impatience or with terror,
the stated returns of the public games and festivals. On those
occasions the inhabitants of the great cities of the empire were
collected in the circus or the theatre, where every circumstance of the place, as well as of the ceremony, contributed
to kindle their devotion, and to extinguish their humanity.
Whilst the numerous spectators, crowned with garlands, per-
fumed with incense, purified with the blood of victims, and
surrounded with the altars and statues of their tutelar deities,
resigned themselves to the enjoyment of pleasures, which they
considered as an essential part of their religious worship,
they recollected, that the Christians alone abhorred the gods
of mankind, and by their absence and melancholy on these
solemn festivals, seemed to insult or to lament the public
felicity. If the empire had been afflicted by any recent calam-

---

[60] Eusebius (Hist. Ecclesiast. l. iv. c. 9) has preserved the edict of
Hadrian. He has likewise (c. 13) given us one still more favorable,
under the name of Antoninus; the authenticity of which is not so
universally allowed. The second Apology of Justin contains some
curious particulars relative to the accusations of Christians.†

---

* The enactment of this 'aw affords strong presumption, that accusa
tions of the " crime of Christianity," were by no means so uncommon, nor
received with so much mistrust and caution by the ruling authorities, as
Gibbon would insinuate. — M.
† Professor Hegelmayer has proved the authenticity of the edict of An
toninus, in his Comm. Hist.-Theol. in Edict. Imp. Antonini. Tubing. 1777,
in 4to. — G.
Neander doubts its authenticity. (vol. i. p. 152.) In my opinion, the
internal evidence is decisive against it. — M.

tiy, by a plague, a famine, or an unsuccessful war; if the Tyber had, or if the Nile had not, risen beyond its banks; if the earth had shaken, or if the temperate order of the seasons had been interrupted, the superstitious Pagans were convinced that the crimes and the impiety of the Christians, who were spared by the excessive lenity of the government, had at length provoked the divine justice. It was not among a licentious and exasperated populace, that the forms of legal proceedings could be observed; it was not in an amphitheatre stained with the blood of wild beasts and gladiators, that the voice of compassion could be heard. The impatient clamors of the multitude denounced the Christians as the enemies of gods and men, doomed them to the severest tortures, and venturing to accuse by name some of the most distinguished of the new sectaries, required with irresistible vehemence that they should be instantly apprehended and cast to the lions.[61] The provincial governors and magistrates who presided in the public spectacles were usually inclined to gratify the inclinations, and to appease the rage, of the people, by the sacrifice of a few obnoxious victims. But the wisdom of the emperors protected the church from the danger of these tumultuous clamors and irregular accusations, which they justly censured as repugnant both to the firmness and to the equity of their administration. The edicts of Hadrian and of Antoninus Pius expressly declared, that the voice of the multitude should never be admitted as legal evidence to convict or to punish those unfortunate persons who had embraced the enthusiasm of the Christians.[62]

III. Punishment was not the inevitable consequence of conviction, and the Christians, whose guilt was the most clearly proved by the testimony of witnesses, or even by their voluntary confession, still retained in their own power the alternative of life or death. It was not so much the past offence, as the actual resistance, which excited the indignation of the magistrate. He was persuaded that he offered them an easy pardon, since, if they consented to cast a few grains of incense upon the altar, they were dismissed from the tribunal in safety and with applause. It was esteemed the duty of a humane

---

[61] See Tertullian, (Apolog. c. 40.) The acts of the martyrdom of Polycarp exhibit a lively picture of these tumults, which were usually fomented by the malice of the Jews.

[62] These regulations are inserted in the above mentioned edicts of Hadrian and Pius. See the apology of Melito, (apud Euseb. l. iv. c 26.)

judge to endeavor to reclaim, rather than to punish, those deluded enthusiasts. Varying his tone according to the age the sex, or the situation of the prisoners, he frequently con descended to set before their eyes every circumstance which could render life more pleasing, or death more terrible; and to solicit, nay, to entreat, them, that they would show some compassion to themselves, to their families, and to their friends.[63] If threats and persuasions proved ineffectual, he had often recourse to violence; the scourge and the rack were called in to supply the deficiency of argument, and every art of cruelty was employed to subdue such inflexible, and, as it appeared to the Pagans, such criminal, obstinacy. The ancient apologists of Christianity have censured, with equal truth and severity, the irregular conduct of their persecutors, who, contrary to every principle of judicial proceeding, ad-mitted the use of torture, in order to obtain, not a confession, but a denial, of the crime which was the object of their inquiry.[64] The monks of succeeding ages, who, in their peaceful solitudes, entertained themselves with diversifying the deaths and sufferings of the primitive martyrs, have fre-quently invented torments of a much more refined and ingenious nature. In particular, it has pleased them to suppose, that the zeal of the Roman magistrates, disdaining every con-sideration of moral virtue or public decency, endeavored to seduce those whom they were unable to vanquish, and that by their orders the most brutal violence was offered to those whom they found it impossible to seduce. It is related, that pious females, who were prepared to despise death, were sometimes condemned to a more severe trial,† and called

---

[63] See the rescript of Trajan, and the conduct of Pliny. The most authentic acts of the martyrs abound in these exhortations.*

[64] In particular, see Tertullian, (Apolog. c. 2, 3,) and Lactantius, (Institut. Divin. v. 9.) Their reasonings are almost the same; but we may discover, that one of these apologists had been a lawyer, and the other a rhetorician.

---

* Pliny's test was the worship of the gods, offerings to the statue of the emperor, and blaspheming Christ — præterea maledicerent Christo. — M.
† The more ancient as well as authentic memorials of the church, relate many examples of the fact, (of these severe trials,) which there is nothing to contradict. Tertullian, among others, says, Nam proximè ad leonem damnando Christianam, potius quam ad leonem, confessi estis labem pudi-citiæ apud nos atrociorem omni pœnâ et omni morte reputari, Apol. cap-ult. Eusebius likewise says, "Other virgins, dragged to brothels, have lost their life rather than defile their virtue." Euseb. Hist. Ecc. viii. 14. — G
The miraculous interpositions were the offspring of the coarse imagina-tions of the monks. — M.

upon to determine whether they set a higher value on their religion or on their chastity. The youths to whose licentious embraces they were abandoned, received a solemn exhortation from the judge, to exert their most strenuous efforts to maintain the honor of Venus against the impious virgin who refused to burn incense on her altars. Their violence, however, was commonly disappointed, and the seasonable interposition of some miraculous power preserved the chaste spouses of Christ from the dishonor even of an involuntary defeat. We should not indeed neglect to remark, that the more ancient as well as authentic memorials of the church are seldom polluted with these extravagant and indecent fictions.[65]

The total disregard of truth and probability in the representation of these primitive martyrdoms was occasioned by a very natural mistake. The ecclesiastical writers of the fourth or fifth centuries ascribed to the magistrates of Rome the same degree of implacable and unrelenting zeal which filled their own breasts against the heretics or the idolaters of their own times. It is not improbable that some of those persons who were raised to the dignities of the empire, might have imbibed the prejudices of the populace, and that the cruel disposition of others might occasionally be stimulated by motives of avarice or of personal resentment.[66] But it is certain, and we may appeal to the grateful confessions of the first Christians, that the greatest part of those magistrates who exercised in the provinces the authority of the emperor, or of the senate, and to whose hands alone the jurisdiction of life and death was intrusted, behaved like men of polished manners and liberal education, who respected the rules of justice, and who were conversant with the precepts of philosophy. They frequently declined the odious task of persecution, dismissed the charge with contempt, or suggested to the accused Christian some legal evasion, by which he might elude the severity of

---

[65] See two instances of this kind of torture in the Acta Sincera Martyrum, published by Ruinart, p. 160, 399. Jerome, in his Legend of Paul the Hermit, tells a strange story of a young man, who was chained naked on a bed of flowers, and assaulted by a beautiful and wanton courtesan. He quelled the rising temptation by biting off his tongue.

[66] The conversion of his wife provoked Claudius Herminianus, governor of Cappadocia, to treat the Christians with uncommon severity Tertullian ad Scapulam, c. 3.

the laws.[67] Whenever they were invested with a discretionary power,[68] they used it much less for the oppression, than for the relief and benefit, of the afflicted church. They were far from condemning all the Christians who were accused before their tribunal, and very far from punishing with death all those who were convicted of an obstinate adherence to the new superstition. Contenting themselves, for the most part, with the milder chastisements of imprisonment, exile, or slavery in the mines,[69] they left the unhappy victims of their justice some reason to hope, that a prosperous event, the accession, the marriage, or the triumph of an emperor, might speedily restore them, by a general pardon, to their former state. The martyrs, devoted to immediate execution by the Roman magistrates, appear to have been selected from the most opposite extremes. They were either bishops and presbyters, the persons the most distinguished among the Christians by their rank and influence, and whose example might strike terror into the whole sect; [70] or else they were the meanest and most abject among them, particularly those of the servile condition, whose lives were esteemed of little value, and whose sufferings were

---

[67] Tertullian, in his epistle to the governor of Africa, mentions several remarkable instances of lenity and forbearance, which had happened within his knowledge.

[68] Neque enim in universum aliquid quod quasi certam formam habeat, constitui potest; an expression of Trajan, which gave a very great latitude to the governors of provinces.*

[69] In Metalla damnamur, in insulas relegamur. Tertullian, Apolog. c. 12. The mines of Numidia contained nine bishops, with a proportionable number of their clergy and people, to whom Cyprian addressed a pious epistle of praise and comfort. See Cyprian. Epistol. 76, 77.

[70] Though we cannot receive with entire confidence either the epistles, or the acts, of Ignatius, (they may be found in the 2d volume of the Apostolic Fathers,) yet we may quote that bishop of Antioch as one of these *exemplary* martyrs. He was sent in chains to Rome as a public spectacle ; and when he arrived at Troas, he received the pleasing intelligence, that the persecution of Antioch was already at an end.†

* Gibbon altogether forgets that Trajan fully approved of the course pursued by Pliny. That course was, to order all who persevered in their faith to be led to execution : perseverantes duci jussi. — M.

† The acts of Ignatius are generally received as authentic, as are seven of his letters. Eusebius and St. Jerome mention them : there are two editions ; in one, the letters are longer, and many passages appear to have been interpolated ; the other edition is that which contains the real letters of St. Ignatius ; such at least is the opinion of the wisest and most enlightened critics (See Lardner, Cred. of Gosp. Hist.) Less uber die

viewed by the ancients with too careless an indifference.[71] The learned Origen, who, from his experience as well as reading, was intimately acquainted with the history of the Christians, declares, in the most express terms, that the number of martyrs was very inconsiderable.[72] His authority would alone be sufficient to annihilate that formidable army of martyrs, whose relics, drawn for the most part from the catacombs of Rome, have replenished so many churches,[73] and whose marvellous achievements have been the subject of so many volumes of Holy Romance.[74] But the general assertion of

[71] Among the martyrs of Lyons, (Euseb. l. v. c. 1,) the slave Blandina was distinguished by more exquisite tortures. Of the five martyrs so much celebrated in the acts of Felicitas and Perpetua, two were of a servile, and two others of a very mean, condition.

[72] Origen. advers. Celsum, l. iii. p. 116. His words deserve to be transcribed. " Ὀλίγοι κατὰ καιρούς, καὶ σφόδρα εὐαρίθμητοι ὑπὲρ τῆς Χριστιανῶν θεοσεβείας τεθνήκασι." *

[73] If we recollect that all the Plebeians of Rome were not Christians, and that all the Christians were not saints and martyrs, we may judge with how much safety religious honors can be ascribed to bones or urns, indiscriminately taken from the public burial-place. After ten centuries of a very free and open trade, some suspicions have arisen among the more learned Catholics. They now require, as a proof of sanctity and martyrdom, the letters B. M., a vial full of red liquor supposed to be blood, or the figure of a palm-tree. But the two former signs are of little weight, and with regard to the last, it is observed by the critics, 1. That the figure, as it is called, of a palm, is perhaps a cypress, and perhaps only a stop, the flourish of a comma used in the monumental inscriptions. 2. That the palm was the symbol of victory among the Pagans. 3. That among the Christians it served as the emblem, not only of martyrdom, but in general of a joyful resurrection. See the epistle of P. Mabillon, on the worship of unknown saints, and Muratori sopra le Antichità Italiane, Dissertat. lviii.

[74] As a specimen of these legends, we may be satisfied with 10,000 Christian soldiers crucified in one day, either by Trajan or Hadrian, on Mount Ararat. See Baronius ad Martyrologium Romanum; Tillemont, Mém. Ecclesiast. tom. ii. part ii. p. 438; and Geddes's Miscel-

Religion, v. i. p. 529. Usser. Diss. de Ign. Epist. Pearson, Vindic. Ignatianæ. It should be remarked, that it was under the reign of Trajan that the bishop Ignatius was carried from Antioch to Rome, to be exposed to the lions in the amphitheatre, the year of J. C. 107, according to some; of 116, according to others. — G.

* The words that follow should be quoted : " God not permitting that all this class of men should be exterminated ; " which appears to indicate that Origen thought the number put to death inconsiderable only when compared to the numbers who had survived. Besides this, he is speaking of the state of the religion under Caracalla, Elagabalus, Alexander Severus, and Philip; who had not persecuted the Christians. It was during the reign of the latter that Origen wrote his books against Celsus. — G.

Or gen may be explained and confirmed by the particular testimony of his friend Dionysius, who, in the immense city of Alexandria, and under the rigorous persecution of Decius, reckons only ten men and seven women who suffered for the profession of the Christian name.[75]

During the same period of persecution, the zealous, the eloquent, the ambitious Cyprian governed the church, not only of Carthage, but even of Africa. He possessed every quality which could engage the reverence of the faithful, or provoke the suspicions and resentment of the Pagan magistrates. His character as well as his station seemed to mark out that holy prelate as the most distinguished object of envy and of danger.[76] The experience, however, of the life of Cyprian, is sufficient to prove that our fancy has exaggerated the perilous situation of a Christian bishop; and that the dangers to which he was exposed were less imminent than those which temporal ambition is always prepared to encounter in the pursuit of honors. Four Roman emperors, with their families, their favorites, and their adherents, perished by the sword in the space of ten years, during which the bishop of Carthage guided by his authority and eloquence the councils of the African church. It was only in the third year of his administration, that he had reason, during a few months, to apprehend

---

lanies, vol. ii. p. 203. The abbreviation of MIL., which may signify either *soldiers* or *thousands*, is said to have occasioned some extraordinary mistakes.

[75] Dionysius ap. Euseb. l. vi. c. 41. One of the seventeen was likewise accused of robbery.*

[76] The letters of Cyprian exhibit a very curious and original picture both of the *man* and of the *times*. See likewise the two lives of Cyprian, composed with equal accuracy, though with very different views; the one by Le Clerc (Bibliothèque Universelle, tom. xii. p. 208—378,) the other by Tillemont, Mémoires Ecclesiastiques, tom. iv. part i. p. 76—459.

---

* Gibbon ought to have said, was falsely accused of robbery, for so it is in the Greek text. This Christian, named Nemesion, falsely accused of robbery before the centurion, was acquitted of a crime altogether foreign to his character, (ἀλλοτριωτάτην,) but he was led before the governor as guilty of being a Christian, and the governor inflicted upon him a double torture. (Euseb. loc. cit.) It must be added, that Saint Dionysius only makes particular mention of the principal martyrs, [this is very doubtful. — M.,] and that he says, in general, that the fury of the Pagans against the Christians gave to Alexandria the appearance of a city taken by storm. [This refers to plunder and ill usage, not to actual slaughter. — M.] Finally, it should be observed that Origen wrote before the persecution of the emperor Decius. — G

the severe edicts of Decius, the vigilance of the magistrate, and the clamors of the multitude, who loudly demanded, that Cyprian, the leader of the Christians, should be thrown to the lions. Prudence suggested the necessity of a temporary retreat, and the voice of prudence was obeyed. He withdrew himself into an obscure solitude, from whence he could main-tain a constant correspondence with the clergy and people of Carthage; and, concealing himself till the tempest was past, he preserved his life, without relinquishing either his power or his reputation. His extreme caution did not, however, escape the censure of the more rigid Christians, who lamented, or the reproaches of his personal enemies, who insulted, a conduct which they considered as a pusillanimous and criminal deser-tion of the most sacred duty.[77] The propriety of reserving himself for the future exigencies of the church, the example of several holy bishops,[78] and the divine admonitions, which, as he declares himself, he frequently received in visions and ecstasies, were the reasons alleged in his justification.[79] But his best apology may be found in the cheerful resolution, with which, about eight years afterwards, he suffered death in the cause of religion. The authentic history of his martyrdom has been recorded with unusual candor and impartiality. A short abstract, therefore, of its most important circumstances, will convey the clearest information of the spirit, and of the forms, of the Roman persecutions.[80]

When Valerian was consul for the third, and Gallienus for the fourth, time, Paternus, proconsul of Africa, summoned Cyprian to appear in his private council-chamber. He there acquainted him with the Imperial mandate which he had just

---

[77] See the polite but severe epistle of the clergy of Rome to the bishop of Carthage. (Cyprian. Epist. 8, 9.) Pontius labors with the greatest care and diligence to justify his master against the general censure.

[78] In particular those of Dionysius of Alexandria, and Gregory Thaumaturgus, of Neo-Cæsarea. See Euseb. Hist. Ecclesiast. l. vi. c. 40; and Mémoires de Tillemont, tom. iv. part ii. p. 685.

[79] See Cyprian. Epist. 16, and his life by Pontius.

[80] We have an original life of Cyprian by the deacon Pontius, the companion of his exile, and the spectator of his death; and we like-wise possess the ancient proconsular acts of his martyrdom. These two relations are consistent with each other, and with probability; and what is somewhat remarkable, they are both unsullied by any miraculous circumstances.

received,[81] that those who had abandoned the Roman religion
should immediately return to the practice of the ceremonies
of their ancestors. Cyprian replied without hesitation, that
he was a Christian and a bishop, devoted to the worship of the
true and only Deity, to whom he offered up his daily supplications for the safety and prosperity of the two emperors, his
lawful sovereigns. With modest confidence he pleaded the
privilege of a citizen, in refusing to give any answer to some
invidious and indeed illegal questions which the proconsul had
proposed. A sentence of banishment was pronounced as the
penalty of Cyprian's disobedience; and he was conducted
without delay to Curubis, a free and maritime city of Zeugi-
tania, in a pleasant situation, a fertile territory, and at the
distance of about forty miles from Carthage.[82] The exiled
bishop enjoyed the conveniences of life and the consciousness
of virtue. His reputation was diffused over Africa and Italy;
an account of his behavior was published for the edification of
the Christian world;[83] and his solitude was frequently interrupted by the letters, the visits, and the congratulations of the
faithful. On the arrival of a new proconsul in the province,
the fortune of Cyprian appeared for some time to wear a still
more favorable aspect. He was recalled from banishment;
and though not yet permitted to return to Carthage, his own
gardens in the neighborhood of the capital were assigned for
the place of his residence.[84]

At length, exactly one year[85] after Cyprian was first

[81] It should seem that these were circular orders, sent at the same
time to all the governors. Dionysius (ap. Euseb. l. vii. c. 11) relates
the history of his own banishment from Alexandria almost in the
same manner. But as he escaped and survived the persecution, we
must account him either more or less fortunate than Cyprian.

[82] See Plin. Hist. Natur. v. 3. Cellarius, Geograph. Antiq. part
iii. p. 96. Shaw's Travels, p. 90; and for the adjacent country, (which
is terminated by Cape Bona, or the promontory of Mercury,) l'Afrique
de Marmol. tom. ii. p. 494. There are the remains of an aqueduct
near Curubis, or Curbis, at present altered into Gurbes; and Dr. Shaw
read an inscription, which styles that city *Colonia Fulvia*. The deacon
Pontius (in Vit. Cyprian. c. 12) calls it "Apricum et competentem
locum, hospitium pro voluntate secretum, et quicquid apponi eis ante
promissum est, qui regnum et justitiam Dei quærunt."

[83] See Cyprian. Epistol. 77, edit. Fell.

[84] Upon his conversion, he had sold those gardens for the benefit
of the poor. The indulgence of God (most probably the liberality of
some Christian friend) restored them to Cyprian. See Pontius, c. 15.

[85] When Cyprian, a twelvemonth before, was sent into exile, he
dreamt that he should be put to death the next day. The event

app:ehended, Galerius Maximus, proconsul of Africa, received .he Imperial warrant for the execution of the Christian teachers. The oishop of Carthage was sensible that he should be singled out for one of the first victims; and the frailty of nature tempted him to withdraw himself, by a secret flight, from the danger and the honor of martyrdom;* but soon recovering that fortitude which his character required, he returned to his gardens, and patiently expected the ministers of death. Two officers of rank, who were intrusted with that commission, placed Cyprian between them in a chariot; and as the proconsul was not then at leisure, they conducted him, not to a prison, but to a private house in Carthage, which belonged to one of them. An elegant supper was provided for the entertainment of the bishop, and his Christian friends were permitted for the last time to enjoy his society, whilst the streets were filled with a multitude of the faithful, anxious and alarmed at the approaching fate of their spiritual father.[86] In the morning he appeared before the tribunal of the proconsul, who, after informing himself of the name and situation of Cyprian, commanded him to offer sacrifice, and pressed him to reflect on the consequences of his disobedience. The refusal of Cyprian was firm and decisive; and the magistrate, when he had taken the opinion of his council, pronounced with some reluctance the sentence of death. It was conceived in the following terms: " That Thascius Cyprianus should be

---

made it necessary to explain that word, as signifying a year. Pontius, c. 12.

[86] Pontius (c. 15) acknowledges that Cyprian, with whom he supped, passed the night custodiâ delicatâ. The bishop exercised a last and very proper act of jurisdiction, by directing that the younger females, who watched in the street, should be removed from the dangers and temptations of a nocturnal crowd. Act. Proconsularia, c. 2.

---

* This was not, as it appears, the motive which induced St. Cyprian to conceal himself for a short time: he was threatened to be carried to Utica: ne preferred remaining at Carthage, in order to suffer martyrdom in the midst of his flock, and in order that his death might conduce to the edification of those whom he had guided during life. Such, at least, is his own explanation of his conduct in one of his letters: Cum perlatum ad nos fuisset, fratres carissimi, frumentarios esse missos qui me Uticam perducerent, consilioque carissimorum persuasum est, ut de hortis interim secederemus, justâ interveniente causâ, consensi; eo quod congruat episcopum in eâ civitate, in quâ Ecclesiæ dominicæ præest, illic Dominum confiteri et plebem universam præpositi præsentis confessione clarificari Ep. 83. -- G.

immediately beheaded, as the enemy of the gods of Rome and as the chief and ringleader of a criminal association, which he had seduced into an impious resistance against the laws of the most holy emperors, Valerian and Gallienus."[87] The manner of his execution was the mildest and least painful that could be inflicted on a person convicted of any capital offence; nor was the use of torture admitted to obtain from the bishop of Carthage either the recantation of his principles, or the discovery of his accomplices.

As soon as the sentence was proclaimed, a general cry of "We will die with him," arose at once among the listening multitude of Christians who waited before the palace gates. The generous effusions of their zeal and their affection were neither serviceable to Cyprian nor dangerous to themselves. He was led away under a guard of tribunes and centurions, without resistance and without insult, to the place of his execution, a spacious and level plain near the city, which was already filled with great numbers of spectators. His faithful presbyters and deacons were permitted to accompany their holy bishop.* They assisted him in laying aside his upper garment, spread linen on the ground to catch the precious relics of his blood, and received his orders to bestow five-and-twenty pieces of gold on the executioner. The martyr then covered his face with his hands, and at one blow his head was separated from his body. His corpse remained during some hours exposed to the curiosity of the Gentiles: but in the night it was removed, and transported in a triumphal procession, and with a splendid illumination, to the burial-place of the Christians. The funeral of Cyprian was publicly celebrated without receiving any interruption from the Roman magistrates; and those among the faithful, who had performed the last offices to his person and his memory, were secure from the danger of inquiry or of punishment. It is remarkable, that of so great a multitude of bishops in the province of

---

[87] See the original sentence in the Acts, c. 4; and in Pontius, c. 17. The latter expresses it in a more rhetorical manner.

---

* There is nothing in the life of St. Cyprian, by Pontius, nor in the ancient manuscripts, which can make us suppose that the presbyters and deacons, in their clerical character, and known to be such, had the permission to attend their holy bishop. Setting aside all religious considerations, it is impossible not to be surprised at the kind of complaisance with which the historian here insists, in favor of the persecutors, on some mitigating circumstances allowed at the death of a man whose only crime was maintaining his own opinions with frankness and courage. - G.

Afri*c*a, Cyprian was the first who was esteemed worthy to obtain the crown of martyrdom.[88]

It was in the choice of Cyprian, either to die a martyr, or to live an apostate : but on that choice depended the alternative of honor or infamy. Could we suppose that the bishop of Carthage had employed the profession of the Christian faith only as the instrument of his avarice or ambition, it was still incumbent on him to support the character he had assumed ;[89] and if he possessed the smallest degree of manly fortitude, rather to expose himself to the most cruel tortures, than by a single act to exchange the reputation of a whole life, for the abhorrence of his Christian brethren, and the contempt of the Gentile world. But if the zeal of Cyprian was supported by the sincere conviction of the truth of those doctrines which he preached, the crown of martyrdom must have appeared to him as an object of desire rather than of terror. It is not easy to extract any distinct ideas from the vague though eloquent declamations of the Fathers, or to ascertain the degree of immortal glory and happiness which they con fidently promised to those who were so fortunate as to shed their blood in the cause of religion.[90] They inculcated with becoming diligence, that the fire of martyrdom supplied every defect and expiated every sin ; that while the souls of ordinary Christians were obliged to pass through a slow and painful

---

[88] Pontius, c. 19. M. de Tillemont (Mémoires, tom. iv. part i. p. 150, note 50) is not pleased with so positive an exclusion of any former martyrs of the episcopal rank.*

[89] Whatever opinion we may entertain of the character or principles of Thomas Becket, we must acknowledge that he suffered death with a constancy not unworthy of the primitive martyrs. See Lord Lyttleton's History of Henry II. vol. ii. p. 592, &c.

[90] See in particular the treatise of Cyprian de Lapsis, p. 87—98, edit. Fell. The learning of Dodwell, (Dissertat. Cyprianic. xii. xiii.,) and the ingenuity of Middleton, (Free Inquiry, p. 162, &c.,) have left scarcely any thing to add concerning the merit, the honors, and the motives of the martyrs.

---

* M. de Tillemont, as an honest writer, explains the difficulties which *h*e felt about the text of Pontius, and concludes by distinctly stating, that without doubt there is some mistake, and that Pontius must have meant only Africa Minor or Carthage; for St. Cyprian. in his 58th (69th) letter addressed to Pupianus, speaks expressly of many bishops his colleagues, qui proscripti sunt, vel apprehensi in carcere et catenis fuerunt; aut qui n exilium relegati, illustri itinere ad Dominum profecti sunt; aut qui quibusdam locis animadversi, coelestes coronas de Domini clarificatione sumpserunt. — G.

purification, the triumphant sufferers entered into the immediate fruition of eternal bliss, where, in the society of the
patriarchs, the apostles, and the prophets, they reigned with
Christ, and acted as his assessors in the universal judgment
of mankind. The assurance of a lasting reputation upon
earth, a motive so congenial to the vanity of human nature,
often served to animate the courage of the martyrs. The
honors which Rome or Athens bestowed on those citizens who
had fallen in the cause of their country, were cold and un-
meaning demonstrations of respect, when compared with the
ardent gratitude and devotion which the primitive church
expressed towards the victorious champions of the faith. The
annual commemoration of their virtues and sufferings was
observed as a sacred ceremony, and at length terminated in
religious worship. Among the Christians who had publicly
confessed their religious principles, those who (as it very
frequently happened) had been dismissed from the tribunal or
the prisons of the Pagan magistrates, obtained such honors as
were justly due to their imperfect martyrdom and their generous resolution. The most pious females courted the permission of imprinting kisses on the fetters which they had
worn, and on the wounds which they had received. Their
persons were esteemed holy, their decisions were admitted
with deference, and they too often abused, by their spiritual
pride and licentious manners, the preëminence which their
zeal and intrepidity had acquired.[91] Distinctions like these,
whilst they display the exalted merit, betray the inconsiderable number of those who suffered, and of those who died, for
the profession of Christianity.

The sober discretion of the present age will more readily

---

[91] Cyprian. Epistol. 5, 6, 7, 22, 24 ; * and de Unitat. Ecclesiæ. The
number of pretended martyrs has been very much multiplied, by the
custom which was introduced of bestowing that honorable name on
confessors.

---

* M. Guizot denies that the letters of Cyprian, to which he refers, bear
out the statement in the text. I cannot scruple to admit the accuracy of
Gibbon's quotation. To take only the fifth letter, we find this passage:
Doleo enim quando audio quosdam improbe et insolenter discurrere, et ad
neptias vel ad discordias vacare, Christi membra et jam Christum confessa
per concubitus illicitos inquinari, nec a diaconis aut presbyteris regi posse,
sed id agere ut per paucorum pravos et malos mores, multorum et bonorum
confessorum gloria honesta maculetur. Gibbon's misrepresentation lies in
the ambiguous expression " too often." Were the epistles arranged in a
different manner in the edition consulted by M. Guizot ? — M.

censure than admire, but can more easily admire than imitate, the fervor of the first Christians, who, according to the lively expression of Sulpicius Severus, desired martyrdom with more eagerness than his own contemporaries solicited a bishopric.[92] The epistles which Ignatius composed as he was carried in chains through the cities of Asia, breathe sentiments the most repugnant to the ordinary feelings of human nature. He earnestly beseeches the Romans, that when he should be exposed in the amphitheatre, they would not, by their kind but unreasonable intercession, deprive him of the crown of glory ; and he declares his resolution to provoke and irritate the wild beasts which might be employed as the instruments of his death.[93] Some stories are related of the courage of martyrs, who actually performed what Ignatius had intended , who exasperated the fury of the lions, pressed the executioner to hasten his office, cheerfully leaped into the fires which were kindled to consume them, and discovered a sensation of joy and pleasure in the midst of the most exquisite tortures. Several examples have been preserved of a zeal impatient of those restraints which the emperors had provided for the security of the church. The Christians sometimes supplied by their voluntary declaration the want of an accuser, rudely disturbed the public service of paganism,[94] and rushing in crowds round the tribunal of the magistrates, called upon them to pronounce and to inflict the sentence of the law. The behavior of the Christians was too remarkable to escape the notice of the ancient philosophers ; but they seem to have considered it with much less admiration than astonishment. Incapable of conceiving the motives which sometimes transported the fortitude of believers beyond the bounds of prudence or reason, they treated such an eagerness to die as the

[92] Certatim gloriosa in certamina ruebatur; multique avidius tum martyria gloriosis mortibus quærebantur, quam nunc Episcopatus pravis ambitionibus appetuntur. Sulpicius Severus, l. ii. He might have omitted the word *nunc.*

[93] See Epist. ad Roman. c. 4, 5, ap. Patres Apostol. tom. ii. p. 27. It suited the purpose of Bishop Pearson (see Vindiciæ Ignatianæ, part ii. c. 9) to justify, by a profusion of examples and authorities, the sentiments of Ignatius.

[94] The story of Polyeuctes, on which Corneille has founded a very beautiful tragedy, is one of the most celebrated, though not perhaps the most authentic, instances of this excessive zeal. We should observe, that the 60th canon of the council of Illiberis refuses the title of martyrs to those who exposed themselves to death, by publicly destroying the idols.

strange result of obstinate despair, of stupid insensibility, or
of superstitious frenzy.[95] " Unhappy men ! " exclaimed
the proconsul Antoninus to the Christians of Asia ; " unhappy
men ! if you are thus weary of your lives, is it so difficult for
you to find ropes and precipices ? " [96] He was extremely
cautious (as it is observed by a learned and pious historian)
of punishing men who had found no accusers but themselves,
the Imperial laws not having made any provision for so
unexpected a case : condemning therefore a few as a warn-
ing to their brethren, he dismissed the multitude with indignation and contempt [97] Notwithstanding this real or affected
disdain, the intrepid constancy of the faithful was productive
of more salutary effects on those minds which nature or grace
had disposed for the easy reception of religious truth.   On
these melancholy occasions, there were many among the
Gentiles who pitied, who admired, and who were converted.
The generous enthusiasm was communicated from the sufferer
to the spectators ; and the blood of martyrs, according to
a well-known observation, became the seed of the church.

But although devotion had raised, and eloquence continued
to inflame, this fever of the mind, it insensibly gave way to
the more natural hopes and fears of the human heart, to the
love of life, the apprehension of pain, and the horror of dissolution. The more prudent rulers of the church found themselves obliged to restrain the indiscreet ardor of their followers,
and to distrust a constancy which too often abandoned them in
the hour of trial.[98] As the lives of the faithful become less

[95] See Epictetus, l. iv. c. 7, (though there is some doubt whether
he alludes to the Christians.)   Marcus Antoninus de Rebus suis,
l. xi. c. 3.   Lucian in Peregrin.
[96] Tertullian ad Scapul. c. 5.   The learned are divided between
three persons of the same name, who were all proconsuls of Asia.   I
am inclined to ascribe this story to Antoninus Pius, who was afterwards emperor ; and who may have governed Asia under the reign
of Trajan.
[97] Mosheim, de Rebus Christ. ante Constantin. p. 235.
[98] See the Epistle of the Church of Smyrna, ap. Euseb. Hist. Eccles.
l. iv. c. 15.*

* The 15th chapter of the 10th book of the Eccles. History of Eusebius
treats principally of the martyrdom of St. Polycarp, and mentions some
other martyrs.   A single example of weakness is related ; it is that of a
Phrygian named Quintus, who, appalled at the sight of the wild beasts
and the tortures, renounced his faith.   This example proves little against
the mass of Christians, and this chapter of Eusebius furnished much
stronger evidence of their courage than of their timidity. — G.
This Quintus had, however, rashly and of his own accord appeared

mortified and austere, they were every day less ambitious of
the honors of martyrdom; and the soldiers of Christ, instead
of distinguishing themselves by voluntary deeds of heroism,
frequently deserted their post, and fled in confusion before the
enemy whom it was their duty to resist. There were three
methods, however, of escaping the flames of persecution,
which were not attended with an equal degree of guilt: the
first, indeed, was generally allowed to be innocent; the second was of a doubtful, or at least of a venial, nature; but the
hird implied a direct and criminal apostasy from the Christian
faith.

I. A modern inquisitor would hear with surprise, that
whenever an information was given to a Roman magistrate
of any person within his jurisdiction who had embraced the
sect of the Christians, the charge was communicated to the
party accused, and that a convenient time was allowed him to
settle his domestic concerns, and to prepare an answer to the
crime which was imputed to him.[99] If he entertained any
doubt of his own constancy, such a delay afforded him the
opportunity of preserving his life and honor by flight, of with-
drawing himself into some obscure retirement or some distant

---

[99] In the second apology of Justin, there is a particular and very
curious instance of this legal delay. The same indulgence was granted to accused Christians, in the persecution of Decius: and Cyprian
(de Lapsis) expressly mentions the " Dies negantibus praestitutus." *

---

before the tribunal; and the church of Smyrna condemn "*his indiscreet
ardor*," coupled as it was with weakness in the hour of trial. — M.

* The examples drawn by the historian from Justin Martyr and Cyprian
relate altogether to particular cases, and prove nothing as to the general
practice adopted towards the accused; it is evident, on the contrary, from
the same apology of St. Justin, that they hardly ever obtained delay. "A
man named Lucius, himself a Christian, present at an unjust sentence
passed against a Christian by the judge Urbicus, asked him why he thus
punished a man who was neither adulterer nor robber, nor guilty of any
other crime but that of avowing himself a Christian." Urbicus answered
only in these words: "Thou also hast the appearance of being a Christian." "Yes, without doubt," replied Lucius. The judge ordered that
he should be put to death on the instant. A third, who came up, was condemned to be beaten with rods. Here, then, are three examples where
no delay was granted. [Surely these acts of a single passionate and irritated judge prove the general practice as little as those quoted by Gibbon. — M.] There exist a multitude of others, such as those of Ptole-
my, Marcellus, &c. Justin expressly charges the judges with ordering
the accused to be executed without hearing the cause. The words of St.
Cyprian are as particular, and simply say, that he had appointed a day by
which the Christians must have renounced their faith; those who had
not done it by that time were condemned. — G. This confirms the state
ment in the text. — M.

province, and of patiently expecting the return of peace and security. A measure so consonant to reason was soon authorized by the advice and example of the most holy prelates, and seems to have been censured by few, except by the Montanists, who deviated into heresy by their strict and obstinate adherence to the rigor of ancient discipline.[100] II. The provincial governors, whose zeal was less prevalent than their avarice, had countenanced the practice of selling certificates, (or libels, as they were called,) which attested, that the persons therein mentioned had complied with the laws, and sacrificed to the Roman deities. By producing these false declarations, the opulent and timid Christians were enabled to silence the malice of an informer, and to reconcile in some measure their safety with their religion. A slight penance atoned for this profane dissimulation.[101] * III. In every persecution there were great numbers of unworthy Christians who publicly disowned or renounced the faith which they had professed; and who confirmed the sincerity of their abjuration, by the legal acts of burning incense or of offering sacrifices. Some of these apostates had yielded on the first menace or exhortation of the magistrate; whilst the patience of others had been subdued by the length and repetition of tortures. The affrighted countenances of some betrayed their inward remorse, while others advanced with confidence and alacrity to the altars of the gods.[102] But the disguise which fear had imposed, subsisted no longer than the present danger. As soon as the severity of the persecution was abated, the doors of the churches were assailed by the returning multitude of

---

[100] Tertullian considers flight from persecution as an imperfect, but very criminal, apostasy, as an impious attempt to elude the will of God, &c., &c. He has written a treatise on this subject, (see p. 536—544, edit. Rigalt.,) which is filled with the wildest fanaticism and the most incoherent declamation. It is, however, somewhat remarkable, hat Tertullian did not suffer martyrdom himself.

[101] The *libellatici*, who are chiefly known by the writings of Cyprian, are described with the utmost precision, in the copious commentary of Mosheim, p. 483—489.

[102] Plin. Epistol. x. 97. Dionysius Alexandrin. ap. Euseb. l. vi. c. 41. Ad prima statim verba minantis inimici maximus fratrum numerus fidem suam prodidit: nec prostratus est persecutionis impetu, sed voluntario lapsu seipsum prostravit. Cyprian. Opera, p. 89. Among these deserters were many priests, and even bishops.

---

* The penance was not so slight, for it was exactly the same with that of apostates who had sacrificed to idols; it lasted several years. See Fleury, Hist. Ecc. v. ii. p. 171.—G.

penitents who detested their idolatrous submission, and who solicited with equal ardor, but with various success, their read-mission into the society of Christians.[103] *

IV. Notwithstanding the general rules established for the conviction and punishment of the Christians, the fate of those sectaries, in an extensive and arbitrary government, must still in a great measure, have depended on their own behavior, the circumstances of the times, and the temper of their supreme as well as subordinate rulers. Zeal might sometimes provoke and prudence might sometimes avert or assuage, the super-stitious fury of the Pagans. A variety of motives might dis-pose the provincial governors either to enforce or to relax the execution of the laws ; and of these motives the most forcible was their regard not only for the public edicts, but for the secret intentions of the emperor, a glance from whose eye was sufficient to kindle or to extinguish the flames of perse-cution. As often as any occasional severities were exercised in the different parts of the empire, the primitive Christians .amented and perhaps magnified their own sufferings ; but the celebrated number of *ten* persecutions has been deter-mined by the ecclesiastical writers of the fifth century, who possessed a more distinct view of the prosperous or adverse fortunes of the church, from the age of Nero to that of Dio-cletian. The ingenious parallels of the *ten* plagues of Egypt, and of the *ten* horns of the Apocalypse, first suggested this calculation to their minds ; and in their application of the faith of prophecy to the truth of history, they were careful to select those reigns which were indeed the most hostile to the

---

[103] It was on this occasion that Cyprian wrote his treatise De Lapsis and many of his epistles. The controversy concerning the treatment of penitent apostates, does not occur among the Christians of the pre-ceding century. Shall we ascribe this to the superiority of their faith and courage, or to our less intimate knowledge of their history ?

---

* Pliny says, that the greater part of the Christians persisted in avow-ing themselves to be so ; the reason for his consulting Trajan was the periclitantium numerus. Eusebius (l. vi. c. 41) does not permit us to doubt that the number of those who renounced their faith was infinitely below the number of those who boldly confessed it. The prefect, he says, and his assessors present at the council, were alarmed at seeing the crowd of Christians ; the judges themselves trembled. Lastly, St. Cyprian in-forms us, that the greater part of those who had appeared weak brethren in the persecution of Decius, signalized their courage in that of Gallus. Steterunt fortes, et ipso dolore pœnitentiæ facti ad prælium fortiores Epist. lx. p. 142 — G.

Christian cause.[104]   But these transient persecutions served
only to revive the zeal and to restore the discipline of the
faithful ; and the moments of extraordinary rigor were compensated by much longer intervals of peace and security.
The indifference of some princes, and the indulgence of
others, permitted the Christians to enjoy, though not perhaps
a legal, yet an actual and public, toleration of their religion.

The apology of Tertullian contains two very ancient, very
singular, but at the same time very suspicious, instances of
Imperial clemency ; the edicts published by Tiberius, and by
Marcus Antoninus, and designed not only to protect the innocence of the Christians, but even to proclaim those stupendous miracles which had attested the truth of their doctrine.
The first of these examples is attended with some difficulties
which might perplex a sceptical mind.[105]   We are required
to believe, *that* Pontius Pilate informed the emperor of the
unjust sentence of death which he had pronounced against an
innocent, and, as it appeared, a divine, person ; and that,
without acquiring the merit, he exposed himself to the danger of martyrdom ; *that* Tiberius, who avowed his contempt
for all religion, immediately conceived the design of placing
the Jewish Messiah among the gods of Rome ; *that* his servile
senate ventured to disobey the commands of their master ;
that Tiberius, instead of resenting their refusal, contented
himself with protecting the Christians from the severity of the
laws, many years before such laws were enacted, or before
the church had assumed any distinct name or existence ; and
lastly, *that* the memory of this extraordinary transaction was
preserved in the most public and authentic records, which
escaped the knowledge of the historians of Greece and Rome,
and were only visible to the eyes of an African Christian, who
composed his apology one hundred and sixty years after the
death of Tiberius.   The edict of Marcus Antoninus is supposed to have been the effect of his devotion and gratitude,
for the miraculous deliverance which he had obtained in the

---

[104] See Mosheim, p. 97.   Sulpicius Severus was the first author of
this computation ; though he seemed desirous of reserving the tenth
and greatest persecution for the coming of the Antichrist.

[105] The testimony given by Pontius Pilate is first mentioned by
Justin.   The successive improvements which the story acquired (as it
has passed through the hands of Tertullian, Eusebius, Epiphanius,
Chrysostom, Orosius, Gregory of Tours, and the authors of the sev-
eral editions of the acts of Pilate) are very fairly stated by Dom
Calmet, Dissertat. sur 'Ecriture, tom. iii p. 651, &c.

Marcomannic war. The distress of the legions, the seasona ble tempest of rain and hail, of thunder and of lightning, and the dismay and defeat of the barbarians, have been celebrated by the eloquence of several Pagan writers. If there were any Christians in that army, it was natural that they should ascribe some merit to the fervent prayers, which, in the moment of danger, they had offered up for their own and the public safety. But we are still assured by monuments of brass and marble, by the Imperial medals, and by the Antonine column, that neither the prince nor the people entertained any sense of this signal obligation, since they unanimously attribute their deliverance to the providence of Jupiter, and to the interposition of Mercury. During the whole course of his reign, Marcus despised the Christians as a philosopher, ana punished them as a sovereign.[106] *

By a singular fatality, the hardships which they had endured under the government of a virtuous prince, immediately ceased on the accession of a tyrant; and as none except themselves had experienced the injustice of Marcus, so they

---

[106] On this miracle, as it is commonly called, of the thundering legion, see the admirable criticism of Mr. Moyle, in his Works, vol. ii. p. 81—390.

---

* Gibbon, with this phrase, and that below, which admits the injustice of Marcus, has dexterously glossed over one of the most remarkable facts in the early Christian history, that the reign of the wisest and most humane of the heathen emperors was the most fatal to the Christians. Most writers have ascribed the persecutions under Marcus to the latent bigotry of his character; Mosheim, to the influence of the philosophic party : but the fact is admitted by all. A late writer (Mr. Waddington, Hist. of the Church, p. 47) has not scrupled to assert, that "this prince polluted every year of a long reign with innocent blood;" but the causes as well as the date of the persecutions authorized or permitted by Marcus are equally uncertain.

Of the Asiatic edict recorded by Melito, the date is unknown, nor is it quite clear that it was an Imperial edict. If it was the act under which Polycarp suffered, his martyrdom is placed by Ruinart in the sixth, by Mosheim in the ninth, year of the reign of Marcus. The martyrs of Vienne and Lyons are assigned by Dodwell to the seventh, by most writers to the seventeenth. In fact, the commencement of the persecutions of the Christians appears to synchronize exactly with the period of the breaking out of the Marcomannic war, which seems to have alarmed the whole empire, and the emperor himself, into a paroxysm of returning piety to their gods, of which the Christians were the victims. See Jul. Capit. Script. Hist. August. p. 181, edit. 1661. It is remarkable that Tertullian (Apologet. c. v.) distinctly asserts that Verus (M. Aurelius) issued no edicts against the Christians, and almost positively exempts him from the charge of persecution. — M.

This remarkable synchronism, which explains the persecutions under M. Aurelius, is shown at length in Milman's History of Christianity, book ii. c. 7. — M. 1845.

alone were protected by the lenity of Commodus. The celebrated Marcia, the most favored of his concubines, and who at length contrived the murder of her Imperial lover, entertained a singular affection for the oppressed church; and though it was impossible that she could reconcile the practice of vice with the precepts of the gospel, she might hope to atone for the frailties of her sex and profession by declaring herself the patroness of the Christians.[107] Under the gracious protection of Marcia, they passed in safety the thirteen years of a cruel tyranny; and when the empire was established in the house of Severus, they formed a domestic but more honorable connection with the new court. The emperor was persuaded, that in a dangerous sickness, he had derived some benefit, either spiritual or physical, from the holy oil, with which one of his slaves had anointed him. He always treated with peculiar distinction several persons of both sexes who had embraced the new religion. The nurse as well as the preceptor of Caracalla were Christians; * and if that young prince ever betrayed a sentiment of humanity, it was occasioned by an incident, which, however trifling, bore some relation to the cause of Christianity.[108] Under the reign of Severus, the fury of the populace was checked; the rigor of ancient laws was for some time suspended; and the provincial governors were satisfied with receiving an annual present from the churches within their jurisdiction, as the price, or as the reward, of their moderation.[109] The controversy concerning the precise time of the celebration of Easter, armed the bishops of Asia and Italy against each other, and was considered as the most important business of

---

[107] Dion Cassius, or rather his abbreviator Xiphilin, l. lxxii. p. 1206. Mr. Moyle (p. 266) has explained the condition of the church under the reign of Commodus.

[108] Compare the life of Caracalla in the Augustan History, with the epistle of Tertullian to Scapula. Dr. Jortin (Remarks on Ecclesiastical History, vol. ii. p. 5, &c.) considers the cure of Severus by the means of holy oil, with a strong desire to convert it into a miracle.

[109] Tertullian de Fugâ, c. 13. The present was made during the feast of the Saturnalia; and it is a matter of serious concern to Tertullian, that the faithful should be confounded with the most infamous professions which purchased the connivance of the government.

---

* The Jews and Christians contest the honor of having furnished a nurse to the fratricide son of Severus Caracalla. Hist. of Jews, iii. 158. — M.

this period of eisure and tranquillity.[110] Nor was the peace of the church interrupted, till the increasing numbers of proselytes seem at length to have attracted the attention, and to have alienated the mind of Severus. With the design of restraining the progress of Christianity, he published an edict which, though it was designed to affect only the new converts, could not be carried into strict execution, without exposing to danger and punishment the most zealous of their teachers and missionaries. In this mitigated persecution we may still discover the indulgent spirit of Rome and of Polytheism, which so readily admitted every excuse in favor of those who practised the religious ceremonies of their fathers.[111]

But the laws which Severus had enacted soon expired with the authority of that emperor ; and the Christians, after this accidental tempest, enjoyed a calm of thirty-eight years.[112] Till this period they had usually held their assemblies in private houses and sequestered places. They were now permitted to erect and consecrate convenient edifices for the purpose of religious worship ; [113] to purchase lands, even at Rome itself, for the use of the community ; and to conduct the elections of their ecclesiastical ministers in so public, but at the same time in so exemplary a manner, as to deserve the respectful attention of the Gentiles.[114] This long repose of the church was accompanied with dignity. The reigns of those princes who derived their extraction from the Asiatic provinces, proved the most favorable to the Christians ; the eminent persons of the sect, instead of being reduced to implore the protection of a slave or concubine, were admitted into the palace in the honorable characters of priests and

---

[110] Euseb. l. v. c. 23, 24. Mosheim, p. 435—447.

[111] Judæos fieri sub gravi pœna vetuit. Idem etiam de Christianis sanxit. Hist. August. p. 70.

[112] Sulpicius Severus, l. ii. p. 384. This computation (allowing for a single exception) is confirmed by the history of Eusebius, and by the writings of Cyprian.

[113] The antiquity of Christian churches is discussed by Tillemont, (Mémoires Ecclesiastiques, tom. iii. part ii. p. 68—72,) and by Mr. Moyle, (vol. i. p. 378—398.) The former refers the first construction of them to the peace of Alexander Severus ; the latter, to the peace of Gallienus.

[114] See the Augustan History, p. 130. The emperor Alexander adopted their method of publicly proposing the names of those persons who were candidates for ordination. It is true, that the honor of this practice is likewise attributed to the Jews.

philosophers; and their mysterious doctrinces, which were already diffused among the people, insensibly attracted the curiosity of their sovereign. When the empress Mammæa passed through Antioch, she expressed a desire of conversing with the celebrated Origen, the fame of whose piety and learning was spread over the East. Origen obeyed so flattering an invitation, and though he could not expect to succeed in the conversion of an artful and ambitious woman, she listened with pleasure to his eloquent exhortations, and honorably dismissed him to his retirement in Palestine.[115] The sentiments of Mammæa were adopted by her son Alexander, and the philosophic devotion of that emperor was marked by a singular but injudicious regard for the Christian religion. In his domestic chapel he placed the statues of Abraham, of Orpheus, of Apollonius, and of Christ, as an honor justly due to those respectable sages who had instructed mankind in the various modes of addressing their homage to the supreme and universal Deity.[116] A purer faith, as well as worship, was openly professed and practised among his household. Bishops, perhaps for the first time, were seen at court; and, after the death of Alexander, when the inhuman Maximin discharged his fury on the favorites and servants of his unfortunate benefactor, a great number of Christians of every rank, and of both sexes, were involved in the promiscuous massacre, which, on their account, has properly received the name of Persecution.[117] *

---

[115] Euseb. Hist. Ecclesiast. l. vi. c. 21. Hieronym. de Script. Eccles. c. 54. Mammæa was styled a holy and pious woman, both by the Christians and the Pagans. From the former, therefore, it was impossible that she should deserve that honorable epithet.

[116] See the Augustan History, p. 123. Mosheim (p. 465) seems to refine too much on the domestic religion of Alexander. His design of building a public temple to Christ, (Hist. August. p. 129,) and the objection which was suggested either to him, or in similar circumstances to Hadrian, appear to have no other foundation than an improbable report, invented by the Christians, and credulously adopted by an historian of the age of Constantine.

[117] Euseb. l. vi. c. 28. It may be presumed that the success of the Christians had exasperated the increasing bigotry of the Pagans.

---

* It is with good reason that this massacre has been called a persecution, for it lasted during the whole reign of Maximin, as may be seen in Eusebius. (l. vi. c. 28.) Rufinus expressly confirms it: Tribus annis a Maximino persecutione commotâ, in quibus finem et persecutionis fecit et vitæ Hist. l. vi. c. 19. — G.

Notwithstanding the cruel disposition of Max min, the effects of his resentment against the Christians were of a very local and temporary nature, and the pious Origen, who had been proscribed as a devoted victim, was still reserved to convey the truths of the gospel to the ear of monarchs.[118] He ad-dressed several edifying letters to the emperor Philip, to h.s wife, and to his mother; and as soon as that prince, who was born in the neighborhood of Palestine, had usurped the Impe-rial sceptre, the Christians acquired a friend and a protector. The public and even partial favor of Philip towards the sec-taries of the new religion, and his constant reverence for the ministers of the church, gave some color to the suspicion, which prevailed in his own times, that the emperor himself was become a convert to the faith;[119] and afforded some grounds for a fable which was afterwards invented, that he had been purified by confession and penance from the guilt

---

Dion Cassius, who composed his history under the former reign, had most probably intended for the use of his master those counsels of persecution, which he ascribes to a better age, and to the favorite of Augustus. Concerning this oration of Mæcenas, or rather of Dion,* I may refer to my own unbiased opinion, (vol. i. c. 1, note 25,) and to the Abbé de la Bleterie (Mémoires de l'Académie, tom. xxiv. p. 303, tom. xxv. p. 432.)

[118] Orosius, l. vii. c. 19, mentions Origen as the object of Maximin's resentment; and Firmilianus, a Cappadocian bishop of that age, gives a just and confined idea of this persecution, (apud Cyprian. Epist. 75.)

[119] The mention of those princes who were publicly supposed to be Christians, as we find it in an epistle of Dionysius of Alexandria, (ap. Euseb. l. vii. c. 10,) evidently alludes to Philip and his family, and forms a contemporary evidence, that such a report had prevailed; but the Egyptian bishop, who lived at an humble distance from the court of Rome, expresses himself with a becoming diffidence concern-ing the truth of the fact. The epistles of Origen (which were extant in the time of Eusebius, see l. vi. c. 36) would most probably decide this curious, rather than important, question.

---

* If this be the case, Dion Cassius must have known the Christians; they must have been the subject of his particular attention, since the author supposes that he wished his master to profit by these " counsels of persecution." How are we to reconcile this necessary consequence with what Gibbon has said of the ignorance of Dion Cassius even of the name of the Christians? (c. xvi. n. 24.) [Gibbon speaks of Dion's *silence*, not of his *ignorance.* — M.] The supposition in this note is supported by no proof; it is probable that Dion Cassius has often designated the Chris-tians by the name of Jews. See Dion Cassius, l. lxvii. c. 14, lxviii. 1 — G.

On this point I should adopt the view of Gibbon rather than that of M Guizot. — M

contracted by the murder of his innocent predecessor.[120]
The fall of Philip introduced, with the change of masters, a
new system of government, so oppressive to the Christians,
that their former condition, ever since the time of Domitian,
was represented as a state of perfect freedom and security
if compared with the rigorous treatment which they experienced under the short reign of Decius.[121]   The virtues of
that prince will scarcely allow us to suspect that he was actuated by a mean resentment against the favorites of his predecessor; and it is more reasonable to believe, that in the prosecution of his general design to restore the purity of Roman
manners, he was desirous of delivering the empire from what
he condemned as a recent and criminal superstition.   The
bishops of the most considerable cities were removed by exile
or death: the vigilance of the magistrates prevented the
clergy of Rome during sixteen months from proceeding to a
new election; and it was the opinion of the Christians, that
the emperor would more patiently endure a competitor for the
purple, than a bishop in the capital.[122]   Were it possible to
suppose that the penetration of Decius had discovered pride
under the disguise of humility, or that he could foresee the
temporal dominion which might insensibly arise from the
claims of spiritual authority, we might be less surprised, that
he should consider the successors of St. Peter as the most
formidable rivals to those of Augustus.

The administration of Valerian was distinguished by a
levity and inconstancy ill suited to the gravity of the *Roman
Censor*.   In the first part of his reign, he surpassed in clemency those princes who had been suspected of an attachment
to the Christian faith.   In the last three years and a half, listening to the insinuations of a minister addicted to the superstitions of Egypt, he adopted the maxims, and imitated the

---

[120] Euseb. l. vi. c. 34.   The story, as is usual, has been embellished
by succeeding writers, and is confuted, with much superfluous learning, by Frederick Spanheim, (Opera Varia, tom. ii. p. 400, &c.)

[121] Lactantius, de Mortibus Persecutorum, c. 3, 4.   After celebrating the felicity and increase of the church, under a long succession
of good princes, he adds, "Extitit post annos plurimos, execrabile
animal, Decius, qui vexaret Ecclesiam."

[122] Euseb. l. vi. c. 39.   Cyprian. Epistol. 55.   The see of Rome remained vacant from the martyrdom of Fabianus, the 20th of January,
A D. 250. till the election of Cornelius, the 4th of June, A. D. 251.
Decius had probably left Rome, since he was killed before the end of
that year.

severity, of his predecessor Decius.[123] The accession of Gallienus, which increased the calamities of the empire, restored
peace to the church ; and the Christians obtained the free
exercise of their religion by an edict addressed to the bishops,
and conceived in such terms as seemed to acknowledge their
office and public character.[124] The ancient laws, without
being formally repealed, were suffered to sink into oblivion ;
and (excepting only some hostile intentions which are attributed to the emperor Aurelian[125]) the disciples of Christ passed
above forty years in a state of prosperity, far more dangerous
to their virtue than the severest trials of persecution.

The story of Paul of Samosata, who filled the metropolitan
see of Antioch, while the East was in the hands of Odena-
thus and Zenobia, may serve to illustrate the condition and
character of the times. The wealth of that prelate was a
sufficient evidence of his guilt, since it was neither derived
from the inheritance of his fathers, nor acquired by the arts
of honest industry. But Paul considered the service of the
church as a very lucrative profession.[126] His ecclesiastical

---

[123] Euseb. l. vii. c. 10. Mosheim (p. 548) has very clearly shown,
that the præfect Macrianus, and the Egyptian *Magus*, are one and the
same person.

[124] Eusebius (l. vii. c. 13) gives us a Greek version of this Latin
edict, which seems to have been very concise. By another edict, he
directed that the *Cœmeteria* should be restored to the Christians.

[125] Euseb. l. vii. c. 30. Lactantius de M. P. c. 6. Hieronym. in
Chron. p. 177. Orosius, l. vii. c. 23. Their language is in general so
ambiguous and incorrect, that we are at a loss to determine how far
Aurelian had carried his intentions before he was assassinated. Most
of the moderns (except Dodwell, Dissertat. Cyprian. xi. 64) have
seized the occasion of gaining a few extraordinary martyrs.*

[126] Paul was better pleased with the title of *Ducenarius*, than with
that of bishop. The *Ducenarius* was an Imperial procurator, so called
from his salary of two hundred *Sestertia*, or 1600*l.* a year. (See Sal
matius ad Hist. August. p. 124.) Some critics suppose that the
bishop of Antioch had actually obtained such an office from Zenobia,

---

* Dr. Lardner has detailed, with his usual impartiality, all that has
come down to us relating to the persecution of Aurelian, and concludes
by saying, "Upon more carefully examining the words of Eusebius, and
observing the accounts of other authors, learned men have generally, and,
as I think, very judiciously, determined, that Aurelian not only intended,
but did actually persecute : but his persecution was short, he having died
soon after the publication of his edicts." Heathen Test. c. xxxvi. — Basnage positively pronounces the same opinion : Non intentatum modo, sed
executum quoque brevissimo tempore mandatum, nobis infixum est in ani
mis. Basn. Ann. 275, No. 2, and compare Pagi Ann. 272, Nos 4, 12,
273. — G.

jurisdiction was venal and rapacious; he extorted frequent contributions from the most opulent of the faithful, and converted to his own use a considerable part of the public revenue. By his pride and luxury, the Christian religion was rendered odious in the eyes of the Gentiles. His council chamber and his throne, the splendor with which he appeared in public, the suppliant crowd who solicited his attention, the multitude of letters and petitions to which he dictated his answers, and the perpetual hurry of business in which he was involved, were circumstances much better suited to the state of a civil magistrate,[127] than to the humility of a primitive bishop. When he harangued his people from the pulpit, Paul affected the figurative style and the theatrical gestures of an Asiatic sophist, while the cathedral resounded with the loudest and most extravagant acclamations in the praise of his divine eloquence. Against those who resisted his power, or refused to flatter his vanity, the prelate of Antioch was arrogant, rigid, and inexorable; but he relaxed the discipline, and lavished the treasures of the church on his dependent clergy, who were permitted to imitate their master in the gratification of every sensual appetite. For Paul indulged himself very freely in the pleasures of the table, and he had received into the episcopal palace two young and beautiful women as the constant companions of his leisure moments.[128]

Notwithstanding these scandalous vices, if Paul of Samosata had preserved the purity of the orthodox faith, his reign over the capital of Syria would have ended only with his life; and had a seasonable persecution intervened, an effort of courage might perhaps have placed him in the rank of saints and martyrs.* Some nice and subtle errors, which he impru-

---

while others consider it only as a figurative expression of his pomp and insolence.

[127] Simony was not unknown in those times; and the clergy sometimes bought what they intended to sell. It appears that the bishopric of Carthage was purchased by a wealthy matron, named Lucilla, for her servant Majorinus. The price was 400 *Folles*. (Monument. Antiq. ad calcem Optati, p. 263.) Every *Follis* contained 125 pieces of silver, and the whole sum may be computed at about 2400*l*.

[128] If we are desirous of extenuating the vices of Paul, we must suspect the assembled bishops of the East of publishing the most malicious calumnies in circular epistles addressed to all the churches of the empire, (ap. Euseb. l. vii. c. 30.)

---

* It appears, nevertheless, that the vices and immoralities of Paul of Samosata had much weight in the sentence pronounced against him by

dently adopted and obstinately maintained, concerning the doctrine of the Trinity, excited the zeal and indignation of the Eastern churches.[129] From Egypt to the Euxine Sea, the bishops were in arms and in motion. Several councils were held, confutations were published, excommunications were pronounced, ambiguous explanations were by turns accepted and refused, treaties were concluded and violated, and at length Paul of Samosata was degraded from his episcopal character, by the sentence of seventy or eighty bishops, who assembled for that purpose at Antioch, and who, without con sulting the rights of the clergy or people, appointed a successor by their own authority. The manifest irregularity of this proceeding increased the numbers of the discontented faction ; and as Paul, who was no stranger to the arts of courts, had insinuated himself into the favor of Zenobia, he maintained above four years the possession of the episcopal house and office.* The victory of Aurelian changed the face of the East, and the two contending parties, who applied to each other the epithets of schism and heresy, were either commanded or permitted to plead their cause before the tribunal of the conqueror. This public and very singular trial affords a convincing proof that the existence, the property, the privileges, and the internal policy of the Christians, were acknowledged, if not by the laws, at least by the magistrates, of the empire. As a Pagan and as a soldier, it could scarcely be expected that Aurelian should enter into the discussion, whether the sentiments of Paul or those of his adversaries were most agreeable to the true standard of the orthodox faith. His determination, however, was founded on the general principles of equity and reason. He considered the

---

[129] His heresy (like those of Noetus and Sabellius, in the same century) tended to confound the mysterious distinction of the divine persons. See Mosheim, p. 702, &c.

---

the bishops. The object of the letter, addressed by the synod to the bish ops of Rome and Alexandria, was to inform them of the change in the faith of Paul, the altercations and discussions to which it had given rise, as well as of his morals and the whole of his conduct. Euseb. Hist. Eccl. l. vii. c. xxx. — G.

* "Her favorite, (Zenobia's,) Paul of Samosata, seems to have enter tained some views of attempting a union between Judaism and Christianity ; both parties rejected the unnatural alliance." Hist. of Jews, iii. 175, and Jost. Geschichte der Israeliter, iv. 167. The protection of the severe Zenobia is the only circumstance which may raise a doubt of the notorious immorality of Paul. — M.

bishops of Italy as the most impartial and respectable judges
among the Christians, and as soon as he was informed that
they had unanimously approved the sentence of the council,
he acquiesced in their opinion, and immediately gave orders
that Paul should be compelled to relinquish the temporal possessions belonging to an office, of which, in the judgment of
his brethren, he had been regularly deprived. But while we
applaud the justice, we should not overlook the policy, of Aurelian, who was desirous of restoring and cementing the dependence of the provinces on the capital, by every means
which could bind the interest or prejudices of any part of his
subjects.[130]

Amidst the frequent revolutions of the empire, the Christians still flourished in peace and prosperity; and notwithstanding a celebrated æra of martyrs has been deduced from
the accession of Diocletian,[131] the new system of policy,
introduced and maintained by the wisdom of that prince,
continued, during more than eighteen years, to breathe the
mildest and most liberal spirit of religious toleration. The
mind of Diocletian himself was less adapted indeed to speculative inquiries, than to the active labors of war and government.
His prudence rendered him averse to any great innovation,
and though his temper was not very susceptible of zeal or
enthusiasm, he always maintained an habitual regard for the
ancient deities of the empire. But the leisure of the two
empresses, of his wife Prisca, and of Valeria, his daughter,
permitted them to listen with more attention and respect to
the truths of Christianity, which in every age has acknowledged its important obligations to female devotion.[132]   The

---

[130] Euseb. Hist. Ecclesiast. l. vii. c. 30. We are entirely indebted
to him for the curious story of Paul of Samosata.

[131] The Æra of Martyrs, which is still in use among the Copts
and the Abyssinians, must be reckoned from the 29th of August,
A. D. 284; as the beginning of the Egyptian year was nineteen days
earlier than the real accession of Diocletian. See Dissertation Pre-
liminaire à l'Art de vérifier les Dates.*

[132] The expression of Lactantius, (de M. P. c. 15,) "sacrificio pollui
coegit," implies their antecedent conversion to the faith, but does not
seem to justify the assertion of Mosheim, (p. 912,) that they had been
privately baptized.

---

* On the æra of martyrs see the very curious dissertations of Mons.
Letronne on some recently discovered inscriptions in Egypt and Nubia, p
102, &c. — M.

principal eunuchs, Lucian [133] and Dorotheus, Gorgonius and Andrew, who attended the person, possessed the favor, and governed the household of Diocletian, protected by their powerful influence the faith which they had embraced. Their example was imitated by many of the most considerable officers of the palace, who, in their respective stations, had the care of the Imperial ornaments, of the robes, of the furniture, of the jewels, and even of the private treasury; and, though it might sometimes be incumbent on them to accompany the emperor when he sacrificed in the temple,[134] they enjoyed with their wives, their children, and their slaves, the free exercise of the Christian religion. Diocletian and his colleagues frequently conferred the most important offices on those persons who avowed their abhorrence for the worship of the gods, but who had displayed abilities proper for the service of the state. The bishops held an honorable rank in their respective provinces, and were treated with distinction and respect, not only by the people, but by the magistrates themselves. Almost in every city, the ancient churches were found insufficient to contain the increasing multitude of proselytes; and in their place more stately and capacious edifices were erected for the public worship of the faithful. The corruption of manners and principles, so forcibly lamented by Eusebius,[135] may be considered, not only as a consequence, but as a proof, of the liberty which the Christians enjoyed and abused under the reign of Diocletian. Prosperity had relaxed the nerves of discipline. Fraud, envy, and malice prevailed in every congregation. The presbyters aspired to the episcopal office, which every day became an object more worthy of their ambition. The bishops, who contended with each other for ecclesiastical preëminence, appeared by their conduct to claim a secular and tyrannical power in the church; and the lively faith which still distinguished the Christians from the Gentiles, was shown much less in their lives, than in their controversial writings.

---

[133] M. de Tillemont (Mémoires Ecclesiastiques, tom. v. part i. p. 11, 12) has quoted from the Spicilegium of Dom Luc d'Archeri a very curious instruction which Bishop Theonas composed for the use of Lucian.

[134] Lactantius, de M. P. c. 10.

[135] Eusebius, Hist. Ecclesiast. l. viii. c. 1. The reader who consults the original will not accuse me of heightening the picture. Eusebius was about sixteen years of age at the accession of the emperor Diocletian.

Notwithstanding this seeming security, an attentive observer might discern some symptoms that threatened the church with a more violent persecution than any which she had yet endured. The zeal and rapid progress of the Christians awakened the Polytheists from their supine indifference in the cause of those deities, whom custom and education had taught them to revere. The mutual provocations of a religious war, which had already continued above two hundred years, exasperated the animosity of the contending parties. The Pagans were incensed at the rashness of a recent and obscure sect, which presumed to accuse their countrymen of error, and to devote their ancestors to eternal misery. The habits of justifying the popular mythology against the invectives of an implacable enemy, produced in their minds some sentiments of faith and reverence for a system which they had been accustomed to consider with the most careless levity. The supernatural powers assumed by the church inspired at the same time terror and emulation. The followers of the established religion intrenched themselves behind a similar fortification of prodigies; invented new modes of sacrifice, of expiation, and of initiation; [136] attempted to revive the credit of their expiring oracles; [137] and listened with eager credulity to every impostor, who flattered their prejudices by a tale of wonders.[138] Both parties seemed to acknowledge the truth of those miracles

---

[136] We might quote, among a great number of instances, the mysterious worship of Mythras,* and the Taurobolia; the latter of which became fashionable in the time of the Antonines, (see a Dissertation of M. de Boze, in the Mémoires de l'Academie des Inscriptions, tom. ii. p. 443.) The romance of Apuleius is as full of devotion as of satire.

[137] The impostor Alexander very strongly recommended the oracle of Trophonius at Mallos, and those of Apollo at Claros and Miletus, (Lucian, tom. ii. p. 236, edit. Reitz.) The last of these, whose singular history would furnish a very curious episode, was consulted by Diocletian before he published his edicts of persecution, (Lactantius, de M. P. c. 11.)

[138] Besides the ancient stories of Pythagoras and Aristeas, the cures performed at the shrine of Æsculapius, and the fables related of Apollonius of Tyana, were frequently opposed to the miracles of Christ; though I agree with Dr. Lardner, (see Testimonies, vol. iii. p. 253, 352,) that when Philostratus composed the life of Apollonius, he had no such intention.

---

* On the extraordinary progress of the Mithriac rites, in the West, see De Guigniaud's translation of Creuzer, vol. i. p. 365, and Note 9, tom. i. part 2, p. 738, &c. — M

which were claimed by their adversaries; and while they were contented with ascribing them to the arts of magic, and to the power of dæmons, they mutually concurred in restoring and establishing the reign of superstition.[139] Philosophy, her most dangerous enemy, was now converted into her most useful ally. The groves of the academy, the gardens of Epicurus, and even the portico of the Stoics, were almost deserted, as so many different schools of scepticism or impiety;[140] and many among the Romans were desirous that the writings of Cicero should be condemned and suppressed by the authority of the senate.[141] The prevailing sect of the new Platonicians judged it prudent to connect themselves with the priests, whom perhaps they despised, against the Christians, whom they had reason to fear. These fashionable Philosophers prosecuted the design of extracting allegorical wisdom from the fictions of the Greek poets; instituted mysterious rites of devotion for the use of their chosen disciples; recommended the worship of the ancient gods as the emblems or ministers of the Supreme Deity, and composed against the faith of the gospel many elaborate treatises,[142] which have since been committed to the flames by the prudence of orthodox emperors.[143]

Although the policy of Diocletian and the humanity of Constantius inclined them to preserve inviolate the maxims of

---

[139] It is seriously to be lamented, that the Christian fathers, by acknowledging the supernatural, 'or, as they deem it, the infernal part of Paganism, destroy with their own hands the great advantage which we might otherwise derive from the liberal concessions of our adversaries.

[140] Julian (p. 301, edit. Spanheim) expresses a pious joy, that the providence of the gods had extinguished the impious sects, and for the most part destroyed the books of the Pyrrhonians and Epicuræans, which had been very numerous, since Epicurus himself composed no less than 300 volumes. See Diogenes Laertius, l. x. c. 26.

[141] Cumque alios audiam mussitare indignanter, et dicere opportere statui per Senatum, aboleantur ut hæc scripta, quibus Christiana Religio comprobetur, et vetustatis opprimatur auctoritas. Arnobius adversus Gentes, l. iii. p. 103, 104. He adds very properly, Erroris convincite Ciceronem . . . nam intercipere scripta, et publicatam velle submergere lectionem, non est Deum defendere sed veritatis testificationem timere.

[142] Lactantius (Divin. Institut. l. v. c. 2, 3) gives a very clear and spirited account of two of these philosophic adversaries of the faith. The large treatise of Porphyry against the Christians consisted of thirty books, and was composed in Sicily about the year 270.

[143] See Socrates, Hist. Ecclesiast. l. i. c. 9, and Codex Justinian. l. i. tit. i. l. 3.

31

toleration, it was soon discovered that their two associates,
Maximian and Galerius, entertained the most implacable aversion for the name and religion of the Christians. The minds
of these princes had never been enlightened by science;
education had never softened their temper. They owed their
greatness to their swords, and in their most elevated fortune
they still retained their superstitious prejudices of soldiers and
peasants. In the general administration of the provinces they
obeyed the laws which their benefactor had established ; but
they frequently found occasions of exercising within their camp
and palaces a secret persecution,[144] for which the imprudent
zeal of the Christians sometimes offered the most specious
pretences. A sentence of death was executed upon Maxi-
milianus, an African youth, who had been produced by his
own father * before the magistrate as a sufficient and legal
recruit, but who obstinately persisted in declaring, that his
conscience would not permit him to embrace the profession
of a soldier.[145] It could scarcely be expected that any government should suffer the action of Marcellus the Centurion to
pass with impunity. On the day of a public festival, that
officer threw away his belt, his arms, and the ensigns of his

---

[144] Eusebius, l. viii. c. 4, c. 17. He limits the number of military
martyrs, by a remarkable expression, (σπανίως τούτων εἴς που καὶ δεύ-
τερος,) of which neither his Latin nor French translator have rendered
the energy. Notwithstanding the authority of Eusebius, and the
silence of Lactantius, Ambrose, Sulpicius, Orosius, &c., it has been
long believed, that the Thebæan legion, consisting of 6000 Christians,
suffered martyrdom by the order of Maximian, in the valley of the
Pennine Alps. The story was first published about the middle of the
5th century, by Eucherius, bishop of Lyons, who received it from
certain persons, who received it from Isaac, bishop of Geneva, who is
said to have received it from Theodore, bishop of Octodurum. The
abbey of St. Maurice still subsists, a rich monument of the credulity
of Sigismund, king of Burgundy. See an excellent Dissertation in
xxxvith volume of the Bibliothèque Raisonnée, p. 427—454.

[145] See the Acta Sincera, p. 299. The accounts of his martyrdom,
and of that of Marcellus, bear every mark of truth and authenticity.

---

* M. Guizot criticizes Gibbon's account of this incident. He supposes
that Maximilian was not "produced by his father as a recruit," but was
obliged to appear by the law, which compelled the sons of soldiers to
serve at 21 years old. Was not this a law of Constantine ? Neither does
this circumstance appear in the acts. His father had clearly expected him
to serve, as he had bought him a new dress for the occasion ; yet he refused
to force the conscience of his son, and when Maximilian was condemned
to death, the father returned home in joy, blessing God for having bestowed upon him such a son. — M.

office, and exclaimed with a loud voice, that he would obey none but Jesus Christ the eternal King, and that he renounced forever the use of carnal weapons, and the service of an idolatrous master. The soldiers, as soon as they recovered from their astonishment, secured the person of Marcellus. He was examined in the city of Tingi by the president of that part of Mauritania ; and as he was convicted by his own confession he was condemned and beheaded for the crime of desertion.[146] Examples of such a nature savor much less of religious persecution than of martial or even civil law ; but they served to alienate the mind of the emperors, to justify the severity of Galerius, who dismissed a great number of Christian officers from their employments; and to authorize the opinion, that a sect of enthusiastics, which avowed principles so repugnant to the public safety, must either remain useless, or would soon become dangerous, subjects of the empire.

After the success of the Persian war had raised the hopes and the reputation of Galerius, he passed a winter with Diocletian in the palace of Nicomedia ; and the fate of Christianity became the object of their secret consultations.[147] The experienced emperor was still inclined to pursue measures of lenity ; and though he readily consented to exclude the Christians from holding any employments in the household or the army, he urged in the strongest terms the danger as well as cruelty of shedding the blood of those deluded fanatics. Galerius at length extorted ‡ from him the permission of

---

[146] Acta Sincera, p. 302.*
[147] De M. P. c. 11. Lactantius (or whoever was the author of this little treatise) was, at that time, an inhabitant of Nicomedia; but it seems difficult to conceive how he could acquire so accurate a knowledge of what passed in the Imperial cabinet.†

---

* M. Guizot here justly observes, that it was the necessity of sacrificing to the gods, which induced Marcellus to act in this manner. — M.
† Lactantius, who was subsequently chosen by Constantine to educate Crispus, might easily have learned these details from Constantine himself, already of sufficient age to interest himself in the affairs of the government, and in a position to obtain the best information. — G.
This assumes the doubtful point of the authorship of the Treatise.—M.
‡ This permission was not extorted from Diocletian; he took the step of his own accord. Lactantius says, in truth, Nec tamen deflectere notuit (Diocletianus) praecipitis hominis insaniam; placuit ergo amicorum sententiam experiri. (De Mort. Pers. c. 11.) But this measure was in accordance with the artificial character of Diocletian, who wished to have the appearance of doing good by his own impulse, and evil by the impulse of others. Nam erat hujus malitiae, cum bonum quid facere decrevisset,

summoning a council, composed of a few persons the most distinguished in the civil and military departments of the state. The important question was agitated in their presence, and those ambitious courtiers easily discerned, that it was incumbent on them to second, by their eloquence, the importunate violence of the Cæsar. It may be presumed, that they insisted on every topic which might interest the pride, the piety, or the fears, of their sovereign in the destruction of Christianity. Perhaps they represented, that the glorious work of the deliverance of the empire was left imperfect, as long as an independent people was permitted to subsist and multiply in the heart of the provinces. The Christians, (it might specially be alleged,) renouncing the gods and the institutions of Rome, had constituted a distinct republic, which might yet be suppressed before it had acquired any military force ; but which was already governed by its own laws and magistrates, was possessed of a public treasure, and was intimately connected in all its parts by the frequent assemblies of the bishops, to whose decrees their numerous and opulent congregations yielded an implicit obedience. Arguments like these may seem to have determined the reluctant mind of Diocletian to embrace a new system of persecution ; but though we may suspect, it is not in our power to relate, the secret intrigues of the palace, the private views and resentments, the jealousy of women or eunuchs, and all those trifling but decisive causes which so often influence the fate of empires, and the councils of the wisest monarchs.[148]

---

[148] The only circumstance which we can discover, is the devotion and jealousy of the mother of Galerius. She is described by Lactantius, as Deorum montium cultrix ; mulier admodum superstitiosa. She had a great influence over her son, and was offended by the disregard of some of her Christian servants.*

---

sine consilio faciebat, ut ipse laudaretur. Cum autem malum, quoniam id reprehendendum sciebat, in consilium multos advocabat, ut aliorum culpæ adscriberetur quicquid ipse deliquerat. Lact. ib. Eutropius says likewise, Miratus callidè fuit, sagax præterea et admodum subtilis ingenio, et qui severitatem suam alienâ invidiâ vellet explere. Eutrop. ix. c. 26. — G.

The manner in which the coarse and unfriendly pencil of the author of the Treatise de Mort. Pers. has drawn the character of Diocletian, seems inconsistent with this profound subtilty. Many readers will perhaps agree with Gibbon. — M.

* This disregard consisted in the Christians fasting and praying instead of participating in the banquets and sacrifices which she celebrated with the Pagans. Dapibus sacrificabat pœne quotidiè, ac vicsriis suis epulis exhibebat. Christiani abstinebant, et illâ cum gentibus epu-

The pleasure of the emperors was at length signified to the Christians, who, during the course of this melancholy winter had expected, with anxiety, the result of so many secret con sultations. The twenty-third of February, which coincided with the Roman festival of the Terminalia,[149] was appointed (whetner from accident or design) to set bounds to the prog. ress of Christianity. At the earliest dawn of day, the Prætorian præfect,[150] accompanied by several generals, tribunes, and officers of the revenue, repaired to the principal church of Nicomedia, which was situated on an eminence in the most populous and beautiful part of the city. The doors were instantly broke open ; they rushed into the sanctuary ; and as they searched in vain for some visible object of worship, they were obliged to content themselves with committing to the flames the volumes of the holy Scripture. The ministers of Diocletian were followed by a numerous body of guards and pioneers, who marched in order of battle, and were provided with all the instruments used in the destruction of fortified cities. By their incessant labor, a sacred edifice, which towered above the Imperial palace, and had long excited the indignation and envy of the Gentiles, was in a few hours levelled with the ground.[151]

The next day the general edict of persecution was pub. ished ;[152] and though Diocletian, still averse to the effusion of blood, had moderated the fury of Galerius, who proposed, that every one refusing to offer sacrifice should immediately be burnt alive, the penalties inflicted on the obstinacy of the Christians might be deemed sufficiently rigorous and effectual. It was enacted, that their churches, in all the provinces of the empire, should be demolished to their foundations ; and the

---

[149] The worship and festival of the god Terminus are elegantly illustrated by M. de Boze, Mém. de l'Academie des Inscriptions, tom. i. p. 50.

[150] In our only MS. of Lactantius, we read *profectus ;* but reason, and the authority of all the critics, allow us, instead of that word, which destroys the sense of the passage, to substitute *præfectus.*

[151] Lactantius, de M. P. c. 12, gives a very lively picture of the destruction of the church.

[152] Mosheim, (p. 922—926,) from many scattered passages f Lactantius and Eusebius, has collected a very just and accurate notion of this edict; though he sometimes deviates into conjecture and refinement.

---

ante, jejuniis hi et orationibus insistebant: hinc concepit odium adversu eos. Lact. de His. Pers. c. 11. — G.

punishment of death was denounced against all who should presume to hold any secret assemblies for the purpose of religious worship. The philosophers, who now assumed the unworthy office of directing the blind zeal of persecution, had diligently studied the nature and genius of the Christian religion; and as they were not ignorant that the speculative doctrines of the faith were supposed to be contained in the writings of the prophets, of the evangelists, and of the apostles they most probably suggested the order, that the bishops and presbyters should deliver all their sacred books into the hands of the magistrates; who were commanded, under the severest penalties, to burn them in a public and solemn manner. By the same edict, the property of the church was at once confiscated; and the several parts of which it might consist were either sold to the highest bidder, united to the Imperial domain, bestowed on the cities and corporations, or granted to the solicitations of rapacious courtiers. After taking such effectual measures to abolish the worship, and to dissolve the government of the Christians, it was thought necessary to subject to the most intolerable hardships the condition of those perverse individuals who should still reject the religion of nature, of Rome, and of their ancestors. Persons of a liberal birth were declared incapable of holding any honors or employments; slaves were forever deprived of the hopes of freedom, and the whole body of the people were put out of the protection of the law. The judges were authorized to hear and to determine every action that was brought against a Christian. But the Christians were not permitted to complain of any injury which they themselves had suffered; and thus those unfortunate sectaries were exposed to the severity, while they were excluded from the benefits, of public justice. This new species of martyrdom, so painful and lingering, so obscure and ignominious, was, perhaps, the most proper to weary the constancy of the faithful: nor can it be doubted that the passions and interest of mankind were disposed on this occasion to second the designs of the emperors. But the policy of a well-ordered government must sometimes have interposed in behalf of the oppressed Christians; * nor was it possible for the Roman princes entirely to remove the apprehension of punishment, or to connive at every act of fraud

---

* This wants proof. The edict of Diocletian was executed in all its rigor during the rest of his reign. Euseb Hist. Eccl. l. viii c. 13. — G

and violence, without exposing their own authority and the rest of their subjects to the most alarming dangers.[153]

This edict was scarcely exhibited to the public view, in the most conspicuous place of Nicomedia, before it was torn down by the hands of a Christian, who expressed at the same time, by the bitterest invectives, his contempt as well as abhorrence for such impious and tyrannical governors. His offence, according to the mildest laws, amounted to treason, and deserved death. And if it be true that he was a person of rank and education, those circumstances could serve only to aggravate his guilt. He was burnt, or rather roasted, by a slow fire and his executioners, zealous to revenge the personal insult which had been offered to the emperors, exhausted every refinement of cruelty, without being able to subdue his patience, or to alter the steady and insulting smile which in his dying agonies he still preserved in his countenance. The Christians, though they confessed that his conduct had not been strictly conformable to the laws of prudence, admired the divine fervor of his zeal; and the excessive commendations which they lavished on the memory of their hero and martyr, contributed to fix a deep impression of terror and hatred in the mind of Diocletian.[154]

His fears were soon alarmed by the view of a danger from which he very narrowly escaped. Within fifteen days the palace of Nicomedia, and even the bed-chamber of Diocletian, were twice in flames; and though both times they were extinguished without any material damage, the singular repetition of the fire was justly considered as an evident proof that it had not been the effect of chance or negligence. The suspicion naturally fell on the Christians; and it was suggested, with some degree of probability, that those desperate fanatics, provoked by their present sufferings, and apprehensive of impending calamities, had entered into a conspiracy with their faithful brethren, the eunuchs of the palace, against the lives of two emperors, whom they detested as the irreconcilable

---

[153] Many ages afterwards, Edward I. practised, with great success, the same mode of persecution against the clergy of England. See Hume's History of England, vol. ii. p 300, last 4to edition.

[154] Lactantius only calls him quidam, et si non recte, magno tamen animo, &c., c. 12. Eusebius (l. viii. c. 5) adorns him with secular honors. Neither have condescended to mention his name; but the Greeks celebrate his memory under that of John. See Tillemont, Mémoires Ecclesiast ques, tom. v. part ii. p. 320.

enemies of the church of God. Jealousy and resentment prevailed in every breast, but especially in that of Diocletian. A great number of persons, distinguished either by the offices which they had filled, or by the favor which they had enjoyed, were thrown into prison. Every mode of torture was put in practice, and the court, as well as city, was polluted with many bloody executions.[155] But as it was found impossible to extort any discovery of this mysterious transaction, it seems incumbent on us either to presume the innocence, or to admire the resolution, of the sufferers. A few days afterwards Galerius hastily withdrew himself from Nicomedia, declaring, that if he delayed his departure from that devoted palace, he should fall a sacrifice to the rage of the Christians. The ecclesiastical historians, from whom alone we derive a partial and imperfect knowledge of this persecution, are at a loss how to account for the fears and dangers of the emperors. Two of these writers, a prince and a rhetorician, were eye-witnesses of the fire of Nicomedia. The one ascribes it to lightning, and the divine wrath; the other affirms, that it was kindled by the malice of Galerius himself.[156]

As the edict against the Christians was designed for a general law of the whole empire, and as Diocletian and Galerius, though they might not wait for the consent, were assured of the concurrence, of the Western princes, it would appear more consonant to our ideas of policy, that the governors of all the provinces should have received secret instructions to

---

[155] Lactantius de M. P. c. 13, 14. Potentissimi quondam Eunuchi necati, per quos Palatium et ipse constabat. Eusebius (l. viii. c. 6) mentions the cruel executions of the eunuchs, Gorgonius and Dorotheus, and of Anthimius, bishop of Nicomedia; and both those writers describe, in a vague but tragical manner, the horrid scenes which were acted even in the Imperial presence.

[156] See Lactantius, Eusebius, and Constantine, ad Coetum Sanctorum, c. xxv. Eusebius confesses his ignorance of the cause of this fire.*

---

* As the history of these times affords us no example of any attempts made by the Christians against their persecutors, we have no reason, not the slightest probability, to attribute to them the fire in the palace; and the authority of Constantine and Lactantius remains to explain it. M. de Tillemont has shown how they can be reconciled. Hist. des Empereurs Vie de Diocletian, xix. — G. Had it been done by a Christian, it would probably have been a fanatic, who would have avowed and gloried in it. Tillemont's supposition that the fire was first caused by lightning and fed and increased by the malice of Galerius, seems singularly improbable. — M.

publish, on one and the same day, this declaration of war within their respective departments. It was at least to be expected, that the convenience of the public highways and established posts would have enabled the emperors to trans-mit their orders with the utmost despatch from the palace of Nicomedia to the extremities of the Roman world; and that they would not have suffered fifty days to elapse, before the edict was published in Syria, and near four months before it was signified to the cities of Africa.[157] This delay may perhaps be imputed to the cautious temper of Diocletian, who had yielded a reluctant consent to the measures of persecu-tion, and who was desirous of trying the experiment under his more immediate eye, before he gave way to the disorders and discontent which it must inevitably occasion in the distant provinces. At first, indeed, the magistrates were restrained from the effusion of blood; but the use of every other severity was permitted, and even recommended to their zeal; nor could the Christians, though they cheerfully resigned the orna-ments of their churches, resolve to interrupt their religious assemblies, or to deliver their sacred books to the flames. The pious obstinacy of Felix, an African bishop, appears to have embarrassed the subordinate ministers of the govern-ment. The curator of his city sent him in chains to the proconsul. The proconsul transmitted him to the Prætorian præfect of Italy; and Felix, who disdained even to give an evasive answer, was at length beheaded at Venusia, in Lucania, a place on which the birth of Horace has conferred fame.[158] This precedent, and perhaps some Imperial rescript, which was issued in consequence of it, appeared to author-ize the governors of provinces, in punishing with death the refusal of the Christians to deliver up their sacred books. There were undoubtedly many persons who embraced this opportunity of obtaining the crown of martyrdom; but there were likewise too many who purchased an ignominious life, by discovering and betraying the holy Scripture into the hands of infidels. A great number even of bishops and presbyters acquired, by this criminal compliance, the opprobrious epithet

---

[157] Tillemont, Mémoires Ecclesiast. tom. v. part i. p. 43.

[158] See the Acta Sincera of Ruinart, p. 353; those of Felix of Thibara or Tibiur, appear much less corrupted than in the other editions, which afford a lively specimen of legendary license.

31 *

of *Traditors;* and their offence was productive of much
present scandal and of much future discord in the African
church.[159]

The copies as well as the versions of Scripture, were
already so multiplied in the empire, that the most severe
inquisition could no longer be attended with any fatal consequences; and even the sacrifice of those volumes, which, in
every congregation, were preserved for public use, required
the consent of some treacherous and unworthy Christians.
But the ruin of the churches was easily effected by the
authority of the government, and by the labor of the Pagans.
In some provinces, however, the magistrates contented themselves with shutting up the places of religious worship. In
others, they more literally complied with the terms of the
edict; and after taking away the doors, the benches, and the
pulpit, which they burnt as it were in a funeral pile, they
completely demolished the remainder of the edifice.[160] It is
perhaps to this melancholy occasion that we should apply a
very remarkable story, which is related with so many circumstances of variety and improbability, that it serves rather
to excite than to satisfy our curiosity. In a small town in
Phrygia, of whose name as well as situation we are left ignorant, it should seem that the magistrates and the body of the
people had embraced the Christian faith; and as some resistance might be apprehended to the execution of the edict,
the governor of the province was supported by a numerous
detachment of legionaries. On their approach the citizens
threw themselves into the church, with the resolution either
of defending by arms that sacred edifice, or of perishing in its
ruins. They indignantly rejected the notice and permission
which was given them to retire, till the soldiers, provoked by
their obstinate refusal, set fire to the building on all sides, and

---

[159] See the first book of Optatus of Milevis against the Donatists.
Paris, 1700, edit. Dupin. He lived under the reign of Valens.

[160] The ancient monuments, published at the end of Optatus,
p. 261, &c. describe, in a very circumstantial manner, the proceedings
of the governors in the destruction of churches. They made a minute
inventory of the plate, &c., which they found in them. That of the
church of Cirta, in Numidia, is still extant. It consisted of two
chalices of gold, and six of silver; six urns, one kettle, seven lamps,
all likewise of silver; besides a large quantity of brass utensils, and
wearing apparel.

consumed, by this extraordinary kind of martyrdom, a great number of Phrygians, with their wives and children.[161]

Some slight disturbances, though they were suppressed almost as soon as excited, in Syria and the frontiers of Armenia, afforded the enemies of the church a very plausible occasion to insinuate, that those troubles had been secretly fomented by the intrigues of the bishops, who had already forgotten their ostentatious professions of passive and unlimited obedience.[162] The resentment, or the fears, of Diocletian, at length transported him beyond the bounds of moderation, which he had hitherto preserved, and he declared in a series of cruel edicts,† his intention of abolishing the Christian name. By the first of these edicts, the governors of the provinces were directed to apprehend all persons of the ecclesiastical order; and the prisons, destined for the vilest criminals, were soon filled with a multitude of bishops, presbyters, deacons, readers, and exorcists. By a second edict, the magistrates were commanded to employ every method

---

[161] Lactantius (Institut. Divin. v. 11) confines the calamity to the *conventiculum*, with its congregation. Eusebius (viii. 11) extends it to a whole city,* and introduces something very like a regular siege. His ancient Latin translator, Rufinus, adds the important circumstance of the permission given to the inhabitants of retiring from thence. As Phrygia reached to the confines of Isauria, it is possible that the restless temper of those independent barbarians may have contributed to this misfortune.

[162] Eusebius, l. viii. c. 6. M. de Valois (with some probability) thinks that he has discovered the Syrian rebellion in an oration of Libanius; and that it was a rash attempt of the tribune Eugenius, who with only five hundred men seized Antioch, and might perhaps allure the Christians by the promise of religious toleration. From Eusebius, (l. ix. c. 8,) as well as from Moses of Chorene, (Hist. Armen. l. ii. 77, &c.,) it may be inferred, that Christianity was already introduced into Armenia.

---

* Universum populum. Lact. Inst. Div. v. 11. — G.

† He had already passed them in his first edict. It does not appear that resentment or fear had any share in the new persecutions: perhaps they originated in superstition, and a specious apparent respect for its ministers. The oracle of Apollo, consulted by Diocletian, gave no answer; and said that just men hindered it from speaking. Constantine, who assisted at the ceremony, affirms, with an oath, that when questioned about these men, the high priest named the Christians. "The Emperor eagerly seized on this answer; and drew against the innocent a sword, destined only to punish the guilty: he instantly issued edicts, written, if I may use the expression, with a poniard; and ordered the judges to employ all their skill to invent new modes of punishment. Euseb. Vit Constant. l. ii. c. 54." — G.

of severity which might reclaim them from their odious
superstition, and oblige them to return to the established
worship of the gods. This rigorous order was extended, by
a subsequent edict, to the whole body of Christians, who were
exposed to a violent and general persecution.[163] Instead of
those salutary restraints, which had required the direct and
solemn testimony of an accuser, it became the duty as well
as the interest of the Imperial officers to discover, to pursue, and to torment the most obnoxious among the faithful.
Heavy penalties were denounced against all who should presume to save a prescribed sectary from the just indignation
of the gods, and of the emperors. Yet, notwithstanding
the severity of this law, the virtuous courage of many of
the Pagans, in concealing their friends or relations, affords
an honorable proof, that the rage of superstition had not
extinguished in their minds the sentiments of nature and
humanity.[164]

Diocletian had no sooner published his edicts against the
Christians, than, as if he had been desirous of committing to
other hands the work of persecution, he divested himself of
the Imperial purple. The character and situation of his col
leagues and successors sometimes urged them to enforce
and sometimes inclined them to suspend, the execution of
hese rigorous laws; nor can we acquire a just and distinct
idea of this important period of ecclesiastical history, unless
we separately consider the state of Christianity, in the different parts of the empire, during the space of ten years, which
elapsed between the first edicts of Diocletian and the final
peace of the church.

The mild and humane temper of Constantius was averse to
the oppression of any part of his subjects. The principal
offices of his palace were exercised by Christians. He loved
their persons, esteemed their fidelity, and entertained not
any dislike to their religious principles. But as long as Constantius remained in the subordinate station of Cæsar, it was
not in his power openly to reject the edicts of Diocletian, or
to disobey the commands of Maximian. His authority con-

---

[163] See Mosheim, p. 938: the text of Eusebius very plainly shows,
that the governors, whose powers were enlarged, not restrained, by
the new laws, could punish with death the most obstinate Christians,
as an example to their brethren.

[164] Athanasius, p. 833, ap. Tillemont, Mém. Ecclesiast. tom. v
part i 90.

tributed, however, to alleviate the sufferings which he pitied and abhorred. He consented with reluctance to the ruin of the churches; but he ventured to protect the Christians themselves from the fury of the populace, and from the rigor of the laws. The provinces of Gaul (under which we may probably include those of Britain) were indebted for the singular tranquillity which they enjoyed, to the gentle interposition of their sovereign.[165] But Datianus, the president or governor of Spain, actuated either by zeal or policy, chose rathe to execute the public edicts of the emperors, than to understand the secret intentions of Constantius; and it can scarcely be doubted, that his provincial administration was stained with the blood of a few martyrs.[166] The elevation of Constantius to the supreme and independent dignity of Augustus, gave a free scope to the exercise of his virtues, and the shortness of his reign did not prevent him from establishing a system of toleration, of which he left the precept and the example to his son Constantine. His fortunate son, from the first moment of his accession, declaring himself the protector of the church at length deserved the appellation of the first emperor who publicly professed and established the Christian religion. The motives of his conversion, as they may variously be deduced from benevolence, from policy, from conviction, or from remorse, and the progress of the revolution, which, under his powerful influence and that of his sons, rendered Christianity the reigning religion of the Roman empire, will form a very interesting and important chapter in the present volume of this history. At present it may be sufficient to observe, that every victory of Constantine was productive of some relief or benefit to the church.

---

[165] Eusebius, l. viii. c. 13. Lactantius de M. P. c. 15. Dodwell (Dissertat. Cyprian. xi. 75) represents them as inconsistent with each other. But the former evidently speaks of Constantius in the station of Cæsar, and the latter of the same prince in the rank of Augustus.

[166] Datianus is mentioned, in Gruter's Inscriptions, as having determined the limits between the territories of Pax Julia, and those of Ebora, both cities in the southern part of Lusitania. If we recollect the neighborhood of those places to Cape St. Vincent, we may suspect that the celebrated deacon and martyr of that name has been inaccurately assigned by Prudentius, &c., to Saragossa, or Valentia. See the pompous history of his sufferings, in the Mémoires de Tillemont, tom. v. part ii. p. 58—85. Some critics are of opinion, that the department of Constantius, as Cæsar, did not include Spain, which still continued under the immediate jurisdiction of Maximian.

The provinces of Italy and Afr:a experienced a short but violent persecution. The rigoro s edicts of Diocletian were strictly and cheerfully executed by his associate Maximian, who had long hated the Christians, and who delighted in acts of blood and violence. In the autumn of the first year of the persecution, the two emperors met at Rome to celebrate their triumph; several oppressive laws appear to have issued from their secret consultations, and the diligence of the magistrates was animated by the presence of their sovereigns. After Diocletian had divested himself of the purple, Italy and Africa were administered under the name of Severus, and were exposed, without defence, to the implacable resentment of his master Galerius. Among the martyrs of Rome, Adauctus deserves the notice of posterity. He was of a noble family in Italy, and had raised himself, through the successive honors of the palace, to the important office of treasurer of the private demesnes. Adauctus is the more remarkable for being the only person of rank and distinction who appears to have suffered death, during the whole course of this general persecution.[167]

The revolt of Maxentius immediately restored peace to the churches of Italy and Africa; and the same tyrant who oppressed every other class of his subjects, showed himself just, humane, and even partial, towards the afflicted Christians. He depended on their gratitude and affection, and very naturally presumed, that the injuries which they had suffered, and the dangers which they still apprehended from his most inveterate enemy, would secure the fidelity of a party already considerable by their numbers and opulence.[168] Even the

---

[167] Eusebius, l. viii. c. 11. Gruter, Inscrip. p. 1171, No. 18. Rufinus has mistaken the office of Adauctus, as well as the place of his martyrdom.*

[168] Eusebius, l. viii. c. 14. But as Maxentius was vanquished by Constantine, it suited the purpose of Lactantius to place his death among those of the persecutors.†

---

* M. Guizot suggests the powerful eunuchs of the palace, Dorotheus, Gorgonius, and Andrew, admitted by Gibbon himself to have been put to death, p. 66.

† M. Guizot directly contradicts this statement of Gibbon, and appeals to Eusebius. Maxentius, who assumed the power in Italy, pretended at first to be a Christian, ($\kappa\alpha\theta\nu\pi\epsilon\kappa\rho\acute{\iota}\nu\alpha\tau\sigma$,) to gain the favor of the Roman people; he ordered his ministers to cease to persecute the Christians, affecting a hypocritical piety, in order to appear more mild than his predecessors; but his actions soon proved that he was very different from what they had at first hoped." The actions of Maxentius were those of a lasciv

conduct of Maxentius towards the bishops of Rome and Carthage may be considered as the proof of his toleration, since it is probable that the most orthodox princes would adopt the same measures with regard to their established clergy. Marcellus, the former of those prelates, had thrown the capital into confusion, by the severe penance which he imposed on a great number of Christians, who, during the late persecution, had renounced or dissembled their religion. The rage of faction broke out in frequent and violent seditions; the blood of the faithful was shed by each other's hands, and the exile of Marcellus, whose prudence seems to have been less eminent than his zeal, was found to be the only measure capable of restoring peace to the distracted church of Rome.[169] The behavior of Mensurius, bishop of Carthage, appears to have been still more reprehensible. A deacon of that city had published a libel against the emperor. The offender took refuge in the episcopal palace ; and though it was somewhat early to advance any claims of ecclesiastical immunities, the bishop refused to deliver him up to the officers of justice. For this treasonable resistance, Mensurius was summoned to court, and instead of receiving a legal sentence of death or banishment, he was permitted, after a short examination, to return to his diocese.[170]

---

[169] The epitaph of Marcellus is to be found in Gruter, Inscrip. p. 1172, No. 3, and it contains all that we know of his history. Marcellinus and Marcellus, whose names follow in the list of popes, are supposed by many critics to be different persons ; but the learned Abbé de Longuerue was convinced that they were one and the same.

> Veridicus rector lapsis quia crimina flere
> Prædixit miseris, fuit omnibus hostis amarus.
> Hinc furor, hinc odium ; sequitur discordia, lites,
> Seditio, cædes ; solvuntur fœdera pacis.
> Crimen ob alterius, Christum qui in pace negavit
> Finibus expulsus patriæ est feritate Tyranni.
> Hæc breviter Damasus voluit comperta referre :
> Marcelli populus meritum cognoscere posset.

We may observe that Damasus was made Bishop of Rome, A. D. 366.

[170] Optatus contr. Donatist. l. i. c. 17, 18.*

---

ious and cruel tyrant, but not those of a persecutor: the Christians, like the rest of his subjects, suffered from his vices, but they were not oppressed as a sect. Christian females were exposed to his lusts, as well as to the brutal violence of his colleague Maximian, but they were not selected as Christians. — M.

* The words of Optatus are, Profectus (Roman) causum dixit ; jussus est reverti Carthaginem ; perhaps, in pleading his cause, he exculpated himself, since he received an order to return to Carthage. — G.

Such was the happy condition of the Christian subjects of Maxentius, that whenever they were desirous of procuring for their own use any bodies of martyrs, they were obliged to purchase them from the most distant provinces of the East. A story is related of Aglae, a Roman lady, descended from a consular family, and possessed of so ample an estate, that it required the management of seventy-three stewards. Among these, Boniface was the favorite of his mistress; and as Aglae mixed love with devotion, it is reported that he was admitted to share her bed. Her fortune enabled her to gratify the pious desire of obtaining some sacred relics from the East. She intrusted Boniface with a considerable sum of gold, and a large quantity of aromatics; and her lover, attended by twelve horsemen and three covered chariots, undertook a remote pilgrimage, as far as Tarsus in Cilicia.[171]

The sanguinary temper of Galerius, the first and principal author of the persecution, was formidable to those Christians whom their misfortunes had placed within the limits of his dominions; and it may fairly be presumed that many persons of a middle rank, who were not confined by the chains either of wealth or of poverty, very frequently deserted their native country, and sought a refuge in the milder climate of the West.† As long as he commanded only the armies and provinces of Illyricum, he could with difficulty either find or make a considerable number of martyrs, in a warlike country, which had entertained the missionaries of the gospel with

---

[171] The Acts of the Passion of St. Boniface, which abound in miracles and declamation, are published by Ruinart, (p. 283—291,) both in Greek and Latin, from the authority of very ancient manuscripts.*

---

* We are ignorant whether Aglae and Boniface were Christians at the time of their unlawful connection. See Tillemont. Mém. Eccles. Note on the Persecution of Domitian, tom. v. note 82. M. de Tillemont proves also that the history is doubtful. — G.

Sir D. Dalrymple (Lord Hailes) calls the story of Aglae and Boniface as of equal authority with our *popular* histories of Whittington and Hickathrift. Christian Antiquities, ii. 64. — M.

† A little after this, Christianity was propagated to the north of the Roman provinces, among the tribes of Germany: a multitude of Christians, forced by the persecutions of the Emperors to take refuge among the Barbarians, were received with kindness. Euseb. de Vit. Constant. ii. 53. Semler, Select. cap. H. E. p. 115. The Goths owed their first knowledge of Christianity to a young girl, a prisoner of war; she continued in the midst of them her exercises of piety: she fasted, prayed, and praised God day and night. When she was asked what good could come of so much painful trouble, she answered, "It is thus that Christ, the Son of God, is to be honored." Sozomen, ii. c. 6. — G.

more coldness and reluctance than any other part of the empire.[172] But when Galerius had obtained the supreme power, and the government of the East, he indulged in their fullest extent his zeal and cruelty, not only in the provinces of Thrace and Asia, which acknowledged his immediate jurisdiction, but in those of Syria, Palestine, and Egypt, where Maximin gratified his own inclination, by yielding a rigorous obedience to the stern commands of his benefactor.[173] The frequent disappointments of his ambitious views, the experience of six years of persecution, and the salutary reflections which a lingering and painful distemper suggested to the mind of Galerius, at length convinced him that the most violent efforts of despotism are insufficient to extirpate a whole people, or to subdue their religious prejudices. Desirous of repairing the mischief that he had occasioned, he published in his own name, and in those of Licinius and Constantine, a general edict, which, after a pompous recital of the Imperial titles, proceeded in the following manner : —

"Among the important cares which have occupied our mind for the utility and preservation of the empire, it was our intention to correct and reëstablish all things according to the ancient laws and public discipline of the Romans. We were particularly desirous of reclaiming into the way of reason and nature, the deluded Christians who had renounced the religion and ceremonies instituted by their fathers ; and presumptuously despising the practice of antiquity, had invented extravagant laws and opinions, according to the dictates of their fancy, and had collected a various society from the different provinces of our empire. The edicts, which we have published to enforce the worship of the gods, having exposed many of the Christians to danger and distress, many having suffered death, and many more, who still persist in their

---

[172] During the four first centuries, there exist few traces of either bishops or bishoprics in the western Illyricum. It has been thought probable that the primate of Milan extended his jurisdiction over Sirmium, the capital of that great province. See the Geographia Sacra of Charles de St. Paul, p. 68—76, with the observations of Lucas Holstenius.

[173] The viiith book of Eusebius, as well as the supplement concerning the martyrs of Palestine, principally relate to the persecution of Galerius and Maximin. The general lamentations with which Lactantius opens the vth book of his Divine Institutions, allude to their cruelty

impious folly, being left destitute of *any* public exercise of religion, we are disposed to extend to those unhappy men the effects of our wonted clemency. We permit them therefore freely to profess their private opinions, and to assemble in their conventicles without fear or molestation, provided always that they preserve a due respect to the established laws and government. By another rescript we shall signify our intentions to the judges and magistrates ; and we hope that our indulgence will engage the Christians to offer up their prayers to the Deity whom they adore, for our safety and prosperity for their own, and for that of the republic."[174] It is not usually in the language of edicts and manifestos that we should search for the real character or the secret motives of princes ; but as these were the words of a dying emperor, his situation, perhaps, may be admitted as a pledge of his sincerity.

When Galerius subscribed this edict of toleration, he was well assured that Licinius would readily comply with the inclinations of his friend and benefactor, and that any measures in favor of the Christians would obtain the approbation of Constantine. But the emperor would not venture to insert in the preamble the name of Maximin, whose consent was of the greatest importance, and who succeeded a few days afterwards to the provinces of Asia. In the first six months, however, of his new reign, Maximin affected to adopt the prudent counsels of his predecessor ; and though he never condescended to secure the tranquillity of the church by a public edict, Sabinus, his Prætorian præfect, addressed a circular letter to all the governors and magistrates of the provinces, expatiating on the Imperial clemency, acknowledging the invincible obstinacy of the Christians, and directing the officers of justice to cease their ineffectual prosecutions, and to connive at the secret assemblies of those enthusiasts. In consequence of these orders, great numbers of Christians were released from prison, or delivered from the mines. The

---

[174] Eusebius (l. viii. c. 17) has given us a Greek version, and Lactantius (de M. P. c. 34) the Latin original, of this memorable edict. Neither of these writers seems to recollect how directly it contradicts whatever they have just affirmed of the remorse and repentance of

[119] Summà igitur ope, et alacri studio has leges nostras accipite ; et Galerius.*

---

* But Gibbon has answered this by his just observation, that it is not in the language of edicts and manifestos that we should search * * for the secret motives of princes. — M

confessors, singing hymns of triumph, returned into their own countries; and those who had yielded to the violence of the tempest, solicited with tears of repentance their readmission into the bosom of the church.[175]

But this treacherous calm was of short duration; nor could the Christians of the East place any confidence in the character of their sovereign. Cruelty and superstition were the ruling passions of the soul of Maximin. The former suggested the means, the latter pointed out the objects of persecution. The emperor was devoted to the worship of the gods, to the study of magic, and to the belief of oracles. The prophets or philosophers, whom he revered as the favorites of Heaven, were frequently raised to the government of provinces, and admitted into his most secret councils. They easily convinced him that the Christians had been indebted for their victories to their regular discipline, and that the weakness of polytheism had principally flowed from a want of union and subordination among the ministers of religion. A system of government was therefore instituted, which was evidently copied from the policy of the church. In all the great cities of the empire, the temples were repaired and beautified by the order of Maximin, and the officiating priests of the various deities were subjected to the authority of a superior pontiff destined to oppose the bishop, and to promote the cause of paganism. These pontiffs acknowledged, in their turn, the supreme jurisdiction of the metropolitans or high priests of the province, who acted as the immediate vice-gerents of the emperor himself. A white robe was the ensign of their dignity; and these new prelates were carefully selected from the most noble and opulent families. By the influence of the magistrates, and of the sacerdotal order, a great number of dutiful addresses were obtained, particularly from the cities of Nicomedia, Antioch, and Tyre, which artfully represented the well-known intentions of the court as the general sense of the people; solicited the emperor to consult the laws of justice rather than the dictates of his clemency; expressed their abhorrence of the Christians, and humbly prayed that those impious sectaries might at least be excluded from the limits of their respective territories. The answer of Maximin to the address which he obtained from the citizens of Tyre is still extant. He praises their zeal and

---

[175] Eusebius, l. ix. c. 1. He inserts the epistle of it

devotion in terms of the highest satisfaction, descants on
the obstinate impiety of the Christians, and betrays, by the
readiness with which he consents to their banishment, that he
considered himself as receiving, rather than as conferring, an
obligation. The priests as well as the magistrates were empowered to enforce the execution of his edicts, which were
engraved on tables of brass ; and though it was recommended
to them to avoid the effusion of blood, the most cruel and
ignominious punishments were inflicted on the refractory
Christians.[176]

The Asiatic Christians had every thing to dread from the
severity of a bigoted monarch who prepared his measures of
violence with such deliberate policy. But a few months had
scarcely elapsed before the edicts published by the two Western emperors obliged Maximin to suspend the prosecution
of his designs : the civil war which he so rashly undertook
against Licinius employed all his attention ; and the defeat
and death of Maximin soon delivered the church from the
last and most implacable of her enemies.[177]

---

[176] See Eusebius, l. viii. c. 14, l. ix. c. 2—8. Lactantius de M. P.
c. 36. These writers agree in representing the arts of Maximin; but
the former relates the execution of several martyrs, while the latter
expressly affirms, occidi servos Dei vetuit. *
[177] A few days before his death, he published a very ample edict of
toleration, in which he imputes all the severities which the Christians
suffered to the judges and governors, who had misunderstood his
intentions. See the edict in Eusebius, l. ix. c. 10.

---

* It is easy to reconcile them ; it is sufficient to quote the entire text of
Lactantius : Nam cum clementiam specie tenus profiteretur, occidi servos Dei vetuit, debilitari jussit. Itaque confessoribus effodiebantur oculi,
amputabantur manus, nares vel auriculæ desecabantur. Hæc ille moliens
Constantini litteris deterretur. Dissimulavit ergo, et tamen, si quis incid-
erit, mari occultè mergebatur. This detail of torments inflicted on the
Christians easily reconciles Lactantius and Eusebius. Those who died in
consequence of their tortures, those who were plunged into the sea, might
well pass for martyrs. The mutilation of the words of Lactantius has
alone given rise to the apparent contradiction. — G.
Eusebius, ch. vi., relates the public martyrdom of the aged bishop of
Emesa, with two others, who were thrown to the wild beasts. the behead-
ing of Peter, bishop of Alexandria, with several others, and the death of
Lucian, presbyter of Antioch, who was carried to Numidia, and put to
death in prison. The contradiction is direct and undeniable, for although
Eusebius may have misplaced the former martyrdoms, it may be doubted
whether the authority of Maximin extended to Nicomedia till after the
death of Galerius. The last edict of toleration issued by Maximin, and
published by Eusebius himself, Eccl. Hist. ix. 9, confirms the statement of
Lactantius. — M.

In this general view of the persecution, which was first authorized by the edicts of Diocletian, I have purposely refrained from describing the particular sufferings and deaths of the Christian martyrs. It would have been an easy task, from the history of Eusebius, from the declamations of Lactantius, and from the most ancient acts, to collect a long series of horrid and disgustful pictures, and to fill many pages with racks and scourges, with iron hooks and red-hot beds, and with all the variety of tortures which fire and steel, savage beasts, and more savage executioners, could inflict upon the human body. These melancholy scenes might be enlivened by a crowd of visions and miracles destined either to delay the death, to celebrate the triumph, or to discover the relics of those canonized saints who suffered for the name of Christ. But I cannot determine what I ought to transcribe, till I am satisfied how much I ought to believe. The gravest of the ecclesiastical historians, Eusebius himself, indirectly confesses that he has related whatever might redound to the glory, and that he has suppressed all that could tend to the disgrace, of religion.[178] Such an acknowledgment will naturally excite a suspicion that a writer who has so openly violated one of the fundamental laws of history, has not paid a very strict regard

---

[178] Such is the *fair* deduction from two remarkable passages in Eusebius, l. viii. c. 2, and de Martyr. Palestin. c. 12. The prudence of the historian has exposed his own character to censure and suspicion. It was well known that he himself had been thrown into prison ; and it was suggested that he had purchased his deliverance by some dishonorable compliance. The reproach was urged in his lifetime, and even in his presence, at the council of Tyre. See Tillemont, Mémoires Ecclesiastiques, tom. viii. part i. p. 67.*

---

* Historical criticism does not consist in rejecting indiscriminately all the facts which do not agree with a particular system, as Gibbon does in this chapter, in which, except at the last extremity, he will not consent to believe a martyrdom. Authorities are to be weighed, not excluded from examination. Now, the Pagan historians justify in many places the details which have been transmitted to us by the historians of the church, concerning the tortures endured by the Christians. Celsus reproaches the Christians with holding their assemblies in secret, on account of the fear inspired by their sufferings, " for when you are arrested," he says, " you are dragged to punishment ; and, before you are put to death, you have to suffer all kinds of tortures." Origen cont. Cels. l. i. ii. vi. viii. passim. Libanius, the panegyrist of Julian, says, while speaking of the Christians, " Those who followed a corrupt religion were in continual apprehensions; they feared lest Julian should invent tortures still more refined than those to which they had been exposed before, as mutilation, burning alive, &c.; for the emperors had inflicted upon them all these barbarities." Lib Parent. in Julian. ap. Fab. Bib. Græc. No. 9, No. 58. p. 283. — G.

to the observance of the other ; and the suspicion will derive additional credit from the character of Eusebius,* which was less tinctured with credulity, and more practised in the arts of courts, than that of almost any of his contemporaries. On some particular occasions, when the magistrates were exasperated by some personal motives of interest or resentment, when the zeal of the martyrs urged them to forget the rules of prudence and perhaps of decency, to overturn the altars, to pour out imprecations against the emperors, or to strike the judge as he sat on his tribunal, it may be presumed, that every mode of torture which cruelty could invent, or constancy could endure, was exhausted on those devoted vic tims.[179] Two circumstances, however, have been unwarily

---

[179] The ancient, and perhaps authentic, account of the sufferings of Tarachus † and his companions, (Acta Sincera Ruinart, p. 419—448,) is filled with strong expressions of resentment and contempt, which could not fail of irritating the magistrate. The behavior of Ædesius to Hierocles, præfect of Egypt, was still more extraordinary. λόγοις τε καὶ ἔργοις τὸν δικαστὴν . . . περιβαλών. Euseb. de Martyr. Palestin. c. 5.‡

---

* This sentence of Gibbon has given rise to several learned disserta tions: Möller, de Fide Eusebii Cæsar, &c., Havniæ, 1813. Danzius, de Eusebio Cæs. Hist. Eccl. Scriptore, ejusque fide historicâ rectè æstimandâ, &c., Jenæ, 1815. Kestner Commentatio de Eusebii Hist. Eccles. conditoris auctoritate et fide, &c. See also Reuterdahl, de Fontibus Historiæ Eccles. Eusebianæ, Lond. Goth., 1826. Gibbon's inference may appear stronger than the text will warrant, yet it is difficult, after reading the passages, to dismiss all suspicion of partiality from the mind. — M.

† M. Guizot states, that the acts of Tarachus and his companion contain nothing that appears dictated by violent feelings, (sentiment outré.) Nothing can be more painful than the constant attempt of Gibbon, throughout this discussion, to find some flaw in the virtue and heroism of the martyrs, some extenuation for the cruelty of the persecutors. But truth must not be sacrificed even to well-grounded moral indignation. Though the language of these martyrs is in great part that of calm defiance, of noble firmness, yet there are many expressions which betray " resentment and contempt." " Children of Satan, worshippers of Devils," is their common appellation of the heathen. One of them calls the judge, ἀναιδέστατε; another, θηρίων ἀναιδέστατε τύραννε : one curses, and declares that he will curse the Emperors, ὕβρισα, καὶ ὑβρίσω λοιμοὺς ὄντας καὶ αἱμοπότας, as pestilential and bloodthirsty tyrants, whom God will soon visit in his wrath. On the other hand, though at first they speak the milder language of persuasion, the cold barbarity of the judges and officers might surely have called forth one sentence of abhorrence from Gibbon. On the first unsatisfactory answer, " Break his jaw," is the order of the judge. They direct and witness the most excruciating tortures ; the people, as M. Guizot observes, were so much revolted by the cruelty of Maximus, that when the martyrs appeared in the amphitheatre, fear seized on all hearts, and general murmurs against the unjust judge ran through the assembly. It is singular, at least, that Gibbon should have quoted " as probably authen tic," acts so much embellished with miracle as these of Tarachus are, par ticularly towards the end. — M.

‡ Scarcely were the authorities informed of this, than the president of

mentioned, which insinuate that the general treatment of the Christians, who had been apprehended by the officers of justice, was less intolerable than it is usually imagined to have been. 1. The confessors who were condemned to work in the mines were permitted by the humanity or the negligence of their keepers to build chapels, and freely to profess their religion in the midst of those dreary habitations.[180] 2. The bishops were obliged to check and to censure the forward zeal of the Christians, who voluntarily threw themselves into the hands of the magistrates. Some of these were persons oppressed by poverty and debts, who blindly sought to terminate a miserable existence by a glorious death. Others were allured by the hope that a short confinement would expiate the sins of a whole life; and others again were actuated by the less honorable motive of deriving a plentiful subsistence, and perhaps a considerable profit, from the alms which the charity of the faithful bestowed on the prisoners.[181] After the church had triumphed over all her enemies, the interest as well as vanity of the captives prompted them to magnify the merit of their respective sufferings. A convenient distance of time or place gave an ample scope to the progress of fiction; and the frequent instances which might be alleged of holy martyrs, whose wounds had been instantly healed, whose strength had been renewed, and whose lost members had miraculously been restored, were extremely convenient for the purpose of removing every difficulty, and of silencing every objection. The most extravagant legends, as they conduced to the honor of the church, were applauded by the credulous multitude, countenanced by the power of the clergy, and attested by the suspicious evidence of ecclesiastical history.

---

[180] Euseb. de Martyr. Palestin. c. 13.

[181] Augustin. Collat. Carthagin. Dei, iii. c. 13, ap. Tillemont, Mémoires Ecclesiastiques, tom. v. part i. p. 46. The controversy with the Donatists has reflected some, though perhaps a partial, light on the history of the African church.

---

the province, a man, says Eusebius, harsh and cruel, banished the confessors, some to Cyprus, others to different parts of Palestine, and ordered them to be tormented by being set to the most painful labors. Four of them, whom he required to abjure their faith, and refused, were burnt alive. Euseb. de Mart. Palest. c xiii. — G. Two of these were bishops; a fifth, Silvanus, bishop of Gaza, was the last martyr; another, named John, was blinded, but used to officiate, and recite from memory long passages of the sacred writings. — M.

The vague descriptions of exile and imprisonment, cf pain
and torture, are so easily exaggerated or softened by the pencil of an artful orator,* that we are naturally induced to inquire into a fact of a more distinct and stubborn kind; the
number of persons who suffered death in consequence of the
edicts published by Diocletian, his associates, and his successors. The recent legendaries record whole armies and cities,
which were at once swept away by the undistinguishing rage
of persecution. The more ancient writers content themselves
with pouring out a liberal effusion of loose and tragical invectives, without condescending to ascertain the precise number
of those persons who were permitted to seal with their blood
their belief of the gospel. From the history of Eusebius, it
may, however, be collected, that only nine bishops were punished with death; and we are assured, by his particular enumeration of the martyrs of Palestine, that no more than
ninety-two Christians were entitled to that honorable appellation.[182] † As we are unacquainted with the degree of epis-

---

[182] Eusebius de Martyr. Palestin. c. 13. He closes his narration by
assuring us that these were the martyrdoms inflicted in Palestine,
during the *whole* course of the persecution. The 9th chapter of his
viiith book, which relates to the province of Thebais in Egypt, may
seem to contradict our moderate computation; but it will only lead
us to admire the artful management of the historian. Choosing for
the scene of the most exquisite cruelty the most remote and sequestered country of the Roman empire, he relates that in Thebais ,from
ten to one hundred persons had frequently suffered martyrdom in the
same day. But when he proceeds to mention his own journey into
Egypt, his language insensibly becomes more cautious and moderate.
Instead of a large, but definite number, he speaks of many Christians
(πλειους), and most artfully selects two ambiguous words, (ιστορησαμεν

* Perhaps there never was an instance of an author committing so
deliberately the fault which he reprobates so strongly in others. What is
the dexterous management of the more inartificial historians of Christianity, in exaggerating the numbers of the martyrs, compared to the unfair
address with which Gibbon here quietly dismisses from the account all the
horrible and excruciating tortures which fell short of death? The reader
may refer to the xiith chapter (book viii.) of Eusebius for the description
and for the scenes of these tortures. — M.

† This calculation is made from the martyrs, of whom Eusebius speaks
by name; but he recognizes a much greater number. Thus the ninth and
tenth chapters of his work are entitled, " Of Antoninus, Zebinus, Ger-
manus, and other martyrs; of Peter the monk, of Asclepius the Maroion-
ite, and other martyrs." [Are these vague contents of chapters very good
authority ? — M.] Speaking of those who suffered under Diocletian, he
says, " I will only relate the death of one of these, from which the reader
may divine what befell the rest." Hist. Eccl. viii. 6. [This relates only to

copal zeal and courage which prevailed at that time, it is not
in our power to draw any useful inferences from the former
of these facts: but the latter may serve to justify a very important and probable conclusion. According to the distribution of Roman provinces, Palestine may be considered as the
sixteenth part of the Eastern empire: [183] and since there were
some governors, who from a real or affected clemency had
preserved their hands unstained with the blood of the faithful, [184] it is reasonable to believe, that the country which had

---

and ὑπομείναντας,) * which may signify either what he had seen, or
what he had heard; either the expectation, or the execution of the
punishment. Having thus provided a secure evasion, he commits the
equivocal passage to his readers and translators; justly conceiving
that their piety would induce them to prefer the most favorable sense.
There was perhaps some malice in the remark of Theodorus Meto-
chita, that all who, like Eusebius, had been conversant with the
Egyptians, delighted in an obscure and intricate style. (See Valesius
ad loc.)

[183] When Palestine was divided into three, the præfecture of the
East contained forty-eight provinces. As the ancient distinctions of
nations were long since abolished, the Romans distributed the provinces according to a general proportion of their extent and opulence.

[184] Ut gloriari possint nullam se innocentium peremisse, nam et

---

the martyrs in the royal household. — M.] Dodwell had made, before Gibbon, this calculation and these objections; but Ruinart (Act. Mart. Pref.
p. 27, et seq.) has answered him in a peremptory manner: Nobis constat
Eusebium in historiâ infinitos passim martyres admisisse, quamvis reverâ
paucorum nomina recensuerit. Nec alium Eusebii interpretem quam
ipsummet Eusebium proferimus, qui (l. iii. c. 33) ait sub Trajano plurimos
ex fidelibus martyrii certamen subiisse (l. v. init.) sub Antonino et Vero
innumerabiles prope martyres per universum orbem enituisse affirmat.
(L. vi. c. 1.) Severum persecutionem concitâsse refert, in qua per omnes
ubique locorum Ecclesias, ab athletis pro pietate certantibus, illustria con-
fecta fuerunt martyria. Sic de Decii, sic de Valeriani, persecutionibus
loquitur, quæ an Dodwelli faveant conjectionibus judicet æquus lector.
Even in the persecutions which Gibbon has represented as much more
mild than that of Diocletian, the number of martyrs appears much greater
than that to which he limits the martyrs of the latter: and this number is
attested by incontestable monuments. I will quote but one example. We
find among the letters of St. Cyprian one from Lucianus to Celerinus,
written from the depth of a prison, in which Lucianus names seventeen
of his brethren dead, some in the quarries, some in the midst of tortures,
some of starvation in prison. Jussi sumus (he proceeds) secundum præ-
ceptum imperatoris, fame et siti necari, et reclusi sumus in duabus cellis
ita ut nos afficerent fame et siti et ignis vapore. — G.

* Those who will take the trouble to consult the text will see that if
the word ὑπομείναντας could be taken for the expectation of punishment,
the passage could have no sense, and become absurd. — G. The many
(πλείους) he speaks of as suffering together in one day; ἀθρόως κατὰ μιαν
ἡμεραν. The fact seems to be, that religious persecution always raged in
Egypt with greater violence than elsewhere. — M.

given birth to Christianity, produced at least the sixteenth part of the martyrs who suffered death within the dominions of Gaierius and Maximin ; the whole might consequently amount to about fifteen hundred, a number which, if it is equally divided between the ten years of the persecution, will allow an annual consumption of one hundred and fifty martyrs. Allotting the same proportion to the provinces of Italy, Africa, and perhaps Spain, where, at the end of two or three years, the rigor of the penal laws was either suspended or abolished, the multitude of Christians in the Roman empire, on whom a capital punishment was inflicted by a judicial sentence, will be reduced to somewhat less than two thousand persons. Since it cannot be doubted that the Christians were more numerous, and their enemies more exasperated, in the time of Diocletian, than they had ever been in any former persecution, this probable and moderate computation may teach us to estimate the number of primitive saints and martyrs who sacrificed their lives for the important purpose of introducing Christianity into the world.

We shall conclude this chapter by a melancholy truth, which obtrudes itself on the reluctant mind ; that even admitting, without hesitation or inquiry, all that history has recorded, or devotion has feigned, on the subject of martyrdoms, it must still be acknowledged, that the Christians, in the course of their intestine dissensions, have inflicted far greater severities on each other, than they had experienced from the zeal of infidels. During the ages of ignorance which followed the subversion of the Roman empire in the West, the bishops of the Imperial city extended their dominion over the laity as well as clergy of the Latin church. The fabric of superstition which they had erected, and which might long have defied the feeble efforts of reason, was at length assaulted by a crowd of daring fanatics, who from the twelfth to the sixteenth century assumed the popular character of reformers. The church of Rome defended by violence the empire which she had acquired by fraud ; a system of peace and benevolence was soon disgraced by proscriptions, war, massacres, and the institution of the holy office. And as the reformers were animated by the love of civil as well as of religious freedom, the Catholic princes connected their own interest

---

ipse audivi aliquos gloriantes, quia administratio sua, in hâc parte, fuerit incruenta. Lactant. Institut. Divin. v. 11.

with that of the clergy, and enforced by fire and the sword the terrors of spiritual censures. In the Netherlands alone more than one hundred thousand of the subjects of Charles V. are said to have suffered by the hand of the executioner; and this extraordinary number is attested by Grotius,[185] a man of genius and learning, who preserved his moderation amidst the fury of contending sects, and who composed the annals of his own age and country, at a time when the invention of printing had facilitated the means of intelligence, and increased the danger of detection. If we are obliged to submit our belief to the authority of Grotius, it must be allowed, that the number of Protestants, who were executed in a single province and a single reign, far exceeded that of the primitive martyrs in the space of three centuries, and of the Roman empire. But if the improbability of the fact itself should prevail over the weight of evidence; if Grotius should be convicted of exaggerating the merit and sufferings of the Reformers; [186] we shall be naturally led to inquire what confidence can be placed in the doubtful and imperfect monuments of ancient credulity; what degree of credit can be assigned to a courtly bishop, and a passionate declaimer,* who, under the protection of Constantine, enjoyed the exclusive privilege of recording the persecutions inflicted on the Christians by the vanquished rivals or disregarded predecessors of their gracious sovereign.

---

[185] Grot. Annal. de Rebus Belgicis, l. i. p. 12, edit. fol.

[186] Fra Paolo (Istoria del Concilio Tridentino, l. iii.) reduces the number of the Belgic martyrs to 50,000. In learning and moderation Fra Paolo was not inferior to Grotius. The priority of time gives some advantage to the evidence of the former, which he loses, on the other hand, by the distance of Venice from the Netherlands.

---

* Eusebius and the author of the Treatise de Mortibus Persecutorum. It is deeply to be regretted that the history of this period rests so much on the loose, and, it must be admitted, by no means scrupulous, authority of Eusebius. Ecclesiastical history is a solemn and melancholy lesson that the best, even the most sacred, cause will eventually suffer by the least departure from truth! — M.

CHAPTER XVII.

FOUNDATION OF CONSTANTINOPLE. — POLITICAL SYSTEM OF CONSTANTINE, AND HIS SUCCESSORS. — MILITARY DISCIPLINE. — THE PALACE. — THE FINANCES.

THE unfortunate Licinius was the last rival who opposed the greatness, and the last captive who adorned the triumph, of Constantine. After a tranquil and prosperous reign, the conqueror bequeathed to his family the inheritance of the Roman empire ; a new capital, a new policy, and a new religion ; and the innovations which he established have been embraced and consecrated by succeeding generations. The age of the great Constantine and his sons is filled with important events ; but the historian must be oppressed by their number and variety, unless he diligently separates from each other the scenes which are connected only by the order of time. He will describe the political institutions that gave strength and stability to the empire, before he proceeds to relate the wars and revolutions which hastened its decline. He will adopt the division unknown to the ancients of civil and ecclesiastical affairs : the victory of the Christians, and their intestine discord, will supply copious and distinct materials both for edification and for scandal.

After the defeat and abdication of Licinius, his victorious rival proceeded to lay the foundations of a city destined to reign in future times, the mistress of the East, and to survive the empire and religion of Constantine. The motives, whether of pride or of policy, which first induced Diocletian to withdraw himself from the ancient seat of government, had acquired additional weight by the example of his successors, and the habits of forty years. Rome was insensibly confounded with the dependent kingdoms which had once acknowledged her supremacy ; and the country of the Cæsars was viewed with cold indifference by a martial prince, born in the neighborhood of the Danube, educated in the courts and armies of Asia, and invested with the purple by the legions of Britain. The Italians, who had received Constantine as their deliverer, submissively obeyed the edicts which he sometimes condescended to address to the senate and people of Rome; but they were seldom honored with the presence of their new sovereign. During the vigor of his age, Constantine, according to the various exigencies of peace and war, moved with slow dignity, or with active diligence, along the frontiers of his extensive dominions; and was always prepared to take the field either against a foreign or a domestic enemy. But as he gradually reached the summit of prosperity and the decline of life, he began to meditate the design of fixing in a more permanent station the strength as well as majesty of the throne. In the choice of an advantageous situation, he preferred the confines of Europe and Asia; to curb with a powerful arm the barbarians who dwelt between the Danube and the Tanais; to watch with an eye of jealousy the conduct of the Persian monarch, who indignantly supported the yoke of an ignominious treaty. With these views, Diocletian had selected and embellished the residence of Nicomedia: but the memory of Diocletian was justly abhorred by the protector of the church; and Constantine was not insensible to the ambition of founding a city which might perpetuate the glory of his own name. During the late operations of the war against Licinius, he had sufficient opportunity to contemplate, both as a soldier and as a statesman, the incomparable position of Byzantium; and to observe how strongly it was guarded by nature against a hostile attack, whilst it was accessible on every side to the benefits of commercial intercourse. Many ages before Constantine, one of the most judicious historians of antiquity[1] had described the advantages of a situation, from whence a feeble colony of Greeks derived the command of the sea, and the honors of a flourishing and independent republic.[2]

If we survey Byzantium in the extent which it acquired with the august name of Constantinople, the figure of the Imperial

---

[1] Polybius, l. iv. p. 423, edit. Casaubon. He observes that the peace of the Byzantines was frequently disturbed, and the extent of their territory contracted, by the inroads of the wild Thracians.

[2] The navigator Byzas, who was styled the son of Neptune, founded the city 656 years before the Christian æra. His followers were drawn from Argos and Megara. Byzantium was afterwards rebuilt and fortified by the Spartan general Pausanias. See Scaliger, Animadvers. ad Euseb. p. 81. Ducange, Constantinopolis, l. i. part i. cap. 15, 16. With regard to the wars of the Byzantines against Philip, the Gauls, and the kings of Bithynia, we should trust none but the ancient writers who lived before the greatness of the Imperial city had excited a spirit of flattery and fiction.

city may be represented under that of an unequal triangle.
The obtuse point, which advances towards the east and the
shores of Asia, meets and repels the waves of the Thracian
Bosphorus. The northern side of the city is bounded by the
harbor; and the southern is washed by the Propontis, or Sea
of Marmara. The basis of the triangle is opposed to the
west, and terminates the continent of Europe. But the admirable form and division of the circumjacent land and water
cannot, without a more ample explanation, be clearly or
sufficiently understood.

The winding channel through which the waters of the
Euxine flow with a rapid and incessant course towards the
Mediterranean, received the appellation of Bosphorus, a name
not less celebrated in the history, than in the fables, of antiquity.[3] A crowd of temples and of votive altars, profusely
scattered along its steep and woody banks, attested the unskil-
fulness, the terrors, and the devotion of the Grecian naviga-
tors, who, after the example of the Argonauts, explored the
dangers of the inhospitable Euxine. On these banks tradition
long preserved the memory of the palace of Phineus, infested
by the obscene harpies;[4] and of the sylvan reign of Amycus,
who defied the son of Leda to the combat of the cestus.[5] The
straits of the Bosphorus are terminated by the Cyanean rocks,
which, according to the description of the poets, had once
floated on the face of the waters; and were destined by the
gods to protect the entrance of the Euxine against the eye of
profane curiosity.[6] From the Cyanean rocks to the point and

---

[3] The Bosphorus has been very minutely described by Dionysius
of Byzantium, who lived in the time of Domitian, (Hudson, Geograph.
Minor, tom. iii.,) and by Gilles or Gyllius, a French traveller of the
XVIth century. Tournefort (Lettre XV.) seems to have used his own
eyes, and the learning of Gyllius. [Add Von Hammer, Constantinopolis und der Bosporos, 8vo. — M.]

[4] There are very few conjectures so happy as that of Le Clerc,
(Bibliothéque Universelle, tom. i. p. 148,) who supposes that the
harpies were only locusts. The Syriac or Phœnician name of those
insects, their noisy flight, the stench and devastation which they
occasion, and the north wind which drives them into the sea, all contribute to form the striking resemblance.

[5] The residence of Amycus was in Asia, between the old and the
new castles, at a place called Laurus Insana. That of Phineus was
in Europe, near the village of Mauromole and the Black Sea. See
Gyllius de Bosph. l. ii. c. 23. Tournefort, Lettre XV.

[6] The deception was occasioned by several pointed rocks, alternately
covered and abandoned by the waves. At present there are two small

harbor of Byzantium, the winding length of the Bosphorus extends about sixteen miles,[7] and its most ordinary breadth may be computed at about one mile and a half. The *new* castles of Europe and Asia are constructed, on either conti· nent, upon the foundations of two celebrated temples, of Sera· pis and of Jupiter Urius. The *old* castles, a work of the Greek emperors, command the narrowest part of the channel, in a place where the opposite banks advance within five hun· dred paces of each other. These fortresses were destroyed and strengthened by Mahomet the Second, when he meditated the siege of Constantinople : [8] but the Turkish conqueror was most probably ignorant, that near two thousand years before his reign, Darius had chosen the same situation to connect the two continents by a bridge of boats.[9] At a small distance from the old castles we discover the little town of Chrysopolis, or Scutari, which may almost be considered as the Asiatic suburb of Constantinople. The Bosphorus, as it begins to open into the Propontis, passes between Byzantium and Chal· cedon. The latter of those cities was built by the Greeks, a few years before the former ; and the blindness of its found· ers, who overlooked the superior advantages of the opposite coast, has been stigmatized by a proverbial expression of contempt.[10]

The harbor of Constantinople, which may be considered as an arm of the Bosphorus, obtained, in a very remote period, the denomination of the *Golden Horn*. The curve which it

---

islands, one towards either shore ; that of Europe is distinguished by the column of Pompey.

[7] The ancients computed one hundred and twenty stadia, or fifteen Roman miles. They measured only from the new castles, but they carried the straits as far as the town of Chalcedon.

[8] Ducas. Hist. c. 34. Leunclavius Hist. Turcica Mussulmanica, l. xv. p. 577. Under the Greek empire these castles were used as state prisons, under the tremendous name of Lethe, or towers of oblivion.

[9] Darius engraved in Greek and Assyrian letters, on two marble columns, the names of his subject nations, and the amazing numbers of his land and sea forces. The Byzantines afterwards transported these columns into the city, and used them for the altars of their tutelar deities. Herodotus, l. iv. c. 87.

[10] Namque arctissimo inter Europam Asiamque divortio Byzantium in extremâ Europâ posuere Greci, quibus, Pythium Apollinem con· sulentibus ubi conderent urbem, redditum oraculum est, quærerent *sedem cæcorum* terris adversam. Eà ambage Chalcedonii monstraban· tur, quod priores illuc advecti, prævisâ locorum utilitate pejora legis· sent. Tacit. Anal. xii. 63.

describes might be compared to the horn of a stag, or as it should seem, with more propriety, to that of an ox.[11] The epithet of *golden* was expressive of the riches which every wind wafted from the most distant countries into the secure and capacious port of Constantinople. The River Lycus, formed by the conflux of two little streams, pours into the harbor a perpetual supply of fresh water, which serves to cleanse the bottom, and to invite the periodical shoals of fish to seek their retreat in that convenient recess. As the vicissitudes of tides are scarcely felt in those seas, the constant depth of the harbor allows goods to be landed on the quays without the assistance of boats; and it has been observed, that in many places the largest vessels may rest their prows against the houses, while their sterns are floating in the water.[12] From the mouth of the Lycus to that of the harbor, this arm of the Bosphorus is more than seven miles in length. The entrance is about five hundred yards broad, and a strong chain could be occasionally drawn across it, to guard the port and city from the attack of a hostile navy.[13]

Between the Bosphorus and the Hellespont, the shores of Europe and Asia, receding on either side, enclose the sea of Marmara, which was known to the ancients by the denomination of Propontis. The navigation from the issue of the Bosphorus to the entrance of the Hellespont is about one hundred and twenty miles. Those who steer their westward course through the middle of the Propontis, may at once descry the high lands of Thrace and Bithynia, and never lose sight of the lofty summit of Mount Olympus, covered with eternal snows.[14] They leave on the left a deep gulf, at the bottom

---

[11] Strabo, l. vii. p. 492, [edit. Casaub.] Most of the antlers are now broken off; or, to speak less figuratively, most of the recesses of the harbor are filled up. See Gill. de Bosphoro Thracio, l. i. c. 5.

[12] Procopius de Ædificiis, l. i. c. 5. His description is confirmed by modern travellers. See Thevenot, part i. l. i. c. 15. Tournefort, Lettre XII. Niebuhr, Voyage d'Arabie, p. 22.

[13] See Ducange, C. P. l. i. part i. c. 16, and his Observations sur Villehardouin, p. 289. The chain was drawn from the Acropolis near the modern Kiosk, to the tower of Galata; and was supported at convenient distances by large wooden piles.

[14] Thevenot (Voyages au Levant, part i. l. i. c. 14) contracts the measure to 125 small Greek miles. Belon (Observations, l. ii. c. 1) gives a good description of the Propontis, but contents himself with the vague expression of one day and one night's sail. When Sandys (Travels, p. 21) talks of 150 furlongs in length, as well as breadth, we

of which Nicomedia was seated, the Imperial residence of Diocletian; and they pass the small islands of Cyzicus and Proconnesus before they cast anchor at Gallipoli; where the sea, which separates Asia from Europe, is again contracted into a narrow channel.

The geographers who, with the most skilful accuracy, have surveyed the form and extent of the Hellespont, assign about sixty miles for the winding course, and about three miles for the ordinary breadth of those celebrated straits.[15] But the narrowest part of the channel is found to the northward of the old Turkish castles between the cities of Sestus and Abydus. It was here that the adventurous Leander braved the passage of the flood for the possession of his mistress.[16] It was here likewise, in a place where the distance between the opposite banks cannot exceed five hundred paces, that Xerxes imposed a stupendous bridge of boats, for the purpose of transporting into Europe a hundred and seventy myriads of barbarians.[17] A sea contracted within such narrow limits may seem but ill to deserve the singular epithet of *broad*, which Homer, as

---

can only suppose some mistake of the press in the text of that judicious traveller.

[15] See an admirable dissertation of M. d'Anville upon the Hellespont or Dardanelles, in the Mémoires de l'Academie des Inscriptions, tom. xxviii. p. 318—346. Yet even that ingenious geographer is too fond of supposing new, and perhaps imaginary *measures*, for the purpose of rendering ancient writers as accurate as himself. The stadia employed by Herodotus in the description of the Euxine, the Bosphorus, &c., (l. iv. c. 85,) must undoubtedly be all of the same species; but it seems impossible to reconcile them either with truth or with each other.

[16] The oblique distance between Sestus and Abydus was thirty stadia. The improbable tale of Hero and Leander is exposed by M. Mahudel, but is defended on the authority of poets and medals by M. de la Nauze. See the Academie des Inscriptions, tom. vii. Hist. p. 74. Mem. p. 240.*

[17] See the seventh book of Herodotus, who has erected an elegant trophy to his own fame and to that of his country. The review appears to have been made with tolerable accuracy; but the vanity, first of the Persians, and afterwards of the Greeks, was interested to magnify the armament and the victory. I should much doubt whether the *invaders* have ever outnumbered the *men* of any country which they attacked.

---

* The practical illustration of the possibility of Leander's feat by Lord Byron and other English swimmers is too well known to need particular reference. — M.

32 *

well as Orpheus, has frequently bestowed on the Hellespont *
But our ideas of greatness are of a relative nature : the traveller, and especially the poet, who sailed along the Hellespont
who pursued the windings of the stream, and contemplated the
rural scenery, which appeared on every side to terminate the
prospect, insensibly lost the remembrance of the sea : and his
fancy painted those celebrated straits, with all the attributes
of a mighty river flowing with a swift current, in the midst of
a woody and inland country, and at length, through a wide
mouth, discharging itself into the Ægean or Archipelago.[18]
Ancient Troy,[19] seated on an eminence at the foot of Mount
Ida, overlooked the mouth of the Hellespont, which scarcely
received an accession of waters from the tribute of those
immortal rivulets the Simois and Scamander. The Grecian
camp had stretched twelve miles along the shore from the
Sigæan to the Rhætean promontory ; and the flanks of the
army were guarded by the bravest chiefs who fought under
the banners of Agamemnon. The first of those promontories
was occupied by Achilles with his invincible myrmidons, and

---

[18] See Wood's Observations on Homer, p. 320. I have, with
pleasure, selected this remark from an author who in general seems
to have disappointed the expectation of the public as a critic, and still
more as a traveller. He had visited the banks of the Hellespont;
he had read Strabo; he ought to have consulted the Roman itineraries. How was it possible for him to confound Ilium and Alexandria Troas, (Observations, p. 340, 341,) two cities which were sixteen
miles distant from each other ? †

[19] Demetrius of Scepsis wrote sixty books on thirty lines of Homer's
catalogue. The XIIIth Book of Strabo is sufficient for *our* curiosity.

---

* Gibbon does not allow greater width between the two nearest points
of the shores of the Hellespont than between those of the Bosphorus ; yet
all the ancient writers speak of the Hellespontic strait as broader than the
other : they agree in giving it seven stadia in its narrowest width, (Herod.
In Melp. c. 85. Polym. c. 34. Strabo, p. 591. Plin. iv. c. 12,) which make
875 paces. It is singular that Gibbon, who in the fifteenth note of this
chapter reproaches d'Anville with being fond of supposing new and perhaps imaginary measures, has here adopted the peculiar measurement
which d'Anville has assigned to the stadium. This great geographer
believes that the ancients had a stadium of fifty-one toises, and it is that
which he applies to the walls of Babylon. Now, seven of these stadia are
equal to about 500 paces, 7 stadia = 2142 feet; 500 paces = 2135 feet
5 inches. — G. See Rennell, Geog. of Herod. p. 121. Add Ukert, Geo
graphie der Griechen und Römer, v. i. p. 2, 71. — M.
† Compare Walpole's Memoirs on Turkey, v. i. p. 101. Dr. Clarke
adopted Mr. Walpole's interpretation of πλάτυς Ἑλλήσποντος, the salt Hellespont. But the old interpretation is more graphic and Homeric. Clarke's
Travels, ii. 70. — M.

the dauntless Ajax pitched his tents on the other. After Ajax had fallen a sacrifice to his disappointed pride, and to the ingratitude of the Greeks, his sepulchre was erected on the ground where he had defended the navy against the rage of Jove and of Hector; and the citizens of the rising town of Rhæteum celebrated his memory with divine honors.[20] Before Constantine gave a just preference to the situation of Byzantium, he had conceived the design of erecting the seat of empire on this celebrated spot, from whence the Romans derived their fabulous origin. The extensive plain which lies below ancient Troy, towards the Rhætean promontory and the tomb of Ajax, was first chosen for his new capital; and though the undertaking was soon relinquished the stately remains of unfinished walls and towers attracted the notice of all who sailed through the straits of the Hellespont.[21]

We are at present qualified to view the advantageous position of Constantinople; which appears to have been formed by nature for the centre and capital of a great monarchy. Situated in the forty-first degree of latitude, the Imperial city commanded, from her seven hills,[22] the opposite shores of Europe and Asia; the climate was healthy and temperate, the soil fertile, the harbor secure and capacious; and the approach on the side of the continent was of small extent and easy defence. The Bosphorus and the Hellespont may be considered as the two gates of Constantinople; and the prince who possessed those important passages could always shut them against a naval enemy, and open them to the fleets of commerce. The preservation of the eastern provinces may, in some degree, be ascribed to the policy of Constantine, as the barbarians of the Euxine, who in the preceding age had

---

[20] Strabo, l. xiii. p. 595, [890, edit. Casaub.] The disposition of the ships, which were drawn upon dry land, and the posts of Ajax and Achilles, are very clearly described by Homer. See Iliad, ix. 220.

[21] Zosim. l. ii. [c. 30,] p. 105. Sozomen, l. ii. c. 3. Theophanes, p. 18. Nicephorus Callistus, l. vii. p. 48. Zonaras, tom. ii. l. xiii. p. 6. Zosimus places the new city between Ilium and Alexandria, but this apparent difference may be reconciled by the large extent of its circumference. Before the foundation of Constantinople, Thessalonica is mentioned by Cedrenus, (p. 283,) and Sardica by Zonaras, as the intended capital. They both suppose, with very little probability, that the emperor, if he had not been prevented by a prodigy, would have repeated the mistake of the *blind* Chalcedonians.

[22] Pocock's Description of the East, vol. ii. part ii. p. 127. His plan of the seven hills is clear and accurate. That traveller is seldom so satisfactory.

poured their armaments into the heart of the Mediterranean soon desisted from the exercise of piracy, and despaired of forcing this insurmountable barrier. When the gates of the Hellespont and Bosphorus were shut, the capital still enjoyed within their spacious enclosure every production which could supply the wants, or gratify the luxury, of its numerous inhabitants. The sea-coasts of Thrace and Bithynia, which languish under the weight of Turkish oppression, still exhibit a rich prospect of vineyards, of gardens, and of plentiful harvests ; and the Propontis has ever been renowned for an inexhaustible store of the most exquisite fish, that are taken in their stated seasons, without skill, and almost without labor.[23] But when the passages of the straits were thrown open for trade, they alternately admitted the natural and artificial riches of the north and south, of the Euxine, and of the Mediterranean. Whatever rude commodities were collected in the forests of Germany and Scythia, and far as the sources of the Tanais and the Borysthenes ; whatsoever was manufactured by the skill of Europe or Asia ; the corn of Egypt, and the gems and spices of the farthest India, were brought by the varying winds into the port of Constantinople, which for many ages attracted the commerce of the ancient world.[24]

The prospect of beauty, of safety, and of wealth, united in a single spot, was sufficient to justify the choice of Constantine. But as some decent mixture of prodigy and fable has, in every age, been supposed to reflect a becoming majesty on the origin of great cities,[25] the emperor was desirous of ascribing his resolution, not so much to the uncertain counsels of human policy, as to the infallible and eternal decrees of divine wisdom. In one of his laws he has been careful to instruct posterity, that in obedience to the commands of God, he laid the everlasting foundations of Constantinople : [26] and though

---

[23] See Belon, Observations, c. 72—73. Among a variety of different species, the Pelamides, a sort of Thunnies, were the most celebrated. We may learn from Polybius, Strabo, and Tacitus, that the profits of the fishery constituted the principal revenue of Byzantium.

[24] See the eloquent description of Busbequius, epistol. i. p. 64. Est in Europa ; habet in conspectu Asiam, Egyptum, Africamque a dextrâ : quæ tametsi contiguæ non sunt, maris tamen navigandique commoditate veluti junguntur. A sinistra vero Pontus est Euxinus, &c.

[25] Datur hæc venia antiquitati, ut miscendo humana divinis, prim ordia urbium augustiora faciat. T. Liv. in prœm.

[26] He says in one of his laws, pro commoditate urbis quam æterno nomine, jubente Deo, donavimus. Cod. Theodos. l. xiii. tit. v. leg. 7

he has not condescended to relate in what manner the celestial inspiration was communicated to his mind, the defect of his modest silence has been liberally supplied by the ingenuity of succeeding writers; who describe the nocturnal vision which appeared to the fancy of Constantine, as he slept within the walls of Byzantium. The tutelar genius of the city, a venerable matron sinking under the weight of years and infirmities, was suddenly transformed into a blooming maid whom his own hands adorned with all the symbols of Imperial greatness.[27] The monarch awoke, interpreted the auspicious omen, and obeyed, without hesitation, the will of Heaven. The day which gave birth to a city or colony was celebrated by the Romans with such ceremonies as had been ordained by a generous superstition; [28] and though Constantine might omit some rites which savored too strongly of their Pagan origin, yet he was anxious to leave a deep impression of hope and respect on the minds of the spectators. On foot, with a lance in his hand, the emperor himself led the solemn procession; and directed the line, which was traced as the boundary of the destined capital: till the growing circumference was observed with astonishment by the assistants, who, at length, ventured to observe, that he had already exceeded the most ample measure of a great city. " I shall still advance," replied Constantine, " till HE, the invisible guide who marches before me, thinks proper to stop." [29] Without presuming to investigate the nature or motives of this extraordinary conductor, we shall content ourselves with the more humble task of describing the extent and limits of Constantinople.[30]

---

[27] The Greeks, Theophanes, Cedrenus, and the author of the Alexandrian Chronicle, confine themselves to vague and general expressions. For a more particular account of the vision, we are obliged to have recourse to such Latin writers as William of Malmesbury. See Ducange, C. P. l. i. p. 24, 25.

[28] See Plutarch in Romul. tom. i. p. 49, edit. Bryan. Among other ceremonies, a large hole, which had been dug for that purpose, was filled up with handfuls of earth, which each of the settlers brought from the place of his birth, and thus adopted his new country.

[29] Philostorgius, l. ii. c. 9. This incident, though borrowed from a suspected writer, is characteristic and probable.

[30] See in the Mémoires de l'Académie, tom. xxxv. p. 747—758, a dissertation of M. d'Anville on the extent of Constantinople. He takes the plan inserted in the Imperium Orientale of Banduri as the most complete; but, by a series of very nice observations, he reduces the extravagant proportion of the scale, and instead of 9500, determines the circumference of the city as consisting of about 7800 French

In the actual state of the city, the palace and gardens of the Seraglio occupy the eastern promontory, the first of the seven hills, and cover about one hundred and fifty acres of our own measure. The seat of Turkish jealousy and despotism is erected on the foundations of a Grecian republic; but it may be supposed that the Byzantines were tempted by the conveniency of the harbor to extend their habitations on that side beyond the modern limits of the Seraglio. The new walls of Constantine stretched from the port to the Propontis across the enlarged breadth of the triangle, at the distance of fifteen stadia from the ancient fortification; and with the city of Byzantium they enclosed five of the seven hills, which, to the eyes of those who approach Constantinople, appear to rise above each other in beautiful order.[31] About a century after the death of the founder, the new buildings, extending on one side up the harbor, and on the other along the Propontis, already covered the narrow ridge of the sixth, and the broad summit of the seventh hill. The necessity of protecting those suburbs from the incessant inroads of the barbarians engaged the younger Theodosius to surround his capital with an adequate and permanent enclosure of walls.[32] From the eastern promontory to the golden gate, the extreme length of Constantinople was about three Roman miles;[33] the circumference measured between ten and eleven; and the surface might be computed as equal to about two thousand English acres. It is impossible to justify the vain and credulous exaggerations of modern travellers, who have sometimes stretched the limits of Constantinople over the adjacent villages of the European, and even of the Asiatic coast.[34] But the suburbs

[31] Codinus, Antiquitat. Const. p. 12. He assigns the church of St. Anthony as the boundary on the side of the harbor. It is mentioned in Ducange, l. iv. c. 6; but I have tried, without success, to discover the exact place where it was situated.

[32] The new wall of Theodosius was constructed in the year 413. In 447 it was thrown down by an earthquake, and rebuilt in three months by the diligence of the præfect Cyrus. The suburb of the Blachernæ was first taken into the city in the reign of Heraclius. Ducange, Const. l. i. c. 10, 11.

[33] The measurement is expressed in the Notitia by 14,075 feet. It is reasonable to suppose that these were Greek feet, the proportion of which has been ingeniously determined by M. d'Anville. He compares the 180 feet with 78 Hashemite cubits, which in different writers are assigned for the heights of St. Sophia. Each of these cubits was equal to 27 French inches.

[34] The accurate Thevenot (l. i. c. 15) walked in one hour and three quarters round two of the sides of the triangle, from the Kiosk of the

of Pera and Galata, though situate beyond the harbor, may deserve to be considered as a part of the city ; [35] and this addition may perhaps authorize the measure of a Byzantine historian, who assigns sixteen Greek (about fourteen Roman) miles for the circumference of his native city.[36] Such an extent may seem not unworthy of an Imperial residence. Yet Constantinople must yield to Babylon and Thebes,[37] to ancien Rome, to London, and even to Paris.[38]

The master of the Roman world, who aspired to erect an eternal monument of the glories of his reign, could employ in the prosecution of that great work the wealth, the labor, and all that yet remained of the genius of obedient millions. Some estimate may be formed of the expense bestowed with Imperial liberality on the foundation of Constantinople, by the allowance of about two millions five hundred thousand pounds for the construction of the walls, the porticos, and the aqueducts.[39] The forests that overshadowed the shores of the Euxine, and the celebrated quarries of white marble in the little island of Proconnesus, supplied an inexhaustible stock of materials, ready to be conveyed, by the convenience of a

---

Seraglio to the seven towers. D'Anville examines with care, and receives with confidence, this decisive testimony, which gives a circumference of ten or twelve miles. The extravagant computation of Tournefort (Lettre XI.) of thirty-four or thirty miles, without including Scutari, is a strange departure from his usual character.

[35] The sycæ, or fig-trees, formed the thirteenth region, and were very much embellished by Justinian. It has since borne the names of Pera and Galata. The etymology of the former is obvious; that of the latter is unknown. See Ducange, Const. l. i. c. 22, and Gyllius de Byzant. l. iv. c. 10.

[36] One hundred and eleven stadia, which may be translated into modern Greek miles each of seven stadia, or 660, sometimes only 600, French toises. See D'Anville, Mesures Itineraires, p. 53.

[37] When the ancient texts, which describe the size of Babylon and Thebes, are settled, the exaggerations reduced, and the measures ascertained, we find that those famous cities filled the great but not incredible circumference of about twenty-five or thirty miles. Compare D'Anville, Mem. de l'Academie, tom. xxviii. p. 235, with his Description de l'Egypte, p. 201, 202.

[38] If we divide Constantinople and Paris into equal squares of 50 French *toises*, the former contains 850, and the latter 1160, of those divisions.

[39] Six hundred centenaries, or sixty thousand pounds' weight of gold. This sum is taken from Codinus, Antiquit. Const. p. 11 ; but unless that contemptible author had derived his information from some purer sources, he would probably have been unacquainted with so obsolete a mode of reckoning.

short water-carriage, to the harbor of Byzantium.[40] A multitude of laborers and artificers urged the conclusion of the work with incessant toil : but the impatience of Constantine soon discovered, that, in the decline of the arts, the skill as well as numbers of his architects bore a very unequal proportion to the greatness of his designs. The magistrates of the most distant provinces were therefore directed to institute schools, to appoint professors, and by the hopes of rewards and privileges, to engage in the study and practice of architecture a sufficient number of ingenious youths, who had received a liberal education.[41] The buildings of the new city were executed by such artificers as the reign of Constantine could afford ; but they were decorated by the hands of the most celebrated masters of the age of Pericles and Alexander. To revive the genius of Phidias and Lysippus, surpassed indeed the power of a Roman emperor ; but the immortal productions which they had bequeathed to posterity were exposed without defence to the rapacious vanity of a despot. By his commands the cities of Greece and Asia were despoiled of their most valuable ornaments.[42] The trophies of memorable wars, the objects of religious veneration, the most finished statues of the gods and heroes, of the sages and poets, of ancient times, contributed to the splendid triumph of Constantinople ; and gave occasion to the remark of the historian Cedrenus,[43] who observes, with some enthusiasm, that nothing seemed wanting except the souls of the illustrious men whom these admirable monuments were intended to represent. But it is not in the city of Constantine, nor in the declining

---

[40] For the forests of the Black Sea, consult Tournefort, Lettre XVI ; for the marble quarries of Proconnesus, see Strabo, l. xiii. p. 588, [881, edit. Casaub.] The latter had already furnished the materials of the stately buildings of Cyzicus.

[41] See the Codex Theodos. l. xiii. tit. iv. leg. 1. This law is dated in the year 334, and was addressed to the præfect of Italy, whose jurisdiction extended over Africa. The commentary of Godefroy on the whole title well deserves to be consulted.

[42] Constantinopolis dedicatur pœne omnium urbium nuditate. Hieronym. Chron. p. 181. See Codinus, p. 8, 9. The author of the Antiquitat. Const. l. iii. (apud Banduri Imp. Orient. tom. i. p. 41) enumerates Rome, Sicily, Antioch, Athens, and a long list of other cities. The provinces of Greece and Asia Minor may be supposed to have yielded the richest booty.

[43] Hist. Compend. p. 369. He describes the statue, or rather bust, of Homer with a degree of taste which plainly indicates that Cedrenus copied the style of a more fortunate age.

period of an empire, when the human mind was depressed by civil and religious slavery, that we should seek for the souls of Homer and of Demosthenes.

During the siege of Byzantium, the conqueror had pitched nis tent on the commanding eminence of the second hill. To perpetuate the memory of his success, he chose the same advantageous position for the principal Forum;[44] which appears to have been of a circular, or rather elliptical form. The two opposite entrances formed triumphal arches; the porticos which enclosed it on every side, were filled with statues; and the centre of the Forum was occupied by a lofty column, of which a mutilated fragment is now degraded by the appellation of the *burnt pillar*. This column was erected on a pedestal of white marble twenty feet high; and was composed of ten pieces of porphyry, each of which measured about ten feet in height, and about thirty-three in circumference.[45] On the summit of the pillar, above one hundred and twenty feet from the ground, stood the colossal statue of Apollo. It was of bronze, had been transported either from Athens or from a town of Phrygia, and was supposed to be the work of Phidias. The artist had represented the god of day, or, as it was afterwards interpreted, the emperor Constantine himself, with a sceptre in his right hand, the globe of the world in his left, and a crown of rays glittering on his head.[46] The Circus, or Hippodrome, was a stately building about four

---

[44] Zosim. l. ii. p. 106. Chron. Alexandrin. vel Paschal. p. 284. Ducange, Const. l. i. c. 24. Even the last of those writers seems to confound the Forum of Constantine with the Augusteum, or court of the palace. I am not satisfied whether I have properly distinguished what belongs to the one and the other.

[45] The most tolerable account of this column is given by Pocock. Description of the East, vol. ii. part ii. p. 131. But it is still in many instances perplexed and unsatisfactory.

[46] Ducange, Const. l. i. c. 24, p. 76, and his notes ad Alexiad. p. 382. The statue of Constantine or Apollo was thrown down under the reign of Alexius Comnenus.*

---

* On this column (says M. von Hammer) Constantine, with singular shamelessness, placed his own statue with the attributes of Apollo and Christ. He substituted the nails of the Passion for the rays of the sun. Such is the direct testimony of the author of the Antiquit. Constantinop. apud Banduri. Constantine was replaced by the "great and religious" Julian; Julian, by Theodosius. A. D. 1412, the key stone was loosened by an earthquake. The statue fell in the reign of Alexius Comnenus, and was replaced by the cross. The Palladium was said to be buried under the pillar. Von Hammer, Constantinopolis und der Bosporos, i. 162. — M

15237

hundred paces in length, and one hundred in breadth.[17] The
space between the two *metæ* or goals was filled with statues
and obelisks; and we may still remark a very singular fragment of antiquity; the bodies of three serpents, twisted into
one pillar of brass. Their triple heads had once supported
the golden tripod which, after the defeat of Xerxes, was consecrated in the temple of Delphi by the victorious Greeks.[48]
The beauty of the Hippodrome has been long since defaced
by the rude hands of the Turkish conquerors;[†] but, under
the similar appellation of Atmeidan, it still serves as a place
of exercise for their horses. From the throne, whence the
emperor viewed the Circensian games, a winding staircase [49]
descended to the palace; a magnificent edifice, which scarcely
yielded to the residence of Rome itself, and which, together
with the dependent courts, gardens, and porticos, covered a
considerable extent of ground upon the banks of the Propontis between the Hippodrome and the church of St. Sophia.[50]

---

[47] Tournefort (Lettre XII.) computes the Atmeidan at four hundred paces. If he means geometrical paces of five feet each, it was
three hundred *toises* in length, about forty more than the great circus
of Rome. See D'Anville, Mesures Itineraires, p. 73.

[48] The guardians of the most holy relics would rejoice if they were
able to produce such a chain of evidence as may be alleged on this
occasion. See Banduri ad Antiquitat. Const. p. 668. Gyllius de
Byzant. l. ii. c. 13.   1. The original consecration of the tripod and
pillar in the temple of Delphi may be proved from Herodotus and
Pausanias.   2. The Pagan Zosimus agrees with the three ecclesiastical
historians, Eusebius, Socrates, and Sozomen, that the sacred ornaments of the temple of Delphi were removed to Constantinople by
the order of Constantine; and among these the serpentine pillar of
the Hippodrome is particularly mentioned.   3. All the European
travellers who have visited Constantinople, from Buondelmonte to
Pocock, describe it in the same place, and almost in the same manner;
the differences between them are occasioned only by the injuries
which it has sustained from the Turks. Mahomet the Second broke
the under-jaw of one of the serpents with a stroke of his battle-axe.
Thevenot, l. i. c. 17.[*]

[49] The Latin name *Cochlea* was adopted by the Greeks, and very
frequently occurs in the Byzantine history. Ducange, Const. l. ii. c.
1, p. 104.

[50] There are three topographical points which indicate the situation

---

[*] See note 75, ch. lxviii. for Dr. Clarke's rejection of Thevenot's authority. Von Hammer, however, repeats the story of Thevenot without ques-
tioning its authenticity. — M.

[†] In 1808 the Janizaries revolted against the vizier Mustapha Baisactar,
who wished to introduce a new system of military organization, besieged
the quarter of the Hippodrome, in which stood the palace of the viziers,
and the Hippodrome was consumed in the conflagration. — G.

We might likewise celebrate the baths, which stiu retained the name of Zeuxippus, after they had been enriched, by the munificence of Constantine, with lofty columns, various marbles, and above threescore statues of bronze.[5]. But we should deviate from the design of this history, if we attempted minutely to describe the different buildings or quarters of the city. It may be sufficient to observe, that whatever could adorn the dignity of a great capital, or contribute to tne benefit or pleasure of its numerous inhabitants, was contained within the walls of Constantinople. A particular description, composed about a century after its foundation, enumerates a capitol or school of learning, a circus, two theatres, eight public, and one hundred and fifty-three private baths, fifty-two porticos, five granaries, eight aqueducts or reservoirs of water, four spacious halls for the meetings of the senate or courts of justice, fourteen churches, fourteen palaces, and four thousand three hundred and eighty-eight houses, which, for their size or beauty, deserved to be distinguished from the multitude of plebeian habitations.[52]

The populousness of his favored city was the next and most serious object of the attention of its founder. In the dark ages which succeeded the translation of the empire, the remote

---

of the palace. 1. The staircase which connected it with the Hippodrome or Atmeidan. 2. A small artificial port on the Propontis, from whence there was an easy ascent, by a flight of marble steps, to the gardens of the palace. 3. The Augusteum was a spacious court, one side of which was occupied by the front of the palace, and another by the church of St. Sophia.

[51] Zeuxippus was an epithet of Jupiter, and the baths were a part of old Byzantium. The difficulty of assigning their true situation has not been felt by Ducange. History seems to connect them with St. Sophia and the palace; but the original plan inserted in Banduri places them on the other side of the city, near the harbor. For their beauties, see Chron. Paschal. p. 285, and Gyllius de Byzant. l. ii. c. 7. Christodorus (see Antiquitat. Const. l. vii.) composed inscriptions in verse for each of the statues. He was a Theban poet in genius as well as in birth : —

Bæotum in crasso jurares aëre natum.*

[52] See the Notitia. Rome only reckoned 1780 large houses, *domus;* but the word must have had a more dignified signification. No *insulæ* are mentioned at Constantinople. The old capital consisted of 424 streets, the new of 322.

---

* Yet, for his age, the description of the statues of Hecuba and of Homer are by no means without merit. See Antholog. Palat. (edit. Jacobs) i. 37. — M.

and the immediate consequences of that memorable event were strangely confounded by the vanity of the Greeks and the credulity of the Latins.[53] It was asserted, and believed, that all the noble families of Rome, the senate, and the equestrian order, with their innumerable attendants, had followed their emperor to the banks of the Propontis; that a spurious race of strangers and plebeians was left to possess the solitude of the ancient capital; and that the lands of Italy, long since converted into gardens, were at once deprived of cultivation and inhabitants.[54] In the course of this history, such exaggerations will be reduced to their just value: yet, since the growth of Constantinople cannot be ascribed to the general increase of mankind and of industry, it must be admitted that this artificial colony was raised at the expense of the ancient cities of the empire. Many opulent senators of Rome, and of the eastern provinces, were probably invited by Constantine to adopt for their country the fortunate spot, which he had chosen for his own residence. The invitations of a master are scarcely to be distinguished from commands; and the liberality of the emperor obtained a ready and cheerful obedience. He bestowed on his favorites the palaces which he had built in the several quarters of the city, assigned them lands and pensions for the support of their dignity,[55] and alienated the demesnes of Pontus and Asia to grant hereditary estates by the easy tenure of maintaining a house in the capital.[56]

---

[53] Liutprand, Legatio ad Imp. Nicephorum, p. 153. The modern Greeks have strangely disfigured the antiquities of Constantinople. We might excuse the errors of the Turkish or Arabian writers; but it is somewhat astonishing, that the Greeks, who had access to the authentic materials preserved in their own language, should prefer fiction to truth, and loose tradition to genuine history. In a single page of Codinus we may detect twelve unpardonable mistakes; the reconciliation of Severus and Niger, the marriage of their son and daughter, the siege of Byzantium by the Macedonians, the invasion of the Gauls, which recalled Severus to Rome, the *sixty* years which elapsed from his death to the foundation of Constantinople, &c.

[54] Montesquieu, Grandeur et Decadence des Romains, c. 17.

[55] Themist. Orat. iii. p. 48, edit. Hardouin.   Sozomen, l. ii. c. 3 Zosim. l. ii. p. 107.   Anonym. Valesian. p. 715.   If we could credit Codinus, (p. 10,) Constantine built houses for the senators on the exact model of their Roman palaces, and gratified them, as well as himself, with the pleasure of an agreeable surprise; but the whole story is full of fictions and inconsistencies.

[56] The law by which the younger Theodosius, in the year 438, abolished this tenure, may be found among the Novellæ of the emperor at the end of the Theodosian Code, tom. vi. nov. 12.   **M. de**

But these encouragements and obligations soon became super-fluous, and were gradually abolished. Wherever the seat of government is fixed, a considerable part of the public revenue will be expended by the prince himself, by his ministers, by the officers of justice, and by the domestics of the palace. The most wealthy of the provincials will be attracted by the powerful motives of interest and duty, of amusement and curiosity. A third and more numerous class of inhabitants will insensibly be formed, of servants, of artificers, and of merchants, who derive their subsistence from their own labor and from the wants or luxury of the superior ranks. In less than a century, Constantinople disputed with Rome itself the preëminence of riches and numbers. New piles of buildings crowded together with too little regard to health or convenience, scarcely allowed the intervals of narrow streets for the per-petual throng of men, of horses, and of carriages. The allotted space of ground was insufficient to contain the increasing people; and the additional foundations, which, on either side, were advanced into the sea, might alone have composed a very considerable city.[57]

The frequent and regular distributions of wine and oil, of corn or bread, of money or provisions, had almost exempted the poorest citizens of Rome from the necessity of labor. The magnificence of the first Cæsars was in some measure imi-tated by the founder of Constantinople:[58] but his liberality,

---

Tillemont (Hist. des Empereurs, tom. iv. p. 371) has evidently mis-taken the nature of these estates. With a grant from the Imperial demesnes, the same condition was accepted as a favor, which would justly have been deemed a hardship, if it had been imposed upon private property.

[57] The passages of Zosimus, of Eunapius, of Sozomen, and of Agathias, which relate to the increase of buildings and inhabitants at Constantinople, are collected and connected by Gyllius de Byzant. l. i. c. 3. Sidonius Apollinaris (in Panegyr. Anthem. 56, p. 279, edit. Sirmond) describes the moles that were pushed forwards into the sea; they consisted of the famous Puzzolan sand, which hardens in the water.

[58] Sozomen, l. ii. c. 3. Philostorg. l. ii. c. 9. Codin. Antiquitat. Const. p. 8. It appears by Socrates, l. ii. c. 13, that the daily allow-ance of the city consisted of eight myriads of σίτου, which we may either translate, with Valesius, by the words modii of corn, or consider as expressive of the number of loaves of bread.*

---

* At Rome the poorer citizens who received these gratuities were inscribed in a register; they had only a personal right. Constantine attached the right to the houses in his new capital, to engage the lower classes of the people to build their houses with expedition. Codex Theo-dos. l. xiv — G.

however it might excite the applause of the people, has in
curred the censure of posterity. A nation of legislators and
conquerors might assert their claim to the harvests of Africa,
which had been purchased with their blood ; and it was art
fully contrived by Augustus, that, in the enjoyment of plenty,
the Romans should lose the memory of freedom. But the
prodigality of Constantine could not be excused by any consideration either of public or private interest ; and the annual
tribute of corn imposed upon Egypt for the benefit of his new
capital, was applied to feed a lazy and insolent populace, at
the expense of the husbandmen of an industrious province.[59] *
Some other regulations of this emperor are less liable to blame
but they are less deserving of notice. He divided Constantinople into fourteen regions or quarters,[60] dignified the public
council with the appellation of senate,[61] communicated to

---

[59] See Cod. Theodos. l. xiii. and xiv., and Cod. Justinian. Edict. xii
tom. ii. p. 648, edit. Genev. See the beautiful complaint of Rome in
the poem of Claudian de Bell. Gildonico, ver. 46—64.

> Cum subiit par Roma mihi, divisaque sumsit
> Æquales aurora togas ; Ægyptia rura
> In partem cessere novam.

[60] The regions of Constantinople are mentioned in the code of
Justinian, and particularly described in the Notitia of the younger
Theodosius ; but as the four last of them are not included within the
wall of Constantine, it may be doubted whether this division of the
city should be referred to the founder.

[61] Senatum constituit secundi ordinis ; *Claros* vocavit. Anonym.
Valesian. p. 715. The senators of old Rome were styled *Clarissimi*.
See a curious note of Valesius ad Ammian. Marcellin. xxii. 9. From
the eleventh epistle of Julian, it should seem that the place of senator
was considered as a burden, rather than as an honor ; but the Abbé
de la Bleterie (Vie de Jovien, tom. ii. p. 371) has shown that this
epistle could not relate to Constantinople. Might we not read,
instead of the celebrated name of Βυζαντίοις, the obscure but more
probable word βισανθίνοις ? Bisanthe or Rhœdestus, now Rhodosto,
was a small maritime city of Thrace. See Stephan. Byz. de Urbibus,
p. 225, and Cellar. Geograph. tom. i. p. 849.

---

* This was also at the expense of Rome. The emperor ordered that the
fleet of Alexandria should transport to Constantinople the grain of Egypt,
which it carried before to Rome : this grain supplied Rome during four
months of the year. Claudian has described with force the famine occasioned by this measure : —

> Hæc nobis, hæc ante dabas ; nunc pabula tantum
> Roma precor : miserere tuæ, pater optime, gentis ·
> Extremam defende famem.

Claud. de Bell. Gildon. v 34

— G

It was scarcely this measure. Gildo had cut off the African as well as
the Egyptian supplies. — M.

the citizens the privileges of Italy,[62] and bestowed on the rising city the title of Colony, the first and most favored daughter of ancient Rome. The venerable parent still maintained the legal and acknowledged supremacy, which was due to her age, to her dignity, and to the remembrance of her former greatness.[63]

As Constantine urged the progress of the work with the impatience of a lover, the walls, the porticos, and the principal edifices were completed in a few years, or, according to another account, in a few months; [64] but this extraordinary diligence should excite the less admiration, since many of the buildings were finished in so hasty and imperfect a manner, that under the succeeding reign, they were preserved with difficulty from impending ruin.[65] But while they dis-

---

[62] Cod. Theodos. l. xiv. 13. The commentary of Godefroy (tom. v. p. 220) is long, but perplexed; nor indeed is it easy to ascertain in what the Jus Italicum could consist, after the freedom of the city had been communicated to the whole empire.*

[63] Julian (Orat. i. p. 8) celebrates Constantinople as not less superior to all other cities than she was inferior to Rome itself. His learned commentator (Spanheim, p. 75, 76) justifies this language by several parallel and contemporary instances. Zosimus, as well as Socrates and Sozomen, flourished after the division of the empire between the two sons of Theodosius, which established a perfect *equality* between the old and the new capital.

[64] Codinus (Antiquitat. p. 8) affirms, that the foundations of Constantinople were laid in the year of the world 5837, (A. D. 329,) on the 26th of September, and that the city was dedicated the 11th of May, 5838, (A. D. 330.) He connects these dates with several characteristic epochs, but they contradict each other; the authority of Codinus is of little weight, and the space which he assigns must appear insufficient. The term of ten years is given us by Julian, (Orat. i. p. 8;) and Spanheim labors to establish the truth of it, (p. 69—75,) by the help of two passages from Themistius, (Orat. iv. p. 58,) and of Philostorgius, (l. ii. c. 9,) which form a period from the year 324 to the year 334. Modern critics are divided concerning this point of chronology, and their different sentiments are very accurately described by Tillemont, Hist. des Empereurs, tom. iv. p. 619—625.

[65] Themistius. Orat. iii. p. 47. Zosim. l. ii. p. 108. Constantine himself, in one of his laws, (Cod. Theod. l. xv. tit. i.,) betrays his impatience.

---

* " This right, (the Jus Italicum,) which by most writers is referred without foundation to the personal condition of the citizens, properly related to the city as a whole, and contained two parts. First, the Roman or quiritarian property in the soil, (commercium,) and its capability of mancipation, usucaption, and vindication; moreover, as an inseparable consequence of this, exemption from land-tax. Then, secondly, a free constitution in the Italian form, with Duumvirs, Quinquennales, and Ædiles, and especially with Jurisdiction." Savigny, Geschichte des Röm. Rechts. b. i. p. 51. — M.

play:.l the vigor and freshness of youth, the founder prepared to celebrate the dedication of his city.[66]   The games and largesses which crowned the pomp of this memorable festival may easily be supposed ; but there is one circumstance of a more singular and permanent nature, which ought not entirely to be overlooked.   As often as the birthday of the city returned, the statue of Constantine, framed by his order, of gilt wood, and bearing in his right hand a small image of the genius of the place, was erected on a triumphal car.   The guards, carrying white tapers, and clothed in their richest apparel, accompanied the solemn procession as it moved through the Hippodrome.   When it was opposite to the throne of the reigning emperor, he rose from his seat, and with grateful reverence adored the memory of his predecessor.[67]   At the festival of the dedication, an edict, engraved on a column of marble, bestowed the title of SECOND or NEW ROME on the city of Constantine.[68]   But the name of Constantinople [69] has prevailed over that honorable epithet ; and after the revolution of fourteen centuries, still perpetuates the fame of its author.[70]

The foundation of a new capital is naturally connected with the establishment of a new form of civil and military administration.   The distinct view of the complicated system of

[66] Cedrenus and Zonaras, faithful to the mode of superstition which prevailed in their own times, assure us that Constantinople was consecrated to the virgin Mother of God.

[67] The earliest and most complete account of this extraordinary ceremony may be found in the Alexandrian Chronicle, p. 285.   Tillemont, and the other friends of Constantine, who are offended with the air of Paganism which seems unworthy of a Christian prince, had a right to consider it as doubtful, but they were not authorized to omit the mention of it.

[68] Sozomen, l. ii. c. 2.   Ducange C. P. l. i. c. 6.   Velut ipsius Romæ filiam, is the expression of Augustin. de Civitat. Dei, l. v. c. 25.

[69] Eutropius, l. x. c. 8.   Julian. Orat. i. p. 8.   Ducange C. P. l. i. c. 5.   The name of Constantinople is extant on the medals of Constantine.

[70] The lively Fontenelle (Dialogues des Morts xii.) affects to deride the vanity of human ambition, and seems to triumph in the disappointment of Constantine, whose immortal name is now lost in the vulgar appellation of Istambol, a Turkish corruption of εἰς τὴν πόλιν. Yet the original name is still preserved, 1. By the nations of Europe. 2. By the modern Greeks. 3. By the Arabs, whose writings are diffused over the wide extent of their conquests in Asia and Africa. See D'Herbelot Bibliothèque Orientale, p. 275. 4. By the more learned Turks, and by the emperor himself in his public mandates. Cantemir's History of the Othman Empire, p. 51.

policy, introduced by Diocletian, improved by Constantine, and completed by his immediate successors, may not only amuse the fancy by the singular picture of a great empire, but will tend to illustrate the secret and internal causes of its rapid decay. In the pursuit of any remarkable institution, we may be frequently led into the more early or the more recent times of the Roman history; but the proper limits of this inquiry will be included within a period of about one hundred and thirty years, from the accession of Constantine to the publication of the Theodosian code; [71] from which, as well as from the *Notitia* * of the East and West,[72] we derive the most copious and authentic information of the state of the empire. This variety of objects will suspend, for some time, the course of the narrative; but the interruption will be censured only by those readers who are insensible to the importance of laws and manners, while they peruse, with eager curiosity, the transient intrigues of a court, or the accidental event of a battle.

The manly pride of the Romans, content with substantial power, had left to the vanity of the East the forms and ceremonies of ostentatious greatness.[73] But when they lost even the semblance of those virtues which were derived from their ancient freedom, the simplicity of Roman manners was insensibly corrupted by the stately affectation of the courts of Asia.

---

[71] The Theodosian code was promulgated A. D. 438. See the Prolegomena of Godefroy, c. i. p. 185.

[72] Pancirolus, in his elaborate Commentary, assigns to the Notitia a date almost similar to that of the Theodosian code; but his proofs, or rather conjectures, are extremely feeble. I should be rather inclined to place this useful work between the final division of the empire (A. D. 395) and the successful invasion of Gaul by the barbarians, (A. D. 407.) See Histoire des Anciens Peuples de l'Europe, tom. vii. p. 40.

[73] Scilicet externæ superbiæ sucto, non inerat notitia nostri, (perhaps *nostræ;*) apud quos vis Imperii valet, inania transmittuntur. Tacit. Annal. xv. 31. The gradation from the style of freedom and simplicity, to that of form and servitude, may be traced in the Epistles of Cicero, of Pliny, and of Symmachus.

---

* The Notitia Dignitatum Imperii is a description of all the offices in the court and the state, of the legions, &c. It resembles our court almanacs, (Red Books,) with this single difference, that our almanacs name the persons in office, the Notitia only the offices. It is of the time of the emperor Theodosius II., that is to say, of the fifth century, when the empire was divided into the Eastern and Western. It is probable that it was not made for the first time, and that descriptions of the same kind existed before. — G.

The distinctions of personal merit and influence, so conspicu ous in a republic, so feeble and obscure under a monarchy, were abolished by the despotism of the emperors; who substituted in their room a severe subordination of rank and office, from the titled slaves who were seated on the steps of the throne, to the meanest instruments of arbitrary power. This multitude of abject dependants was interested in the support of the actual government from the dread of a revolution, which might at once confound their hopes and intercept the reward of their services. In this divine hierarchy (for such it is frequently styled) every rank was marked with the most scrupulous exactness, and its dignity was displayed in a variety of trifling and solemn ceremonies, which it was a study to learn, and a sacrilege to neglect.[74] The purity of the Latin language was debased, by adopting, in the intercourse of pride and flattery, a profusion of epithets, which Tully would scarcely have understood, and which Augustus would have rejected with indignation. The principal officers of the empire were saluted, even by the sovereign himself, with the deceitful titles of your *Sincerity*, your *Gravity*, your *Excellency*, your *Eminence*, your *sublime and wonderful Magnitude*, your *illustrious and magnificent Highness*.[75] The codicils or patents of their office were curiously emblazoned with such emblems as were best adapted to explain its nature and high dignity; the image or portrait of the reigning emperors; a triumphal car; the book of mandates placed on a table, covered with a rich carpet, and illuminated by four tapers; the allegorical figures of the provinces which they governed; or the appellations and standards of the troops whom they commanded. Some of these official ensigns were really exhibited in their hall of audience; others preceded their pompous march when-

---

[74] The emperor Gratian, after confirming a law of precedency published by Valentinian, the father of his *Divinity*, thus continues: Siquis igitur indebitum sibi locum usurpaverit, nulla se ignoratione defendat; sitque plane *sacrilegii* reus, qui *d'vina* præcepta neglexerit Cod. Theod. l. vi. tit. v. leg. 2.

[75] Consult the *Notitia Dignitatum* at the end of the Theodosian code, tom. vi. p. 316.*

* Constantin, qui remplaça le grand Patriciat par une noblesse titrée, et qui changea avec d'autres institutions la nature de la société Latine, est le véritable fondateur de la royauté moderne, dans ce qu'elle conserva de Romain. Chateaubriand, Etud. Histor. Preface, i. 151. Manso, (Leben Constantins des Grossen,) p. 153, &c., has given a lucid view of the dignities and duties of the officers in the Imperial court — M.

ever they appeared in public; and every circumstance of their demeanor, their dress, their ornaments, and their train, was calculated to inspire a deep reverence for the representatives of supreme majesty. By a philosophic observer, the system of the Roman government might have been mistaken for a splendid theatre, filled with players of every character and degree, who repeated the language, and imitated the passions, of their original model.[76]

All the magistrates of sufficient importance to find a place in the general state of the empire, were accurately divided into three classes. 1. The *Illustrious*. 2. The *Spectabiles*, or *Respectable*. And, 3. The *Clarissimi*; whom we may translate by the word *Honorable*. In the times of Roman simplicity, the last-mentioned epithet was used only as a vague expression of deference, till it became at length the peculiar and appropriated title of all who were members of the senate,[77] and consequently of all who, from that venerable body, were selected to govern the provinces. The vanity of those who, from their rank and office, might claim a superior distinction above the rest of the senatorial order, was long afterwards indulged with the new appellation of *Respectable*: but the title of *Illustrious* was always reserved to some eminent personages who were obeyed or reverenced by the two subordinate classes. It was communicated only, I. To the consuls and patricians; II. To the Prætorian præfects, with the præfects of Rome and Constantinople; III. To the masters-general of the cavalry and the infantry; and, IV. To the seven ministers of the palace, who exercised their *sacred* functions about the person of the emperor.[78] Among those illustrious magistrates who were esteemed coördinate with each other, the seniority of appointment gave place to the union of dignities.[79] By the expedient of honorary codicils, the emperors, who were fond of multiplying their favors, might

---

[76] Pancirolus ad Notitiam utriusque Imperii, p. 39. But his explanations are obscure, and he does not sufficiently distinguish the painted emblems from the effective ensigns of office.

[77] In the Pandects, which may be referred to the reigns of the Antonines, *Clarissimus* is the ordinary and legal title of a senator.

[78] Pancirol. p. 12—17. I have not taken any notice of the two inferior ranks, *Prefectissimus* and *Egregius*, which were given to many persons who were not raised to the senatorial dignity.

[79] Cod. Theodos. l. vi. tit. vi. The rules of precedence are ascertained with the most minute accuracy by the emperors, and illustrated with equal prolixity by their learned interpreter.

sometimes gratify the vanity, though not the ambition, of impatient courtiers.[80]

I. As long as the Roman consuls were the first magistrates of a free state, they derived their right to power from the choice of the people. As long as the emperors condescended to disguise the servitude which they imposed, the consuls were still elected by the real or apparent suffrage of the senate. From the reign of Diocletian, even these vestiges of liberty were abolished, and the successful candidates who were invested with the annual honors of the consulship, affected to deplore the humiliating condition of their predecessors. The Scipios and the Catos had been reduced to solicit the votes of plebeians, to pass through the tedious and expensive forms of a popular election, and to expose their dignity to the shame of a public refusal; while their own happier fate had reserved them for an age and government in which the rewards of virtue were assigned by the unerring wisdom of a gracious sovereign.[81] In the epistles which the emperor addressed to the two conslus elect, it was declared, that they were created by his sole authority.[82] Their names and portraits, engraved on gilt tablets of ivory, were dispersed over the empire as presents to the provinces, the cities, the magistrates, the senate, and the people.[83] Their solemn inauguration was performed at the place of the Imperial residence; and during a period of one hundred and twenty years, Rome was constantly deprived of the presence of her ancient magistrates.[84] On the morning of the first of January, the consuls assumed the ensigns of their dignity. Their dress was a robe of purple,

---

[80] Cod. Theodos. l. vi. tit. xxii.

[81] Ausonius (in Gratiarum Actione) basely expatiates on this unworthy topic, which is managed by Mamertinus (Panegyr. Vet. xi. [x.] 16, 19) with somewhat more freedom and ingenuity.

[82] Cum de Consulibus in annum creandis, solus mecum volutarem .... te Consulem et designavi, et declaravi, et priorem nuncupavi; are some of the expressions employed by the emperor Gratian to his preceptor, the poet Ausonius.

[83]   Immanesque .... dentes
    Qui secti ferro in tabulas auroque micantes,
    Inscripti rutilum cœlato Consule nomen
    Per proceres et vulgus eant.

                        Claud. in ii Cons. Stilichon. 456.

Montfaucon has represented some of these tablets or dypticks; see Supplement à l'Antiquité expliquée, tom. iii. p. 220.

[84] Consule lætatur post plurima secula viso
     Pallanteus apex; agnoscunt rostra curules

embroidered in silk and gold, and sometimes oramented with costly gems.[85] On the morning of the first of January, the consuls assumed the ensigns of their dignity. Their dress was a robe of purple, embroidered in silk and gold, and sometimes ornamented with costly gems.[85] On this solemn occasion they were attended by the most eminent officers of the state and army, in the habit of senators; and the useless fasces, armed with the once formidable axes, were borne before them by the lictors.[86] The procession moved from the palace [87] to the Forum or principal square of the city; where the consuls ascended their tribunal, and seated themselves in the curule chairs, which were framed after the fashion of ancient times. They immediately exercised an act of jurisdiction, by the manumission of a slave, who was brought before them for that purpose; and the ceremony was intended to represent the celebrated action of the elder Brutus, the author of liberty and of the consulship, when he admitted among his fellow-citizens the faithful Vindex, who had revealed the conspiracy of the Tarquins.[88] The public festival

Auditas quondam proavis : desuetaque cingit
Regius auratis Fora fascibus Ulpia lictor.
Claud. in vi Cons. Honorii, 643.

From the reign of Carus to the sixth consulship of Honorius, there was an interval of one hundred and twenty years, during which the emperors were always absent from Rome on the first day of January. See the Chronologie de Tillemont, tom. iii. iv. and v.

[85] See Claudian in Cons. Prob. et Olybrii, 178, &c.; and in iv Cons. Honorii, 585, &c.; though in the latter it is not easy to separate the ornaments of the emperor from those of the consul. Ausonius received from the liberality of Gratian a *vestis palmata*, or robe of state, in which the figure of the emperor Constantius was embroidered.

[86] Cernis et armorum proceres legumque potentes :
Patricios sumunt habitus; et more Gabino
Discolor incedit legio, positisque parumper
Bellorum signis, sequitur vexilla Quirini.
Lictori cedunt aquilæ, ridetque togatus
Miles, et in mediis effulget curia castris.
Claud. in iv Cons. Honorii, &.

—— *strictasque* procul radiare *secures.*
In Cons. Prob. 229

[87] See Valesius ad Ammian. Marcellin. l. xxii. c. 7.

[88] Auspice mox læto sonuit clamore tribunal;
Te fastos ineunte quater; solemnia ludit
Omnia libertas: deductum Vindice morem
Lex servat, famulusque jugo laxatus herili
Ducitur, et grato remeat securior ictu.
Claud. in iv Cons. Honorii, 611

was continued during several days in all the principal cities, in Rome, from custom; in Constantinople, from imitation; in Carthage, Antioch, and Alexandria, from the love of pleasure, and the superfluity of wealth.[89] In the two capitals of the empire the annual games of the theatre, the circus, and the amphitheatre,[90] cost four thousand pounds of gold, (about) one hundred and sixty thousand pounds sterling: and if so heavy an expense surpassed the faculties or the inclination of the magistrates themselves, the sum was supplied from the Imperial treasury.[91] As soon as the consuls had discharged these customary duties, they were at liberty to retire into the shade of private life, and to enjoy, during the remainder of the year, the undisturbed contemplation of their own greatness. They no longer presided in the national councils; they no longer executed the resolutions of peace or war. Their abilities (unless they were employed in more effective offices) were of little moment; and their names served only as the legal date of the year in which they had filled the chair of Marius and of Cicero. Yet it was still felt and acknowledged, in the last period of Roman servitude, that this empty name might be compared, and even preferred, to the possession of substantial power. The title of consul was still the most splendid object of ambition, the noblest reward of virtue and loyalty. The emperors themselves, who disdained the faint shadow of the republic, were conscious that they acquired an additional splendor and majesty as often as they assumed the annual honors of the consular dignity.[92]

The proudest and most perfect separation which can be found in any age or country, between the nobles and the

---

[89] Celebrant quidem solemnes istos dies omnes ubique urbes quæ sub legibus agunt; et Roma de more, et Constantinopolis de imitatione, et Antiochia pro luxu, et discincta Carthago, et domus fluminis Alexandria, sed Treviri Principis beneficio. Ausonius in Grat. Actione.

[90] Claudian (in Cons. Mall. Theodori, 279—331) describes, in a lively and fanciful manner, the various games of the circus, the theatre, and the amphitheatre, exhibited by the new consul. The sanguinary combats of gladiators had already been prohibited.

[91] Procopius in Hist. Arcana, c. 26.

[92] In Consulatu honos sine labore suscipitur. (Mamertin. in Panegyr. Vet. xi. [x.] 2.) This exalted idea of the consulship is borrowed from an Oration (iii. p. 107) pronounced by Julian in the servile court of Constantius. See the Abbé de la Bleterie, (Mémoires de l'Academie, tom. xxiv. p. 289,) who delights to pursue the vestiges of the old constitution, and who sometimes finds them in his copious fancy

people, is perhaps that of the Patricians and the Plebeians as it was established in the first age of the Roman republic Wealth and honors, the offices of the state, and the ceremonies of religion, were almost exclusively possessed by the former; who, preserving the purity of their blood with the most insulting jealousy,[93] held their clients in a condition of specious vassalage. But these distinctions, so incompatible with the spirit of a free people, were removed, after a long struggle, by the persevering efforts of the Tribunes. The most active and successful of the Plebeians accumulated wealth, aspired to honors, deserved triumphs, contracted alliances, and, after some generations, assumed the pride of ancient nobility.[94] The Patrician families, on the other hand, whose original number was never recruited till the end of the commonwealth, either failed in the ordinary course of nature or were extinguished in so many foreign and domestic wars, or, through a want of merit or fortune, insensibly mingled with the mass of the people.[95] Very few remained who could derive their pure and genuine origin from the infancy of the city, or even from that of the republic, when Cæsar and Augustus, Claudius and Vespasian, created from the body of the senate a competent number of new Patrician families, in the hope of perpetuating an order, which was still considered as honorable and sacred.[96] But these artificial supplies (in which the reign-

---

[93] Intermarriages between the Patricians and Plebeians were prohibited by the laws of the XII. Tables; and the uniform operations of human nature may attest that the custom survived the law. See in Livy (iv. 1—6) the pride of family urged by the consul, and the rights of mankind asserted by the tribune Canuleius.

[94] See the animated picture drawn by Sallust, in the Jugurthine war, of the pride of the nobles, and even of the virtuous Metellus, who was unable to brook the idea that the honor of the consulship should be bestowed on the obscure merit of his lieutenant Marius. (c. 64.) Two hundred years before, the race of the Metelli themselves were confounded among the Plebeians of Rome; and from the etymology of their name of *Cæcilius*, there is reason to believe that those haughty nobles derived their origin from a sutler.

[95] In the year of Rome 800, very few remained, not only of the old Patrician families, but even of those which had been created by Cæsar and Augustus. (Tacit. Annal. xi. 25.) The family of Scaurus (a branch of the Patrician Æmilii) was degraded so low that his father, who exercised the trade of a charcoal merchant, left him only ten slaves, and somewhat less than three hundred pounds sterling. (Valerius Maximus, l. iv. c. 4. n, 11. Aurel. Victor in Scauro) The family was saved from oblivion by the merit of the son.

[96] Tacit. Annal. xi. 25. Dion Cassius, l. iii. p. 693. The virtues

ing house was always included) were rapidly swept away by the rage of tyrants, by frequent revolutions, by the change of manners, and by the intermixture of nations.[97] Little more was left when Constantine ascended the throne, than a vague and imperfect tradition, that the Patricians had once been the first of the Romans. To form a body of nobles, whose influence may restrain, while it secures the authority of the monarch, would have been very inconsistent with the character and policy of Constantine; but had he seriously entertained such a design, it might have exceeded the measure of his power to ratify, by an arbitrary edict, an institution which must expect the sanction of time and of opinion. He revived, indeed, the title of PATRICIANS, but he revived it as a personal, not as an hereditary distinction. They yielded only to the transient superiority of the annual consuls; but they enjoyed the preeminence over all the great officers of state, with the most familiar access to the person of the prince. This honorable rank was bestowed on them for life; and as they were usually favorites, and ministers who had grown old in the Imperial court, the true etymology of the word was perverted by ignorance and flattery; and the Patricians of Constantine were reverenced as the adopted *Fathers* of the emperor and the republic.[98]

II. The fortunes of the Prætorian præfects were essentially different from those of the consuls and Patricians. The latter saw their ancient greatness evaporate in a vain title. The former, rising by degrees from the most humble condition, were invested with the civil and military administration of the Roman world. From the reign of Severus to that of Diocletian, the guards and the palace, the laws and the finances, the armies and the provinces, were intrusted to their superintending care; and, like the Viziers of the East, they held with one hand the seal, and with the other the standard, of the empire. The ambition of the præfects, always formidable, and some-

---

of Agricola, who was created a Patrician by the emperor Vespasian, reflected honor on that ancient order; but his ancestors had not any claim beyond an Equestrian nobility.

[97] This failure would have been almost impossible if it were true, as Casaubon compels Aurelius Victor to affirm (ad Sueton. in Cæsar c. 42. See Hist. August. p. 203, and Casaubon Comment., p. 220) that Vespasian created at once a thousand Patrician families. But this extravagant number is too much even for the whole Senatorial order, unless we should include all the Roman knights who were distinguished by the permission of wearing the laticlave.

[98] Zosimus, l. ii. p. 118; and Gᵢ defroy ad Cod. Theodos. l. vi. tit. vi

times fatal to the masters whom they served, was supported by the strength of the Prætorian bands; but after those haughty troops had been weakened by Diocletian, and finally suppressed by Constantine, the præfects, who survived their fall, were reduced without difficulty to the station of useful and obedient ministers. When they were no longer responsible for the safety of the emperor's person, they resigned the jurisdiction which they had hitherto claimed and exercised over all the departments of the palace. They were deprived by Constantine of all military command, as soon as they had ceased to lead into the field, under their immediate orders, the flower of the Roman troops; and at length, by a singular revolution, the captains of the guards were transformed into the civil magistrates of the provinces. According to the plan of government instituted by Diocletian, the four princes had each their Prætorian præfect; and after the monarchy was once more united in the person of Constantine, he still continued to create the same number of FOUR PRÆFECTS, and intrusted to their care the same provinces which they already administered. 1. The præfect of the East stretched his ample jurisdiction into the three parts of the globe which were subject to the Romans, from the cataracts of the Nile to the banks of the Phasis, and from the mountains of Thrace to the frontiers of Persia. 2. The important provinces of Pannonia, Dacia, Macedonia, and Greece, once acknowledged the authority of the præfect of Illyricum. 3. The power of the præfect of Italy was not confined to the country from whence he derived his title; it extended over the additional territory of Rhætia as far as the banks of the Danube, over the dependent islands of the Mediterranean, and over that part of the continent of Africa which lies between the confines of Cyrene and those of Tingitania. 4. The præfect of the Gauls comprehended under that plural denomination the kindred provinces of Britain and Spain, and his authority was obeyed from the wall of Antoninus to the foot of Mount Atlas.[99]

After the Prætorian præfects had been dismissed from all military command, the civil functions which they were ordained to exercise over so many subject nations, were

---

[99] Zosimus, l. ii. p. 109, 110. If we had not fortunately possessed this satisfactory account of the division of the power and provinces of the Prætorian præfects, we should frequently have been perplexed amidst the copious details of the Code, and the circumstantial minuteness of the Notitia.

adequate to the ambition and abilities of the most consummate ministers To their wisdom was committed the supreme administration of justice and of the finances, the two objects which, in a state of peace, comprehend almost all the respective duties of the sovereign and of the people; of the former, to protect the citizens who are, obedient to the laws; of the latter, to contribute the share of their property which is required for the expenses of the state. The coin, the highways, the posts, the granaries, the manufactures, whatever could interest the public prosperity, was moderated by the authority of the Prætorian præfects. As the immediate representatives of the Imperial majesty, they were empowered to explain, to enforce, and on some occasions to modify, the general edicts by their discretionary proclamations. They watched over the conduct of the provincial governors, removed the negligent, and inflicted punishments on the guilty. From all the inferior jurisdictions, an appeal in every matter of importance, either civil or criminal, might be brought before the tribunal of the præfect; but *his* sentence was final and absolute; and the emperors themselves refused to admit any complaints against the judgment or the integrity of a magistrate whom they honored with such unbounded confidence.[100] His appointments were suitable to his dignity;[101] and if avarice was his ruling passion, he enjoyed frequent opportunities of collecting a rich harvest of fees, of presents, and of perquisites. Though the emperors no longer dreaded the ambition of their præfects, they were attentive to counterbalance the power of this great office by the uncertainty and shortness of its duration.[102]

---

[100] See a law of Constantine himself. A præfectis autem prætorio provocare, non sinimus. Cod. Justinian. l. vii. tit. lxii. leg. 19. Charisius, a lawyer of the time of Constantine, (Heinec. Hist. Juris Romani, p. 349,) who admits this law as a fundamental principle of jurisprudence, compares the Prætorian præfects to the masters of the horse of the ancient dictators. Pandect. l. i. tit. xi.

[101] When Justinian, in the exhausted condition of the empire, instituted a Prætorian præfect for Africa, he allowed him a salary of one hundred pounds of gold. Cod. Justinian. l. i. tit. xxvii. leg. i.

[102] For this, and the other dignities of the empire, it may be sufficient to refer to the ample commentaries of Pancirolus and Godefroy, who have diligently collected and accurately digested in their proper order all the legal and historical materials. From those authors, Dr. Howell (History of the World, vol. ii. p. 24—77) has deduced a very distinct abridgment of the state of the

From their superior importance and digni y, Rome and Constantinople were alone excepted from the jurisdiction of the Prætorian præfects. The immense size of the city, and the experience of the tardy, ineffectual operation of the laws had furnished the policy of Augustus with a specious pretence for introducing a new magistrate, who alone could restrain a servile and turbulent populace by the strong arm of arbitrary power.[103]   Valerius Messalla was appointed the first præfect of Rome, that his reputation might countenance so invidious a measure ; but, at the end of a few days, that accomplished citizen [104] resigned his office, declaring, with a spirit worthy of the friend of Brutus, that he found himself incapable of exer· cising a power incompatible with public freedom.[105] As the sense of liberty became less exquisite, the advantages of order were more clearly understood ; and the præfect, who seemed to have been designed as a terror only to slaves and vagrants, was permitted to extend his civil and criminal jurisdiction over the equestrian and noble families of Rome.   The prætors, annually created as the judges of law and equity, could not long dispute the possession of the Forum with a vigorous and permanent magistrate, who was usually admitted into the confidence of the prince.   Their courts were deserted, their number, which had once fluctuated between twelve and eighteen,[106] was gradually reduced to two or three, and their important functions were confined to the expensive obligation [107] of exhibiting games for the amusement of the people.

---

103 Tacit. Annal. vi. 11. Euseb. in Chron. p. 155. Dion Cassius, in the oration of Mæcenas, (l. lvii. p. 675,) describes the prerogatives of the præfect of the city as they were established in his own time.

104 The fame of Messalla has been scarcely equal to his merit.   In the earliest youth he was recommended by Cicero to the friendship of Brutus.   He followed the standard of the republic till it was broken in the fields of Philippi ; he then accepted and deserved the favor of the most moderate of the conquerors ; and uniformly asserted his freedom and dignity in the court of Augustus.   The triumph of Messalla was justified by the conquest of Aquitain.   As an orator, he disputed the palm of eloquence with Cicero himself.   Messalla cultivated every muse, and was the patron of every man of genius.   He spent his evenings in philosophic conversation with Horace ; assumed his place at table between Delia and Tibullus ; and amused his leisure by encouraging the poetical talents of young Ovid.

105 Incivilem esse potestatem contestans, savs the translator of Eusebius.   Tacitus expresses the same idea in other words : quasi nescius exercendi.

106 See Lipsius, Excursus D. ad 1 lib. Tacit. Annal.

107 Heineccii Element. Juris Civilis secund. ordinem Pandect. tom.

After the office of the Roman consuls had been changed into a vain pageant, which was rarely displayed in the capital, the præfects assumed their vacant place in the senate, and were soon acknowledged as the ordinary presidents of that venerable assembly. They received appeals from the distance of one hundred miles; and it was allowed as a principle of jurisprudence, that all municipal authority was derived from them alone.[108] In the discharge of his laborious employment, the governor of Rome was assisted by fifteen officers, some of whom had been originally his equals, or even his superiors. The principal departments were relative to the command of a numerous watch, established as a safeguard against fires, robberies, and nocturnal disorders; the custody and distribution of the public allowance of corn and provisions; the care of the port, of the aqueducts, of the common sewers, and of the navigation and bed of the Tyber; the inspection of the markets, the theatres, and of the private as well as public works. Their vigilance insured the three principal objects of a regular police, safety, plenty, and cleanliness; and as a proof of the attention of government to preserve the splendor and ornaments of the capital, a particular inspector was appointed for the statues; the guardian, as it were, of that inanimate people, which, according to the extravagant computation of an old writer, was scarcely inferior in number to the living inhabitants of Rome. About thirty years after the foundation of Constantinople, a similar magistrate was created in that rising metropolis, for the same uses and with the same powers. A perfect equality was established between the dignity of the *two* municipal, and that of the *four* Prætorian præfects.[109]

Those who, in the Imperial hierarchy, were distinguished by

---

i. p. 70. See, likewise, Spanheim de Usu Numismatum, tom. ii. dissertat. x. p. 119. In the year 450, Marcian published a law, that *three* citizens should be annually created Prætors of Constantinople by the choice of the senate, but with their own consent. Cod. Justinian. li. i. tit. xxxix. leg. 2.

[108] Quidquid igitur intra urbem admittitur, ad P. U. videtur pertinere; sed et siquid intra centesimum milliarium. Ulpian in Pandect. l. i. tit. xiii. n. 1. He proceeds to enumerate the various offices of the præfect, who, in the code of Justinian, (l. i. tit. xxxix. leg. 3,) is declared to precede and command all city magistrates sine injuriâ ac detrimento honoris alieni.

[109] Besides our usual guides, we may observe that Felix Cantelorius has written a separate treatise, De Præfecto Urbis; and that many curious details concerning the police of Rome and Constantinople are contained in the fourteenth book of the Theodosian Code.

the title of *Respectable*, formed an intermediate class between the *illustrious* præfects, and the *honorable* magistrates of the provinces. In this class the proconsuls of Asia, Achaia, and Africa, claimed a preëminence, which was yielded to the remembrance of their ancient dignity; and the appeal from their tribunal to that of the præfects was almost the only mark of their dependence.[110] But the civil government of the empire was distributed into thirteen great DIOCESES, each of which equalled the just measure of a powerful kingdom. The first of these dioceses was subject to the jurisdiction of the *count* of the east; and we may convey some idea of the importance and variety of his functions, by observing, that six hundred apparitors, who would be styled at present either secretaries, or clerks, or ushers, or messengers, were employed in his immediate office.[111] The place of *Augustal præfect* of Egypt was no longer filled by a Roman knight; but the name was retained; and the extraordinary powers which the situation of the country, and the temper of the inhabitants, had once made indispensable, were still continued to the governor. The eleven remaining dioceses, of Asiana, Pontica, and Thrace; of Macedonia, Dacia, and Pannonia, or Western Illyricum; of Italy and Africa; of Gaul, Spain, and Britain; were governed by twelve *vicars* or *vice-præfects*,[112] whose name sufficiently explains the nature and dependence of their office. It may be added, that the lieutenant-generals of the Roman armies, the military counts and dukes, who will be hereafter mentioned, were allowed the rank and title of *Respectable*.

As the spirit of jealousy and ostentation prevailed in the councils of the emperors, they proceeded with anxious diligence to divide the substance and to multiply the titles of power. The vast countries which the Roman conquerors had united under the same simple form of administration, were imperceptibly crumbled into minute fragments; till at length the

---

[110] Eunapius affirms, that the proconsul of Asia was independent of the præfect; which must, however, be understood with some allowance: the jurisdiction of the vice-præfect he most assuredly disclaimed. Pancirolus, p. 161.

[111] The proconsul of Africa had four hundred apparitors; and they all received large salaries, either from the treasury or the province. See Pancirol. p. 26, and Cod. Justinian. l. xii. tit. lvi. lvii.

[112] In Italy there was likewise the *Vicar of Rome*. It has been much disputed, whether his jurisd'ction measured one hundred miles from the city, or whether it stretched over the ten southern provinces of Italy.

whole empire was distributed into one hundred and sixteen provinces, each of which supported an expensive and splendid establishment. Of these, three were governed by *proconsuls* thirty-seven by *consulars*, five by *correctors*, and seventy-one by *presidents*. The appellations of these magistrates were different; they ranked in successive order, the ensigns of their dignity were curiously varied, and their situation, from accidental circumstances, might be more or less agreeable or advantageous. But they were all (excepting only the proconsuls) alike included in the class of *honorable* persons ; and they were alike intrusted, during the pleasure of the prince, and under the authority of the præfects or their deputies, with the administration of justice and the finances in their respective districts. The ponderous volumes of the Codes and Pandects [113] would furnish ample materials for a minute inquiry into the system of provincial government, as in the space of six centuries it was improved by the wisdom of the Roman statesmen and lawyers. It may be sufficient for the historian to select two singular and salutary provisions, intended to restrain the abuse of authority. 1. For the preservation of peace and order, the governors of the provinces were armed with the sword of justice. They inflicted corporal punishments, and they exercised, in capital offences, the power of life and death. But they were not authorized to indulge the condemned criminal with the choice of his own execution, or to pronounce a sentence of the mildest and most honorable kind of exile. These prerogatives were reserved to the præfects, who alone could impose the heavy fine of fifty pounds of gold : their vicegerents were confined to the trifling weight of a few ounces.[114] This distinction, which seems to grant the larger, while it denies the smaller degree of authority, was founded on a very rational motive. The smaller degree was infinitely more liable to abuse. The passions of a provincial magistrate might frequently provoke him into acts of oppression, which affected only the freedom or the fortunes of the subject ;

---

[113] Among the works of the celebrated Ulpian, there was one in ten books, concerning the office of a proconsul, whose duties in the most essential articles were the same as those of an ordinary governor of a province.

[114] The presidents, or consulars, could impose only two ounces; the vice-præfects, three; the proconsuls, count of the east, and præfect of Egypt, six. See Heineccii Jur. Civil. tom. i. p. 75. Pandect. l. xlviii. tit. xix. n. 8.   Cod. Justinian. l. i. tit. liv. leg. 4, ?

though, fi m a principle of prudence, perhaps of humanity, he might still be terrified by the guilt of innocent blood. It may likewise be considered, that exile, considerable fines, or the choice of an easy death, relate more particularly to the rich and the noble ; and the persons the most exposed to the avarice or resentment of a provincial magistrate, were thus removed from his obscure persecution to the more august and impartial tribunal of the Prætorian præfect. 2. As it was reasonably apprehended that the integrity of the judge might be biased, if his interest was concerned, or his affections were engaged, the strictest regulations were established, to exclude any person, without the special dispensation of the emperor, from the government of the province where he was born ; [115] and to prohibit the governor or his son from contracting marriage with a native, or an inhabitant ; [116] or from purchasing slaves, lands, or houses, within the extent of his jurisdiction.[117] Notwithstanding these rigorous precautions, the emperor Constantine, after a reign of twenty-five years, still deplores the venal and oppressive administration of justice, and expresses the warmest indignation that the audience of the judge, his despatch of business, his seasonable delays, and his final sentence, were publicly sold, either by himself or by the officers of his court. The continuance, and perhaps the impunity, of these crimes, is attested by the repetition of impotent laws and ineffectual menaces.[118]

All the civil magistrates were drawn from the profession of the law. The celebrated Institutes of Justinian are addressed

---

[115] Ut nulli patriæ suæ administratio sine speciali principis permissu permittatur. Cod. Justinian. l. i. tit. xli. This law was first enacted by the emperor Marcus, after the rebellion of Cassius. (Dion. l. lxxi.) The same regulation is observed in China, with equal strictness, and with equal effect.

[116] Pandect. l. xxiii. tit. ii. n. 38, 57, 63.

[117] In jure continetur, ne quis in administratione constitutus aliquid compararet. Cod. Theod. l. viii. tit. xv. leg.1. This maxim of common law was enforced by a series of edicts (see the remainder of the title) from Constantine to Justin. From this prohibition, which is extended to the meanest officers of the governor, they except only clothes and provisions. The purchase within five years may be recovered ; after which, on information, it devolves to the treasury.

[118] Cessent rapaces jam nunc officialium manus ; cessent, inquam, nam si moniti non cessaverint, gladiis præcidentur, &c. Cod. Theod. l. i. tit. vii. leg. 1. Zeno enacted that all governors should remain in the province, to answer any accusations, fifty days after the expiration of their power Cod. Justinian. l. ii. tit. xlix. leg. 1

to the youth of his dominions, who had devoted themselves to the study of Roman jurisprudence; and the sovereign condescends to animate their diligence, by the assurance that their skill and ability would in time be rewarded by an adequate share in the government of the republic.[119] The rudiments of this lucrative science were taught in all the considerable cities of the east and west; but the most famous school was that of Berytus,[120] on the coast of Phœnicia; which flourished above three centuries from the time of Alexander Severus, the author perhaps of an institution so advantageous to his native country. After a regular course of education, which lasted five years, the students dispersed themselves through the provinces, in search of fortune and honors; nor could they want an inexhaustible supply of business in a great empire, already corrupted by the multiplicity of laws, of arts, and of vices. The court of the Prætorian præfect of the east could alone furnish employment for one hundred and fifty advocates, sixty-four of whom were distinguished by peculiar privileges; and two were annually chosen, with a salary of sixty pounds of gold, to defend the causes of the treasury. The first experiment was made of their judicial talents, by appointing them to act occasionally as assessors to the magistrates; from thence they were often raised to preside in the tribunals before which they had pleaded. They obtained the government of a province; and, by the aid of merit, of reputation, or of favor, they ascended, by successive steps, to the *illustrious* dignities of the state.[121] In the practice of the bar, these men had

---

[119] Summâ igitur ope, et alacri studio has leges nostras accipite; et vosmetipsos sic eruditos ostendite, ut spes vos pulcherrima foveat; noto legitimo opere perfecto, posse etiam nostram rempublicam in partibus ejus vobis credendis gubernari. Justinian. in proem. Institutionum.

[120] The splendor of the school of Berytus, which preserved in the east the language and jurisprudence of the Romans, may be computed to have lasted from the third to the middle of the sixth century. Heinecc. Jur. Rom. Hist. p. 351—356.

[121] As in a former period I have traced the civil and military promotion of Pertinax, I shall here insert the civil honors of Mallius Theodorus. 1. He was distinguished by his eloquence, while he pleaded as an advocate in the court of the Prætorian præfect. 2. He governed one of the provinces of Africa, either as president or consular, and deserved, by his administration, the honor of a brass statue. 3. He was appointed vicar, or vice-præfect, of Macedonia. 4. Quæstor. 5. Count of the sacred largesses. 6. Prætorian præfect of the Gauls; whilst he might yet be represented as a young man. 7. After a

considered reason as the instrument of dispute; they interpreted the laws according to the dictates of private interest; and the same pernicious habits might still adhere to their characters in the public administration of the state. The honor of a liberal profession has indeed been vindicated by ancient and modern advocates, who have filled the most important stations, with pure integrity and consummate wisdom: but in the decline of Roman jurisprudence, the ordinary promotion of lawyers was pregnant with mischief and disgrace. The noble art, which had once been preserved as the sacred inheritance of the patricians, was fallen into the hands of freedmen and plebeians,[122] who, with cunning rather than with skill, exercised a sordid and pernicious trade. Some of them procured admittance into families for the purpose of fomenting differences, of encouraging suits, and of preparing a harvest of gain for themselves or their brethren. Others, recluse in their chambers, maintained the dignity of legal professors, by furnishing a rich client with subtleties to confound the plainest truths, and with arguments to color the most unjustifiable pretensions. The splendid and popular class was composed of the advocates, who filled the Forum with the sound of their turgid and loquacious rhetoric. Careless of fame and of justice, they are described, for the most part, as ignorant and rapacious guides, who conducted their clients through a maze of expense, of delay, and of disappointment; from whence, after a tedious series of years, they were at length dismissed, when their patience and fortune were almost exhausted.[123]

---

retreat, perhaps a disgrace, of many years, which Mallius (confounded by some critics with the poet Manilius; see Fabricius Bibliothec. Latin. Edit. Ernest. tom. i. c. 18, p. 501) employed in the study of the Grecian philosophy, he was named Prætorian præfect of Italy, in the year 397. 8. While he still exercised that great office, he was created, in the year 399, consul for the West; and his name, on account of the infamy of his colleague, the eunuch Eutropius, often stands alone in the Fasti. 9. In the year 408, Mallius was appointed a second time Prætorian præfect of Italy. Even in the venal panegyric of Claudian, we may discover the merit of Mallius Theodorus, who, by a rare felicity, was the intimate friend, both of Symmachus and of St. Augustin. See Tillemont, Hist. des Emp. tom. v. p. 1110—1114.

[122] Mamertinus in Panegyr. Vet. xi. [x.] 20. Asterius apud Photium, p. 1500.

[123] The curious passage of Ammianus, (l. xxx. c. 4,) in which he paints the manners of contemporary lawyers affords a strange mix

III. In the system of policy introduced by Augustus, the governors, those at least of the Imperial provinces, were invested with the full powers of the sovereign himself. Ministers of peace and war, the distribution of rewards and punishments depended on them alone, and they successively appeared on their tribunal in the robes of civil magistracy, and in complete armor at the head of the Roman legions.[124] The influence of the revenue, the authority of law, and the command of a military force, concurred to render their power supreme and absolute ; and whenever they were tempted to violate their allegiance, the loyal province which they involved in their rebellion was scarcely sensible of any change in its political state. From the time of Commodus to the reign of Constantine, near one hundred governors might be enumerated, who, with various success, erected the standard of revolt; and though the innocent were too often sacrificed, the guilty might be sometimes prevented, by the suspicious cruelty of their master.[125] To secure his throne and the public tranquillity from these formidable servants, Constantine resolved to divide the military from the civil administration, and to establish, as a permanent and professional distinction, a practice which had been adopted only as an occasional expedient. The supreme jurisdiction exercised by the Prætorian præfects over the armies of the empire, was transferred to the two *masters-general* whom he instituted, the one for the *cavalry*, the other for the *infantry ;* and though each of these *illustrious* officers was more peculiarly responsible for the discipline of those troops which were under his immediate inspection, they both indifferently commanded in the field the several bodies, whether of horse or foot, which were united in the

---

ture of sound sense, false rhetoric, and extravagant satire. Godefroy (Prolegom. ad Cod. Theod. c. i. p. 185) supports the historian by similar complaints and authentic facts. In the fourth century, many camels might have been laden with law-books. Eunapius in Vit. Ædesii, p. 72.

[124] See a very splendid example in the life of Agricola, particularly c. 20, 21. The lieutenant of Britain was intrusted with the same powers which Cicero, proconsul of Cilicia, had exercised in the name of the senate and people.

[125] The Abbé Dubos, who has examined with accuracy (see Hist. de la Monarchie Françoise, tom. i. p. 41—100, edit. 1742) the institutions of Augustus and of Constantine, observes, that if Otho had been put to death the day before he executed his conspiracy, Otho would now appear in history as innocent as Corbulo.

same army.[126] Their number was soon doubled by the division of the east and west; and as separate generals of the same rank and title were appointed on the four important frontiers of the Rhine, of the Upper and the Lower Danube, and of the Euphrates, the defence of the Roman empire was at length committed to eight masters-general of the cavalry and infantry. Under their orders, thirty-five military commanders were stationed in the provinces : three in Britain, six in Gaul, one in Spain, one in Italy, five on the Upper, and four on the Lower Danube; in Asia, eight, three in Egypt, and four in Africa. The titles of *counts*, and *dukes*,[127] by which they were properly distinguished, have obtained in modern languages so very different a sense, that the use of them may occasion some surprise. But it should be recollected, that the second of those appellations is only a corruption of the Latin word, which was indiscriminately applied to any military chief. All these provincial generals were therefore *dukes ;* but no more than ten among them were dignified with the rank of *counts* or companions, a title of honor, or rather of favor, which had been recently invented in the court of Constantine. A gold belt was the ensign which distinguished the office of the counts and dukes ; and besides their pay, they received a liberal allowance sufficient to maintain one hundred and ninety servants, and one hundred and fifty-eight horses. They were strictly prohibited from interfering in any matter which related to the administration of justice or the revenue ; but the command which they exercised over the troops of their department, was independent of the authority of the magistrates. About the same time that Constantine gave a legal sanction to the ecclesiastical order, he instituted in the Roman empire the nice balance of the civil and the military powers. The emulation, and sometimes the discord, which reigned between two professions of opposite interests and incompatible manners, was productive of beneficial and of pernicious consequences. It was seldom to be expected

---

[126] Zosimus, l. ii. p. 110. Before the end of the reign of Constantius, the *magistri militum* were already increased to four. See Velesius ad Ammian. l. xvi. c. 7.

[127] Though the military counts and dukes are frequently mentioned, both in history and the codes, we must have recourse to the Notitia for the exact knowledge of their number and stations. For the institution, rank, privileges, &c., of the counts in general, see Cod Theod. l. vi. tit. xii—xx., with the commentary of Godefroy.

that the general and the civil governor of a province should either conspire for the disturbance, or should unite for the service, of their country. While the one delayed to offer the assistance which the other disdained to solicit, the troops very frequently remained without orders or without supplies ; the public safety was betrayed, and the defenceless subjects were left exposed to the fury of the Barbarians. The divided administration, which had been formed by Constantine, relaxed the vigor of the state, while it secured the tranquillity of the monarch.

The memory of Constantine has been deservedly censured for another innovation, which corrupted military discipline and prepared the ruin of the empire. The nineteen years which preceded his final victory over Licinius, had been a period of license and intestine war. The rivals who contended for the possession of the Roman world, had withdrawn the greatest part of their forces from the guard of the general frontier; and the principal cities which formed the boundary of their respective dominions were filled with soldiers, who considered their countrymen as their most implacable enemies. After the use of these internal garrisons had ceased with the civil war, the conqueror wanted either wisdom or firmness to revive the severe discipline of Diocletian, and to suppress a fatal indulgence, which habit had endeared and almost confirmed to the military order. From the reign of Constantine, a popular and even legal distinction was admitted between the *Palatines* [123] and the *Borderers ;* the troops of the court, as they were improperly styled, and the troops of the frontier. The former, elevated by the superiority of their pay and privileges, were permitted, except in the extraordinary emergencies of war, to occupy their tranquil stations in the heart of the provinces. The most flourishing cities were oppressed by the intolerable weight of quarters. The soldiers insensibly forgot the virtues of their profession, and contracted only the vices of civil life. They were either degraded by the industry of mechanic trades, or enervated by the luxury of baths and theatres. They soon became careless of their martial exercises, curious in their diet and apparel; and while they inspired

---

[123] Zosimus, l. ii. p. 111. The distinction between the two classes of Roman troops is very darkly expressed in the historians, the laws, and the Notitia. Consult, however, the copious *paratitlon,* or abstract, which Godefroy has drawn up of the seventh book, de Re Militari, of the Theodosian Code, l. vii. tit. i. leg. 18, l. viii. tit. i. leg. 10.

terror to the subjects of the empire, they trembled at the hostile approach of the Barbarians.[129] The chain of fortifications which Diocletian and his colleagues had extended along the banks of the great rivers, was no longer maintained with the same care, or defended with the same vigilance. The numbers which still remained under the name of the troops of the frontier, might be sufficient for the ordinary defence; but their spirit was degraded by the humiliating reflection, that *they* who were exposed to the hardships and dangers of a perpetual warfare, were rewarded only with about two thirds of the pay and emoluments which were lavished on the troops of the court. Even the bands or legions that were raised the nearest to the level of those unworthy favorites, were in some measure disgraced by the title of honor which they were allowed to assume. It was in vain that Constantine repeated the most dreadful menaces of fire and sword against the Borderers who should dare to desert their colors, to connive at the inroads of the Barbarians, or to participate in the spoil.[130] The mischiefs which flow from injudicious counsels are seldom removed by the application of partial severities: and though succeeding princes labored to restore the strength and numbers of the frontier garrisons, the empire, till the last moment of its dissolution, continued to languish under the mortal wound which had been so rashly or so weakly inflicted by the hand of Constantine.

The same timid policy, of dividing whatever is united, of reducing whatever is eminent, of dreading every active power, and of expecting that the most feeble will prove the most obedient, seems to pervade the institutions of several princes, and particularly those of Constantine. The martial pride of the legions, whose victorious camps had so often been the scene of rebellion, was nourished by the memory of their past exploits, and the consciousness of their actual strength. As long as they maintained their ancient establishment of six thousand men, they subsisted, under the reign of Diocletian, each of them singly, a visible and important object in the

---

[129] Ferox erat in suos miles et rapax, ignavus vero in hostes et fractus. Ammian. l. xxii. c. 4. He observes, that they loved downy beds and houses of marble; and that their cups were heavier than their swords.

[130] Cod. Theod. l. vii. tit. i. leg. 1, tit. xii. leg. i. See Howell s Hist. of the World, vol. ii. p. 19. That learned historian, who is not sufficiently known, labors to justify the character and policy of Constantine

military history of the Roman empire.   A few years afterwards, these gigantic bodies were shrunk to a very diminutive size ; and when *seven* legions, with some auxiliaries, defended the city of Amida against the Persians, the total garrison, with the inhabitants of both sexes, and the peasants of the deserted country, did not exceed the number of twenty thousand persons.[131]   From this fact, and from similar examples, there is reason to believe, that the constitution of the legionary troops, to which they partly owed their valor and discipline, was dissolved by Constantine ; and that the bands of Roman infantry, which still assumed the same names and the same honors, consisted only of one thousand or fifteen hundred men.[132]   The conspiracy of so many separate detachments, each of which was awed by the sense of its own weakness, could easily be checked ; and the successors of Constantine might indulge their love of ostentation, by issuing their orders to one hundred and thirty-two legions, inscribed on the muster-roll of their numerous armies.   The remainder of their troops was distributed into several hundred cohorts of infantry, and squadrons of cavalry.   Their arms, and titles, and ensigns, were calculated to inspire terror, and to display the variety of nations who marched under the Imperial standard.   And not a vestige was left of that severe simplicity, which, in the ages of freedom and victory, had distinguished he line of battle of a Roman army from the confused host of an Asiatic monarch.[133]   A more particular enumeration, drawn from the *Notitia*, might exercise the diligence of an antiquary ; but the historian will content himself with observing, that the number of permanent stations or garrisons established on the frontiers of the empire, amounted to five hundred and eighty-three ; and that, under the successors of Constantine, the complete force of the military establishment was computed at six hundred and forty-five thousand soldiers.[134]

---

[131] Ammian. l. xix. c. 2.   He observes, (c. 5,) that the desperate sallies of two Gallic legions were like a handful of water thrown on a great conflagration.

[132] Pancirolus ad Notitiam, p. 96.   Memoires de l'Academie des Inscriptions, tom. xxv. p. 491.

[133] Romana acies unius prope formæ erat et hominum et armorum genere. — Regia acies varia magis multis gentibus dissimilitudine armorum auxiliorumque erat.   T. Liv. l. xxxvii. c. 39, 40.   Flaminius, even before the event, had compared the army of Antiochus to a supper, in which the flesh of one vile animal was diversified by the skill of the cooks.   See the Life of Flaminius in Plutarch.

[134] Agathias, l. v. p 157, edit. Louvre.

An effort so prodigious surpassed the wants of a more ancient, and the faculties of a later, period.

In the various states of society, armies are recruited from very different motives. Barbarians are urged by the love of war; the citizens of a free republic may be prompted by a principle of duty; the subjects, or at least the nobles, of a monarchy, are animated by a sentiment of honor; but the timid and luxurious inhabitants of a declining empire must be allured into the service by the hopes of profit, or compelled by the dread of punishment. The resources of the Roman treasury were exhausted by the increase of pay, by the repetition of donatives, and by the invention of new emoluments and indulgences, which, in the opinion of the provincial youth, might compensate the hardships and dangers of a military life. Yet, although the stature was lowered,[135] although slaves, at least by a tacit connivance, were indiscriminately received into the ranks, the insurmountable difficulty of procuring a regular and adequate supply of volunteers, obliged the emperors to adopt more effectual and coercive methods. The lands bestowed on the veterans, as the free reward of their valor, were henceforward granted under a condition which contains the first rudiments of the feudal tenures; that their sons, who succeeded to the inheritance, should devote themselves to the profession of arms, as soon as they attained the age of manhood; and their cowardly refusal was punished by the loss of honor, of fortune, or even of life.[136] But as the annual growth of the sons of the veterans bore a very small proportion to the demands of the service, levies of men were frequently required from the provinces, and every proprietor was obliged either to take up arms, or to procure a substitute, or to purchase his exemption by the payment of a heavy fine. The sum of forty-two pieces of gold, to which it was *reduced* ascertains the exorbitant price of volunteers, and the reluctance

---

[135] Valentinian (Cod. Theodos. l. vii. tit. xiii. leg. 3) fixes the standard at five feet seven inches, about five feet four inches and a half, English measure. It had formerly been five feet ten inches, and in the best corps, six Roman feet. Sed tunc erat amplior multitudo, et plures sequebantur militiam armatam. Vegetius de Re Militari, l. i. c. v.

[136] See the two titles, De Veteranis and De Filiis Veteranorum, in the seventh book of the Theodosian Code. The age at which their military service was required, varied from twenty-five to sixteen. If the sons of the veterans appeared with a horse, they had a right to serve in the cavalry; two horses gave them some valuable privileges

with which the government admitted of this alternative.[137]
Such was the horror for the profession of a soldier, which had
affected the minds of the degenerate Romans, that many of
the youth of Italy and the provinces chose to cut off the
fingers of their right hand, to escape from being pressed into
the service; and this strange expedient was so commonly
practised, as to deserve the severe animadversion of the laws,[138]
and a peculiar name in the Latin language.[139]

The introduction of Barbarians into the Roman armies
became every day more universal, more necessary, and more
fatal. The most daring of the Scythians, of the Goths, and
of the Germans, who delighted in war, and who found it more
profitable to defend than to ravage the provinces, were en-
rolled, not only in the auxiliaries of their respective nations, but
in the legions themselves, and among the most distinguished
of the Palatine troops. As they freely mingled with the subjects of the empire, they gradually learned to despise their
manners, and to imitate their arts. They abjured the implicit
reverence which the pride of Rome had exacted from their
ignorance, while they acquired the knowledge and possession
of those advantages by which alone she supported her declining greatness. The Barbarian soldiers, who displayed any
military talents, were advanced, without exception, to the most
important commands; and the names of the tribunes, of the

---

[137] Cod. Theod. l. vii. tit. xiii. leg. 7. According to the historian
Socrates, (see Godefroy ad loc.,) the same emperor Valens sometimes
required eighty pieces of gold for a recruit. In the following law it
is faintly expressed, that slaves shall not be admitted inter optimas
lectissimorum militum turmas.

[138] The person and property of a Roman knight, who had mutilated his two sons, were sold at public auction by order of Augustus.
(Sueton. in August. c. 27.) The moderation of that artful usurper
proves, that this example of severity was justified by the spirit of the
times. Ammianus makes a distinction between the effeminate Italians and the hardy Gauls. (L. xv. c. 12.) Yet only 15 years afterwards, Valentinian, in a law addressed to the præfect of Gaul, is
obliged to enact that these cowardly deserters shall be burnt alive.
(Cod. Theod. l. vii. tit. xiii. leg. 5.) Their numbers in Illyricum were
so considerable, that the province complained of a scarcity of recruits.
(Id. leg. 10.)

[139] They were called Murci. Murcidus is found in Plautus and
Festus, to denote a lazy and cowardly person, who, according to Arnobius and Augustin, was under the immediate protection of the goddess Murcia. From this particular instance of cowardice, murcare is
used as synonymous to mutilare, by the writers of the middle Latinity.
See Lindenbrogius, and Valesius ad Ammian. Marcellin, l. xv. c 12

counts and dukes, and of the generals themselves, betray a foreign origin, which they no longer condescended to disguise. They were often intrusted with the conduct of a war against their countrymen; and though most of them preferred the ties of allegiance to those of blood, they did not always avoid the guilt, or at least the suspicion, of holding a treasonable correspondence with the enemy, of inviting his invasion, or of sparing his retreat. The camps and the palace of the son of Constantine were governed by the powerful faction of the Franks, who preserved the strictest connection with each other, and with their country, and who resented every personal affront as a national indignity.[140] When the tyrant Caligula was suspected of an intention to invest a very extraordinary candidate with the consular robes, the sacrilegious profanation would have scarcely excited less astonishment, if, instead of a horse, the noblest chieftain of Germany or Britain had been the object of his choice. The revolution of three centuries had produced so remarkable a change in the prejudices of the people, that, with the public approbation, Constantine showed his successors the example of bestowing the honors of the consulship on the Barbarians, who, by their merit and services had deserved to be ranked among the first of the Romans.[141] But as these hardy veterans, who had been educated in the ignorance or contempt of the laws, were incapable of exercising any civil offices, the powers of the human mind were contracted by the irreconcilable separation of talents as well as of professions. The accomplished citizens of the Greek and Roman republics, whose characters could adapt themselves to the bar, the senate, the camp, or the schools, had learned to write, to speak, and to act with the same spirit, and with equal abilities.

IV. Besides the magistrates and generals, who at a distance from the court diffused their delegated authority over the provinces and armies, the emperor conferred the rank of *Illus-*

---

[140] Malarichus — adhibitis Francis quorum ea tempestate in palatio multitudo florebat, erectius jam loquebatur tumultuabaturque. Ammian. l. xv. c. 5.

[141] Barbaros omnium primus, ad usque fasces auxerat et trabeas consulares. Ammian. l. xx. c. 10. Eusebius (in Vit. Constantin. l. iv. c. 7) and Aurelius Victor seem to confirm the truth of this assertion: yet in the thirty-two consular Fasti of the reign of Constantine, I cannot discover the name of a single Barbarian. I should therefore interpret the liberality of that prince as relative to the ornaments, rather than to the office of the consulship.

trious on seven of his more immediate servants, to whose
fidelity he intrusted his safety, or his counsels, or his treasures.
1. The private apartments of the palace were governed by a
favorite eunuch, who, in the language of that age, was styled
the *prœpositus*, or præfect of the sacred bed-chamber. His
duty was to attend the emperor in his hours of state, or in
those of amusement, and to perform about his person all those
menial services, which can only derive their splendor from
the influence of royalty Under a prince who deserved to
reign, the great chambellain (for such we may call him) was
a useful and humble domestic; but an artful domestic, who
improves every occasion of unguarded confidence, will insensibly acquire over a feeble mind that ascendant which harsh
wisdom and uncomplying virtue can seldom obtain. The
degenerate grandsons of Theodosius, who were invisible to
their subjects, and contemptible to their enemies, exalted the
præfects of their bed-chamber above the heads of all the
ministers of the palace;[142] and even his deputy, the first of
the splendid train of slaves who waited in the presence, was
thought worthy to rank before the *respectable* proconsuls of
Greece or Asia. The jurisdiction of the chamberlain was
acknowledged by the *counts*, or superintendents, who regulated
the two important provinces of the magnificence of the ward-
robe, and of the luxury of the Imperial table.[143] 2. The
principal administration of public affairs was committed to the
diligence and abilities of the *master of the offices*.[144] He was
the supreme magistrate of the palace, inspected the discipline
of the civil and military *schools*, and received appeals from all
parts of the empire, in the causes which related to that numerous army of privileged persons, who, as the servants of the

---

[142] Cod. Theod. l. vi. tit. 8.

[143] By a very singular metaphor, borrowed from the military character of the first emperors, the steward of their household was styled
the count of their camp, (comes castrensis.) Cassiodorus very seriously represents to him, that his own fame, and that of the empire,
must depend on the opinion which foreign ambassadors may conceive
of the plenty and magnificence of the royal table. (Variar. l. vi.
epistol. 9.)

[144] Gutherius (de Officiis Domûs Augustæ, l. ii. c. 20, l. iii.) has
very accurately explained the functions of the master of the offices,
and the constitution of the subordinate *scrinia*. But he vainly attempts, on the most doubtful authority, to deduce from the time of
the Antonines, or even of Nero, the origin of a magistrate who cannot
be found in history before the reign of Constantine.

court, had obtained, for themselves and families, a right to decline the authority of the ordinary judges. The correspondence between the prince and his subjects was managed by the four *scrinia*, or offices of this minister of state. The first was appropriated to memorials, the second to epistles, the third to petitions, and the fourth to papers and orders of a miscellaneous kind. Each of these was directed by an inferior *master* of *respectable* dignity, and the whole business was despatched by a hundred and forty-eight secretaries, chosen for the most part from the profession of the law, on account of the variety of abstracts of reports and references which frequently occurred in the exercise of their several functions. From a condescension, which in former ages would have been esteemed unworthy of the Roman majesty, a particular secretary was allowed for the Greek language; and interpreters were appointed to receive the ambassadors of the Barbarians; but the department of foreign affairs, which constitutes so essential a part of modern policy, seldom diverted the attention of the master of the offices. His mind was more seriously engaged by the general direction of the posts and arsenals of the empire. There were thirty-four cities, fifteen in the East, and nineteen in the West, in which regular companies of workmen were perpetually employed in fabricating defensive armor, offensive weapons of all sorts, and military engines, which were deposited in the arsenals, and occasionally delivered for the service of the troops. 3. In the course of nine centuries, the office of *quæstor* had experienced a very singular revolution. In the infancy of Rome, two inferior magistrates were annually elected by the people, to relieve the consuls from the invidious management of the public treasure; [145] a similar assistant was granted to every proconsul and to every prætor, who exercised a military or provincial command; with the extent of conquest, the two quæstors were gradually multiplied to the number of four, of eight, of twenty, and, for a short time, perhaps, of forty; [146] and the

---

[145] Tacitus (Anual. xi. 22) says, that the first quæstors were elected by the people, sixty-four years after the foundation of the republic; but he is of opinion, that they had, long before that period, been annually appointed by the consuls, and even by the kings. But this obscure point of antiquity is contested by other writers.

[146] Tacitus (Annal. xi. 22) seems to consider twenty as the highest number of quæstors; and Dion (l. xliii. p. 374) insinuates, that if the dictator Cæsar once created forty, it was only to facilitate the pay

noblest citizens ambitiously solicited an office which gave them
a seat in the senate, and a just hope of obtaining the honors
of the republic. Whilst Augustus affected to maintain the
freedom of election, he consented to accept the annual privilege of recommending, or rather indeed of nominating, a
certain proportion of candidates; and it was his custom to
select one of these distinguished youths, to read his orations
or epistles in the assemblies of the senate.[147] The practice
of Augustus was imitated by succeeding princes; the occasional commission was established as a permanent office; and
the favored quæstor, assuming a new and more illustrious
character, alone survived the suppression of his ancient and
useless colleagues.[148] As the orations which he composed in
the name of the emperor,[149] acquired the force, and, at length,
the form, of absolute edicts, he was considered as the representative of the legislative power, the oracle of the council,
and the original source of the civil jurisprudence. He was
sometimes invited to take his seat in the supreme judicature
of the Imperial consistory, with the Prætorian præfects, and
the master of the offices; and he was frequently requested to
resolve the doubts of inferior judges : but as he was not

ment of an immense debt of gratitude. Yet the augmentation which
he made of prætors subsisted under the succeeding reigns.

[147] Sueton. in August. c. 65, and Torrent. ad loc. Dion. Cas. p. 755.

[148] The youth and inexperience of the quæstors, who entered on
that important office in their twenty-fifth year, (Lips. Excurs. ad
Tacit. l. iii. D.,) engaged Augustus to remove them from the management of the treasury; and though they were restored by Claudius,
they seem to have been finally dismissed by Nero. (Tacit. Annal.
xiii. 29. Sueton. in Aug. c. 36, in Claud. c. 24. Dion, p. 696, 961,
&c. Plin. Epistol. x. 20, et alibi.) In the provinces of the Imperial
division, the place of the quæstors was more ably supplied by the
procurators, (Dion Cas. p. 707. Tacit. in Vit. Agricol. c. 15;) or, as
they were afterwards called, *rationales*. (Hist. August. p. 130.) But
in the provinces of the senate we may still discover a series of quæstors till the reign of Marcus Antoninus. (See the Inscriptions of
Gruter, the Epistles of Pliny, and a decisive fact in the Augustan
History, p. 64.) From Ulpian we may learn, (Pandect. l. i. tit. 13,)
that under the government of the house of Severus, their provincial
administration was abolished; and in the subsequent troubles, the
annual or triennial elections of quæstors must have naturally ceased.

[149] Cum patris nomine et epistolas ipse dictaret, et edicti conscrib-
eret, orationesque in senatu recitaret, etiam quæstoris vice. Sueton.
in Tit. c. 6. The office must have acquired new dignity, which was
occasionally executed by the heir apparent of the empire. Trajan
intrusted the same care to Hadrian, his quæstor and cousin. See
Dodwell, Prælection. Cambden, x. xi p. 362—394.

oppressed with a variety of subordinate business, nis eisure and talents were employed to cultivate that dignified style of eloquence, which, in the corruption of taste and language still preserves the majesty of the Roman laws.[150] In some respects, the office of the Imperial quæstor may be compared with that of a modern chancellor; but the use of a great seal, which seems to have been adopted by the illiterate barbarians was never introduced to attest the public acts of the emperors. 4. The extraordinary title of *count of the sacred largesses* was bestowed on the treasurer-general of the revenue, with the intention perhaps of inculcating, that every payment flowed from the voluntary bounty of the monarch. To conceive the almost infinite detail of the annual and daily expense of the civil and military administration in every part of a great empire, would exceed the powers of the most vigorous imagination. The actual account employed several hundred persons, distributed into eleven different offices, which were artfully contrived to examine and control their respective oper ations. The multitude of these agents had a natural tendency to increase; and it was more than once thought expedient to dismiss to their native homes the useless supernumeraries, who, deserting their honest labors, had pressed with too much eagerness into the lucrative profession of the finances.[151] Twenty-nine provincial receivers, of whom eighteen were honored with the title of count, corresponded with the treasurer; and he extended his jurisdiction over the mines from whence the precious metals were extracted, over the mints, in which they were converted into the current coin, and over the public treasuries of the most important cities, where they were deposited for the service of the state. The foreign trade of the empire was regulated by this minister, who directed likewise all the linen and woollen manufactures, in which the successive operations of spinning, weaving, and dyeing were executed, chiefly by women of a servile condition for the use of the palace and army. Twenty-six of these institutions are enumerated in the West, where the arts had been

---

[150] ———————— Terris edicta daturus;
Supplicibus responsa. — Oracula regis
Eloquio crevere tuo; nec dignius unquam
Majestas meminit sese Romana locutam.

Claudian in Consulat. Mall. Theodor. 33. See likewise Symmachus 'Epistol. i. 17) and Cassiodorus. (Variar. vi. 5.)
[151] Cod. Theod. l. vi. tit. 30. Cod. Justinian. l. xii. tit. 24.

more recently introduced, and a still larger proportion may be allowed for the industrious provinces of the East.[152]   5. Besides the public revenue, which an absolute monarch might levy and expend according to his pleasure, the emperors, in the capacity of opulent citizens, possessed a very extensive property, which was administered by the *count* or treasurer of *the private estate.*   Some part had perhaps been the ancient demesnes of kings and republics ; some accessions might be derived from the families which were successively invested with the purple ; but the most considerable portion flowed from the impure source of confiscations and forfeitures.   The Imperial estates were scattered through the provinces, from Mauritania to Britain ; but the rich and fertile soil of Cappadocia tempted the monarch to acquire in that country his fairest possessions,[153] and either Constantine or his successors embraced the occasion of justifying avarice by religious zeal. They suppressed the rich temple of Comana, where the high-priest of the goddess of war supported the dignity of a sovereign prince ; and they applied to their private use the consecrated lands, which were inhabited by six thousand subjects or slaves of the deity and her ministers.[154]   But these were not the valuable inhabitants : the plains that stretch from the foot of Mount Argæus to the banks of the Sarus, bred a generous race of horses, renowned above all others in the ancient world for their majestic shape and incomparable swiftness.   These *sacred* animals, destined for the service of the palace and the Imperial games, were protected by the laws from the profanation of a vulgar master.[155]   The demesnes of Cappadocia

---

[152] In the departments of the two counts of the treasury, the eastern part of the *Notitia* happens to be very defective.   It may be observed, that we had a treasury chest in London, and a gynæceum or manufacture at Winchester.   But Britain was not thought worthy either of a mint or of an arsenal.   Gaul alone possessed three of the former, and eight of the latter.

[153] Cod. Theod. l. vi. tit. xxx. leg. 2, and Godefroy ad loc.

[154] Strabon. Geograph. l. xii. p. 809, [edit. Casaub.]   The other temple of Comana, in Pontus, was a colony from that of Cappadocia, l. xii. p. 835.   The President Des Brosses (see his Saluste, tom. ii. p. 21, [edit. Casaub.]) conjectures that the deity adored in both Comanas was Beltis, the Venus of the east, the goddess of generation ; a very different being indeed from the goddess of war.

[155] Cod. Theod. l. x. tit. vi. de Grege Dominico.   Godefroy has collected every circumstance of antiquity relative to the Cappadocian horses.   One of the finest breeds, the Palmatian, was the forfeiture of a rebel, whose estate lay about sixteen miles from Tyana, near the great road between Constantinople and Antioch.

were important enough to require the inspection of a *count* ; [156]
officers of an inferior rank were stationed in the other parts of
the empire ; and the deputies of the private, as well as those
of the public, treasurer were maintained in the exercise of
their independent functions, and encouraged to control the
authority of the provincial magistrates. [157] 6, 7. The chosen
bands of cavalry and infantry, which guarded the person of
the emperor, were under the immediate command of the *two
counts of the domestics.* The whole number consisted of three
thousand five hundred men, divided into seven *schools*, or
troops, of five hundred each ; and in the East, this honorable
service was almost entirely appropriated to the Armenians.
Whenever, on public ceremonies, they were drawn up in the
courts and porticos of the palace, their lofty stature, silent
order, and splendid arms of silver and gold, displayed a
martial pomp not unworthy of the Roman majesty. [158] From
the seven schools two companies of horse and foot were
selected, of the *protectors*, whose advantageous station was
the hope and reward of the most deserving soldiers. They
mounted guard in the interior apartments, and were occasionally despatched into the provinces, to execute with celerity
and vigor the orders of their master. [159] The counts of the
domestics had succeeded to the office of the Prætorian præfects ; like the præfects, they aspired from the service of the
palace to the command of armies.

The perpetual intercourse between the court and the provinces was facilitated by the construction of roads and the institution of posts. But these beneficial establishments were
accidentally connected with a pernicious and intolerable abuse.
Two or three hundred *agents* or messengers were employed,
under the jurisdiction of the master of the offices, to announce
the names of the annual consuls, and the edicts or victories
of the emperors. They insensibly assumed the license of

---

[156] Justinian (Novell. 30) subjected the province of the count of
Cappadocia to the immediate authority of the favorite eunuch, who
presided over the sacred bed-chamber.

[157] Cod. Theod. l. vi. tit. xxx. leg. 4, &c.

[158] Pancirolus, p. 102, 136. The appearance of these military domestics is described in the Latin poem of Corippus, de Laudibus Justin. l. iii. 157—179. p. 419, 420 of the Appendix Hist. Byzantin.
Rom. 177.

[159] Ammianus Marcellinus, who served so many years, obtained
only the rank of a protector. The first ten among these honorable
soldiers were *Clarissimi.*

reporting whatever they could observe of the conduct either of magistrates or of private citizens; and were soon considered as the eyes of the monarch,[160] and the scourge of the people. Under the warm influence of a feeble reign, they multiplied to the incredible number of ten thousand, disdained the mild though frequent admonitions of the laws, and exercised in the profitable management of the posts a rapacious and insolent oppression. These official spies, who regularly corresponded with the palace, were encouraged, by favor and reward, anxiously to watch the progress of every treasonable design, from the faint and latent symptoms of disaffection, to the actual preparation of an open revolt. Their careless or criminal violation of truth and justice was covered by the consecrated mask of zeal; and they might securely aim their poisoned arrows at the breast either of the guilty or the innocent, who had provoked their resentment, or refused to purchase their silence. A faithful subject, of Syria perhaps, or of Britain, was exposed to the danger, or at least to the dread, of being dragged in chains to the court of Milan or Constantinople, to defend his life and fortune against the malicious charge of these privileged informers. The ordinary administration was conducted by those methods which extreme necessity can alone palliate; and the defects of evidence were diligently supplied by the use of torture.[161]

The deceitful and dangerous experiment of the criminal *quaestion*, as it is emphatically styled, was admitted, rather than approved, in the jurisprudence of the Romans. They applied this sanguinary mode of examination only to servile bodies, whose sufferings were seldom weighed by those haughty republicans in the scale of justice or humanity; but they would never consent to violate the sacred person of a citizen, till they possessed the clearest evidence of his guilt.[162]

---

[160] Xenophon, Cyropaed. l. viii. Brisson, de Regno Persico, l. i. No. 190, p. 264. The emperors adopted with pleasure this Persian metaphor.

[161] For the *Agentes in Rebus*, see Ammian. l. xv. c. 3, l. xvi. *l.* 5, l. xxii. c. 7, with the curious annotations of Valesius. Cod. Theod. l. vi. tit. xxvii. xxviii. xxix. Among the passages collected in the Commentary of Godefroy, the most remarkable is one from Libanius, in his discourse concerning the death of Julian.

[162] The Pandects (l. xlviii. tit. xviii.) contain the sentiments of the most celebrated civilians on the subject of torture. They strictly confine it to slaves; and Ulpian himself is ready to acknowledge, that Res est fragilis, et periculosa, et quae veritatem fallat.

The annals of tyranny, from the reign of Tiberius to that of Domitian, circumstantially relate the executions of many innocent victims; but, as long as the faintest remembrance was kept alive of the national freedom and honor, the last hours of a Roman were secure from the danger of ignominious torture.[163] The conduct of the provincial magistrates was not, however, regulated by the practice of the city, or the strict maxims of the civilians. They found the use of torture established not only among the slaves of oriental despotism, but among the Macedonians, who obeyed a limited monarch · among the Rhodians, who flourished by the liberty of commerce; and even among the sage Athenians, who had asserted and adorned the dignity of human kind.[164] The acquiescence of the provincials encouraged their governors to acquire, or perhaps to usurp, a discretionary power of employing the rack to extort from vagrants or plebeian criminals the confession of their guilt, till they insensibly proceeded to confound the distinction of rank, and to disregard the privileges of Roman citizens. The apprehensions of the subjects urged them to solicit, and the interest of the sovereign engaged him to grant, a variety of special exemptions, which tacitly allowed, and even authorized, the general use of torture. They protected all persons of illustrious or honorable rank, bishops and their presbyters, professors of the liberal arts, soldiers and their families, municipal officers, and their posterity to the third generation, and all children under the age of puberty.[165] But a fatal maxim was introduced into the new jurisprudence of the empire, that in the case of treason, which included every offence that the subtlety of lawyers could derive from a *hostile intention* towards the prince or republic,[166] all privileges

---

[163] In the conspiracy of Piso against Nero, Epicharis (libertina mulier) was the only person tortured: the rest were *intacti tormentis*. It would be superfluous to add a weaker, and it would be difficult to find a stronger, example. Tacit. Annal. xv. 57.

[164] Dicendum . . . de Institutis Atheniensium, Rhodiorum, doctissimorum hominum, apud quos etiam (id quod acerbissimum est) liberi, civesque torquentur. Cicero, Partit. Orat. c. 34. We may learn from the trial of Philotas the practice of the Macedonians. (Diodor. Sicul. l. xvii. p. 604. Q. Curt. l. vi. c. 11.

[165] Heineccius (Element. Jur. Civil. part vii. p. 81) has collected these exemptions into one view.

[166] This definition of the sage Ulpian (Pandect. l. xlviii. tit. iv.) seems to have been adapted to the court of Caracalla, rather than to that of Alexander Severus. See the Codes of Theodosius and Justinian ad leg. Juliam majestatis.

34*

were suspended, and all conditions were reduced to the same ignominious level. As the safety of the emperor was avowedly preferred to every consideration of justice or humanity the dignity of age and the tenderness of youth were alike exposed to the most cruel tortures ; and the terrors of a malicious information, which might select them as the accomplices, or even as the witnesses, perhaps, of an imaginary crime, perpetually hung over the heads of the principal citizens of the Roman world.[167]

These evils, however terrible they may appear, were confined to the smaller number of Roman subjects, whose dangerous situation was in some degree compensated by the enjoyment of those advantages, either of nature or of fortune, which exposed them to the jealousy of the monarch. The obscure millions of a great empire have much less to dread from the cruelty than from the avarice of their masters, and *their* humble happiness is principally affected by the grievance of excessive taxes, which, gently pressing on the wealthy, descend with accelerated weight on the meaner and more indigent classes of society. An ingenious philosopher [168] has calculated the universal measure of the public impositions by the degrees of freedom and servitude ; and ventures to assert, that, according to an invariable law of nature, it must always increase with the former, and diminish in a just proportion to the latter. But this reflection, which would tend to alleviate the miseries of despotism, is contradicted at least by the history of the Roman empire ; which accuses the same princes of despoiling the senate of its authority, and the provinces of their wealth. Without abolishing all the various customs and duties on merchandises, which are imperceptibly discharged by the apparent choice of the purchaser, the policy of Constantine and his successors preferred a simple and direct mode of taxation, more congenial to the spirit of an arbitrary government.[169]

---

[167] Arcadius Charisius is the oldest lawyer quoted in the Pandects to justify the universal practice of torture in all cases of treason ; but this maxim of tyranny, which is admitted by Ammianus (l. xix. c. 12) with the most respectful terror, is enforced by several laws of the successors of Constantine. See Cod. Theod. l. ix. tit. xxxv. In majestatis crimine omnibus æqua est conditio.

[168] Montesquieu, Esprit des Loix, l. xii. c. 13.

[169] Mr. Hume (Essays, vol. i. p 389) has seen this important truth with some degree of perplexity.

The name and use of the *indictions*,[170] which serve to ascertain the chronology of the middle ages, were derived from the regular practice of the Roman tributes.[171] The emperor subscribed with his own hand, and in purple ink, the solemn edict, or indiction, which was fixed up in the principal city of each diocese, during two months previous to the first day of September. And by a very easy connection of ideas, the word *indiction* was transferred to the measure of tribute which it prescribed, and to the annual term which it allowed for the payment. This general estimate of the supplies was proportioned to the real and imaginary wants of the state ; but as often as the expense exceeded the revenue, or the revenue fell short of the computation, an additional tax, under the name of *superindiction*, was imposed on the people, and the most valuable attribute of sovereignty was communicated to the Prætorian præfects, who, on some occasions, were permitted to provide for the unforeseen and extraordinary exigencies of the public service. The execution of these laws (which it would be tedious to pursue in their minute and intricate detail) consisted of two distinct operations : the resolving the general imposition into its constituent parts, which were assessed on the provinces, the cities, and the individuals of the Roman world ; and the collecting the separate contributions of the individuals, the cities, and the provinces, till the accumulated sums were poured into the Imperial treasuries. But as the account between the monarch and the subject was perpetually

---

[170] The cycle of indictions, which may be traced as high as the reign of Constantius, or perhaps of his father, Constantine, is still employed by the Papal court : but the commencement of the year has been very reasonably altered to the first of January. See l'Art de Verifier les Dates, p. xi. ; and Dictionnaire Raison. de la Diplomatique, tom. ii. p. 25 ; two accurate treatises, which come from the workshop of the Benedictines.*

[171] The first twenty-eight titles of the eleventh book of the Theodosian Code are filled with the circumstantial regulations on the important subject of tributes ; but they suppose a clearer knowledge of fundamental principles than it is at present in our power to attain.

---

* It does not appear that the establishment of the indiction is to be attributed to Constantine : it existed before he had been created *Augustus* at Rome, and the remission granted by him to the city of Autun is the proof. He would not have ventured while only *Cæsar*, and under the necessity of courting popular favor, to establish such an odious impost. Aurelius Victor and Lactantius agree in designating Diocletian as the author of this despotic institution. Aur. Vict. de Cæs. c. 39. Lactant de Mort. Pers c 7. — G.

open, and as the renewal of the demand anticipated the perfect discharge of the preceding obligation, the weighty machine of the finances was moved by the same hands round the circle of its yearly revolution. Whatever was honorable or important in the administration of the revenue, was committed to the wisdom of the præfects, and their provincial representatives; the lucrative functions were claimed by a crowd of subordinate officers, some of whom depended on the treasurer, others on the governor of the province; and who, in the inevitable conflicts of a perplexed jurisdiction, had frequent opportunities of disputing with each other the spoils of the people. The laborious offices, which could be productive only of envy and reproach, of expense and danger, were imposed on the *Decurions*, who formed the corporations of the cities, and whom the severity of the Imperial laws had condemned to sustain the burdens of civil society.[172] The whole landed property of the empire (without excepting the patrimonial estates of the monarch) was the object of ordinary taxation; and every new purchaser contracted the obligations of the former proprietor. An accurate *census*,[173] or survey, was the only equitable mode of acertaining the proportion which every citizen should be obliged to contribute for the public service; and from the well-known period of the indictions, there is reason to believe that this difficult and expensive operation was repeated at the regular distance of fifteen

---

[172] The title concerning the Decurions (l. xii. tit. i.) is the most ample in the whole Theodosian Code; since it contains not less than one hundred and ninety-two distinct laws to ascertain the duties and privileges of that useful order of citizens.*

[173] Habemus enim et hominum numerum qui delati sunt, et agrûm modum. Eumenius in Panegyr. Vet. viii. 6. See Cod. Theod. l. xiii. tit. x. xi., with Godefroy's Commentary.

---

* The Decurions were charged with assessing, according to the census of property prepared by the tabularii, the payment due from each proprietor. This odious office was authoritatively imposed on the richest citizens of each town; they had no salary, and all their compensation was, to be exempt from certain corporal punishments, in case they should have incurred them. The Decurionate was the ruin of all the rich. Hence they tried every way of avoiding this dangerous honor; they concealed themselves, they entered into military service; but their efforts were unavailing; they were seized, they were compelled to become Decurions, and the dread inspired by this title was termed *Impiety*. — G.

The Decurions were mutually responsible; they were obliged to undertake for pieces of ground abandoned by their owners on account of the pressure of the taxes, and, finally, to make up all deficiencies. Savigny, Geschichte des Röm. Rechts, i. 25. -- M.

years. The lands were measured by surveyors, who were
sent into the provinces; their nature, whether arable or pas-
ture, or vineyards or woods, was distinctly reported; and an
estimate was made of their common value from the average
produce of five years. The numbers of slaves and of cattle
constituted an essential part of the report; an oath was administered to the proprietors, which bound them to disclose the
true state of their affairs; and their attempts to prevaricate, or
elude the intention of the legislator, were severely watched,
and punished as a capital crime, which included the double
guilt of treason and sacrilege.[174] A large portion of the
tribute was paid in money; and of the current coin of the
empire, gold alone could be legally accepted.[175] The remainder of the taxes, according to the proportions determined
by the annual indiction, was furnished in a manner still more
direct, and still more oppressive. According to the different
nature of lands, their real produce in the various articles of
wine or oil, corn or barley, wood or iron, was transported by
the labor or at the expense of the provincials* to the Imperial
magazines, from whence they were occasionally distributed,
for the use of the court, of the army, and of the two capitals,
Rome and Constantinople. The commissioners of the revenue
were so frequently obliged to make considerable purchases,
that they were strictly prohibited from allowing any compensation, or from receiving in money the value of those sup-

---

[174] Siquis sacrilegâ vitem falce succiderit, aut feracium ramorum
fœtus hebetaverit, quo delinet fidem Censuum, et mentiatur callide
paupertatis ingenium, mox detectus capitale subibit exitium, et bona
ejus in Fisci jura migrabunt.   Cod. Theod. l. xiii. tit. xi. leg. 1.   Although this law is not without its studied obscurity, it is, however,
clear enough to prove the minuteness of the inquisition, and the disproportion of the penalty.

[175] The astonishment of Pliny would have ceased.   Equidem miror
P. R. victis gentibus argentum semper imperitasse non aurum.   Hist.
Natur. xxxiii. 15.

---

* The proprietors were not charged with the expense of this transport:
in the provinces situated on the sea-shore or near the great rivers, there
were companies of boatmen, and of masters of vessels, who had this commission, and furnished the means of transport at their own expense.   In
return, they were themselves exempt altogether, or in part, from the indiction and other imposts.   They had certain privileges; particular regulations determined their rights and obligations.   (Cod. Theod. l. xiii. tit. v
ix.)   The transports by land were made in the same manner, by the inter-
vention of a privileged company called Bastaga; the members were called
Bastagarii   Cod. Theod. l. viii. tit. v. — G.

plies which were exacted in kind. In the primitive simplicity of small communities, this method may be well adapted to collect the almost voluntary offerings of the people; but it is at once susceptible of the utmost latitude, and of the utmost strictness, which in a corrupt and absolute monarchy must introduce a perpetual contest between the power of oppression and the arts of fraud.[176]   The agriculture of the Roman provinces was insensibly ruined, and, in the progress of despotism, which tends to disappoint its own purpose, the emperors were obliged to derive some merit from the forgiveness of debts, or the remission of tributes, which their subjects were utterly incapable of paying.   According to the new division of Italy, the fertile and happy province of Campania, the scene of the early victories and of the delicious retirements of the citizens of Rome, extended between the sea and the Apennine from the Tiber to the Silarus.   Within sixty years after the death of Constantine, and on the evidence of an actual survey, an exemption was granted in favor of three hundred and thirty thousand English acres of desert and uncultivated land; which amounted to one eighth of the whole surface of the province.   As the footsteps of the Barbarians had not yet been seen in Italy, the cause of this amazing desolation, which is recorded in the laws, can be ascribed only to the administration of the Roman emperors.[177]

Either from design or from accident, the mode of assessment seemed to unite the substance of a land tax with the forms of a capitation.[178]   The returns which were sent of every province or district, expressed the number of tributary

---

[176] Some precautions were taken (see Cod. Theod. l. xi. tit. ii. and Cod. Justinian. l. x. tit. xxvii. leg. 1, 2, 3) to restrain the magistrates from the abuse of their authority, either in the exaction or in the purchase of corn : but those who had learning enough to read the orations of Cicero against Verres, (iii. de Frumento,) might instruct themselves in all the various arts of oppression, with regard to the weight, the price, the quality, and the carriage.   The avarice of an unlettered governor would supply the ignorance of precept or precedent.

[177] Cod. Theod. l. xi. tit. xxviii. leg. 2, published the 24th of March, A. D. 395, by the emperor Honorius, only two months after the death of his father, Theodosius.   He speaks of 528,042 Roman ugera, which I have reduced to the English measure.   The jugerum contained 28,800 square Roman feet.

[178] Godefroy (Cod. Theod. tom. vi. p. 116) argues with weight and learning on the subject of the capitation ; but while he explains the caput, as a share or measure of property, he too absolutely excludes the idea of a personal assessment.

subjects, and the amount of the public impositions. The latter of these sums was divided by the former; and the estimate, that such a province contained so many *capita*, or heads of tribute; and that each *head* was rated at such a price, was universally received, not only in the popular, but even in the legal computation. The value of a tributary head must have varied, according to many accidental, or at least fluctuating circumstances; but some knowledge has been preserved of a very curious fact, the more important, since it relates to one of the richest provinces of the Roman empire, and which now flourishes as the most splendid of the European kingdoms. The rapacious ministers of Constantius had exhausted the wealth of Gaul, by exacting twenty-five pieces of gold for the annual tribute of every head. The humane policy of his successor reduced the capitation to seven pieces.[179] A moderate proportion between these opposite extremes of extraordinary oppression and of transient indulgence, may therefore be fixed at sixteen pieces of gold, or about nine pounds sterling, the common standard, perhaps, of the impositions of Gaul.[180] But this calculation, or rather indeed the facts from whence it is deduced, cannot fail of suggesting two difficulties to a think-

---

[179] Quid profuerit (*Julianus*) anhelantibus extremâ penuriâ Gallis, hinc maxime claret, quod primitus partes eas ingressus, pro *capitibus* singulis tributi nomine vicenos quinos aureos reperit flagitari; discedens vero septenos tantum numera universa complentes. Ammian. l. xvi. c. 5.

[180] In the calculation of any sum of money under Constantine and his successors, we need only refer to the excellent discourse of Mr. Greaves on the Denarius, for the proof of the following principles: 1. That the ancient and modern Roman pound, containing 5256 grains of Troy weight, is about one twelfth lighter than the English pound, which is composed of 5760 of the same grains. 2. That the pound of gold, which had once been divided into forty-eight *aurei*, was at this time coined into seventy-two smaller pieces of the same denomination. 3. That five of these aurei were the legal tender for a pound of silver, and that consequently the pound of gold was exchanged for fourteen pounds eight ounces of silver, according to the Roman, or about thirteen pounds according to the English weight. 4. That the English pound of silver is coined into sixty-two shillings. From these elements we may compute the Roman pound of gold, the usual method of reckoning large sums, at forty pounds sterling, and we may fix the currency of the *aureus* at some what more than eleven shillings.*

---

* See, likewise, a Dissertation of M. Letronne, "Considérations Générales sur l'Evaluation les Monnaies Grecques et Romaines. Paris, 1817 — M.

ing mind, who will be at once surprised by the *equality*, and by the *enormity*, of the capitation. An attempt to explain them may perhaps reflect some light on the interesting subjec of the finances of the declining empire.

I. It is obvious, that, as long as the immutable constitution of human nature produces and maintains so unequal a division of property, the most numerous part of the community would be deprived of their subsistence, by the equal assessment of a tax from which the sovereign would derive a very trifling revenue. Such indeed might be the theory of the Roman capitation ; but in the practice, this unjust equality was no longer felt, as the tribute was collected on the principle of a *real*, not of a *personal* imposition.* Several indigent citizens contributed to compose a single *head*, or share of taxation ; while the wealthy provincial, in proportion to his fortune, alone represented several of those imaginary beings. In a poetical request, addressed to one of the last and most deserving of the Roman princes who reigned in Gaul, Sidonius Apollinaris personifies his tribute under the figure of a triple monster, the Geryon of the Grecian fables, and entreats the new Hercules that he would most graciously be pleased to save his life by cutting off three of his heads.[181]   The fortune of Sidonius far

---

[181]   Geryones nos esse puta, monstrumque tributum,
     Hic *capita* ut vivam, tu mihi tolle *tria*.
                    Sidon. Apollinar. Carm. xiii.

The reputation of Father Sirmond led me to expect more satisfaction than I have found in his note (p. 144) on this remarkable passage.   The words, suo vel *suorum* nomine, betray the perplexity of the commentator.

---

* Two masterly dissertations of M. Savigny, in the Mem. of the Berlin Academy (1822 and 1823) have thrown new light on the taxation system of the Empire.   Gibbon, according to M. Savigny, is mistaken in supposing that there was but one kind of capitation tax ; there was a land tax, and a capitation tax, strictly so called.   The land tax was, in its operation, a proprietor's or landlord's tax.   But, besides this, there was a direct capitation tax on all who were not possessed of landed property. This tax dates from the time of the Roman conquests ; its amount is not clearly known.   Gradual exemptions released different persons and classes from this tax.   One edict exempts painters.   In Syria, all under twelve or fourteen, or above sixty-five, were exempted ; at a later period, all under twenty, and all unmarried females ; still later, all under twenty-five, widows and nuns, soldiers, veterani and clerici — whole dioceses, that of Thrace and Illyricum.   Under Galerius and Licinius, the plebs urbana became exempt ; though this, perhaps, was only an ordinance for the East. By degrees, however, the exemption was extended to all the inhabitants of towns ; and as it was strictly capitatio plebeia, from which all possessors were exempted, it fell at length altogether on the coloni and agricultural

exceeded the customary wealth of a poet; but if he had pur sued the allusion, he might have painted many of the Gallic nobles with the hundred heads of the deadly Hydra, spreading over the face of the country, and devouring the substance of a hundred families. II. The difficulty of allowing an annual sum of about nine pounds sterling, even for the average of the capitation of Gaul, may be rendered more evident by the comparison of the present state of the same country, as it is now governed by the absolute monarch of an industrious, wealthy, and affectionate people. The taxes of France cannot be magnified, either by fear or by flattery, beyond the annual amount of eighteen millions sterling, which ought perhaps to be shared among four and twenty millions of inhabitants.[182] Seven millions of these, in the capacity of fathers, or brothers, or husbands, may discharge the obligations of the remaining multitude of women and children.; yet the equal proportion of each tributary subject will scarcely rise above fifty shillings of our money, instead of a proportion almost four times as considerable, which was regularly imposed on their Gallic ancestors. The reason of this difference may be found, not so much in the relative scarcity or plenty of gold and silver, as in the different state of society, in ancient Gaul and in modern France. In a country where

---

[182] This assertion, however formidable it may seem, is founded on the original registers of births, deaths, and marriages, collected by public authority, and now deposited in the *Contrôlee General* at Paris. The annual average of births throughout the whole kingdom, taken in five years, (from 1770 to 1774, both inclusive,) is 479,649 boys, and 449,269 girls, in all 928,918 children. The province of French Hainault alone furnishes 9906 births; and we are assured, by an actual enumeration of the people, annually repeated from the year 1773 to the year 1776, that upon an average, Hainault contains 257,097 inhabitants. By the rules of fair analogy, we might infer, that the ordinary proportion of annual births to the whole people, is about 1 to 26; and that the kingdom of France contains 24,151,868 persons of both sexes and of every age. If we content ourselves with the more moderate proportion of 1 to 25, the whole population will amount to 23,222,950. From the diligent researches of the French Government, (which are not unworthy of our own imitation,) we may hope to obtain a still greater degree of certainty on this important subject.*

---

slaves. These were registered in the same cataster (capitastrum) with the land tax. It was paid by the proprietor, who raised it again from his coloni and laborers. — M.

* On no subject has so much valuable information been collected since the time of Gibbon, as the statistics of the different cou itries of Europe, but much is still wanting as to our own. — M.

personal freedom is the privilege of every subject, the whole
mass of taxes, whether they are levied on property or on consumption, may be fairly divided among the whole body of the
nation. But the far greater part of the lands of ancient Gaul,
as well as of the other provinces of the Roman world, were
cultivated by slaves, or by peasants, whose dependent condition was a less rigid servitude.[183] In such a state the poor
were maintained at the expense of the masters who enjoyed
the fruits of their labor ; and as the rolls of tribute were filled
only with the names of those citizens who possessed the
means of an honorable, or at least of a decent subsistence,
the comparative smallness of their numbers explains and justifies the high rate of their capitation. The truth of this assertion may be illustrated by the following example : The Ædui,
one of the most powerful and civilized tribes or *cities* of Gaul,
occupied an extent of territory, which now contains about five
hundred thousand inhabitants, in the two ecclesiastical dioceses of Autun and Nevers ; [184] and with the probable accession of those of Châlons and Mâcon,[185] the population would
amount to eight hundred thousand souls. In the time of Constantine, the territory of the Ædui afforded no more than
twenty-five thousand *heads* of capitation, of whom seven

---

[183] Cod. Theod. l. v. tit. ix. x. xi. Cod. Justinian. l. xi. tit. lxiii.
Coloni appellantur qui conditionem debent genitali solo, propter agri-
culturum sub dominio possessorum. Augustin. de Civitate Dei,
l. x. c. i.

[184] The ancient jurisdiction of (*Augustodunum*) Autun in Burgundy,
the capital of the Ædui, comprehended the adjacent territory of (*No-
viodunum*) Nevers. See D'Anville, Notice de l'Ancienne Gaule, p.
491. The two dioceses of Autun and Nevers are now composed, the
former of 610, and the latter of 160 parishes. The registers of births,
taken during eleven years, in 476 parishes of the same province of
Burgundy, and multiplied by the moderate proportion of 25, (see
Messance Recherches sur la Population, p. 142,) may authorize us to
assign an average number of 656 persons for each parish, which being
again multiplied by the 770 parishes of the dioceses of Nevers and
Autun, will produce the sum of 505,120 persons for the extent of
country which was once possessed by the Ædui.

[185] We might derive an additional supply of 301,750 inhabitants
from the dioceses of Châlons (*Cabillonum*) and of Mâcon, (*Matisco*,)
since they contain, the one 200, and the other 260 parishes. This
accession of territory might be justified by very specious reasons.
1. Châlons and Mâcon were undoubtedly within the original jurisdiction of the Ædui. (See D'Anville, Notice, p. 187, 443.) 2. In the
Notitia of Gaul, they are enumerated not as *Civitates* but merely as
Castra. 3. They do not appear to have been episcopal seats before

thousand were discharged by that prince from the intolerable weight of tribute.[186]   A just analogy would seem to countenance the opinion of an ingenious historian,[187] that the free and tributary citizens did not surpass the number of half a million ; and if, in the ordinary administration of government, their annual payments may be computed at about four millions and a half of our money, it would appear, that although the share of each individual was four times as considerable, a fourth part only of the modern taxes of France was levied on the Imperial province of Gaul.   The exactions of Constantius may be calculated at seven millions sterling, which were reduced to two millions by the humanity or the wisdom of Julian.

But this tax, or capitation, on the proprietors of land, would have suffered a rich and numerous class of free citizens to escape.   With the view of sharing that species of wealth which is derived from art or labor, and which exists in money or in merchandise, the emperors imposed a distinct and personal tribute on the trading part of their subjects.[188]   Some exemptions, very strictly confined both in time and place, were allowed to the proprietors who disposed of the produce of their own estates.   Some indulgence was granted to the profession of the liberal arts : but every other branch of commercial industry was affected by the severity of the law. The honorable merchant of Alexandria, who imported the gems and spices of India for the use of the western world ; the usurer, who derived from the interest of money a silent and ignominious profit ; the ingenious manufacturer, the diligent mechanic, and even the most obscure retailer of a sequestered village, were obliged to admit the officers of the revenue into the partnership of their gain ; and the sovereign of the Roman empire, who tolerated the profession, consented to share the infamous salary, of public prostitutes.†   As this

---

the fifth and sixth centuries.   Yet there is a passage in Eumenius (Panegyr. Vet. viii. 7) which very forcibly deters me from extending the territory of the Ædui, in the reign of Constantine, along the beautiful banks of the navigable Saône.*

[186] Eumenius in Panegyr. Vet. viii. 11.
[187] L'Abbé du Bos, Hist. Critique de la M. F. tom. i. p. 121.
[188] See Cod. Theod. l. xiii. tit. i. and iv.

---

* In this passage of Eumenius, Savigny supposes the original number to have been 32,000 : 7000 being discharged, there remained 25,000 liable to the tribute.   See Mem. quoted above. — M.
† The emperor Theodosius put an end by a law, to this disgraceful

general tax upon industry was collected every fourth year, it was styled the *Lustral Contribution :* and the historian Zosimus [189] laments that the approach of the fatal period was announced by the tears and terrors of the citizens, who were often compelled by the impending scourge to embrace the most abhorred and unnatural methods of procuring the sum at which their property had been assessed. The testimony of Zosimus cannot indeed be justified from the charge of passion and prejudice ; but, from the nature of this tribute, it seems reasonable to conclude, that it was arbitrary in the distribution, and extremely rigorous in the mode of collecting. The secret wealth of commerce, and the precarious profits of art or labor, are susceptible only of a discretionary valuation, which is seldom disadvantageous to the interest of the treasury ; and as the person of the trader supplies the want of a visible and permanent security, the payment of the imposition, which, in the case of a land tax, may be obtained by the seizure of property, can rarely be extorted by any other means than those of corporal punishments. The cruel treatment of the insolvent debtors of the state, is attested, and was perhaps mitigated by a very humane edict of Constantine, who, disclaiming the use of racks and of scourges, allots a spacious and airy prison for the place of their confinement.[190]

These general taxes were imposed and levied by the absolute authority of the monarch ; but the occasional offerings of the *coronary gold* still retained the name and semblance of popular consent. It was an ancient custom that the allies of the republic, who ascribed their safety or deliverance to the success of the Roman arms, and even the cities of Italy, who admired the virtues of their victorious general, adorned the pomp of his triumph by their voluntary gifts of crowns of gold, which after the ceremony were consecrated in the

---

[189] Zosimus, l. ii. p. 115. There is probably as much passion and prejudice in the attack of Zosimus, as in the elaborate defence of the memory of Constantine by the zealous Dr. Howell. Hist. of the World, vol. ii. p. 20.

[190] Cod. Theod. l. xi. tit. vii. leg. 3.

---

source of revenue. (Godef. ad Cod. Theod. xiii. tit. i. c. 1.) But before he deprived himself of it, he made sure of some way of replacing this deficit. A rich patrician, Florentius, indignant at this legalized licentiousness, had made representations on the subject to the emperor. To induce him to tolerate it no longer, he offered his own property to supply the dim inution of the revenue. The emperor had the baseness to accept his offer —G.

temple of Jupiter to remain a lasting monument of his glory to future ages. The progress of zeal and flattery soon multiplied the number, and increased the size, of these popular donations; and the triumph of Cæsar was enriched with two thousand eight hundred and twenty-two massy crowns, whose weight amounted to twenty thousand four hundred and fourteen pounds of gold. This treasure was immediately melted down by the prudent dictator, who was satisfied that it would be more serviceable to his soldiers than to the gods: his example was imitated by his successors; and the custom was introduced of exchanging these splendid ornaments for the more acceptable present of the current gold coin of the empire.[191] The spontaneous offering was at length exacted as the debt of duty; and instead of being confined to the occasion of a triumph, it was supposed to be granted by the several cities and provinces of the monarchy, as often as the emperor condescended to announce his accession, his consulship, the birth of a son, the creation of a Cæsar, a victory over the Barbarians, or any other real or imaginary event which graced the annals of his reign. The peculiar free gift of the senate of Rome was fixed by custom at sixteen hundred pounds of gold, or about sixty-four thousand pounds sterling. The oppressed subjects celebrated their own felicity, that their sovereign should graciously consent to accept this feeble but voluntary testimony of their loyalty and gratitude.[192]

A people elated by pride, or soured by discontent, are seldom qualified to form a just estimate of their actual situation. The subjects of Constantine were incapable of discerning the decline of genius and manly virtue, which so far degraded them below the dignity of their ancestors; but they could feel and lament the rage of tyranny, the relaxation of discipline, and the increase of taxes. The impartial historian, who acknowl-

---

[191] See Lipsius de Magnitud. Romana, l. ii. c. 9. The Tarragonese Spain presented the emperor Claudius with a crown of gold of seven, and Gaul with another of nine, *hundred* pounds weight. I have followed the rational emendation of Lipsius.*

[192] Cod. Theod. l. xii. tit. xiii. The senators were supposed to be exempt from the *Aurum Coronarium;* but the *Auri Oblatio,* which was required at their hands, was precisely of the same nature.

---

* This custom is of still earlier date; the Romans had borrowed it from Greece. Who is not acquainted with the famous oration of Demosthenes for the golden crown, which his citizens wished to bestow, and Æschines to deprive him of?—G

edges the justice of their complaints, will observe some favorable circumstances which tended to alleviate the misery of their condition. The threatening tempest of Barbarians, which so soon subverted the foundations of Roman greatness, was still repelled, or suspended, on the frontiers. The arts of luxury and literature were cultivated, and the elegant pleasures of society were enjoyed, by the inhabitants of a considerable portion of the globe. The forms, the pomp, and the expense of the civil administration contributed to restrain the irregular license of the soldiers ; and although the laws were violated by power, or perverted by subtlety, the sage principles of the Roman jurisprudence preserved a sense of order and equity, unknown to the despotic governments of the East. The rights of mankind might derive some protection from religion and philosophy ; and the name of freedom, which could no longer alarm, might sometimes admonish, the successors of Augustus that they did not reign over a nation of Slaves or Barbarians.[193]

---

[193] The great Theodosius, in his judicious advice to his son, (Claudian in iv Consulat. Honorii, 214, &c.,) distinguishes the station of a Roman prince from that of a Parthian monarch. Virtue was necessary for the one ; birth might suffice for the other.

CHAPTER XVIII.

CHARACTER OF CONSTANTINE. — GOTHIC WAR. — DEATH OF
CONSTANTINE. — DIVISION OF THE EMPIRE AMONG HIS THREE
SONS. — PERSIAN WAR. — TRAGIC DEATHS OF CONSTANTINE
THE YOUNGER AND CONSTANS. — USURPATION OF MAGNEN-
TIUS. — CIVIL WAR. — VICTORY OF CONSTANTIUS.

THE character of the prince who removed the seat of empire, and introduced such important changes into the civil and religious constitution of his country, has fixed the attention, and divided the opinions, of mankind. By the grateful zeal of the Christians, the deliverer of the church has been decorated with every attribute of a hero, and even of a saint ; while the discontent of the vanquished party has compared Constantine to the most abhorred of those tyrants, who, by their vice and weakness, dishonored the Imperial purple. The same passions have in some degree been perpetuated to succeeding generations, and the character of Constantine is considered, even in the present age, as an object either of satire or of panegyric. By the impartial union of those defects which are confessed by his warmest admirers, and of those virtues which are acknowledged by his most implacable enemies, we might hope to delineate a just portrait of that extraordinary man, which the truth and candor of history should adopt without a blush.[1] But it would soon appear, that the vain attempt to blend such discordant colors, and to reconcile such inconsistent qualities, must produce a figure monstrous rather than human, unless it is viewed in its proper and distinct lights, by a careful separation of the different periods of the reign of Constantine.

The person, as well as the mind, of Constantine, had been enriched by nature with her choicest endowments. His

---

[1] On ne se trompera point sur Constantin, en croyant tout le mal qu'en dit Eusebe, et tout le bien qu'en dit Zosime. Fleury, Hist. Ecclesiastique, tom. iii. p. 233. Eusebius and Zosimus form indeed the two extremes of flattery and invective. The intermediate shades are expressed by those writers, whose character or situation variously tempered the influence of their religious zeal.

stature was lofty, his countenance majestic, his deportment graceful , his strength and activity were displayed in every manly exercise, and from his earliest youth, to a very advanced season of life, he preserved the vigor of his constitution by a strict adherence to the domestic virtues of chastity and temperance.   He delighted in the social intercourse of familiar conversation ; and though he might sometimes indulge his disposition to raillery with less reserve than was required by the severe dignity of his station, the courtesy and liberality of his manners gained the hearts of all who approached him.   The sincerity of his friendship has been suspected ; yet he showed, on some occasions, that he was not incapable of a warm and lasting attachment.   The disadvantage of an illiterate education had not prevented him from forming a just estimate of the value of learning ; and the arts and sciences derived some encouragement from the munificent protection of Constantine. In the despatch of business, his diligence was indefatigable ; and the active powers of his mind were almost continually exercised in reading, writing, or meditating, in giving audience to ambassadors, and in examining the complaints of his subjects.   Even those who censured the propriety of his measures were compelled to acknowledge, that he possessed magnanimity to conceive, and patience to execute, the most arduous designs, without being checked either by the prejudices of education, or by the clamors of the multitude.   In the field, he infused his own intrepid spirit into the troops, whom he conducted with the talents of a consummate general ; and to his abilities, rather than to his fortune, we may ascribe the signal victories which he obtained over the foreign and domestic foes of the republic.   He loved glory as the reward, perhaps as the motive, of his labors.   The boundless ambition, which, from the moment of his accepting the purple at York, appears as the ruling passion of his soul, may be justified by the dangers of his own situation, by the character of his rivals, by the consciousness of superior merit, and by the prospect that his success would enable him to restore peace and order to the distracted empire.   In his civil wars against Maxentius and Licinius, he had engaged on his side the inclinations of the people, who compared the undissembled vices of those tyrants with the spirit of wisdom and justice which seemed to direct the general tenor of the administration of Constantine.[2]

* The virtues of Constantine are collected for the most part from

Had Constantine fallen on the banks of the Tyber, or even in the plains of Hadrianople, such is the character which, with a few exceptions, he might have transmitted to posterity. But the conclusion of his reign (according to the moderate and indeed tender sentence of a writer of the same age) degraded him from the rank which he had acquired among the most deserving of the Roman princes.[3] In the life of Augustus, we behold the tyrant of the republic, converted, almost by imperceptible degrees, into the father of his country, and of human kind. In that of Constantine, we may contemplate a hero, who had so long inspired his subjects with love, and his enemies with terror, degenerating into a cruel and dissolute monarch, corrupted by his fortune, or raised by conquest above the necessity of dissimulation. The general peace which he maintained during the last fourteen years of his reign, was a period of apparent splendor rather than of real prosperity ; and the old age of Constantine was disgraced by the opposite yet reconcilable vices of rapaciousness and prodigality. The accumulated treasures found in the palaces of Maxentius and Licinius, were lavishly consumed ; the various innovations introduced by the conqueror, were attended with an increasing expense ; the cost of his buildings, his court, and his festivals, required an immediate and plentiful supply ; and the oppression of the people was the only fund which could support the magnificence of the sovereign.[4] His unworthy favorites, enriched by the boundless liberality of their master, usurped with impunity the privilege of rapine

---

Eutropius and the younger Victor, two sincere pagans, who wrote after the extinction of his family. Even Zosimus, and the Emperor Julian, acknowledge his personal courage and military achievements.

[3] See Eutropius, x. 6. In primo Imperii tempore optimis principibus, ultimo mediis comparandus. From the ancient Greek version of Pœanius, (edit. Havercamp. p. 697,) I am inclined to suspect that Eutropius had originally written vix mediis ; and that the offensive monosyllable was dropped by the wilful inadvertency of transcribers. Aurelius Victor expresses the general opinion by a vulgar and indeed obscure proverb. Trachala decem annis præstantissimus ; duodecim sequentibus latro ; decem novissimis pupillus ob immodicas profusiones.

[4] Julian, Orat. i. p. 8, in a flattering discourse pronounced before the son of Constantine ; and Cæsares, p. 335. Zosimus, p. 114, 115. The stately buildings of Constantinople, &c., may be quoted as a lasting and unexceptionable proof of the profuseness of their founder.

and corruption.[5] A secret but universal decay was felt in
every part of the public administration, and the emperor himself, though he still retained the obedience, gradually lost the
esteem, of his subjects. The dress and manners, which,
towards the decline of life, he chose to affect, served only to
degrade him in the eyes of mankind. The Asiatic pomp,
which had been adopted by the pride of Diocletian, assumed
an air of softness and effeminacy in the person of Constantine.
He is represented with false hair of various colors, laboriously
arranged by the skilful artists of the times; a diadem of a
new and more expensive fashion; a profusion of gems and
pearls, of collars and bracelets, and a variegated flowing robe
of silk, most curiously embroidered with flowers of gold. In
such apparel, scarcely to be excused by the youth and folly
of Elagabalus, we are at a loss to discover the wisdom of an
aged monarch, and the simplicity of a Roman veteran.[6] A
mind thus relaxed by prosperity and indulgence was incapable
of rising to that magnanimity which disdains suspicion, and
dares to forgive. The deaths of Maximian and Licinius may
perhaps be justified by the maxims of policy, as they are
taught in the schools of tyrants; but an impartial narrative of
the executions, or rather murders, which sullied the declining
age of Constantine, will suggest to our most candid thoughts
the idea of a prince who could sacrifice without reluctance
the laws of justice, and the feelings of nature, to the dictates
either of his passions or of his interest.

The same fortune which so invariably followed the standard
of Constantine, seemed to secure the hopes and comforts of
his domestic life. Those among his predecessors who had
enjoyed the longest and most prosperous reigns, Augustus,
Trajan, and Diocletian, had been disappointed of posterity;
and the frequent revolutions had never allowed sufficient time
for any Imperial family to grow up and multiply under the

---

[5] The impartial Ammianus deserves all our confidence. Proximo-
rum fauces aperuit primus omnium Constantinus. L. xvi. c. 8. Eusebius himself confesses the abuse, (Vit. Constantin. l. iv. c. 29, 54;)
and some of the Imperial laws feebly point out the remedy. See
above, p. 146 of this volume.

[6] Julian, in the Cæsars, attempts to ridicule his uncle. His suspicious testimony is confirmed, however, by the learned Spanheim, with
the authority of medals, (see Commentaire, p. 156, 299, 397, 459.)
Eusebius (Orat. c. 5) alleges, that Constantine dressed for the public,
not for himself. Were this admitted, the vainest coxcomb could
never want an excuse.

shade of the purple. But the royalty of the Flavian line, which had been first ennobled by the Gothic Claudius, descended through several generations; and Constantine himself derived from his royal father the hereditary honors which he transmitted to his children. The emperor had been twice married. Minervina, the obscure but lawful object of his youthful attachment,[7] had left him only one son, who was called Crispus. By Fausta, the daughter of Maximian, he had three daughters, and three sons known by the kindred names of Constantine, Constantius, and Constans. The unambitious brothers of the great Constantine, Julius Constantius, Dalmatius, and Hannibalianus,[8] were permitted to enjoy the most honorable rank, and the most affluent fortune, that could be consistent with a private station. The youngest of the three lived without a name, and died without posterity. His two elder brothers obtained in marriage the daughters of wealthy senators, and propagated new branches of the Imperial race. Gallus and Julian afterwards became the most illustrious of the children of Julius Constantius, the *Patrician*. The two sons of Dalmatius, who had been decorated with the vain title of *Censor*, were named Dalmatius and Hannibalianus. The two sisters of the great Constantine, Anastasia and Eutropia, were bestowed on Optatus and Nepotianus, two senators of noble birth and of consular dignity. His third sister, Constantia, was distinguished by her preëminence of greatness and of misery. She remained the widow of the vanquished Licinius; and it was by her entreaties, that an innocent boy, the offspring of their marriage, preserved for some time, his life, the title of Cæsar, and a precarious hope of the succession. Besides the females, and the allies of the Flavian house, ten or twelve males, to whom the language of modern courts would apply the title of princes of the blood, seemed, according to the order of their birth, to be destined either to inherit or to support the throne of Constantine. But in less than thirty years, this numerous and increasing family

---

[7] Zosimus and Zonaras agree in representing Minervina as the concubine of Constantine; but Ducange has very gallantly rescued her character, by producing a decisive passage from one of the panegyrics: " Ab ipso fine pueritiæ te matrimonii legibus dedisti."

[8] Ducange (Familiæ Byzantinæ, p. 44) bestows on him, after Zonaras, the name of Constantine; a name somewhat unlikely, as it was already occupied by the elder brother. That of Hannibalianus is mentioned in the Paschal Chronicle, and is approved by Tillemont. Hist. des Empereurs, tom. iv. p. 527

was reduced to the persons of Constantius and Julian, who alone had survived a series of crimes and calamities, such as the tragic poets have deplored in the devoted lines of Pelops and of Cadmus.

Crispus, the eldest son of Constantine, and the presumptive heir of the empire, is represented by impartial historians as an amiable and accomplished youth. The care of his education, or at least of his studies, was intrusted to Lactantius, the most eloquent of the Christians; a preceptor admirably qualified to form the taste, and to excite the virtues, of his illustrious disciple.[9] At the age of seventeen, Crispus was invested with the title of Cæsar, and the administration of the Gallic provinces, where the inroads of the Germans gave him an early occasion of signalizing his military prowess. In the civil war which broke out soon afterwards, the father and son divided their powers; and this history has already celebrated the valor as well as conduct displayed by the latter, in forcing the straits of the Hellespont, so obstinately defended by the superior fleet of Licinius. This naval victory contributed to determine the event of the war; and the names of Constantine and of Crispus were united in the joyful acclamations of their eastern subjects; who loudly proclaimed, that the world had been subdued, and was now governed, by an emperor endowed with every virtue; and by his illustrious son, a prince beloved of Heaven, and the lively image of his father's perfections. The public favor, which seldom accompanies old age, diffused its lustre over the youth of Crispus. He deserved the esteem, and he engaged the affections, of the court, the army, and the people. The experienced merit of a reigning monarch is acknowledged by his subjects with reluctance, and frequently denied with partial and discontented murmurs; while, from the opening virtues of his successor, they fondly conceive the most unbounded hopes of private as well as public felicity.[10]

This dangerous popularity soon excited the attention of Constantine, who, both as a father and as a king, was impa-

---

[9] Jerom. in Chron. The poverty of Lactantius may be applied either to the praise of the disinterested philosopher, or to the shame of the unfeeling patron. See Tillemont, Mem. Ecclesiast. tom. vi. part i. p. 345. Dupin, Bibliothèque Ecclesiast. tom. i. ɪ. 205. Lardner's Credibility of the Gospel History, part ii. vol. vii. p. 66.

[10] Euseb. Hist. Ecclesiast. l. x. c. 9. Eutropius (x. 6) styles him "egregium virum;" and Julian (Orat. i.) very plainly alludes to the exploits of Crispus in the civil war. See Spanheim, Comment. p. 92.

tient of an equal. Instead of attempting to secure the allegiance of his son by the generous ties of confidence and gratitude, he resolved to prevent the mischiefs which might be apprehended from dissatisfied ambition. Crispus soon had reason to complain, that while his infant brother Constantius was sent, with the title of Cæsar, to reign over his peculiar department of the Gallic provinces,[11] he, a prince of mature years, who had performed such recent and signal services, instead of being raised to the superior rank of Augustus, was confined almost a prisoner to his father's court; and exposed, without power or defence, to every calumny which the malice of his enemies could suggest. Under such painful circumstances, the royal youth might not always be able to compose his behavior, or suppress his discontent; and we may be assured, that he was encompassed by a train of indiscreet or perfidious followers, who assiduously studied to inflame, and who were perhaps instructed to betray, the unguarded warmth of his resentment. An edict of Constantine, published about this time, manifestly indicates his real or affected suspicions, that a secret conspiracy had been formed against his person and government. By all the allurements of honors and rewards, he invites informers of every degree to accuse without exception his magistrates or ministers, his friends or his most intimate favorites, protesting, with a solemn asseveration, that he himself will listen to the charge, that he himself will revenge his injuries; and concluding with a prayer, which discovers some apprehension of danger, that the providence of the Supreme Being may still continue to protect the safety of the emperor and of the empire.[12]

The informers, who complied with so liberal an invitation, were sufficiently versed in the arts of courts to select the friends and adherents of Crispus as the guilty persons; nor is there any reason to distrust the veracity of the emperor, who had promised an ample measure of revenge and punishment. The policy of Constantine maintained, however, the same

[11] Compare Idatius and the Paschal Chronicle, with Ammianus, (l. xiv. c. 5.) The year in which Constantius was created Cæsar seems to be more accurately fixed by the two chronologists; but the historian who lived in his court could not be ignorant of the day of the anniversary. For the appointment of the new Cæsar to the provinces of Gaul, see Julian, Orat. i. p. 12, Godefroy, Chronol. Legum, p. 26, and Blondel, de Primauté de l'Eglise, p. 1183.

[12] Cod. Theod. l. ix. tit. iv. Godefroy suspected the secret motives of this law. Comment. tom. iii. p. 9

appearances of regard and confidence towards a son, whom he began to consider as his most irreconcilable enemy. Medals were struck with the customary vows for the long and auspicious reign of the young Cæsar; [13] and as the people, who were not admitted into the secrets of the palace, still loved his virtues, and respected his dignity, a poet who solicits his recall from exile, adores with equal devotion the majesty of the father and that of the son. [14] The time was no'v arrived for celebrating the august ceremony of the twentieth year of the reign of Constantine; and the emperor, for that purpose, removed his court from Nicomedia to Rome, where the most splendid preparations had been made for his reception. Every eye, and every tongue, affected to express their sense of the general happiness, and the veil of ceremony and dissimulation was drawn for a while over the darkest designs of revenge and murder. [15] In the midst of the festival, the unfortunate Crispus was apprehended by order of the emperor, who laid aside the tenderness of a father, without assuming the equity of a judge. The examination was short and private; [16] and as it was thought decent to conceal the fate of the young prince from the eyes of the Roman people he was sent under a strong guard to Pola, in Istria, where soon afterwards, he was put to death, either by the hand of the executioner, or by the more gentle operation of poison. [17] The Cæsar Licinius, a youth of amiable manners, was involved in the ruin of Crispus: [18] and the stern jealousy of Constantine

[13] Ducange, Fam. Byzant. p. 28. Tillemont, tom. iv. p. 610.

[14] His name was Porphyrius Optatianus. The date of his panegyric, written, according to the taste of the age, in vile acrostics, is settled by Scaliger ad Euseb. p. 250, Tillemont, tom. iv. p. 607, and Fabricius, Biblioth. Latin, l. iv. c. 1.

[15] Zosim. l. ii. p. 103. Godefroy, Chronol. Legum, p. 28.

[16] 'Αχρίτως, without a trial, is the strong and most probably the just expression of Suidas. The elder Victor, who wrote under the next reign, speaks with becoming caution. " Natû grandior incertum quâ causâ, patris judicio occidisset." If we consult the succeeding writers, Eutropius, the younger Victor, Orosius, Jerom, Zosimus, Philostorgius, and Gregory of Tours, their knowledge will appear gradually to increase, as their means of information must have diminished — a circumstance which frequently occurs in historical disquisition.

[17] Ammianus (l. xiv. c. 11) uses the general expression of peremptum. Codinus (p. 34) beheads the young prince; but Sidonius Apollinaris (Epistol. v. 8,) for the sake perhaps of an antithesis to Fausta's warm bath, chooses to administer a draught of cold poison.

[18] Sororis filium, commodæ indolis juvenem. Eutropius, x. 6. May I not be permitted to conjecture that Crispus had married Hele-

was unmoved by the prayers and tears of his favorite sister pleading for the life of a son, whose rank was his only crime and whose loss she did not long survive. The story of these unhappy princes, the nature and evidence of their guilt, the forms of their trial, and the circumstances of their death, were buried in mysterious obscurity; and the courtly bishop, who has celebrated in an elaborate work the virtues and piety of his hero, observes a prudent silence on the subject of these tragic events.[19] Such haughty contempt for the opinion of mankind, whilst it imprints an indelible stain on the memory of Constantine, must remind us of the very different behavior of one of the greatest monarchs of the present age. The Czar Peter, in the full possession of despotic power, submitted to the judgment of Russia, of Europe, and of posterity, the reasons which had compelled him to subscribe the condemnation of a criminal, or at least of a degenerate, son.[20]

The innocence of Crispus was so universally acknowledged that the modern Greeks, who adore the memory of their founder, are reduced to palliate the guilt of a parricide, which the common feelings of human nature forbade them to justify. They pretend, that as soon as the afflicted father discovered the falsehood of the accusation by which his credulity had been so fatally misled, he published to the world his repentance and remorse; that he mourned forty days, during which he abstained from the use of the bath, and all the ordinary comforts of life; and that, for the lasting instruction of posterity, he erected a golden statue of Crispus, with this memorable inscription: TO MY SON, WHOM I UNJUSTLY CONDEMNED.[21] A tale so moral and so interesting would deserve

---

na, the daughter of the emperor Licinius, and that on the happy delivery of the princess, in the year 322, a general pardon was granted by Constantine? See Ducange, Fam. Byzant. p. 47, and the law (l. ix. tit. xxxvii.) of the Theodosian code, which has so much embarrassed the interpreters. Godefroy, tom. iii. p. 267.*

[19] See the life of Constantine, particularly l. ii. c. 19, 20. Two hundred and fifty years afterwards, Evagrius (l. iii. c. 41) deduced from the silence of Eusebius a vain argument against the reality of the fact.

[20] Histoire de Pierre le Grand, par Voltaire, part ii. c. 10.

[21] In order to prove that the statue was erected by Constantine, and afterwards concealed by the malice of the Arians, Codinus very

---

* This conjecture is very doubtful. The obscurity of the law quoted from the Theodosian code scarcely allows any inference, and there is extant but one medal which can be attributed to a Helena, wife of Crispus. See Eckhel, Doct. Num. Vet. t. viii. p. 102 and 145. — G.

to be suppor ed by less exceptionable authority; but if we consult the more ancient and authentic writers, they will inform us, that the repentance of Constantine was manifested only in acts of blood and revenge ; and that he atoned for the murder of an innocent son, by the execution, perhaps, of a guilty wife. They ascribe the misfortunes of Crispus to the arts of his step-mother Fausta, whose implacable hatred, or whose disappointed love, renewed in the palace of Constantine the ancient tragedy of Hippolitus and of Phædra.[22] Like the daughter of Minos, the daughter of Maximian accused her son in-law of an incestuous attempt on the chastity of his father's wife ; and easily obtained, from the jealousy of the emperor, a sentence of death against a young prince, whom she considered with reason as the most formidable rival of her own children. But Helena, the aged mother of Constantine, lamented and revenged the untimely fate of her grandson Crispus ; nor was it long before a real or pretended discovery was made, that Fausta herself entertained a criminal connection with a slave belonging to the Imperial stables.[23] Her condemnation and punishment were the instant consequences of the charge ; and the adulteress was suffocated by the steam of a bath, which, for that purpose, had been heated to an ex traordinary degree.[24] By some it will perhaps be thought, that the remembrance of a conjugal union of twenty years, and the honor of their common offspring, the destined heirs of the throne, might have softened the obdurate heart of Constantine, and persuaded him to suffer his wife, however guilty she might appear, to expiate her offences in a solitary prison. But it seems a superfluous labor to weigh the propriety, unless we could ascertain the truth, of this singular event, which is

readily creates (p. 34) two witnesses, Hippolitus, and the younger Herodotus, to whose imaginary histories he appeals with unblushing confidence.

[22] Zosimus (l. ii. p. 103) may be considered as our original. The ingenuity of the moderns, assisted by a few hints from the ancients, has illustrated and improved his obscure and imperfect narrative.

[23] Philostorgius, l. ii. c. 4. Zosimus (l. ii. p. 104, 116) imputes to Constantine the death of two wives, of the innocent Fausta, and of an adulteress, who was the mother of his three successors. According to Jerom, three or four years elapsed between the death of Crispus and that of Fausta. The elder Victor is prudently silent.

[24] If Fausta was put to death, it is reasonable to believe that the private apartments of the palace were the scene of her execution. The orator Chrysostom indulges his fancy by exposing the naked empress on a desert mountain to be devoured by wild beasts.

attended with some circumstances of doubt and perplexity Those who have attacked, and those who have defended, the character of Constantine, have alike disregarded two very remarkable passages of two orations pronounced under the succeeding reign. The former celebrates the virtues, the beauty, and the fortune of the empress Fausta, the daughter, wife, sister, and mother of so many princes.[25] The latter asserts, in explicit terms, that the mother of the younger Constantine, who was slain three years after his father's death, survived to weep over the fate of her son.[26] Notwithstanding the positive testimony of several writers of the Pagan as well as of the Christian religion, there may still remain some reason to believe, or at least to suspect, that Fausta escaped the blind and suspicious cruelty of her husband.* The deaths of a son and a nephew, with the execution of a great number of respectable, and perhaps innocent friends,[27] who were involved in their fall, may be sufficient, however, to justify the discontent of the Roman people, and to explain the satirical verses affixed to the palace gate, comparing the splendid and bloody reigns of Constantine and Nero.[28]

By the death of Crispus, the inheritance of the empire seemed to devolve on the three sons of Fausta, who have been already mentioned under the names of Constantine, of Constantius, and of Constans. These young princes were suc-

---

[25] Julian. Orat. i. He seems to call her the mother of Crispus. She might assume that title by adoption. At least, she was not considered as his mortal enemy. Julian compares the fortune of Fausta with that of Parysatis, the Persian queen. A Roman would have more naturally recollected the second Agrippina : —

> Et moi, qui sur le trone ai suivi mes ancêtres :
> Moi, fille, femme, sœur, et mere de vos maitres.

[26] Monod. in Constantin. Jun. c. 4, ad Calcem Eutrop. edit. Havercamp. The orator styles her the most divine and pious of queens

[27]   Interfecit numerosos amicos. Eutrop. xx. 6.
[28]   Saturni aurea sæcula quis requirat ?
> Sunt hæc gemmea, sed Neroniana.
>   Sidon. Apollinar. v. 8.

It is somewhat singular that these satirical lines should be attributed, not to an obscure libeller, or a disappointed patriot, but to Ablavius, prime minister and favorite of the emperor. We may now perceive that the imprecations of the Roman people were dictated by humanity, as well as by superstition. Zosim. l. ii. p. 105.

---

* Manso (Leben Constantins, p. 65) treats this inference of Gibbon, and the authorities to which he appeals, with too much contempt, considering the general scantiness of proof on this curious question. — M.

35 *

cessively invested with the title of Cæsar; and the dates of
their promotion may be referred to the tenth, the twentieth,
and the thirtieth years of the reign of their father.[29] This
conduct, though it tended to multiply the future masters of the
Roman world, might be excused by the partiality of paternal
affection; but it is not so easy to understand the motives of the
emperor, when he endangered the safety both of his family
and of his people, by the unnecessary elevation of his two
nephews, Dalmatius and Hannibalianus. The former was
raised, by the title of Cæsar, to an equality with his cousins.
In favor of the latter, Constantine invented the new and singular appellation of *Nobilissimus;*[30] to which he annexed the
flattering distinction of a robe of purple and gold. But of the
whole series of Roman princes in any age of the empire
Hannibalianus alone was distinguished by the title of KING;
a name which the subjects of Tiberius would have detested,
as the profane and cruel insult of capricious tyranny. The
use of such a title, even as it appears under the reign of Constantine, is a strange and unconnected fact, which can scarcely
oe admitted on the joint authority of Imperial medals and contemporary writers.[31]

The whole empire was deeply interested in the education
of these five youths, the acknowledged successors of Constantine. The exercises of the body prepared them for the
fatigues of war and the duties of active life. Those who occa

---

[29] Euseb. Orat. in Constantin. c. 3. These dates are sufficiently
correct to justify the orator.

[30] Zosim. l. ii. p. 117. Under the predecessors of Constantine, *Nobilissimus* was a vague epithet, rather than a legal and determined
title.

[31] Adstruunt nummi veteres ac singulares. Spanheim de Usu
Numismat. Dissertat. xii. vol. ii. p. 357. Ammianus speaks of this
Roman king (l. xiv. c. 1, and Valesius ad loc.) The Valesian fragment styles him King of kings; and the Paschal Chronicle, (p.
286,) by employing the word, *Ρηγα,* acquires the weight of Latin
evidence.*

---

* Hannibalianus is always designated in these authors by the title of
king. There still exist medals struck to his honor, on which the same
title is found, FL. HANNIBALIANO REGI. See Eckhel, Doct. Num. t. viii.
204. Armeniam nationesque circum socias habebat, says Aur. Victor, p.
225. The writer means the Lesser Armenia. Though it is not possible to
question a fact supported by such respectable authorities, Gibbon considers it inexplicable and incredible. It is a strange abuse of the privilege
of doubting, to refuse all belief in a fact of such little importance in itself,
and attested thus formally by contemporary authors and public monuments. St Martin, note to Le Beau, i. 341. — M.

sionally mention the education or talents of Constantius, allow
that he excelled in the gymnastic arts of leaping and running;
that he was a dexterous archer, a skilful horseman, and a
master of all the different weapons used in the service either
of the cavalry or of the infantry.[32] The same assiduous
cultivation was bestowed, though not perhaps with equal success, to improve the minds of the sons and nephews of Constantine.[33] The most celebrated professors of the Christian
faith, of the Grecian philosophy, and of the Roman jurisprudence, were invited by the liberality of the emperor, who
reserved for himself the important task of instructing the royal
youths in the science of government, and the knowledge of
mankind. But the genius of Constantine himself had been
formed by adversity and experience. In the free intercourse
of private life, and amidst the dangers of the court of Galerius, he had learned to command his own passions, to encounter those of his equals, and to depend for his present safety
and future greatness on the prudence and firmness of his personal conduct. His destined successors had the misfortune of
being born and educated in the Imperial purple. Incessantly
surrounded with a train of flatterers, they passed their youth
in the enjoyment of luxury, and the expectation of a throne;
nor would the dignity of their rank permit them to descend
from that elevated station from whence the various characters
of human nature appear to wear a smooth and uniform
aspect. The indulgence of Constantine admitted them, at a
very tender age, to share the administration of the empire;
and they studied the art of reigning, at the expense of the
people intrusted to their care. The younger Constantine was
appointed to hold his court in Gaul; and his brother Constantius exchanged that department, the ancient patrimony of
their father, for the more opulent, but less martial, countries
of the East. Italy, the Western Illyricum, and Africa, were
accustomed to revere Constans, the third of his sons, as the
representative of the great Constantine. He fixed Dalmatius
on the Gothic frontier, to which he annexed the government

---

[32] His dexterity in martial exercises is celebrated by Julian, (Orat. i.
p. 11, Orat. ii. p, 53,) and allowed by Ammianus, (l. xxi. c. 16.)
[33] Euseb. in Vit. Constantin. l. iv. c. 51. Julian, Orat. i. p. 11—16,
with Spanheim's elaborate Commentary. Libanius, Orat. iii. p. 100.
Constantius studied with laudable diligence; but the dulness of his
fancy prevented him from succeeding in the art of poetry, or even of
rhetoric.

of Thrace, Macedonia, and Greece. The city of Cæsarea
was chosen for the residence of Hannibalianus; and the prov
inces of Pontus, Cappadocia, and the Lesser Armenia, were
destined to form the extent of his new kingdom. For each
of these princes a suitable establishment was provided. A just
proportion of guards, of legions, and of auxiliaries, was allotted for their respective dignity and defence. The ministers
and generals, who were placed about their persons, were such
as Constantine could trust to assist, and even to control, these
youthful sovereigns in the exercise of their delegated power.
As they advanced in years and experience, the limits of their
authority were insensibly enlarged : but the emperor always
reserved for himself the title of Augustus ; and while he
showed the *Cæsars* to the armies and provinces, he maintained every part of the empire in equal obedience to its
supreme head.[34] The tranquillity of the last fourteen years
of his reign was scarcely interrupted by the contemptible
insurrection of a camel-driver in the Island of Cyprus,[35] or by
the active part which the policy of Constantine engaged him
to assume in the wars of the Goths and Sarmatians.

Among the different branches of the human race, the Sarmatians form a very remarkable shade ; as they seem to unite
the manners of the Asiatic barbarians with the figure and
complexion of the ancient inhabitants of Europe. According
to the various accidents of peace and war, of alliance or conquest, the Sarmatians were sometimes confined to the banks
of the Tanais ; and they sometimes spread themselves over
the immense plains which lie between the Vistula and the
Volga.[36] The care of their numerous flocks and herds, the
pursuit of game, and the exercises of war, or rather of rapine,
directed the vagrant motions of the Sarmatians. The movable

---

[34] Eusebius, (l. iv. c. 51, 52,) with a design of exalting the authority
and glory of Constantine, affirms, that he divided the Roman empire
as a private citizen might have divided his patrimony. His distribution of the provinces may be collected from Eutropius, the two Victors, and the Valesian fragment.
[35] Calocerus, the obscure leader of this rebellion, or rather tumult,
was apprehended and burnt alive in the market-place of Tarsus, by
the vigilance of Dalmatius. See the elder Victor, the Chronicle of
Jerom, and the doubtful traditions of Theophanes and Cedrenus.
[36] Cellarius has collected the opinions of the ancients concerning
the European and Asiatic Sarmatia ; and M. D Anville has applied
them to modern geography with the skill and accuracy which always
distinguish that excellent writer.

camps or cities, the ordinary residence of their wives and children, consisted only of large wagons drawn by oxen, and covered in the form of tents. The military strength of the nation was composed of cavalry; and the custom of their warriors, to lead in their hand one or two spare horses, ena bled them to advance and to retreat with a rapid diligence, which surprised the security, and eluded the pursuit, of a distant enemy.[37] Their poverty of iron prompted their rude industry to invent a sort of cuirass, which was capable of resisting a sword or javelin, though it was formed only of horses' hoofs, cut into thin and polished slices, carefully laid over each other in the manner of scales or feathers, and strongly sewed upon an under garment of coarse linen.[38] The offensive arms of the Sarmatians were short daggers, long lances, and a weighty bow with a quiver of arrows. They were reduced to the necessity of employing fish-bones for the points of their weapons; but the custom of dipping them in a venomous liquor, that poisoned the wounds which they inflicted, is alone sufficient to prove the most savage manners, since a people impressed with a sense of humanity would have abhorred so cruel a practice, and a nation skilled in the arts of war would have disdained so impotent a resource.[39] Whenever these Barbarians issued from their deserts in quest of prey, their shaggy beards, uncombed locks, the furs with which they were covered from head to foot, and their fierce countenances, which seemed to express the innate cruelty of their minds, inspired the more civilized provincials of Rome with horror and dismay.

The tender Ovid, after a youth spent in the enjoyment of

---

[37] Ammian. l. xvii. c. 12. The Sarmatian horses were castrated to prevent the mischievous accidents which might happen from the noisy and ungovernable passions of the males.

[38] Pausanius, l. i. p. 50, edit. Kuhn. That inquisitive traveller had carefully examined a Sarmatian cuirass, which was preserved in the temple of Æsculapius at Athens.

[39]   Aspicis et mitti sub adunco toxica ferro,
         Et telum causas mortis habere duas.
                                   Ovid, ex Ponto, l. iv. ep. 7, ver. 7.

See in the Recherches sur les Americains, tom. ii. p. 236—271, a very curious dissertation on poisoned darts. The venom was commonly extracted from the vegetable reign : but that employed by the Scythians appears to have been drawn from the viper, and a mixture of human blood. The use of poisoned arms, which has been spread over both worlds, never preserved a savage tribe from the arms of a disciplined enemy.

fame and luxury, was condemned to a hopeless exile on the frozen banks of the Danube, where he was exposed, almost without defence, to the fury of these monsters of the desert, with whose stern spirits he feared that his gentle shade might hereafter be confounded. In his pathetic, but sometimes unmanly lamentations,[40] he describes in the most lively colors the dress and manners, the arms and inroads, of the Getæ and Sarmatians, who were associated for the purposes of destruction; and from the accounts of history there is some reason to believe that these Sarmatians were the Jazygæ, one of the most numerous and warlike tribes of the nation. The allurements of plenty engaged them to seek a permanent establishment on the frontiers of the empire. Soon after the reign of Augustus, they obliged the Dacians, who subsisted by fishing on the banks of the River Teyss or Tibiscus, to retire into the hilly country, and to abandon to the victorious Sarmatians the fertile plains of the Upper Hungary, which are bounded by the course of the Danube and the semicircular enclosure of the Carpathian Mountains.[41] In this advantageous position, they watched or suspended the moment of attack, as they were provoked by injuries or appeased by presents, they gradually acquired the skill of using more dangerous weapons; and although the Sarmatians did not illustrate their name by any memorable exploits, they occasionally assisted their eastern and western neighbors, the Goths and the Germans, with a formidable body of cavalry. They lived under the irregular aristocracy of their chieftains;[42] but after they had received

---

[40] The nine books of Poetical Epistles which Ovid composed during the seven first years of his melancholy exile, possess, besides the merit of elegance, a double value. They exhibit a picture of the human mind under very singular circumstances; and they contain many curious observations, which no Roman, except Ovid, could have an opportunity of making. Every circumstance which tends to illustrate the history of the Barbarians, has been drawn together by the very accurate Count de Buat. Hist. Ancienne des Peuples de l'Europe, tom. iv. c. xvi. p. 286—317.

[41] The Sarmatians Jazygæ were settled on the banks of Pathissus or Tibiscus, when Pliny, in the year 79, published his Natural History. See l. iv. c. 25. In the time of Strabo and Ovid, sixty or seventy years before, they appear to have inhabited beyond the Getæ, along the coast of the Euxine.

[42] Principes Sarmaturum Jazygum penes quos civitatis regimen plebem quoque et vim equitum, quâ solâ valent, offerebant. Tacit Hist. iii. 5. This offer was made in the civil war between Vitellius and Vespasian.

into their bosom the fugitive Vandals, who yielded to the pressure of the Gothic power, they seem to have chosen a king from that nation, and from the illustrious race of the Astingi, who had formerly dwelt on the shores of the northern ocean.[43]

This motive of enmity must have inflamed the subjects of contention, which perpetually arise on the confines of warlike and independent nations. The Vandal princes were stimulated by fear and revenge; the Gothic kings aspired to extend their dominion from the Euxine to the frontiers of Germany; and the waters of the Maros, a small river which falls into the Teyss, were stained with the blood of the contending Barbarians. After some experience of the superior strength and numbers of their adversaries, the Sarmatians implored the protection of the Roman monarch, who beheld with pleasure the discord of the nations, but who was justly alarmed by the progress of the Gothic arms. As soon as Constantine had declared himself in favor of the weaker party, the haughty Araric, king of the Goths, instead of expecting the attack of the legions, boldly passed the Danube, and spread terror and devastation through the province of Mæsia. To oppose the inroad of this destroying host, the aged emperor took the field in person; but on this occasion either his conduct or his fortune betrayed the glory which he had acquired in so many foreign and domestic wars. He had the mortification of seeing his troops fly before an inconsiderable detachment of the Barbarians, who pursued them to the edge of their fortified camp, and obliged him to consult his safety by a precipitate

---

[43] This hypothesis of a Vandal king reigning over Sarmatian subjects, seems necessary to reconcile the Goth Jornandes with the Greek and Latin historians of Constantine. It may be observed that Isidore, who lived in Spain under the dominion of the Goths, gives them for enemies, not the Vandals, but the Sarmatians. See his Chronicle in Grotius, p. 709.*

---

* I have already noticed the confusion which must necessarily arise in history, when names purely *geographical*, as this of Sarmatia, are taken for *historical* names belonging to a single nation. We perceive it here; it has forced Gibbon to suppose, without any reason but the necessity of extricating himself from his perplexity, that the Sarmatians had taken a king from among the Vandals; a supposition entirely contrary to the usages of Barbarians. Dacia, at this period, was occupied, not by Sarmatians, who have never formed a distinct race, but by Vandals, whom the ancients have often confounded under the general term Sarmatians. See Gatterer's Welt-Geschichte, p. 464. — G.

and ignominious retreat.* The event of a second and more successful action retrieved the honor of the Roman name and the powers of art and discipline prevailed, after an obstinate contest, over the efforts of irregular valor. The broken army of the Goths abandoned the field of battle, the wasted province, and the passage of the Danube : and although the eldest of the sons of Constantine was permitted to supply the place of his father, the merit of the victory, which diffused universal joy, was ascribed to the auspicious counsels of the emperor himself.

He contributed at least to improve this advantage, by his negotiations with the free and warlike people of Chersonesus,[44] whose capital, situate on the western coast of the Tauric or Crimæan peninsula, still retained some vestiges of a Grecian colony, and was governed by a perpetual magistrate, assisted by a council of senators, emphatically styled the Fathers of the City. The Chersonites were animated against the Goths, by the memory of the wars, which, in the preceding century they had maintained with unequal forces against the invaders of their country. They were connected with the Romans by the mutual benefits of commerce ; as they were supplied from

---

[44] I may stand in need of some apology for having used, without scruple, the authority of Constantine Porphyrogenitus, in all that relates to the wars and negotiations of the Chersonites. I am aware that he was a Greek of the tenth century, and that his accounts of ancient history are frequently confused and fabulous. But on this occasion his narrative is, for the most part, consistent and probable ; nor is there much difficulty in conceiving that an emperor might have access to some secret archives, which had escaped the diligence of meaner historians. For the situation and history of Chersone, see Peyssonel, des Peuples barbares qui ont habité les Bords du Danube, c. xvi. 84—90.†

---

* Gibbon states, that Constantine was defeated by the Goths in a first battle. No ancient author mentions such an event. It is, no doubt, a mistake in Gibbon. St. Martin, note to Le Beau, i. 324. — M.

† Gibbon has confounded the inhabitants of the city of Cherson, the ancient Chersonesus, with the people of the Chersonesus Taurica. If he had read with more attention the chapter of Constantinus Porphyrogenitus, from which this narrative is derived, he would have seen that the author clearly distinguishes the republic of Cherson from the rest of the Tauric Peninsula, then possessed by the kings of the Cimmerian Bosphorus, and that the city of Cherson alone furnished succors to the Romans. The English historian is also mistaken in saying that the Steph anephoros of the Chersonites was a perpetual magistrate ; since it is easy to discover from the great number of Stephanephoroi mentioned by Constantine Porphyrogenitus, that they were annual magistrates, like almost all those which governed the Grecian republics. St. Martin, note to Le Beau, i. 326. — M.

the provinces of Asia with corn and manufa.ures, which they purchased with their only productions, salt, wax, and hides. Obedient to the requisition of Constantine, they prepared, under the conduct of their magistrate Diogenes, a considerable army, of which the principal strength consisted in cross-bows and military chariots. The speedy march and intrepid attack of the Chersonites, by diverting the attention of the Goths, assisted the operations of the Imperial generals. The Goths, vanquished on every side, were driven into the mountains, where, in the course of a severe campaign, above a hundred thousand were computed to have perished by cold and hunger. Peace was at length granted to their humble supplications; the eldest son of Araric was accepted as the most valuable hostage; and Constantine endeavored to convince their chiefs, by a liberal distribution of honors and rewards, how far the friendship of the Romans was preferable to their enmity. In the expressions of his gratitude towards the faithful Chersonites, the emperor was still more magnificent. The pride of the nation was gratified by the splendid and almost royal decorations bestowed on their magistrate and his successors. A perpetual exemption from all duties was stipulated for their vessels which traded to the ports of the Black Sea. A regular subsidy was promised, of iron, corn, oil, and of every supply which could be useful either in peace or war. But it was thought that the Sarmatians were sufficiently rewarded by their deliverance from impending ruin; and the emperor, perhaps with too strict an economy, deducted some part of the expenses of the war from the customary gratifications which were allowed to that turbulent nation.

Exasperated by this apparent neglect, the Sarmatians soon forgot, with the levi'y of barbarians, the services which they had so lately received, and the dangers which still threatened their safety. Their inroads on the territory of the empire provoked the indignation of Constantine to leave them to their fate; and he no longer opposed the ambition of Geberic, a renowned warrior, who had recently ascended the Gothic throne. Wisumar, the Vandal king, whilst alone, and unassisted, he defended his dominions with undaunted courage, was vanquished and slain in a decisive battle, which swept away the flower of the Sarmatian youth.* The remainder of

* Gibbon supposes that this war took place because Constantine had deducted a part of the customary gratifications, granted by his predecessors to the Sarmatians. Nothing of this kind appears in the authors. We see on the contrary, that after his victory, and to punish the Sarmatians

the nation embraced the desperate expedient of arming their
slaves, a hardy race of hunters and herdsmen, by whose
tumultuary aid they revenged their defeat, and expelled the
invader from their confines.   But they soon discovered that
they had exchanged a foreign for a domestic enemy, more
dangerous and more implacable.   Enraged by their former
servitude, elated by their present glory, the slaves, under the
name of Limigantes, claimed and usurped the possession of
the country which they had saved.   Their masters, unable to
withstand the ungoverned fury of the populace, preferred the
hardships of exile to the tyranny of their servants.   Some of
the fugitive Sarmatians solicited a less ignominious dependence, under the hostile standard of the Goths.   A more
numerous band retired beyond the Carpathian Mountains,
among the Quadi, their German allies, and were easily admitted to share a superfluous waste of uncultivated land.
But the far greater part of the distressed nation turned their
eyes towards the fruitful provinces of Rome.   Imploring the
protection and forgiveness of the emperor, they solemnly
promised, as subjects in peace, and as soldiers in war, the
most inviolable fidelity to the empire which should graciously
receive them into its bosom.   According to the maxims
adopted by Probus and his successors, the offers of this barbarian colony were eagerly accepted ; and a competent portion of lands in the provinces of Pannonia, Thrace, Macedonia,
and Italy, were immediately assigned for the habitation and
subsistence of three hundred thousand Sarmatians.[45]

By chastising the pride of the Goths, and by accepting the
homage of a suppliant nation, Constantine asserted the majesty

---

[45] The Gothic and Sarmatian wars are related in so broken and imperfect a manner, that I have been obliged to compare the following
writers, who mutually supply, correct, and illustrate each other.
Those who will take the same trouble, may acquire a right of criticiz-
ing my narrative.   Ammianus, l. xvii. c. 12.   Anonym. Valesian. p.
715.   Eutropius, x. 7.   Sextus Rufus de Provinciis, c. 26.   Julian
Orat. i. p. 9, and Spanheim, Comment. p. 94.   Hieronym. in Chron.
Euseb. in Vit. Constantin l. iv. c. 6.   Socrates, l. i. c. 18.   Sozomen,
l. i. c. 8.   Zosimus, l. ii. p. 108.   Jornandes de Reb. Geticis, c. 22.
Isidorus in Chron. p. 709 ; in Hist. Gothorum Grotii.   Constantin.
Porphyrogenitus de Administrat. Imperii, c. 53, p. 208, edit. Meursii.*

---

for the ravages they had committed, he withheld the sums which it had
been the custom to bestow.   St. Martin, note to Le Beau, i. 327. — M.
    * Compare, on this very obscure but remarkable war, Manso, Leben Con-
stantins p 195. — M.

of the Roman empire; and the ambassadors of Æthiopia, Persia, and the most remote countries of India, congratulated the peace and prosperity of his government.[46] If he reckoned, among the favors of fortune, the death of his eldest son, of his nephew, and perhaps of his wife, he enjoyed an uninterrupted flow of private as well as public felicity, till the thirtieth year of his reign; a period which none of his predecessors, since Augustus, had been permitted to celebrate. Constantine survived that solemn festival about ten months; and at the mature age of sixty-four, after a short illness, he ended his memorable life at the palace of Aquyrion, in the suburbs of Nicomedia, whither he had retired for the benefit of the air, and with the hope of recruiting his exhausted strength by the use of the warm baths. The excessive demonstrations of grief, or at least of mourning, surpassed whatever had been practised on any former occasion. Notwithstanding the claims of the senate and people of ancient Rome, the corpse of the deceased emperor, according to his last request, was transported to the city, which was destined to preserve the name and memory of its founder. The body of Constantine, adorned with the vain symbols of greatness, the purple and diadem, was deposited on a golden bed in one of the apartments of the palace, which for that purpose had been splendidly furnished and illuminated. The forms of the court were strictly maintained. Every day, at the appointed hours, the principal officers of the state, the army, and the household, approaching the person of their sovereign with bended knees and a composed countenance, offered their respectful homage as seriously as if he had been still alive. From motives of policy, this theatrical representation was for some time continued; nor could flattery neglect the opportunity of remarking that Constantine alone, by the peculiar indulgence of Heaven, had reigned after his death.[47]

But this reign could subsist only in empty pageantry; and

---

[46] Eusebius (in Vit. Const. l. iv. c. 50) remarks three circumstances relative to these Indians. 1. They came from the shores of the eastern ocean; a description which might be applied to the coast of China or Coromandel. 2. They presented shining gems, and unknown animals. 3. They protested their kings had erected statues to represent the supreme majesty of Constantine.

[47] Funus relatum in urbem sui nominis, quod sane P. R. ægerrime tulit. Aurelius Victor. Constantine prepared for himself a stately tomb in the church of the Holy Apostles. Euseb. l. iv. c. 60. The best, and indeed almost the only account of the sickness, death, and

it was soon discovered that the will of the most absolute monarch is seldom obeyed, when his subjects have no longer anything to hope from his favor, or to dread from his resentment. The same ministers and generals, who bowed with such reverential awe before the inanimate corpse of their deceased sovereign, were engaged in secret consultations to exclude his two nephews, Dalmatius and Hannibalianus, from the share which he had assigned them in the succession of the empire. We are too imperfectly acquainted with the court of Constantine to form any judgment of the real motives which influenced the leaders of the conspiracy; unless we should suppose that they were actuated by a spirit of jealousy and revenge against the præfect Ablavius, a proud favorite, who had long directed the counsels and abused the confidence of the late emperor. The arguments, by which they solicited the concurrence of the soldiers and people, are of a more obvious nature; and they might with decency, as well as truth, insist on the superior rank of the children of Constantine, the danger of multiplying the number of sovereigns, and the impending mischiefs which threatened the republic, from the discord of so many rival princes, who were not connected by the tender sympathy of fraternal affection. The intrigue was conducted with zeal and secrecy, till a loud and unanimous declaration was procured from the troops, that they would suffer none except the sons of their lamented monarch to reign over the Roman empire.[48] The younger Dalmatius, who was united with his collateral relations by the ties of friendship and interest, is allowed to have inherited a considerable share of the abilities of the great Constantine: but, on this occasion he does not appear to have concerted any measure for supporting, by arms, the just claims which himself and his royal brother derived from the liberality of their uncle. Astonished and overwhelmed by the tide of popular fury, they seem to have remained, without the power of flight or of resistance, in the hands of their implacable enemies. Their fate was suspended till the arrival of Constantius, the second,[49] and perhaps the most favored, of the sons of Constantine.

---

funeral of Constantine, is contained in the fourth book of his Life, by Eusebius.

[48] Eusebius (l. iv. c. 6) terminates his narrative by this loyal declaration of the troops, and avoids all the invidious circumstances of the subsequent massacre.

[49] The character of Dalmatius is advantageously, though concisely,

The voice of the dying emperor had recommended the care of his funeral to the piety of Constantius ; and that prince, by the vicinity of his eastern station, could easily prevent the diligence of his brothers, who resided in their distant government of Italy and Gaul. As soon as he had taken possession of the palace of Constantinople, his first care was to remove the apprehensions of his kinsmen, by a solemn oath which he pledged for their security. His next employment was to find some specious pretence which might release his conscience from the obligation of an imprudent promise. The arts of fraud were made subservient to the designs of cruelty ; and a manifest forgery was attested by a person of the most sacred character. From the hands of the Bishop of Nicomedia, Constantius received a fatal scroll, affirmed to be the genuine testament of his father ; in which the emperor expressed his suspicions that he had been poisoned by his brothers ; and conjured his sons to revenge his death, and to consult their own safety, by the punishment of the guilty.[50] Whatever reasons might have been alleged by these unfortunate princes to defend their life and honor against so incredible an accusation, they were silenced by the furious clamors of the soldiers, who declared themselves, at once, their enemies, their judges, and their executioners. The spirit, and even the forms of legal proceedings were repeatedly violated in a promiscuous massacre ; which involved the two uncles of Constantius, seven of his cousins, of whom Dalmatius and Hannibalianus were the most illustrious, the Patrician Optatus, who had married a sister of the late emperor, and the Præfect Ablavius, whose power and riches had inspired him with some hopes of obtain-

---

drawn by Eutropius. (x. 9.) Dalmatius Cæsar prosperrimâ indole, neque patruo absimilis, *haud multo* post oppressus est factione militari. As both Jerom and the Alexandrian Chronicle mention the third year of the Cæsar, which did not commence till the 18th or 24th of September, A. D. 337, it is certain that these military factions continued above four months.

[50] I have related this singular anecdote on the authority of Philostorgius, l. ii. c. 16. But if such a pretext was ever used by Constantius and his adherents, it was laid aside with contempt, as soon as it served their immediate purpose. Athanasius (tom. i. p. 856) mentions the oath which Constantius had taken for the security of his kinsmen.*

---

* The authority of Philostorgius is so suspicious, as not to be sufficient to establish this fact, which Gibbon has inserted in his history as certain while in the note he appears to doubt it. — G.

ing the purple If it were necessary to aggravate the horrors
of this bloody scene we might add, that Constantius himself
had espoused the daughter of his uncle Julius, and that he had
bestowed his sister in marriage on his cousin Hannibalianus.
These alliances, which the policy of Constantine, regardless
of the public prejudice,[51] had formed between the several
branches of the Imperial house, served only to convince mankind, that these princes were as cold to the endearments of
conjugal affection, as they were insensible to the ties of con-
sanguinity, and the moving entreaties of youth and innocence.
Of so numerous a family, Gallus and Julian alone, the two
youngest children of Julius Constantius, were saved from the
hands of the assassins, till their rage, satiated with slaughter,
had in some measure subsided. The emperor Constantius,
who, in the absence of his brothers, was the most obnoxious
to guilt and reproach, discovered, on some future occasions, a
faint and transient remorse for those cruelties which the perfidious counsels of his ministers, and the irresistible violence
of the troops, had extorted from his unexperienced youth.[52]

The massacre of the Flavian race was succeeded by a new
division of the provinces; which was ratified in a personal
interview of the three brothers. Constantine, the eldest of
the Cæsars, obtained, with a certain preëminence of rank,

---

[51] Conjugia sobrinarum diu ignorata, tempore addito percrebuisse.
Tacit. Annal. xii. 6, and Lipsius ad loc. The repeal of the ancient
law, and the practice of five hundred years, were insufficient to eradicate the prejudices of the Romans, who still considered the marriages
of cousins-german as a species of imperfect incest, (Augustin de Civitate Dei, xv. 6;) and Julian, whose mind was biased by superstition
and resentment, stigmatizes these unnatural alliances between his own
cousins with the opprobrious epithet of γαμῶν τε οὐ γαμῶν, (Orat. vii.
p. 228.) The jurisprudence of the canons has since revived and
enforced this prohibition, without being able to introduce it either into
the civil or the common law of Europe. See on the subject of these
marriages, Taylor's Civil Law, p. 331. Brouer de Jure Connub. l. ii.
c. 12. Hericourt des Loix Ecclesiastiques part iii. c. 5. Fleury,
Institutions du Droit Canonique, tom. i. p. 331. Paris, 1767, and
Fra Paolo, Istoria del Concilio Trident. l. viii.

[52] Julian (ad S. P. Q. Athen. p. 270) charges his cousin Constantius with the whole guilt of a massacre, from which he himself so
narrowly escaped. His assertion is confirmed by Athanasius, who,
for reasons of a very different nature, was not less an enemy of Constantius, (tom. i. p. 856.) Zosimus joins in the same accusation. But
the three abbreviators, Eutropius and the Victors, use very qualifying
expressions : " sinente potius quam jubente ; " " incertum quo sua-
sore ; " " vi militum."

the possession of the new capital, which bore his own name and that of his father. Thrace, and the countries of the East, were allotted for the patrimony of Constantius; and Constans was acknowledged as the lawful sovereign of Italy, Africa, and the Western Illyricum. The armies submitted to their hereditary right; and they condescended, after some delay, to accept from the Roman senate the title of *Augustus*. When they first assumed the reins of government, the eldest of these princes was twenty-one, the second twenty, and the third only seventeen, years of age.[53]

While the martial nations of Europe followed the standards of his brothers, Constantius, at the head of the effeminate troops of Asia, was left to sustain the weight of the Persian war. At the decease of Constantine, the throne of the East was filled by Sapor, son of Hormouz, or Hormisdas, and grandson of Narses, who, after the victory of Galerius, had humbly confessed the superiority of the Roman power. Although Sapor was in the thirtieth year of his long reign, he was still in the vigor of youth, as the date of his accession, by a very strange fatality, had preceded that of his birth. The wife of Hormouz remained pregnant at the time of her husband's death; and the uncertainty of the sex, as well as of the event, excited the ambitious hopes of the princes of the house of Sassan. The apprehensions of civil war were at length removed, by the positive assurance of the Magi, that the widow of Hormouz had conceived, and would safely produce a son. Obedient to the voice of superstition, the Persians prepared, without delay, the ceremony of his coronation. A royal bed, on which the queen lay in state, was exhibited in the midst of the palace; the diadem was placed on the spot, which might be supposed to conceal the future heir of Artaxerxes, and the prostrate satraps adored the majesty of their invisible and insensible sovereign.[54] If any credit can

---

[53] Euseb. in Vit. Constantin. l. iv. c. 69. Zosimus, l. ii. p. 117. Idat. in Chron. See two notes of Tillemont, Hist. des Empereurs, tom. iv. p. 1086—1091. The reign of the eldest brother at Constantinople is noticed only in the Alexandrian Chronicle.

[54] Agathias, who lived in the sixth century, is the author of this story, (l. iv. p. 135, edit. Louvre.) He derived his information from some extracts of the Persian Chronicles, obtained and translated by the interpreter Sergius, during his embassy at that court. The coronation of the mother of Sapor is likewise mentioned by Schikard, (Tarikh. p. 116,) and D'Herbelot (Bibliothèque Orientale, p. 763.) *

---

* The author of the Zenut-ul-Tarikh states, that the lady herself af

be given to this marvellous tale, which seems, however, to be countenanced by the manners of the people, and by the extraordinary duration of his reign, we must admire not only the fortune, but the genius, of Sapor. In the soft, sequestered education of a Persian harem, the royal youth could discover the importance of exercising the vigor of his mind and body; and, by his personal merit, deserved a throne, on which he had been seated, while he was yet unconscious of the duties and temptations of absolute power. His minority was exposed to the almost inevitable calamities of domestic discord; his capital was surprised and plundered by Thair, a powerful king of Yemen, or Arabia; and the majesty of the royal family was degraded by the captivity of a princess, the sister of the deceased king. But as soon as Sapor attained the age of manhood, the presumptuous Thair, his nation, and his country, fell beneath the first effort of the young warrior; who used his victory with so judicious a mixture of rigor and clemency, that he obtained from the fears and gratitude of the Arabs the title of *Dhoulacnaf*, or protector of the nation.[55]

The ambition of the Persian, to whom his enemies ascribe the virtues of a soldier and a statesman, was animated by the desire of revenging the disgrace of his fathers, and of wresting from the hands of the Romans the five provinces beyond the Tigris. The military fame of Constantine, and the real or apparent strength of his government, suspended the attack; and while the hostile conduct of Sapor provoked the resentment, his artful negotiations amused the patience of the Imperial court. The death of Constantine was the signal of war,[56] and the actual condition of the Syrian and Armenian

---

[55] D'Herbelot, Bibliothèque Orientale, p. 764.*

[56] Sextus Rufus, (c. 26,) who on this occasion is no contemptible authority, affirms, that the Persians sued in vain for peace, and that Constantine was preparing to march against them: yet the superior

---

firmed her belief of this from the extraordinary liveliness of the infant, and its lying on the right side. Those who are sage on such subjects must determine what right she had to be positive from these symptoms. Malcolm, Hist. of Persia, i. 83. — M.

* Gibbon, according to Sir J. Malcolm, has greatly mistaken the derivation of this name; it means Zoolaktaf, the Lord of the Shoulders, from his directing the shoulders of his captives to be pierced and then dislocated by a string passed through them. Eastern authors are agreed with respect to the origin of this title. Malcolm, i. 84. Gibbon took his derivation from D'Herbelot, who gives both, the latter on the authority of the Leb Tarikh. — M.

frontier seemed to encourage the Persians by the prospect of a rich spoil and an easy conquest. The example of the mas-sacres of the palace diffused a spirit of licentiousness and sedition among the troops of the East, who were no longer restrained by their habits of obedience to a veteran command-er. By the prudence of Constantius, who, from the interview with his brothers in Pannonia, immediately hastened to the banks of the Euphrates, the legions were gradually restored to a sense of duty and discipline; but the season of anarchy had permitted Sapor to form the siege of Nisibis, and to occupy several of the most important fortresses of Mesopo-tamia.[57] In Armenia, the renowned Tiridates had long enjoyed the peace and glory which he deserved by his valor and fidelity to the cause of Rome.† The firm alliance which he maintained with Constantine was productive of spiritual as well as of temporal benefits; by the conversion of Tiridates, the charac-ter of a saint was applied to that of a hero, the Christian faith was preached and established from the Euphrates to the shores of the Caspian, and Armenia was attached to the empire by the double ties of policy and religion. But as many of the Armenian nobles still refused to abandon the plurality of their gods and of their wives, the public tranquillity was disturbed by a discontented faction, which insulted the feeble age of their sovereign, and impatiently expected the hour of his death. He died at length after a reign of fifty-six years, and the fortune of the Armenian monarchy expired with Tiridates. His lawful heir was driven into exile, the Christian priests were either murdered or expelled from their churches, the barbarous tribes of Albania were solicited to descend from their mountains; and two of the most powerful governors,

---

weight of the testimony of Eusebius obliges us to admit the prelim-inaries, if not the ratification, of the treaty. See Tillemont, Hist. des Empereurs, tom. iv. p. 420.*

[57] Julian. Orat. i. p. 20.

---

* Constantine had endeavored to allay the fury of the persecutions, which, at the instigation of the Magi and the Jews, Sapor had commenced against the Christians. Euseb. Vit. Hist. Theod. i. 25. Sozom. ii. c. 8, 15. — M.

† Tiridates had sustained a war against Maximin, caused by the hatred of the latter against Christianity. Armenia was the first *nation* which embraced Christianity. About the year 276 it was the religion of the king, the nobles, and the people of Armenia. From St. Martin, Supplement to Le Beau, v. i. p. 78. Compare Preface to History of Vartan, by Professor Neumann, p. ix. — M.

usurping the ensigns or the powers of royalty, implored the
assistance of Sapor, and opened the gates of their cities to the
Persian garrisons. The Christian party, under the guidance
of the Archbishop of Artaxata, the immediate successor of
St. Gregory the Illuminator, had recourse to the piety of Constantius. After the troubles had continued about three years,
Antiochus, one of the officers of the household, executed with
success the Imperial commission of restoring Chosroes,* the
son of Tiridates, to the throne of his fathers, of distributing
honors and rewards among the faithful servants of the house
of Arsaces, and of proclaiming a general amnesty, which was
accepted by the greater part of the rebellious satraps. But
the Romans derived more honor than advantage from this
revolution. Chosroes was a prince of a puny stature and a
pusillanimous spirit. Unequal to the fatigues of war, averse
to the society of mankind, he withdrew from his capital to a
retired palace, which he built on the banks of the River Eleu-
therus, and in the centre of a shady grove; where he consumed his vacant hours in the rural sports of hunting and
hawking. To secure this inglorious ease, he submitted to the
conditions of peace which Sapor condescended to impose; the
payment of an annual tribute, and the restitution of the fertile
province of Atropatene, which the courage of Tiridates, and

---

* Chosroes was restored probably by Licinius, between 314 and 319.
There was an Antiochus who was præfectus vigilum at Rome, as appears
from the Theodosian Code, (l. iii. de inf. his quæ sub ty.,) in 326, and from
a fragment of the same work published by M. Amédée Peyron, in 319. He
may before this have been sent into Armenia. St. M. p. 407. [Is it not
more probable that Antiochus was an officer in the service of the Cæsar
who ruled in the East? — M.] Chosroes was succeeded in the year 322
by his son Diran. Diran was a weak prince, and in the sixteenth year of
his reign, A. D. 337, was betrayed into the power of the Persians by the
treachery of his chamberlain and the Persian governor of Atropatene or
Aderbidjan. He was blinded: his wife and his son Arsaces shared his
captivity, but the princes and nobles of Armenia claimed the protection of
Rome; and this was the cause of Constantine's declaration of war against
the Persians.—The king of Persia attempted to make himself master of
Armenia; but the brave resistance of the people, the advance of Constantius, and a defeat which his army suffered at Oskha in Armenia, and the
failure before Nisibis, forced Shahpour to submit to terms of peace. Varaz-
Shahpour, the perfidious governor of Atropatene, was flayed alive; Diran
and his son were released from captivity; Diran refused to ascend the
throne, and retired to an obscure retreat: his son Arsaces was crowned
king of Armenia. Arsaces pursued a vacillating policy between the influence of Rome and Persia, and the war recommenced in the year
345. At least, that was the period of the expedition of Constantius to the
East. See St. Martin, additions to Le Beau, i. 442. The Persians have
made an extraordinary romance out of the history of Shahpour, who went
as a spy to Constantinople, was taken, harnessed like a horse, and carried to witness the devastation of his kingdom. Malcolm, i. 84. — M

the victorious arms of Galerius, had annexed to the Armenian monarchy.[58]

During the long period of the reign of Constantius, the provinces of the East were afflicted by the calamities of the Persian war.† The irregular incursions of the light troops alternately spread terror and devastation beyond the Tigris and beyond the Euphrates, from the gates of Ctesiphon to those of Antioch; and this active service was performed by the Arabs of the desert, who were divided in their interest and affections; some of their independent chiefs being enlisted in the party of Sapor, whilst others had engaged their doubtful

---

[58] Julian. Orat. i. p. 20, 21. Moses of Chorene, l. ii. c. 89, l. iii. c. 1—9, p. 226—240. The perfect agreement between the vague hints of the contemporary orator, and the circumstantial narrative of the national historian, gives light to the former, and weight to the latter. For the credit of Moses, it may be likewise observed, that the name of Antiochus is found a few years before in a civil office of inferior dignity. See Godefroy, Cod. Theod. tom. vi. p. 350.*

---

* Gibbon has endeavored, in his History, to make use of the information furnished by Moses of Chorene, the only Armenian historian then translated into Latin. Gibbon has not perceived all the chronological difficulties which occur in the narrative of that writer. He has not thought of all the critical discussions which his text ought to undergo before it can be combined with the relations of the western writers. From want of this attention, Gibbon has made the facts which he has drawn from this source more erroneous then they are in the original. This judgment applies to all which the English historian has derived from the Armenian author. I have made the History of Moses a subject of particular attention; and it is with confidence that I offer the results, which I insert here, and which will appear in the course of my notes. In order to form a judgment of the difference which exists between me and Gibbon, I will content myself with remarking, that throughout he has committed an anachronism of thirty years, from whence it follows, that he assigns to the reign of Constantius many events which took place during that of Constantine. He could not, therefore, discern the true connection which exists between the Roman history and that of Armenia, or form a correct notion of the reasons which induced Constantine, at the close of his life, to make war upon the Persians, or of the motives which detained Constantius so long in the East; he does not even mention them. St. Martin, note on Le Beau, i. 406. I have inserted M. St. Martin's observations, but I must add, that the chronology which he proposes, is not generally received by Armenian scholars, not, I believe, by Professor Neumann — M.

† It was during this war that a bold flatterer (whose name is unknown) published the Itineraries of Alexander and Trajan, in order to direct the victorious Constantius in the footsteps of those great conquerors of the East. The former of these has been published for the first time by M Angelo Mai, (Milan, 1817, reprinted at Frankfort, 1818.) It adds so little to our knowledge of Alexander's campaigns, that it only excites our regret that it is not the Itinerary of Trajan, of whose eastern victories we have no distinct record. — M.

fidelity to the emperor.[59] The more grave and important operations of the war were conducted with equal vigor; and the armies of Rome and Persia encountered each other in nine bloody fields, in two of which Constantius himself commanded in person.[60] The event of the day was most commonly adverse to the Romans, but in the battle of Singara, their imprudent valor had almost achieved a signal and decisive victory. The stationary troops of Singara * retired on the approach of Sapor, who passed the Tigris over three bridges, and occupied near the village of Hilleh an advantageous camp, which, by the labor of his numerous pioneers, he surrounded in one day with a deep ditch and a lofty rampart. His formidable host, when it was drawn out in order of battle, covered the banks of the river, the adjacent heights, and the whole extent of a plain of above twelve miles, which separated the two armies. Both were alike impatient to engage; but the Barbarians, after a slight resistance, fled in disorder; unable to resist, or desirous to weary, the strength of the heavy legions, who, fainting with heat and thirst, pursued them across the plain, and cut in pieces a line of cavalry, clothed in complete armor, which had been posted before the gates of the camp to protect their retreat. Constantius, who was hurried along in the pursuit, attempted, without effect, to restrain the ardor of his troops, by representing to them the dangers of the approaching night, and the certainty of completing their success with the return of day. As they depended much

---

[59] Ammianus (xiv. 4) gives a lively description of the wandering and predatory life of the Saracens, who stretched from the confines of Assyria to the cataracts of the Nile. It appears from the adventures of Malchus, which Jerom has related in so entertaining a manner, that the high road between Berœa and Edessa was infested by these robbers. See Hieronym. tom. i. p. 256.

[60] We shall take from Eutropius the general idea of the war, (x. 10.) A Persis enim multa et gravia perpessus, sæpe captis, oppidis, obsessis urbibus, cæsis exercitibus, nullumque ei contra Saporem prosperum prælium fuit, nisi quod apud Singaram, &c. This honest account is confirmed by the hints of Ammianus, Rufus, and Jerom. The two first orations of Julian, and the third oration of Libanius, exhibit a more flattering picture; but the recantation of both those orators, after the death of Constantius, while it restores us to the possession of the truth, degrades their own character, and that of the emperor. The Commentary of Spanheim on the first oration of Julian is profusely learned. See likewise the judicious observations of Tillemont, Hist. des Empereurs, tom. iv. p. 656.

* Now Sinjar, on the River Chaboras.—M

more on their own valor than on the experience or the abilities of their chief, they silenced by their clamors his timid remonstrances, and rushing with fury to the charge, filled up the ditch, broke down the rampart, and dispersed themselves through the tents to recruit their exhausted strength, and to enjoy the rich harvest of their labors. But the prudent Sapor had watched the moment of victory. His army, of which the greater part, securely posted on the heights, had been spectators of the action, advanced in silence, and under the shadow of the night; and his Persian archers, guided by the illumination of the camp, poured a shower of arrows on a disarmed and licentious crowd. The sincerity of history [61] declares, that the Romans were vanquished with a dreadful slaughter, and that the flying remnant of the legions was exposed to the most intolerable hardships. Even the tenderness of panegyric, confessing that the glory of the emperor was sullied by the disobedience of his soldiers, chooses to draw a veil over the circumstances of this melancholy retreat. Yet one of those venal orators, so jealous of the fame of Constantius, relates, with amazing coolness, an act of such incredible cruelty, as, in the judgment of posterity, must imprint a far deeper stain on the honor of the Imperial name. The son of Sapor, the heir of his crown, had been made a captive in the Persian camp. The unhappy youth, who might have excited the compassion of the most savage enemy, was scourged, tortured, and publicly executed by the inhuman Romans. [62]

Whatever advantages might attend the arms of Sapor in the field, though nine repeated victories diffused among the nations the fame of his valor and conduct, he could not hope to succeed in the execution of his designs, while the fortified towns of Mesopotamia, and, above all, the strong and ancient city of Nisibis, remained in the possession of the Romans. In the space of twelve years, Nisibis, which, since the time of Lu-

---

[6] Acerrimâ nocturnâ concertatione pugnatum est, nostrorum copiis ingenti strage confossis. Ammian. xviii. 5. See likewise Eutropius, x. 10, and S. Rufus, c. 27.*

[62] Libanius, Orat. iii. p. 133, with Julian. Orat. i. p. 24, and Spanheim's Commentary, p. 179.

---

* The Persian historians, or romancers, do not mention the battle of Singara, but make the captive Shahpour escape, defeat, and take prisoner the Roman emperor. The Roman captives were forced to repair all the ravages they had committed, even o replanting the smallest trees Malcolm, i. 85. — M.

cullus, had been deservedly esteemed the bulwark of the East sustained three memorable sieges against the power of Sapor; and the disappointed monarch, after urging his attacks above sixty, eighty, and a hundred days, was thrice repulsed with loss and ignominy.[63] This large and populous city was situate about two days' journey from the Tigris, in the midst of a pleasant and fertile plain at the foot of Mount Masius. A treble enclosure of brick walls was defended by a deep ditch;[64] and the intrepid resistance of Count Lucilianus, and his garrison, was seconded by the desperate courage of the people. The citizens of Nisibis were animated by the exhortations of their bishop,[65] inured to arms by the presence of danger, and convinced of the intentions of Sapor to plant a Persian colony in their room, and to lead them away into distant and barbarous captivity. The event of the two former sieges elated their confidence, and exasperated the haughty spirit of the Great King, who advanced a third time towards Nisibis, at the head of the united forces of Persia and India. The ordinary machines, invented to batter or undermine the walls, were rendered ineffectual by the superior skill of the Romans; and many days had vainly elapsed, when Sapor embraced a resolution worthy of an eastern monarch, who believed that the elements themselves were subject to his power. At the stated season of the melting of the snows in Armenia, the River Mygdonius, which divides the plain and the city of Nisibis, forms, like the Nile,[66] an inundation over the adjacent country.

[63] See Julian. Orat. i. p. 27, Orat. ii. p. 62, &c., with the Commentary of Spanheim, (p. 188—202,) who illustrates the circumstances, and ascertains the time of the three sieges of Nisibis. Their dates are likewise examined by Tillemont, (Hist. des Empereurs, tom. iv. p. 668, 671, 674.) Something is added from Zosimus, l. iii. p. 151, and the Alexandrine Chronicle, p. 290.

[64] Sallust. Fragment. lxxxiv. edit. Brosses, and Plutarch in Lucull. tom. iii. p. 184. Nisibis is now reduced to one hundred and fifty houses: the marshy lands produce rice, and the fertile meadows, as far as Mosul and the Tigris, are covered with the ruins of towns and villages. See Niebuhr, Voyages, tom. ii. p. 300—309.

[65] The miracles which Theodoret (l. ii. c. 30) ascribes to St. James, Bishop of Edessa, were at least performed in a worthy cause, the defence of his country. He appeared on the walls under the figure of the Roman emperor, and sent an army of gnats to sting the trunks of the elephants, and to discomfit the host of the new Sennacherib.

[66] Julian. Orat. i. p. 27. Though Niebuhr (tom. ii. p. 307) allows a very considerable swell to the Mygdonius, over which he saw a bridge of *twelve* arches: it is difficult, however, to understand thus

By the labor of the Persians, the course of the river was stopped below the town, and the waters were confined on every side by solid mounds of earth. On this artificial lake, a fleet of armed vessels filled with soldiers, and with engines which discharged stones of five hundred pounds weight, advanced in order of battle, and engaged, almost upon a level, the troops which defended the ramparts.* The irresistible force of the waters was alternately fatal to the contending parties, till at length a portion of the walls, unable to sustain the accumulated pressure, gave way at once, and exposed an ample breach of one hundred and fifty feet. The Persians were instantly driven to the assault, and the fate of Nisibis depended on the event of the day. The heavy-armed cavalry, who led the van of a deep column, were embarrassed in the mud, and great numbers were drowned in the unseen holes which had been filled by the rushing waters. The elephants, made furious by their wounds, increased the disorder, and trampled down thousands of the Persian archers. The Great King, who, from an exalted throne, beheld the misfortunes of his arms, sounded, with reluctant indignation, the signal of the retreat, and suspended for some hours the prosecution of the attack. But the vigilant citizens improved the opportunity of the night; and the return of day discovered a new wall of six feet in height, rising every moment to fill up the interval of the breach. Notwithstanding the disappointment of his hopes, and the loss of more than twenty thousand men, Sapor still pressed the reduction of Nisibis, with an obstinate firmness, which could have yielded only to the necessity of defending the eastern provinces of Persia against a formidable invasion of the Massagetæ.[67] Alarmed by this intelligence, he hastily

parallel of a trifling rivulet with a mighty river. There are many circumstances obscure, and almost unintelligible, in the description of these stupendous water-works.

[67] We are obliged to Zonaras (tom. ii. l. xiii. p. 11,) for this invasion of the Massagetæ, which is perfectly consistent with the general series of events, to which we are darkly led by the broken history of Ammianus.

* Macdonald Kinnier observes on these floating batteries, "As the elevation of place is considerably above the level of the country in its immediate vicinity, and the Mygdonius is a very insignificant stream, it is difficult to imagine how this work could have been accomplished, even with the wonderful resources which the king must have had at his disposal." Geographical Memoir, p. 262. —M.

relinquished the siege, and marched with rapid diligence from the banks of the Tigris to those of the Oxus. The danger and difficulties of the Scythian war engaged him soon after-vards to conclude, or at least to observe, a truce with the Roman emperor, which was equally grateful to both princes; as Constantius himself, after the death of his two brothers, was involved, by the revolutions of the West, in a civil contest, which required and seemed to exceed the most vigorous exertion of his undivided strength.

After the partition of the empire, three years had scarcely elapsed before the sons of Constantine seemed impatient to convince mankind that they were incapable of contenting themselves with the dominions which they were unqualified to govern. The eldest of those princes soon complained, that he was defrauded of his just proportion of the spoils of their murdered kinsmen; and though he might yield to the superior guilt and merit of Constantius, he exacted from Constans the cession of the African provinces, as an equivalent for the rich countries of Macedonia and Greece, which his brother had acquired by the death of Dalmatius. The want of sincerity, which Constantine experienced in a tedious and fruitless negotiation, exasperated the fierceness of his temper; and he eagerly listened to those favorites, who suggested to him that his honor, as well as his interest, was concerned in the prosecution of the quarrel. At the head of a tumultuary band, suited for rapine rather than for conquest, he suddenly broke into the dominions of Constans, by the way of the Julian Alps, and the country round Aquileia felt the first effects of his resentment. The measures of Constans, who then resided in Dacia, were directed with more prudence and ability. On the news of his brother's invasion, he detached a select and disciplined body of his Illyrian troops, proposing to follow them in person, with the remainder of his forces. But the conduct of his lieutenants soon terminated the unnatural contest. By the artful appearances of flight, Constantine was betrayed into an ambuscade, which had been concealed in a wood, where the rash youth, with a few attendants, was surprised, surrounded, and slain. His body, after it had been found in the obscure stream of the Alsa, obtained the honors of an Imperial sepulchre; but his provinces transferred their allegiance to the conqueror, who, refusing to admit his elder brother Constantius to any share in these new acquisitions, maintained the undisputed possession of more than two thirds of the Roman empire.[68]

The fate of Constans himself was delayed about ten years longer, and the revenge of his brother's death was reserved for the more ignoble hand of a domestic traitor. The pernicious tendency of the system introduced by Constantine was displayed in the feeble administration of his sons; who, by their vices and weakness, soon lost the esteem and affections of their people. The pride assumed by Constans, from the unmerited success of his arms, was rendered more contemptible by his want of abilities and application. His fond partiality towards some German captives, distinguished only by the charms of youth, was an object of scandal to the people;[69] and Magnentius, an ambitious soldier, who was himself of Barbarian extraction, was encouraged by the public discontent to assert the honor of the Roman name.[70] The chosen bands of Jovians and Herculians, who acknowledged Magnentius as their leader, maintained the most respectable and important station in the Imperial camp. The friendship of Marcellinus, count of the sacred largesses, supplied with a liberal hand the means of seduction. The soldiers were convinced by the most specious arguments, that the republic summoned them to break the bonds of hereditary servitude; and, by the choice of an active and vigilant prince, to reward the same virtues which had raised the ancestors of the degenerate Constans from a private condition to the throne of the world. As soon as the conspiracy was ripe for execution, Marcellinus, under

---

[68] The causes and the events of this civil war are related with much perplexity and contradiction. I have chiefly followed Zonaras and the younger Victor. The monody (ad Calcem Eutrop. edit. Havercamp.) pronounced on the death of Constantine, might have been very instructive; but prudence and false taste engaged the orator to involve himself in vague declamation.

[69] Quarum (*gentium*) obsides pretio quæsitos pueros venustiores quod cultius habuerat libidine hujusmodi arsisse *pro certo* habetur. Had not the depraved taste of Constans been publicly avowed, the elder Victor, who held a considerable office in his brother's reign, would not have asserted it in such positive terms.

[70] Julian. Orat i. and ii. Zosim. l. ii. p. 134. Victor in Epitome. There is reason to believe that Magnentius was born in one of those Barbarian colonies which Constantius Chlorus had established in Gaul, (see this History, vol. i. p. 414.) His behavior may remind us of the patriot earl of Leicester, the famous Simon de Montfort, who could persuade the good people of England, that he, a Frenchman by birth, had taken arms to deliver them from foreign favorites.

tne pretence of celebrating his son's birthday, gave a splen
did entertainment to the *illustrious* and *honorable* persons of
the court of Gaul, which then resided in the city of Autun.
The intemperance of the feast was artfully protracted till a
very late hour of the night; and the unsuspecting guests were
tempted to indulge themselves in a dangerous and guilty freedom of conversation. On a sudden the doors were thrown
open, and Magnentius, who had retired for a few moments,
returned into the apartment, invested with the diadem and
purple. The conspirators instantly saluted him with the titles
of Augustus and Emperor. The surprise, the terror, the
intoxication, the ambitious hopes, and the mutual ignorance of
the rest of the assembly, prompted them to join their voices to
the general acclamation. The guards hastened to take the
oath of fidelity; the gates of the town were shut; and before
the dawn of day, Magnentius became master of the troops
and treasure of the palace and city of Autun. By his secrecy
and diligence he entertained some hopes of surprising the
person of Constans, who was pursuing in the adjacent forest
his favorite amusement of hunting, or perhaps some pleasures
of a more private and criminal nature. The rapid progress
of fame allowed him, however, an instant for flight, though
the desertion of his soldiers and subjects deprived him of the
power of resistance. Before he could reach a seaport in
Spain, where he intended to embark, he was overtaken near
Helena,[71] at the foot of the Pyrenees, by a party of light
cavalry, whose chief, regardless of the sanctity of a temple,
executed his commission by the murder of the son of Constantine.[72]

As soon as the death of Constans had decided this easy but
important revolution, the example of the court of Autun was
imitated by the provinces of the West. The authority of
Magnentius was acknowledged through the whole extent of
the two great præfectures of Gaul and Italy; and the usurper

---

[71] This ancient city had once flourished under the name of Illiberis.
(Pomponius Mela, ii. 5.) The munificence of Constantine gave it
new splendor, and his mother's name. Helena (it is still called Elne)
became the seat of a bishop, who long afterwards transferred his residence to Perpignan, the capital of modern Rousillon. See D'Anville,
Notice de l'Ancienne Gaule, p. 380. Longuerue, Description de la
France, p. 223, and the Marca Hispanica, l. i. c. 2.

[72] Zosimus, l. ii. p. 119, 120. Zonaras, tom. ii. l. xiii. p. 13, and the
Abbreviators.

prepared, by every act of oppression, to collect a treasure, which might discharge the obligation of an immense donative, and supply the expenses of a civil war. The martial countries of Illyricum, from the Danube to the extremity of Greece, had long obeyed the government of Vetranio, an aged general, beloved for the simplicity of his manners, and who had acquired some reputation by his experience and services in war.[73] Attached by habit, by duty, and by gratitude, to the house of Constantine, he immediately gave the strongest assurances to the only surviving son of his late master, that he would expose, with unshaken fidelity, his person and his troops, to inflict a just revenge on the traitors of Gaul. But the legions of Vetranio were seduced, rather than provoked, by the example of rebellion; their leader soon betrayed a want of firmness, or a want of sincerity; and his ambition derived a specious pretence from the approbation of the princess Constantina. That cruel and aspiring woman, who had obtained from the great Constantine, her father, the rank of *Augusta*, placed the diadem with her own hands on the head of the Illyrian general; and seemed to expect from his victory the accomplishment of those unbounded hopes, of which she had been disappointed by the death of her husband Hannibalianus. Perhaps it was without the consent of Constantina, that the new emperor formed a necessary, though dishonorable, alliance with the usurper of the West, whose purple was so recently stained with her brother's blood.[74]

The intelligence of these important events, which so deeply affected the honor and safety of the Imperial house, recalled the arms of Constantius from the inglorious prosecution of the Persian war. He recommended the care of the East to his lieutenants, and afterwards to his cousin Gallus, whom he raised from a prison to a throne; and marched towards Europe, with a mind agitated by the conflict of hope and fear, of grief and indignation. On his arrival at Heraclea in Thrace, the emperor gave audience to the ambassadors of

---

[73] Eutropius (x. 10) describes Vetranio with more temper, and probably with more truth, than either of the two Victors. Vetranio was born of obscure parents in the wildest parts of Mœsia; and so much had his education been neglected, that, after his elevation, he studied the alphabet.

[74] The doubtful, fluctuating conduct of Vetranio is described by Julian in his first oration, and accurately explained by Spanheim, who discusses the situation and behavior of Constantina.

Magnentius and Vetranio. The first author of the conspiracy Marcellinus, who in some measure had bestowed the purple on his new master, boldly accepted this dangerous commission ; and his three colleagues were selected from the illustrious personages of the state and army. These deputies were instructed to soothe the resentment, and to alarm the fears, of Constantius. They were empowered to offer him the friendship and alliance of the western princes, to cement their union by a double marriage ; of Constantius with the daughter of Magnentius, and of Magnentius himself with the ambitious Constantina ; and to acknowledge in the treaty the preëminence of rank, which might justly be claimed by the emperor of the East. Should pride and mistaken piety urge him to refuse these equitable conditions, the ambassadors were ordered to expatiate on the inevitable ruin which must attend his rashness, if he ventured to provoke the sovereigns of the West to exert their superior strength ; and to employ against him that valor, those abilities, and those legions, to which the house of Constantine had been indebted for so many triumphs. Such propositions and such arguments appeared to deserve the most serious attention ; the answer of Constantius was deferred till the next day ; and as he had reflected on the importance of justifying a civil war in the opinion of the people, he thus addressed his council, who listened with real or affected credulity : " Last night," said he, " after I retired to rest, the shade of the great Constantine, embracing the corpse of my murdered brother, rose before my eyes ; his well-known voice awakened me to revenge, forbade me to despair of the republic, and assured me of the success and immortal glory which would crown the justice of my arms." The authority of such a vision, or rather of the prince who alleged it, silenced every doubt, and excluded all negotiation. The ignominious terms of peace were rejected with disdain. One of the ambassadors of the tyrant was dismissed with the haughty answer of Constantius ; his colleagues, as unworthy of the privileges of the law of nations, were put in irons ; and the contending powers prepared to wage an implacable war.[75]

Such was the conduct, and such perhaps was the duty, of the brother of Constans towards the perfidious usurper of Gaul. The situation and character of Vetranio admitted of milder measures ; and the policy of the Eastern emperor was directed

---

[75] See Peter the Patrician, in the Excerpta Legationem, p. 27.

to disunite his antagonists, and to separate the forces of Illyricum from the cause of rebellion. It was an easy task to deceive the frankness and simplicity of Vetranio, who, fluctuating some time between the opposite views of honor and interest, displayed to the world the insincerity of his temper, and was insensibly engaged in the snares of an artful negotiation. Constantius acknowledged him as a legitimate and equal colleague in the empire, on condition that he would renounce his disgraceful alliance with Magnentius, and appoint a place of interview on the frontiers of their respective provinces ; where they might pledge their friendship by mutual vows of fidelity, and regulate by common consent the future operations of the civil war. In consequence of this agreement, Vetranio advanced to the city of Sardica,[76] at the head of twenty thousand horse, and of a more numerous body of infantry ; a power so far superior to the forces of Constantius, that the Illyrian emperor appeared to command the life and fortunes of his rival, who, depending on the success of his private negotiations, had seduced the troops, and undermined the throne, of Vetranio. The chiefs, who had secretly embraced the party of Constantius, prepared in his favor a public spectacle, calculated to discover and inflame the passions of the multitude.[77] The united armies were commanded to assemble in a large plain near the city. In the centre, according to the rules of ancient discipline, a military tribunal, or rather scaffold, was erected, from whence the emperors were accustomed, on solemn and important occasions, to harangue the troops. The well-ordered ranks of Romans and Barbarians, with drawn swords, or with erected spears, the squadrons of cavalry, and the cohorts of infantry, distinguished by the variety of their arms and ensigns, formed an immense circle round the tribunal ; and the attentive silence which they preserved was sometimes interrupted by loud bursts of clamor or of applause. In the presence of this formidable assembly, the two emperors were called upon to explain the situation of public affairs : the precedency of rank was yielded to the royal birth of

---

[76] Zonaras, tom. ii. l. xiii. p. 16. The position of Sardica, near the modern city of Sophia, appears better suited to this interview than the situation of either Naissus or Sirmium, where it is placed by Jerom, Socrates, and Sozomen.

[77] See the two first orations of Julian, particularly p. 31 ; and Zosimus, l. ii. p. 122. The distinct narrative of the historian serves to illustrate the diffuse but vague descriptions of the orator.

Constantius, and though he was indifferently skilled in the arts of rhetoric, he acquitted himself, under these difficult circumstances, with firmness, dexterity, and eloquence. The first part of his oration seemed to be pointed only against the tyrant of Gaul; but while he tragically lamented the cruel murder of Constans, he insinuated, that none, except a brother, could claim a right to the succession of his brother. He displayed, with some complacency, the glories of his Imperial race; and recalled to the memory of the troops the valor, the triumphs, the liberality of the great Constantine, to whose sons they had engaged their allegiance by an oath of fidelity, which the ingratitude of his most favored servants had tempted them to violate. The officers, who surrounded the tribunal, and were instructed to act their parts in this extraordinary scene, confessed the irresistible power of reason and eloquence, by saluting the emperor Constantius as their lawful sovereign. The contagion of loyalty and repentance was communicated from rank to rank; till the plain of Sardica resounded with the universal acclamation of " Away with these upstart usurpers! Long life and victory to the son of Constantine! Under his banners alone we will fight and conquer." The shout of thousands, their menacing gestures, the fierce clashing of their arms, astonished and subdued the courage of Vetranio, who stood, amidst the defection of his followers, in anxious and silent suspense. Instead of embracing the last refuge of generous despair, he tamely submitted to his fate; and taking the diadem from his head, in the view of both armies fell prostrate at the feet of his conqueror. Constantius used his victory with prudence and moderation; and raising from the ground the aged suppliant, whom he affected to style by the endearing name of Father, he gave him his hand to descend from the throne. The city of Prusa was assigned for the exile or retirement of the abdicated monarch, who lived six years in the enjoyment of ease and affluence. He often expressed his grateful sense of the goodness of Constantius, and, with a very amiable simplicity, advised his benefactor to resign the sceptre of the world, and to seek for content (where alone it could be found) in the peaceful obscurity of a private condition.[78]

---

[78] The younger Victor assigns to his exile the emphatical appellation of "Voluptarium otium." Socrates (l. ii. c. 28) is the voucher for the correspondence with the emperor, which would seem to prove that Vetranio was, indeed, prope ad stultitiam simplicissimus.

The behavior of Constantius on this memorable occasion was celebrated with some appearance of justice ; and his cour tiers compared the studied orations which a Pericles or a Demosthenes addressed to the populace of Athens, with the victorious eloquence which had persuaded an armed multitude to desert and depose the object of their partial choice.[79] The approaching contest with Magnentius was of a more serious and bloody kind. The tyrant advanced by rapid marches to encounter Constantius, at the head of a numerous army, com posed of Gauls and Spaniards, of Franks and Saxons ; of those provincials who supplied the strength of the legions, and of those barbarians who were dreaded as the most formidable enemies of the republic. The fertile plains [80] of the Lower Pannonia, between the Drave, the Save, and the Danube, pre- sented a spacious theatre ; and the operations of the civil war were protracted during the summer months by the skill or timidity of the combatants.[81] Constantius had declared his intention of deciding the quarrel in the fields of Cibalis, a name that would animate his troops by the remembrance of the victory, which, on the same auspicious ground, had been obtained by the arms of his father Constantine. Yet by the impregnable fortifications with which the emperor encompassed his camp, he appeared to decline, rather than to invite, a gen- eral engagement. It was the object of Magnentius to tempt or to compel his adversary to relinquish this advantageous position ; and he employed, with that view, the various marches evolutions, and stratagems, which the knowledge of the art of war could suggest to an experienced officer. He carried by assault the important town of Siscia ; made an attack on the

---

[79] Eum Constantius . . . . . facundiæ vi dejectum Imperio in privatum otium removit. Quæ gloria post natum Imperium soli pro- cessit eloquio clementiâque, &c. Aurelius Victor, Julian, and The- mistius (Orat. iii. and iv.) adorn this exploit with all the artificial and gaudy coloring of their rhetoric.

[80] Busbequius (p. 112) traversed the Lower Hungary and Sclavonia at a time when they were reduced almost to a desert, by the recipro cal hostilities of the Turks and Christians. Yet he mentions with admiration the unconquerable fertility of the soil ; and observes that the height of the grass was sufficient to conceal a loaded wagon from his sight. See likewise Browne's Travels, in Harris's Collection, vol ii. p. 762, &c.

[81] Zosimus gives a very large account of the war, and the negotia- tion, (l. ii. p. 123—130.) But as he neither shows himself a soldier nor a politician, his narrative must be weighed with attention, and received with caution.

city of Sirmium, which lay in the rear of the Imperial camp, attempted to force a passage over the Save into the eastern provinces of Illyricum ; and cut in pieces a numerous detachment, which he had allured into the narrow passes of Adarne. During the greater part of the summer, the tyrant of Gaul showed himself master of the field. The troops of Constantius were harassed and dispirited ; his reputation declined in the eye of the world ; and his pride condescended to solicit a treaty of peace, which would have resigned to the assassin of Constans the sovereignty of the provinces beyond the Alps. These offers were enforced by the eloquence of Philip the Imperial ambassador ; and the council as well as the army of Magnentius were disposed to accept them. But the haughty usurper, careless of the remonstrances of his friends, gave orders that Philip should be detained as a captive, or, at least, as a hostage ; while he despatched an officer to reproach Constantius with the weakness of his reign, and to insult him by the promise of a pardon if he would instantly abdicate the purple. " That he should confide in the justice of his cause, and the protection of an avenging Deity," was the only answer which honor permitted the emperor to return. But he was so sensible of the difficulties of his situation, that he no longer dared to retaliate the indignity which had been offered to his representative. The negotiation of Philip was not, however, ineffectual, since he determined Sylvanus the Frank, a general of merit and reputation, to desert with a considerable body of cavalry, a few days before the battle of Mursa.

The city of Mursa, or Essek, celebrated in modern times for a bridge of boats, five miles in length, over the River Drave, and the adjacent morasses,[82] has been always considered as a place of importance in the wars of Hungary. Magnentius, directing his march towards Mursa, set fire to the gates, and, by a sudden assault, had almost scaled the walls of the town The vigilance of the garrison extinguished the flames ; the approach of Constantius left him no time to continue the operations of the siege ; and the emperor soon removed the only obstacle that could embarrass his motions, by forcing a body of troops which had taken post in an adjoining amphitheatre.

---

[82] This remarkable bridge, which is flanked with towers, and supported on large wooden piles, was constructed A. D. 1566, by Sultan Soliman, to facilitate the march of his armies into Hungary. See Browne's Travels, and Busching's System of Geography, vol i. p 90.

The field of battle round Mursa was a naked and level plain: on this ground the army of Constantius formed, with the Drave on their right; while their left, either from the nature of their disposition, or from the superiority of their cavalry, extended far beyond the right flank of Magnentius.[83] The troops on both sides remained under arms, in anxious expectation, during the greatest part of the morning; and the son of Constantine, after animating his soldiers by an eloquent speech, retired into a church at some distance from the field of battle, and committed to his generals the conduct of this decisive day.[84] They deserved his confidence by the valor and military skill which they exerted. They wisely began the action upon the left; and advancing their whole wing of cavalry in an oblique line, they suddenly wheeled it on the right flank of the enemy, which was unprepared to resist the impetuosity of their charge. But the Romans of the West soon rallied, by the habits of dis cipline; and the Barbarians of Germany supported the renown of their national bravery. The engagement soon became general; was maintained with various and singular turns of fortune; and scarcely ended with the darkness of the night. The signal victory which Constantius obtained is attributed to the arms of his cavalry. His cuirassiers are described as so many massy statues of steel, glittering with their scaly armor, and breaking with their ponderous lances the firm array of the Gallic legions. As soon as the legions gave way, the lighter and more active squadrons of the second line rode sword in hand into the intervals, and completed the disorder. In the mean while, the huge bodies of the Germans were exposed almost naked to the dexterity of the Oriental archers; and whole troops of those Barbarians were urged by anguish and despair to precipitate themselves into the broad and rapid stream of the Drave.[85] The number of the slain was com-

---

[83] This position, and the subsequent evolutions, are clearly, though concisely, described by Julian, Orat. i. p. 36.

[84] Sulpicius Severus, l. ii. p. 405. The emperor passed the day in prayer with Valens, the Arian bishop of Mursa, who gained his confidence by announcing the success of the battle. M. de Tillemont (Hist. des Empereurs, tom. iv. p. 1110) very properly remarks the silence of Julian with regard to the personal prowess of Constantius in the battle of Mursa. The silence of flattery is sometimes equal to the most positive and authentic evidence.

[85] Julian. Orat. i. p. 36, 37; and Orat. ii. p. 59, 60. Zonaras, tom. ii. l. xiii. p. 17. Zosimus, l. ii. p. 130—133. The last of these celebrates the dexterity of the archer Menelaus, who could discharge

puted at fifty-four thousand men, and the slaughter of the con
querors was more considerable than that of the vanquished ;[86]
a circumstance which proves the obstinacy of the contest, and
justifies the observation of an ancient writer, that the forces
of the empire were consumed in the fatal battle of Mursa, by
the loss of a veteran army, sufficient to defend the frontiers,
or to add new triumphs to the glory of Rome.[87]   Notwithstanding the invectives of a servile orator, there is not the least
reason to believe that the tyrant deserted his own standard in
the beginning of the engagement.   He seems to have displayed the virtues of a general and of a soldier till the day
was irrecoverably lost, and his camp in the possession of the
enemy.   Magnentius then consulted his safety, and throwing
away the Imperial ornaments, escaped with some difficulty
from the pursuit of the light horse, who incessantly followed
his rapid flight from the banks of the Drave to the foot of the
Julian Alps.[88]

The approach of winter supplied the indolence of Constantius with specious reasons for deferring the prosecution of the
war till the ensuing spring.   Magnentius had fixed his residence
in the city of Aquileia, and showed a seeming resolution to
dispute the passage of the mountains and morasses which fortified the confines of the Venetian province.   The surprisal
of a castle in the Alps by the secret march of the Imperialists,
could scarcely have determined him to relinquish the possession

---

three arrows at the same time ; an advantage which, according to his
apprehension of military affairs, materially contributed to the victory
of Constantius.

[86] According to Zonaras, Constantius, out of 80,000 men, lost 30,000;
and Magnentius lost 24,000 out of 36,000.   The other articles of this
account seem probable and authentic, but the numbers of the tyrant's
army must have been mistaken, either by the author or his transcribers.   Magnentius had collected the whole force of the West, Romans and Barbarians, into one formidable body, which cannot fairly
be estimated at less than 100,000 men.   Julian. Orat. i. p. 34, 35.

[87] Ingentes R. I. vires eâ dimicatione consumptæ sunt, ad quælibet
bella externa idoneæ, quæ multum triumphorum possent securita-
tisque conferre.   Eutropius, x. 13.   The younger Victor expresses
himself to the same effect.

[88] On this occasion, we must prefer the unsuspected testimony of
Zosimus and Zonaras to the flattering assertions of Julian.   The
younger Victor paints the character of Magnentius in a singular
light : " Sermonis acer, animi tumidi, et immodice timidus ; artifex
tamen ad occultandam audaciæ specie formidinem."   Is it most likely
that in the battle of Mursa his behavior was governed by nature or
by art ?   I should incline for the latter.

of Italy, if the inclinations of the people had supported the cause of their tyrant.[89] But the memory of the cruelties exercised by his ministers, after the unsuccessful revolt of Nepotian, had left a deep impression of horror and resentment on the minds of the Romans. That rash youth, the son of the princess Eutropia, and the nephew of Constantine, had seen with indignation the sceptre of the West usurped by a perfidious barbarian. Arming a desperate troop of slaves and gladiators, he overpowered the feeble guard of the domestic tranquillity of Rome, received the homage of the senate, and assuming the title of Augustus, precariously reigned during a tumult of twenty-eight days. The march of some regular forces put an end to his ambitious hopes: the rebellion was extinguished in the blood of Nepotian, of his mother Eutropia, and of his adherents; and the proscription was extended to all who had contracted a fatal alliance with the name and family of Constantine.[90] But as soon as Constantius, after the battle of Mursa, became master of the sea-coast of Dalmatia, a band of noble exiles, who had ventured to equip a fleet in some harbor of the Adriatic, sought protection and revenge in his victorious camp. By their secret intelligence with their countrymen, Rome and the Italian cities were persuaded to display the banners of Constantius on their walls. The grateful veterans, enriched by the liberality of the father, signalized their gratitude and loyalty to the son. The cavalry, the legions, and the auxiliaries of Italy, renewed their oath of allegiance to Constantius; and the usurper, alarmed by the general desertion, was compelled, with the remains of his faithful troops, to retire beyond the Alps into the provinces of Gaul. The detachments, however, which were ordered either to press or to intercept the flight of Magnentius, conducted themselves with the usual imprudence of success; and allowed him, in the plains of Pavia, an opportunity of turning on his pur-

---

[89] Julian. Orat. i. p. 38, 39. In that place, however, as well as in Oration ii. p. 97, he insinuates the general disposition of the senate, the people, and the soldiers of Italy, towards the party of the emperor.

[90] The elder Victor describes, in a pathetic manner, the miserable condition of Rome : " Cujus stolidum ingenium adeo P. R. patribusque exitio fuit, uti passim domus, fora, viæ, templaque, cruore, cadaveribusque opplerentur bustorum modo." Athanasius (tom. i. p. 677) deplores the fate of several illustrious victims, and Julian (Orat. ii. p. 58) execrates the cruelty of Marcellinus, the implacable enemy of the house of Constantine.

suers, and of gratifying his despair by the carnage of a useless victory.[91]

The pride of Magnentius was reduced, by repeated misfortunes, to sue, and to sue in vain, for peace. He first despatched a senator, in whose abilities he confided, and afterwards several bishops, whose holy character might obtain a more favorable audience, with the offer of resigning the purple, and the promise of devoting the remainder of his life to the service of the emperor. But Constantius, though he granted fair terms of pardon and reconciliation to all who abandoned the standard of rebellion,[92] avowed his inflexible resolution to inflict a just punishment on the crimes of an assassin, whom he prepared to overwhelm on every side by the effort of his victorious arms. An Imperial fleet acquired the easy possession of Africa and Spain, confirmed the wavering faith of the Moorish nations, and landed a considerable force, which passed the Pyrenees, and advanced towards Lyons, the last and fatal station of Magnentius.[93] The temper of the tyrant, which was never inclined to clemency, was urged by distress to exercise every act of oppression which could extort an immediate supply from the cities of Gaul.[94] Their patience was at length exhausted ; and Treves, the seat of Prætorian government, gave the signal of revolt, by shutting her gates against Decentius, who had been raised by his brother to the rank either of Cæsar or of Augustus.[95] From Treves, Decentius was obliged to retire to Sens, where he was soon surrounded by an army of Germans, whom the pernicious arts of Constantius had introduced into the civil dissensions of Rome.[96]

---

[91] Zosim. l. ii. p. 133. Victor in Epitome. The panegyrists of Constantius, with their usual candor, forget to mention this accidental defeat.

[92] Zonaras, tom. ii. l. xiii. p. 17. Julian, in several places of the two orations, expatiates on the clemency of Constantius to the rebels.

[93] Zosim. l. ii. p. 133. Julian. Orat. i. p. 40, ii. p. 74.

[94] Ammian. xv. 6. Zosim. l. ii. p. 123. Julian, who (Orat. i. p. 40) inveighs against the cruel effects of the tyrant's despair, mentions (Orat i. p. 34) the oppressive edicts which were dictated by his necessities, or by his avarice. His subjects were compelled to purchase the Imperial demesnes ; a doubtful and dangerous species of property, which, in case of a revolution, might be imputed to them as a treasonable usurpation.

[95] The medals of Magnentius celebrate the victories of the *two* Augusti, and of the Cæsar. The Cæsar was another brother, named Desiderius. See Tillemont, Hist. des Empereurs, tom. iv. p. 757.

[96] Julian. Orat. i. p. 40, ii. p. 74; with Spanheim, p. 263. His

In the mean time, the Imperial troops forced the passages of the Cottian Alps, and in the bloody combat of Mount Seleucus irrevocably fixed the title of rebels on the party of Magnentius.[97] He was unable to bring another army into the field; the fidelity of his guards was corrupted; and when he appeared in public to animate them by his exhortations, he was saluted with a unanimous shout of "Long live the emperor Constantius!" The tyrant, who perceived that they were preparing to deserve pardon and rewards by the sacrifice of the most obnoxious criminal, prevented their design by falling on his sword;[98] a death more easy and more honorable than he could hope to obtain from the hands of an enemy, whose revenge would have been colored with the specious pretence of justice and fraternal piety. The example of suicide was imitated by Decentius, who strangled himself on the news of his brother's death. The author of the conspiracy, Marcellinus, had long since disappeared in the battle of Mursa,[99] and the public tranquillity was confirmed by the execution of the surviving leaders of a guilty and unsuccessful faction. A severe inquisition was extended over all who, either from

---

Commentary illustrates the transactions of this civil war. Mons Seleuci was a small place in the Cottian Alps, a few miles distant from Vapincum, or Gap, an episcopal city of Dauphiné. See D'Anville, Notice de la Gaule, p. 464; and Longuerue, Description de la France, p. 327.*

[97] Zosimus, l. ii. p. 134. Liban. Orat. x. p. 268, 269. The latter most vehemently arraigns this cruel and selfish policy of Constantius.

[98] Julian. Orat. i. p. 40. Zosimus, l. ii. p. 134. Socrates, l. ii. c. 32. Sozomen, l. iv. c. 7. The younger Victor describes his death with some horrid circumstances: Transfosso latere, ut erat vasti corporis, vulnere naribusque et ore cruorem effundens, exspiravit. If we can give credit to Zonaras, the tyrant, before he expired, had the pleasure of murdering, with his own hand, his mother and his brother Desiderius.

[99] Julian (Orat. i. p. 58, 59) seems at a loss to determine, whether he inflicted on himself the punishment of his crimes, whether he was drowned in the Drave, or whether he was carried by the avenging dæmons from the field of battle to his destined place of eternal tortures.

---

* The Itinerary of Antoninus (p. 357, ed. Wess.) places Mons Seleucus twenty-four miles from Vapinicum, (Gap,) and twenty-six from Lucus, (le Luc,) on the road to Die, (Dea Vocontiorum.) The situation answers to Mont Saleon, a little place on the right of the small river Buech, which falls into the Durance Roman antiquities have been found in this place St. Martin Note to Le Beau, ii. 47. — M.

choice or from compulsion, had been involved in the cause of rebellion. Paul, surnamed Catena from his superior skill in the judicial exercise of tyranny,* was sent to explore the latent remains of the conspiracy in the remote province of Britain. The honest indignation expressed by Martin, vice-præfect of the island, was interpreted as an evidence of his own guilt; and the governor was urged to the necessity of turning against his breast the sword with which he had been provoked to wound the Imperial minister. The most innocent subjects of the West were exposed to exile and confiscation, to death and torture; and as the timid are always cruel, the mind of Constantius was inaccessible to mercy.[100]

---

[100] Ammian. xiv. 5, xxi. 16.

---

* This is scarcely correct, ut erat in complicandis negotiis artifex dirus, unde ei Catenæ inditum est cognomentum. Amm. Mar. loc. cit. — M.

CHAPTER XIX.

THE divided provinces of the empire were again united by
the victory of Constantius ; but as that feeble prince was destitute of personal merit, either in peace or war ; as he feared
his generals, and distrusted his ministers ; the triumph of his
arms served only to establish the reign of the *eunuchs* over the
Roman world. Those unhappy beings, the ancient production of Oriental jealousy and despotism,[1] were introduced
into Greece and Rome by the contagion of Asiatic luxury.[2]
Their progress was rapid ; and the eunuchs, who, in the time
of Augustus, had been abhorred, as the monstrous retinue of
an Egyptian queen,[3] were gradually admitted into the families
of matrons, of senators, and of the emperors themselves.[4]

---

[1] Ammianus (l. xiv. c. 6) imputes the first practice of castration to
the cruel ingenuity of Semiramis, who is supposed to have reigned
above nineteen hundred years before Christ. The use of eunuchs is of
high antiquity, both in Asia and Egypt. They are mentioned in the
law of Moses, Deuteron. xxiii. 1. See Goguet, Origines des Loix,
&c., Part i. l. i. c. 3.

[2]
> Eunuchum dixti velle te ;
> Quia solæ utuntur his reginæ ——
>> Terent. Eunuch. act i. scene 2.

This play is translated from Meander, and the original must have
appeared soon after the eastern conquests of Alexander.

[3]
> Miles....spadonibus
> Servire rugosis potest.
>> Horat. Carm. v. 9, and Dacier ad loc.

By the word *spado*, the Romans very forcibly expressed their
abhorrence of this mutilated condition. The Greek appellation of
eunuchs, which insensibly prevailed, had a milder sound, and a more
ambiguous sense.

[4] We need only mention Posides, a freedman and eunuch of Claudius, in whose favor the emperor prostituted some of the most honorable rewards of military valor. See Sueton. in Claudio, c 28.
Posides employed a great part of his wealth in building.

> Ut *Spado* vincebat Capitolia nostra
> Posides.

Rest:ained by the severe edicts of Domitian and Nerva,[5] cherished by the pride of Diocletian, reduced to an humble station by the prudence of Constantine,[6] they multiplied in the palaces of his degenerate sons, and insensibly acquired the knowledge, and at length the direction, of the secret councils of Constantius. The aversion and contempt which mankind has so uniformly entertained for that imperfect species, appears to have degraded their character, and to have rendered them almost as incapable as they were supposed to be, of conceiving any generous sentiment, or of performing any worthy action.[7] But the eunuchs were skilled in the arts of flattery and intrigue ; and they alternately governed the mind of Constantius by his fears, his indolence, and his vanity.[8] Whilst he viewed in a deceitful mirror the fair appearance of public prosperity, he supinely permitted them to intercept the complaints of the injured provinces, to accumulate immense treasures by the sale of justice and of honors ; to disgrace the most important dignities, by the promotion of those who had purchased at their hands the powers of oppression,[9] and to gratify

---

[5] Castrari mares vetuit. Sueton. in Domitian. c. 7. See Dion Cassius, l. lxvii. p. 1107, l. lxviii. p. 1119.

[6] There is a passage in the Augustan History, p. 137, in which Lampridius, whilst he praises Alexander Severus and Constantine for restraining the tyranny of the eunuchs, deplores the mischiefs which they occasioned in other reigns. Huc accedit quod eunuchos nec in consiliis nec in ministeriis habuit ; qui soli principes perdunt, dum eos more gentium aut regum Persarum volunt vivere; qui a populo etiam amicissimum semovent ; qui internuntii sunt, aliud quàm respondetur, referentes ; claudentes principem suum, et agentes ante omnia ne quid sciat.

[7] Xenophon (Cyropædia, l. viii. p. 540) has stated the specious reasons which engaged Cyrus to intrust his person to the guard of eunuchs. He had observed in animals, that although the practice of castration might tame their ungovernable fierceness, it did not diminish their strength or spirit ; and he persuaded himself, that those who were separated from the rest of human kind, would be more firmly attached to the person of their benefactor. But a long experience has contradicted the judgment of Cyrus. Some particular instances may occur of eunuchs distinguished by their fidelity, their valor, and their abilities ; but if we examine the general history of Persia, India, and China, we shall find that the power of the eunuchs has uniformly marked the decline and fall of every dynasty.

[8] See Ammianus Marcellinus, l. xxi. c. 16, l. xxii. c. 4. The whole tenor of his impartial history serves to justify the invectives of Mamertinus, of Libanius, and of Julian himself, who have insulted the vices of the court of Constantius.

[9] Aurelius Victor censures the negligence of his sovereign in choos

their resentment against the few independent spirits, who
arrogantly refused to solicit the protection of slaves. Of these
slaves the most distinguished was the chamberlain Eusebius,
who ruled the monarch and the palace with such absolute
sway, that Constantius, according to the sarcasm of an impartial historian, possessed some credit with this haughty favorite.[10]
By his artful suggestions, the emperor was persuaded to subscribe the condemnation of the unfortunate Gallus, and to add
a new crime to the long list of unnatural murders which pollute
the honor of the house of Constantine.

When the two nephews of Constantine, Gallus and Julian,
were saved from the fury of the soldiers, the former was about
twelve, and the latter about six, years of age; and, as the
eldest was thought to be of a sickly constitution, they obtained
with the less difficulty a precarious and dependent life, from
the affected pity of Constantius, who was sensible that the
execution of these helpless orphans would have been esteemed,
by all mankind, an act of the most deliberate cruelty.[11] *
Different cities of Ionia and Bithynia were assigned for the
places of their exile and education; but as soon as their growing years excited the jealousy of the emperor, he judged it
more prudent to secure those unhappy youths in the strong
castle of Macellum, near Cæsarea. The treatment which they
experienced during a six years' confinement, was partly such
as they could hope from a careful guardian, and partly such
as they might dread from a suspicious tyrant.[12] Their prison

ing the governors of the provinces, and the generals of the army, and
concludes his history with a very bold observation, as it is much
more dangerous under a feeble reign to attack the ministers than the
master himself. " Uti verum absolvam brevi, ut Imperatore ipso cla-
rius ita apparitorum plerisque magis atrox nihil."

[10] Apud quem (si vere dici debeat) multum Constantius potuit.
Ammian. l. xviii. c. 4.

[11] Gregory Nazianzen (Orat. iii. p. 90) reproaches the apostate with
his ingratitude towards Mark, bishop of Arethusa, who had contributed to save his life; and we learn, though from a less respectable authority, (Tillemont, Hist. des Empereurs, tom. iv. p. 916,) that
Julian was concealed in the sanctuary of a church.

[12] The most authentic account of the education and adventures
of Julian is contained in the epistle or manifesto which he himself
addressed to the Senate and people of Athens. Libanius, (Orat. Parentalis,) on the side of the Pagans, and Socrates, (l. iii. c. 1,) on that
of the Christians, have preserved several interesting circumstances.

* Gallus and Julian were not sons of the same mother. Their father
Julius Constantius, had had Gallus by his first wife, named Galla: Julian
was the son of Basilina, whom he had espoused in a second marriage.
Tillemont. Hist. des Emp. Vie de Constantin. art. 3. — G.
37

was an ancient palace, the residence of the kings of Cappadocia; the situation was pleasant, the building stately, the
enclosure spacious. They pursued their studies, and practised
their exercises, under the tuition of the most skilful masters;
and the numerous household appointed to attend, or rather to
guard, the nephews of Constantine, was not unworthy of the
dignity of their birth. But they could not disguise to themselves that they were deprived of fortune, of freedom, and of
safety; secluded from the society of all whom they could
trust or esteem, and condemned to pass their melancholy hours
in the company of slaves devoted to the commands of a
tyrant who had already injured them beyond the hope of
reconciliation. At length, however, the emergencies of the
state compelled the emperor, or rather his eunuchs, to invest
Gallus, in the twenty-fifth year of his age, with the title of
Cæsar, and to cement this political connection by his marriage
with the princess Constantina. After a formal interview, in
which the two princes mutually engaged their faith never to
undertake any thing to the prejudice of each other, they
repaired without delay to their respective stations. Constantius continued his march towards the West, and Gallus fixed
his residence at Antioch; from whence, with a delegated
authority, he administered the five great dioceses of the eastern præfecture.[13] In this fortunate change, the new Cæsar
was not unmindful of his brother Julian, who obtained the
honors of his rank, the appearances of liberty, and the restitution of an ample patrimony.[14]

The writers the most indulgent to the memory of Gallus.
and even Julian himself, though he wished to cast a veil over
the frailties of his brother, are obliged to confess that the
Cæsar was incapable of reigning. Transported from a prison
to a throne, he possessed neither genius nor application, nor
docility to compensate for the want of knowledge and experience. A temper naturally morose and violent, instead of being

---

[13] For the promotion of Gallus, see Idatius, Zosimus, and the two
Victors. According to Philostorgius, (l. iv. c. 1,) Theophilus, an
Arian bishop, was the witness, and, as it were, the guarantee of this
solemn engagement. He supported that character with generous
firmness; but M. de Tillemont (Hist. des Empereurs, tom. iv. p. 1120'
thinks it very improbable that a heretic should have possessed such
virtue.

[14] Julian was at first permitted to pursue his studies at Constanti
nople, but the reputation which he acquired soon excited the jealousy
of Constantius; and the young prince was advised to withdraw him
self to the less conspicuous scenes of Bithynia and Ionia.

corrected, was soured by solitude and adversity; the remembrance of what he had endured disposed him to retaliation rather than to sympathy; and the ungoverned sallies of his rage were often fatal to those who approached his person, or were subject to his power.[15] Constantina, his wife, is described, not as a woman, but as one of the infernal furies tormented with an insatiate thirst of human blood.[16] Instead of employing her influence to insinuate the mild counsels of prudence and humanity, she exasperated the fierce passions of her husband; and as she retained the vanity, though she had renounced the gentleness, of her sex, a pearl necklace was esteemed an equivalent price for the murder of an innocent and virtuous nobleman.[17] The cruelty of Gallus was sometimes displayed in the undissembled violence of popular or military executions; and was sometimes disguised by the abuse of law, and the forms of judicial proceedings. The private houses of Antioch, and the places of public resort, were besieged by spies and informers; and the Cæsar himself, concealed in a plebeian habit, very frequently condescended to assume that odious character. Every apartment of the palace was adorned with the instruments of death and torture, and a general consternation was diffused through the capital of Syria. The prince of the East, as if he had been conscious how much he had to fear, and how little he deserved to reign, selected for the objects of his resentment the provincials accused of some imaginary treason, and his own courtiers, whom with more reason he suspected of incensing, by their secret correspondence, the timid and suspicious mind of Constantius. But he forgot that he was depriving himself of his only support, the affection of the people; whilst he furnished the malice of his

[15] See Julian. ad S. P. Q. A. p. 271. Jerom. in Chron. Aurelius Victor, Eutropius, x. 14. I shall copy the words of Eutropius, who wrote his abridgment about fifteen years after the death of Gallus, when there was no longer any motive either to flatter or to depreciate his character. "Multis incivilibus gestis Gallus Cæsar.... vir naturâ ferox et ad tyrannidem pronior, si suo jure imperare licuisset."

[16] Megæra quidem mortalis, inflammatrix sævientis assidua, humani cruoris avida, &c. Ammian. Marcellin. l. xiv. c. 1. The sincerity of Ammianus would not suffer him to misrepresent facts or characters, but his love of ambitious ornaments frequently betrayed him into an unnatural vehemence of expression.

[17] His name was Clematius of Alexandria, and his only crime was a refusal to gratify the desires of his mother-in-law; who solicited his death, because she had been disappointed of his love. Ammian. xiv. c. 1.

enemies with the arms of truth, and afforded the emperor the fairest pretence of exacting the forfeit of his purple, and of his life.[18]

As long as the civil war suspended the fate of the Roman world, Constantius dissembled his knowledge of the weak and cruel administration to which his choice had subjected the East; and the discovery of some assassins, secretly despatched to Antioch by the tyrant of Gaul, was employed to convince the public, that the emperor and the Cæsar were united by the same interest, and pursued by the same enemies.[19] But when the victory was decided in favor of Constantius, his dependent colleague became less useful and less formidable. Every circumstance of his conduct was severely and suspiciously examined, and it was privately resolved, either to deprive Gallus of the purple, or at least to remove him from the indolent luxury of Asia to the hardships and dangers of a German war. The death of Theophilus, consular of the province of Syria, who in a time of scarcity had been massacred by the people of Antioch, with the connivance, and almost at the instigation, of Gallus, was justly resented, not only as an act of wanton cruelty, but as a dangerous insult on the supreme majesty of Constantius. Two ministers of illustrious rank, Domitian the Oriental præfect, and Montius, quæstor of the palace, were empowered by a special commission * to visit and reform the state of the East. They were instructed to behave towards Gallus with moderation and respect, and, by the gentlest arts of persuasion, to engage him to comply with the invitation of his brother and colleague. The rashness of the præfect disappointed these prudent measures, and hastened his own ruin as well as that of his enemy. On his arrival at Antioch, Domitian passed disdainfully before the gates of the palace and alleging a slight pretence of indisposition, continued several days in sullen retirement, to prepare an inflammatory

---

[18] See in Ammianus (l. xiv. c. 1, 7) a very ample detail of the cruelties of Gallus. His brother Julian (p. 272) insinuates, that a secret conspiracy had been formed against him; and Zosimus names (l. ii. p. 135) the persons engaged in it; a minister of considerable rank, and two obscure agents, who were resolved to make their fortune.

[19] Zonaras, l. xiii. tom. ii. p. 17, 18. The assassins had seduced a great number of legionaries; but their designs were discovered and revealed by an old woman in whose cottage they lodged

---

* The commission seems to have been granted to Domitian alone Montius interfered to support his authority. Amm. Marc. loc. cit. — M.

memorial, which he transmitted to the Imperial court. Yielding at length to the pressing solicitations of Gallus, the præfect condescended to take his seat in council; but his first step was to signify a concise and haughty mandate, importing that the Cæsar should immediately repair to Italy, and threatening that he himself would punish his delay or hesitation, by suspending the usual allowance of his household. The nephew and daughter of Constantine, who could ill brook the insolence of a subject, expressed their resentment by instantly delivering Domitian to the custody of a guard. The quarrel still admitted of some terms of accommodation. They were rendered impracticable by the imprudent behavior of Montius, a statesman whose art and experience were frequently betrayed by the levity of his disposition.[20] The quæstor reproached Gallus in haughty language, that a prince who was scarcely authorized to remove a municipal magistrate, should presume to imprison a Prætorian præfect; convoked a meeting of the civil and military officers; and required them, in the name of their sovereign, to defend the person and dignity of his representatives. By this rash declaration of war, the impatient temper of Gallus was provoked to embrace the most desperate counsels. He ordered his guards to stand to their arms, assembled the populace of Antioch, and recommended to their zeal the care of his safety and revenge. His commands were too fatally obeyed. They rudely seized the præfect and the quæstor, and tying their legs together with ropes, they dragged them through the streets of the city, inflicted a thousand insults and a thousand wounds on these unhappy victims, and at last precipitated their mangled and lifeless bodies into the stream of the Orontes.[21]

After such a deed, whatever might have been the designs of Gallus, it was only in a field of battle that he could assert

[20] In the present text of Ammianus, we read *Asper*, quidem, sed ad *lenitatem* propensior; which forms a sentence of contradictory nonsense. With the aid of an old manuscript, Valesius has rectified the first of these corruptions, and we perceive a ray of light in the substitution of the word *vafer*. If we venture to change *lenitatem* into *levitatem*, this alteration of a single letter will render the whole passage clear and consistent.

[21] Instead of being obliged to collect scattered and imperfect hints from various sources, we now enter into the full stream of the history of Ammianus, and need only refer to the seventh and ninth chapters of his fourteenth book. Philostorgius, however, (l. iii. c. 28,) though partial to Gallus, should not be entirely overlooked.

his innocence with any hope of success. But the mind of that prince was formed of an equal mixture of violence and weakness. Instead of assuming the title of Augustus, instead of employing in his defence the troops and treasures of the East, he suffered himself to be deceived by the affected tranquillity of Constantius, who, leaving him the vain pageanty of a court, imperceptibly recalled the veteran legions from the provinces of Asia. But as it still appeared dangerous to arrest Gallus in his capital, the slow and safer arts of dissimulation were practised with success. The frequent and pressing epistles of Constantius were filled with professions of confidence and friendship; exhorting the Cæsar to discharge the duties of his high station, to relieve his colleague from a part of the public cares, and to assist the West by his presence, his counsels, and his arms. After so many reciprocal injuries, Gallus had reason to fear and to distrust. But he had neglected the opportunities of flight and of resistance; he was seduced by the flattering assurances of the tribune Scudilo, who, under the semblance of a rough soldier, disguised the most artful insinuation; and he depended on the credit of his wife Constantina, till the unseasonable death of that princess completed the ruin in which he had been involved by her impetuous passions.[22]

After a long delay, the reluctant Cæsar set forwards on his journey to the Imperial court. From Antioch to Hadrianople ne traversed the wide extent of his dominions with a numerous and stately train; and as he labored to conceal his apprehensions from the world, and perhaps from himself, he entertained the people of Constantinople with an exhibition of the games of the circus. The progress of the journey might, however, have warned him of the impending danger. In all the principal cities he was met by ministers of confidence, commissioned to seize the offices of government, to observe his motions, and to prevent the hasty sallies of his despair. The persons despatched to secure the provinces which he left behind, passed him with cold salutations, or affected disdain; and the troops, whose station lay along the public road, were studiously removed on his approach, lest they might be tempted to offer their swords for the service of a civil war.[23]

---

[22] She had preceded her husband, but died of a fever on the road, at a little place in Bithynia, called Cœnum Gallicanum.

[23] The Thebæan legions, which were then quartered at Hadrianople, sent a deputation to Gallus, with a tender of their services

After Gallus had been permitted to repose himself a few days at Hadrianople, he received a mandate, expressed in the most haughty and absolute style, that his splendid retinue should halt in that city, while the Cæsar himself, with only ten post carriages, should hasten to the Imperial residence at Milan In this rapid journey, the profound respect which was due to the brother and colleague of Constantius, was insensibly changed into rude familiarity; and Gallus, who discovered in the countenances of the attendants that they already considered themselves as his guards, and might soon be employed as his executioners, began to accuse his fatal rashness, and to recollect, with terror and remorse, the conduct by which he had provoked his fate. The dissimulation which had hitherto been preserved, was laid aside at Petovio,* in Pannonia. He was conducted to a palace in the suburbs, where the general Barbatio, with a select band of soldiers, who could neither be moved by pity, or corrupted by rewards, expected the arrival of his illustrious victim. In the close of the evening he was arrested, ignominiously stripped of the ensigns of Cæsar, and hurried away to Pola,† in Istria, a sequestered prison, which had been so recently polluted with royal blood. The horror which he felt was soon increased by the appearance of his implacable enemy the eunuch Eusebius, who, with the assistance of a notary and a tribune, proceeded to interrogate him concerning the administration of the East. The Cæsar sank under the weight of shame and guilt, confessed all the criminal actions and all the treasonable designs with which he was charged; and by imputing them to the advice of his wife, exasperated the indignation of Constantius, who reviewed with partial prejudice the minutes of the examination. The emperor was easily convinced, that his own safety was incompatible with the life of his cousin: the sentence of death was signed, despatched, and executed; and the nephew of Constantine, with his hands tied behind his back, was beheaded in

Ammian. l. xiv. c. 11. The Notitia (s. 6, 20, 38, edit Labb.) mentions three several legions which bore the name of Thebæan. The zeal of M. de Voltaire to destroy a despicable though celebrated legion, has tempted him on the slightest grounds to deny the existence of a Thebæan legion in the Roman armies. See Œuvres de Voltaire, tom. xv. p. 414, quarto edition.

---

* Pettan in Styria. — M.
† Rather to Flanonia, now Fianone, near Pola. St. Martin. — M

prison like the vilest malefactor.[24]   Those who are inclined to
palliate the cruelties of Constantius, assert that he soon re-
lented, and endeavored to recall the bloody mandate ; but that
the second messenger, intrusted with the reprieve, was detained by the eunuchs, who dreaded the unforgiving temper
of Gallus, and were desirous of reuniting to *their* empire the
wealthy provinces of the East.[25]

Besides the reigning emperor, Julian alone survived, of all
the numerous posterity of Constantius Chlorus.   The misfortune of his royal birth involved him in the disgrace of Gallus.
From his retirement in the happy country of Ionia, he was
conveyed under a strong guard to the court of Milan ; where
he languished above seven months, in the continual apprehension of suffering the same ignominious death, which was daily
inflicted, almost before his eyes, on the friends and adherents
of his persecuted family.   His looks, his gestures, his silence,
were scrutinized with malignant curiosity, and he was perpetually assaulted by enemies whom he had never offended, and
by arts to which he was a stranger.[26]   But in the school of
adversity, Julian insensibly acquired the virtues of firmness
and discretion.   He defended his honor, as well as his life,
against the insnaring subtleties of the eunuchs, who endeavored to extort some declaration of his sentiments ; and whilst
he cautiously suppressed his grief and resentment, he nobly
disdained to flatter the tyrant, by any seeming approbation of
his brother's murder.   Julian most devoutly ascribes his miraculous deliverance to the protection of the gods, who had
exempted his innocence from the sentence of destruction pronounced by their justice against the impious house of Constan-

---

[24] See the complete narrative of the journey and death of Gallus
in Ammianus, l. xiv. c. 11.   Julian complains that his brother was
put to death without a trial ; attempts to justify, or at least to excuse,
the cruel revenge which he had inflicted on his enemies ; but seems
at last to acknowledge that he might justly have been deprived of the
purple.

[25] Philostorgius, l. iv. c. 1.   Zonaras, l. xiii. tom. ii. p. 19.   But the
former was partial towards an Arian monarch, and the latter transcribed, without choice or criticism, whatever he found in the writings
of the ancients.

[26] See Ammianus Marcellin. l. xv. c. 1, 3, 8.   Julian himself, in his
epistle to the Athenians, draws a very lively and just picture of his
own danger, and of his sentiments.   He shows, however, a tendency
to exaggerate his sufferings, by insinuating, though in obscure terms,
that they lasted above a year ; a period which cannot be reconciled
with the truth of chronology.

tine.[27] As the most effectual instrument of their providence, he gratefully acknowledges the steady and generous friendship of the empress Eusebia,[28] a woman of beauty and merit, who, by the ascendant which she had gained over the mind of her husband, counterbalanced, in some measure, the powerful conspiracy of the eunuchs. By the intercession of his patroness, Julian was admitted into the Imperial presence : he pleaded his cause with a decent freedom, he was heard with favor ; and, notwithstanding the efforts of his enemies, who urged the danger of sparing an avenger of the blood of Gallus, the milder sentiment of Eusebia prevailed in the council. But the effects of a second interview were dreaded by the eunuchs ; and Julian was advised to withdraw for a while into the neighborhood of Milan, till the emperor thought proper to assign the city of Athens for the place of his honorable exile. As he had discovered, from his earliest youth, a propensity, or rather passion, for the language, the manners, the learning, and the religion of the Greeks, he obeyed with pleasure an order so agreeable to his wishes. Far from the tumult of arms, and the treachery of courts, he spent six months amidst the groves of the academy, in a free intercourse with the philosophers of the age, who studied to cultivate the genius, to encourage the vanity, and to inflame the devotion of their royal pupil. Their labors were not unsuccessful ; and Julian inviolably preserved for Athens that tender regard which seldom fails to arise in a liberal mind, from the recollection of the place where it has discovered and exercised its growing powers. The gentleness and affability of manners, which his temper suggested and his situation imposed, insensibly engaged the affections of the strangers, as well as citizens, with whom he conversed. Some of his fellow-students might perhaps examine his behavior with an eye of prejudice and aversion ; but Julian established, in the

---

[27] Julian has worked the crimes and misfortunes of the family of Constantine into an allegorical fable, which is happily conceived and agreeably related. It forms the conclusion of the seventh Oration, from whence it has been detached and translated by the Abbé de la Bleterie, Vie de Jovien, tom. ii. p. 385—408.

[28] She was a native of Thessalonica, in Macedonia, of a noble family, and the daughter, as well as sister, of consuls. Her marriage with the emperor may be placed in the year 352. In a divided age, the historians of all parties agree in her praises. See their testimonies collected by Tillemont, Hist. des Empereurs, tom. iv. p. 750 754.

37 *

schools of Athens, a general prepossession in favor of his virtues and talents, which was soon diffused over the Roman world.[29]

Whilst his hours were passed in studious retirement, the empress, resolute to achieve the generous design which she had undertaken, was not unmindful of the care of his fortune. The death of the late Cæsar had left Constantius invested with the sole command, and oppressed by the accumulated weight of a mighty empire. Before the wounds of civil discord could be healed, the provinces of Gaul were overwhelmed by a deluge of Barbarians. The Sarmatians no longer respected the barrier of the Danube. The impunity of rapine had increased the boldness and numbers of the wild Isaurians : those robbers descended from their craggy mountains to ravage the adjacent country, and had even presumed, though without success, to besiege the important city of Seleucia, which was defended by a garrison of three Roman legions. Above all, the Persian monarch, elated by victory, again threatened the peace of Asia, and the presence of the emperor was indispensably required, both in the West and in the East. For the first time, Constantius sincerely acknowledged, that his single strength was unequal to such an extent of care and of dominion.[30] Insensible to the voice of flattery, which assured him that his all-powerful virtue, and celestial fortune, would still continue to triumph over every obstacle, he listened with complacency to the advice of Eusebia, which gratified his indolence, without offending his suspicious pride. As she perceived that the remembrance of Gallus dwelt on the emperor's mind, she artfully turned his attention to the opposite characters of the two brothers, which from their infancy had been compared to those of Domitian

---

[29] Libanius and Gregory Nazianzen have exhausted the arts as well as the powers of their eloquence, to represent Julian as the first of heroes, or the worst of tyrants. Gregory was his fellow-student at Athens.; and the symptoms which he so tragically describes, of the future wickedness of the apostate, amount only to some bodily imperfections, and to some peculiarities in his speech and manner. He protests, however, that he *then* foresaw and foretold the calamities of the church and state. (Greg. Nazianzen, Orat. iv. p. 121, 122.)

[30] Succumbere tot necessitatibus tamque crebris unum se, quod nunquam fecerat, aperte demonstrans. Ammian. l. xv. c. 8. He then expresses, in their own words, the flattering assurances of the courtiers.

and of Titus.[31] She accustomed her husband to consider Julian as a youth of a mild, unambitious disposition, whose allegiance and gratitude might be secured by the gift of the purple, and who was qualified to fill with honor a subordinate station, without aspiring to dispute the commands, or to shade the glories, of his sovereign and benefactor. After an obstinate, though secret struggle, the opposition of the favorite eunuchs submitted to the ascendency of the empress; and it was resolved that Julian, after celebrating his nuptials with Helena, sister of Constantius, should be appointed, with the title of Cæsar, to reign over the countries beyond the Alps.[32]

Although the order which recalled him to court was probably accompanied by some intimation of his approaching greatness, he appeals to the people of Athens to witness his tears of undissembled sorrow, when he was reluctantly torn away from his beloved retirement [33] He trembled for his life, for his fame, and even for his virtue; and his sole confidence was derived from the persuasion, that Minerva inspired all his actions, and that he was protected by an invisible guard of angels, whom for that purpose she had borrowed from the Sun and Moon. He approached, with horror, the palace of Milan; nor could the ingenuous youth conceal his indignation, when he found himself accosted with false and servile respect by the assassins of his family. Eusebia, rejoicing in the success of her benevolent schemes, embraced him with the tenderness of a sister; and endeavored, by the most soothing caresses, to dispel his terrors, and reconcile him to his fortune. But the ceremony of shaving his beard, and his awkward demeanor, when he first exchanged the cloak of a Greek philosopher for the military habit of a Roman prince, amused, during a few days, the levity of the Imperial court.[34]

---

[31] Tantum a temperatis moribus Juliani differens fratris quantum inter Vespasiani filios fuit, Domitianum et Titum. Ammian. l. xiv. c. 11. The circumstances and education of the two brothers were so nearly the same, as to afford a strong example of the innate difference of characters.

[32] Ammianus, l. xv. c. 8. Zosimus, l. iii. p. 137, 138.

[33] Julian. ad S. P. Q. A. p. 275, 276. Libanius, Orat. x. p. 268. Julian did not yield till the gods had signified their will by repeated visions and omens. His piety then forbade him to resist.

[34] Julian himself relates, (p. 274,) with some humor, the circumstances of his own metamorphosis, his downcast looks, and his perplexity at being thus suddenly transported into a new world, where every object appeared strange and hostile.

The emperors of the age of Constantine no longer deigned to consult with the senate in the choice of a colleague ; but they were anxious that their nomination should be ratified by the consent of the army. On this solemn occasion, the guards, with the other troops whose stations were in the neighborhood of Milan, appeared under arms ; and Constantius ascended his lofty tribunal, holding by the hand his cousin Julian, who entered the same day into the twenty-fifth year of his age.[35] In a studied speech, conceived and delivered with dignity, the emperor represented the various dangers which threatened the prosperity of the republic, the necessity of naming a Cæsar for the administration of the West, and his own intention, if it was agreeable to their wishes, of rewarding with the honors of the purple the promising virtues of the nephew of Constantine. The approbation of the soldiers was testified by a respectful murmur ; they gazed on the manly countenance of Julian, and observed with pleasure, that the fire which sparkled in his eyes was tempered by a modest blush, on being thus exposed, for the first time, to the public view of mankind. As soon as the ceremony of his investiture had been performed, Constantius addressed him with the tone of authority which his superior age and station permitted him to assume ; and exhorting the new Cæsar to deserve, by heroic deeds, that sacred and immortal name, the emperor gave his colleague the strongest assurances of a friendship which should never be impaired by time, nor interrupted by their separation into the most distant climates. As soon as the speech was ended, the troops, as a token of applause, clashed their shields against their knees ;[36] while the officers who surrounded the tribunal expressed, with decent reserve, their sense of the merits of the representative of Constantius.

The two princes returned to the palace in the same chariot ; and during the slow procession, Julian repeated to himself a verse of his favorite Homer, which he might equally apply to his fortune and to his fears.[37] The four-and-twenty days which

---

[35] See Ammian. Marcellin. l. xv. c. 8. Zosimus, l. iii. p 139. Aurelius Victor. Victor Junior in Epitom. Eutrop. x. 14.

[36] Militares omnes horrendo fragore scuta genibus illidentes ; quod est prosperitatis indicium plenum ; nam contra cum hastis clypei feriuntur, iræ documentum est et doloris. . . . . Ammianus adds, with a nice distinction, Eumque ut potiori reverentia servaretur, nec supra modum laudabant nec infra quam decebat.

[37] Ἔλλαβε πορφύρεος θάνατος, καὶ μοῖρα κραταιή. The word purple,

the Cæsar spent at Milan after his investiture, and the first months of his Gallic reign, were devoted to a splendid but severe captivity; nor could the acquisition of honor compensate for the loss of freedom.[38] His steps were watched, his correspondence was intercepted; and he was obliged, by prudence, to decline the visits of his most intimate friends. Of his former domestics, four only were permitted to attend him; two pages, his physician, and his librarian; the last of whom was employed in the care of a valuable collection of books, the gift of the empress, who studied the inclinations as well as the interest of her friend. In the room of these faithful servants, a household was formed, such indeed as became the dignity of a Cæsar; but it was filled with a crowd of slaves, destitute, and perhaps incapable, of any attachment for their new master, to whom, for the most part, they were either unknown or suspected. His want of experience might require the assistance of a wise council; but the minute instructions which regulated the service of his table, and the distribution of his hours, were adapted to a youth still under the discipline of his preceptors, rather than to the situation of a prince intrusted with the conduct of an important war. If he aspired to deserve the esteem of his subjects, he was checked by the fear of displeasing his sovereign; and even the fruits of his marriage-bed were blasted by the jealous artifices of Eusebia [39] herself, who, on this occasion alone, seems to have been

which Homer had used as a vague but common epithet for death, was applied by Julian to express, very aptly, the nature and object of his own apprehensions.

[38] He represents, in the most pathetic terms, (p. 277,) the distress of his new situation. The provision for his table was, however, so elegant and sumptuous, that the young philosopher rejected it with disdain. Quum legeret libellum assidue, quem Constantius ut privignum ad studia mittens manû suâ conscripserat, prælicenter disponens quid in convivio Cæsaris impendi deberet: Phasianum, et vulvam et sumen exigi vetuit et inferri. Ammian. l. xvi. c. 5.

[39] If we recollect that Constantine the father of Helena, died above eighteen years before, in a mature old age, it will appear probable, that the daughter, though a virgin, could not be very young at the time of her marriage. She was soon afterwards delivered of a son, who died immediately, quòd obstetrix corrupta mercede, mox natum præsecto plusquam convenerat umbilico necavit. She accompanied the emperor and empress in their journey to Rome, and the latter, quæsitum venenum bibere per fraudem illexit, ut quotiescunque concepisset, immaturum abjicerit partum. Ammian. l. xvi. c. 10. Our physicians will determine whether there exists such a poison. For my own part, I am inclined to hope that the public malignity imputed the effects of accident as the guilt of Eusebia.

unmindful of the tenderness of her sex, and the generosity of her character. The memory of his father and of his brothers reminded Julian of his own danger, and his apprehensions were increased by the recent and unworthy fate of Sylvanus. In the summer which preceded his own elevation, that general had been chosen to deliver Gaul from the tyranny of the Barbarians; but Sylvanus soon discovered that he had left his most dangerous enemies in the Imperial court. A dexterous informer, countenanced by several of the principal ministers, procured from him some recommendatory letters; and erasing the whole of the contents, except the signature, filled up the vacant parchment with matters of high and treasonable import. By the industry and courage of his friends, the fraud was however detected, and in a great council of the civil and military officers, held in the presence of the emperor himself, the innocence of Sylvanus was publicly acknowledged. But the discovery came too late; the report of the calumny, and the hasty seizure of his estate, had already provoked the indignant chief to the rebellion of which he was so unjustly accused. He assumed the purple at his head-quarters of Cologne, and his active powers appeared to menace Italy with an invasion, and Milan with a siege. In this emergency, Ursicinus, a general of equal rank, regained, by an act of treachery, the favor which he had lost by his eminent services in the East. Exasperated, as he might speciously allege, by injuries of a similar nature, he hastened with a few followers to join the standard, and to betray the confidence, of his too credulous friend. After a reign of only twenty-eight days, Sylvanus was assassinated: the soldiers who, without any criminal intention, had blindly followed the example of their leader, immediately returned to their allegiance; and the flatterers of Constantius celebrated the wisdom and felicity of the monarch who had extinguished a civil war without the hazard of a battle.[40]

The protection of the Rhætian frontier, and the persecution of the Catholic church, detained Constantius in Italy above eighteen months after the departure of Julian. Before the emperor returned into the East, he indulged his pride and curiosity in a visit to the ancient capital.[41] He proceeded

---

[40] Ammianus (xv. v.) was perfectly well informed of the conduct and fate of Sylvanus. He himself was one of the few followers who attended Ursicinus in his dangerous enterprise.

[41] For the particulars of the visit of Constantius to Rome, see

from Milan to Rome along the Æmilian and Flaminian ways; and as soon as he approached within forty miles of the city, the march of a prince who had never vanquished a foreign enemy, assumed the appearance of a triumphal procession. His splendid train was composed of all the ministers of luxury; but in a time of profound peace, he was encompassed by the glittering arms of the numerous squadrons of his guards and cuirassiers. Their streaming banners of silk, embossed with gold, and shaped in the form of dragons, waved round the person of the emperor. Constantius sat alone in a lofty car, resplendent with gold and precious gems : and, except when he bowed his head to pass under the gates of the cities, he affected a stately demeanor of inflexible, and, as it might seem, of insensible gravity. The severe discipline of the Persian youth had been introduced by the eunuchs into the Imperial palace ; and such were the habits of patience which they had inculcated, that during a slow and sultry march, he was never seen to move his hand towards his face, or to turn his eyes either to the right or to the left. He was received by the magistrates and senate of Rome ; and the emperor surveyed, with attention, the civil honors of the republic, and the consular images of the noble families. The streets were lined with an innumerable multitude. Their repeated acclamations expressed their joy at beholding, after an absence of thirty-two years, the sacred person of their sovereign ; and Constantius himself expressed, with some pleasantry, his affected surprise that the human race should thus suddenly be collected on the same spot. The son of Constantine was lodged in the ancient palace of Augustus : he presided in the senate, harangued the people from the tribunal which Cicero had so often ascended, assisted with unusual courtesy at the games of the Circus, and accepted the crowns of gold, as well as the Panegyrics which had been prepared for the ceremony by the deputies of the principal cities. His short visit of thirty days was employed in viewing the monuments of art and power, which were scattered over the seven hills and the interjacent valleys. He admired the awful majesty of the Capitol, the vast extent of the baths of Caracalla and Diocletian, the severe simplicity of the Pantheon, the massy greatness of the

---

Ammianus, l. xvi. c. 10. We have only to add. that Themistius was appointed deputy from Constantinople, and that he composed his fourth oration for this ceremony.

amphitheatre of Titus, the elegant architecture of the theatre of Pompey and the Temple of Peace, and, above all, the stately structure of the Forum and column of Trajan; acknowledging that the voice of fame, so prone to invent and to magnify, had made an inadequate report of the metropolis of the world. The traveller, who has contemplated the ruins of ancient Rome, may conceive some imperfect idea of the sentiments which they must have inspired when they reared their heads in the splendor of unsullied beauty.

The satisfaction which Constantius had received from this journey excited him to the generous emulation of bestowing on the Romans some memorial of his own gratitude and munificence. His first idea was to imitate the equestrian and colossal statue which he had seen in the Forum of Trajan; but when he had maturely weighed the difficulties of the execution,[42] he chose rather to embellish the capital by the gift of an Egyptian obelisk. In a remote but polished age, which seems to have preceded the invention of alphabetical writing, a great number of these obelisks had been erected, in the cities of Thebes and Heliopolis, by the ancient sovereigns of Egypt, in a just confidence that the simplicity of their form, and the hardness of their substance, would resist the injuries of time and violence.[43] Several of these extraordinary columns had been transported to Rome by Augustus and his successors, as the most durable monuments of their power and victory;[44] but there remained one obelisk, which, from its size or sanctity, escaped for a long time the rapacious vanity of the conquerors. It was designed by Constantine to adorn his new city;[45] and, after being removed by his order

---

[42] Hormisdas, a fugitive prince of Persia, observed to the emperor, that if he made such a horse, he must think of preparing a similar stable, (the Forum of Trajan.) Another saying of Hormisdas is recorded, " that one thing only had *displeased* him, to find that men died at Rome as well as elsewhere." If we adopt this reading of the text of Ammianus, (*displicuisse*, instead of *placuisse*, we may consider it as a reproof of Roman vanity. The contrary sense would be that of a misanthrope.

[43] When Germanicus visited the ancient monuments of Thebes, the eldest of the priests explained to him the meaning of these hieroglyphics. Tacit. Annal. ii. c. 60. But it seems probable, that before the useful invention of an alphabet, these natural or arbitrary signs were the common characters of the Egyptian nation. See Warburton's Divine Legation of Moses, vol. iii. p. 69—243.

[44] See Plin. Hist. Natur. l. xxxvi. c. 14, 15.

[45] Ammian. Marcellin. l. xvii. c. 4. He gives us a Greek interpreta

from the pedestal where it stood before the Temple of the Sun at Heliopolis, was floated down the Nile to Alexandria. The death of Constantine suspended the execution of his purpose, and this obelisk was destined by his son to the ancient capital of the empire. A vessel of uncommon strength and capaciousness was provided to convey this enormous weight of granite, at least a hundred and fifteen feet in length, from the banks of tne Nile to those of the Tyber. The obelisk of Constantius was landed about three miles from the city, and elevated, by the efforts of art and labor, in the great Circus of Rome.[46]

The departure of Constantius from Rome was hastened by .he alarming intelligence of the distress and danger of the Illyrian provinces. The distractions of civil war, and the irreparable loss which the Roman legions had sustained in the battle of Mursa, exposed those countries, almost without defence, to the light cavalry of the Barbarians; and particularly to the inroads of the Quadi, a fierce and powerful nation, who seem to have exchanged the institutions of Germany for the arms and military arts of their Sarmatian allies.[47] The garrisons of the frontier were insufficient to check their progress; and the indolent monarch was at length compelled to assemble, from the extremities of his dominions, the flower of the Palatine troops, to take the field in person, and to employ a whole campaign, with the preceding autumn and the ensuing

---

tion of the hieroglyphics, and his commentator Lindenbrogius adds a Latin inscription, which, in twenty verses of the age of Constantius, contain a short history of the obelisk.

[46] See Donat. Roma. Antiqua, l. iii. c. 14. l. iv. c. 12, and the learned, though confused, Dissertation of Bargæus on Obelisks, inserted in the fourth volume of Grævius's Roman Antiquities, p. 1897—1936. This dissertation is dedicated to Pope Sixtus V., who erected the obelisk of Constantius in the square before the patriarchal church of St. John Lateran.*

[47] The events of this Quadian and Sarmatian war are related by Ammianus, xvi. 10, xvii. 12, 13, xix. 11.

---

* It is doubtful whether the obelisk transported by Constantius to Rome now exists. Even from the text of Ammianus, it is uncertain whether the interpretation of Hermapion refers to the older obelisk, (obelisco incisus est veteri quem videmus in Circo,) raised, as he himself states, in the Circus Maximus, long before, by Augustus, or to the one brought by Constantius. The obelisk in the square before the church of St. John Lateran is ascribed, not to Rameses the Great, but to Thoutmos II. Champollion, 1 Lettre à M. de Blacas, p. 32. —M.

spring, in the serious prosecution of the war. The emperor passed the Danube on a bridge of boats, cut in pieces all that encountered his march, penetrated into the heart of the country of the Quadi, and severely retaliated the calamities which they had inflicted on the Roman province. The dismayed Barbarians were soon reduced to sue for peace : they offered the restitution of his captive subjects as an atonement for the past, and the noblest hostages as a pledge of their future conduct. The generous courtesy which was shown to the first among their chieftains who implored the clemency of Constantius, encouraged the more timid, or the more obstinate, to imitate their example ; and the Imperial camp was crowded with the princes and ambassadors of the most distant tribes who occupied the plains of the Lesser Poland, and who might have deemed themselves secure behind the lofty ridge of the Carpathian Mountains. While Constantius gave laws to the Barbarians beyond the Danube, he distinguished, with specious compassion, the Sarmatian exiles, who had been expelled from their native country by the rebellion of their slaves, and who formed a very considerable accession to the power of the Quadi. The emperor, embracing a generous but artful system of policy, released the Sarmatians from the bands of this humiliating dependence, and restored them, by a separate treaty, to the dignity of a nation united under the government of a king, the friend and ally of the republic. He declared his resolution of asserting the justice of their cause, and of securing the peace of the provinces by the extirpation, or at least the banishment, of the Limigantes, whose manners were still infected with the vices of their servile origin. The execution of this design was attended with more difficulty than glory. The territory of the Limigantes was protected against the Romans by the Danube, against the hostile Barbarians by the Teyss. The marshy lands which lay between those rivers, and were often covered by their inundations, formed an intricate wilderness, pervious only to the inhabitants, who were acquainted with its secret paths and inaccessible fortresses. On the approach of Constantius, the Limigantes tried the efficacy of prayers, of fraud, and of arms ; but he sternly rejected their supplications, defeated their rude stratagems, and repelled with skill and firmness the efforts of their irregular valor. One of their most warlike tribes, established in a small island towards the conflux of the Teyss and the Danube, consented to pass the river with the intention of surprising the emperor during the security of an amicable conference. They soon became the victims of the perfidy which they meditated. Encompassed on every side, trampled down by the cavalry, slaughtered by the swords of the legions, they disdained to ask for mercy; and with an undaunted countenance, still grasped their weapons in the agonies of death. After this victory, a considerable body of Romans was landed on the opposite banks of the Danube; the Taifalæ, a Gothic tribe engaged in the service of the empire, invaded the Limigantes on the side of the Teyss; and their former masters, the free Sarmatians, animated by hope and revenge, penetrated through the hilly country, into the heart of their ancient possessions. A general conflagration revealed the huts of the Barbarians, which were seated in the depth of the wilderness; and the soldier fought with confidence on marshy ground, which it was dangerous for him to tread. In this extremity, the bravest of the Limigantes were resolved to die in arms, rather than to yield: but the milder sentiment, enforced by the authority of their elders, at length prevailed; and the suppliant crowd, followed by their wives and children, repaired to the Imperial camp, to learn their fate from the mouth of the conqueror. After celebrating his own clemency, which was still inclined to pardon their repeated crimes, and to spare the remnant of a guilty nation, Constantius assigned for the place of their exile a remote country, where they might enjoy a safe and honorable repose. The Limigantes obeyed with reluctance; but before they could reach, at least before they could occupy, their destined habitations, they returned to the banks of the Danube, exaggerating the hardships of their situation, and requesting, with fervent professions of fidelity, that the emperor would grant them an undisturbed settlement within the limits of the Roman provinces. Instead of consulting his own experience of their incurable perfidy, Constantius listened to his flatterers, who were ready to represent the honor and advantage of accepting a colony of soldiers, at a time when it was much easier to obtain the pecuniary contributions than the military service of the subjects of the empire. The Limigantes were permitted to pass the Danube; and the emperor gave audience to the multitude in a large plain near the modern city of Buda. They surrounded the tribunal, and seemed to hear with respect an oration full of mildness and dignity, when one of the Barbarians, casting his shoe into the air,

exclaimed with a loud voice, *Marha! Marha!*[*] a word of
defiance, which was received as a signal of the tumult. They
rushed with fury to seize the person of the emperor; his
royal throne and golden couch were pillaged by these rude
hands; but the faithful defence of his guards, who died at his
feet, allowed him a moment to mount a fleet horse, and to
escape from the confusion. The disgrace which had been
incurred by a treacherous surprise was soon retrieved by the
numbers and discipline of the Romans; and the combat was
only terminated by the extinction of the name and nation of
the Limigantes. The free Sarmatians were reinstated in the
possession of their ancient seats; and although Constantius
distrusted the levity of their character, he entertained some
hopes that a sense of gratitude might influence their future
conduct. He had remarked the lofty stature and obsequious
demeanor of Zizais, one of the noblest of their chiefs. He
conferred on him the title of King; and Zizais proved that he
was not unworthy to reign, by a sincere and lasting attachment to the interest of his benefactor, who, after this splendid
success, received the name of *Sarmaticus* from the acclamations of his victorious army.[48]

While the Roman emperor and the Persian monarch, at the
distance of three thousand miles, defended their extreme limits against the Barbarians of the Danube and of the Oxus,
their intermediate frontier experienced the vicissitudes of a
languid war, and a precarious truce. Two of the eastern
ministers of Constantius, the Prætorian præfect Musonian,
whose abilities were disgraced by the want of truth and
integrity, and Cassian, duke of Mesopotamia, a hardy and
veteran soldier, opened a secret negotiation with the satrap
Tamsapor.[49][†] These overtures of peace, translated into the
servile and flattering language of Asia, were transmitted to the
camp of the Great King; who resolved to signify, by an ambassador, the terms which he was inclined to grant to the suppliant
Romans. Narses, whom he invested with that character, was

---

[48] Genti Sarmatarum magno decori confidens apud eos regem dedit.
Aurelius Victor. In a pompous oration pronounced by Constantius
nimself, he expatiates on his own exploits with much vanity, and
some truth.

[49] Ammian. xvi. 9.

---

[*] Reinesius reads Warrha, Warrha, Guerre, War. **Wagner note on**
Amm. Marc. xix. 11.—M.
[†] In Persian, Ten-schah-pour. St. Martin, ii. 177.—M.

honorably received in his passage through Antioch and Constantinople : he reached Sirmium after a long journey, and, at his first audience, respectfully unfolded the silken veil which covered the haughty epistle of his sovereign. Sapor, King of Kings, and Brother of the Sun and Moon, (such were the lofty titles affected by Oriental vanity,) expressed his satisfaction that his brother, Constantius Cæsar, had been taught wisdom by adversity. As the lawful successor of Darius Hystaspes, Sapor asserted, that the River Strymon, in Macedonia, was the true and ancient boundary of his empire ; declaring, however, that as an evidence of his moderation, he would content himself with the provinces of Armenia and Mesopotamia, which had been fraudulently extorted from his ancestors. He alleged, that, without the restitution of these disputed countries, it was impossible to establish any treaty on a solid and permanent basis ; and he arrogantly threatened, that if his ambassador returned in vain, he was prepared to take the field in the spring, and to support the justice of his cause by the strength of his invincible arms. Narses, who was endowed with the most polite and amiable manners, endeavored, as far as was consistent with his duty, to soften the harshness of the message.[50] Both the style and substance were maturely weighed in the Imperial council, and he was dismissed with the following answer : " Constantius had a right to disclaim the officiousness of his ministers, who had acted without any specific orders from the throne : he was not, however, averse to an equal and honorable treaty ; but it was highly indecent, as well as absurd, to propose to the sole and victorious emperor of the Roman world, the same conditions of peace which he had indignantly rejected at the time when his power was contracted within the narrow limits of the East : the chance of arms was uncertain ; and Sapor should recollect, that if the Romans had sometimes been vanquished in battle, they had almost always been successful in the event of the war." A few days after the departure of Narses, three ambassadors were sent to the court of Sapor, who was already returned from the Scythian expedition to his ordinary residence of Ctesiphon. A count, a notary, and a sophist, had been selected for this important

---

[50] Ammianus (xvii. 5) transcribes the haughty letter. Themistius (Orat. iv. p. 57, edit. Petav.) takes notice of the silken covering. Idatius and Zonaras mention the journey of the ambassador ; and Peter the Patrician (in Excerpt. Legat. p. 28) has informed us of has conciliating behavior.

commission, and Constantius, who was secretly anxious for the conclusion of the peace, entertained some hopes that the dignity of the first of these ministers, the dexterity of the second, and the rhetoric of the third,[51] would persuade the Persian monarch to abate of the rigor of his demands. But the progress of their negotiation was opposed and defeated by the hostile arts of Antoninus,[52] a Roman subject of Syria, who had fled from oppression, and was admitted into the councils of Sapor, and even to the royal table, where, according to the custom of the Persians, the most important business was frequently discussed.[53] The dexterous fugitive promoted his interest by the same conduct which gratified his revenge. He incessantly urged the ambition of his new master to embrace the favorable opportunity when the bravest of the Palatine troops were employed with the emperor in a distant war on the Danube. He pressed Sapor to invade the exhausted and defenceless provinces of the East, with the numerous armies of Persia, now fortified by the alliance and accession of the fiercest Barbarians. The ambassadors of Rome retired without success, and a second embassy, of a still more honorable rank, was detained in strict confinement, and threatened either with death or exile.

The military historian,[54] who was himself despatched to observe the army of the Persians, as they were preparing to construct a bridge of boats over the Tigris, beheld from an eminence the plain of Assyria, as far as the edge of the horizon, covered with men, with horses, and with arms. Sapor

---

[51] Ammianus, xvii. 5, and Valesius ad loc. The sophist, or philosopher, (in that age these words were almost synonymous,) was Eustathius the Cappadocian, the disciple of Jamblichus, and the friend of St. Basil. Eunapius (in Vit. Ædesii, p. 44—47) fondly attributes to this philosophic ambassador the glory of enchanting the Barbarian king by the persuasive charms of reason and eloquence. See Tillemont, Hist. des Empereurs, tom. iv. p. 828, 1132.

[52] Ammian. xviii. 5, 6, 8. The decent and respectful behavior of Antoninus towards the Roman general, sets him in a very interesting light; and Ammianus himself speaks of the traitor with some compassion and esteem.

[53] This circumstance, as it is noticed by Ammianus, serves to prove the veracity of Herodotus, (l. i. c. 133,) and the permanency of the Persian manners. In every age the Persians have been addicted to intemperance, and the wines of Shiraz have triumphed over the law of Mahomet. Brisson de Regno Pers. l. ii. p. 462—472, and Chardin. Voyages en Perse, tom. iii. p. 90.

[54] Ammian. lxviii. 6, 7, 8, 10.

appeared in the front, conspicuous by the splendor of his purple. On his left hand, the place of honor among the Orientals, Grumbates, king of the Chionites, displayed the stern countenance of an aged and renowned warrior. The monarch had reserved a similar place on his right hand for the king of the Albanians, who led his independent tribes from the shores of the Caspian.* The satraps and generals were distributed according to their several ranks, and the whole army, besides the numerous train of Oriental luxury, consisted of more than one hundred thousand effective men, inured to fatigue, and selected from the bravest nations of Asia. The Roman deserter, who in some measure guided the councils of Sapor, had prudently advised, that, instead of wasting the summer in tedious and difficult sieges, he should march directly to the Euphrates, and press forwards without delay to seize the feeble and wealthy metropolis of Syria. But the Persians were no sooner advanced into the plains of Mesopotamia, than they discovered that every precaution had been used which could retard their progress, or defeat their design. The inhabitants, with their cattle, were secured in places of strength, the green forage throughout the country was set on fire, the fords of the rivers were fortified by sharp stakes; military engines were planted on the opposite banks, and a seasonable swell of the waters of the Euphrates deterred the Barbarians from attempting the ordinary passage of the bridge of Thapsacus. Their skilful guide, changing his plan of operations, then conducted the army by a longer circuit, but through a fertile territory, towards the head of the Euphrates, where the infant river is reduced to a shallow and accessible stream. Sapor overlooked, with prudent disdain, the strength of Nisibis; but as he passed under the walls of Amida, he resolved to try whether the majesty of his presence would not awe the garrison into immediate submission. The sacrilegious insult of a random dart, which glanced against the royal tiara, convinced him of his error; and the indignant monarch listened with impatience to the advice of his ministers, who conjured him not to sacri-

---

* These perhaps were the barbarous tribes who inhabit the northern part of the present Schirwan, the Albania of the ancients. This country, now inhabited by the Lezghis, the terror of the neighboring districts, was then occupied by the same people, called by the ancients Legæ, by the Armenians Gheg, or Leg. The latter represent them as constant allies of the Persians in their wars against Armenia and the Empire. A little after this period, a certain Schergir was their king, and it is of him doubtless that Ammianus Marcellinus speaks St. Martin, ii. 285. — M.

fice the success of his ambition to the gratification of his resentment. The following day Grumbates advanced towards the gates with a select body of troops, and required the instant surrender of the city, as the only atonement which could be accepted for such an act of rashness and insolence. His proposals were answered by a general discharge, and his only son, a beautiful and valiant youth, was pierced through the heart by a javelin, shot from one of the balistæ. The funeral of the prince of the Chionites was celebrated according to the rites of his country; and the grief of his aged father was alleviated by the solemn promise of Sapor, that the guilty city of Amida should serve as a funeral pile to expiate the death, and to perpetuate the memory, of his son.

The ancient city of Amid or Amida,[55] which sometimes assumes the provincial appellation of Diarbekir,[56] is advantageously situate in a fertile plain, watered by the natural and artificial channels of the Tigris, of which the least inconsiderable stream bends in a semicircular form round the eastern part of the city. The emperor Constantius had recently conferred on Amida the honor of his own name, and the additional fortifications of strong walls and lofty towers. It was provided with an arsenal of military engines, and the ordinary garrison

---

[55] For the description of Amida, see D'Herbelot, Bibliothèque Orientale, p. 108. Histoire de Timur Bec, par Cherefeddin Ali, l. iii. c. 41. Ahmed Arabsiades, tom. i. p. 331, c. 43. Voyages de Tavernier, tom. i. p. 301. Voyages d'Otter, tom. ii. p. 273, and Voyages de Niebuhr, tom. ii. p. 324—328. The last of these travellers, a learned and accurate Dane, has given a plan of Amida, which illustrates the operations of the siege.

[56] Diarbekir, which is styled Amid, or Kara Amid, in the public writings of the Turks, contains above 16,000 houses, and is the residence of a pacha with three tails. The epithet of *Kara* is derived from the *blackness* of the stone which composes the strong and ancient wall of Amida.*

---

* In my Mem. Hist. sur l'Armenie, l. i. p. 166, 173, I conceive that I have proved this city, still called, by the Armenians, Dirkranagerd, the city of Tigranes, to be the same with the famous Tigranocerta, of which the situation was unknown. St. Martin, i. 432. On the siege of Amida, see St. Martin's Notes, ii. 290. Faustus of Byzantium, nearly a contemporary, (Armenian,) states that the Persians, on becoming masters of it, destroyed 40,000 houses; though Ammianus describes the city as of no great extent, (civitatis ambitum non nimium amplæ.) Besides the ordinary population, and those who took refuge from the country, it contained 20,000 soldiers St. Martin, ii. 290. This interpretation is extremely doubtful. Wagner (note on Ammianus) considers the whole population to amount only to 20,000. — M.

had been reënforced to the amount of seven legions, when the place was invested by the arms of Sapor.[57] His first and most sanguine hopes depended on the success of a general assault. To the several nations which followed his standard, their respective posts were assigned; the south to the Vertæ; the north to the Albanians; the east to the Chionites, inflamed with grief and indignation; the west to the Segestans, the bravest of his warriors, who covered their front with a formidable line of Indian elephants.[58] The Persians, on every side, supported their efforts, and animated their courage; and the monarch himself, careless of his rank and safety, displayed, in the prosecution of the siege, the ardor of a youthful soldier. After an obstinate combat, the Barbarians were repulsed; they incessantly returned to the charge; they were again driven back with a dreadful slaughter, and two rebel legions of Gauls, who had been banished into the East, signalized their undisciplined courage by a nocturnal sally into the heart of the Persian camp. In one of the fiercest of these repeated assaults, Amida was betrayed by the treachery of a deserter, who indicated to the Barbarians a secret and neglected staircase, scooped out of the rock that hangs over the stream of

---

[57] The operations of the siege of Amida are very minutely described by Ammianus, (xix. 1—9,) who acted an honorable part in the defence, and escaped with difficulty when the city was stormed by the Persians.

[58] Of these four nations, the Albanians are too well known to require any description. The Segestans [*Sacastenè. St. Martin.*] inhabited a large and level country, which still preserves their name, to the south of Khorasan, and the west of Hindostan. (See Geographia Nubiensis, p. 133, and D'Herbelot, Bibliothèque Orientale, p. 797.) Notwithstanding the boasted victory of Bahram, (vol. i. p. 410,) the Segestans, above fourscore years afterwards, appear as an independent nation, the ally of Persia. We are ignorant of the situation of the Vertæ and Chionites, but I am inclined to place them (a least the latter) towards the confines of India and Scythia. See Ammian. xvi. 9.*

---

* Klaproth considers the real Albanians the same with the ancient Alani, and quotes a passage of the emperor Julian in support of his opinion. They are the Ossetæ, now inhabiting part of Caucasus. Tableaux Hist de l'Asie, p. 179, 180. — M.

The Vertæ are still unknown. It is possible that the Chionites are the same as the Huns. These people were already known; and we find from Armenian authors that they were making, at this period, incursions into Asia. They were often at war with the Persians. The name was perhaps pronounced differently in the East and in the West, and this prevents us from recognizing it. St. Martin, ii. 177. — M.

the Tigris. Seventy chosen archers of the royal guard ascended in silence to the third story of a lofty tower, which
commanded the precipice, they elevated on high the Persian
banner, the signal of confidence to the assailants, and of dismay to the besieged ; and if this devoted band could have
maintained their post a few minutes longer, the reduction of
the place might have been purchased by the sacrifice of their
lives After Sapor had tried, without success, the efficacy of
force and of stratagem, he had recourse to the slower bi
more certain operations of a regular siege, in the conduct of
which he was instructed by the skill of the Roman deserters.
The trenches were opened at a convenient distance, and the
troops destined for that service advanced under the portable
cover of strong hurdles, to fill up the ditch, and undermine
the foundations of the walls. ' Wooden towers were at the
same time constructed, and moved forwards on wheels, till the
soldiers, who were provided with every species of missile
weapons, could engage almost on level ground with the troops
who defended the rampart. Every mode of resistance which
art could suggest, or courage could execute, was employed in
the defence of Amida, and the works of Sapor were more
than once destroyed by the fire of the Romans. But the
resources of a besieged city may be exhausted. The Persians
repaired their losses, and pushed their approaches ; a large
breach was made by the battering-ram, and the strength of
the garrison, wasted by the sword and by disease, yielded to
the fury of the assault. The soldiers, the citizens, their wives,
their children, all who had not time to escape through the
opposite gate, were involved by the conquerors in a promiscuous massacre.

But the ruin of Amida was the safety of the Roman provinces. As soon as the first transports of victory had subsided,
Sapor was at leisure to reflect, that to chastise a disobedient
city, he had lost the flower of his troops, and the most favorable season for conquest.[59] Thirty thousand of his veterans

---

[59] Ammianus has marked the chronology of this year by three
signs, which do not perfectly coincide with each other, or with the
series of the history. i. The corn was ripe when Sapor invaded
Mesopotamia; " Cum jam stipulâ flavente turgerent ; " a circumstance,
which, in the latitude of Aleppo, would naturally refer us to the
month of April or May. See Harmer's Observations on Scripture,
vol. i. p. 41. Shaw's Travels, p. 335, edit. 4to. 2. The progress of
Sapor was checked by the overflowing of the Euphrates, which gen-

had fallen under the walls of Amida, during the continuance of a siege, which lasted seventy-three days; and the disappointed monarch returned to his capital with affected triumph and secret mortification. It is more than probable, that the inconstancy of his Barbarian allies was tempted to relinquish a war in which they had encountered such unexpected difficulties; and that the aged king of the Chionites, satiated with revenge, turned away with horror from a scene of action where he had been deprived of the hope of his family and nation. The strength as well as the spirit of the army with which Sapor took the field in the ensuing spring was no longer equal to the unbounded views of his ambition. Instead of aspiring to the conquest of the East, he was obliged to content himself with the reduction of two fortified cities of Mesopotamia, Singara and Bezabde; [60] the one situate in the midst of a sandy desert, the other in a small peninsula, surrounded almost on every side by the deep and rapid stream of the Tigris. Five Roman legions, of the diminutive size to which they had been reduced in the age of Constantine, were made prisoners, and sent into remote captivity on the extreme confines of Persia. After dismantling the walls of Singara, the conqueror abandoned that solitary and sequestered place; but he carefully restored the fortifications of Bezabde, and fixed in that important post a garrison or colony of veterans; amply supplied with every means of defence, and animated by high sentiments of honor and fidelity. Towards the close of the campaign, the arms of Sapor incurred some disgrace by an unsuccessful enterprise against Virtha, or Tecrit, a strong, or, as it was universally esteemed till the age of Tamerlane, an impregnable fortress of the independent Arabs. [61]

---

erally happens in July and August. Plin. Hist. Nat. v. 21. Viaggi di Pietro della Valle, tom. i. p. 696. 3. When Sapor had taken Amida, after a siege of seventy-three days, the autumn was far advanced. "Autumno præcipiti hædorumque improbo sidere exorto." To reconcile these apparent contradictions, we must allow for some delay in the Persian king, some inaccuracy in the historian, and some disorder in the seasons.

[60] The account of these sieges is given by Ammianus, xx. 6, 7.*

[61] For the identity of Virtha and Tecrit, see D'Anville, Geographie Ancienne, tom. ii. p. 201. For the siege of that castle by Timur Bec,

---

* The Christian bishop of Bezabde went to the camp of the king of Persia, to persuade him to check the waste of human blood. Amm. Marc xx. 7. — M.

The defence of the East against the arms of Sapor required and would have exercised, the abilities of the most consummate general ; and it seemed fortunate for the state, that it was the actual province of the brave Ursicinus, who alone deserved the confidence of the soldiers and people.   In the hour of danger, Ursicinus [62] was removed from his station by the intrigues of the eunuchs ; and the military command of the East was bestowed, by the same influence, on Sabinian a wealthy and subtle veteran, who had attained the infirmities, without acquiring the experience, of age.   By a second order, which issued from the same jealous and inconstant councils, Ursicinus was again despatched to the frontier of Mesopotamia, and condemned to sustain the labors of a war, the honors of which had been transferred to his unworthy rival. Sabinian fixed his indolent station under the walls of Edessa ; and while he amused himself with the idle parade of military exercise, and moved to the sound of flutes in the Pyrrhic dance, the public defence was abandoned to the boldness and diligence of the former general of the East.   But whenever Ursicinus recommended any vigorous plan of operations ; when he proposed, at the head of a light and active army, to wheel round the foot of the mountains, to intercept the convoys of the enemy, to harass the wide extent of the Persian lines, and to relieve the distress of Amida ; the timid and envious commander alleged, that he was restrained by his positive orders from endangering the safety of the troops. Amida was at length taken ; its bravest defenders, who had escaped the sword of the Barbarians, died in the Roman camp by the hand of the executioner ; and Ursicinus himself, after supporting the disgrace of a partial inquiry, was punished for the misconduct of Sabinian by the loss of his military rank. But Constantius soon experienced the truth of the prediction which honest indignation had extorted from his injured lieu-

---

or Tamerlane, see Cherefeddin, l. iii. c. 33.   The Persian biographer exaggerates the merit and difficulty of this exploit, which delivered the caravans of Bagdad from a formidable gang of robbers.*

[62] Ammianus (xviii. 5, 6, xix. 3, xx. 2) represents the merit and disgrace of Ursicinus with that faithful attention which a soldier owed to his general.   Some partiality may be suspected, yet the whole account is consistent and probable.

---

* St. Martin doubts whether it lay so much to the south.   "The word Birtha means in Syriac a castle or fortress, and might be applied to many places."   Note ii. p. 344.   M.

tenant, that as long as such maxims of government were suffered to prevail, the emperor himself would find it no easy task to defend his eastern dominions from the invasion of a foreign enemy. When he had subdued or pacified the Barbarians of the Danube, Constantius proceeded by slow marches into the East; and after he had wept over the smoking ruins of Amida, he formed, with a powerful army, the siege of Bezabde. The walls were shaken by the reiterated efforts of the most enormous of the battering-rams; the town was reduced to the last extremity; but it was still defended by the patient and intrepid valor of the garrison, till the approach of the rainy season obliged the emperor to raise the siege, and ingloriously to retreat into his winter quarters at Antioch.[63] The pride of Constantius, and the ingenuity of his courtiers, were at a loss to discover any materials for panegyric in the events of the Persian war; while the glory of his cousin Julian, to whose military command he had intrusted the provinces of Gaul, was proclaimed to the world in the simple and concise narrative of his exploits.

In the blind fury of civil discord, Constantius had abandoned to the Barbarians of Germany the countries of Gaul, which still acknowledged the authority of his rival. A numerous swarm of Franks and Alemanni were invited to cross the Rhine by presents and promises, by the hopes of spoil, and by a perpetual grant of all the territories which they should be able to subdue.[64] But the emperor, who for a temporary service had thus imprudently provoked the rapacious spirit of the Barbarians, soon discovered and lamented the difficulty of dismissing these formidable allies, after they had tasted the richness of the Roman soil. Regardless of the nice distinction of loyalty and rebellion, these undisciplined robbers treat-

---

[63] Ammian. xx. 11. Omisso vano incepto, hiematurus Antiochiæ redit in Syriam ærumnosam, perpessus et ulcerum sed et atrocia, diuque deflenda. It is *thus* that James Gronovius has restored an obscure passage; and he thinks that this correction alone would have deserved a new edition of his author; whose sense may now be darkly perceived. I expected some additional light from the recent labors of the learned Ernestus. (Lipsiæ, 1773.)*

[64] The ravages of the Germans, and the distress of Gaul may be collected from Julian himself. Orat. ad S. P. Q. Athen. p. 277. Ammian. xv. 11. Libanius, Orat. x. Zosimus, l. iii. p. 140. Sozomen, l. iii. c. 1 [Mamertin. Grat. Art. c. iv.]

---

* The late editor (Wagner) has nothing better to suggest, and laments with Gibbon, the silence of Ernesi. — M.

ed as their natural enemies all the subjects of the empire, who possessed any property which they were desirous of acquiring. Forty-five flourishing cities, Tongres, Cologne, Treves, Worms, Spires, Strasburgh, &c., besides a far greater number of towns and villages, were pillaged, and for the most part reduced to ashes. The Barbarians of Germany, still faithful to the maxims of their ancestors, abhorred the confinement of walls, to which they applied the odious names of prisons and sepulchres; and fixing their independent habitations on the banks of rivers, the Rhine, the Moselle, and the Meuse, they secured themselves against the danger of a surprise, by a rude and hasty fortification of large trees, which were felled and thrown across the roads. The Alemanni were established in the modern countries of Alsace and Lorraine; the Franks occupied the island of the Batavians, together with an extensive district of Brabant, which was then known by the appellation of Toxandria,[65] and may deserve to be considered as the original seat of their Gallic monarchy.[66] From the sources, to the mouth, of the Rhine, the conquests of the Germans extended above forty miles to the west of that river, over a country peopled by colonies of their own name and nation; and the scene of their devastations was three times more extensive than that of their conquests. At a still greater distance the open towns of Gaul were deserted, and the inhabitants of the fortified cities, who trusted to their strength and vigilance, were obliged to content themselves with such supplies of corn as they could raise on the vacant land within the enclosure of their walls. The diminished legions, destitute of pay and provisions, of arms and discipline, trembled at the approach, and even at the name, of the Barbarians.

---

[65] Ammianus, xvi. 8. This name seems to be derived from the Toxandri of Pliny, and very frequently occurs in the histories of the middle age. Toxandria was a country of woods and morasses, which extended from the neighborhood of Tongres to the conflux of the Vahal and the Rhine. See Valesius, Notit. Galliar. p. 558.

[66] The paradox of P. Daniel, that the Franks never obtained any permanent settlement on this side of the Rhine before the time of Clovis, is refuted with much learning and good sense by M. Biet, who has proved, by a chain of evidence, their uninterrupted possession of Toxandria, one hundred and thirty years before the accession of Clovis. The Dissertation of M. Biet was crowned by the Academy of Soissons, in the year 1736, and seems to have been justly preferred to the discourse of his more celebrated competitor, the Abbé le Bœuf, an antiquarian, whose name was happily expressive of his talents.

Under these melancholy circumstances, an unexperienced youth was appointed to save and to govern the provinces of Gaul, or rather, as he expresses it himself, to exhibit the vain image of Imperial greatness. The retired scholastic education of Julian, in which he had been more conversant with books than with arms, with the dead than with the living, left him in profound ignorance of the practical arts of war and government: and when he awkwardly repeated some military exercise which it was necessary for him to learn, he exclaimed with a sigh, " O Plato, Plato, what a task for a philosopher!" Yet even this speculative philosophy, which men of business are too apt to despise, had filled the mind of Julian with the noblest precepts and the most shining examples; had animated him with the love of virtue, the desire of fame, and the contempt of death. The habits of temperance recommended in the schools, are still more essential in the severe discipline of a camp. The simple wants of nature regulated the measure of his food and sleep. Rejecting with disdain the delicacies provided for his table, he satisfied his appetite with the coarse and common fare which was allotted to the meanest soldiers. During the rigor of a Gallic winter, he never suffered a fire in his bed-chamber; and after a short and interrupted slumber, he frequently rose in the middle of the night from a carpet spread on the floor, to despatch any urgent business, to visit his rounds, or to steal a few moments for the prosecution of his favorite studies.[67] The precepts of eloquence, which he had hitherto practised on fancied topics of declamation, were more usefully applied to excite or to assuage the passions of an armed multitude: and although Julian, from his early habits of conversation and literature, was more familiarly acquainted with the beauties of the Greek language, he had attained a competent knowledge of the Latin tongue.[68] Since Julian was not originally designed for the character of a legislator, or a judge, it is probable that the civil jurisprudence of the Romans had not engaged any consider-

[67] The private life of Julian in Gaul, and the severe discipline which he embraced, are displayed by Ammianus, (xvi. 5,) who professes to praise, and by Julian himself, who affects to ridicule, (Misopogon, p. 340,) a conduct, which, in a prince of the house of Constantine, might justly excite the surprise of mankind.

[68] Aderat Latine quoque disserenti sufficiens sermo. Ammianus, xvi. 5. But Julian, educated in the schools of Greece, always considered the language of the Romans as a foreign and popular dialect, which he might use on necessary occasions.

able share of his attention : but he derived from his philosophic studies an inflexible regard for justice, tempered by a disposition to clemency ; the knowledge of the general principles of equity and evidence, and the faculty of patiently investigating the most intricate and tedious questions which could be proposed for his discussion. The measures of policy, and the operations of war, must submit to the various accidents of circumstance and character, and the unpractised student will often be perplexed in the application of the most perfect theory. But in the acquisition of this important science, Julian was assisted by the active vigor of his own genius, as well as by the wisdom and experience of Sallust, an officer of rank, who soon conceived a sincere attachment for a prince so worthy of his friendship ; and whose incorruptible integrity was adorned by the talent of insinuating the harshest truths without wounding the delicacy of a royal ear.[69]

Immediately after Julian had received the purple at Milan, he was sent into Gaul with a feeble retinue of three hundred and sixty soldiers. At Vienna, where he passed a painful and anxious winter, in the hands of those ministers to whom Constantius had intrusted the direction of his conduct, the Cæsar was informed of the siege and deliverance of Autun. That large and ancient city, protected only by a ruined wall and pusillanimous garrison, was saved by the generous resolution of a few veterans, who resumed their arms for the defence of their country. In his march from Autun, through the heart of the Gallic provinces, Julian embraced with ardor the earliest opportunity of signalizing his courage. At the head of a small body of archers and heavy cavalry, he preferred the shorter but the more dangerous of two roads ; * and sometimes eluding, and sometimes resisting, the attacks of the

---

[69] We are ignorant of the actual office of this excellent minister, whom Julian afterwards created præfect of Gaul. Sallust was speedily recalled by the jealousy of the emperor; and we may still read a sensible but pedantic discourse, (p. 240—252,) in which Julian deplores the loss of so valuable a friend, to whom he acknowledges himself indebted for his reputation. See La Bleterie, Preface à la Vie de Jovien, p. 20.

---

* Aliis per Arbor — quibusdam per Sedelaucum et Coram iri debere firmantibus. Amm. Marc. xvi. 2. I do not know what place can be meant by the mutilated name Arbor. Sedelanus is Saulieu, a small town of the department of the Côte d'Or, six leagues from Autun. Cora answers to the village of Cure, on the river of the same name, between Autun and Nevers. St. Martin, ii. 162. — M.

Barbarians, who were masters of the field, he arrived with honor and safety at the camp near Rheims, where the Roman troops had been ordered to assemble. The aspect of their young prince revived the drooping spirit of the soldiers, and they marched from Rheims in search of the enemy, with a confidence which had almost proved fatal to them. The Alemanni, familiarized to the knowledge of the country, secretly collected their scattered forces, and seizing the opportunity of a dark and rainy day, poured with unexpected fury on the rear-guard of the Romans. Before the inevitable disorder could be remedied, two legions were destroyed; and Julian was taught by experience, that caution and vigilance are the most important lessons of the art of war. In a second and more successful action,* he recovered and established his military fame; but as the agility of the Barbarians saved them from the pursuit, his victory was neither bloody nor decisive. He advanced, however, to the banks of the Rhine, surveyed the ruins of Cologne, convinced himself of the difficulties of the war, and retreated on the approach of winter, discontented with the court, with his army, and with his own success.[70] The power of the enemy was yet unbroken; and the Cæsar had no sooner separated his troops, and fixed his own quarters at Sens, in the centre of Gaul, than he was surrounded and besieged by a numerous host of Germans. Reduced, in this extremity, to the resources of his own mind, he displayed a prudent intrepidity, which compensated for all the deficiencies of the place and garrison; and the Barbarians, at the end of thirty days, were obliged to retire with disappointed rage.

The conscious pride of Julian, who was indebted only to his sword for this signal deliverance, was imbittered by the reflection, that he was abandoned, betrayed, and perhaps devoted to destruction, by those who were bound to assist him by every tie of honor and fidelity. Marcellus, master-general of the cavalry in Gaul, interpreting too strictly the jealous orders of the court, beheld with supine indifference the distress of Julian, and had restrained the troops under his command from

---

[70] Ammianus (xvi. 2, 3) appears much better satisfied with the success of this first campaign than Julian himself; who very fairly owns that he did nothing of consequence, and that he fled before the enemy.

---

* At Brocomagus, Brumat, near Strasburgh. St. Martin, ii. 164. — M.

38 *

marching to the relief of Sens. If the Cæsar had dissembled in silence so dangerous an insult, his person and authority would have been exposed to the contempt of the world; and if an action so criminal had been suffered to pass with impunity, the emperor would have confirmed the suspicions, which received a very specious color from his past conduct towards the princes of the Flavian family. Marcellus was recalled, and gently dismissed from his office.[71] In his room Severus was appointed general of the cavalry; an experienced soldier, of approved courage and fidelity, who could advise with respect, and execute with zeal; and who submitted, without reluctance, to the supreme command which Julian, by the interest of his patroness Eusebia, at length obtained over the armies of Gaul.[72] A very judicious plan of operations was adopted for the approaching campaign. Julian himself, at the head of the remains of the veteran bands, and of some new levies which he had been permitted to form, boldly penetrated into the centre of the German cantonments, and carefully reëstablished the fortifications of Saverne, in an advantageous post, which would either check the incursions, or intercept the retreat, of the enemy. At the same time, Barbatio, general of the infantry, advanced from Milan with an army of thirty thousand men, and passing the mountains, prepared to throw a bridge over the Rhine, in the neighborhood of Basil. It was reasonable to expect that the Alemanni, pressed on either side by the Roman arms, would soon be forced to evacuate the provinces of Gaul, and to hasten to the defence of their native country. But the hopes of the campaign were defeated by the incapacity, or the envy, or the secret instructions, of Barbatio; who acted as if he had been the enemy of the Cæsar, and the secret ally of the Barbarians. The negligence with which he permitted a troop of pillagers freely to pass, and to return almost before the gates of his camp, may be imputed to his want of abilities; but the treasonable act of burning a number of boats, and a superfluous stock of provisions, which would have been of the most essential service to the army of Gaul,

---

[71] Ammian. xvi. 7. Libanius speaks rather more advantageously of the military talents of Marcellus, Orat. x. p. 272. And Julian insinuates, that he would not have been so easily recalled, unless he had given other reasons of offence to the court, p. 278.

[72] Severus, non discors, non arrogans, sed longa militiæ frugalitate compertus; et cum recta præeuntem secuturus, ut ductorem morigerus miles. Ammian. xvi. 11. Zosimus, l. iii. p. 140.

was an evidence of his hostile and criminal intentions. The Germans despised an enemy who appeared destitute either of power or of inclination to offend them ; and the ignominious retreat of Barbatio deprived Julian of the expected support ; and left him to extricate himself from a hazardous situation, where he could neither remain with safety, nor retire with honor.[73]

As soon as they were delivered from the fears of invasion, the Alemanni prepared to chastise the Roman youth, who presumed to dispute the possession of that country, which they claimed as their own by the right of conquest and of treaties They employed three days, and as many nights, in transporting over the Rhine their military powers. The fierce Chnodomar, shaking the ponderous javelin which he had victoriously wielded against the brother of Magnentius, led the van of the Barbarians, and moderated by his experience the martial ardor which his example inspired.[74] He was followed by six other kings, by ten princes of regal extraction, by a long train of high-spirited nobles, and by thirty-five thousand of the bravest warriors of the tribes of Germany. The confidence derived from the view of their own strength, was increased by the intelligence which they received from a deserter, that the Cæsar, with a feeble army of thirteen thousand men, occupied a post about one-and-twenty miles from their camp of Strasburgh. With this inadequate force, Julian resolved to seek and to encounter the Barbarian host ; and the chance of a general action was preferred to the tedious and uncertain operation of separately engaging the dispersed parties of the Alemanni. The Romans marched in close order, and in two columns ; the cavalry on the right, the infantry on the left ; and the day was so far spent when they appeared in sight of the enemy, that Julian was desirous of deferring the battle till the next morning, and of allowing his troops to

---

[73] On the design and failure of the coöperation between Julian and Barbatio, see Ammianus (xvi. 11) and Libanius, (Orat. x. p. 273.)*

[74] Ammianus (xvi. 12) describes with his inflated eloquence the figure and character of Chnodomar. Audax et fidens ingenti robore lacertorum, ubi ardor proelii sperabatur immanis, equo spumante sublimior, erectus in jaculum formidandæ vastitatis, armorumque nitore conspicuus : antea strenuus et miles, et utilis præter cæteros ductor . . . Decentium Cæsarem superavit æquo marte congressus.

* Barbatio seems to have allowed himself to be surprised and defeated
— M

recruit their exhausted strength by the necessary refreshments of sleep and food. Yielding, however, with some reluctance, to the clamors of the soldiers, and even to the opinion of his council, he exhorted them to justify by their valor the eager impatience, which, in case of a defeat, would be universally branded with the epithets of rashness and presumption. The trumpets sounded, the military shout was heard through the field, and the two armies rushed with equal fury to the charge. The Cæsar, who conducted in person his right wing, depended on the dexterity of his archers, and the weight of his cuirassiers. But his ranks were instantly broken by an irregular mixture of light horse and of light infantry, and he had the mortification of beholding the flight of six hundred of his mos renowned cuirassiers.[75] The fugitives were stopped and rallied by the presence and authority of Julian, who, careless of his own safety, threw himself before them, and urging every motive of shame and honor, led them back against the victorious enemy. The conflict between the two lines of infantry was obstinate and bloody. The Germans possessed the superiority of strength and stature, the Romans that of discipline and temper; and as the Barbarians, who served under the standard of the empire, united the respective advantages of both parties, their strenuous efforts, guided by a skilful leader at length determined the event of the day. The Romans lost four tribunes, and two hundred and forty-three soldiers, in this memorable battle of Strasburgh, so glorious to the Cæsar,[76] and so salutary to the afflicted provinces of Gaul. Six thousand of the Alemanni were slain in the field, without including those who were drowned in the Rhine, or transfixed with darts while they attempted to swim across the river.[77] Chnodomar

[75] After the battle, Julian ventured to revive the rigor of ancient discipline, by exposing these fugitives in female apparel to the derision of the whole camp. In the next campaign, these troops nobly retrieved their honor. Zosimus, l. iii. p. 142.

[76] Julian himself (ad S. P. Q. Athen. p. 279) speaks of the battle of Strasburgh with the modesty of conscious merit; ἐμαχεσάμην ουκ ἀκλεῶς, ἴσως καὶ εἰς ὑμᾶς αφίχετο ἡ τοιαύτη μάχη. Zosimus compares it with tne victory of Alexander over Darius; and yet we are at a loss to discover any of those strokes of military genius which fix the attention of ages on the conduct and success of a single day.

[77] Ammianus, xvi. 12. Libanius adds 2000 more to the number of the slain, (Orat. x. p. 274.) But these trifling differences disappear before the 60,000 Barbarians, whom Zosimus has sacrificed to the glory of his hero, (l. iii. p. 141.) We might attribute this extravagant number to the carelessness of transcribers, if this credulous or partial

himself was surrounded and taken prisoner, with three of his brave companions, who had devoted themselves to follow in life or death the fate of their chieftain. Julian received him with military pomp in the council of his officers; and expressing a generous pity for the fallen state, dissembled his inward contempt for the abject humiliation, of his captive. Instead of exhibiting the vanquished king of the Alemanni, as a grateful spectacle to the cities of Gaul, he respectfully laid at the feet of the emperor this splendid trophy of his victory. Chnodomar experienced an honorable treatment: but the impatient Barbarian could not long survive his defeat, his confinement, and his exile.[78]

After Julian had repulsed the Alemanni from the provinces of the Upper Rhine, he turned his arms against the Franks, who were seated nearer to the ocean, on the confines of Gaul and Germany; and who, from their numbers, and still more from their intrepid valor, had ever been esteemed the most formidable of the Barbarians.[79] Although they were strongly actuated by the allurements of rapine, they professed a disinterested love of war; which they considered as the supreme honor and felicity of human nature; and their minds and bodies were so completely hardened by perpetual action, that, according to the lively expression of an orator, the snows of winter were as pleasant to them as the flowers of spring. In the month of December, which followed the battle of Strasburgh, Julian attacked a body of six hundred Franks, who had thrown themselves into two castles on the Meuse.[80] In the midst of that severe season they sustained, with inflexible constancy, a siege of fifty-four days; till at length, exhausted by hunger, and satisfied that the vigilance of the enemy, in breaking the ice of the river, left them no hopes of escape, the Franks

---

historian had not swelled the army of 35,000 Alemanni to an innumerable multitude of Barbarians, πλῆθος ἄπειρον βαρβάρων. It is our own fault if this detection does not inspire us with proper distrust on similar occasions.

[78] Ammian. xvi. 12. Libanius, Orat. x. p. 276.

[79] Libanius (Orat. iii. p. 137) draws a very lively picture of the manners of the Franks.

[80] Ammianus, xvii. 2. Libanius, Orat. x. p. 278. The Greek orator, by misapprehending a passage of Julian, has been induced to represent the Franks as consisting of a thousand men; and as his head was always full of the Peloponnesian war, he compares them to the Lacedæmonians, who were besieged and taken in the Island of Sphacteria.

consented, for the first time, to dispense with the ancient law which commanded them to conquer or to die. The Cæsar immediately sent his captives to the court of Constantius, who, accepting them as a valuable present,[81] rejoiced in the opportunity of adding so many heroes to the choicest troops of his domestic guards. The obstinate resistance of this handful of Franks apprised Julian of the difficulties of the expedition which he meditated for the ensuing spring, against the whole body of the nation. His rapid diligence surprised and astonished the active Barbarians. Ordering his soldiers to provide themselves with biscuit for twenty days, he suddenly pitched his camp near Tongres, while the enemy still supposed him in his winter quarters of Paris, expecting the slow arrival of his convoys from Aquitain. Without allowing the Franks to unite or deliberate, he skilfully spread his legions from Cologne to the ocean; and by the terror, as well as by the success, of his arms, soon reduced the suppliant tribes to implore the clemency, and to obey the commands, of their conqueror. The Chamavians submissively retired to their former habitations beyond the Rhine; but the Salians were permitted to possess their new establishment of Toxandria, as the subjects and auxiliaries of the Roman empire.[82] The treaty was ratified by solemn oaths; and perpetual inspectors were appointed to reside among the Franks, with the authority of enforcing the strict observance of the conditions. An incident is related, inter-

---

[81] Julian. ad S. P. Q. Athen. p. 280. Libanius, Orat. x. p. 278. According to the expression of Libanius, the emperor δῶρα ὠνομάζε, which La Bleterie understands (Vie de Julien, p. 118) as an honest confession, and Valesius (ad Ammian. xvii. 2) as a mean evasion, of the truth. Dom Bouquet, (Historiens de France, tom. i. p. 733,) by substituting another word, ἐνόμισε, would suppress both the difficulty and the spirit of this passage.

[82] Ammian. xvii. 8. Zosimus, l. iii. p. 146—150, (his narrative is darkened by a mixture of fable,) and Julian. ad S. P. Q. Athen. p. 280. His expression, ὑπεδεξάμην μὲν μοῖραν τοῦ Σαλίων ἔθνους, Χαμαιβους δὲ ἐξήλασα. This difference of treatment confirms the opinion that the Salian Franks were permitted to retain the settlements in Toxandria.*

---

* A newly discovered fragment of Eunapius, whom Zosimus probably transcribed, illustrates this transaction. "Julian commanded the Romans to abstain from all hostile measures against the Salians, neither to waste or ravage *their own* country, for he called every country *their own* which was surrendered without resistance or toil on the part of the conquerors." Mai, Script. Vet. Nov. Collect. ii. 256, and Eunapius in Niebuhr, Byzant. Hist. p. 86. — M.

esting enough in itself, and by no means repugnant to the character of Julian, who ingeniously contrived both the plot and the catastrophe of the tragedy. When the Chamavians sued for peace, he required the son of their king, as the only hostage on whom he could rely. A mournful silence, interrupted by tears and groans, declared the sad perplexity of the Barbarians; and their aged chief lamented in pathetic language, that his private loss was now imbittered by a sense of the public calamity. While the Chamavians lay prostrate at the foot of his throne, the royal captive, whom they believed to have been slain, unexpectedly appeared before their eyes; and as soon as the tumult of joy was hushed into attention, the Cæsar addressed the assembly in the following terms: " Behold the son, the prince, whom you wept. You had lost him by your fault. God and the Romans have restored him to you. I shall still preserve and educate the youth, rather as a monument of my own virtue, than as a pledge of your sincerity. Should you presume to violate the faith which you have sworn, the arms of the republic will avenge the perfidy, not on the innocent, but on the guilty." The Barbarians withdrew from his presence, impressed with the warmest sentiments of gratitude and admiration.[83]

It was not enough for Julian to have delivered the provinces of Gaul from the Barbarians of Germany. He aspired to emulate the glory of the first and most illustrious of the emperors; after whose example, he composed his own commentaries of the Gallic war.[84] Cæsar has related, with conscious pride, the manner in which he *twice* passed the Rhine. Julian could boast, that before he assumed the title of Augustus he had carried the Roman eagles beyond that great river in *three* successful expeditions.[85] The consternation of the Germans,

[83] This interesting story, which Zosimus has abridged, is related by Eunapius, (in Excerpt. Legationum, p. 15, 16, 17,) with all the amplifications of Grecian rhetoric: but the silence of Libanius, of Ammianus, and of Julian himself, renders the truth of it extremely suspicious.

[84] Libanius, the friend of Julian, clearly insinuates (Orat. iv. p. 178) that his hero had composed the history of his Gallic campaigns. But Zosimus (l. iii. p. 140) seems to have derived his information only from the Orations (λόγοι) and the Epistles of Julian. The discourse which is addressed to the Athenians contains an accurate, though general, account of the war against the Germans.

[85] See Ammian. xvii. 1, 10, xviii. 2, and Zosim. l. iii. p. 144. Julian ad S. P. Q Athen. p. 280.

after the battle of Strasburgh, encouraged him to the first attempt; and the reluctance of the troops soon yielded to the persuasive eloquence of a leader, who shared the fatigues and dangers which he imposed on the meanest of the soldiers. The villages on either side of the Meyn, which were plentifully stored with corn and cattle, felt the ravages of an invading army. The principal houses, constructed with some imitation of Roman elegance, were consumed by the flames; and the Cæsar boldly advanced about ten miles, till his progress was stopped by a dark and impenetrable forest, undermined by subterraneous passages, which threatened with secret snares and ambush every step of the assailants. The ground was already covered with snow; and Julian, after repairing an ancient castle which had been erected by Trajan, granted a truce of ten months to the submissive Barbarians. At the expiration of the truce, Julian undertook a second expedition beyond the Rhine, to humble the pride of Surmar and Hortaire, two of the kings of the Alemanni, who had been present at the battle of Strasburg. They promised to restore all the Roman captives who yet remained alive; and as the Cæsar had pro cured an exact account from the cities and villages of Gaul, of the inhabitants whom they had lost, he detected every attempt to deceive him, with a degree of readiness and accu racy, which almost established the belief of his supernatural knowledge. His third expedition was still more splendid and important than the two former. The Germans had collected their military powers, and moved along the opposite banks of the river, with a design of destroying the bridge, and of pre venting the passage of the Romans. But this judicious plan of defence was disconcerted by a skilful diversion. Three hundred light-armed and active soldiers were detached in forty small boats, to fall down the stream in silence, and to land at some distance from the posts of the enemy. They executed their orders with so much boldness and celerity, that they had almost surprised the Barbarian chiefs, who returned in the fearless confidence of intoxication from one of their nocturnal festivals. Without repeating the uniform and disgusting tale of slaughter and devastation, it is sufficient to observe, that Julian dictated his own conditions of peace to six of the haughtiest kings of the Alemanni, three of whom were per mitted to view the severe discipline and martial pomp of a Roman camp. Followed by twenty thousand captives, whom he had rescued from the chains of the Barbarians, the Cæsar repassed the Rhine, after terminating a war, the success of which has been compared to the ancient glories of the Punic and Cimbric victories.

As soon as the valor and conduct of Julian had secured an interval of peace, he applied himself to a work more congenial to his humane and philosophic temper. The cities of Gaul, which had suffered from the inroads of the Barbarians, he diligently repaired; and seven important posts, between Mentz and the mouth of the Rhine, are particularly mentioned, as having been rebuilt and fortified by the order of Julian.[86] The vanquished Germans had submitted to the just but humiliating condition of preparing and conveying the necessary materials. The active zeal of Julian urged the prosecution of the work; and such was the spirit which he had diffused among the troops, that the auxiliaries themselves, waiving their exemption from any duties of fatigue, contended in the most servile labors with the diligence of the Roman soldiers. It was incumbent on the Cæsar to provide for the subsistence, as well as for the safety, of the inhabitants and of the garrisons. The desertion of the former, and the mutiny of the latter, must have been the fatal and inevitable consequences of famine. The tillage of the provinces of Gaul had been interrupted by the calamities of war; but the scanty harvests of the continent were supplied, by his paternal care, from the plenty of the adjacent island. Six hundred large barks, framed in the forest of the Ardennes, made several voyages to the coast of Britain; and returning from thence, laden with corn, sailed up the Rhine, and distributed their cargoes to the several towns and fortresses along the banks of the river.[87] The arms of Julian

---

[86] Ammian. xviii. 2. Libanius, Orat. x. p. 279, 280. Of these seven posts, four are at present towns of some consequence; Bingen, Andernach, Bonn, and Nuyss. The other three, Tricesimæ, Quadriburgium, and Castra Herculis, or Heraclea, no longer subsist; but there is room to believe, that on the ground of Quadriburgium the Dutch have constructed the fort of Schenk, a name so offensive to the fastidious delicacy of Boileau. See D'Anville, Notice de l'Ancienne Gaule, p. 183. Boileau, Epitre iv. and the notes.*

[87] We may credit Julian himself, (Orat. ad S. P. Q. Atheniensem, p. 280,) who gives a very particular account of the transaction. Zosimus adds two hundred vessels more, (l. iii. p. 145.) If we compute the 600 corn ships of Julian at only seventy tons each, they were capable

---

* Tricesimæ, Kellen, Mannert, quoted by Wagner. Heraclea, Erkelens in the district of Juliers. St. Martin, ii. 311. — M.

had restored a free and secure navigation, which Constantius had offered to purchase at the expense of his dignity, and of a tributary present of two thousand pounds of silver. The emperor parsimoniously refused to his soldiers the sums which he granted with a lavish and trembling hand to the Barbarians. The dexterity, as well as the firmness, of Julian was put to a severe trial, when he took the field with a discontented army, which had already served two campaigns, without receiving any regular pay or any extraordinary donative.[88]

A tender regard for the peace and happiness of his subjects was the ruling principle which directed, or seemed to direct, the administration of Julian.[89] He devoted the leisure of his winter quarters to the offices of civil government; and affected to assume, with more pleasure, the character of a magistrate than that of a general. Before he took the field, he devolved on the provincial governors most of the public and private causes which had been referred to his tribunal; but, on his return, he carefully revised their proceedings, mitigated the rigor of the law, and pronounced a second judgment on the judges themselves. Superior to the last temptation of virtuous minds, an indiscreet and intemperate zeal for justice, he restrained, with calmness and dignity, the warmth of an advocate, who prosecuted, for extortion, the president of the Narbonnese province. "Who will ever be found guilty," exclaimed the vehement Delphidius, "if it be enough to deny?" "And who," replied Julian, "will ever be innocent, if it be sufficient to affirm?" In the general administration of peace and war, the interest of the sovereign is commonly the same as that of his people; but Constantius would have thought himself deeply injured, if the virtues of Julian had defrauded him of any part of the tribute which he extorted from an oppressed and exhausted country. The prince who was invested with the ensigns of royalty, might sometimes presume to correct the rapacious insolence of his inferior agents, to expose their corrupt arts, and to introduce an equal and easier mode of collection. But the management of the finances was more safely intrusted to Florentius, Prætorian præfect of Gaul,

---

of exporting 120,000 quarters, (see Arbuthnot's Weights and Measures, p. 237;) and the country which could bear so large an exportation, must already have attained an improved state of agriculture.

[88] The troops once broke out into a mutiny, immediately before the second passage of the Rhine. Ammian. xvii. 9.

[89] Ammian. xvi. 5, xviii. 1 Mamertinus in Panegyr. Vet. xi. 4.

an effeminate tyrant, incapable of pity or remorse : and the haughty minister complained of the most decent and gentle opposition, while Julian himself was rather inclined to censure the weakness of his own behavior. The Cæsar had rejected with abhorrence, a mandate for the levy of an extraordinary tax ; a new superindiction, which the præfect had offered for his signature ; and the faithful picture of the public misery, by which he had been obliged to justify his refusal, offended the court of Constantius. We may enjoy the pleasure of reading the sentiments of Julian, as he expresses them with warmth and freedom in a letter to one of his most intimate friends. After stating his own conduct, he proceeds in the following terms : " Was it possible for the disciple of Plato and Aristotle to act otherwise than I have done ? Could I abandon the unhappy subjects intrusted to my care ? Was I not called upon to defend them from the repeated injuries of these unfeeling robbers ? A tribune who deserts his post is punished with death, and deprived of the honors of burial. With what justice could I pronounce *his* sentence, if, in the hour of danger, I myself neglected a duty far more sacred and far more important ? God has placed me in this elevated post ; his providence will guard and support me. Should I be condemned to suffer, I shall derive comfort from the testimony of a pure and upright conscience. Would to Heaven that I still possessed a counsellor like Sallust ! If they think proper to send me a successor, I shall submit without reluctance ; and had much rather improve the short opportunity of doing good, than enjoy a long and lasting impunity of evil." [90] The precarious and dependent situation of Julian displayed his virtues and concealed his defects. The young hero who supported, in Gaul, the throne of Constantius, was not permitted to reform the vices of the government ; but he had courage to alleviate or to pity the distress of the people. Unless he had been able to revive the martial spirit of the Romans, or to introduce the arts of industry and refinement among their savage enemies, he could not entertain any rational hopes of securing the public tranquillity, either by the peace or conquest of Germany. Yet the victories of Julian suspended, for

---

[90] Ammian. xvii. 3. Julian. Epistol. xv. edit. Spanheim. Such a conduct almost justifies the encomium of Mamertinus. Ita illi anni spatia divisa sunt, ut aut Barbaros domitet, aut civibus jura restituat ; perpetuum professus, aut contra hostem, aut contra vitia, certamen.

a short time, the inroads of the Barbarians, and delayed the ruin of the Western Empire.

His salutary influence restored the cities of Gaul, which had been so long exposed to the evils of civil discord, Barbarian war, and domestic tyranny; and the spirit of industry was revived with the hopes of enjoyment. Agriculture, manufactures, and commerce, again flourished under the protection of the laws; and the *curiæ*, or civil corporations, were again filled with useful and respectable members: the youth were no longer apprehensive of marriage; and married persons were no longer apprehensive of posterity: the public and private festivals were celebrated with customary pomp; and the frequent and secure intercourse of the provinces displayed the image of national prosperity.[91] A mind like that of Julian must have felt the general happiness of which he was the author; but he viewed, with peculiar satisfaction and complacency, the city of Paris; the seat of his winter residence, and the object even of his partial affection.[92] That splendid capital, which now embraces an ample territory on either side of the Seine, was originally confined to the small island in the midst of the river, from whence the inhabitants derived a supply of pure and salubrious water. The river bathed the foot of the walls; and the town was accessible only by two wooden bridges. A forest overspread the northern side of the Seine, but on the south, the ground, which now bears the name of the University, was insensibly covered with houses, and adorned with a palace and amphitheatre, baths, an aqueduct, and a field of Mars for the exercise of the Roman troops. The severity of the climate was tempered by the neighborhood of the ocean; and with some precautions, which experience had taught, the vine and fig-tree were successfully cultivated. But, in remarkable winters, the Seine was deeply frozen; and the huge pieces of ice that floated down the stream, might be compared, by an Asiatic, to the blocks of white marble which were extracted from the quarries of Phrygia. The licentiousness and corruption of Antioch recalled to the memory of

[91] Libanius, Orat. Parental. in Imp. Julian. c. 38, in Fabricius Bibliothec. Græc. tom. vii. p. 263, 264.

[92] See Julian. in Misopogon. p. 340, 341. The primitive state of Paris is illustrated by Henry Valesius, (ad Ammian. xx. 4,) his brother Hadrian Valesius, or de Valois, and M. D'Anville, (in their respective Notitias of ancient Gaul,) the Abbé de Longuerue, (Description de la France, tom. i. p. 12, 13,) and M. Bonamy, (in the Mém. de l'Academie des Inscriptions, tom. xv. p. 656—691.)

Julian the severe and simple manners of his beloved Lutetia;[93] where the amusements of the theatre were unknown or despised. He indignantly contrasted the effeminate Syrians with the brave and honest simplicity of the Gauls, and almost forgave the intemperance, which was the only stain of the Celtic character.[94] If Julian could now revisit the capital of France, he might converse with men of science and genius, capable of understanding and of instructing a disciple of the Greeks; he might excuse the lively and graceful follies of a nation, whose martial spirit has never been enervated by the indulgence of luxury; and he must applaud the perfection of that inestimable art, which softens and refines and embellishes the intercourse of social life.

---

[93] Τὴν φίλην Λευκετίαν. Julian. in Misopogon. p. 340. Leucetia, or Lutetia, was the ancient name of the city which, according to the fashion of the fourth century, assumed the territorial appellation of Parisii.

[94] Julian. in Misopogon. p. 859, 860.

CHAPTER XX.

THE public establishment of Christianity may be considered
as one of those important and domestic revolutions which
excite the most lively curiosity, and afford the most valuable
instruction. The victories and the civil policy of Constantine
no longer influence the state of Europe; but a considerable
portion of the globe still retains the impression which it received from the conversion of that monarch; and the ecclesiastical institutions of his reign are still connected, by an indissoluble chain, with the opinions, the passions, and the interests
of the present generation.

In the consideration of a subject which may be examined
with impartiality, but cannot be viewed with indifference, a
difficulty immediately arises of a very unexpected nature;
that of ascertaining the real and precise date of the conversion
of Constantine. The eloquent Lactantius, in the midst of his
court, seems impatient [1] to proclaim to the world the glorious
example of the sovereign of Gaul; who, in the first moments
of his reign, acknowledged and adored the majesty of the true
and only God.[2] The learned Eusebius has ascribed the faith

---

[1] The date of the Divine Institutions of Lactantius has been accurately discussed, difficulties have been started, solutions proposed, and
an expedient imagined of two *original* editions; the former published
during the persecution of Diocletian, the latter under that of Licinius. See Dufresnoy, Prefat. p. v. Tillemont, Mem. Ecclesiast. tom.
vi. p. 465—470. Lardner's Credibility, part ii. vol. vii. p. 78—86. For
my own part, I am *almost* convinced that Lactantius dedicated his
Institutions to the sovereign of Gaul, at a time when Galerius, Maximin, and even Licinius, persecuted the Christians; that is, between
the years 306 and 311.

[2] Lactant. Divin. Instit. i. 1, vii. 27. The first and most important
of these passages is indeed wanting in twenty-eight manuscripts; but
it is found in nineteen. If we weigh the comparative value of those
manuscripts, one of 900 years old, in the king of France's library, may
be alleged in its favor; but the passage is omitted in the correct man-

ot Constantine to the miraculous sign which was displayed in the heavens whilst he meditated and prepared the Italian expedition.[3] The historian Zosimus maliciously asserts, that the emperor had imbrued his hands in the blood of his eldest son, before he publicly renounced the gods of Rome and of his ancestors.[4] The perplexity prod.ced by these discordant authorities is derived from the behavior of Constantine himself. According to the strictness of ecclesiastical language, the first of the *Christian* emperors was unworthy of that name, till the moment of his death; since it was only during his last illness that he received, as a catechumen, the imposition of hands,[5] and was afterwards admitted, by the initiatory rites of baptism, into the number of the faithful.[6] The Christianity of Constantine must be allowed in a much more vague and qualified sense; and the nicest accuracy is required in tracing the slow and almost imperceptible gradations by which the monarch declared himself the protector, and at length the proselyte, of the church. It was an a' .uous task to eradicate the habits and prejudices of his education, to acknowledge the divine power of Christ, and to understand that the truth of *his* revelation was incompatible with the worship of the gods. The obstacles which he had probably experienced in his own mind, instructed him to proceed with caution in the momentous

uscript of Bologna, which the P. de Montfaucon ascribes to the sixth or seventh century (Diarium Italic. p. 409.) The taste of most of the editors (except Isæus; see Lactant. edit. Dufresnoy, tom. i. p. 596) has felt the genuine style of Lactantius.

[3] Euseb. in Vit. Constant. l. i. c. 27—32.

[4] Zosimus, l. ii. p. 104.

[5] That rite was *always* used in making a catechumen, (see Bingham's Antiquities, l. x. c. i. p. 419. Dom Chardon, Hist. des Sacramens, tom. i. p. 62,) and Constantine received it for the *first* time (Euseb. in Vit. Constant. l. iv. c. 61) immediately before his baptism and death From the connection of these two facts, Valesius (ad loc. Euseb.) ha drawn the conclusion which is reluctantly admitted by Tillemont (Hist. des Empereurs, tom. iv. p. 628,) and opposed with feeble arguments by Mosheim, (p. 968.)

[6] Euseb. in Vit. Constant. l. iv. c. 61, 62, 63. The legend of Constantine's baptism at Rome, thirteen years before his death, was invented in the eighth century, as a proper motive for his *donation*. Such has been the gradual progress of knowledge, that a story, of which Cardinal Baronius (Annal. Ecclesiast. A. D. 324, No. 43—49) declared himself the unblushing advocate, is now feebly supported, even within the verge of the Vatican. See the Antiquitates Christianæ, tom. ii. p. 232; a work published with six approbations at Rome, in the year 1751, by Father Mamachi, a learned Dominican.

change of a national religion; and he insensibly discovered his new opinions, as far as he could enforce them with safety and with effect. During the whole course of his reign, the stream of Christianity flowed with a gentle, though accelerated motion : but its general direction was sometimes checked, and sometimes diverted, by the accidental circumstances of the times, and by the prudence, or possibly by the caprice, of the monarch. His ministers were permitted to signify the intentions of their master in the various language which was best adapted to their respective principles;[7] and he artfully balanced the hopes and fears of his subjects, by publishing in the same year two edicts; the first of which enjoined the solemn observance of Sunday,[8] and the second directed the regular consultation of the Aruspices.[9] While this important revolution yet remained in suspense, the Christians and the Pagans watched the conduct of their sovereign with the same anxiety, but with very opposite sentiments. The former were prompted by every motive of zeal, as well as vanity, to exaggerate the marks of his favor, and the evidences of his faith. The latter, till their just apprehensions were changed into despair and resentment, attempted to conceal from the world, and from themselves, that the gods of Rome could no longer reckon the emperor in the number of their votaries. The same passions and prejudices have engaged the partial writers of the times to connect the public profession of Christianity with the most glorious or the most ignominious æra of the reign of Constantine.

Whatever symptoms of Christian piety might transpire in the discourses or actions of Constantine, he persevered till he was near forty years of age in the practice of the established religion;[10] and the same conduct which in the court of

---

[7] The quæstor, or secretary, who composed the law of the Theodosian Code, makes his master say with indifference, "hominibus supradictæ religionis," (l. xvi. tit. ii. leg 1.) The minister of ecclesiastical affairs was allowed a more devout and respectful style, τῆς ἐνθέσμου καί ἁγιωτάτης καθολικῆς θρησκείας; the legal, most holy, and Catholic worship. See Euseb. Hist. Eccles. l. x. c. 6.

[8] Cod. Theodos. l. ii. viii. tit. leg. 1. Cod. Justinian. l. iii. tit. xii. leg. 3. Constantine styles the Lord's day dies solis, a name which could not offend the ears of his pagan subjects.

[9] Cod. Theodos. l. xvi. tit. x. leg. 1. Godefroy, in the character of a commentator, endeavors (tom. vi. p. 257) to excuse Constantine; out the more zealous Baronius (Annal. Eccles. A. D. 321, No. 18) censures his profane conduct with truth and asperity.

[10] Theodoret (l. i. c. 18) seems to insinuate that Helena gave her

Nicomedia might be imputed to his fear, could be ascribed only to the inclination or policy of the sovereign of Gaul. His liberality restored and enriched the temples of the gods; the medals which issued from his Imperial mint are impressed with the figures and attributes of Jupiter and Apollo, of Mars and Hercules; and his filial piety increased the council of Olympus by the solemn apotheosis of his father Constantius.[11] But the devotion of Constantine was more peculiarly directed to the genius of the Sun, the Apollo of Greek and Roman mythology; and he was pleased to be represented with the symbols of the God of Light and Poetry. The unerring shafts of that deity, the brightness of his eyes, his laurel wreath, immortal beauty, and elegant accomplishments, seem to point him out as the patron of a young hero. The altars of Apollo were crowned with the votive offerings of Constantine; and the credulous multitude were taught to believe, that the emperor was permitted to behold with mortal eyes the visible majesty of their tutelar deity; and that, either walking or in a vision, he was blessed with the auspicious omens of a long and victorious reign. The Sun was universally celebrated as the invincible guide and protector of Constantine; and the Pagans might reasonably expect that the insulted god would pursue with unrelenting vengeance the impiety of his ungrateful favorite.[12]

As long as Constantine exercised a limited sovereignty over the provinces of Gaul, his Christian subjects were protected by the authority, and perhaps by the laws, of a prince, who wisely left to the gods the care of vindicating their own honor. If we may credit the assertion of Constantine himself, he had

---

son a Christian education; but we may be assured, from the superior authority of Eusebius, (in Vit. Constant. l. iii. c. 47,) that she herself was indebted to Constantine for the knowledge of Christianity.

[11] See the medals of Constantine in Ducange and Banduri. As few cities had retained the privilege of coining, almost all the medals of that age issued from the mint under the sanction of the Imperial authority.*

[12] The panegyric of Eumenius, (vii. inter Panegyr. Vet.,) which was pronounced a few months before the Italian war, abounds with the most unexceptionable evidence of the Pagan superstition of Constantine, and of his particular veneration for Apollo, or the Sun; to which Julian alludes, (Orat. vii. p. 228, ἀπολείπων σέ.) See Commentaire de Spanheim sur les Césars, p. 317.

---

* Eckhel. Doctrin. Num. vol. viii. — M.

been an indignant spectator of the savage cruelties which were inflicted, by the hands of Roman soldiers, on those citizens whose religion was their only crime.[13] In the East and in the West, he had seen the different effects of severity and indulgence ; and as the former was rendered still more odious by the example of Galerius, his implacable enemy, the latter was recommended to his imitation by the authority and advice of a dying father. The son of Constantius immediately suspended or repealed the edicts of persecution, and granted the free exercise of their religious ceremonies to all those who had already professed themselves members of the church. They were soon encouraged to depend on the favor as well as on the justice of their sovereign, who had imbibed a secret and sincere reverence for the name of Christ, and for the God of the Christians.[14]

About five months after the conquest of Italy, the emperor made a solemn and authentic declaration of his sentiments by the celebrated edict of Milan, which restored peace to the Catholic church. In the personal interview of the two western princes, Constantine, by the ascendant of genius and power, obtained the ready concurrence of his colleague, Licinius ; the union of their names and authority disarmed the fury of Maximin ; and after the death of the tyrant of the East, the edict of Milan was received as a general and fundamental law of the Roman world.[15]

The wisdom of the emperors provided for the restitution of all the civil and religious rights of which the Christians had been so unjustly deprived. It was enacted that the places of worship, and public lands, which had been confiscated, should be restored to the church, without dispute, without delay, and without expense ; and this severe injunction was accompanied with a gracious promise, that if any of the purchasers had paid a fair and adequate price, they should be indemnified

---

[13] Constantin. Orat. ad Sanctos, c. 25. But it might easily be shown, that the Greek translator has improved the sense of the Latin original; and the aged emperor might recollect the persecution of Diocletian with a more lively abhorrence than he had actually felt in the days of his youth and Paganism.

[14] See Euseb. Hist. Eccles. l. viii. 13, l. ix. 9, and in Vit. Const. l. i. c. 16, 17. Lactant. Divin. Institut. i. 1. Cæcilius de Mort. Persecut. c. 25.

[15] Cæcilius (de Mort. Persecut. c. 48) has preserved the Latin original ; and Eusebius (Hist. Eccles. l. x. c. 5) has given a Greek translation of this perpetual edict, which refers to some provisional regulations.

from the Imperial treasury. The salutary regulations which guard the future tranquillity of the faithful are framed on the principles of enlarged and equal toleration ; and such an equality must have been interpreted by a recent sect as an advantageous and honorable distinction. The two emperors proclaim to the world, that they have granted a free and absolute power to the Christians, and to all others, of following the religion which each individual thinks proper to prefer, to which he has addicted his mind, and which he may deem the best adapted to his own use. They carefully explain every ambiguous word, remove every exception, and exact from the governors of the provinces a strict obedience to the true and simple meaning of an edict, which was designed to establish and secure, without any limitation, the claims of religious liberty. They condescend to assign two weighty reasons which have induced them to allow this universal toleration : the humane intention of consulting the peace and happiness of their people ; and the pious hope, that, by such a conduct, they shall appease and propitiate *the Deity*, whose seat is in heaven. They gratefully acknowledge the many signal proofs which they have received of the divine favor ; and they trust .nat the same Providence will forever continue to protect the prosperity of the prince and people. From these vague and indefinite expressions of piety, three suppositions may be deduced, of a different, but not of an incompatible nature. The mind of Constantine might fluctuate between the Pagan ·and the Christian religions. According to the loose and complying notions of Polytheism, he might acknowledge the God of the Christians as *one* of the *many* deities who compose the hierarchy of heaven. Or perhaps he might embrace the philosophic and pleasing idea, that, notwithstanding the variety of names, of rites, and of opinions, all the sects, and all the nations of mankind, are united in the worship of the common Father and Creator of the universe.[16]

But the counsels of princes are more frequently influenced by views of temporal advantage, than by considerations of

---

[16] A panegyric of Constantine, pronounced seven or eight months after the edict of Milan, (see Gothofred. Chronolog. Legum, p. 7, and Tillemont, Hist. des Empereurs, tom. iv. p. 246,) uses the following remarkable expression : " Summe rerum sator, cujus tot nomina sunt, quot linguas gentium esse voluisti, quem enim te ipse dici velis, scire non possumus." (Panegyr. Vet. ix. 26.) In explaining Constantine's progress in the faith, Mosheim (p 971, &c.) is ingenious, subtle, prolix.

abstract and speculative truth. The partial and increasing favor of Constantine may naturally be referred to the esteem which he entertained for the moral character of the Christians; and to a persuasion, that the propagation of the gospel would inculcate the practice of private and public virtue. Whatever latitude an absolute monarch may assume in his own conduct, whatever indulgence he may claim for his own passions, it is undoubtedly his interest that all his subjects should respect the natural and civil obligations of society. But the operation of the wisest laws is imperfect and precarious. They seldom inspire virtue, they cannot always restrain vice. Their power is insufficient to prohibit all that they condemn, nor can they always punish the actions which they prohibit. The legislators of antiquity had summoned to their aid the powers of education and of opinion. But every principle which had once maintained the vigor and purity of Rome and Sparta, was long since extinguished in a declining and despotic empire. Philosophy still exercised her temperate sway over the human mind, but the cause of virtue derived very feeble support from the influence of the Pagan superstition. Under these discouraging circumstances, a prudent magistrate might observe with pleasure the progress of a religion which diffused among the people a pure, benevolent, and universal system of ethics, adapted to every duty and every condition of life; recommended as the will and reason of the supreme Deity, and enforced by the sanction of eternal rewards or punishments. The experience of Greek and Roman history could not inform the world how far the system of national manners might be reformed and improved by the precepts of a divine revelation; and. Constantine might listen with some confidence to the flattering, and indeed reasonable, assurances of Lactantius. The eloquent apologist seemed firmly to expect, and almost ventured to promise, *that* the establishment of Christianity would restore the innocence and felicity of the primitive age; *that* the worship of the true God would extinguish war and dissension among those who mutually considered themselves as the children of a common parent; *that* every impure desire, every angry or selfish passion, would be restrained by the knowledge of the gospel; and *that* the magistrates might sheath the sword of justice among a people who would be universally actuated by the sentiments of truth and piety, of equity and moderation, of harmony and universal love.[17]

---

[17] See the elegant description of Lactantius, (Divin. Institut. v. 8,)

The passive and unresisting obedience, which bows under the yoke of authority, or even of oppression, must have appeared, in the eyes of an absolute monarch, the most conspicuous and useful of the evangelic virtues.[18] The primitive Christians derived the institution of civil government, not from the consent of the people, but from the decrees of Heaven. The reigning emperor, though he had usurped the sceptre by treason and murder, immediately assumed the sacred character of vicegerent of the Deity. To the Deity alone he was accountable for the abuse of his power ; and his subjects were indissolubly bound, by their oath of fidelity, to a tyrant, who had violated every law of nature and society. The humble Christians were sent into the world as sheep among wolves ; and since they were not permitted to employ force, even in the defence of their religion, they should be still more criminal if they were tempted to shed the blood of their fellow-creatures, in disputing the vain privileges, or the sordid possessions, of this transitory life. Faithful to the doctrine of the apostle, who in the reign of Nero had preached the duty of unconditional submission, the Christians of the three first centuries preserved their conscience pure and innocent of the guilt of secret conspiracy, or open rebellion. While they experienced the rigor of persecution, they were never provoked either to meet their tyrants in the field, or indignantly to withdraw themselves into some remote and sequestered corner of the globe.[19] The Protestants of France, of Germany, and of Britain, who asserted with such intrepid courage their civil and religious freedom, have been insulted by the invidious comparison between the conduct of the primitive and of the reformed Christians.[20] Perhaps, instead of censure, some

---

who is much more perspicuous and positive than becomes a discreet prophet.

[18] The political system of the Christians is explained by Grotius, de Jure Belli et Pacis, l. i. c. 3, 4. Grotius was a republican and an exile, but the mildness of his temper inclined him to support the established powers.

[19] Tertullian. Apolog. c. 32, 34, 35, 36. Tamen nunquam Albiniani, nec Nigriani vel Cassiani inveniri potuerunt Christiani. Ad Scapulam, c. 2. If this assertion be strictly true, it excludes the Christians of that age from all civil and military employments, which would have compelled them to take an active part in the service of their respective governors. See Moyle's Works, vol. ii. p. 349.

[20] See the artful Bossuet, (Hist. des Variations des Eglises Protestantes, tom. ii. p. 210—258,) and the malicious Bayle, (tom. ii. p.

applause may be due to the superior sense and spirit of our ancestors, who had convinced themselves that religion cannot abolish the unalienable rights of human nature.[21] Perhaps the patience of the primitive church may be ascribed to its weakness, as well as to its virtue. A sect of unwarlike plebeians, without leaders, without arms, without fortifications, must have encountered inevitable destruction in a rash and fruitless resistance to the master of the Roman legions. But the Christians, when they deprecated the wrath of Diocletian, or solicited the favor of Constantine, could allege, with truth and confidence, that they held the principle of passive obedience, and that, in the space of three centuries, their conduct had always been conformable to their principles. They might add, that the throne of the emperors would be established on a fixed and permanent basis, if all their subjects, embracing the Christian doctrine, should learn to suffer and to obey.

In the general order of Providence, princes and tyrants are considered as the ministers of Heaven, appointed to rule or to chastise the nations of the earth. But sacred history affords many illustrious examples of the more immediate interposition of the Deity in the government of his chosen people. The sceptre and the sword were committed to the hands of Moses, of Joshua, of Gideon, of David, of the Maccabees ; the virtues of those heroes were the motive or the effect of the divine favor, the success of their arms was destined to achieve the deliverance or the triumph of the church. If the judges of Israel were occasional and temporary magistrates, the kings of Judah derived from the royal unction of their great ancestor an hereditary and indefeasible right, which could not be forfeited by their own vices, nor recalled by the caprice of their subjects. The same extraordinary providence, which was no longer confined to the Jewish people, might elect Constantine and his family as the protectors of the Christian world ; and the devout Lactantius announces, in a prophetic tone, the future glories of his long and universal reign.[22] Galerius and

---

620). I *name* Bayle, for he was certainly the author of the Avis aux Refugiés; consult the Dictionnaire Critique de Chauffepié, tom. i. part. ii. p. 145.

[21] Buchanan is the earliest, or at least the most celebrated, of the reformers, who has justified the theory of resistance. See his Dialogue de Jure Regni apud Scotos, tom. ii. p. 28, 30, edit. fol. Ruddiman.

[22] Lactant. Divin. Institut. i. 1. Eusebius, in the course of his

Maximin, Maxentius and Licinius, were the rivals who shared with the favorite of Heaven the provinces of the empire. The tragic deaths of Galerius and Maximin soon gratified the resentment, and fulfilled the sanguine expectations, of the Christians. The success of Constantine against Maxentius and Licinius removed the two formidable competitors who still opposed the triumph of the second David, and his cause might seem to claim the peculiar interposition of Providence. The character of the Roman tyrant disgraced the purple and human nature ; and though the Christians might enjoy his precarious favor, they were exposed, with the rest of his subjects, to the effects of his wanton and capricious cruelty. The conduct of Licinius soon betrayed the reluctance with which he had consented to the wise and humane regulations of the edict of Milan. The convocation of provincial synods was prohibited in his dominions; his Christian officers were ignominiously dismissed ; and if he avoided the guilt, or rather danger, of a general persecution, his partial oppressions were rendered still more odious by the violation of a solemn and voluntary engagement.[23] While the East, according to the lively expression of Eusebius, was involved in the shades of infernal darkness, the auspicious rays of celestial light warmed and illuminated the provinces of the West. The piety of Constantine was admitted as an unexceptionable proof of the justice of his arms ; and his use of victory confirmed the opinion of the Christians, that their hero was inspired, and conducted, by the Lord of Hosts. The conquest of Italy produced a general edict of toleration ; and as soon as the defeat of Licinius had invested Constantine with the sole dominion of the Roman world, he immediately, by circular letters, exhorted all his subjects to imitate, without delay, the example of their sovereign, and to embrace the divine truth of Christianity.[24]

The assurance that the elevation of Constantine was intimately connected with the designs of Providence, instilled into the minds of the Christians two opinions, which, by very

history, his life, and his oration, repeatedly inculcates the divine right of Constantine to the empire.

[23] Our imperfect knowledge of the persecution of Licinius is derived from Eusebius, (Hist. Eccles. l. x. c. 8. Vit. Constantin. l. i. c 49—56, l. ii. c. 1, 2.) Aurelius Victor mentions his cruelty in general terms.

[24] Euseb. in Vit. Constant. l. i. c. 24—42, 48—60.

different means, assisted the accomplishment of the prophecy Their warm and active loyalty exhausted in his favor every resource of human industry; and they confidently expected that their strenuous efforts would be seconded by some divine and miraculous aid. The enemies of Constantine have imputed to interested motives the alliance which he insensibly contracted with the Catholic church, and which apparently contributed to the success of his ambition. In the beginning of the fourth century, the Christians still bore a very inadequate proportion to the inhabitants of the empire; but among a degenerate people, who viewed the change of masters with the indifference of slaves, the spirit and union of a religious party might assist the popular leader, to whose service, from a principle of conscience, they had devoted their lives and fortunes.[25] The example of his father had instructed Constantine to esteem and to reward the merit of the Christians; and in the distribution of public offices, he had the advantage of strengthening his government, by the choice of ministers or generals, in whose fidelity he could repose a just and unreserved confidence. By the influence of these dignified missionaries, the proselytes of the new faith must have multiplied in the court and army; the Barbarians of Germany, who filled the ranks of the legions, were of a careless temper, which acquiesced without resistance in the religion of their commander; and when they passed the Alps, it may fairly be presumed, that a great number of the soldiers had already consecrated their swords to the service of Christ and of Constantine.[26] The habits of mankind and the interest of religion gradually abated the horror of war and bloodshed, which had so long prevailed among the Christians; and in the councils which were assembled under the gracious protection of Constantine, the authority of the bishops was seasonably employed

---

[25] In the beginning of the last century, the Papists of England were only a *thirtieth*, and the Protestants of France only a *fifteenth*, part of the respective nations, to whom their spirit and power were a constant object of apprehension. See the relations which Bentivoglio (who was then nuncio at Brussels, and afterwards cardinal) transmitted to the court of Rome, (Relazione, tom. ii. p. 211, 241,) Bentivoglio was curious, well informed, but somewhat partial.

[26] This careless temper of the Germans appears almost uniformly in the history of the conversion of each of the tribes. The legions of Constantine were recruited with Germans, (Zosimus, l. ii. p. 86;) and the court even of his father had been filled with Christians. See the first book of the Life of Constantine, by Eusebius.

to ratify the obligation of the military oath, and to inflict the penalty of excommunication on those soldiers who threw away their arms during the peace of the church.[27] While Cons.antine, in his own dominions, increased the number and zeal of his faithful adherents, he could depend on the support of a powerful faction in those provinces which were still possessed or usurped by his rivals. A secret disaffection was diffused among the Christian subjects of Maxentius and Licinius; and the resentment, which the latter did not attempt to conceal, served only to engage them still more deeply in the interest of his competitor. The regular correspondence which connected the bishops of the most distant provinces, enabled them freely to communicate their wishes and their designs and to transmit without danger any useful intelligence, or any pious contributions, which might promote the service of Constantine, who publicly declared that he had taken up arms for the deliverance of the church.[28]

The enthusiasm which inspired the troops, and perhaps the emperor himself, had sharpened their swords while it satisfied their conscience. They marched to battle with the full assurance, that the same God, who had formerly opened a passage to the Israelites through the waters of Jordan, and had thrown down the walls of Jericho at the sound of the trumpets of Joshua, would display his visible majesty and power in the victory of Constantine. The evidence of ecclesiastical history is prepared to affirm, that their expectations were justified by the conspicuous miracle to which the conversion of the first Christian emperor has been almost unanimously ascribed. The real or imaginary cause of so important an event, deserves and demands the attention of posterity; and I shall endeavor to form a just estimate of the famous vision of Constantine, by a distinct consideration of the *standard*, the *dream*,

---

[27] De his qui arma projiciunt in *pace*, placuit eos abstinere a communione. Concil. Arelat. Canon. iii. The best critics apply these words to the *peace of the church*.

[28] Eusebius always considers the second civil war against Licinius as a sort of religious crusade. At the invitation of the tyrant, some Christian officers had resumed their *zones;* or, in other words, had returned to the military service. Their conduct was afterwards censured by the twelfth canon of the Council of Nice; if this particular application may be received, instead of the loose and general sense of the Greek interpreters, Balsamon, Zonaras, and Alexis Aristenus. See Beveridge, Pandect. Eccles. Græc. tom. i. p. 72, tom. ii. p. 78, Annotation.

and the *celestial sign;* by separating the historical, the natural, and the marvellous parts of this extraordinary story which, in the composition of a specious argument, have been artfully confounded in one splendid and brittle mass.

I An instrument of the tortures which were inflicted only on slaves and strangers, became an object of horror in the eyes of a Roman citizen; and the ideas of guilt, of pain, and of ignominy, were closely united with the idea of the cross.[29] The piety, rather than the humanity, of Constantine soon abolished in his dominions the punishment which the Savior of mankind had condescended to suffer;[30] but the emperor had already learned to despise the prejudices of his education, and of his people, before he could erect in the midst of Rome his own statue, bearing a cross in its right hand; with an inscription, which referred the victory of its arms, and the deliverance of Rome, to the virtue of that salutary sign, the true symbol of force and courage.[31] The same symbol sanctified the arms of the soldiers of Constantine; the cross glittered on their helmet, was engraved on their shields, was interwoven into their banners; and the consecrated emblems which adorned the person of the emperor himself, were distinguished only by richer materials and more exquisite workmanship.[32] But the principal standard which displayed the

---

[29] Nomen ipsum *crucis* absit non modo a corpore civium Romanorum, sed etiam a cogitatione, oculis, auribus. Cicero pro Raberio, c. 5. The Christian writers, Justin, Minucius Felix, Tertullian, Jerom, and Maximus of Turin, have investigated with tolerable success the figure or likeness of a cross in almost every object of nature or art; in the intersection of the meridian and equator, the human face, a bird flying, a man swimming, a mast and yard, a plough, a *standard*, &c., &c., &c. See Lipsius de Cruce, l. i. c. 9.

[30] See Aurelius Victor, who considers this law as one of the examples of Constantine's piety. An edict so honorable to Christianity deserved a place in the Theodosian Code, instead of the indirect mention of it, which seems to result from the comparison of the fifth and eighteenth titles of the ninth book.

[31] Eusebius, in Vit. Constantin. l. i. c. 40. This statue, or at least the cross and inscription, may be ascribed with more probability to the second, or even third, visit of Constantine to Rome. Immediately after the defeat of Maxentius, the minds of the senate and people were scarcely ripe for this public monument.

[32] Agnoscas, regina, libens mea signa necesse est;
In quibus effigies *crucis* aut gemmata refulget
Aut longis solido ex auro præfertur in hastis.
Hoc signo invictus, transmissis Alpibus Ultor

triumph of the cross was styled the *Labarum*,[33] an obscure, though celebrated, name, which has been vainly derived from almost all the languages of the world. It is described [34] as a long pike intersected by a transversal beam. The silken veil, which hung down from the beam, was curiously inwrought with the images of the reigning monarch and his children. The summit of the pike supported a crown of gold which enclosed the mysterious monogram, at once expressive of the figure of the cross, and the initial letters, of the name of Christ.[35] The safety of the labarum was intrusted to fifty guards, of approved valor and fidelity; their station was marked by honors and emoluments; and some fortunate accidents soon introduced an opinion, that as long as the guards of the labarum were engaged in the execution of their office hey were secure and invulnerable amidst the darts of the enemy. In the second civil war, Licinius felt and dreaded the power of this consecrated banner, the sight of which, in the distress of battle, animated the soldiers of Constantine with an invincible enthusiasm, and scattered terror and dismay through the ranks of the adverse legions.[36] The Christian emperors,

---

Servitium solvit miserabile Constantius.
* * * * *

Christus *purpureum* gemmanti textus in auro
Signabat *Labarum*, clypeorum insignia Christus
Scripserat; ardebat summis *crux* addita cristis.
Prudent. in Symmachum, l. ii. 464, 486.

[33] The derivation and meaning of the word *Labarum* or *Laborum*, which is employed by Gregory Nazianzen, Ambrose, Prudentius, &c., still remain totally unknown, in spite of the efforts of the critics, who have ineffectually tortured the Latin, Greek, Spanish, Celtic, Teutonic, Illyric, Armenian, &c., in search of an etymology. See Ducange, in Gloss. Med. et infim. Latinitat. sub voce *Labarum*, and Godefroy, ad Cod. Theodos. tom. ii. p. 143.

[34] Euseb. in Vit. Constantin. l. i. c. 30, 31. Baronius (Annal. Eccles. A. D. 312, No. 26) has engraved a representation of the Labarum.

[35] Transversâ X literâ, summo capite circumflexo, Christum in scutis notat. Cæcilius dé M. P. c. 44, Cuper, (ad M. P. in edit. Lactant. tom. ii. p. 500,) and Baronius (A. D. 312, No. 25) have engraved from ancient monuments several specimens (as thus of these monograms) which became extremely fashionable in the Christian world.

[36] Euseb. in Vit. Constantin. l. ii. c. 7, 8, 9. He introduces the Labarum before the Italian expédition; but his narrative seems to indicate that it was never shown at the head of an army, till Constantine, above ten years afterwards, declared himself the enemy of Licinius, and the deliverer of the church.

who respected the example of Constantine, displayed in all
their military expeditions the standard of the cross; but when
the degenerate successors of Theodosius had ceased to appear
in person at the head of their armies, the labarum was deposited as a venerable but useless relic in the palace of Constan
tinople.[37] Its honors are still preserved on the medals of the
Flavian family. Their grateful devotion has placed the monogram of Christ in the midst of the ensigns of Rome. The
solemn epithets of, safety of the republic, glory of the army,
restoration of public happiness, are equally applied to the
religious and military trophies; and there is still extant a
medal of the emperor Constantius, where the standard of the
labarum is accompanied with these memorable words, BY
THIS SIGN THOU SHALT CONQUER.[38]

II. In all occasions of danger and distress, it was the practice of the primitive Christians to fortify their minds and
bodies by the sign of the cross, which they used, in all their
ecclesiastical rites, in all the daily occurrences of life, as an
infallible preservative against every species of spiritual or
temporal evil.[39] The authority of the church might alone
have had sufficient weight to justify the devotion of Constantine, who in the same prudent and gradual progress acknowledged the truth, and assumed the symbol, of Christianity.
But the testimony of a contemporary writer, who in a formal
treatise has avenged the cause of religion, bestows on the
piety of the emperor a more awful and sublime character.
He affirms, with the most perfect confidence, that in the night
which preceded the last battle against Maxentius, Constantine
was admonished in a dream * to inscribe the shields of his

---

[37] See Cod. Theod. l. vi. tit. xxv. Sozomen, l. i. c. 2. Theophan.
Chronograph. p. 11. Theophanes lived towards the end of the eighth
century, almost five hundred years after Constantine. The modern
Greeks were not inclined to display in the field the standard of the
empire and of Christianity; and though they depended on every
superstitious hope of *defence*, the promise of *victory* would have
appeared too bold a fiction.

[38] The Abbé du Voisin, p. 103, &c., alleges several of these medals,
and quotes a particular dissertation of a Jesuit, the Père de Grain-
ville, on this subject.

[39] Tertullian de Corona, c. 3. Athanasius, tom. i. p. 101. The
learned Jesuit Petavius (Dogmata Theolog. l. xv. c. 9, 10) has collected many similar passages on the virtues of the cross, which in
the last age embarrassed our Protestant disputants.

---

* Manso has observed, that Gibbon ought not to have separated the
vision of Constantine from the wonderful apparition in the sky, as the two

soldiers with the *celestial sign of God*, the sacred monogram of the name of Christ; that he executed the commands of Heaven, and that his valor and obedience were rewarded by the decisive victory of the Milvian Bridge. Some considerations might perhaps incline a sceptical mind to suspect the judgment or the veracity of the rhetorician, whose pen, either from zeal or interest, was devoted to the cause of the prevailing faction.[40] He appears to have published his deaths of the persecutors at Nicomedia about three years after the Roman victory; but the interval of a thousand miles, and a thousand days, will allow an ample latitude for the invention of declaimers, the credulity of party, and the tacit approbation of the emperor himself; who might listen without indignation to a marvellous tale, which exalted his fame, and promoted his designs. In favor of Licinius, who still dissembled his animosity to the Christians, the same author has provided a similar vision, of a form of prayer, which was communicated by an angel, and repeated by the whole army before they engaged the legions of the tyrant Maximin. The frequent repetition of miracles serves to provoke, where it does not subdue, the reason of mankind; [41] but if the dream of Constantine is separately considered, it may be naturally explained either by the policy or the enthusiasm of the emperor Whilst his anxiety for the approaching day, which must decide the

---

[40] Cæcilius de M. P. c. 44. It is certain, that this historical declamation was composed and published while Licinius, sovereign of the East, still preserved the friendship of Constantine and of the Christians. Every reader of taste must perceive that the style is of a very different and inferior character to that of Lactantius; and such indeed is the judgment of Le Clerc and Lardner, (Bibliothèque Ancienne et Moderne, tom. iii. p. 438. Credibility of the Gospel, &c., part ii. vol. vii. p. 94.) Three arguments from the title of the book, and from the names of Donatus and Cæcilius, are produced by the advocates for Lactantius. (See the P. Lestocq, tom. ii. p. 46—60.) Each of these proofs is singly weak and defective; but their concurrence has great weight. I have often fluctuated, and shall *tamely* follow the Colbert MS. in calling the author (whoever he was) Cæcilius.

[41] Cæcilius de M. P. c. 46. There seems to be some reason in the observation of M. de Voltaire, (Œuvres, tom. xiv. p. 307,) who ascribes to the success of Constantine the superior fame of his Labarum above the angel of Licinius. Yet even this angel is favorably entertained by Pagi, Tillemont, Fleury, &c., who are fond of increasing their stock of miracles.

---

wonders are closely connected in Eusebius. Mans Leben Constantins, p 82.—M.

fate of the empire, was suspended by a short and interrupted slumber, the venerable form of Christ, and the well-known symbol of his religion, might forcibly offer themselves to the active fancy of a prince who reverenced the name, and had perhaps secretly implored the power, of the God of the Christians. As readily might a consummate statesman indulge himself in the use of one of those military stratagems, one of those pious frauds, which Philip and Sertorius had employed with such art and effect.[42] The præternatural origin of dreams was universally admitted by the nations of antiquity and a considerable part of the Gallic army was already prepared to place their confidence in the salutary sign of the Christian religion. The secret vision of Constantine could be disproved only by the event; and the intrepid hero who had passed the Alps and the Apennine, might view with careless despair the consequences of a defeat under the walls of Rome. The senate and people, exulting in their own deliverance from an odious tyrant, acknowledged that the victory of Constantine surpassed the powers of man, without daring to insinuate that it had been obtained by the protection of the *Gods*. The triumphal arch, which was erected about three years after the event, proclaims, in ambiguous language, that by the greatness of his own mind, and by an *instinct* or impulse of the Divinity, he had saved and avenged the Roman republic.[43] The Pagan orator, who had seized an earlier opportunity of celebrating the virtues of the conqueror, supposes that he alone enjoyed a secret and intimate commerce with the Supreme Being, who delegated the care of mortals to his subordinate deities; and thus assigns a very plausible reason why the subjects of Constantine should not presume to embrace the new religion of their sovereign.[44]

---

[42] Besides these well-known examples, Tollius (Preface to Boileau's translation of Longinus) has discovered a vision of Antigonus, who assured his troops that he had seen a pentagon (the symbol of safety) with these words, "In this conquer." But Tollius has most inexcusably omitted to produce his authority, and his own character, literary as well as moral, is not free from reproach. (See Chauffepié, Dictionnaire Critique, tom. iv. p. 460.) Without insisting on the silence of Diodorus, Plutarch, Justin, &c., it may be observed that Polyænus, who in a separate chapter (l. iv. c. 6) has collected nineteen military stratagems of Antigonus, is totally ignorant of this remarkable vision.

[43] Instinctu Divinitatis, mentis magnitudine. The inscription on the triumphal arch of Constantine, which has been copied by Baronius, Gruter, &c., may still be perused by every curious traveller.

[44] Habes profecto aliquid cum illa mente Divinâ secretum; quæ

III. The philosopher, who with calm suspicion examines the dreams and omens, the miracles and prodigies, of profane or even of ecclesiastical history, will probably conclude, that if the eyes of the spectators have sometimes been deceived by fraud, the understanding of the readers has much more frequently been insulted by fiction. Every event, or appearance, or accident, wh:ch seems to deviate from the ordinary course of nature, has been rashly ascribed to the immediate action of the Deity; and the astonished fancy of the multitude has sometimes given shape and color, language and motion, to the fleeting but uncommon meteors of the air.[45] Nazarius and Eusebius are the two most celebrated orators, who, in studied panegyrics, have labored to exalt the glory of Constantine. Nine years after the Roman victory, Nazarius [46] describes an army of divine warriors, who seemed to fall from the sky : he marks their beauty, their spirit, their gigantic forms, the stream of light which beamed from their celestial armor, their patience in suffering themselves to be heard, as well as seen, by mortals; and their declaration that they were sent, that they flew, to the assistance of the great Constantine. For the truth of this prodigy, the Pagan orator appeals to the whole Gallic nation, in whose presence he was then speaking ; and seems to hope that the ancient apparitions [47] would now obtain credit from this recent and public event. The Chris-

---

delegatâ nostrâ Diis Minoribus curâ uni se tibi dignatur ostendere. Panegyr. Vet. ix. 2.

[45] M. Freret (Memoires de l'Academie des Inscriptions, tom. iv. p. 411—437) explains, by physical causes, many of the prodigies of antiquity; and Fabricius, who is abused by both parties, vainly tries to introduce the celestial cross of Constantine among the solar halos. Bibliothec. Græc. tom. iv. p. 8—29.*

[46] Nazarius inter Panegyr. Vet. x. 14, 15. It is unnecessary to name the moderns, whose undistinguishing and ravenous appetite has swallowed even the Pagan bait of Nazarius.

[47] The apparitions of Castor and Pollux, particularly to announce the Macedonian victory, are attested by historians and public monuments. See Cicero de Natura Deorum, ii. 2, iii. 5, 6. Florus, ii. 12. Valerius Maximus, l. i. c. 8, No. 1. Yet the most recent of these miracles is omitted, and indirectly denied, by Livy, (xlv. i.)

---

* The great difficulty in resolving it into a natural phenomenon, arises from the inscription ; even the most heated or awe-struck imagination would hardly discover distinct and legible letters in a solar halo. But the inscription may have been a later embellishment, or an interpretation of the meaning, which the sign was construed to convey. Compare Heinichen, Excursus in locum Eusebii, and the authors quoted. — M

tian fable of Eusebius, which, in the space of twenty-six years, might arise from the original dream, is cast in a much more correct and elegant mould. In one of the marches of Constantine, he is reported to have seen with his own eyes the luminous trophy of the cross, placed above the meridian sun, and inscribed with the following words: BY THIS CONQUER. This amazing object in the sky astonished the whole army, as well as the emperor himself, who was yet undetermined in the choice of a religion: but his astonishment was converted into faith by the vision of the ensuing night. Christ appeared before his eyes; and displaying the same celestial sign of the cross, he directed Constantine to frame a similar standard, and to march, with an assurance of victory, against Maxentius and all his enemies.[48] The learned bishop of Cæsarea appears to be sensible, that the recent discovery of this marvellous anec- dote would excite some surprise and distrust among the most pious of his readers.   Yet, instead of ascertaining the precise circumstances of time and place, which always serve to detect falsehood or establish truth; [49] instead of collecting and recording the evidence of so many living witnesses, who must have been spectators of this stupendous miracle; [50] Eu- sebius contents himself with alleging a very singular testi- mony; that of the deceased Constantine, who, many years after the event, in the freedom of conversation, had related to him this extraordinary incident of his own life, and had attest- ed the truth of it by a solemn oath. The prudence and grat- itude of the learned prelate forbade him to suspect the veracity of his victorious master; but he plainly intimates, that in a fact of such a nature, he should have refused his assent to any meaner authority. This motive of credibility could not survive the power of the Flavian family; and the celestial sign, which the Infidels might afterwards deride,[51] was disre- garded by the Christians of the age which immediately

---

[48] Eusebius, l. i. c. 28, 29, 30. The silence of the same Eusebius, in his Ecclesiastical History, is deeply felt by those advocates for the miracle who are not absolutely callous.

[49] The narrative of Constantine seems to indicate, that he saw the cross in the sky before he passed the Alps against Maxentius. The scene has been fixed by provincial vanity at Treves, Besançon, &c. See Tillemont, Hist. des Empereurs, tom. iv. p. 573.

[50] The pious Tillemont (Mem. Eccles. tom. vii. p. 1317) rejects with a sigh the useful Acts of Artemius, a veteran and a martyr, who attests as an eye-witness the vision of Constantine.

[51] Gelasius Cyzic. in Act. Concil. Nicen. l. i. c 4.

followed the conversion of Constantine.[52] But the Catholic church, both of the East and of the West, has adopted a prodigy, which favors, or seems to favor, the popular worship of the cross. The vision of Constantine maintained an honorable place in the legend of superstition, till the bold and sagacious spirit of criticism presumed to depreciate the triumph, and to arraign the truth, of the first Christian emperor.[53]

The Protestant and philosophic readers of the present age will incline to believe, that in the account of his own conversion, Constantine attested a wilful falsehood by a solemn and deliberate perjury. They may not hesitate to pronounce, that in the choice of a religion, his mind was determined only by a sense of interest; and that (according to the expression of a profane poet[54]) he used the altars of the church as a con-

---

[52] The advocates for the vision are unable to produce a single testimony from the Fathers of the fourth and fifth centuries, who, in their voluminous writings, repeatedly celebrate the triumph of the church and of Constantine. As these venerable men had not any dislike to a miracle, we may suspect, (and the suspicion is confirmed by the ignorance of Jerom,) that they were all unacquainted with the life of Constantine by Eusebius. This tract was recovered by the diligence of those who translated or continued his Ecclesiastical History, and who have represented in various colors the vision of the cross.

[53] Godefroy was the first, who, in the year 1643, (Not. ad Philostorgium, l. i. c. 6, p. 16,) expressed any doubt of a miracle which had been supported with equal zeal by Cardinal Baronius, and the Centuriators of Magdeburgh. Since that time, many of the Protestant critics have inclined towards doubt and disbelief. The objections are urged, with great force, by M. Chauffepié, (Dictionnaire Critique, tom. iv. p. 6—11;) and, in the year 1774, a doctor of Sorbonne, the Abbé du Voisin, published an apology, which deserves the praise of learning and moderation.*

[54]   Lors Constantin dit ces propres paroles :
       J'ai renversé le culte des idoles :
       Sur les debris de leurs temples fumans
       Au Dieu du Ciel j'ai prodigué l'encens.
       Mais tous mes soins pour sa grandeur supreme
       N'eurent jamais d'autre objêt que moi-même ;
       Les saints autels n'etoient à mes regards
       Qu'un marchepié du trône des Césars.
       L'ambition, la fureur, les delices
       Etoient mes Dieux, avoient mes sacrifices.
       L'or des Chrêtiens, leur intrigues, leur sang
       Ont cimenté ma fortune et mon rang.

The poem which contains these lines may be read with pleasure, but cannot be named with decency.

---

* The first Excursus of Heinichen (in Vitam Constantini, p. 507) contains a full summary of the opinions and arguments of the later writers

venient footstool to the throne of the empire. A conclusion so harsh and so absolute, is not, however, warranted by our knowledge of human nature, of Constantine, or of Christianity. In an age of religious fervor, the most artful statesmen are observed to feel some part of the enthusiasm which they inspire; and the most orthodox saints assume the dangerous privilege of defending the cause of truth by the arms of deceit and false-hood. Personal interest is often the standard of our belief, as well as of our practice; and the same motives of temporal advantage which might influence the public conduct and pro-fessions of Constantine, would insensibly dispose his mind to embrace a religion so propitious to his fame and fortunes. His vanity was gratified by the flattering assurance, that he had been chosen by Heaven to reign over the earth; success had justified his divine title to the throne, and that title was founded on the truth of the Christian revelation. As real virtue is sometimes excited by undeserved applause, the spe-cious piety of Constantine, if at first it was only specious, might gradually, by the influence of praise, of habit, and of example, be matured into serious faith and fervent devotion. The bishops and teachers of the new sect, whose dress and man-ners had not qualified them for the residence of a court, were admitted to the Imperial table; they accompanied the monarch in his expeditions; and the ascendant which one of them, an Egyptian or a Spaniard,[55] acquired over his mind, was im-puted by the Pagans to the effect of magic.[56] Lactantius, who has adorned the precepts of the gospel with the eloquence of Cicero,[57] and Eusebius, who has consecrated the learning and

---

[55] This favorite was probably the great Osius, bishop of Cordova who preferred the pastoral care of the whole church to the govern-ment of a particular diocese. His character is magnificently, though concisely, expressed by Athanasius, (tom. i. p. 703.) See Tillemont, Mém. Eccles. tom. vii. p. 524–561. Osius was accused, perhaps unjustly, of retiring from court with a very ample fortune.

[56] See Eusebius (in Vit. Constant. passim) and Zosimus, l. ii. p 104.

[57] The Christianity of Lactantius was of a moral rather than of a mysterious cast. " Erat pæne rudis (says the orthodox Bull) disci-plinæ Christianæ, et in rhetoricà melius quam in theologià versatus." Defensio Fidei Nicenæ, sect. ii. c. 14.

---

who have discussed this interminable subject. As to his conversion, where interest and inclination, state policy, and, if not a sincere conviction of its truth, at least a respect, an esteem, an awe of Christianity, thus coincided, Constantine himself would probably have been unable to trace the actual history of the workings of his own mind, or to assign its real influence to ea h concurrent motive. — M.

philosophy of the Greeks to the service of religion,[58] were both received into the friendship and familiarity of their sovereign; and those able masters of controversy could patiently watch the soft and yielding moments of persuasion, and dexterously apply the arguments which were the best adapted to his character and understanding. Whatever advantages might be derived from the acquisition of an Imperial proselyte, he was distinguished by the splendor of his purple, rather than by the superiority of wisdom, or virtue, from the many thousands of his subjects who had embraced the doctrines of Christianity. Nor can it be deemed incredible, that the mind of an unlettered soldier should have yielded to the weight of evidence, which, in a more enlightened age, has satisfied or subdued the reason of a Grotius, a Pascal, or a Locke. In the midst of the incessant labors of his great office, this soldier employed, or affected to employ, the hours of the night in the diligent study of the Scriptures, and the composition of theological discourses; which he afterwards pronounced in the presence of a numerous and applauding audience. In a very long discourse, which is still extant, the royal preacher expatiates on the various proofs of religion; but he dwells with peculiar complacency on the Sibylline verses,[59] and the fourth eclogue of Virgil.[60] Forty years before the birth of Christ, the Mantuan bard, as if inspired by the celestial muse of Isaiah, had celebrated, with all the pomp of oriental metaphor, the return of the Virgin, the fall of the serpent, the approaching birth of a godlike child, the offspring of the great Jupiter, who should expiate the guilt of human kind, and govern the peaceful universe with the virtues of his father; the rise and appearance of a heavenly race, a primitive nation throughout the world; and the gradual restoration of the innocence and felicity of the golden age. The poet was perhaps unconscious of the secret sense and object of these sublime predictions, which have been so unworthily

---

[58] Fabricius, with his usual diligence, has collected a list of between three and four hundred authors quoted in the Evangelical Preparation of Eusebius. See Bibl. Græc. l. v. c. 4, tom. vi. p. 37—56.

[59] See Constantin. Orat. ad Sanctos, c. 19, 20. He chiefly depends on a mysterious acrostic, composed in the sixth age after the Deluge, by the Erythræan Sibyl, and translated by Cicero into Latin. The initial letters of the thirty-four Greek verses form this prophetic sentence: JESUS CHRIST, SON OF GOD, SAVIOR OF THE WORLD.

[60] In his paraphrase of Virgil, the emperor has frequently assisted and improved the literal sense of the Latin text. See Blondel des Sibylles, l. i c. 14, 15, 16.

applied to the infant son of a consul, or a triumvir ; [61] but if a more splendid, and indeed specious, interpretation of the fourth eclogue contributed to the conversion of the first Christian emperor, Virgil may deserve to be ranked among the most successful missionaries of the gospel.[62]

The awful mysteries of the Christian faith and worship were concealed from the eyes of strangers, and even of catechumens, with an affected secrecy, which served to excite their wonder and curiosity.[63] But the severe rules of discipline which the prudence of the bishops had instituted, were relaxed by the same prudence in favor of an Imperial proselyte, whom it was so important to allure, by every gentle condescension, into the pale of the church ; and Constantine was permitted, at least by a tacit dispensation, to enjoy *most* of the privileges, before he had contracted *any* of the obligations, of a Christian. Instead of retiring from the congregation, when the voice of the deacon dismissed the profane multitude, he prayed with the faithful, disputed with the bishops, preached on the most sublime and intricate subjects of theology, celebrated with sacred rites the vigil of Easter, and publicly declared himself, not only a partaker, but, in some measure, a priest and hierophant of the Christian mysteries.[64] The pride of Constantine might assume, and his services had deserved, some extraordinary distinction : and ill-timed rigor might have blasted the

---

[61] The different claims of an elder and younger son of Pollio, of Julia, of Drusus, of Marcellus, are found to be incompatible with chronology, history, and the good sense of Virgil.

[62] See Lowth de Sacra Poesi Hebræorum Prælect. xxi. p. 289—293. In the examination of the fourth eclogue, the respectable bishop of London has displayed learning, taste, ingenuity, and a temperate enthusiasm, which exalts his fancy without degrading his judgment.

[63] The distinction between the public and the secret parts of divine service, the *missa catechumenorum* and the *missa fidelium*, and the mysterious veil which piety or policy had cast over the latter, are very judiciously explained by Thiers, Exposition du Saint Sacrament, l. i. c. 8—12, p. 59—91 : but as, on this subject, the Papists may reasonably be suspected, a Protestant reader will depend with more confidence on the learned Bingham, Antiquities, l. x. c. 5.

[64] See Eusebius in Vit. Const. l. iv. c. 15—32, and the whole tenor of Constantine's Sermon. The faith and devotion of the emperor has furnished Baronius with a specious argument in favor of his early baptism.*

---

* Compare Heinichen, Excursus iv. et v., where these questions are examined with candor and acuteness, and with constant reference to the opinions of more modern writers. — M.

unripened fruits of his conversion; and if the doors of the church had been strictly closed against a prince who had deserted the altars of the gods, the master of the empire would have been left destitute of any form of religious worship. In his last visit to Rome, he piously disclaimed and insulted the superstition of his ancestors, by refusing to lead the military procession of the equestrian order, and to offer the public vows to the Jupiter of the Capitoline Hill.[65] Many years before his baptism and death, Constantine had proclaimed to the world, that neither his person nor his image should ever more be seen within the walls of an idolatrous temple; while he distributed through the provinces a variety of medals and pictures, which represented the emperor in an humble and suppliant posture of Christian devotion.[66]

The pride of Constantine, who refused the privileges of a catechumen, cannot easily be explained or excused; but the delay of his baptism may be justified by the maxims and the practice of ecclesiastical antiquity. The sacrament of baptism[67] was regularly administered by the bishop himself, with his assistant clergy, in the cathedral church of the diocese, during the fifty days between the solemn festivals of Easter and Pentecost; and this holy term admitted a numerous band of infants and adult persons into the bosom of the church. The discretion of parents often suspended the baptism of their children till they could understand the obligations which they contracted: the severity of ancient bishops exacted from the new converts a novitiate of two or three years; and the catechumens themselves, from different motives of a temporal or a spiritual nature, were seldom impatient to assume the character of perfect and initiated Christians. The sacrament of baptism was supposed to contain a full and absolute expiation of sin; and the soul was instantly restored to its original purity, and entitled to the promise of eternal salvation. Among the prose-

---

[65] Zosimus, l. ii. p. 105.

[66] Eusebius in Vit. Constant. l. iv. c. 15, 16.

[67] The theory and practice of antiquity, with regard to the sacrament of baptism, have been copiously explained by Dom Chardon. Hist. des Sacremens, tom. i. p. 3—405; Dom Martenne de Ritibus Ecclesiæ Antiquis, tom. i.; and by Bingham, in the tenth and eleventh books of his Christian Antiquities. One circumstance may be observed, in which the modern churches have materially departed from the ancient custom. The sacrament of baptism (even when it was administered to infants) was immediately followed by confirmation and the holy communion.

lytes of Christianity, there were many who judged it imprudent to precipitate a salutary rite, which could not be repeated ; to throw away an inestimable privilege, which could never be recovered. By the delay of their baptism, they could venture freely to indulge their passions in the enjoyments of this world, while they still retained in their own hands the means of a sure and easy absolution.[68] The sublime theory of the gospel had made a much fainter impression on the heart than on the understanding of Constantine himself. He pursued tho great object of his ambition through the dark and bloody paths of war and policy ; and, after the victory, he abandoned himself, without moderation, to the abuse of his fortune. Instead of asserting his just superiority above the imperfect heroism and profane philosophy of Trajan and the Antonines, the mature age of Constantine forfeited the reputation which he had acquired in his youth. As he gradually advanced in the knowledge of truth, he proportionally declined in the practice of virtue ; and the same year of his reign in which he convened the council of Nice, was polluted by the execution, or rather murder, of his eldest son. This date is alone sufficient to refute the ignorant and malicious suggestions of Zosimus,[69]

---

[68] The Fathers, who censured this criminal delay, could not deny the certain and victorious efficacy even of a death-bed baptism. The ingenious rhetoric of Chrysostom could find only three arguments against these prudent Christians. 1. That we should love and pursue virtue for her own sake, and not merely for the reward. 2. That we may be surprised by death without an opportunity of baptism. 3. That although we shall be placed in heaven, we shall only twinkle like little stars, when compared to the suns of righteousness who have run their appointed course with labor, with success, and with glory. Chrysostom in Epist. ad Hebræos, Homil. xiii. apud Chardon, Hist. des Sacremens, tom. i. p. 49. I believe that this delay of baptism, though attended with the most pernicious consequences, was never condemned by any general or provincial council, or by any public act or declaration of the church. The zeal of the bishops was easily kindled on much slighter occasions.*

[69] Zosimus, l. ii. p. 104. For this disingenuous falsehood he has deserved and experienced the harshest treatment from all the ecclesiastical writers, except Cardinal Baronius, (A. D. 324, No. 15—28,) who had occasion to employ the infidel on a particular service against the Arian Eusebius.†

---

* This passage of Chrysostom, though not in his more forcible manner, is not quite fairly represented. He is stronger in other places, in Act. Hom. xxiii. — and Hom. i. Compare, likewise, the sermon of Gregory of Nyssa on this subject, and Gregory Nazianzen. After all, to those who believed in the efficacy of baptism, what argument could be more conclusive. than the danger of dying without it ? Orat. xl. — M.

† Heyne. in a valuable note on this passage of Zosimus, has shown

who affirms, that, after the death of Crispus, the remorse of his father accepted from the ministers of Christianity the expiation which he had vainly solicited from the Pagan pontiffs. At the time of the death of Crispus, the emperor could no longer hesitate in the choice of a religion; he could no longer be ignorant that the church was possessed of an infallible remedy, though he chose to defer the application of it till the approach of death had removed the temptation and danger of a relapse. The bishops whom he summoned, in his last illness, to the palace of Nicomedia, were edified by the fervor with which he requested and received the sacrament of baptism, by the solemn protestation that the remainder of his life should be worthy of a disciple of Christ, and by his humble refusal to wear the Imperial purple after he had been clothed in the white garment of a Neophyte. The example and reputation of Constantine seemed to countenance the delay of baptism.[70] Future tyrants were encouraged to believe, that the innocent blood which they might shed in a long reign would instantly be washed away in the waters of regeneration; and the abuse of religion dangerously undermined the foundations of moral virtue.

The gratitude of the church has exalted the virtues and excused the failings of a generous patron, who seated Christianity on the throne of the Roman world; and the Greeks, who celebrate the festival of the Imperial saint, seldom mention the name of Constantine without adding the title of *equal to the Apostles*.[71] Such a comparison, if it allude to the character of those divine missionaries, must be imputed to the extravagance of impious flattery. But if the parallel be confined to the extent and number of their evangelic victories, the success of Constantine might perhaps equal that of the Apostles themselves. By the edicts of toleration, he removed the temporal disadvantages which had hitherto retarded the

[70] Eusebius, l. iv. c. 61, 62, 63. The bishop of Cæsarea supposes the salvation of Constantine with the most perfect confidence.
[71] See Tillemont, Hist. des Empereurs, tom. iv. p. 429. The Greeks, the Russians, and, in the darker ages, the Latins themselves, have been desirous of placing Constantine in the catalogue of saints.

decisively that this malicious way of accounting for the conversion of Constantine was not an invention of Zosimus. It appears to have been the current calumny, eagerly adopted and propagated by the exasperated Pagan party. Reitemeier, a later editor of Zosimus, whose notes are retained in the recent edition, in the collection of the Byzantine historians, has a disquisition on the passage, as candid, but not more conclusive than some which have preceded him. —M.

progress of Christianity ; and its active and numerous ministers received a free permission, a liberal encouragement, to
recommend the salutary truths of revelation by every argument which could affect the reason or piety of mankind.   The
exact balance of the two religions continued but a moment ;
and the piercing eye of ambition and avarice soon discovered,
that the profession of Christianity might contribute to the
interest of the present, as well as of a future life.[72]   The
hopes of wealth and honors, the example of an emperor, his
exhortations, his irresistible smiles, diffused conviction among
the venal and obsequious crowds which usually fill the apartments of a palace.   The cities which signalized a forward
zeal by the voluntary destruction of their temples, were distinguished by municipal privileges, and rewarded with popular
donatives ; and the new capital of the East gloried in the
singular advantage that Constantinople was never profaned by
the worship of idols.[73]   As the lower ranks of society are
governed by imitation, the conversion of those who possessed
any eminence of birth, of power, or of riches, was soon followed by dependent multitudes.[74]   The salvation of the common people was purchased at an easy rate, if it be true that,
in one year, twelve thousand men were baptized at Rome,
besides a proportionable number of women and children, and
that a white garment, with twenty pieces of gold, had been
promised by the emperor to every convert.[75]   The powerful

---

[72] See the third and fourth books of his life. He was accustomed
to say, that whether Christ was preached in pretence, or in truth, he
should still rejoice, (l. iii. c. 58.)

[73] M. de Tillemont (Hist. des Empereurs, tom. iv. p. 374, 616) has
defended, with strength and spirit, the virgin purity of Constantinople against some malevolent insinuations of the Pagan Zosimus.

[74] The author of the Histoire Politique et Philosophique des deux
Indes (tom. i. p. 9) condemns a law of Constantine, which gave freedom to all the slaves who should embrace Christianity. The emperor
did indeed publish a law, which restrained the Jews from circumcising, perhaps from keeping, any Christian slave. (See Euseb. in Vit.
Constant. l. iv. c. 27, and Cod. Theod. l. xvi. tit. ix., with Godefroy's
Commentary, tom. vi. p. 247.) But this imperfect exception related
only to the Jews ; and the great body of slaves, who were the property of Christian or Pagan masters, could not improve their temporal
condition by changing their religion. I am ignorant by what guides
the Abbé Raynal was deceived ; as the total absence of quotations is
the unpardonable blemish of his entertaining history

[75] See Acta S^{ti} Silvestri, and Hist. Eccles. Nicephor. Callist l. vii.
c. 34, ap. Baronium Annal. Eccles. A. D. 324, No. 67, 74. Such evi
dence is contemptible enough ; but these circumstances are in them

influence of Constantine was not circumscribed by the narrow limits of his life, or of his dominions. The education which he bestowed on his sons and nephews secured to the empire a race of princes, whose faith was still more lively and sincere, as they imbibed, in their earliest infancy, the spirit, or at least the doctrine, of Christianity. War and commerce had spread the knowledge of the gospel beyond the confines of the Roman provinces ; and the Barbarians, who had disdained an humble and proscribed sect, soon learned to esteem a religion which had been so lately embraced by the greatest monarch, and the most civilized nation, of the globe.[76] The Goths and Germans, who enlisted under the standard of Rome, revered the cross which glittered at the head of the legions, and their fierce countrymen received at the same time the lessons of faith and of humanity. The kings of Iberia and Armenia * worshipped the god of their protector ; and their subjects, who have invariably preserved the name of Christians, soon formed a sacred and perpetual connection with their Roman brethren. The Christians of Persia were suspected, in time of war, of preferring their religion to their

---

selves so probable, that the learned Dr. Howell (History of the World, vol. iii. p. 14) has not scrupled to adopt them.

[76] The conversion of the Barbarians under the reign of Constantine is celebrated by the ecclesiastical historians. (See Sozomen, l. ii. c. 6, and Theodoret. l. i. c. 23, 24.) But Rufinus, the Latin translator of Eusebius, deserves to be considered as an original authority. His information was curiously collected from one of the companions of the Apostle of Æthiopia, and from Bacurius, an Iberian prince, who was count of the domestics. Father Mamachi has given an ample compilation on the progress of Christianity, in the first and second volumes of his great but imperfect work.

---

* According to the Georgian chronicles, Iberia (Georgia) was converted by the virgin Nino, who effected an extraordinary cure on the wife of the king, Mihran. The temple of the god Aramazt, or Armaz, not far from the capital Mtskitha, was destroyed, and the cross erected in its place. Le Beau, i. 202, with St. Martin's Notes.

St. Martin has likewise clearly shown (St. Martin, Ad i. to Le Beau, i. 291) that Armenia was the first *nation* which embraced Christianity, (Addition to Le Beau, i. 76, and Mémoires sur l'Armenie, i. 305.) Gibbon himself suspected this truth. — "Instead of maintaining that the conversion of Armenia was not attempted with any degree of success, till the sceptre was in the hands of an orthodox emperor," I ought *to have said, that the seeds of the faith were deeply sown during the season of the last and greatest persecution, that many Roman exiles might assist the labors of Gregory, and that the renowned Tiridates, the hero of the East, may dispute with Constantine the honor of being the first sovereign who embraced the Christian religion. Vindication, Misc Works, iv. 577. — M.

40

country ; but as long as peace subsisted between the two
empires, the persecuting spirit of the Magi was effectually
restrained by the interposition of Constantine.[77] The rays
of the gospel illuminated the coast of India. The colonies
of Jews, who had penetrated into Arabia and Ethiopia,[78] op
posed the progress of Christianity ; but the labor of the missionaries was in some measure facilitated by a previous
knowledge of the Mosaic revelation ; and Abyssinia still
reveres the memory of Frumentius,* who, in the time of
Constantine, devoted his life to the conversion of those
sequestered regions. Under the reign of his son Constantius,
Theophilus,[79] who was himself of Indian extraction, was invested with the double character of ambassador and bishop.
He embarked on the Red Sea with two hundred horses of the
purest breed of Cappadocia, which were sent by the emperor
to the prince of the Sabæans, or Homerites. Theophilus was
intrusted with many other useful or curious presents, which
might raise the admiration, and conciliate the friendship, of
the Barbarians ; and he successfully employed several years
in a pastoral visit to the churches of the torrid zone.[80]

The irresistible power of the Roman emperors was dis-

---

[77] See, in Eusebius, (in Vit. Constant. l. iv. c. 9,) the pressing and
pathetic epistle of Constantine in favor of his Christian brethren of
Persia.

[78] See Basnage, Hist. des Juifs, tom. vii. p. 182, tom. viii. p. 333,
tom. ix. p. 810. The curious diligence of this writer pursues the Jewish exiles to the extremities of the globe.

[79] Theophilus had been given in his infancy as a hostage by his
countrymen of the Isle of Diva, and was educated by the Romans in
learning and piety. The Maldives, of which Male, or *Diva*, may be
the capital, are a cluster of 1900 or 2000 minute islands in the Indian
Ocean. The ancients were imperfectly acquainted with the Maldives ;
but they are described in the two Mahometan travellers of the ninth
century, published by Renaudot, Geograph. Nubiensis, p. 30, 31.
D'Herbelot, Bibliothèque Orientale, p. 704. Hist. Generale des Voyages, tom. viii.†

[80] Philostorgius, l. iii. c. 4, 5, 6, with Godefroy's learned observations. The historical narrative is soon lost in an inquiry concerning
the seat of Paradise, strange monsters, &c.

---

* Abba Salama, or Fremonatos, is mentioned in the Tareek Negushti,
or Chronicle of the kings of Abyssinia. Salt's Travels, vol. ii. p. 464. — M.
† See the dissertation of M. Letronne on this question. He conceives
that Theophilus was born in the Island of Dahlak, in the Arabian Gulf
His embassy was to Abyssinia rather than to India. Letronne, Matériaux
pour l'Hist. du Christianisme en Egypte, Indie, et Abyssinie. Paris, 1832.
3d Dissert — M.

played in the important and dangerous change of the national religion. The terrors of a military force silenced the faint and unsupported murmurs of the Pagans, and there was reason to expect, that the cheerful submission of the Christian clergy, as well as people, would be the result of conscience and gratitude. It was long since established, as a fundamental maxim of the Roman constitution, that every rank of citizens was alike subject to the laws, and that the care of religion was the right as well as duty of the civil magistrate. Constantine and his successors could not easily persuade themselves that they had forfeited, by their conversion, any branch of the Imperial prerogatives, or that they were incapable of giving laws to a religion which they had protected and embraced. The emperors still continued to exercise a supreme jurisdiction over the ecclesiastical order ; and the sixteenth book of the Theodosian code represents, under a variety of titles, the authority which they assumed in the government of the Catholic church.

But the distinction of the spiritual and temporal powers,[81] which had never been imposed on the free spirit of Greece and Rome, was introduced and confirmed by the legal establishment of Christianity. The office of supreme pontiff, which, from the time of Numa to that of Augustus, had always been exercised by one of the most eminent of the senators, was at length united to the Imperial dignity. The first magistrate of the state, as often as he was prompted by superstition or policy, performed with his own hands the sacerdotal functions ;[82] nor was there any order of priests, either at Rome or in the provinces, who claimed a more sacred character among men, or a more intimate communication with the gods. But in the Christian church, which intrusts the service of the altar to a perpetual succession of consecrated ministers, the monarch, whose spiritual rank is less honorable than that of the meanest deacon, was seated below the rails of the sanctuary, and confounded with the

---

[81] See the epistle of Osius, ap. Athanasium, vol. i. p. 840. The public remonstrance which Osius was forced to address to the son, contained the same principles of ecclesiastical and civil government which he had secretly instilled into the mind of the father.

[82] M. de la Bastiel (Mémoires de l'Academie des Inscriptions, tom. xv. p. 38—61) has evidently proved, that Augustus and his successors exercised in person all the sacred functions of pontifex maximus, or high priest, of the Roman empire.

rest of the faithful multitude.[83] The emperor might be saluted as the father of his people, but he owed a filial duty and reverence to the fathers of the church ; and the same marks of respect, which Constantine had paid to the persons of saints and confessors, were soon exacted by the pride of the episcopal order.[84] A secret conflict between the civil and ecclesiastical jurisdictions embarrassed the operations of the Roman government ; and a pious emperor was alarmed by the guilt and danger of touching with a profane hand the ark of the covenant. The separation of men into the two orders of the clergy and of the laity was, indeed, familiar to many nations of antiquity ; and the priests of India, of Persia, of Assyria, of Judea, of Æthiopia, of Egypt, and of Gaul, derived from a celestial origin the temporal power and possessions which they had acquired. These venerable institutions had gradually assimilated themselves to the manners and government of their respective countries ; [85] but the opposition or contempt of the civil power served to cement the discipline of the primitive church. The Christians had been obliged to elect their own magistrates, to raise and distribute a peculiar revenue, and to regulate the internal policy of their republic by a code of laws, which were ratified by the consent of the people, and the practice of three hundred years. When Constantine embraced the faith of the Christians, he seemed to contract a perpetual alliance with a distinct and independent society ; and the privileges granted or confirmed by that emperor, or by his successors, were accepted, not as the precarious favors

---

[83] Something of a contrary practice had insensibly prevailed in the church of Constantinople; but the rigid Ambrose commanded Theodosius to retire below the rails, and taught him to know the difference between a king and a priest. See Theodoret, l. v. c. 18.

[84] At the table of the emperor Maximus, Martin, bishop of Tours, received the cup from an attendant, and gave it to the presbyter, his companion, before he allowed the emperor to drink ; the empress waited on Martin at table. Sulpicius Severus, in Vit. S^d Martin, c. 23, and Dialogue ii. 7. Yet it may be doubted, whether t ese extraordinary compliments were paid to the bishop or the saint. The honors usually granted to the former character may be seen in Bingham's Antiquities, l. ii. c. 9, and Vales. ad Theodoret, l. iv. c. 6. See the haughty ceremonial which Leontius, bishop of Tripoli, imposed on the empress. Tillemont, Hist. des Empereurs, tom. iv. p. 754. (Patres Apostol. tom. ii. p. 179.)

[85] Plutarch, in his treatise of Isis and Osiris, informs us, that the kings of Egypt, who were not already priests, were initiated, after their election, into the sacerdotal order.

of the court, but as the just and inalienable rights of the ecclesiastical order.

The Catholic church was administered by the spiritual and legal jurisdiction of eighteen hundred bishops ; [86] of whom one thousand were seated in the Greek, and eight hundred in the Latin, provinces of the empire. The extent and boundaries of their respective dioceses had been variously and accidentally decided by the zeal and success of the first missionaries, by the wishes of the people, and by the propagation of the gospel. Episcopal churches were closely planted along the banks of the Nile, on the sea-coast of Africa, in the proconsular Asia, and through the southern provinces of Italy. The bishops of Gaul and Spain, of Thrace and Pontus reigned over an ample territory, and delegated their rural suffragans to execute the subordinate duties of the pastoral office. [87] A Christian diocese might be spread over a province, or reduced to a village ; but all the bishops possessed an equal and indelible character. they all derived the same powers and privileges from the apostles, from the people and from the laws. While the *civil* and *military* professions were separated by the policy of Constantine, a new and perpetual order of *ecclesiastical* ministers, always respectable, sometimes dangerous, was established in the church and state. The important review of their station and attributes may be distributed under the following heads : I. Popular Election. II. Ordination of the Clergy. III. Property. IV. Civil Jurisdiction. V. Spiritual censures. VI. Exercise of public oratory. VII. Privilege of legislative assemblies.

I. The freedom of election subsisted long after the legal establishment of Christianity ; [88] and the subjects of Rome

---

[86] The numbers are not ascertained by any ancient writer or original catalogue ; for the partial lists of the eastern churches are comparatively modern. The patient diligence of Charles a Sᵗᵒ Paolo, of Luke Holstenius, and of Bingham, has laboriously investigated all the episcopal sees of the Catholic church, which was almost commensurate with the Roman empire. The ninth book of the Christian Antiquities is a very accurate map of ecclesiastical geography.

[87] On the subject of rural bishops, or *Chorepiscopi*, who voted in synods, and conferred the minor orders, see Thomassin, Discipline de l'Eglise, tom. i. p. 447, &c., and Chardon, Hist. des Sacremens, tom. v. p 395, &c. They do not appear till the fourth century ; and this equivocal character, which had excited the jealousy of the prelates, was abolished before the end of the tenth, both in the East and the West.

[88] Thomassin (Discipline de l'Eglise, tom. ii. l. ii. c. 1—8, p. 673—

enjoyed in the church the privilege which they had lost in the republic, of choosing the magistrates whom they were bound to obey. As soon as a bishop had closed his eyes, the metropolitan issued a commission to one of his suffragans to administer the vacant see, and prepare, within a limited time, the future election. The right of voting was vested in the inferior clergy, who were best qualified to judge of the merit of the candidates; in the senators or nobles of the city, all those who were distinguished by their rank or property; and finally in the whole body of the people, who, on the appointed day, flocked in multitudes from the most remote parts of the diocese,[89] and sometimes silenced, by their tumultuous acclamations, the voice of reason and the laws of discipline. These acclamations might accidentally fix on the head of the most deserving competitor; of some ancient presbyter, some holy monk, or some layman, conspicuous for his zeal and piety. But the episcopal chair was solicited, especially in the great and opulent cities of the empire, as a temporal rather than as a spiritual dignity. The interested views, the selfish and angry passions, the arts of perfidy and dissimulation, the secret corruption, the open and even bloody violence which had formerly disgraced the freedom of election in the commonwealths of Greece and Rome, too often influenced the choice of the successors of the apostles. While one of the candidates boasted the honors of his family, a second allured his judges by the delicacies of a plentiful table, and a third

---

721) has copiously treated of the election of bishops during the five first centuries, both in the East and in the West; but he shows a very partial bias in favor of the episcopal aristocracy. Bingham (l. iv. c. 2) is moderate; and Chardon (Hist. des Sacremens, tom. v. p. 108—128) is very clear and concise.*

[89] Incredibilis multitudo, non solum ex eo oppido, (*Tours*,) sed etiam ex vicinis urbibus ad suffragia ferenda convenerat, &c. Sulpicius Severus, in Vit. Martin. c. 7. The council of Laodicea (canon xiii.) prohibits mobs and tumults; and Justinian confines the right of election to the nobility. Novel. cxxiii. 1.

---

* This freedom was extremely limited, and soon annihilated: already, from the third century, the deacons were no longer nominated by the members of the community, but by the bishops. Although it appears by the letters of Cyprian, that even in his time, no priest could be elected without the consent of the community, (Ep. 68,) that election was far from being altogether free. The bishop proposed to his parishioners the candidate whom he had chosen, and they were permitted to make such objections as might be suggested by his conduct and morals. (St. Cyprian, Ep. 33.) They lost this last right towards the middle of the fourth century. — G.

more guilty than his rivals, offered to share the plunder of the church among the accomplices of his sacrilegious hopes.[90] The civil as well as ecclesiastical laws attempted to exclude the populace from this solemn and important transaction The canons of ancient discipline, by requiring several episcopal qualifications of age, station, &c., restrained, in some measure, the indiscriminate caprice of the electors. The authority of the provincial bishops, who were assembled in the vacant church to consecrate the choice of the people, was interposed to moderate their passions, and to correct their mistakes. The bishops could refuse to ordain an unworthy candidate, and the rage of contending factions sometimes accepted their impartial mediation. The submission, or the resistance, of the clergy and people, on various occasions, afforded different precedents, which were insensibly converted into positive laws and provincial customs ; [91] but it was every where admitted, as a fundamental maxim of religious policy, that no bishop could be imposed on an orthodox church, without the consent of its members. The emperors, as the guardians of the public peace, and as the first citizens of Rome and Constantinople, might effectually declare their wishes in the choice of a primate : but those absolute monarchs respected the freedom of ecclesiastical elections ; and while they distributed and resumed the honors of the state and army, they allowed eighteen hundred perpetual magistrates to receive their important offices from the free suffrages of the people.[92] It was agreeable to the dictates of justice, that these magistrates should not desert an honorable station from

[90] The epistles of Sidonius Apollinaris (iv. 25, vii. 5, 9) exhibit some of the scandals of the Gallican church ; and Gaul was less polished and less corrupt than the East.

[91] A compromise was sometimes introduced by law or by consent ; either the bishops or the people chose one of the three candidates who had been named by the other party.

[92] All the examples quoted by Thomassin (Discipline de l'Eglise, tom. ii. l. ii. c. vi. p. 704—714) appear to be extraordinary acts of power, and even of oppression. The confirmation of the bishop of Alexandria is mentioned by Philostorgius as a more regular proceeding. (Hist. Eccles. l. ii. 11.)*

* The statement of Planck is more consistent with history : " From the middle of the fourth century, the bishops of some of the larger churches, particularly those of the Imperial residence, were almost always chosen under the influence of the court, and often directly and immediately nominated by the emperor." Planck, Geschichte der Christlich-kirchlichen Gesellschafts-verfassung, vol. i. p. 263. — M.

which they could not be removed, but the wisdom of councils
endeavored, without much success, to enforce the residence
and to prevent the translation, of bishops. The discipline of
the West was indeed less relaxed than that of the East; bu'
the same passions which made those regulations necessary,
rendered them ineffectual. The reproaches which angry
prelates have so vehemently urged against each other, serve
only to expose their common guilt, and their mutual indiscretion.

II. The bishops alone possessed the faculty of *spiritual*
generation: and this extraordinary privilege might compensate, in some degree, for the painful celibacy [93] which was
imposed as a virtue, as a duty, and at length as a positive obligation. The religions of antiquity, which established a separate
order of priests, dedicated a holy race, a tribe or family, to the
perpetual service of the gods.[94] Such institutions were founded
for possession, rather than conquest. The children of the priests
enjoyed, with proud and indolent security, their sacred inheritance; and the fiery spirit of enthusiasm was abated by the
cares, the pleasures, and the endearments of domestic life.
But the Christian sanctuary was open to every ambitious candidate, who aspired to its heavenly promises or temporal possessions. This office of priests, like that of soldiers or magistrates, was strenuously exercised by those men, whose temper
and abilities had prompted them to embrace the ecclesiastical

---

[93] The celibacy of the clergy during the first five or six centuries,
is a subject of discipline, and indeed of controversy, which has been
very diligently examined. See, in particular, Thomassin, Discipline
de l'Eglise, tom. i. l. ii. c. lx. lxi. p. 886—902, and Bingham's Antiquities, l. iv. c. 5. By each of these learned but partial critics, on
half of the truth is produced, and the other is concealed.*

[94] Diodorus Siculus attests and approves the hereditary succession
of the priesthood among the Egyptians, the Chaldeans, and the
Indians, (l. i. p. 84, l. ii. p. 142, 153, edit. Wesseling.) The magi are
described by Ammianus as a very numerous family: "Per sæcula
multa ad præsens unâ eâdemque prosapiâ multitudo creata, Deorum
cultibus dedicata." (xxiii. 6.) Ausonius celebrates the *Stirps Drui-
darum,* (De Professorib. Burdigal. iv.;) but we may infer from the
remark of Cæsar, (vi. 13,) that in the Celtic hierarchy, some room
was left for choice and emulation.

---

* Compare Planck, (vol. i. p. 348.) This century, the third, first brought
forth the monks, and the monks, or the spirit of monkery, the celibacy of
the clergy. Planck likewise observes, that from the history of Eusebius
alone, names of married bishops and presbyters may be adduced by doz
: — M.

profession, or who had been selected by a discerning bishop, as the best qualified to promote the glory and interest of the churca. The bishops[95] (till the abuse was restrained by the prudence of the laws) might constrain the reluctant, and protect the distressed ; and the imposition of hands forever be stowed some of the most valuable privileges of civil society The whole body of the Catholic clergy, more numerous perhaps than the legions, was exempted * by the emperors from all service, private or public, all municipal offices, and all personal taxes and contributions, which pressed on their fellow-citizens with intolerable weight ; and the duties of their holy profession were accepted as a full discharge of their obligations to the republic.[96] Each bishop acquired an absolute and indefeasible right to the perpetual obedience of the clerk whom he ordained : the clergy of each episcopal church with its dependent parishes, formed a regular and permanent society ; and the cathedrals of Constantinople[97] and Car-

---

[95] The subject of the vocation, ordination, obedience, &c., of the clergy, is laboriously discussed by Thomassin) Discipline de l'Eglise, tom. ii. p. 1—83) and Bingham, (in the 4th book of his Antiquities, more especially the 4th, 6th, and 7th chapters.) When the brother of St. Jerom was ordained in Cyprus, the deacons forcibly stopped his mouth, lest he should make a solemn protestation, which might invalidate the holy rites.

[96] The charter of immunities, which the clergy obtained from the Christian emperors, is contained in the 16th book of the Theodosian code; and is illustrated with tolerable candor by the learned Godefroy, whose mind was balanced by the opposite prejudices of a civilian and a Protestant.

[97] Justinian. Novell. ciii. Sixty presbyters, or priests, one hundred deacons, forty deaconesses, ninety sub-deacons, one hundred and ten readers, twenty-five chanters, and one hundred door-keepers ; in all, five hundred and twenty-five. This moderate number was fixed by the emperor to relieve the distress of the church, which had been involved in debt and usury by the expense of a much higher establishment.

---

* This exemption was very much limited. The municipal offices were of two kinds ; the one attached to the individual in his character of inhabitant, the other in that of *proprietor.* Constantine had exempted ecclesiastics from offices of the first description. (Cod. Theod. xvi. t. ii. leg. 1, 2. Eusebius, Hist. Eccles. l. x. c. vii.) They sought, also, to be exempted from those of the second, (munera patrimoniorum.) The rich, to obtain this privilege, obtained subordinate situations among the clergy. Constantine published in 320 an edict, by which he prohibited the more opulent citizens (decuriones and curiales) from embracing the ecclesiastical profession, and the bishops from admitting new ecclesiastics, before a place should be vacant by the death of the occupant, (Godefroy ad Cod. Theod.

40 *

thage [98] maintained their peculiar establishment of five hundred ecclesiastical ministers. Their ranks [99] and numbers were insensibly multiplied by the superstition of the times, which introduced into the church the splendid ceremonies of a Jewish or Pagan temple ; and a long train of priests, deacons, sub-deacons, acolythes, exorcists, readers, singers, and door-keepers, contributed, in their respective stations, to swell the pomp and harmony of religious worship. The clerical name and privilege were extended to many pious fraternities, who devoutly supported the ecclesiastical throne.[100] Six hundred *parabolani*, or adventurers, visited the sick at Alexandria; eleven hundred *copiatæ*, or grave-diggers, buried the dead at Constantinople; and the swarms of monks, who arose from the Nile, overspread and darkened the face of the Christian world.

III. The edict of Milan secured the revenue as well as the peace of the church.[101] The Christians not only recovered the lands and houses of which they had been stripped by the persecuting laws of Diocletian, but they acquired a perfect title to all the possessions which they had hitherto enjoyed by the connivance of the magistrate. As soon as Christianity became the religion of the emperor and the empire, the national

---

[98] Universus clerus ecclesiæ Carthaginiensis . . . fere *quingenti* vel amplius ; inter quos quamplurima erant lectores infantuli. Victor Vitensis, de Persecut. Vandal. v. 9, p. 78, edit. Ruinart. This remnant of a more prosperous state still subsisted under the oppression of the Vandals.

[99] The number of *seven* orders has been fixed in the Latin church, exclusive of the episcopal character. But the four inferior ranks, the minor orders, are now reduced to empty and useless titles.

[100] See Cod. Theodos. l. xvi. tit. ii. leg. 42, 43. Godefroy's Commentary, and the Ecclesiastical History of Alexandria, show the danger of these pious institutions, which often disturbed the peace of that turbulent capital.

[101] The edict of Milan (de M. P. c. 48) acknowledges, by reciting, that there existed a species of landed property, ad jus corporis eorum, id est, ecclesiarum non hominum singulorum pertinentia. Such a solemn declaration of the supreme magistrate must have been received in all the tribunals as a maxim of civil law.

---

l. xii. t. i. de Decur.) Valentinian the First, by a rescript sti'l more general, enacted that no rich citizen should obtain a situation in the church, (De Episc. l. lxvii.) He also enacted that ecclesiastics, who wished to be exempt from offices which they were bound to discharge as proprietors, should be obliged to give up their property to their relations. Cod. Theodos. l. xii. t. i, leg. 49. — G.

clergy might claim a decent and honorable maintenance : and
the payment of an annual tax might have delivered the people
from the more oppressive tribute, which superstition imposes
on her votaries. But as the wants and expenses of the church
increased with her prosperity, the ecclesiastical order was still
supported and enriched by the voluntary oblations of the
faithful. Eight years after the edict of Milan, Constantine
granted to all his subjects the free and universal permission
of bequeathing their fortunes to the holy Catholic church ; [102]
and their devout liberality, which during their lives was
checked by luxury or avarice, flowed with a profuse stream
at the hour of their death. The wealthy Christians were
encouraged by the example of their sovereign. An absolute
monarch, who is rich without patrimony, may be charitable
without merit ; and Constantine too easily believed that he
should purchase the favor of Heaven, if he maintained the
idle at the expense of the industrious ; and distributed among
the saints the wealth of the republic. The same messenger
who carried over to Africa the head of Maxentius, might be
intrusted with an epistle to Cæcilian, bishop of Carthage. The
emperor acquaints him, that the treasurers of the province are
directed to pay into his hands the sum of three thousand *folles*,
or eighteen thousand pounds sterling, and to obey his further
requisitions for the relief of the churches of Africa, Numidia,
and Mauritania.[103] The liberality of Constantine increased in
a just proportion to his faith, and to his vices. He assigned
in each city a regular allowance of corn, to supply the fund
of ecclesiastical charity ; and the persons of both sexes who
embraced the monastic life became the peculiar favorites of
their sovereign. The Christian temples of Antioch, Alexandria, Jerusalem, Constantinople, &c., displayed the ostentatious piety of a prince, ambitious in a declining age to equal
the perfect labors of antiquity.[104] The form of these religious

---

[102] Habeat unusquisque licentiam sanctissimo Catholicæ (*ecclesiæ*)
venerabilique concilio, decedens bonorum quod optavit relinquere.
Cod. Theodos. l. xvi. tit. ii. leg. 4. This law was published at Rome,
A. D. 321, at a time when Constantine might foresee the probability
of a rupture with the emperor of the East.

[103] Eusebius, Hist. Eccles. l. x. 6 ; in Vit. Constantin. l. iv. c. 28.
He repeatedly expatiates on the liberality of the Christian hero, which
the bishop himself had an opportunity of knowing, and even of tast-
ing.

[104] Eusebius, Hist. Eccles. l. x. c. 2, 3, 4. The bishop of Cæsarea,
who studied and gratified the taste of his master, pronounced so

edific:s was simple and oblong; though they might sometimes swell into the shape of a dome, and sometimes branch into the figure of a cross. The timbers were framed for the most part of cedars of Libanus; the roof was covered with tiles, perhaps of gilt brass; and the walls, the columns, the pavement, were encrusted with variegated marbles. The most precious ornaments of gold and silver, of silk and gems, were profusely dedicated to the service of the altar; and this specious magnificence was supported on the solid and perpetual basis of landed property. In the space of two centuries, from the reign of Constantine to that of Justinian, the eighteen hundred churches of the empire were enriched by the frequent and unalienable gifts of the prince and people. An annual income of six hundred pounds sterling may be reasonably assigned to the bishops, who were placed at an equal distance between riches and poverty,[105] but the standard of their wealth insensibly rose with the dignity and opulence of the cities which they governed. An authentic but imperfect [106] rent-roll specifies some houses, shops, gardens, and farms, which belonged to the three *Basilicæ* of Rome, St. Peter, St. Paul, and St. John Lateran, in the provinces of Italy, Africa, and the East. They produce, besides a reserved rent of oil, linen, paper, aromatics, &c., a clear annual revenue of twenty-two thousand pieces of gold, or twelve thousand pounds sterling. In the age of Constantine and Justinian, the bishops no longer possessed, perhaps they no longer deserved, the unsuspecting confidence of their clergy and people. The ecclesiastical revenues of each diocese were divided into four parts; for the respective uses of the bishop himself, of his inferior clergy, of the poor, and of the public worship; and the abuse

---

public an elaborate description of the church of Jerusalem, (in Vit. Cons. l. iv. c. 46.) It no longer exists, but he has inserted in the life of Constantine (l. iii. c. 36) a short account of the architecture and ornaments. He likewise mentions the church of the Holy Apostles at Constantinople, (l. iv. c. 59.)

[105] See Justinian. Novell. cxxiii. 3. The revenue of the patriarchs, and the most wealthy bishops, is not expressed: the highest annual valuation of a bishopric is stated at *thirty*, and the lowest at *two*, pounds of gold; the medium might be taken at *sixteen*, but these valuations are much below the real value.

[106] See Baronius, (Annal. Eccles. A. D. 324, No. 58, 65, 70, 71.) Every record which comes from the Vatican is justly suspected; yet these rent-rolls have an ancient and authentic color; and it is at least evident, that, if forged, they were forged in a period when *farms*, not *kingdoms*, were the objects of papal avarice.

of this sacred trust was strictly and repeatedly checked.[107] The patrimony of the church was still subject to all the public impositions of the state.[108] The clergy of Rome, Alexandria, Thessalonica, &c., might solicit and obtain some partial exemptions ; but the premature attempt of the great council of Rimini, which aspired to universal freedom, was successfully resisted by the son of Constantine.[109]

IV. The Latin clergy, who erected their tribunal on the ruins of the civil and common law, have modestly accepted, as the gift of Constantine,[110] the independent jurisdiction, which was the fruit of time, of accident, and of their own industry. But the liberality of the Christian emperors had actually endowed them with some legal prerogatives, which secured and dignified the sacerdotal character [111] 1. Under a despotic government, the bishops alone enjoyed and asserted

---

[107] See Thomassin, Discipline de l'Eglise, tom. iii. l. ii. c. 13, 14, 15, p. 689—706. The legal division of the ecclesiastical revenue does not appear to have been established in the time of Ambrose and Chrysostom. Simplicius and Gelasius, who were bishops of Rome in the latter part of the fifth century, mention it in their pastoral letters as a general law, which was already confirmed by the custom of Italy.

[108] Ambrose, the most strenuous assertor of ecclesiastical privileges, submits without a murmur to the payment of the land tax. " Si tributum petit Imperator, non negamus ; agri ecclesiæ solvunt tributum ; solvimus quæ sunt Cæsaris Cæsari, et quæ sunt Dei Deo ; tributum Cæsaris est ; non negatur." Baronius labors to interpret this tribute as an act of charity rather than of duty, (Annal. Eccles. A. D. 387; but the words, if not the intentions, of Ambrose are more candidly explained by Thomassin, Discipline de l'Eglise, tom. iii. l. i. c. 34, p. 268.

[109] In Ariminense synodo super ecclesiarum et clericorum privilegiis tractatû habito, usque eo dispositio progressa est, ut juga quæ viderentur ad ecclesiam pertinere, a publicâ functione cessarent inquietudine desistente ; quod nostra videtur dudum sanctio repulsisse Cod. Theod. l. xvi. tit. ii. leg. 15. Had the synod of Rimini carried this point, such practical merit might have atoned for some speculative heresies.

[110] From Eusebius (in Vit. Constant. l. iv. c. 27) and Sozomen (l. i c. 9) we are assured that the episcopal jurisdiction was extended and confirmed by Constantine ; but the forgery of a famous edict, which was never fairly inserted in the Theodosian Code, (see at the end, tom. vi. p. 303,) is demonstrated by Godefroy in the most satisfactory manner. It is strange that M. de Montesquieu, who was a lawyer as well as a philosopher, should allege this edict of Constantine (Esprit des Loix, l. xxix. c. 16) without intimating any suspicion.

[111] The subject of ecclesiastical jurisdiction has been involved in a mist of passion, of prejudice, and of interest. Two of the fairest

the inestimable privilege of being tried only by their *peers*; and even in a capital accusation, a synod of their brethren were the sole judges of their guilt or innocence. Such a tribunal, unless it was inflamed by personal resentment or religious discord, might be favorable, or even partial, to the sacerdotal order: but Constantine was satisfied,[112] that secret impunity would be less pernicious than public scandal: and the Nicene council was edified by his public declaration, that if he surprised a bishop in the act of adultery, he should cast his Imperial mantle over the episcopal sinner.   2. The domestic jurisdiction of the bishops was at once a privilege and a restraint of the ecclesiastical order, whose civil causes were decently withdrawn from the cognizance of a secular judge. Their venial offences were not exposed to the shame of a public trial or punishment; and the gentle correction which the tenderness of youth may endure from its parents or instructors, was inflicted by the temperate severity of the bishops. But if the clergy were guilty of any crime which could not be sufficiently expiated by their degradation from an honorable and beneficial profession, the Roman magistrate drew the sword of justice, without any regard to ecclesiastical immunities.   3. The arbitration of the bishops was ratified by a positive law; and the judges were instructed to execute, without appeal or delay, the episcopal decrees, whose validity had hitherto depended on the consent of the parties. The conversion of the magistrates themselves, and of the whole empire, might gradually remove the fears and scruples of the Christians. But they still resorted to the tribunal of the bishops, whose abilities and integrity they esteemed; and the venerable Austin enjoyed the satisfaction of complaining that his spiritual functions were perpetually interrupted by the invidious labor of deciding the claim or the possession of

books which have fallen into my hands, are the Institutes of Canon Law, by the Abbé de Fleury, and the Civil History of Naples, by Giannone. Their moderation was the effect of situation as well as of temper. Fleury was a French ecclesiastic, who respected the authority of the parliaments; Giannone was an Italian lawyer, who dreaded the power of the church. And here let me observe, that as the general propositions which I advance are the result of *many* particular and imperfect facts, I must either refer the reader to those modern authors who have expressly treated the subject, or swell these notes to a disagreeable and disproportioned size.

[112] Tillemont has collected from Rufinus, Theodoret, &c., the sentiments and language of Constantine. Mém. Eccles. tom. iii. p. 749, 750.

silver and gold, of lands and cattle. 4. The ancient privilege of sanctuary was transferred to the Christian temples, and extended, by the liberal piety of the younger Theodosius, to the precincts of consecrated ground.[113] The fugitive, and even guilty, suppliants were permitted to implore either the justice, or the mercy, of the Deity and his ministers. The rash violence of despotism was suspended by the mild interposition of the church; and the lives or fortunes of the most eminent subjects might be protected by the mediation of the bishop.

V. The bishop was the perpetual censor of the morals of his people. The discipline of penance was digested into a system of canonical jurisprudence,[114] which accurately defined the duty of private or public confession, the rules of evidence, the degrees of guilt, and the measure of punishment. It was impossible to execute this spiritual censure, if the Christian pontiff, who punished the obscure sins of the multitude, respected the conspicuous vices and destructive crimes of the magistrate : but it was impossible to arraign the conduct of the magistrate, without controlling the administration of civil government. Some considerations of religion, or loyalty, or fear, protected the sacred persons of the emperors from the zeal or resentment of the bishops ; but they boldly censured and excommunicated the subordinate tyrants, who were not invested with the majesty of the purple. St. Athanasius excommunicated one of the ministers of Egypt; and the interdict which he pronounced, of fire and water, was solemnly transmitted to the churches of Cappadocia.[115] Under

---

[113] See Cod. Theod. l. ix. tit. xlv. leg. 4. In the works of Fra Paolo, (tom. iv. p. 192, &c.,) there is an excellent discourse on the origin, claims, abuses, and limits of sanctuaries. He justly observes, that ancient Greece might perhaps contain fifteen or twenty *azyla* or sanctuaries ; a number which at present may be found in Italy within the walls of a single city.

[114] The penitential jurisprudence was continually improved by the canons of the councils. But as many cases were still left to the discretion of the bishops, they occasionally published, after the example of the Roman Prætor, the rules of discipline which they proposed to observe. Among the canonical epistles of the fourth century, those of Basil the Great were the most celebrated. They are inserted in the Pandects of Beveridge, (tom. ii. p. 47—151,) and are translated by Chardon, Hist. des Sacremens, tom. iv. p. 219—277.

[115] Basil, Epistol. xlvii. in Baronius, (Annal. Eccles. A. D. 370. N°. 91,) who declares that he purposely relates it, to convince governors that they were not exempt from a sentence of excommunication. In

the reign of the younger Theodosius, the polite and eloquent Synesius, one of the descendants of Hercules,[116] filled the episcopal seat of Ptolemais, near the ruins of ancient Cyrene,[117] and the philosophic bishop supported with dignity the character which he had assumed with reluctance.[118] He vanquished the monster of Libya, the president Andronicus, who abused the authority of a venal office, invented new modes of rapine and torture, and aggravated the guilt of oppression by that of sacrilege.[119] After a fruitless attempt to reclaim the haughty magistrate by mild and religious admonition, Synesius proceeds to inflict the last sentence of ecclesiastial justice,[120]

---

his opinion, even a royal head is not safe from the thunders of the Vatican; and the cardinal shows himself much more consistent than the lawyers and theologians of the Gallican church.

[116] The long series of his ancestors, as high as Eurysthenes, the first Doric king of Sparta, and the fifth in lineal descent from Hercules, was inscribed in the public registers of Cyrene, a Lacedæmonian colony. (Synes. Epist. lvii. p. 197, edit. Petav.) Such a pure and illustrious pedigree of seventeen hundred years, without adding the royal ancestors of Hercules, cannot be equalled in the history of mankind.

[117] Synesius (de Regno, p. 2) pathetically deplores the fallen and ruined state of Cyrene, πόλις Ἑλληνὶς, παλαιὸν ὄνομα καὶ σεμνὸν, καὶ ἐν ᾠδῇ μυρίᾳ τῶν πάλαι σόφων, νῦν πένης καὶ κατηφῆς, καὶ μέγα ἐρειπιῶν. Ptolemais, a new city, 82 miles to the westward of Cyrene, assumed the metropolitan honors of the Pentapolis, or upper Libya, which were afterwards transferred to Sozusa. See Wesseling, Itinerar. p. 67, 68, 732. Celarius, Geograph. tom. ii, part ii. 72 74. Carolus a Sto Paulo, Geograph. Sacra, p. 273. D'Anville, Geographie Ancienne, tom. iii. p. 43, 44. Mémoires de l'Acad. des Inscriptions, tom. xxxvii. p. 363—391.

[118] Synesius had previously represented his own disqualifications, (Epist. c. v. p. 246—250.) He loved profane studies and profane sports; he was incapable of supporting a life of celibacy; he disbelieved the resurrection; and he refused to preach *fables* to the people, unless he might be permitted to *philosophize* at home. Theophilus, primate of Egypt, who knew his merit, accepted this extraordinary compromise. See the life of Synesius in Tillemont, Mém. Eccles tom. xii. p. 499—554.

[119] See the invective of Synesius, Epist. lvii. p. 191—201. The promotion of Andronicus was illegal; since he was a native of Berenice in the same province The instruments of torture are curiously specified; the κιεστήριον, or press, the δακτυλήθρα, the ποδοστράβη, the ῥινολάβις, the ὤταγρα, and the χειλοτρόφιον, that variously pressed or distended the fingers, the feet, the nose, the ears, and the lips of the victims.

[120] The sentence of excommunication is expressed in a rhetorical style. (Synesius, Epist. lviii. p. 201—203.) The method of involving whole families, though somewhat unjust, was improved into national interdicts

which devotes Andronicus, with his associates and their *families*, to the abhorrence of earth and heaven. The impenitent sinners, more cruel than Phalaris or Sennacherib, more destructive than war, pestilence, or a cloud of locusts, are deprived of the name and privileges of Christians, of the participation of the sacraments, and of the hope of Paradise. The bishop exhorts the clergy, the magistrates, and the people, to renounce all society with the enemies of Christ; to exclude them from their houses and tables; and to refuse them the common offices of life, and the decent rites of burial. The church of Ptolemais, obscure and contemptible as she may appear, addresses this declaration to all her sister churches of the world; and the profane who reject her decrees, will be involved in the guilt and punishment of Andronicus and his impious followers. These spiritual terrors were enforced by a dexterous application to the Byzantine court; the trembling president implored the mercy of the church; and the descendant of Hercules enjoyed the satisfaction of raising a prostrate tyrant from the ground.[121] Such principles and such examples insensibly prepared the triumph of the Roman pontiffs, who have trampled on the necks of kings.

VI. Every popular government has experienced the effects of rude or artificial eloquence. The coldest nature is animated, the firmest reason is moved, by the rapid communication of the prevailing impulse; and each hearer is affected by his own passions, and by those of the surrounding multitude. The ruin of civil liberty had silenced the demagogues of Athens, and the tribunes of Rome; the custom of preaching, which seems to constitute a considerable part of Christian devotion, had not been introduced into the temples of antiquity; and the ears of monarchs were never invaded by the harsh sound of popular eloquence, till the pulpits of the empire were filled with sacred orators, who possessed some advantages unknown to their profane predecessors.[122] The arguments and rhetoric of the tribune were instantly opposed, with equal arms, by skilful and resolute antagonists; and the

---

[121] See Synesius, Epist. xlvii. p. 186, 187. Epist. lxxii. p. 218, 219. Epist. lxxxix. p 230, 231.

[122] See Thomassin (Discipline de l'Eglise, tom. ii. l. iii. c. 83, p. 1761—1770,) and Bingham, (Antiquities, vol. i. l. xiv. c. 4, p. 688 – 717.) Preaching was considered as the most important office of the bishop; but this function was sometimes intrusted to such presbyters as Chrysostom and Augustin.

cause of truth and reason might derive an accidental support from the conflict of hostile passions. The bishop, or some distinguished presbyter, to whom he cautiously delegated the powers of preaching, harangued, without the danger of interruption or reply, a submissive multitude, whose minds had been prepared and subdued by the awful ceremonies of religion. Such was the strict subordination of the Catholic church, that the same concerted sounds might issue at once from a hundred pulpits of Italy or Egypt, if they were *tuned*[123] by the master hand of the Roman or Alexandrian primate. The design of this institution was laudable, but the fruits were not always salutary. The preachers recommended the practice of the social duties ; but they exalted the perfection of monastic virtue, which is painful to the individual, and useless to mankind. Their charitable exhortations betrayed a secret wish, that the clergy might be permitted to manage the wealth of the faithful, for the benefit of the poor. The most sublime representations of the attributes and laws of the Deity were sullied by an idle mixture of metaphysical subtleties, puerile rites, and fictitious miracles : and they expatiated, with the most fervent zeal, on the religious merit of hating the adversaries, and obeying the ministers of the church. When the public peace was distracted by heresy and schism, the sacred orators sounded the trumpet of discord, and, perhaps, of sedition. The understandings of their congregations were perplexed by mystery, their passions were inflamed by invectives ; and they rushed from the Christian temples of Antioch or Alexandria, prepared either to suffer or to inflict martyrdom. The corruption of taste and language is strongly marked in the vehement declamations of the Latin bishops ; but the compositions of Gregory and Chrysostom have been compared with the most splendid models of Attic, or at least of Asiatic, eloquence.[124]

VII. The representatives of the Christian republic were regularly assembled in the spring and autumn of each year ,

---

[123] Queen Elizabeth used this expression, and practised this art, whenever she wished to prepossess the minds of her people in favor of any extraordinary measure of government. The hostile effects of this *music* were apprehended by her successer, and severely felt by his son. " When pulpit, drum ecclesiastic," &c. See Heylin's Life of Archbishop Laud, p. 153.

[124] Those modest orators acknowledged, that, as they were destitute of the gift of miracles, they endeavored to acquire the arts of eloquence

and these synods diffused the spirit of ecclesiastical discipline and legislation through the hundred and twenty provinces of the Roman world.[125] The archbishop or metropolitan was empowered, by the laws, to summon the suffragan bishops of his province; to revise their conduct, o vindicate their rights, to declare their faith, and to examine the merit of the candidates who were elected by the clergy and people to supply the vacancies of the episcopal college. The primates of Rome, Alexandria, Antioch, Carthage, and afterwards Constantinople, who exercised a more ample jurisdiction, convened the numerous assembly of their dependent bishops. But the convocation of great and extraordinary synods was the prerogative of the emperor alone. Whenever the emergencies of the church required this decisive measure, he despatched a peremptory summons to the bishops, or the deputies of each province, with an order for the use of post-horses, and a competent allowance for the expenses of their journey. At an early period, when Constantine was the protector, rather than the proselyte, of Christianity, he referred the African controversy to the council of Arles; in which the bishops of York, of Trèves, of Milan, and of Carthage, met as friends and brethren, to debate in their native tongue on the common interest of the Latin or Western church.[126] Eleven years afterwards, a more numerous and celebrated assembly was convened at Nice in Bithynia, to extinguish, by their final sentence, the subtle disputes which had arisen in Egypt on the subject of the Trinity. Three hundred and eighteen bishops obeyed the summons of their indulgent master; the ecclesiastics of every rank, and sect, and denomination, have been computed at two thousand and forty-eight persons;[127] the Greeks appeared in person; and the consent of the Latins was

---

[125] The council of Nice, in the fourth, fifth, sixth, and seventh canons, has made some fundamental regulations concerning synods, metropolitans, and primates. The Nicene canons have been variously tortured, abused, interpolated, or forged, according to the interest of the clergy. The *Suburbicarian* churches, assigned (by Rufinus) to the bishop of Rome, have been made the subject of vehement controversy. (See Sirmond, Opera, tom. iv. p. 1—238.)

[126] We have only thirty-three or forty-seven episcopal subscriptions: but Ado, a writer indeed of small account, reckons six hundred bishops in the council of Arles. Tillemont, Mém. Eccles. tom. vi. p. 422.

[127] See Tillemont, tom. vi. p. 915, and Beausobre, Hist. du Manicheisme, tom i. p. 529. The name of *bishop*, which is given by Eu-

expressed by the legates of the Roman pontiff. The session which lasted about two months, was frequently honored by the presence of the emperor. Leaving his guards at the door, he seated himself (with the permission of the council) on a low stool in the midst of the hall. Constantine listened with patience, and spoke with modesty: and while he influenced the debates, he humbly professed that he was the minister, not the judge, of the successors of the apostles, who had been established as priests and as gods upon earth.[128] Such profound reverence of an absolute monarch towards a feeble and unarmed assembly of his own subjects, can only be compared to the respect with which the senate had been treated by the Roman princes who adopted the policy of Augustus. Within the space of fifty years, a philosophic spectator of the vicissitudes of human affairs might have contemplated Tacitus in the senate of Rome, and Constantine in the council of Nice. The fathers of the Capitol and those of the church had alike degenerated from the virtues of their founders; but as the bishops were more deeply rooted in the public opinion, they sustained their dignity with more decent pride, and sometimes opposed with a manly spirit the wishes of their sovereign. The progress of time and superstition erased the memory of the weakness, the passion, the ignorance, which disgraced these ecclesiastical synods; and the Catholic world has unanimously submitted[129] to the *infallible* decrees of the general councils.[130]

---

tychius to the 2048 ecclesiastics, (Annal. tom. i. p. 440, vers. Pocock,) must be extended far beyond the limits of an orthodox or even episcopal ordination.

[128] See Euseb. in Vit. Constantin. l. iii. c. 6—21. Tillemont, Mém. Ecclesiastiques, tom. vi. p. 669—759.

[129] Sancimus igitur vicem legum obtinere, quæ a quatuor Sanctis Conciliis . . . . expositæ sunt aut firmatæ. Prædictarum enim quatuor synodorum dogmata sicut sanctas Scripturas et regulas sicut leges observamus. Justinian. Novell. cxxxi. Beveridge (ad Pandect. proleg. p. 2) remarks, that the emperors never made new laws in ecclesiastical matters; and Giannone observes, in a very different spirit, that they gave a legal sanction to the canons of councils. Istoria Civile di Napoli, tom. i. p. 136.

[130] See the article CONCILE in the Encyclopedie, tom. iii. p. 668—679, edition de Lucques. The author, M. de docteur Bouchaud, has discussed, according to the principles of the Gallican church, the principal questions which relate to the form and constitution of general, national, and provincial councils. The editors (see Preface, p. xvi.) have reason to be proud of *this* article. Those who consult their immense compilation, seldom depart so well satisfied.

CHAPTER XXI.

PERSECUTION OF HERESY. — THE SCHISM OF THE DONATISTS. — THE ARIAN CONTROVERSY. — ATHANASIUS. — DISTRACTED STATE OF THE CHURCH AND EMPIRE UNDER CONSTANTINE AND HIS SONS. — TOLERATION OF PAGANISM.

THE grateful applause of the clergy has consecrated the memory of a prince who indulged their passions and promoted their interest. Constantine gave them security, wealth, honors, and revenge; and the support of the orthodox faith was considered as the most sacred and important duty of the civil magistrate. The edict of Milan, the great charter of toleration, had confirmed to each individual of the Roman world the privilege of choosing and professing his own religion. But this inestimable privilege was soon violated; with the knowledge of truth, the emperor imbibed the maxims of persecution; and the sects which dissented from the Catholic church were afflicted and oppressed by the triumph of Christianity. Constantine easily believed that the Heretics, who presumed to dispute *his* opinions, or to oppose *his* commands, were guilty of the most absurd and criminal obstinacy; and that a seasonable application of moderate severities might save those unhappy men from the danger of an everlasting condemnation. Not a moment was lost in excluding the ministers and teachers of the separated congregations from any share of the rewards and immunities which the emperor had so liberally bestowed on the orthodox clergy. But as the sectaries might still exist under the cloud of royal disgrace, the conquest of the East was immediately followed by an edict which announced their total destruction.[1] After a preamble filled with passion and reproach, Constantine absolutely prohibits the assemblies of the Heretics, and confiscates their public property to the use either of the revenue or of the Catholic church. The sects against whom the Imperial severity was directed, appear to have been the adherents of Paul of Samosata; the Montanists of Phrygia, who maintained an enthusiastic succession of

---

[1] Eusebius in Vit. Constantin. l. iii. c. 63, 64, 65, 66

295

prophecy ; the Novatians, who sternly rejected the temporal efficacy of repentance ; the Marcionites and Valentinians, under whose leading banners the various Gnostics of Asia and Egypt had insensibly rallied ; and perhaps the Manichæans, who had recently imported from Persia a more artful composition of Oriental and Christian theology.[2] The design of extirpating the name, or at least of restraining the progress, of these odious Heretics, was prosecuted with vigor and effect. Some of the penal regulations were copied from the edicts of Diocletian ; and this method of conversion was applauded by the same bishops who had felt the hand of oppression, and pleaded for the rights of humanity. Two immaterial circumstances may serve, however, to prove that the mind of Constantine was not entirely corrupted by the spirit of zeal and bigotry. Before he condemned the Manichæans and their kindred sects, he resolved to make an accurate inquiry into the nature of their religious principles. As if he distrusted the impartiality of his ecclesiastical counsellors, this delicate commission was intrusted to a civil magistrate, whose learning and moderation he justly esteemed, and of whose venal character he was probably ignorant.[3] The emperor was soon convinced, that he had too hastily proscribed the orthodox faith and the exemplary morals of the Novatians, who had dissented from the church in some articles of discipline which were not perhaps essential to salvation. By a particular edict, he exempted them from the general penalties of the law ; [4] allowed them to build a church at Constantinople, respected the miracles of their saints, invited their bishop Acesius to the council of Nice ; and gently ridiculed the narrow tenets of his sect by a familiar

---

[2] After some examination of the various opinions of Tillemont, Beausobre, Lardner, &c., I am convinced that Manes did not propagate his sect, even in Persia, before the year 270. It is strange, that a philosophic and foreign heresy should have penetrated so rapidly into the African provinces ; yet I cannot easily reject the edict of Diocletian against the Manichæans, which may be found in Baronius. (Annal. Eccl. A. D. 287.)

[3] Constantinus enim, cum limatius superstitionum quæreret sectas, Manichæorum et similium, &c. Ammian. xv. 15. Strategius, who from this commission obtained the surname of *Musonianus*, was a Christian of the Arian sect. He acted as one of the counts at the council of Sardica. Libanius praises his mildness and prudence. Vales. ad locum Ammian.

[4] Cod. Theod. l. xvi. tit. 5, leg. 2. As the general law is not inserted in the Theodosian Code, it is probable that, in the year 438, the sects which it had condemned were already extinct.

iest; which, from the mouth of a sovereign, must have been
received with applause and gratitude.[5]

The complaints and mutual accusations which assailed the
throne of Constantine, as soon as the death of Maxentius had
submitted Africa to his victorious arms, were ill adapted to
edify an imperfect proselyte. He learned, with surprise, that the
provinces of that great country, from the confines of Cyrene to
the columns of Hercules, were distracted with religious discord.[6] The source of the division was derived from a double
election in the church of Carthage; the second, in rank and
opulence, of the ecclesiastical thrones of the West. Cæcilian
and Majorinus were the two rival primates of Africa; and the
death of the latter soon made room for Donatus, who, by his
superior abilities and apparent virtues, was the firmest support
of his party. The advantage which Cæcilian might claim
from the priority of his ordination, was destroyed by the illegal,
or at least indecent, haste, with which it had been performed,
without expecting the arrival of the bishops of Numidia. The
authority of these bishops, who, to the number of seventy, condemned Cæcilian, and consecrated Majorinus, is again weakened by the infamy of some of their personal characters; and
by the female intrigues, sacrilegious bargains, and tumultuous
proceedings, which are imputed to this Numidian council.[7]
The bishops of the contending factions maintained, with equal

---

[5] Sozomen, l. i. c. 22. Socrates, l. i. c. 10. These historians have
been suspected, but I think without reason, of an attachment to the
Novatian doctrine. The emperor said to the bishop, "Acesius, take
a ladder, and get up to heaven by yourself." Most of the Christian
sects have, by turns, borrowed the ladder of Acesius.

[6] The best materials for this part of ecclesiastical history may be
found in the edition of Optatus Milevitanus, published (Paris, 1700)
by M. Dupin, who has enriched it with critical notes, geographical
discussions, original records, and an accurate abridgment of the whole
controversy. M. de Tillemont has bestowed on the Donatists the
greatest part of a volume, (tom. vi. part i.;) and I am indebted to him
for an ample collection of all the passages of his favorite St. Augustin,
which relate to those heretics.

[7] Schisma igitur illo tempore confusæ mulieris iracundia peperit,
ambitus nutrivit; avaritia roboravit. Optatus, l. i. c. 19. The language of Purpurius is that of a furious madman. Dicitur te necasse
filios sororis tuæ duos. Purpurius respondit: Putas me terreri à te
. . . occidi; et occido eos qui contra me faciunt. Acta Concil. Cirten-
sis, ad calc. Optat. p. 274. When Cæcilian was invited to an assembly of bishops, Purpurius said to his brethren, or rather to his accomplices, "Let him come hither to receive our imposition of hands;
and we will break his head by way of penance." Optat. l. i. c. 19

ardor and obstinacy, that their adversaries were degraded, or at least dishonored, by the odious crime of delivering the Holy Scriptures to the officers of Diocletian. From their mutual reproaches, as well as from the story of this dark transaction, it may justly be inferred, that the late persecution had imbittered the zeal, without reforming the manners, of the African Christians. That divided church was incapable of affording an impartial judicature; the controversy was solemnly tried in five successive tribunals, which were appointed by the emperor; and the whole proceeding, from the first appeal to the final sentence, lasted above three years. A severe inquisition, which was taken by the Prætorian vicar, and the proconsul of Africa, the report of two episcopal visitors who had been sent to Carthage, the decrees of the councils of Rome and of Arles, and the supreme judgment of Constantine himself in his sacred consistory, were all favorable to the cause of Cæcilian; and he was unanimously acknowledged by the civil and ecclesiastical powers, as the true and lawful primate of Africa. The honors and estates of the church were attributed to *his* suffragan bishops, and it was not without difficulty, that Constantine was satisfied with inflicting the punishment of exile on the principal leaders of the Donatist faction. As their cause was examined with attention, perhaps it was determined with justice. Perhaps their complaint was not without foundation, that the credulity of the emperor had been abused by the insidious arts of his favorite Osius. The influence of falsehood and corruption might procure the condemnation of the innocent, or aggravate the sentence of the guilty. Such an act, however, of injustice, if it concluded an importunate dispute, might be numbered among the transient evils of a despotic administration, which are neither felt nor remembered by posterity.

But this incident, so inconsiderable that it scarcely deserves a place in history, was productive of a memorable schism, which afflicted the provinces of Africa above three hundred years, and was extinguished only with Christianity itself. The inflexible zeal of freedom and fanaticism animated the Donatists to refuse obedience to the usurpers, whose election they disputed, and whose spiritual powers they denied. Excluded from the civil and religious communion of mankind, they boldly excommunicated the rest of mankind, who had embraced the impious party of Cæcilian, and of the Traditors, from which he derived his pretended ordination. They asserted with confidence, and almost with exultation, that the

Apostolical succession was interrupted; that *all* the bishops of Europe and Asia were infected by the contagion of guilt and schism; and that the prerogatives of the Catholic church were confined to the chosen portion of the African believers, who alone had preserved inviolate the integrity of their faith and discipline. This rigid theory was supported by the most uncharitable conduct. Whenever they acquired a proselyte, even from the distant provinces of the East, they carefully repeated the sacred rites of baptism[8] and ordination; as they rejected the validity of those which he had already received from the hands of heretics or schismatics. Bishops, virgins, and even spotless infants, were subjected to the disgrace of a public penance, before they could be admitted to the communion of the Donatists. If they obtained possession of a church which had been used by their Catholic adversaries, they purified the unhallowed building with the same zealous care which a temple of idols might have required. They washed the pavement, scraped the walls, burnt the altar, which was commonly of wood, melted the consecrated plate, and cast the Holy Eucharist to the dogs, with every circumstance of ignominy which could provoke and perpetuate the animosity of religious factions.[9] Notwithstanding this irreconcilable aversion, the two parties, who were mixed and separated in all the cities of Africa, had the same language and manners, the same zeal and learning, the same faith and worship. Proscribed by the civil and ecclesiastical powers of the empire, the Donatists still maintained in some provinces, particularly in Numidia, their superior numbers; and four hundred bishops acknowledged the jurisdiction of their primate. But the invincible spirit of the sect sometimes preyed on its own vitals: and the bosom of their schismatical church was torn by intestine divisions. A fourth part of the Donatist bishops followed the independent standard of the Maximianists. The narrow and solitary path which their first leaders had marked out, continued to deviate from the great society

---

[8] The councils of Arles, of Nice, and of Trent, confirmed the wise and moderate practice of the church of Rome. The Donatists, however, had the advantage of maintaining the sentiment of Cyprian, and of a considerable part of the primitive church. Vincentius Lirinesis (p. 332, ap. Tillemont, Mém. Eccles. tom. vi. p. 138) has explained why the Donatists are eternally burning with the Devil, while St. Cyprian reigns in heaven with Jesus Christ.

[9] See the sixth book of Optatus Milevitanus, p. 91—100.

of mankind. Even the imperceptible sect of the Rogatians could affirm, without a blush, that when Christ should descend to judge the earth, he would find his true religion preserved only in a few nameless villages of the Cæsarean Mauritania.[10]

The schism of the Donatists was confined to Africa: the more diffusive mischief of the Trinitarian controversy successively penetrated into every part of the Christian world. The former was an accidental quarrel, occasioned by the abuse of freedom; the latter was a high and mysterious argument, derived from the abuse of philosophy. From the age of Constantine to that of Clovis and Theodoric, the temporal interests both of the Romans and Barbarians were deeply involved in the theological disputes of Arianism. The historian may therefore be permitted respectfully to withdraw the veil of the sanctuary; and to deduce the progress of reason and faith, of error and passion, from the school of Plato, to the decline and fall of the empire.

The genius of Plato, informed by his own meditation, or by the traditional knowledge of the priests of Egypt,[11] had ventured to explore the mysterious nature of the Deity. When he had elevated his mind to the sublime contemplation of the first self-existent, necessary cause of the universe, the Athenian sage was incapable of conceiving *how* the simple unity of his essence could admit the infinite variety of distinct and successive ideas which compose the model of the intellectual world; *how* a Being purely incorporeal could execute that perfect model, and mould with a plastic hand the rude and independent chaos. The vain hope of extricating himself from these difficulties, which must ever oppress the feeble powers of the human mind, might induce Plato to consider the divine nature under the threefold modification — of the first cause, the reason, or *Logos*, and the soul or spirit of the

---

[10] Tillemont, Mém. Ecclesiastiques, tom. vi. part i. p. 253. He laughs at their partial credulity. He revered Augustin, the great doctor of the system of predestination.

[11] Plato Ægyptum peragravit ut a sacerdotibus Barbaris numeros et *cœlestia* acciperet. Cicero de Finibus, v. 25. The Egyptians might still preserve the traditional creed of the Patriarchs. Josephus has persuaded many of the Christian fathers, that Plato derived a part of his knowledge from the Jews; but this vain opinion cannot be reconciled with the obscure state and unsocial manners of the Jewish people, whose scriptures were not accessible to Greek curiosity till more than one hundred years after the death of Plato. See Marsham, Canon. Chron. p. 144. Le Clerc, Epistol. Critic. vii. p. 177—194.

universe. His poetical imagination sometimes fixed and animated these metaphysical abstractions; the three *archicai* or original principles were represented in the Platonic system as three Gods, united with each other by a mysterious and ineffable generation; and the Logos was particularly considered under the more accessible character of the Son of an Eternal Father, and the Creator and Governor of the world. Such appear to have been the secret doctrines which were cautiously whispered in the gardens of the academy; and which, according to the more recent disciples of Plato,* could not be

---

* This exposition of the doctrine of Plato appears to me contrary to the true sense of that philosopher's writings. The brilliant imagination which he carried into metaphysical inquiries, his style, full of allegories and figures, have misled those interpreters who did not seek, from the whole tenor of his works and beyond the images which the writer employs, the system of this philosopher. In my opinion, there is no Trinity in Plato : he has established no mysterious generation between the three pretended principles which he is made to distinguish. Finally, he conceived only as *attributes* of the Deity, or of matter, those ideas, of which it is supposed that he made *substances*, real beings.

According to Plato, God and matter existed from all eternity. Before the creation of the world, matter had in itself a principle of motion, but without end or laws : it is this principle which Plato calls the irrational soul of the world, (ἄλογος ψυχη;) because, according to his doctrine, every spontaneous and original principle of motion is called soul. God wished to impress *form* upon matter, that is to say, 1. To mould matter, and make it into a body; 2. To regulate its motion, and subject it to some end and to certain laws. The Deity, in this operation, could not act but according to the ideas existing in his intelligence : their union filled this, and formed the ideal type of the world. It is this ideal world, this divine intelligence, existing with God from all eternity, and called by Plato νους or λόγος, which he is supposed to personify, to substantialize; while an attentive examination is sufficient to convince us that he has never assigned it an existence external to the Deity, (hors de la Divinité,) and that he considered the λόγος as the aggregate of the ideas of God, the divine understanding in its relation to the world. The contrary opinion is irreconcilable with all his philosophy : thus he says (Timæus, p. 348, edit. Bip.) that to the idea of the Deity is essentially united that of an intelligence, of a *logos*. He would thus have admitted a double *logos ;* one inherent in the Deity as an attribute, the other independently existing as a substance. He affirms (Timæus, 316, 337, 348, Sophista, v. ii. p. 265, 266) that the intelligence, the principle of order, νους or λόγος, cannot exist but as an attribute of a soul, (ψυχη,) the principle of motion and of life, of which the nature is unknown to us. How, then, according to this, could he consider the *logos* as a substance endowed with an independent existence ? In other places he explains it by these two words, ἐπιστήμη, (knowledge, science,) and διά νοια, (intelligence,) which signify the attributes of the Deity. (Sophist. v. ii. p. 299.) Lastly, it follows from several passages, among others from Phileb. v. iv. p. 247, 248, that Plato has never given to the words νους, λόγος, but one of these two meanings : 1. *The result of the action of the Deity ;* that is, order, the collective laws which govern the world : and 2. The rational soul of the world, (λογιστίκη ψυχη,) or the cause of this result, that is to say, the divine intelligence. When he separates God, the ideal archetype of the world and matter, it is to explain how, according to his system, God has proceeded, at the creation, to unite the principle of

perfectly understood, till after an assidious study of thirty years.[12]

The arms of the Macedonians diffused over Asia and Egypt the language and learning of Greece; and the theological system of Plato was taught, with less reserve, and perhaps with some improvements, in the celebrated school of Alexandria.[13]

---

[12] The modern guides who lead me to the knowledge of the Platonic system are Cudworth, (Intellectual System, p. 568—620,) Basnage, (Hist. des Juifs, l. iv. c. 4, p. 53—86,) Le Clerc, (Epist. Crit. vii. p. 194—209,) and Brucker, (Hist. Philosoph. tom. i. p. 675—706.) As the learning of these writers was equal, and their intention different, an inquisitive observer may derive instruction from their disputes, and certainty from their agreement.

[13] Brucker, Hist. Philosoph. tom. i. p. 1349—1357. The Alexandrian school is celebrated by Strabo (l. xvii.) and Ammianus, (xxii. 6.)*

---

order, which he had within himself, his proper intelligence, the λόγος, the principle of motion, to the principle of motion, the irrational soul, the ἄλογος ψῦχη, which was in matter. When he speaks of the place occupied by the ideal world, (τόπος νοητός,) it is to designate the divine intelligence, which is its cause. Finally, in no part of his writings do we find a true personification of the pretended beings of which he is said to have formed a trinity: and if this personification existed, it would equally apply to many other notions, of which might be formed many different trinities.

This error into which many ancient as well as modern interpreters of Plato have fallen, was very natural. Besides the snares which were concealed in his figurative style; besides the necessity of comprehending as a whole the system of his ideas, and not to explain isolated passages, the nature of his doctrine itself would conduce to this error. When Plato appeared, the uncertainty of human knowledge, and the continual illusions of the senses were acknowledged, and had given rise to a general scepticism. Socrates had aimed at raising morality above the influence of this scepticism: Plato endeavored to save metaphysics, by seeking in the human intellect a source of certainty which the senses could not furnish. He invented the system of innate ideas, of which the aggregate formed, according to him, the ideal world, and affirmed that these ideas were real attributes, not only attached to our conceptions of objects, but to the nature of the objects themselves; a nature of which from them we might obtain a knowledge. He gave, then, to these ideas a positive existence as attributes; his commentators could easily give them a real existence as substances; especially as the terms which he used to designate them, ἄυτο το κάλον, ἄυτο τὸ ἀγαθον, essential beauty, essential goodness, lent themselves to this substantialization, (hypostasis.) — G.

We have retained this view of the original philosophy of Plato, in which there is probably much truth. The genius of Plato was rather metaphysical than impersonative: his poetry was in his language, rather than, like that of the Orientals, in his conceptions. — M.

* The philosophy of Plato was not the only source of that professed in the school of Alexandria. That city, in which Greek, Jewish, and Egyptian men of letters were assembled, was the scene of a strange fusion of the system of these three people. The Greeks brought a Platonism, already much changed; the Jews, who had acquired at Babylon a great number of Oriental notions, and whose theological opinions had undergone great changes by this intercourse, endeavored to reconcile Platonism with their

A numerous colony of Jews had been invited, by the favor of the Ptolemies, to settle in their new capital.[14] While the bulk of the nation practised the legal ceremonies, and pursued the lucrative occupations of commerce, a few Hebrews, of a more liberal spirit, devoted their lives to religious and philosophical contemplation.[15] They cultivated with diligence, and embraced with ardor, the theological system of the Athenian sage. But their national pride would have been mortified by

---

[14] Joseph. Antiquitat. l. xii. c. 1, 3. Basnage, Hist. des Juifs, l. vii. c. 7.

[15] For the origin of the Jewish philosophy, see Eusebius, Præparat. Evangel. viii. 9, 10. According to Philo, the Therapeutæ studied philosophy ; and Brucker has proved (Hist. Philosoph. tom. ii. p. 787) that they gave the preference to that of Plato.

---

new doctrine, and disfigured it entirely: lastly, the Egyptians, who were not willing to abandon notions for which the Greeks themselves entertained respect, endeavored on their side to reconcile their own with those of their neighbors. It is in Ecclesiasticus and the Wisdom of Solomon that we trace the influence of Oriental philosophy rather than that of Platonism. We find in these books, and in those of the later prophets, as in Ezekiel, notions unknown to the Jews before the Babylonian captivity, of which we do not discover the germ in Plato, but which are manifestly derived from the Orientals. Thus God represented under the image of light, and the principle of evil under that of darkness ; the history of the good and bad angels ; paradise and hell, &c., are doctrines of which the origin, or at least the positive determination, can only be referred to the Oriental philosophy. Plato supposed matter eternal ; the Orientals and the Jews considered it as a creation of God, who alone was eternal. It is impossible to explain the philosophy of the Alexandrian school solely by the blending of the Jewish theology with the Greek philosophy. The Oriental philosophy, however little it may be known, is recognized at every instant. Thus, according to the Zend Avesta, it is by the Word (honover) more ancient than the world, that Ormuzd created the universe. This word is the *logos* of Philo, consequently very different from that of Plato. I have shown that Plato never personified the logos as the ideal archetype of the world : Philo ventured this personification. The Deity, according to him, has a double logos ; the first (λόγος ενδιάθετος) is the ideal archetype of the world, the ideal world, the *first-born* of the Deity ; the second (λόγο. προφόρικος) is the word itself of God, personified under the image of a being acting to create the sensible world, and to make it like to the ideal world : it is the second-born of God. Following out his imaginations, Philo went so far as to personify anew the ideal world, under the image of a celestial man, (δυράιιος άνφρωπος,) the primitive type of man, and the sensible world under the image of another man less perfect than the celestial man. Certain notions of the Oriental philosophy may have given rise to this strange abuse of allegory, which it is sufficient to relate, to show what alterations Platonism had already undergone, and what was their source. Philo, moreover, of all the Jews of Alexandria, is the one whose Platonism is the most pure. (See Buhle, Introd. to Hist. of Mod. Philosophy Michaelis, Introd. to New Test. in German, part ii. p. 973.) It is from this mixture of Orientalism, Platonism, and Judaism, that Gnosticism arose, which has produced so many theological and philosophical extravagancies, and in which Oriental notions evidently predominate. — G.

a fair confession of their former poverty: and they boldly
marked, as the sacred inheritance of their ancestors, the gold
and jewels which they had so lately stolen from their Egyptian
masters. One hundred years before the birth of Christ, a
philosophical treatise, which manifestly betrays the style and
sentiments of the school of Plato, was produced by the Alexandrian Jews, and unanimously received as a genuine and
valuable relic of the inspired Wisdom of Solomon.[16] A similar union of the Mosaic faith and the Grecian philosophy,
distinguishes the works of Philo, which were composed, for
the most part, under the reign of Augustus.[17] The material
soul of the universe [18] might offend the piety of the Hebrews:
but they applied the character of the Logos to the Jehovah of
Moses and the patriarchs; and the Son of God was introduced
upon earth under a visible, and even human appearance, to
perform those familiar offices which seem incompatible with
the nature and attributes of the Universal Cause.[19]

   The eloquence of Plato, the name of Solomon, the authority

---

[16] See Calmet, Dissertations sur la Bible, tom. ii. p. 277. The book
of the Wisdom of Solomon was received by many of the fathers as the
work of that monarch; and although rejected by the Protestants for
want of a Hebrew original, it has obtained, with the rest of the Vul-
gate, the sanction of the council of Trent.

[17] The Platonism of Philo, which was famous to a proverb, is proved
beyond a doubt by Le Clerc, (Epist. Crit. viii. p. 211—228.) Basnage
(Hist. des Juifs, l. iv. c. 5) has clearly ascertained, that the theological works of Philo were composed before the death, and most
probably before the birth, of Christ. In such a time of darkness, the
knowledge of Philo is more astonishing than his errors. Bull,
Defens. Fid. Nicen. s. i. c. i. p. 12.

[18] Mens agitat molem, et magno se corpore *miscet.*
   Besides this material soul, Cudworth has discovered (p. 562) in
Amelius, Porphyry, Plotinus, and, as he thinks, in Plato himself, a
superior, spiritual *upercosmian* soul of the universe. But this double
soul is exploded by Brucker, Basnage, and Le Clerc, as an idle fancy
of the latter Platonists.

[19] Petav. Dogmata Theologica, tom. ii. l. viii. c. 2, p. 791. Bull,
Defens. Fid. Nicen. s. i. c. l. p. 8, 13. This notion, till it was abused
by the Arians, was freely adopted in the Christian theology. Tertullian (adv. Praxeam, c. 16) has a remarkable and dangerous passage.
After contrasting, with indiscreet wit, the nature of God, and the
actions of Jehovah, he concludes: Scilicet ut hæc de filio Dei non
credenda fuisse, si non scripta essent; fortasse non credenda de Patre
licet scripta.*

---

* Tertullian is here arguing against the Patripassians; those who asserted that the Father was born of the Virgin, died and was buried. — M.

of the school of Alexandria, and the consent of the Jews and Greeks, were insufficient to establish the truth of a mysterious doctrine, which might please, but could not satisfy, a rational mind. A prophet, or apostle, inspired by the Deity, can alone exercise a lawful dominion over the faith of mankind: and the theology of Plato might have been forever confounded with the philosophical visions of the Academy, the Porch, and the Lycæum, if the name and divine attributes of the *Logos* had not been confirmed by the celestial pen of the last and most sublime of the Evangelists.[20] The Christian Revelation,

---

[20] The Platonists admired the beginning of the Gospel of St. John, as containing an exact transcript of their own principles. Augustin. de Civitat. Dei, x. 29. Amelius apud Cyril. advers. Julian. l. viii. p. 283. But in the third and fourth centuries, the Platonists of Alexandria might improve their Trinity, by the secret study of the Christian theology.*

---

* A short discussion on the sense in which St. John has used the word Logos, will prove that he has not borrowed it from the philosophy of Plato. The evangelist adopts this word without previous explanation, as a term with which his contemporaries were already familiar, and which they could at once comprehend. To know the sense which he gave to it, we must inquire that which it generally bore in his time. We find two: the one attached to the word *logos* by the Jews of Palestine, the other by the school of Alexandria, particularly by Philo. The Jews had feared at all times to pronounce the name of Jehovah; they had formed a habit of designating God by one of his attributes; they called him sometimes Wisdom, sometimes the Word. *By the word of the Lord were the heavens made.* (Psalm xxxiii. 6.) Accustomed to allegories, they often addressed themselves to this attribute of the Deity as a real being. Solomon makes Wisdom say, " The Lord possessed me in the beginning of his way, before his works of old. I was set up from everlasting, from the beginning, or ever the earth was." (Prov. viii. 22, 23.) Their residence in Persia only increased this inclination to sustained allegories. In the Ecclesiasticus of the Son of Sirach, and the Book of Wisdom like the following: " I came out of the mouth of the Most High; I covered the earth as a cloud; . . . I alone compassed the circuit of heaven, and walked in the bottom of the deep . . . The Creator created me from the beginning, before the world, and I shall never fail." (Eccles. xxiv. 35—39.) See also the Wisdom of Solomon, c. vii. v. 9. [The latter book is clearly Alexandrian. — M.] We see from this that the Jews understood from the Hebrew and Chaldaic words which signify Wisdom, the Word, and which were translated into Greek by σοφία, λόγος, a simple attribute of the Deity, allegorically personified, but of which they did not make a real particular being, separate from the Deity.

The school of Alexandria, on the contrary, and Philo among the rest, mingling Greek with Jewish and Oriental notions, and abandoning himself to his inclination to mysticism, personified the *logos*, and represented it (see note, p. 307) as a distinct being, created by God, and intermediate between God and man. This is the second *logos* of Philo, (λόγος προφόρικος,) that which acts from the beginning of the world, alone in its kind, (μονογενης,) creator of the sensible world, (κόσμος αἰσθητὸς,) formed by God according to the ideal world (κόσμος νόητος) which he had in himself, and

which was consummated under the reign of Nerva, disclosed to the world the amazing secret, that the LOGOS, who was with God from the beginning, and was God, who had made all things, and for whom all things had been made, was incarnate in the person of Jesus of Nazareth; who had been born of a virgin, and suffered death on the cross. Besides the general design of fixing on a perpetual basis the divine honors of Christ, the most ancient and respectable of the ecclesiastical writers have ascribed to the evangelic theologian a particular intention to confute two opposite heresies, which disturbed the

which was the first logos, (ὁ ἀνωτάτω,) the first-born (ὁ πρεσβύτερος υἱος) of the Deity. The *logos* taken in this sense, then, was a created being, but, anterior to the creation of the world, near to God, and charged with his revelations to mankind.

Which of these two senses is that which St. John intended to assign to the word logos in the first chapter of his Gospel, and in all his writings?

St. John was a Jew, born and educated in Palestine; he had no knowledge, at least very little, of the philosophy of the Greeks, and that of the Grecizing Jews: he would naturally, then, attach to the word *logos* the sense attached to it by the Jews of Palestine. If, in fact, we compare the attributes which he assigns to the *logos* with those which are assigned to it in Proverbs, in the Wisdom of Solomon, in Ecclesiasticus, we shall see that they are the same. The Word was in the world, and the world was made by him; in him was life, and the life was the light of men, (c. i. v. 10—14.) It is impossible not to trace in this chapter the ideas which the Jews had formed of the allegorized logos. The evangelist afterwards really personifies that which his predecessors have personified only poetically; for he affirms "*that the Word became flesh*," (v. 14.) It was to prove this that he wrote. Closely examined, the ideas which he gives of the *logos* cannot agree with those of Philo and the school of Alexandria; they correspond, on the contrary, with those of the Jews of Palestine. Perhaps St. John, employing a well-known term to explain a doctrine which was yet unknown, has slightly altered the sense; it is this alteration which we appear to discover on comparing different passages of his writings.

It is worthy of remark, that the Jews of Palestine, who did not perceive this alteration, could find nothing extraordinary in what St. John said of the Logos; at least they comprehended it without difficulty, while the Greeks and Grecizing Jews, on their part, brought to it prejudices and preconceptions easily reconciled with those of the evangelist, who did not expressly contradict them. This circumstance must have much favored the progress of Christianity. Thus the fathers of the church in the two first centuries and later, formed almost all in the school of Alexandria, gave to the Logos of St. John a sense nearly similar to that which it received from Philo. Their doctrine approached very near to that which in the fourth century the council of Nice condemned in the person of Arius. — G.

M. Guizot has forgotten the long residence of St. John at Ephesus, the centre of the mingling opinions of the East and West, which were gradually growing up into Gnosticism. (See Matter. Hist. du Gnosticisme, vol. i. p. 154.) St. John's sense of the Logos seems as far removed from the simple allegory ascribed to the Palestinian Jews as from the Oriental impersonation of the Alexandrian. The simple truth may be, that St. John took the familiar term, and, as it were, infused into it the peculiar and Christian sense in which it is used in his writings. — M.

peace of the primitive church.[21]   I. The faith of the Ebionites,[22] perhaps of the Nazarenes,[23] was gross and imperfect
They revered Jesus as the greatest of the prophets, endowed
with supernatural virtue and power. They ascribed to his
person and to his future reign all the predictions of the
Hebrew oracles which relate to the spiritual and everlasting
kingdom of the promised Messiah.[24] Some of them might
confess that he was born of a virgin; but they obstinately
rejected the preceding existence and divine perfections of the
Logos, or Son of God, which are so clearly defined in the
Gospel of St. John. About fifty years afterwards, the Ebionites, whose errors are mentioned by Justin Martyr with less
severity than they seem to deserve,[25] formed a very inconsiderable portion of the Christian name. II. The Gnostics, who
were distinguished by the epithet of *Docetes*, deviated into
the contrary extreme; and betrayed the human, while they
asserted the divine, nature of Christ. Educated in the school
of Plato, accustomed to the sublime idea of the *Logos*, they
readily conceived that the brightest *Æon*, or *Emanation* of the
Deity, might assume the outward shape and visible appearances of a mortal;[26] but they vainly pretended, that the
imperfections of matter are incompatible with the purity of a

---

[21] See Beausobre, Hist. Critique du Manicheisme, tom. i. p. 377.
The Gospel according to St. John is supposed to have been published
about seventy years after the death of Christ.

[22] The sentiments of the Ebionites are fairly stated by Mosheim (p.
331) and Le Clerc, (Hist. Eccles. p. 535.) The Clementines, published among the apostolical fathers, are attributed by the critics to
one of these sectaries.

[23] Stanch polemics, like a Bull, (Judicium Eccles. Cathol. c. 2,)
insist on the orthodoxy of the Nazarenes; which appears less pure
and certain in the eyes of Mosheim, (p. 330.)

[24] The humble condition and sufferings of Jesus have always been
a stumbling-block to the Jews. "Deus . . . contrariis coloribus
Messiam depinxerat; futurus erat Rex, Judex, Pastor," &c. See
Limborch et Orobio Amica Collat. p. 8, 19, 53—76, 192—234. But
this objection has obliged the believing Christians to lift up their eyes
to a spiritual and everlasting kingdom.

[25] Justin Martyr, Dialog. cum Tryphonte, p. 143, 144. See Le Clerc,
Hist. Eccles. p. 615. Bull and his editor Grabe (Judicium Eccles.
Cathol. c. 7, and Appendix) attempt to distort either the sentiments or
the words of Justin; but their violent correction of the text is rejected
even by the Benedictine editors.

[26] The Arians reproached the orthodox party with borrowing their
Trinity from the Valentinians and Marcionites. See Beausobre, Hist.
du Manicheisme, l. iii. c. 5, 7.

celestial substance. While the blood of Christ yet smoked on Mount Calvary, the Docetes invented the impious and extravagant hypothesis, that, instead of issuing from the womb of the Virgin,[27] he had descended on the banks of the Jordan in the form of perfect manhood; that he had imposed on the senses of his enemies, and of his disciples; and that the ministers of Pilate had wasted their impotent rage on an airy phantom, who *seemed* to expire on the cross, and, after three days, to rise from the dead.[28]

---

[27] Non dignum est ex utero credere Deum, et Deum Christum . . . . non dignum est ut tanta majestas per sordes et squalores mulieris transire credatur. The Gnostics asserted the impurity of matter and of marriage; and they were scandalized by the gross interpretations of the fathers, and even of Augustin himself. See Beausobre, tom. ii. p. 523.*

[28] Apostolis adhuc in sæculo superstitibus apud Judæam Christi sanguine recente, et *phantasma* corpus Domini asserebatur. Cotelerius thinks (Patres Apostol. tom. ii. p. 24) that those who will not allow the *Docetes* to have arisen in the time of the Apostles, may with equal reason deny that the sun shines at noonday. These *Docetes*, who formed the most considerable party among the Gnostics, were so called, because they granted only a *seeming* body to Christ.†

---

* The greater part of the Docetæ rejected the true divinity of Jesus Christ, as well as his human nature. They belonged to the Gnostics, whom some philosophers, in whose party Gibbon has enlisted, make to derive their opinions from those of Plato. These philosophers did not consider that Platonism had undergone continual alterations, and that those which gave it some analogy with the notions of the Gnostics were later in their origin than most of the sects comprehended under this name. Mosheim has proved (in his Instit. Histor. Eccles. Major. s. i. p 136, sqq. and p. 339, sqq.) that the Oriental philosophy, combined with the cabalistical philosophy of the Jews, had given birth to Gnosticism. The relations which exist between this doctrine and the records which remain to us of that of the Orientals, the Chaldean and Persian, have been the source of the errors of the Gnostic Christians, who wished to reconcile their ancient notions with their new belief. It is on this account that, denying the human nature of Christ, they also denied his intimate union with God, and took him for one of the substances (æons) created by God. As they believed in the eternity of matter, and considered it to be the principle of evil, in opposition to the Deity, the first cause and principle of good, they were unwilling to admit that one of the pure substances, one of the æons which came forth from God, had, by partaking in the material nature, allied himself to the principle of evil; and this was their motive for rejecting the real humanity of Jesus Christ. See Ch. G. F Walch, Hist. of Heresies in Germ. t. i. p. 217, sqq. Brucker, Hist. Crit. Phil. ii. p. 639. — G.

† The name of Docetæ was given to these sectaries only in the course of the second century: this name did not designate a sect, properly so called; it applied to all the sects who taught the non-reality of the material body of Christ; of this number were the Valentinians, the Basilidians, the Ophites, the Marcionites, (against whom Tertullian wrote his

The divine sanction, which the Apostle had bestowed on the fundamental principle of the theology of Plato, encouraged the learned proselytes of the second and third centuries to admire and study the writings of the Athenian sage, who had thus marvellously anticipated one of the most surprising discoveries of the Christian revelation. The respectable name of Plato was used by the orthodox,[29] and abused by the heretics,[30] as the common support of truth and error: the authority of his skilful commentators, and the science of dialectics, were employed to justify the remote consequences of his opinions and to supply the discreet silence of the inspired writers. The same subtle and profound questions concerning the nature, the generation, the distinction, and the equality of the three divine persons of the mysterious *Triad*, or *Trinity*,[31] were agitated in the philosophical and in the Christian schools of Alexandria. An eager spirit of curiosity urged them to explore the secrets of the abyss; and the pride of the profes-

---

[29] Some proofs of the respect which the Christians entertained for the person and doctrine of Plato may be found in De la Mothe le Vayer, tom. v. p. 135, &c., edit. 1757; and Basnage, Hist. des Juifs, tom. iv. p. 29, 79, &c.

[30] Doleo bona fide, Platonem omnium hæreticorum condimentarium factum. Tertullian. de Anima, c. 23. Petavius (Dogm. Theolog. tom. iii. proleg. 2) shows that this was a general complaint. Beausobre (tom. i. l. iii. c. 9, 10) has deduced the Gnostic errors from Platonic principles; and as, in the school of Alexandria, those principles were blended with the Oriental philosophy, (Brucker, tom. i. p. 1356,) the sentiment of Beausobre may be reconciled with the opinion of Mosheim, (General History of the Church, vol. i. p. 37.)

[31] If Theophilus, bishop of Antioch, (see Dupin, Bibliothèque Ecclesiastique, tom. i. p. 66,) was the first who employed the word *Triad*, *Trinity*, that abstract term, which was already familiar to the schools of philosophy, must have been introduced into the theology of the christians after the middle of the second century.

---

book, De Carne Christi,) and other Gnostics. In truth, Clement of Alexandria (l. iii. Strom. c. 13, p. 552) makes express mention of a sect of Docetæ, and even names as one of its heads a certain Cassianus; but every thing leads us to believe that it was not a distinct sect. Fhilastrius (de Hæres, c. 31) reproaches Saturninus with being a Docete. Irenæus (adv. Hær. c. 23) makes the same reproach against Basilides. Epiphanius and Philastrius, who have treated in detail on each particular heresy, do not specially name that of the Docetæ. Serapion, bishop of Antioch, (Euseb. Hist. Eccles. l. vi. c. 12,) and Clement of Alexandria, (l. vii. Strom. p. 900,) appear to be the first who have used the generic name. It is not found in any earlier record, though the error which it points out existed even in the time of the Apostles. See Ch. G. F. Walch, Hist. of Her v. i. p. 283. Tillemont, Mém. pour servir à la Hist. Eccles. ii. p. 50. Bud deus de Eccles. Apost. c. 5, § 7. — G.

sors, and of their disciples, was satisfied with the science of words. But the most sagacious of the Christian theologians the great Athanasius himself, has candidly confessed,[32] that whenever he forced his understanding to meditate on the divinity of the *Logos*, his toilsome and unavailing efforts recoiled on themselves; that the more he thought, the less he comprehended; and the more he wrote, the less capable was he of expressing his thoughts. In every step of the inquiry, we are compelled to feel and acknowledge the immeasurable disproportion between the size of the object and the capacity of the human mind. We may strive to abstract the notions of time, of space, and of matter, which so closely adhere to all the perceptions of our experimental knowledge. But as soon as we presume to reason of infinite substance, of spiritual generation; as often as we deduce any positive conclusions from a negative idea, we are involved in darkness, perplexity, and inevitable contradiction. As these difficulties arise from the nature of the subject, they oppress, with the same insuperable weight, the philosophic and the theological disputant; but we may observe two essential and peculiar circumstances, which discriminated the doctrines of the Catholic church from the opinions of the Platonic school.

I. A chosen society of philosophers, men of a liberal education and curious disposition, might silently meditate, and temperately discuss in the gardens of Athens or the library of Alexandria, the abstruse questions of metaphysical science. The lofty speculations, which neither convinced the understanding, nor agitated the passions, of the Platonists themselves, were carelessly overlooked by the idle, the busy, and even the studious part of mankind.[33] But after the *Logos* had been revealed as the sacred object of the faith, the hope, and the religious worship of the Christians, the mysterious system was embraced by a numerous and increasing multitude in every province of the Roman world. Those persons who, from their age, or sex, or occupations, were the least qualified to judge,

[32] Athanasius, tom. i. p. 808. His expressions have an uncommon energy; and as he was writing to monks, there could not be any occasion for him to *affect* a rational language.

[33] In a treatise, which professed to explain the opinions of the ancient philosophers concerning the nature of the gods, we might expect to discover the theological Trinity of Plato. But Cicero very honestly confessed, that although he had translated the Timæus, he could never understand that mysterious dialogue. See Hieronym. præf. ad l. xii. in Isaiam, tom. v. p. 154.

who were .he least exercised in the habits of abstract reasoning, aspired to contemplate the economy of the Divine
Nature: and it is the boast of Tertullian,[34] that a Christian
mechanic could readily answer such questions as had perplexed the wisest of the Grecian sages. Where the subject
lies so far beyond our reach, the difference between the highest and the lowest of human understandings may indeed be
calculated as infinitely small; yet the degree of weakness
may perhaps be measured by the degree of obstinacy and
dogmatic confidence. These speculations, instead of being
treated as the amusement of a vacant hour, became the most
serious business of the present, and the most useful prepara
tion for a future, life. A theology, which it was incumbent
to believe, which it was impious to doubt, and which it might
be dangerous, and even fatal, to mistake, became the familiar
topic of private meditation and popular discourse. The cold
indifference of philosophy was inflamed by the fervent spirit
of devotion; and even the metaphors of common language
suggested the fallacious prejudices of sense and experience.
The Christians, who abhorred the gross and impure generation
of the Greek mythology,[35] were tempted to argue from the
familiar analogy of the filial and paternal relations. The
character of *Son* seemed to imply a perpetual subordination
to the voluntary author of his existence;[36] but as the act of
generation, in the most spiritual and abstracted sense, must be
supposed to transmit the properties of a common nature,[37]
they durst not presume to circumscribe the powers or the
duration of the Son of an eternal and omnipotent Father.
Fourscore years after the death of Christ, the Christians of

[34] Tertullian. in Apolog. c. 46. See Bayle, Dictionnaire, au mot
Simonide. His remarks on the presumption of Tertullian are profound
and interesting.

[35] Lactantius, iv. 8. Yet the *Probole*, or *Prolatio*, which the most
orthodox divines borrowed without scruple from the Valentinians, and
illustrated by the comparisons of a fountain and stream, the sun and
its rays, &c., either meant nothing, or favored a material idea of the
divine generation. See Beausobre, tom. i. l. iii. c. 7, p. 548.

[36] Many of the primitive writers have frankly confessed, that the
Son owed his being to the *will* of the Father. See Clarke's Scripture
Trinity, p. 280—287. On the other hand, Athanasius and his followers seem unwilling to grant what they are afraid to deny. The
schoolmen extricate themselves from this difficulty by the distinction
of a *preceding* and a *concomitant* will. Petav. Dogm. Theolog. tom. ii
l. vi. c. 8, p. 587—603.

[37] See Petav Dogm. Theolog. tom. ii. l. ii. c. 10, p. 158

Bithynia declared before the tribunal of Pliny, that they invoked him as a god : and his divine honors have been perpetuated in every age and country, by the various sects who assume the name of his disciples.[38] Their tender reverence for the memory of Christ, and their horror for the profane worship of any created being, would have engaged them to assert the equal and absolute divinity of the *Logos*, if their rapid ascent towards the throne of heaven had not been imperceptibly checked by the apprehension of violating the unity and sole supremacy of the great Father of Christ and of the Universe. The suspense and fluctuation produced in the minds of the Christians by these opposite tendencies, may be observed in the writings of the theologians who flourished after the end of the apostolic age, and before the origin of the Arian controversy. Their suffrage is claimed, with equal confidence, by the orthodox and by the heretical parties ; and the most inquisitive critics have fairly allowed, that if they had the good fortune of possessing the Catholic verity, they have delivered their conceptions in loose, inaccurate, and sometimes contradictory language.[39]

II. The devotion of individuals was the first circumstance which distinguished the Christians from the Platonists : the second was the authority of the church. The disciples of philosophy asserted the rights of intellectual freedom, and their respect for the sentiments of their teachers was a liberal and voluntary tribute, which they offered to superior reason. But the Christians formed a numerous and disciplined society ; and the jurisdiction of their laws and magistrates was strictly exercised over the minds of the faithful. The loose wanderings of the imagination were gradually confined by creeds and

---

[38] Carmenque Christo quasi Deo dicere secum invicem. Plin. Epist. x. 97. The sense of *Deus*, Θεός, *Elohim*, in the ancient languages, is critically examined by Le Clerc, (Ars Critica, p. 150—156,) and the propriety of worshipping a very excellent creature is ably defended by the Socinian Emlyn, (Tracts, p. 29—36, 51—145.)

[39] See Daillé de Usu Patrum, and Le Clerc, Bibliothèque Universelle, tom. x. p. 409. To arraign the faith of the Ante-Nicene fathers, was the object, or at least has been the effect, of the stupendous work of Petavius on the Trinity, (Dogm. Theolog. tom. ii. ;) nor has the deep impression been erased by the learned defence of Bishop Bull.*

---

* Dr. Burton's work on the doctrine of the Ante-Nicene fathers must be consulted by those who wish to obtain clear notions on this subject. — M.

confessions ;[40] the freedom of private judgment submitted to the public wisdom of synods ; the authority of a theologian was determined by his ecclesiastical rank ; and the episcopal successors of the apostles inflicted the censures of the church on those who deviated from the orthodox belief. But in an age of religious controversy, every act of oppression adds new force to the elastic vigor of the mind ; and the zeal or obstinacy of a spiritual rebel was sometimes stimulated by secret motives of ambition or avarice. A metaphysical argument became the cause or pretence of political contests ; the subtleties of the Platonic school were used as the badges of popular factions, and the distance which separated their respective tenets was enlarged or magnified by the acrimony of dispute. As long as the dark heresies of Praxeas and Sabellius labored to confound the *Father* with the *Son*,[41] the orthodox party might be excused if they adhered more strictly and more earnestly to the *distinction*, than to the *equality*, of the divine persons. But as soon as the heat of controversy had subsided, and the progress of the Sabellians was no longer an object of terror to the churches of Rome, of Africa, or of Egypt, the tide of theological opinion began to flow with a gentle but steady motion towards the contrary extreme ; and the most orthodox doctors allowed themselves the use of the terms and definitions which had been censured in the mouth of the sectaries.[42] After the edict of toleration had restored peace and leisure to the Christians, the Trinitarian controversy was revived in the ancient seat of Platonism, the learned, the opulent, the tumultuous city of Alexandria ; and the flame of religious discord was rapidly communicated from the schools to the clergy, the people, the province, and the East. The abstruse question of the eternity of the *Logos* was agitated in ecclesiastic conferences and popular sermons ; and the heterodox opinions

---

[40] The most ancient creeds were drawn up with the greatest latitude. See Bull, (Judicium Eccles. Cathol.,) who tries to prevent Episcopius from deriving any advantage from this observation.

[41] The heresies of Praxeas, Sabellius, &c., are accurately explained by Mosheim, (p. 425, 680—714.) Praxeas, who came to Rome about the end of the second century, deceived, for some time, the simplicity of the bishop, and was confuted by the pen of the angry Tertullian.

[42] Socrates acknowledges, that the heresy of Arius proceeded from his strong desire to embrace an opinion the most diametrically opposite to that of Sabellius.

of Arius[43] were soon made public by his own zeal, and by that of his adversaries. His most implacable adversaries have acknowledged the learning and blameless life of that eminent presbyter, who, in a former election, had declared, and perhaps generously declined, his pretensions to the episcopal throne.[44] His competitor Alexander assumed the office of his judge. The important cause was argued before him; and if at first he seemed to hesitate, he at length pronounced his final sentence, as an absolute rule of faith.[45] The undaunted presbyter, who presumed to resist the authority of his angry bishop, was separated from the community of the church. But the pride of Arius was supported by the applause of a numerous party. He reckoned among his immediate followers two bishops of Egypt, seven presbyters, twelve deacons, and (what may appear almost incredible) seven hundred virgins. A large majority of the bishops of Asia appeared to support or favor his cause; and their measures were conducted by Eusebius of Cæsarea, the most learned of the Christian prelates; and by Eusebius of Nicomedia, who had acquired the reputation of a statesman without forfeiting that of a saint. Synods in Palestine and Bithynia were opposed to the synods of Egypt. The attention of the prince and people was attracted by this theological dispute; and the decision, at the end of six years,[46] was referred to the supreme authority of the general council of Nice.

When the mysteries of the Christian faith were dangerously exposed to public debate, it might be observed, that the human

---

[43] The figure and manners of Arius, the character and numbers of his first proselytes, are painted in very lively colors by Epiphanius, (tom. i. Hæres. lxix. 3, p. 729,) and we cannot but regret that he should soon forget the historian, to assume the task of controversy.

[44] See Philostorgius l. i. c. 3,) and Godefroy's ample Commentary. Yet the credibility of Philostorgius is lessened, in the eyes of the orthodox, by his Arianism; and in those of rational critics, by his passion, his prejudice, and his ignorance.

[45] Sozomen l. (i. c. 15) represents Alexander as indifferent, and even ignorant, in the beginning of the controversy; while Socrates (l. i. c 5) ascribes the origin of the dispute to the vain curiosity of his theological speculations. Dr. Jortin (Remarks on Ecclesiastical History, vol. ii. p. 178) has censured, with his usual freedom, the conduct of Alexander; πρὸς ὀργὴν ἐξαπτέται . . . . ὁμοίως φρόνειν ἐκέλευσε.

[46] The flames of Arianism might burn for some time in secret; but there is reason to believe that they burst out with violence as early as the year 319. Tillemont, Mém. Eccles. tom. vi. p. 774—780.

understanding was capable of forming three distinct, though imperfect systems, concerning the nature of the Divine Trinity and it was pronounced, that none of these systems, in a pure and absolute sense, were exempt from heresy and error.[47] I. According to the first hypothesis, which was maintained by Arius and his disciples, the *Logos* was a dependent and spontaneous production, created from nothing by the will of the father. The Son, by whom all things were made,[48] had been begotten before all worlds, and the longest of the astronomical periods could be compared only as a fleeting moment to the extent of his duration; yet this duration was not infinite,[49] and there *had* been a time which preceded the ineffable generation of the *Logos*. On this only-begotten Son, the Almighty Father had transfused his ample spirit, and impressed the effulgence of his glory. Visible image of invisible perfection, he saw, at an immeasurable distance beneath his feet, the thrones of the brightest archangels; yet he shone only with a reflected light, and, like the sons of the Roman emperors, who were invested with the titles of Cæsar or Augustus,[50] he governed the universe in obedience to the will of his Father and Monarch. II. In the second hypothesis, the *Logos* possessed all the inherent, incommunicable perfections, which religion and philosophy appropriate to the Supreme God. Three distinct and infinite minds or substances, three coëqual and coëternal beings, composed the Divine Essence;[51] and it would have implied con-

---

[47] Quid credidit? Certe, *aut* tria nomina audiens tres Deos esse credidit, et idololatra effectus est; *aut* in tribus vocabulis trinominem credens Deum, in Sabellii hæresim incurrit; *aut* edoctus ab Arianis unum esse verum Deum Patrem, filium et spiritum sanctum credidit creaturas. Aut extra hæc quid credere potuerit nescio. Hieronym. adv. Luciferianos. Jerom reserves for the last the orthodox system, which is more complicated and difficult.

[48] As the doctrine of absolute creation from nothing was gradually introduced among the Christians, (Beausobre, tom ii. p. 165—215,) the dignity of the *workman* very naturally rose with that of the *work*.

[49] The metaphysics of Dr. Clarke (Scripture Trinity, p. 276—280) could digest an eternal generation from an infinite cause.

[50] This profane and absurd simile is employed by several of the primitive fathers, particularly by Athenagoras, in his Apology to the emperor Marcus and his son; and it is alleged, without censure, by Bull himself. See Defens. Fid. Nicen. sect. iii. c. 5, No. 4.

[51] See Cudworth's Intellectual System, p. 559, 579. This dangerous hypothesis was countenanced by the two Gregories, of Nyssa and Nazianzen, by Cyril of Alexandria, John of Damascus, &c. See Cudworth, p. 603. Le Clerc, Bibliothèque Universelle, tom. xviii. p. 97 -105.

tradiction, that any of them should not have existed, or tha.
they should ever cease to exist.[52]   The advocates of a system
which seemed to establish three independent Deities, attempted
to preserve the unity of the First Cause, so conspicuous in the
design and order of the world, by the perpetual concord of
their administration, and the essential agreement of their will.
A faint resemblance of this unity of action may be discovered
in the societies of men, and even of animals.   The causes
which disturb their harmony, proceed only from the imper-
fection and inequality of their faculties; but the omnipotence
which is guided by infinite wisdom and goodness, cannot fail
of choosing the same means for the accomplishment of the
same ends.   III.   Three beings, who, by the self-derived
necessity of their existence, possess all the divine attributes
in the most perfect degree; who are eternal in duration,
infinite in space, and intimately present to each other, and to
the whole universe; irresistibly force themselves on the astonished mind, as one and the same being,[53] who, in the œconomy
of grace, as well as in that of nature, may manifest himself under different forms, and be considered under different
aspects.   By this hypothesis, a real substantial trinity is refined
into a trinity of names, and abstract modifications, that subsist
only in the mind which conceives them.   The *Logos* is no
longer a person, but an attribute; and it is only in a figurative
sense that the epithet of Son can be applied to the eternal
reason, which was with God from the beginning, and by *which*,
not by *whom*, all things were made.   The incarnation of the
Logos is reduced to a mere inspiration of the Divine Wisdom,
which filled the soul, and directed all the actions, of the man
Jesus.   Thus, after revolving round the theological circle, we
are surprised to find that the Sabellian ends where the Ebion-
ite had begun; and that the incomprehensible mystery which
excites our adoration, eludes our inquiry.[54]

---

[52] Augustin seems to envy the freedom of the Philosophers.   Lib-
eris verbis loquuntur philosophi . . . . Nos autem non dicimus duo
vel tria principia, duos vel tres Deos.   De Civitat. Dei, x. 23.

[53] Boetius, who was deeply versed in the philosophy of Plato and
Aristotle, explains the unity of the Trinity by the *indifference* of the
three persons.   See the judicious remarks of Le Clerc, Bibliothèque
Choisie, tom. xvi. p. 225, &c.

[54] If the Sabellians were startled at this conclusion, they were driven
down another precipice into the confession, that the Father was born
of a virgin, that *he* had suffered on the cross; and thus deserved the
odious epithet of *Patripassians*, with which they were branded by

If the bishops of the council of Nice [55] had been permitted to follow the unbiased dictates of their conscience, Arius and his associates could scarcely have flattered themselves with the hopes of obtaining a majority of votes, in favor of an hypothesis so directly adverse to the two most popular opinions of the Catholic world. The Arians soon perceived the danger of their situation, and prudently assumed those modest virtues, which, in the fury of civil and religious dissensions, are seldom practised, or even praised, except by the weaker party. They recommended the exercise of Christian charity and moderation; urged the incomprehensible nature of the controversy; disclaimed the use of any terms or definitions which could not be found in the Scriptures; and offered, by very liberal concessions, to satisfy their adversaries without renouncing the integrity of their own principles. The victorious faction received all their proposals with haughty suspicion; and anxiously sought for some irreconcilable mark of distinction, the rejection of which might involve the Arians in the guilt and consequences of heresy. A letter was publicly read, and ignominiously torn, in which their patron, Eusebius of Nicomedia, ingenuously confessed, that the admission of the HOMOOUSION, or Consubstantial, a word already familiar to the Platonists, was incompatible with the principles of their theological system. The fortunate opportunity was eagerly embraced by the bishops, who governed the resolutions of the synod; and, according to the lively expression of Ambrose, [56] they used the sword, which heresy itself had drawn from the scabbard, to cut off the head of the hated monster. The consubstantiality of the Father and the Son was established by the council of Nice, and has been unanimously received as a

---

their adversaries. See the invectives of Tertullian against Praxeas, and the temperate reflections of Mosheim, (p. 423, 681;) and Beausobre, tom. i. l. iii. c. 6, p. 533.

[55] The transactions of the council of Nice are related by the ancients, nʹt only in a partial, but in a very imperfect manner. Such a picture as Fra Paolo would have drawn, can never be recovered; but such rude sketches as have been traced by the pencil of bigotry, and that of reason, may be seen in Tillemont, (Mém. Eccles. tom. v p. 669—759,) and in Le Clerc, (Bibliothèque Universelle, tom. x. p 435—454.)

[56] We are indebted to Ambrose (De Fide, l. iii. cap. ult.) for the knowledge of this curious anecdote. Hoc verbum posuerunt Patres, quod viderunt adversariis esse formidini; ut tanquam evaginato ab ipsis gladio, ipsum nefandæ caput hæreseos amputarent.

fundamental article of the Christian faith, by the consent of the Greek, the Latin, the Oriental, and the Protestant churches But if the same word had not served to stigmatize the heretics and to unite the Catholics, it would have been inadequate to the purpose of the majority, by whom it was introduced into the orthodox creed. This majority was divided into two parties, distinguished by a contrary tendency to the sentiments of the Tritheists and of the Sabellians. But as those opposite extremes seemed to overthrow the foundations either of natural or revealed religion, they mutually agreed to qualify the rigor of their principles; and to disavow the just, but invidious, consequences, which might be urged by their antagonists. The interest of the common cause inclined them to join their numbers, and to conceal their differences; their animosity was softened by the healing counsels of toleration, and their disputes were suspended by the use of the mysterious *Homoousion*, which either party was free to interpret according to their peculiar tenets. The Sabellian sense, which, about fifty years before, had obliged the council of Antioch[57] to prohibit this celebrated term, had endeared it to those theologians who entertained a secret but partial affection for a nominal Trinity. But the more fashionable saints of the Arian times, the intrepid Athanasius, the learned Gregory Nazianzen, and the other pillars of the church, who supported with ability and success the Nicene doctrine, appeared to consider the expression of *substance* as if it had been synonymous with that of *nature*; and they ventured to illustrate their meaning, by affirming that three men, as they belong to the same common species, are consubstantial, or homoousian to each other.[58] This pure and distinct equality was tempered, on the one hand, by the internal connection, and spiritual penetration which indissolubly unites the divine persons;[59] and, on the other, by the preëminence

---

[57] See Bull, Defens. Fid. Nicen. sect. ii. c. i. p. 25—36. He thinks it his duty to reconcile two orthodox synods.

[58] According to Aristotle, the stars were homoousian to each other. "That *Homoousios* means of one substance in *kind*, hath been shown by Petavius, Curcellæus, Cudworth, Le Clerc, &c., and to prove it would be *actum agere.*" This is the just remark of Dr. Jortin, (vol. ii. p. 212,) who examines the Arian controversy with learning, candor, and ingenuity.

[59] See Petavius, (Dogm. Theolog. tom. ii. l. iv. c. 16, p. 453, &c.,) Cudworth, (p. 559,) Bull, (sect. iv. p. 285--290, edit. Grab.) The περιχώρησις, or *circumincessio*, is perhaps the deepest and darkest corner of the whole theological abyss.

of the Father which was acknowledged as far as it is com-
patible with the independence of the Son.[60] Within these
limits, the almost invisible and tremulous ball of orthodoxy
was allowed securely to vibrate. On either side, beyond this
consecrated ground, the heretics and the dæmons lurked in
ambush to surprise and devour the unhappy wanderer. But
as the degrees of theological hatred depend on the spirit of the
war, rather than on the importance of the controversy, the
heretics who degraded, were treated with more severity than
those who annihilated, the person of the Son. The life of
Athanasius was consumed in irreconcilable opposition to the
impious *madness* of the Arians;[61] but he defended above
twenty years the Sabellianism of Marcellus of Ancyra; and
when at last he was compelled to withdraw himself from his
communion, he continued to mention, with an ambiguous smile,
the venial errors of his respectable friend.[62]

The authority of a general council, to which the Arians
themselves had been compelled to submit, inscribed on the
banners of the orthodox party the mysterious characters of
the word *Homoousion*, which essentially contributed, notwithstanding some obscure disputes, some nocturnal combats, to
maintain and perpetuate the uniformity of faith, or at least of
language. The Consubstantialists, who by their success have
deserved and obtained the title of Catholics, gloried in the
simplicity and steadiness of their own creed, and insulted the
repeated variations of their adversaries, who were destitute of
any certain rule of faith. The sincerity or the cunning of
the Arian chiefs, the fear of the laws or of the people, their
reverence for Christ, their hatred of Athanasius, all the causes,
human and divine, that influence and disturb the counsels of a
theological faction, introduced among the sectaries a spirit of
discord and inconstancy, which, in the course of a few years,
erected eighteen different models of religion,[63] and avenged

[60] The third section of Bull's Defence of the Nicene Faith, which
some of his antagonists have called nonsense, and others heresy, is
consecrated to the supremacy of the Father.

[61] The ordinary appellation with which Athanasius and his followers chose to compliment the Arians, was that of *Ariomanites*.

[62] Epiphanius, tom. i. Hæres. lxxii. 4, p. 837. See the adventures
of Marcellus, in Tillemont, (Mém. Eccles. tom. vii. p. 880—899.)
His work, in *one* book, of the unity of God, was answered in the *three*
books, which are still extant, of Eusebius. After a long and careful
examination, Petavius (tom. ii. l. i. c. 14, p. 78) has reluctantly pronounced the condemnation of Marcellus.

[63] Athanasius, in his epistle concerning the Synods of Seleucia and

the violated dignity of the church. The zealous Hilary,[64] who, from the peculiar hardships of his situation, was inclined to extenuate rather than to aggravate the errors of the Oriental clergy, declares, that in the wide extent of the ten provinces of Asia, to which he had been banished, there could be found very few prelates who had preserved the knowledge of the true God.[65] The oppression which he had felt, the disorders of which he was the spectator and the victim, appeased, during a short interval, the angry passions of his soul; and in the following passage, of which I shall transcribe a few lines, the bishop of Poitiers unwarily deviates into the style of a Christian philosopher. " It is a thing," says Hilary, " equally deplorable and dangerous, that there are as many creeds as opinions among men, as many doctrines as inclinations, and as many sources of blasphemy as there are faults among us; because we make creeds arbitrarily, and explain them as arbitrarily. The Homoousion is rejected, and received, and explained away by successive synods. The partial or total resemblance of the Father and of the Son is a subject of dispute for these unhappy times. Every year, nay, every moon, we make new creeds to describe invisible mysteries. We repent of what we have done, we defend those who repent, we anathematize those whom we defended. We condemn either the doctrine of others in ourselves, or our own in that of others; and reciprocally tearing one another to pieces we have been the cause of each other's ruin." [66]

It will not be expected, it would not perhaps be endured

Rimini, (tom. i. p. 886—905,) has given an ample list of Arian creeds which has been enlarged and improved by the labors of the indefatigable Tillemont, (Mém. Eccles. tom. vi. p. 477.)

[64] Erasmus, with admirable sense and freedom, has delineated the just character of Hilary. To revise his text, to compose the annals of his life, and to justify his sentiments and conduct, is the province of the Benedictine editors.

[65] Absque episcopo Eleusio et paucis cum eo, ex majore parte Asianæ decem provinciæ, inter quas consisto, vere Deum nesciunt. Atque utinam penitus nescirent! cum procliviore enim veniâ ignorarent quam obtrectarent. Hilar. de Synodis, sive de Fide Orientalium, c. 63, p. 1186, edit. Benedict. In the celebrated parallel between atheism and superstition. the bishop of Poitiers would have been surprised in the philosophic society of Bayle and Plutarch.

[66] Hilarius ad Constantium, l. i. c. 4, 5, p. 1227, 1228. This remarkable passage deserved the attention of Mr. Locke, who has transcribed it (vol. iii. p. 470) into the model of his new commonplace book.

that I should swell this theolog'cal digression, by a minute examination of the eighteen creeds, the authors of which, for the most part, disclaimed the odious name of their parent Arius. It is amusing enough to delineate the form, and to trace the vegetation, of a singular plant; but the tedious detail of leaves without flowers, and of branches without fruit, would soon exhaust the patience, and disappoint the curiosity, of the laborious student. One question, which gradually arose from the Arian controversy, may, however, be noticed, as it served to produce and discriminate the three sects, who were united only by their common aversion to the Homoousion of the Nicene synod. 1. If they were asked whether the Son was *like* unto the Father, the question was resolutely answered in the negative, by the heretics who adhered to the principles of Arius, or indeed to those of philosophy; which seem to establish an infinite difference between the Creator and the most excellent of his creatures. This obvious consequence was maintained by Ætius,[67] on whom the zeal of his adversaries bestowed the surname of the Atheist. His restless and aspiring spirit urged him to try almost every profession of human life. He was successively a slave, or at least a husbandman, a travelling tinker, a goldsmith, a physician, a schoolmaster, a theologian, and at last the apostle of a new church, which was propagated by the abilities of his disciple Eunomius.[68] Armed with texts of Scripture, and with captious syllogisms from the logic of Aristotle, the subtle Ætius had acquired the fame of an invincible disputant, whom it was impossible either to silence or to convince. Such talents engaged the friendship of the Arian bishops, till they were forced to renounce, and even to persecute, a dangerous ally, who, by the accuracy of his reasoning, had prejudiced their cause in the popular opinion, and offended the piety of their most devoted

---

[67] In Philostorgius (l. iii. c. 15) the character and adventures of Ætius appear singular enough, though they are carefully softened by the hand of a friend. The editor, Godefroy, (p. 153,) who was more attached to his principles than to his author, has collected the odious circumstances which his various adversaries have preserved or invented.

[68] According to the judgment of a man who respected both these sectaries, Ætius had been endowed with a stronger understanding, and Eunomius had acquired more art and learning. (Philostorgius, l. viii. c. 18.) The confession and apology of Eunomius (Fabricius, Bibliot. Græc. tom. viii. p. 258—305) is one of the few heretical pieces which have escaped.

followers. 2. The omnipotence of the Creator suggested a specious and respectful solution of the *likeness* of the Father and the Son ; and faith might humbly receive what reason could not presume to deny, that the Supreme God might communicate his infinite perfections, and create a being similar only to himself.[69] These Arians were powerfully supported by the weight and abilities of their leaders, who had succeeded to the management of the Eusebian interest, and who occupied the principal thrones of the East. They detested, perhaps with some affectation, the impiety of Ætius ; they professed to believe, either without reserve, or according to the Scriptures, that the Son was different from all *other* creatures, and similar only to the Father. But they denied, that he was either of the same, or of a similar substance ; sometimes boldly justifying their dissent, and sometimes objecting to the use of the word substance, which seems to imply an adequate, or at least a distinct, notion of the nature of the Deity. 3. The sect which asserted the doctrine of a similar substance, was the most numerous, at least in the provinces of Asia ; and when the leaders of both parties were assembled in the council of Seleucia,[70] *their* opinion would have prevailed by a majority of one hundred and five to forty-three bishops. The Greek word, which was chosen to express this mysterious resemblance, bears so close an affinity to the orthodox symbol, that the profane of every age have derided the furious contests which the difference of a single diphthong excited between the Homoousians and the Homoiousians. As it frequently happens, that the sounds and characters which approach the nearest to each other accidentally represent the most opposite ideas, the observation would be itself ridiculous, if it were possible to mark any real and sensible distinction between the doctrine of the Semi-Arians, as they were improperly styled, and that of the Catholics themselves. The bishop of Poitiers, who in his Phrygian exile very wisely

---

[69] Yet, according to the opinion of Estius and Bull, (p. 297,) there is one power — that of creation — which God *cannot* communicate to a creature. Estius, who so accurately defined the limits of Omnipotence, was a Dutchman by birth, and by trade a scholastic divine. Dupin, Bibliot. Eccles. tom. xvii. p. 45.

[70] Sabinus ap. Socrat. (l. ii. c. 39) had copied the acts : Athanasius and Hilary have explained the divisions of this Arian synod ; the other circumstances which are relative to it are carefully collected by Baronius and Tillemont.

aimed at a coalition of parties, endeavors to prove that, by a pious and faithful interpretation,[71] the *Homoiousion* may be reduced to a consubstantial sense. Yet he confesses that the word has a dark and suspicious aspect ; and, as if darkness were congenial to theological disputes, the Semi-Arians, who advanced to the doors of the church, assailed them with the most unrelenting fury.

The provinces of Egypt and Asia, which cultivated the language and manners of the Greeks, had deeply imbibed the venom of the Arian controversy. The familiar study of the Platonic system, a vain and argumentative disposition, a copious and flexible idiom, supplied the clergy and people of the East with an inexhaustible flow of words and distinctions; and, in the midst of their fierce contentions, they easily forgot the doubt which is recommended by philosophy, and the submission which is enjoined by religion. The inhabitants of the West were of a less inquisitive spirit ; their passions were not so forcibly moved by invisible objects, their minds were less frequently exercised by the habits of dispute ; and such was the happy ignorance of the Gallican church, that Hilary himself, above thirty years after the first general council, was still a stranger to the Nicene creed.[72] The Latins had received the rays of divine knowledge through the dark and doubtful medium of a translation. The poverty and stubbornness of their native tongue was not always capable of affording just equivalents for the Greek terms, for the technical words of the Platonic philosophy,[73] which had been consecrated, by the gospel or by the church, to express the mysteries of the Christian faith ; and a verbal defect might

---

[71] Fideli et piâ intelligentiâ. . . De Synod. ⟨. 77, p. 1193. In his short apologetical notes (first published by the Benedictines from a MS. of Chartres) he observes, that he used this cautious expression, qui intelligentium et impiam, p. 1206. See p. 1146. Philostorgius, who saw those objects through a different medium, is inclined to forget the difference of the important diphthong. See in particular viii. 17, and Godefroy, p. 352.

[72] Testor Deum cœli atque terræ me cum neutrum audissem, semper tamen utrumque sensisse. . . . Regeneratus pridem et in episcopatu aliquantisper manens fidem Nicenam nunquam nisi exsulaturus audivi. Hilar. de Synodis, c. xci. p. 1205. The Benedictines are persuaded that he governed the diocese of Poitiers several years before his exile.

[73] Seneca (Epist. lviii.) complains that even the τὸ ὄν of the Platonists (the *ens* of the bolder schoolmen) could not be expressed by a Latin noun.

42

introduce into the Latin theology a long train of error or per plexity.[74]   But as the western provincials had the good for tune of deriving their religion from an orthodox source they preserved with steadiness the doctrine which they had accepted with docility; and when the Arian pestilence ap proached their frontiers, they were supplied with the season able preservative of the Homoousion, by the paternal care of the Roman pontiff.   Their sentiments and their temper were displayed in the memorable synod of Rimini, which surpassed in numbers the council of Nice, since it was composed of above four hundred bishops of Italy, Africa, Spain, Gaul, Britain, and Illyricum.   From the first debates it appeared, that only fourscore prelates adhered to the party, though *they* affected to anathematize the name and memory, of Arius. But this inferiority was compensated by the advantages of skill, of experience, and of discipline; and the minority was conducted by Valens and Ursacius, two bishops of Illyricum, who had spent their lives in the intrigues of courts and coun cils, and who had been trained under the Eusebian banner in the religious wars of the East.   By their arguments and nego tiations, they embarrassed, they confounded, they at last deceived, the honest simplicity of the Latin bishops; who suffered the palladium of the faith to be extorted from their hand by fraud and importunity, rather than by open violence. The council of Rimini was not allowed to separate, till the members had imprudently subscribed a captious creed, in which some expressions, susceptible of an heretical sense, were inserted in the room of the Homoousion.   It was on this occasion, that, according to Jerom, the world was surprised to find itself Arian.[75]   But the bishops of the Latin provinces had no sooner reached their respective dioceses, than they dis covered their mistake, and repented of their weakness.   The ignominious capitulation was rejected with disdain and abhor rence; and the Homoousian standard, which had been shaken but not overthrown, was more firmly replanted in all the churches of the West.[76]

---

[74] The preference which the fourth council of the Lateran at length gave to a *numerical* rather than a *generical* unity (see Petav. tom. ii. l. iv. c. 13, p. 424) was favored by the Latin language: τριας seems to excite the idea of substance, *trinitas* of qualities.

[75] Ingemuit totus orbis, et Arianum se esse miratus est.   Hiero nym. adv. Lucifer. tom. i. p. 145.

[76] The story of the council of Rimini is very elegantly told by Sul

Such was the rise and progress, and such were the natural revolutions of those theological disputes, which disturbed the peace of Christianity under the reigns of Constantine and of his sons. But as those princes presumed to extend their despotism over the faith, as well as over the lives and fortunes, of their subjects, the weight of their suffrage sometimes inclined the ecclesiastical balance : and the prerogatives of the King of Heaven were settled, or changed, or modified, in the cabinet of an earthly monarch.

The unhappy spirit of discord which pervaded the provinces of the East, interrupted the triumph of Constantine ; but the emperor continued for some time to view, with cool and careless indifference, the object of the dispute. As he was yet ignorant of the difficulty of appeasing the quarrels of theologians, he addressed to the contending parties, to Alexander and to Arius, a moderating epistle ;[77] which may be ascribed, with far greater reason, to the untutored sense of a soldier and statesman, than to the dictates of any of his episcopal counsellors. He attributes the origin of the whole controversy to a trifling and subtle question, concerning an incomprehensible point of the law, which was foolishly asked by the bishop, and imprudently resolved by the presbyter. He laments that the Christian people, who had the same God, the same religion, and the same worship, should be divided by such inconsiderable distinctions ; and he seriously recommends to the clergy of Alexandria the example of the Greek philosophers ; who could maintain their arguments without losing their temper, and assert their freedom without violating their friendship. The indifference and contempt of the sovereign would have been, perhaps, the most effectual method of

---

picius Severus, (Hist. Sacra, l. ii. p. 419—430, edit. Lugd. Bat. 1647,) and by Jerom, in his dialogue against the Luciferians. The design of the latter is to apologize for the conduct of the Latin bishops, who were deceived, and who repented.

[77] Eusebius, in Vit. Constant. l. ii. c. 64—72. The principles of toleration and religious indifference, contained in this epistle, have given great offence to Baronius, Tillemont, &c., who suppose that the emperor had some evil counsellor, either Satan or Eusebius at his elbow. See Jortin's Remarks, tom. ii. p. 183.*

---

* Heinichen (Excursus xi.) quotes with approbation the term "golden words," applied by Ziegler to this moderate and tolerant letter of Constantine. May an English clergyman venture to express his regret, that " the fine gold so soon became dim " in the Christian church ? — M.

silencing the dispute, if the popular current had been less rapid and impetuous, and if Constantine himself, in the midst of faction and fanaticism, could have preserved the calm possession of his own mind. But his ecclesiastical ministers soon contrived to seduce the impartiality of the magistrate, and to awaken the zeal of the proselyte. He was provoked by the insults which had been offered to his statues; he was alarmed by the real, as well as the imaginary magnitude of the spreading mischief; and he extinguished the hope of peace and toleration, from the moment that he assembled three hundred bishops within the walls of the same palace. The presence of the monarch swelled the importance of the debate; his attention multiplied the arguments; and he exposed his person with a patient intrepidity, which animated the valor of the combatants. Notwithstanding the applause which has been bestowed on the eloquence and sagacity of Constantine,[78] a Roman general, whose religion might be still a subject of doubt, and whose mind had not been enlightened either by study or by inspiration, was indifferently qualified to discuss in the Greek language, a metaphysical question, or an article of faith. But the credit of his favorite Osius, who appears to have presided in the council of Nice, might dispose the emperor in favor of the orthodox party; and a well-timed insinuation, that the same Eusebius of Nicomedia, who now protected the heretic, had lately assisted the tyrant,[79] might exasperate him against their adversaries. The Nicene creed was ratified by Constantine; and his firm declaration, that those who resisted the divine judgment of the synod, must prepare themselves for an immediate exile, annihilated the murmurs of a feeble opposition; which, from seventeen, was almost instantly reduced to two, protesting bishops. Eusebius of Cæsarea yielded a reluctant and ambiguous consent to the Homoousion;[80] and the wavering conduct of the Nicomedian

---

[78] Eusebius in Vit. Constantin. l. iii. c. 13.

[79] Theodoret has preserved (l. i. c. 20) an epistle from Constantine to the people of Nicomedia, in which the monarch declares himself the public accuser of one of his subjects; he styles Eusebius ὁ τῆς τυραννίκης ὠμότητος συμμύστης; and complains of his hostile behavior during the civil war.

[80] See in Socrates, (l. i. c. 8,) or rather in Theodoret, (l. i. c. 12,) an original letter of Eusebius of Cæsarea, in which he attempts to justify his subscribing the Homoousion. The character of Eusebius has always been a problem: but those who have read the second critical epistle of Le Clerc, Ars Critica, tom. iii. p. 30—69,) must entertain

Eusebius served only to delay, about three months, his disgrace and exile.[81] The impious Arius was banished into one of the remote provinces of Illyricum; his person and disciples were branded, by law, with the odious name of Porphyrians; his writings were condemned to the flames, and a capital punishment was denounced against those in whose possession they should be found. The emperor had now imbibed the spirit of controversy, and the angry, sarcastic style of his edicts was designed to inspire his subjects with the hatred which he had conceived against the enemies of Christ.[82]

But, as if the conduct of the emperor had been guided by passion instead of principle, three years from the council of Nice were scarcely elapsed before he discovered some symptoms of mercy, and even of indulgence, towards the proscribed sect, which was secretly protected by his favorite sister. The exiles were recalled: and Eusebius, who gradually resumed his influence over the mind of Constantine, was restored to the episcopal throne, from which he had been ignominiously degraded. Arius himself was treated by the whole court with the respect which would have been due to an innocent and oppressed man. His faith was approved by the synod of Jerusalem; and the emperor seemed impatient to repair his injustice, by issuing an absolute command, that he should be solemnly admitted to the communion in the cathedral of Constantinople. On the same day, which had been fixed for the triumph of Arius, he expired; and the strange and horrid circumstances of his death might excite a suspicion, that the orthodox saints had contributed more efficaciously than by their prayers, to deliver the church from the most formidable of her enemies.[83] The three principal leaders of the Catholics, Athanasius of Alexandria, Eustathius of Antioch, and

a very unfavorable opinion of the orthodoxy and sincerity of the bishop of Cæsarea.

[81] Athanasius, tom. i. p. 727. Philostorgius, l. i. c. 10, and Godefroy's Commentary, p. 41.

[82] Socrates, l. i. c. 9. In his circular letters, which were addressed to the several cities, Constantine employed against the heretics the arms of ridicule and comic raillery.

[83] We derive the original story from Athanasius, (tom. i. p. 670,) who expresses some reluctance to stigmatize the memory of the dead. He might exaggerate; but the perpetual commerce of Alexandria and Constantinople would have rendered it dangerous to invent. Those who press the literal narrative of the death of Arius (his bowels suddenly burst out in a privy) must make their option between poison and miracle.

Paul of Constantinople, were deposed on various accusations
by the sentence of numerous councils; and were afterwards
banished into distant provinces by the first of the Christian
emperors, who, in the last moments of his life, received the
rites of baptism from the Arian bishop of Nicomedia. The
ecclesiastical government of Constantine cannot be justified
from the reproach of levity and weakness. But the credulous
monarch, unskilled in the stratagems of theological warfare,
might be deceived by the modest and specious professions of
the heretics, whose sentiments he never perfectly understood;
and while he protected Arius, and persecuted Athanasius, he
still considered the council of Nice as the bulwark of the
Christian faith, and the peculiar glory of his own reign.[84]

The sons of Constantine must have been admitted from
their childhood into the rank of catechumens; but they imitated, in the delay of their baptism, the example of their father.
Like him, they presumed to pronounce their judgment on
mysteries into which they had never been regularly initiated;[85]
and the fate of the Trinitarian controversy depended, in a
great measure, on the sentiments of Constantius; who inherited the provinces of the East, and acquired the possession of
the whole empire. The Arian presbyter or bishop, who had
secreted for his use the testament of the deceased emperor,
improved the fortunate occasion which had introduced him to
the familiarity of a prince, whose public counsels were always
swayed by his domestic favorites. The eunuchs and slaves
diffused the spiritual poison through the palace, and the dangerous infection was communicated by the female attendants
to the guards, and by the empress to her unsuspicious husband.[86] The partiality which Constantius always expressed

---

[84] The change in the sentiments, or at least in the conduct, of Constantine, may be traced in Eusebius, (in Vit. Constant. l. iii. c. 23, l.
iv. c. 41,) Socrates, (l. i. c. 23—39,) Sozomen, (l. ii. c. 16—34,) Theodoret, (l. i. c. 14—34,) and Philostorgius, (l. ii. c. 1—17.) But the first
of these writers was too near the scene of action, and the others were
too remote from it. It is singular enough, that the important task of
continuing the history of the church should have been left for two
laymen and a heretic.

[85] Quia etiam tum catechumenus sacramentum fidei merito videre-
tur potuisse nescire. Sulp. Sever. Hist. Sacra, l. ii. p. 410.

[86] Socrates, l. ii. c. 2. Sozomen, l. iii. c. 18. Athanas. tom. i. p.
813, 834. He observes that the eunuchs are the natural enemies of
the *Son.* Compare Dr. Jortin's Remarks on Ecclesiastical History,
vol. iv. p. 3, with a certain genealogy in *Candide,* (ch. iv.,) which ends
with one of the first companions of Christopher Columbus.

towards the Eusebian faction, was insensibly fortified by the dexterous management of their leaders; and his victory over the tyrant Magnentius increased his inclination, as well as ability, to employ the arms of power in the cause of Arianism. While the two armies were engaged in the plains of Mursa, and the fate of the two rivals depended on the chance of war, the son of Constantine passed the anxious moments in a church of the martyrs, under the walls of the city. His spiritual comforter, Valens, the Arian bishop of the diocese, employed the most artful precautions to obtain such early intelligence as might secure either his favor or his escape. A secret chain of swift and trusty messengers informed him of the vicissitudes of the battle; and while the courtiers stood trembling round their affrighted master, Valens assured him that the Gallic legions gave way; and insinuated with some presence of mind, that the glorious event had been revealed to him by an angel. The grateful emperor ascribed his success to the merits and intercession of the bishop of Mursa, whose faith had deserved the public and miraculous approbation of Heaven.[87] The Arians, who considered as their own the victory of Constantius, preferred his glory to that of his father.[88] Cyril, bishop of Jerusalem, immediately composed the description of a celestial cross, encircled with a splendid rainbow; which during the festival of Pentecost, about the third hour of the day, had appeared over the Mount of Olives, to the edification of the devout pilgrims, and the people of the holy city.[89] The size of the meteor was gradually magnified; and the Arian historian has ventured to affirm, that it was conspicuous to the two armies in the plains of Pannonia; and that the tyrant, who is purposely represented as an idolater, fled before the auspicious sign of orthodox Christianity.[90]

---

[87] Sulpicius Severus in Hist. Sacra, l. ii. p. 405, 406.

[88] Cyril (apud Baron. A. D. 353, No. 26) expressly observes that in the reign of Constantine, the cross had been found in the bowels of the earth; but that it had appeared, in the reign of Constantius, in the midst of the heavens. This opposition evidently proves, that Cyril was ignorant of the stupendous miracle to which the conversion of Constantine is attributed; and this ignorance is the more surprising, since it was no more than twelve years after his death that Cyril was consecrated bishop of Jerusalem, by the immediate successor of Eusebius of Cæsarea. See Tillemont, Mém. Eccles. tom. viii. p. 715.

[89] It is not easy to determine how far the ingenuity of Cyril might be assisted by some natural appearances of a solar halo.

[90] Philostorgius, l. iii. c. 26. He is followed by the author of the

The sentiments of a judicious stranger, who has impartially considered the progress of civil or ecclesiastical discord, are always entitled to our notice : and a short passage of Ammianus, who served in the armies, and studied the character of Constantius, is perhaps of more value than many pages of theological invectives. " The Christian religion, which, in itself," says that moderate historian, " is plain and simple, he confounded by the dotage of superstition. Instead of reconciling the parties by the weight of his authority, he cherished and propagated, by verbal disputes, the differences which his vain curiosity had excited. The highways were covered with troops of bishops galloping from every side to the assemblies, which they call synods ; and while they labored to reduce the whole sect to their own particular opinions, the public establishment of the posts was almost ruined by their hasty and repeated journeys." [91] Our more intimate knowledge of the ecclesiastical transactions of the reign of Constantius would furnish an ample commentary on this remarkable passage ; which justifies the rational apprehensions of Athanasius, that the restless activity of the clergy, who wandered round the empire in search of the true faith, would excite the contempt and laughter of the unbelieving world.[92] As soon as the emperor was relieved from the terrors of the civil war, he devoted the leisure of his winter quarters at Arles, Milan, Sirmium, and Constantinople, to the amusement or toils of controversy : the sword of the magistrate, and even of the tyrant, was unsheathed, to enforce the reasons of the theologian ; and as he opposed the orthodox faith of Nice, it is readily confessed that his incapacity and ignorance were equal to his presumption.[93] The eunuchs, the women, and the bishops,

---

Alexandrian Chronicle, by Cedrenus, and by Nicephorus. (See Gothofred. Dissert. p. 188.) They could not refuse a miracle, even from the hand of an enemy.

[91] So curious a passage well deserves to be transcribed. Christianam religionem absolutam et simplicem, anili superstitione confundens ; in quâ scrutandâ perplexius, quam componendâ gravius excitaret discidia plurima ; quæ progressa fusius aluit concertatio o verborum, ut catervis antistium jumentis publicis ultro citroque discurrentibus, per synodos (quas appellant) dum ritum omnem ad suum trahere conantur (Valesius reads conatur) rei vehiculariæ consideret nervos. Ammianus, xxi. 16.

[92] Athanas. tom. i. p. 870.

[93] Socrates, l. ii. c. 35—47. Sozomen, l. iv. c. 12—30. Theodoret, l. ii. c. 18—32. Philostorg. l. iv. c. 4 —12, l. v. c. 1—4, l. vi c. 1—6.

who governed the vain and feeble mind of the emperor, had inspired him with an insuperable dislike to the Homoousion ; bu his timid conscience was alarmed by the impiety of Ætius. The guilt of that atheist was aggravated by the suspicious favor of the unfortunate Gallus; and even the deaths of the Imperial ministers, who had been massacred at Antioch, were imputed to the suggestions of that dangerous sophist. The mind of Constantius, which could neither be moderated by reason, nor fixed by faith, was blindly impelled to either side of the dark and empty abyss, by his horror of the opposite extreme ; he alternately embraced and condemned the sentiments, he successively banished and recalled the leaders, of the Arian and Semi-Arian factions.[94] During the season of public business or festivity, he employed whole days, and even nights, in selecting the words, and weighing the syllables, which composed his fluctuating creeds. The subject of his meditations still pursued and occupied his slumbers : the incoherent dreams of the emperor were received as celestial visions, and he accepted with complacency the lofty title of bishop of bishops, from those ecclesiastics who forgot the interest of their order for the gratification of their passions. The design of establishing a uniformity of doctrine, which had engaged him to convene so many synods in Gaul, Italy, Illyricum, and Asia, was repeatedly baffled by his own levity, by the divisions of the Arians, and by the resistance of the Catholics ; and he resolved, as the last and decisive effort, imperiously to dictate the decrees of a general council. The destructive earthquake of Nicomedia, the difficulty of finding a convenient place, and perhaps some secret motives of policy, produced an alteration in the summons. The bishops of the East were directed to meet at Seleucia, in Isauria ; while those of the West held their deliberations at Rimini, on the coast of the Hadriatic ; and instead of two or three deputies from each province, the whole episcopal body was ordered to march. The Eastern council, after consuming four days in fierce and unavailing debate, separated without any definitive conclusion. The council of the West was protracted till the seventh month.

---

[94] Sozomen, l. iv. c. 23. Athanas. tom. i. p. 831. Tillemont (Mém. Eccles. tom. vii. p. 947) has collected several instances of the haughty fanaticism of Constantius from the detached treatises of Lucifer of Cagliar The very titles of these treatises inspire zeal and terror ; " Moriendum pro Dei Filio." " De Regibus Apostaticis." " De non conveniendo cum Hæretico." " De non parcendo in Deum delinquentibus.'
22 *

Taurus, the Prætorian præfect, was instructed not to dismiss the prelates till they should all be united in the same opinion and his efforts were supported by the power of banishing fifteen of the most refractory, and a promise of the consulship if he achieved so difficult an adventure. His prayers and threats, the authority of the sovereign, the sophistry of Valens and Ursacius, the distress of cold and hunger, and the tedious melancholy of a hopeless exile, at length extorted the reluctant consent of the bishops of Rimini. The deputies of the East and of the West attended the emperor in the palace of Constantinople, and he enjoyed the satisfaction of imposing on the world a profession of faith which established the *likeness*, without expressing the *consubstantiality*, of the Son of God.[95] But the triumph of Arianism had been preceded by the removal of the orthodox clergy, whom it was impossible either to intimidate or to corrupt; and the reign of Constantius was disgraced by the unjust and ineffectual persecution of the great Athanasius.

We have seldom an opportunity of observing, either in active or speculative life, what effect may be produced, or what obstacles may be surmounted, by the force of a single mind, when it is inflexibly applied to the pursuit of a single object. The immortal name of Athanasius[96] will never be separated from the Catholic doctrine of the Trinity, to whose defence he consecrated every moment and every faculty of his being. Educated in the family of Alexander, he had vigorously opposed the early progress of the Arian heresy: he exercised the important functions of secretary under the aged prelate; and the fathers of the Nicene council beheld with surprise and respect the rising virtues of the young deacon. In a time of public danger, the dull claims of age and of rank are sometimes superseded; and within five months after his return from Nice, the deacon Athanasius was

[95] Sulp. Sever. Hist. Sacra, l. ii. p. 418—430. The Greek historians were very ignorant of the affairs of the West.

[96] We may regret that Gregory Nazianzen composed a panegyric instead of a life of Athanasius; but we should enjoy and improve the advantage of drawing our most authentic materials from the rich fund of his own epistles and apologies, (tom. i. p. 670—951.) I shall not imitate the example of Socrates, (l. ii. c. 1,) who published the first edition of his history without giving himself the trouble to consult the writings of Athanasius. Yet even Socrates, the more curious Sozomen, and the learned Theodoret, connect the life of Athanasius with the series of ecclesiastical history. The diligence of Tillemont, (tom. viii.,) and of the Benedictine editors, has collected every fact, and examined every difficulty.

seated cn the archiepiscopal throne of Egypt. He filled that eminent station above forty-six years, and his long administration was spent in a perpetual combat against the powers of Arianism. Five times was Athanasius expelled from his throne; twenty years he passed as an exile or a fugitive; and almost every province of the Roman empire was successively witness to his merit, and his sufferings in the cause of the Homoousion, which he considered as the sole pleasure and business, as the duty, and as the glory of his life. Amidst the storms of persecution, the archbishop of Alexandria was patient of labor, jealous of fame, careless of safety; and although his mind was tainted by the contagion of fanaticism, Athanasius displayed a superiority of character and abilities, which would have qualified him, far better than the degenerate sons of Constantine, for the government of a great monarchy. His learning was much less profound and extensive than that of Eusebius of Cæsarea, and his rude eloquence could not be compared with the polished oratory of Gregory of Basil; but whenever the primate of Egypt was called upon to justify his sentiments, or his conduct, his unpremeditated style, either of speaking or writing, was clear, forcible, and persuasive. He has always been revered, in the orthodox school, as one of the most accurate masters of the Christian theology: and he was supposed to possess two profane sciences, less adapted to the episcopal character, the knowledge of jurisprudence,[97] and that of divination.[98] Some fortunate conjectures of future events, which impartial reasoners might ascribe to the experience and judgment of Athanasius, were attributed by his friends to heavenly inspiration, and imputed by his enemies to infernal magic.

But as Athanasius was continually engaged with the prejudices and passions of every order of men, from the monk to the emperor, the knowledge of human nature was his first and most important science. He preserved a distinct and unbroken view of a scene which was incessantly shifting; and

---

[97] Sulpicius Severus (Hist. Sacra, l. ii. p. 396) calls him a lawyer, a jurisconsult. This character cannot now be discovered either in the life or writings of Athanasius.

[98] Dicebatur enim fatidicarum sortium fidem, quæve augurales portenderent alites scientissime callens aliquoties prædixisse futura Ammianus, xv. 7. A prophecy, or rather a joke, is related by Sozomen, (l. iv. c. 10,) which evidently proves (if the crows speak Latin) that Athanasius understood the language of the crows.

never failed to improve those decisive moments which are irrecoverably past before they are perceived by a common eye. The archbishop of Alexandria was capable of distinguishing how far he might ooldly command, and where he must dexterously insinuate ; how long he might contend with power, and when he must withdraw from persecution ; and while he directed the thunders of the church against heresy and rebellion, he could assume, in the bosom of his own party, the flexible and indulgent temper of a prudent leader. The election of Athanasius has not escaped the reproach of irregularity and precipitation ;[99] but the propriety of his behavior conciliated the affections both of the clergy and of the people. The Alexandrians were impatient to rise in arms for the defence of an eloquent and liberal pastor. In his distress he always derived support, or at least consolation, from the faithful attachment of his parochial clergy ; and the hundred bishops of Egypt adhered, with unshaken zeal, to the cause of Athanasius. In the modest equipage which pride and policy would affect, he frequently performed the episcopal visitation of his provinces, from the mouth of the Nile to the confines of Æthiopia ; familiarly conversing with the meanest of the populace, and humbly saluting the saints and hermits of the desert.[100] Nor was it only in ecclesiastical assemblies, among men whose education and manners were similar to his own, that Athanasius displayed the ascendency of his genius. He appeared with easy and respectful firmness in the courts of princes ; and in the various turns of his prosperous and adverse fortune he never lost the confidence of his friends, or the esteem of his enemies.

In his youth, the primate of Egypt resisted the great Constantine, who had repeatedly signified his will, that Arius should be restored to the Catholic communion.[101] The em-

---

[99] The irregular ordination of Athanasius was slightly mentioned in the councils which were held against him. See Philostorg. l. ii. c. 11, and Godefroy, p. 71; but it can scarcely be supposed that the assembly of the bishops of Egypt would solemnly attest a *public* falsehood. Athanas. tom. i. p. 726.

[100] See the history of the Fathers of the Desert, published by Rosweide ; and Tillemont, Mém. Eccles. tom. vii., in the lives of Antony, Pachomius, &c. Athanasius himself, who did not disdain to compose the life of his friend Antony, has carefully observed how often the holy monk deplored and prophesied the mischiefs of the Arian heresy. Athanas. tom. ii. p. 492, 498, &c.

[101] At first Constantine threatened in *speaking*, but requested in

peror respected, and might forgive, this inflexible resolution and the faction who considered Athanasius as their most formidable enemy, was constrained to dissemble their hatred, and silently to prepare an indirect and distant assault. They scattered rumors and suspicions, represented the archbishop as a proud and oppressive tyrant, and boldly accused him of violating the treaty which had been ratified in the Nicene council, with the schismatic followers of Meletius.[102] Athanasius had openly disapproved that ignominious peace, and the emperor was disposed to believe that he had abused his ecclesiastical and civil power, to persecute those odious sectaries ; that he had sacrilegiously broken a chalice in one of their churches of Mareotis ; that he had whipped or imprisoned six of their bishops ; and that Arsenius, a seventh bishop of the same party, had been murdered, or at least mutilated, by the cruel hand of the primate.[103] These charges, which affected his honor and his life, were referred by Constantine to his brother Dalmatius the censor, who resided at Antioch ; the synods of Cæsarea and Tyre were successively convened ; and the bishops of the East were instructed to judge the cause of Athanasius, before they proceeded to consecrate the new church of the Resurrection at Jerusalem. The primate might be conscious of his innocence ; but he was sensible that the same implacable spirit which had dictated the accusation, would direct the proceeding, and pronounce the sentence. He

writing, καὶ ἀγράφως μὲν ἠπείλει, γράφων δὲ, ἠξίου. His letters gradually assumed a menacing tone; but while he required that the entrance of the church should be open to _all_, he avoided the odious name of Arius. Athanasius, like a skilful politician, has accurately marked these distinctions, (tom. i. p. 788,) which allowed him some scope for excuse and delay.

[102] The Meletians in Egypt, like the Donatists in Africa, were produced by an episcopal quarrel which arose from the persecution. I have not leisure to pursue the obscure controversy, which seems to have been misrepresented by the partiality of Athanasius and the ignorance of Epiphanius. See Mosheim's General History of the Church, vol. i. p. 201.

[103] The treatment of the six bishops is specified by Sozomen, (l. ii. c. 25 ;) but Athanasius himself, so copious on the subject of Arsenius and the chalice, leaves this grave accusation without a reply.*

---

* This grave charge, if made, (and it rests entirely on the authority of Sozomen,) seems to have been silently dropped by the parties themselves. it is never alluded to in the subsequent investigations. From Sozomen himself, who gives the unfavorable report of the commission of inquiry sent to Egypt: concerning the cup, it does not appear that they noticed this accusation of personal violence. — M.

prudently declined the tribunal of his enemies; despised the
summons of the synod of Cæsarea; and, after a long and
artful delay, submitted to the peremptory commands of the
emperor, who threatened to punish his criminal disobedience
if he refused to appear in the council of Tyre.[104] Before
Athanasius, at the head of fifty Egyptian prelates, sailed from
Alexandria, he had wisely secured the alliance of the Meletians ; and Arsenius himself, his imaginary victim, and his
secret friend, was privately concealed in his train. The synod
of Tyre was conducted by Eusebius of Cæsarea, with more passion, and with less art, than his learning and experience might
promise ; his numerous faction repeated the names of homi-
cide and tyrant ; and their clamors were encouraged by the
seeming patience of Athanasius, who expected the decisive
moment to produce Arsenius alive and unhurt in the midst of
the assembly. The nature of the other charges did not admit
of such clear and satisfactory replies ; yet the archbishop was
able to prove, that in the village, where he was accused of
breaking a consecrated chalice, neither church nor altar nor
chalice could really exist. The Arians who had secretly
determined the guilt and condemnation of their enemy,
attempted, however, to disguise their injustice by the imitation
of judicial forms : the synod appointed an episcopal commission of six delegates to collect evidence on the spot ; and this
measure, which was vigorously opposed by the Egyptian
bishops, opened new scenes of violence and perjury.[105] After
the return of the deputies from Alexandria, the majority of
the council pronounced the final sentence of degradation and
exile against the primate of Egypt. The decree, expressed
in the fiercest language of malice and revenge, was communicated to the emperor and the Catholic church ; and the
bishops immediately resumed a mild and devout aspect, such
as became their holy pilgrimage to the Sepulchre of Christ.[106]

---

[104] Athanas. tom. i. p. 788. Socrates, l. i. c. 28. Sozomen, l. ii. c.
25. The emperor, in his Epistle of Convocation, (Euseb. in Vit. Constant. l. iv. c. 42,) seems to prejudge some members of the clergy,
and it was more than probable that the synod would apply those
reproaches to Athanasius.

[105] See, in particular, the second Apology of Athanasius, (tom. i.
p. 763—808,) and his Epistles to the Monks, (p. 808—866.) They
are justified by original and authentic documents ; but they would
inspire more confidence if he appeared less innocent, and his enemies
less absurd.

[106] Eusebius in Vit. Constantin. l. iv. c. 41—47.

But the injustice of these ecclesiastical judges had not been countenanced by the submission, or even by the presence, of Athanasius. He resolved to make a bold and dangerous experiment, whether the throne was inaccessible to the voice of truth, and before the final sentence could be pronounced at Tyre, the intrepid primate threw himself into a bark which was ready to hoist sail for the Imperial city. The request of a formal audience might have been opposed or eluded ; but Athanasius concealed his arrival, watched the moment of Constantine's return from an adjacent villa, and boldly encountered his angry sovereign as he passed on horseback through the principal street of Constantinople. So strange an apparition excited his surprise and indignation ; and the guards were ordered to remove the importunate suitor; but his resentment was subdued by involuntary respect ; and the haughty spirit of the emperor was awed by the courage and eloquence of a bishop, who implored his justice and awakened his conscience.[107] Constantine listened to the complaints of Athanasius with impartial and even gracious attention ; the members of the synod of Tyre were summoned to justify their proceedings ; and the arts of the Eusebian faction would have been confounded, if they had not aggravated the guilt of the primate, by the dexterous supposition of an unpardonable offence ; a criminal design to intercept and detain the corn-fleet of Alexandria, which supplied the subsistence of the new capital.[108] The emperor was satisfied that the peace of Egypt would be secured by the absence of a popular leader ; but he refused to fill the vacancy of the archiepiscopal throne ; and the sentence, which, after long hesitation, he pronounced, was that of a jealous ostracism, rather than of an ignominious exile. In the remote province of Gaul, but in the hospitable

---

[107] Athanas. tom. i. p. 804. In a church dedicated to St. Athanasius, this situation would afford a better subject for a picture, than most of the stories of miracles and martyrdoms.

[108] Athanas. tom. i. p. 729. Eunapius has related (in Vit. Sophist. p. 36, 37, edit. Commelin) a strange example of the cruelty and credulity of Constantine on a similar occasion. The eloquent Sopater, a Syrian philosopher, enjoyed his friendship, and provoked the resentment of Ablavius, his Prætorian præfect. The corn-fleet was detained for want of a south wind; the people of Constantinople were discontented; and Sopater was beheaded, on a charge that he had bound the winds by the power of magic. Suidas adds, that Constantine wished to prove, by this execution, that he had absolutely renounced the superstition of the Gentiles.

court of Treves, Athanasius passed about twenty-eight months,
The death of the emperor changed the face of public affairs;
and, amidst the general indulgence of a young reign, the primate was restored to his country by an honorable edict of the
younger Constantine, who expressed a deep sense of the innocence and merit of his venerable guest.[109]

The death of that prince exposed Athanasius to a second
persecution; and the feeble Constantius, the sovereign of the
East, soon became the secret accomplice of the Eusebians.
Ninety bishops of that sect or faction assembled at Antioch,
under the specious pretence of dedicating the cathedral. They
composed an ambiguous creed, which is faintly tinged with
the colors of Semi-Arianism, and twenty-five canons, which
still regulate the discipline of the orthodox Greeks.[110] It was
decided, with some appearance of equity, that a bishop,
deprived by a synod, should not resume his episcopal functions till he had been absolved by the judgment of an equal
synod; the law was immediately applied to the case of Athanasius; the council of Antioch pronounced, or rather confirmed, his degradation: a stranger, named Gregory, was
seated on his throne; and Philagrius,[111] the praefect of Egypt,
was instructed to support the new primate with the civil and
military powers of the province. Oppressed by the conspiracy
of the Asiatic prelates, Athanasius withdrew from Alexandria,
and passed three years[112] as an exile and a suppliant on the

---

[109] In his return he saw Constantius twice, at Viminiacum, and at
Caesarea in Cappadocia, (Athanas. tom. i. p. 676.) Tillemont supposes
that Constantine introduced him to the meeting of the three royal
brothers in Pannonia, (Mémoires Eccles. tom. viii. p. 69.)

[110] See Beveridge, Pandect. tom. i. p. 429—452, and tom. ii. Annotation. p. 182. Tillemont, Mém. Eccles. tom. vi. p. 310—324. St.
Hilary of Poitiers has mentioned this synod of Antioch with too
much favor and respect. He reckons ninety-seven bishops.

[111] This magistrate, so odious to Athanasius, is praised by Gregory
Nazianzen, tom. i. Orat. xxi. p. 390, 391.

Sæpe premente Deo fert Deus alter opem.

For the credit of human nature, I am always pleased to discover
some good qualities in those men whom party has represented as
tyrants and monsters.

[112] The chronological difficulties which perplex the residence of
Athanasius at Rome, are strenuously agitated by Valesius (Observat.
ad Calcem, tom. ii. Hist. Eccles. l. i. c. 1—5) and Tillemont, (Mem.
Eccles. tom. viii. p. 674, &c.) I have followed the simple hypothesis
of Valesius, who allows only one journey, after the intrusion of
Gregory.

holy threshold of the Vatican.[113] By the assiduous study of the Latin language, he soon qualified himself to negotiate with the western clergy; his decent flattery swayed and directed the haughty Julius; the Roman pontiff was persuaded to consider his appeal as the peculiar interest of the Apostolic see, and his innocence was unanimously declared in a council of fifty bishops of Italy. At the end of three years, the primate was summoned to the court of Milan by the emperor Constans, who, in the indulgence of unlawful pleasures, still professed a lively regard for the orthodox faith. The cause of truth and justice was promoted by the influence of gold,[114] and the ministers of Constans advised their sovereign to require the convocation of an ecclesiastical assembly, which might act as the representatives of the Catholic church. Ninety-four bishops of the West, seventy-six bishops of the East, encountered each other at Sardica, on the verge of the two empires, but in the dominions of the protector of Athanasius. Their debates soon degenerated into hostile altercations; the Asiatics, apprehensive for their personal safety, retired to Philippopolis in Thrace; and the rival synods reciprocally hurled their spiritual thunders against their enemies, whom they piously condemned as the enemies of the true God. Their decrees were published and ratified in their respective provinces: and Athanasius, who in the West was revered as a saint, was exposed as a criminal to the abhorrence of the East.[115] The council of Sardica reveals the first symptoms

---

[113] I cannot forbear transcribing a judicious observation of Wetstein, (Prolegomen. N. T. p. 19:) Si tamen Historiam Ecclesiasticam velimus consulere, patebit jam inde a seculo quarto, cum, ortis controversiis, ecclesiæ Græciæ doctores in duas partes scinderentur, ingenio, eloquentiâ, numero, tantum non æquales, eam partem quæ vincere cupiebat Romam confugisse, majestatemque pontificis comitei coluisse, eoque pacto oppressis per pontificem et episcopos Latinos adversariis prævaluisse, atque orthodoxiam in conciliis stabilivisse. Eam ob causam Athanasius, non sine comitatu, Romam petiit, pluresque annos ibi hæsit.

[114] Philostorgius, l. iii. c. 12. If any corruption was used to promote the interest of religion, an advocate of Athanasius might justify or excuse this questionable conduct, by the example of Cato and Sidney; the former of whom is *said* to have given, and the latter to have received, a bribe in the cause of liberty.

[115] The canon which allows appeals to the Roman pontiffs, has almost raised the council of Sardica to the dignity of a general council; and its acts have been ignorantly or artfully confounded with those of the Nicene synod. See Tillemont, tom. vii. p. 689, and Geddes's Tracts, vol. ii. p. 419—460.

of discord and schism between the Greek and Latin churches which were separated by the accidental difference of faith and the permanent distinction of language.

During his second exile in the West, Athanasius was frequently admitted to the Imperial presence; at Capua, Lodi, Milan, Verona, Padua, Aquileia, and Treves. The bishop of the diocese usually assisted at these interviews; the master of the offices stood before the veil or curtain of the sacred apartment; and the uniform moderation of the primate might be attested by these respectable witnesses, to whose evidence he solemnly appeals.[116] Prudence would undoubtedly suggest the mild and respectful tone that became a subject and a bishop. In these familiar conferences with the sovereign of the West, Athanasius might lament the error of Constantius, but he boldly arraigned the guilt of his eunuchs and his Arian prelates; deplored the distress and danger of the Catholic church; and excited Constans to emulate the zeal and glory of his father. The emperor declared his resolution of employing the troops and treasures of Europe in the orthodox cause; and signified, by a concise and peremptory epistle to his brother Constantius, that unless he consented to the immediate restoration of Athanasius, he himself, with a fleet and army, would seat the archbishop on the throne of Alexandria.[117] But this religious war, so horrible to nature, was prevented by the timely compliance of Constantius; and the emperor of the East condescended to solicit a reconciliation with a subject whom he had injured. Athanasius waited with decent pride, till he had received three successive epistles full of the strongest assurances of the protection, the favor, and the esteem of his sovereign; who invited him to resume his episcopal seat, and who added the humiliating precaution of engaging his principal ministers to attest the sincerity of his intentions. They were manifested in a still more public manner, by the strict orders which were despatched into Egypt to recall the adherents of Athanasius, to restore their

---

[116] As Athanasius dispersed secret invectives against Constantius, (see the Epistle to the Monks,) at the same time that he assured him of his profound respect, we might distrust the professions of the archbishop.   Tom. i. p. 677.

[117] Notwithstanding the discreet silence of Athanasius, and the manifest forgery of a letter inserted by Socrates, these menaces are proved by the unquestionable evidence of Lucifer of Cagliari, and even of Constantius himself.   See Tillemont, tom. viii. p. 693.

privileges, to proclaim their innocence, and to erase from the public registers the illegal proceedings which had been obtained during the prevalence of the Eusebian faction. After every satisfaction and security had been given, which justice or even delicacy could require, the primate proceeded, by slow journeys, through the provinces of Thrace, Asia, and Syria; and his progress was marked by the abject homage of the Oriental bishops, who excited his contempt without deceiving his penetration.[118]   At Antioch he saw the emperor Constantius; sustained, with modest firmness, the embraces and protestations of his master, and eluded the proposal of allowing the Arians a single church at Alexandria, by claiming, in the other cities of the empire, a similar toleration for his own party; a reply which might have appeared just and moderate in the mouth of an independent prince.   The entrance of the archbishop into his capital was a triumphal procession; absence and persecution had endeared him to the Alexandrians; his authority, which he exercised with rigor, was more firmly established; and his fame was diffused from Æthiopia to Britain, over the whole extent of the Christian world.[119]

But the subject who has reduced his prince to the necessity of dissembling, can never expect a sincere and lasting forgiveness; and the tragic fate of Constans soon deprived Athanasius of a powerful and generous protector.   The civil war between the assassin and the only surviving brother of Constans, which afflicted the empire above three years, secured

---

[118] I have always entertained some doubts concerning the retraction of Ursacius and Valens, (Athanas. tom. i. p. 776.)   Their epistles to Julius, bishop of Rome, and to Athanasius himself, are of so different a cast from each other, that they cannot both be genuine.   The one speaks the language of criminals who confess their guilt and infamy; the other of enemies, who solicit on equal terms an honorable reconciliation.*

[119] The circumstances of his second return may be collected from Athanasius himself, tom. i. p. 769, and 822, 843.   Socrates, l. ii. c. 18.   Sozomen, l. iii. c. 19.   Theodoret, l. ii. c. 11, 12.   Philostorgius l. iii. c. 12.

---

* I cannot quite comprehend the ground of Gibbon's doubts.   Athanasius distinctly asserts the fact of their retractation.   (Athan. Op. i. p. 124, edit Benedict.)   The epistles are apparently translations from the Latin, if, in fact, more than the substance of the epistles.   That to Athanasius is brief, almost abrupt.   Their retractation is likewise mentioned in the address of the orthodox bishops of Rimini to Constantius.   Athan. de Synodis. Op. t. i. p. 723. — M.

an interval of repose to the Catholic church; and the two contending parties were desirous to conciliate the friendship of a bishop, who, by the weight of his personal authority might determine the fluctuating resolutions of an important province. He gave audience to the ambassadors of the tyrant, with whom he was aftewards accused of holding a secret correspondence; [120] and the emperor Constantius repeatedly assured his dearest father, the most reverend Athanasius, that, notwithstanding the malicious rumors which were circulated by their common enemies, he had inherited the sentiments, as well as the throne, of his deceased brother.[121] Gratitude and humanity would have disposed the primate of Egypt to deplore the untimely fate of Constans, and to abhor the guilt of Magnentius; but as he clearly understood that the apprehensions of Constantius were his only safeguard, the fervor of his prayers for the success of the righteous cause might perhaps be somewhat abated. The ruin of Athanasius was no longer contrived by the obscure malice of a few bigoted or angry bishops, who abused the authority of a credulous monarch. The monarch himself avowed the resolution, which he had so long suppressed, of avenging his private injuries; [122] and the first winter after his victory, which he passed at Arles, was employed against an enemy more odious to him than the vanquished tyrant of Gaul.

If the emperor had capriciously decreed the death of the most eminent and virtuous citizen of the republic, the cruel order would have been executed without hesitation, by the ministers of open violence or of specious injustice. The caution, the delay, the difficulty with which he proceeded in the condemnation and punishment of a popular bishop, discovered to the world that the privileges of the church had already revived a sense of order and freedom in the Roman government. The sentence which was pronounced in the synod of Tyre, and subscribed by a large majority of the

---

[120] Athanasius (tom. i. p. 677, 678) defends his innocence by pathetic complaints, solemn assertions, and specious arguments. He admits that letters had been forged in his name, but he requests that his own secretaries and those of the tyrant might be examined, whether those letters had been written by the former, or received by the latter.

[121] Athanas. tom. i. p. 825—844.

[122] Athanas. tom. i. p. 861. Theodoret, l. ii. c. 16. The emperor declared, that he was more desirous to subdue Athanasius, than he had been to vanquish Magnentius or Sylvanus.

Eastern bishops, had never been expressly repealed ; and as Athanasius had been once degraded from his episcopal dignity by the judgment of his brethren, every subsequent act might be considered as irregular, and even criminal. But the memory of the firm and effectual support which the primate of Egypt had derived from the attachment of the Western church, engaged Constantius to suspend the execution of the sentence till he had obtained the concurrence of the Latin bishops. Two years were consumed in ecclesiastical negotiations ; and the important cause between the emperor and one of his subjects was solemnly debated, first in the synod of Arles, and afterwards in the great council of Milan,[123] which consisted of above three hundred bishops. Their integrity was gradually undermined by the arguments of the Arians, the dexterity of the eunuchs, and the pressing solicitations of a prince who gratified his revenge at the expense of his dignity, and exposed his own passions, whilst he influenced those of the clergy. Corruption, the most infallible symptom of constitutional liberty, was successfully practised ; honors, gifts, and immunities were offered and accepted as the price of an episcopal vote ;[124] and the condemnation of the Alexandrian primate was artfully represented as the only measure which could restore the peace and union of the Catholic church. The friends of Athanasius were not, however, wanting to their leader, or to their cause. With a manly spirit, which the sanctity of their character rendered less dangerous, they maintained, in public debate, and in private conference with the emperor, the eternal obligation of religion and justice. They declared, that neither the hope of his favor, nor the fear of his displeasure, should prevail on them to join in the condemnation of an absent, an innocent, a respectable brother.[125] They affirmed, with apparent reason, that the illegal

---

[123] The affairs of the council of Milan are so imperfectly and erroneously related by the Greek writers, that we must rejoice in the supply of some letters of Eusebius, extracted by Baronius from the archives of the church of Vercellæ, and of an old life of Dionysius of Milan, published by Bollandus. See Baronius, A. D. 355, and Tillemont, tom. vii. p. 1415.

[124] The honors, presents, feasts, which seduced so many bishops, are mentioned with indignation by those who were too pure or too proud to accept them. " We combat (says Hilary of Poitiers) against Constantius the Antichrist ; who strokes the belly instead of scourging the back ; " qui non dorsa cædit ; sed ventrem palpat. Hilarius contra Constant. c. 5, p. 1240.

[125] Something of this opposition is mentioned by Ammianus, (xv

and obsolete decrees of the council of Tyre had long since been tacitly abolished by the Imperial edicts, the honorable reëstablishment of the archbishop of Alexandria, and the silence or recantation of his most clamorous adversaries. They alleged, that his innocence had been attested by the unanimous bishops of Egypt, and had been acknowledged in the councils of Rome and Sardica,[126] by the impartial judgment of the Latin church. They deplored the hard condition of Athanasius, who, after enjoying so many years his seat, his reputation, and the seeming confidence of his sovereign, was again called upon to confute the most groundless and extravagant accusations. Their language was specious; their conduct was honorable: but in this long and obstinate contest, which fixed the eyes of the whole empire on a single bishop, the ecclesiastical factions were prepared to sacrifice truth and justice to the more interesting object of defending or removing the intrepid champion of the Nicene faith. The Arians still thought it prudent to disguise, in ambiguous language, their real sentiments and designs; but the orthodox bishops, armed with the favor of the people, and the decrees of a general council, insisted on every occasion, and particularly at Milan, that their adversaries should purge themselves from the suspicion of heresy, before they presumed to arraign the conduct of the great Athanasius.[127]

But the voice of reason (if reason was indeed on the side of Athanasius) was silenced by the clamors of a factious or venal majority; and the councils of Arles and Milan were not dissolved, till the archbishop of Alexandria had been solemnly condemned and deposed by the judgment of the Western, as well as of the Eastern, church. The bishops who had opposed, were required to subscribe, the sentence, and to unite in religious communion with the suspected leaders of

---

7,) who had a very dark and superficial knowledge of ecclesiastical history. Liberius ... perseveranter renitebatur, nec visum hominem, nec auditum damnare, nefas ultimum sæpe exclamans; aperte scilicet recalcitrans Imperatoris arbitrio. Id enim ille Athanasio semper infestus, &c.

[126] More properly by the orthodox part of the council of Sardica. If the bishops of both parties had fairly voted, the division would have been 94 to 76. M. de Tillemont (see tom. viii. p. 1147—1158) is justly surprised that so small a majority should have proceeded so vigorously against their adversaries, the principal of whom they immediately deposed.

[127] Sulp. Severus in Hist. Sacra l. ii. p. 112.

the adverse party. A formulary of consent was transmitted by the messengers of state to the absent bishops: and all those who refused to submit their private opinion to the public and inspired wisdom of the councils of Arles and Milan, were immediately banished by the emperor, who affected to execute the decrees of the Catholic church. Among those prelates who led the honorable band of confessors and exiles, Liberius of Rome, Osius of Cordova, Paulinus of Treves, Dionysius of Milan, Eusebius of Vercellæ, Lucifer of Cagliari, and Hilary of Poitiers, may deserve to be particularly distinguished. The eminent station of Liberius, who governed the capital of the empire; the personal merit and long experience of the venerable Osius, who was revered as the favorite of the great Constantine, and the father of the Nicene faith, placed those prelates at the head of the Latin church: and their example, either of submission or resistance, would probably be imitated by the episcopal crowd. But the repeated attempts of the emperor to seduce or to intimidate the bishops of Rome and Cordova, were for some time ineffectual. The Spaniard declared himself ready to suffer under Constantius, as he had suffered threescore years before under his grandfather Maximian. The Roman, in the presence of his sovereign, asserted the innocence of Athanasius and his own freedom. When he was banished to Berœa in Thrace, he sent back a large sum which had been offered for the accommodation of his journey; and insulted the court of Milan by the haughty remark, that the emperor and his eunuchs might want that gold to pay their soldiers and their bishops.[128] The resolution of Liberius and Osius was at length subdued by the hardships of exile and confinement. The Roman pontiff purchased his return by some criminal compliances; and afterwards expiated his guilt by a seasonable repentance. Persuasion and violence were employed to extort the reluctant signature of the decrepit bishop of Cordova, whose strength was broken, and whose faculties were perhaps impaired by the weight of a hundred years; and the insolent triumph of the Arians provoked some of the orthodox party to treat with inhuman severity the character, or rather the memory, of an

---

[128] The exile of Liberius is mentioned by Ammianus, xv. 7. See Theodoret, l. ii. c. 16. Athanas. tom. i. p. 834—837 Hilar. Fragment i.

unfortunate old man, to whose former services Christianity itself was so deeply indebted.[129]

The fall of Liberius and Osius reflected a brighter lustre on the firmness of those bishops who still adhered, with unshaken fidelity, to the cause of Athanasius and religious truth. The ingenious malice of their enemies had deprived them of the benefit of mutual comfort and advice, separated those illustrious exiles into distant provinces, and carefully selected the most inhospitable spots of a great empire.[130]   Yet they soon experienced that the deserts of Libya, and the most barbarous tracts of Cappadocia, were less inhospitable than the residence of those cities in which an Arian bishop could satiate, without restraint, the exquisite rancor of theological hatred.[131]   Their consolation was derived from the consciousness of rectitude and independence, from the applause, the visits, the letters, and the liberal alms of their adherents,[132] and from the satisfaction which they soon enjoyed of observing the intestine divisions of the adversaries of the Nicene faith.   Such was the nice and capricious taste of the emperor Constantius ; and so easily was he offended by the slightest deviation from his imaginary standard of Christian truth, that he persecuted, with equal zeal, those who defended the *consubstantiality*, those who asserted the *similar substance*, and those who denied the *likeness* of the Son of God.   Three bishops, degraded and banished for those adverse opinions, might possibly meet in the same place of exile ; and, according to the difference of their temper, might either pity or

---

[129] The life of Osius is collected by Tillemont, (tom. vii. p. 524—561,) who in the most extravagant terms first admires, and then reprobates, the bishop of Cordova.   In the midst of their lamentations on his fall, the prudence of Athanasius may be distinguished from the blind and intemperate zeal of Hilary.

[130] The confessors of the West were successively banished to the deserts of Arabia or Thebais, the lonely places of Mount Taurus, the wildest parts of Phrygia, which were in the possession of the impious Montanists, &c.   When the heretic Ætius was too favorably entertained at Mopsuestia in Cilicia, the place of his exile was changed, by the advice of Acacius, to Amblada, a district inhabited by savages, and infested by war and pestilence. Philostorg. l. v. c. 2.

[131] See the cruel treatment and strange obstinacy of Eusebius, in his own letters, published by Baronius, A. D. 356, No. 92—102.

[132] Cæterum exules satis constat, totius orbis studiis celebratos, pecuniasque eis in sumptum affatim congestas, legationibus quoque eos plebis Catholicæ ex omnibus fere provinciis frequentatos. Sulp. Sever. Hist. Sacra, p. 414.   Athanas. tom. i. p. 836, 840.

insult the blind enthusiasm of their antagonists, whose present sufferings would never be compensated by future happiness.

The disgrace and exile of the orthodox bishops of the West were designed as so many preparatory steps to the ruin of Athanasius himself.[133] Six-and-twenty months had elapsed, during which the Imperial court secretly labored, by the most insidious arts, to remove him from Alexandria, and to withdraw the allowance which supplied his popular liberality. But when the primate of Egypt, deserted and proscribed by the Latin church, was left destitute of any foreign support, Constantius despatched two of his secretaries with a verbal commission to announce and execute the order of his banishment. As the justice of the sentence was publicly avowed by the whole party the only motive which could constrain Constantius from giving his messengers the sanction of a written mandate, must be imputed to his doubt of the event ; and to a sense of the danger to which he might expose the second city, and the most fertile province of the empire, if the people should persist in the resolution of defending, by force of arms, the innocence of their spiritual father. Such extreme caution afforded Athanasius a specious pretence respectfully to dispute the truth of an order, which he could not reconcile, either with the equity, or with the former declarations, of his gracious master. The civil powers of Egypt found themselves inadaquate to the task of persuading or compelling the primate to abdicate his episcopal throne; and they were obliged to conclude a treaty with the popular leaders of Alexandria, by which it was stipulated, that all proceedings and all hostilities should be suspended till the emperor's pleasure had been more distinctly ascertained. By this seeming moderation, the Catholics were deceived into a false and fatal security ; while the legions of the Upper Egypt, and of Libya, advanced, by secret orders and hasty marches, to besiege, or rather to surprise, a capital habituated to sedition, and inflamed by religious zeal.[134] The position of

---

[133] Ample materials for the history of this third persecution of Athanasius may be found in his own works. See particularly his very able Apology to Constantius, (tom. i. p. 673 ,) his first Apology for his flight (p. 701,) his prolix Epistle to the Solitaries, (p. 808,) and the original protest of the people of Alexandria against the violences committed by Syrianus, (p. 866.) Sozomen (l. iv. c. 9) has thrown into the narrative two or three luminous and important circumstances.

[134] Athanasius had lately sent for Antony, and some of his chosen monks. They descended from their mountain, announced to the

43

Alexandria, between the sea and the Lake Mareotis, facilitated the approach and landing of the troops ; who were introduced into the heart of the city, before any effectual measures could be taken, either to shut the gates or to occupy the important posts of defence.　At the hour of midnight, twenty-three days after the signature of the treaty, Syrianus, duke of Egypt. at the head of five thousand soldiers, armed and prepared for an assault, unexpectedly invested the church of St. Theonas, where the archbishop, with a part of his clergy and people, performed their nocturnal devotions.　The doors of the sacred edifice yielded to the impetuosity of the attack, which was accompanied with every horrid circumstance of tumult and bloodshed ; but, as the bodies of the slain, and the fragments of military weapons, remained the next day an unexceptionable evidence in the possession of the Catholics. the enterprise of Syrianus may be considered as a successful irruption rather than an absolute conquest.　The other churches of the city were profaned by similar outrages ; and, during at least four months, Alexandria was exposed to the insults of a licentious army, stimulated by the ecclesiastics of a hostile faction. Many of the faithful were killed ; who may deserve the name of martyrs, if their deaths were neither provoked or revenged ; bishops and presbyters were treated with cruel ignominy ; consecrated virgins were stripped naked, scourged and violated ; the houses of wealthy citizens were plundered ; and, under the mask of religious zeal, lust, avarice, and private resentment, were gratified with impunity, and even with applause.　The Pagans of Alexandria, who still formed a numerous and discontented party, were easily persuaded to desert a bishop whom they feared and esteemed.　The hopes of some peculiar favors, and the apprehension of being involved in the general penalties of rebellion, engaged them to promise their support to the destined successor of Athanasius, the famous George of Cappadocia.　The usurper, after receiving the consecration of an Arian synod, was placed on the episcopal throne by the arms of Sebastian, who had been appointed Count of Egypt for the execution of that important design. In the use, as well as in the acquisition, of power, the tyrant

---

Alexandrians the sanctity of Athanasius. and were honorably conducted by the archbishop as far as the gates of the city.　Athanas, tom. ii. p. 491, 492. See likewise Rufinus, iii. 164, in Vit. Patr. p. 254.

George disregarded the laws of religion, of justice, and of humanity; and the same scenes of violence and scandal which had been exhibited in the capital, were repeated in more than ninety episcopal cities of Egypt. Encouraged by success, Constantius ventured to approve the conduct of his ministers. By a public and passionate epistle, the emperor congratulates the deliverance of Alexandria from a popular tyrant, who deluded his blind votaries by the magic of his eloquence; expatiates on the virtues and piety of the most reverend George, the elected bishop; and aspires, as the patron and benefactor of the city, to surpass the fame of Alexander himself. But he solemnly declares his unalterable resolution to pursue with fire and sword the seditious adherents of the wicked Athanasius, who, by flying from justice, has confessed his guilt, and escaped the ignominious death which he had so often deserved.[135]

Athanasius had indeed escaped from the most imminent dangers; and the adventures of that extraordinary man deserve and fix our attention. On the memorable night when the church of St. Theonas was invested by the troops of Syrianus, the archbishop, seated on his throne, expected, with calm and intrepid dignity, the approach of death. While the public devotion was interrupted by shouts of rage and cries of terror, he animated his trembling congregation to express their religious confidence, by chanting one of the psalms of David which celebrates the triumph of the God of Israel over the haughty and impious tyrant of Egypt. The doors were at length burst open: a cloud of arrows was discharged among the people; the soldiers, with drawn swords, rushed forwards into the sanctuary; and the dreadful gleam of their arms was reflected by the holy luminaries which burnt round the altar.[136] Athanasius still rejected the pious importunity of the monks and presbyters, who were attached to his person; and nobly refused to desert his episcopal station, till he had dismissed in safety the last of the congregation. The darkness and tumult of the night favored the retreat of the archbishop; and though he

---

[135] Athanas. tom. i. p. 694. The emperor, or his Arian secretaries, while they express their resentment, betray their fears and esteem of Athanasius.

[136] These minute circumstances are curious, as they are literally transcribed from the protest, which was publicly presented three days afterwards by the Catholics of Alexandria. See Athanas. tom. i. p. 867.

was oppressed by the waves of an agitated multitude, though he was thrown to the ground, and left without sense or motion, he still recovered his undaunted courage, and eluded the eager search of the soldiers, who were instructed by their Arian guides, that the head of Athanasius would be the most acceptable present to the emperor. From that moment the primate of Egypt disappeared from the eyes of his enemies, and remained above six years concealed in impenetrable obscurity.[137]

The despotic power of his implacable enemy filled the whole extent of the Roman world; and the exasperated monarch had endeavored, by a very pressing epistle to the Christian princes of Ethiopia,* to exclude Athanasius from the most remote and sequestered regions of the earth. Counts, præfects, tribunes, whole armies, were successively employed to pursue a bishop and a fugitive; the vigilance of the civil and military powers was excited by the Imperial edicts; liberal rewards were promised to the man who should produce Athanasius, either alive or dead; and the most severe penalties were denounced against those who should dare to protect the public enemy.[138] But the deserts of Thebais were now

---

[137] The Jansenists have often compared Athanasius and Arnauld, and have expatiated with pleasure on the faith and zeal, the merit and exile, of those celebrated doctors. This concealed parallel is very dextorously managed by the Abbé de la Bleterie, Vie de Jovien. tom. i. p. 130.

[138] Hinc jam toto orbe profugus Athanasius, nec ullus ei tutus ad latendum supererat locus. Tribuni, Præfecti, Comites, exercitus quoque, ad pervestigandum eum moventur edictis Imperialibus; præmia delatoribus proponuntur, si quis eum vivum, si id minus, caput certe Athanasii detulisset. Rufin. l. i. c. 16.

---

* These princes were called Aeizanas and Saiazanas. Athanasius calls them the kings of Axum, (ὅτι ἐν Αὐξούμει Τύραννοι.) In the superscription of his letter, Constantius gives them no title, Νικήτης Κονστάντιος μέγιστος σέβαστος Αἰζανᾷ καὶ Σαζανᾷ. Mr. Salt, during his first journey in Ethiopia, (in 1806,) discovered, in the ruins of Axum, a long and very interesting inscription relating to these princes. It was erected to commemorate the victory of Aeizanas over the Bougaitæ, (St. Martin considers them the Blemmyes, whose true name is Bedjah or Bodjah.) Aeizanas is styled king of the Axumites, the Homerites, of Raeidan, of the Ethiopians, of the Sabarites, of Silea, of Tiamo, of the Bougaites, and of Kaei. It appears that at this time the king of the Ethiopians ruled over the Homerites, the inhabitants of Yemen. He was not yet a Christian, as he calls himself son of the invincible Mars, υἱὸς θεοῦ ἀνικήτου Ἄρεως. Another brother besides Saiazanas, named Adephas, is mentioned, though Aeizanas seems to have been sole king. See St. Martin, note on Le Beau, ii. 151 Salt's Travels. Silv. de Sacy, note in Annales des Voyages, xi p 53.—M

peopled by a race of wild, yet submissive fanatics, who preferred the commands of their abbot to the laws of their sovereign. The numerous disciples of Antony and Pachomius
received the fugitive primate as their father, admired the
patience and humility with which he conformed to their strictest
institutions, collected every word which dropped from his lips
as the genuine effusions of inspired wisdom ; and persuaded
themselves, that their prayers, their fasts, and their vigils, were
less meritorious than the zeal which they expressed, and the
dangers which they braved, in the defence of truth and innocence.[139] The monasteries of Egypt were seated in lonely
and desolate places, on the summit of mountains, or in the
islands of the Nile ; and the sacred horn or trumpet of Tabenne
was the well-known signal which assembled several thousand
robust and determined monks, who, for the most part, had
been the peasants of the adjacent country. When their dark
retreats were invaded by a military force, which it was impossible to resist, they silently stretched out their necks to the
executioner ; and supported their national character, that
tortures could never wrest from an Egyptian the confession
of a secret which he was resolved not to disclose.[140] The
archbishop of Alexandria, for whose safety they eagerly devoted their lives, was lost among a uniform and well-disciplined
multitude ; and on the nearer approach of danger, he was
swiftly removed by their officious hands, from one place of
concealment to another, till he reached the formidable deserts,
which the gloomy and credulous temper of superstition had
peopled with dæmons and savage monsters. The retirement of
Athanasius, which ended only with the life of Constantius, was
spent, for the most part, in the society of the monks, who faithfully served him as guards, as secretaries, and as messengers ;
but the importance of maintaining a more intimate connection
with the Catholic party tempted him, whenever the diligence
of the pursuit was abated, to emerge from the desert, to introduce himself into Alexandria, and to trust his person to the
discretion of his friends and adherents. His various adventures
might have furnished the subject of a very entertaining ro-

---

[139] Gregor. Nazianzen. tom. i. Orat. xxi. p. 384, 385. See Tillemont, Mém. Eccles. tom. vii. p. 176—410, 820—880.

[140] Et nulla tormentorum vis inveniri adhuc potuit; quæ obdurato
illius tractûs latroni invito elicere potuit, ut nomen proprium dicat.
Ammian. xxii. 16, and Valesius ad locum

mance. He was once secreted in a dry cistern, which he had scarcely left before he was betrayed by the treachery of a female slave ; [141] and he was once concealed in a still more extraordinary asylum, the house of a virgin, only twenty years of age, and who was celebrated in the whole city for her exquisite beauty. At the hour of midnight, as she related the story many years afterwards, she was surprised by the appearance of the archbishop in a loose undress, who, advancing with hasty steps, conjured her to afford him the protection which he had been directed by a celestial vision to seek under her hospitable roof. The pious maid accepted and preserved the sacred pledge which was intrusted to her prudence and courage. Without imparting the secret to any one, she instantly conducted Athanasius into her most secret chamber, and watched over his safety with the tenderness of a friend and the assiduity of a servant. As long as the danger continued, she regularly supplied him with books and provisions, washed his feet, managed his correspondence, and dexterously concealed from the eye of suspicion this familiar and solitary intercourse between a saint whose character required the most unblemished chastity, and a female whose charms might excite the most dangerous emotions.[142] During the six years of persecution and exile, Athanasius repeated his visits to his fair and faithful companion ; and the formal declaration, that he *saw* the councils of Rimini and Seleucia,[143] forces us to believe that he was secretly present at the time and place of their convocation. The advantage of personally negotiating with his friends, and of observing and improving the divisions of his enemies, might justify, in a prudent statesman, so bold and dangerous an enterprise : and Alexandria was connected by trade and navigation with every seaport of the Mediterranean.

---

[141] Rufin. l. i. c. 18. Sozomen, l. iv. c. 10. This and the following story will be rendered impossible, if we suppose that Athanasius always inhabited the asylum which he accidentally or occasionally had used.

[142] Paladius, (Hist. Lausiac. c. 136, in Vit. Patrum, p. 776,) the original author of this anecdote, had conversed with the damsel, who in her old age still remembered with pleasure so pious and honorable a connection. I cannot indulge the delicacy of Baronius, Valesius, Tillemont, &c., who almost reject a story so unworthy, as they deem it, of the gravity of ecclesiastical history.

[143] Athanas. tom. i. p. 869. I agree with Tillemont, (tom. viii. p 1197,) that his expressions imply a personal, though perhaps secret, visit to the synods.

From the depth of his inaccessible retreat the intrepid primate waged an incessant and offensive war against the protector of the Arians; and his seasonable writings, which were diligently circulated and eagerly perused, contributed to unite and animate the orthodox party. In his public apologies, which he addressed to the emperor himself, he sometimes affected the praise of moderation; whilst at the same time, in secret and vehement invectives, he exposed Constantius as a weak and wicked prince, the executioner of his family, the tyrant of the republic, and the Antichrist of the church. In the height of his prosperity, the victorious monarch, who had chastised the rashness of Gallus, and suppressed the revolt of Sylvanus, who had taken the diadem from the head of Vetranio, and vanquished in the field the legions of Magnentius, received from an invisible hand a wound, which he could neither heal nor revenge; and the son of Constantine was the first of the Christian princes who experienced the strength of those principles, which, in the cause of religion, could resist the most violent exertions [144] of the civil power.

The persecution of Athanasius, and of so many respectable bishops, who suffered for the truth of their opinions, or at least for the integrity of their conscience, was a just subject of indignation and discontent to all Christians, except those who were blindly devoted to the Arian faction. The people regretted the loss of their faithful pastors, whose banishment was usually followed by the intrusion of a stranger [145] into the episcopal chair; and loudly complained, that the right of election was violated, and that they were condemned to obey a mercenary usurper, whose person was unknown, and whose principles were suspected. The Catholics might prove to the world, that they were not involved in the guilt and heresy of

---

[144] The epistle of Athanasius to the monks is filled with reproaches, which the public must feel to be true, (vol. i. p. 834, 856;) and, in compliment to his readers, he has introduced the comparisons of Pharaoh, Ahab, Belshazzar, &c. The boldness of Hilary was attended with less danger, if he published his invective in Gaul after the revolt of Julian; but Lucifer sent his libels to Constantius, and almost challenged the reward of martyrdom. See Tillemont, tom. vii. p. 905.

[145] Athanasius (tom. i. p. 811) complains in general of this practice, which he afterwards exemplifies (p. 861) in the pretended election of Fælix. Three eunuchs represented the Roman people, and three prelates, who followed the court, assumed the functions of the bishops of the Suburbicarian provinces.

their ecclesiastical governor, by publicly testifying their dis
sent, or by totally separating themselves from his communion
The first of these methods was invented at Antioch, and practised with such success, that it was soon diffused over the
Christian world. The doxology, or sacred hymn, which cele
brates the *glory* of the Trinity, is susceptible of very nice, but
material, inflections ; and the substance of an orthodox, or an
heretical, creed, may be expressed by the difference of a dis-
junctive, or a copulative, particle. Alternate responses, and a
more regular psalmody,[146] were introduced into the public
service by Flavianus and Diodorus, two devout and active lay
men, who were attached to the Nicene faith. Under their
conduct a swarm of monks issued from the adjacent desert,
bands of well-disciplined singers were stationed in the cathedral of Antioch, the Glory to the Father, AND the Son, AND
the Holy Ghost,[147] was triumphantly chanted by a full chorus
of voices; and the Catholics insulted, by the purity of their
doctrine, the Arian prelate, who had usurped the throne of the
venerable Eustathius. The same zeal which inspired their
songs prompted the more scrupulous members of the orthodox
party to form separate assemblies, which were governed by
the presbyters, till the death of their exiled bishop allowed the
election and consecration of a new episcopal pastor.[148] The

---

[146] Thomassin (Discipline de l'Eglise, tom. i. l. ii. c. 72, 73, p. 966—
384) has collected many curious facts concerning the origin and
progress of church singing, both in the East and West.*

[147] Philostorgius, l. iii. c. 13. Godefroy has examined this subject
with singular accuracy, (p. 147, &c.) There were three heterodox
forms : "To the Father *by* the Son, *and* in the Holy Ghost;" "To
the Father, *and* the Son *in* the Holy Ghost;" and "To the Father *in*
the Son *and* the Holy Ghost."

[148] After the exile of Eustathius, under the reign of Constantine,
the rigid party of the orthodox formed a separation which afterwards
degenerated into a schism, and lasted about fourscore years. See
Tillemont, Mém. Eccles. tom. vii. p. 35—54, 1137—1158, tom. viii.
p. 537—632, 1314—1332. In many churches, the Arians and
Homoousians, who had renounced each other's *communion*, continued
for some time to join in prayer. Philostorgius, l. iii. c. 14.

---

* Arius appears to have been the first who availed himself of this means
of impressing his doctrines on the popular ear: he composed songs for
sailors, millers, and travellers, and set them to common airs ; "beguiling
the ignorant, by the sweetness of his music, into the impiety of his doctrines.' Philostorgius, ii. 2. Arian singers used to parade the streets
of Constantinople by night, till Chrysostom arrayed against them a band
of orthodox choristers. Sozomen, viii. 8. — M.

revolutions of the court multiplied the number of pretenders ; and the same city was often disputed, under the reign of Constantius, by two, or three, or even four, bishops, who exercised their spiritual jurisdiction over their respective followers, and alternately lost and regained the temporal possessions of the church. The abuse of Christianity introduced into the Roman government new causes of tyranny and sedition ; the bands of civil society were torn asunder by the fury of religious factions ; and the obscure citizen, who might calmly have surveyed the elevation and fall of successive emperors, imagined and experienced, that his own life and fortune were connected with the interests of a popular ecclesiastic. The example of the two capitals, Rome and Constantinople, may serve to represent the state of the empire, and the temper of mankind, under the reign of the sons of Constantine.

I. The Roman pontiff, as long as he maintained his station and his principles, was guarded by the warm attachment of a great people ; and could reject with scorn the prayers, the menaces, and the oblations of an heretical prince. When the eunuchs had secretly pronounced the exile of Liberius, the well-grounded apprehension of a tumult engaged them to use the utmost precautions in the execution of the sentence. The capital was invested on every side, and the præfect was commanded to seize the person of the bishop, either by stratagem or by open force. The order was obeyed, and Liberius, with the greatest difficulty, at the hour of midnight, was swiftly conveyed beyond the reach of the Roman people, before their consternation was turned into rage. As soon as they were informed of his banishment into Thrace, a general assembly was convened, and the clergy of Rome bound themselves, by a public and solemn oath, never to desert their bishop, never to acknowledge the usurper Fælix ; who, by the influence of the eunuchs, had been irregularly chosen and consecrated within the walls of a profane palace. At the end of two years, their pious obstinacy subsisted entire and unshaken ; and when Constantius visited Rome, he was assailed by the importunate solicitations of a people, who had preserved, as the last remnant of their ancient freedom, the right of treating their sovereign with familiar insolence. The wives of many of the senators and most honorable citizens, after pressing their husbands to intercede in favor of Liberius, were advised to undertake a commission, which in their hands would be less dangerous, and might prove more successful. The em-

43 *

peror received with politeness these female deputies, whose wealth and dignity were displayed in the magnificence of their dress and ornaments: he admired their inflexible resolution of following their beloved pastor to the most distant regions of the earth; and consented that the two bishops, Liberius and Fælix, should govern in peace their respective congregations. But the ideas of toleration were so repugnant to the practice, and even to the sentiments, of those times, that when the answer of Constantius was publicly read in the Circus of Rome, so reasonable a project of accommodation was rejected with contempt and ridicule. The eager vehemence which animated the spectators in the decisive moment of a horse-race, was now directed towards a different object; and the Circus resounded with the shout of thousands, who repeatedly exclaimed, " One God, One Christ, One Bishop!" The zeal of the Roman people in the cause of Liberius was not confined to words alone; and the dangerous and bloody sedition which they excited soon after the departure of Constantius determined that prince to accept the submission of the exiled prelate, and to restore him to the undivided dominion of the capital. After some ineffectual resistance, his rival was expelled from the city by the permission of the emperor and the power of the opposite faction; the adherents of Fælix were inhumanly murdered in the streets, in the public places, in the baths, and even in the churches; and the face of Rome, upon the return of a Christian bishop, renewed the horrid image of the massacres of Marius, and the proscriptions of Sylla.[149]

II. Notwithstanding the rapid increase of Christians under the reign of the Flavian family, Rome, Alexandria, and the other great cities of the empire, still contained a strong and powerful faction of Infidels, who envied the prosperity, and who ridiculed, even in their theatres, the theological disputes of the church. Constantinople alone enjoyed the advantage of being born and educated in the bosom of the faith. The capital of the East had never been polluted by the worship of idols; and the whole body of the people had deeply imbibed the opinions, the virtues, and the passions, which distinguished

---

[149] See, on this ecclesiastical revolution of Rome, Ammianus, xv. 7. Athanas. tom. i. p. 834, 861. Sozomen, l. iv. c. 15. Theodoret, l. ii. c. 17. Sulp. Sever. Hist. Sacra, l. ii. p. 413. Hieronym. Chron. Marcellin. et Faustin. Libell. p. 3, 4. Tillemont, Mém. Eccles. tom. vi. p. 336.

the Christians of that age from the rest of mankind. After the death of Alexander, the episcopal throne was disputed by Paul and Macedonius. By their zeal and abilities they both deserved the eminent station to which they aspired; and if the moral character of Macedonius was less exceptionable, his competitor had the advantage of a prior election and a more orthodox doctrine. His firm attachment to the Nicene creed, which has given Paul a place in the calendar among saints and martyrs, exposed him to the resentment of the Arians. In the space of fourteen years he was five times driven from his throne; to which he was more frequently restored by the violence of the people, than by the permission of the prince; and the power of Macedonius could be secured only by the death of his rival. The unfortunate Paul was dragged in chains from the sandy deserts of Mesopotamia to the most desolate places of Mount Taurus,[150] confined in a dark and narrow dungeon, left six days without food, and at length strangled, by the order of Philip, one of the principal ministers of the emperor Constantius.[151] The first blood which stained the new capital was spilt in this ecclesiastical contest; and many persons were slain on both sides, in the furious and obstinate seditions of the people. The commission of enforcing a sentence of banishment against Paul, had been intrusted to Hermogenes, the master-general of the cavalry; but the execution of it was fatal to himself. The Catholics rose in the defence of their bishop; the palace of Hermogenes was consumed; the first military officer of the empire was dragged by the heels through the streets of Constantinople, and, after he expired, his lifeless corpse was exposed to their wanton

---

[150] Cucusus was the last stage of his life and sufferings. The situation of that lonely town, on the confines of Cappadocia, Cilicia, and the Lesser Armenia, has occasioned some geographical perplexity; but we are directed to the true spot by the course of the Roman road from Cæsarea to Anazarbus. See Cellarii Geograph. tom. ii. p. 213. Wesseling ad Itinerar. p. 179, 703.

[151] Athanasius (tom. i. p. 703, 813, 814) affirms, in the most positive terms, that Paul was murdered; and appeals, not only to common fame, but even to the unsuspicious testimony of Philagrius, one of the Arian persecutors. Yet he acknowledges that the heretics attributed to disease the death of the bishop of Constantinople. Athanasius is servilely copied by Socrates, (l. ii. c. 26;) but Sozomen, who discovers a more liberal temper, presumes (l. iv. c. 2) to insinuate a prudent doubt.

insults.[152] The fate of Hermogenes instructed Philip, the Prætorian præfect, to act with more precaution on a similar occasion. In the most gentle and honorable terms, he required the attendance of Paul in the baths of Zeuxippus, which had a private communication with the palace and the sea. A vessel, which lay ready at the garden stairs, immediately hoisted sail; and, while the people were still ignorant of the meditated sacrilege, their bishop was already embarked on his voyage to Thessalonica. They soon beheld, with surprise and indignation, the gates of the palace thrown open, and the usurper Macedonius seated by the side of the præfect on a lofty chariot, which was surrounded by troops of guards with drawn swords. The military procession advanced towards the cathedral; the Arians and the Catholics eagerly rushed to occupy that important post; and three thousand one hundred and fifty persons lost their lives in the confusion of the tumult. Macedonius, who was supported by a regular force, obtained a decisive victory; but his reign was disturbed by clamor and sedition; and the causes which appeared the least connected with the subject of dispute, were sufficient to nourish and to kindle the flame of civil discord. As the chapel in which the body of the great Constantine had been deposited was in a ruinous condition, the bishop transported those venerable remains into the church of St. Acacius. This prudent and even pious measure was represented as a wicked profanation by the whole party which adhered to the Homoousian doctrine. The factions immediately flew to arms, the consecrated ground was used as their field of battle; and one of the ecclesiastical historians has observed, as a real fact, not as a figure of rhetoric, that the well before the church overflowed with a stream of blood, which filled the porticos and the adjacent courts. The writer who should impute these tumults solely to a religious principle, would betray a very imperfect knowledge of human nature; yet it must be confessed that the motive which misled the sincerity of zeal, and the pretence which disguised the licentiousness of passion, suppressed the

[152] Ammianus (xiv. 10) refers to his own account of this tragic event. But we no longer possess that part of his history.*

---

* The murder of Hermogenes took place at the first expulsion of Paul from the see of Constantinople. — M.

remorse which, in another cause, would have succeeded to the rage of the Christians of Constantinople.[153]

The cruel and arbitrary disposition of Constantius, which did not always require the provocations of guilt and resistance, was justly exasperated by the tumults of his capital, and the criminal behavior of a faction, which opposed the authority and religion of their sovereign. The ordinary punishments of death, exile, and confiscation, were inflicted with partial rigor; and the Greeks still revere the holy memory of two clerks, a reader, and a sub-deacon, who were accused of the murder of Hermogenes, and beheaded at the gates of Constantinople. By an edict of Constantius against the Catholics, which has not been judged worthy of a place in the Theodosian code, those who refused to communicate with the Arian bishops, and particularly with Macedonius, were deprived of the immunities of ecclesiastics, and of the rights of Christians; they were compelled to relinquish the possession of the churches and were strictly prohibited from holding their assemblies within the walls of the city. The execution of this unjust law, in the provinces of Thrace and Asia Minor, was committed to the zeal of Macedonius; the civil and military powers were directed to obey his commands; and the cruelties exercised by this Semi-Arian tyrant in the support of the *Homoiousion*, exceeded the commission, and disgraced the reign, of Constantius. The sacraments of the church were administered to the reluctant victims, who denied the vocation, and abhorred the principles, of Macedonius. The rites of baptism were conferred on women and children, who, for that purpose, had been torn from the arms of their friends and parents; the mouths of the communicants were held open by a wooden engine, while the consecrated bread was forced down their throat; the breasts of tender virgins were either burnt with red-hot egg-shells, or inhumanly compressed between sharp and heavy boards.[154] The Novatians of Constantinople and

[153] See Socrates, l. ii. c. 6, 7, 12, 13, 15, 16, 26, 27, 38, and Sozomen, l. iii. 3, 4, 7, 9, l. iv. c. ii. 21. The acts of St. Paul of Constantinople, of which Photius has made an abstract, (Phot. Bibliot. p. 1419—1430,) are an indifferent copy of these historians; but a modern Greek, who could write the life of a saint without adding fables and miracles, is entitled to some commendation.

[154] Socrates, l. ii. c. 27, 38. Sozomen, l. iv. c. 21. The principal assistants of Macedonius, in the work of persecution, were the two bishops of Nicomedia and Cyzicus, who were esteemed for their virtues, and especially for their charity. I cannot forbear reminding the

the adjacent country, by their firm attachment to the Homoousian standard, deserved to be confounded with the Catholics themselves. Macedonius was informed, that a large district of Paphlagonia[155] was almost entirely inhabited by those sectaries. He resolved either to convert or to extirpate them; and as he distrusted, on this occasion, the efficacy of an ecclesiastical mission, he commanded a body of four thousand legionaries to march against the rebels, and to reduce the territory of Mantinium under his spiritual dominion. The Novatian peasants, animated by despair and religious fury, boldly encountered the invaders of their country; and though many of the Paphlagonians were slain, the Roman legions were vanquished by an irregular multitude, armed only with scythes and axes; and, except a few who escaped by an ignominious flight, four thousand soldiers were left dead on the field of battle. The successor of Constantius has expressed, in a concise but lively manner, some of the theological calamities which afflicted the empire, and more especially the East, in the reign of a prince who was the slave of his own passions, and of those of his eunuchs : " Many were imprisoned, and persecuted, and driven into exile. Whole troops of those who are styled heretics, were massacred, particularly at Cyzicus, and at Samosata. In Paphlagonia, Bithynia, Gallatia, and in many other provinces, towns and villages were laid waste, and utterly destroyed.[156]

While the flames of the Arian controversy consumed the vitals of the empire, the African provinces were infested by their peculiar enemies, the savage fanatics, who, under the name of *Circumcellions*, formed the strength and scandal of the Donatist party.[157] The severe execution of the laws of

reader, that the difference between the *Homoousion* and *Homoiousion*, is almost invisible to the nicest theological eye.

[155] We are ignorant of the precise situation of Mantinium. In speaking of these *four* bands of legionaries, Socrates, Sozomen, and the author of the acts of St. Paul, use the indefinite terms of ἀριθμοι, φάλαγγες, τάγματα, which Nicephorus very properly translates *thousands*. Vales. ad Socrat. l. ii. c. 38.

[156] Julian. Epistol. lii. p. 436, edit. Spanheim.

[157] See Optatus Milevitanus, (particularly iii. 4,) with the Donatist history, by M. Dupin, and the original pieces at the end of his edition. The numerous circumstances which Augustin has mentioned, of the fury of the Circumcellions against others, and against themselves, have been laboriously collected by Tillemont, Mém. Eccles tom. vi. p. 147—165; and he has often, though without design exposed the injuries which had provoked those fanatics.

Constantine had excited a spirit of discontent and resistance; the strenuous efforts of his son Constans, to restore the unity of the church, exasperated the sentiments of mutual hatred, which had first occasioned the separation ; and the methods of force and corruption employed by the two Imperial commissioners, Paul and Macarius, furnished the schismatics with a specious contrast between the maxims of the apostles and the conduct of their pretended successors.[158] The peasants who inhabited the villages of Numidia and Mauritania, were a ferocious race, who had been imperfectly reduced under the authority of the Roman laws ; who were imperfectly converted to the Christian faith ; but who were actuated by a blind and furious enthusiasm in the cause of their Donatist teachers.   They indignantly supported the exile of their bishops, the demolition of their churches, and the interruption of their secret assemblies. The violence of the officers of justice, who were usually sustained by a military guard, was sometimes repelled with equal violence ; and the blood of some popular ecclesiastics, which had been shed in the quarrel, inflamed their rude followers with an eager desire of revenging the death of these holy martyrs. By their own cruelty and rashness, the ministers of persecution sometimes provoked their fate ; and the guilt of an accidental tumult precipitated the criminals into despair and rebellion. Driven from their native villages, the Donatist peasants assembled in formidable gangs on the edge of the Getulian desert ; and readily exchanged the habits of labor for a life of idleness and rapine, which was consecrated by the name of religion, and faintly condemned by the doctors of the sect.   The leaders of the Circumcellions assumed the title of captains of the saints ; their principal weapon, as they were indifferently provided with swords and spears, was a huge and weighty club,

---

[158] It is amusing enough to observe the language of opposite parties, when they speak of the same men and things. Gratus, bishop of Carthage, begins the acclamations of an orthodox synod, " Gratias Deo omnipotenti et Christû Jesu . . . qui imperavit religiosissimo Constanti Imperatori, ut votum gereret unitatis, et mitteret ministros sancti operis *famulos Dei* Paulum et Macarium." Monument. Vet. ad Calcem Optati, p. 313. "Ecce subito," (says the Donatist author of the Passion of Marculus, " de Constantis regis tyrannicâ domo. . . pollutum Macarianæ persecutionis murmur increpuit, et *duabus bestiis* ad Africam missis, eodem scilicet Macario et Paulo, execrandum prorsus ac dirum ecclesiæ certamen indictum est ; ut populus Christ-t.anus ad unionem cum traditoribus faciendam, nudatis militum gla-diis et draconum præsentibus signis, et tubarum vocibus cogeretur." Monument. p. 304.

which they termed an *Israelite;* and the well-known sound of ' Praise be to God," which they used as their cry of war diffused consternation over the unarmed provinces of Africa. At first their depredations were colored by the plea of necessity ; but they soon exceeded the measure of subsistence, indulged without control their intemperance and avarice, burnt the villages which they had pillaged, and reigned the licentious tyrants of the open country. The occupations of husbandry, and the administration of justice, were interrupted ; and as the Circumcellions pretended to restore the primitive equality of mankind, and to reform the abuses of civil society they opened a secure asylum for the slaves and debtors, who flocked in crowds to their holy standard. When they were not resisted, they usually contented themselves with plunder, but the slightest opposition provoked them to acts of violence and murder ; and some Catholic priests, who had imprudently signalized their zeal, were tortured by the fanatics with the most refined and wanton barbarity. The spirit of the Circumcellions was not always exerted against their defenceless enemies ; they engaged, and sometimes defeated, the troops of the province ; and in the bloody action of Bagai, they attacked in the open field, but with unsuccessful valor, an advanced guard of the Imperial cavalry. The Donatists who were taken in arms, received, and they soon deserved, the same treatment which might have been shown to the wild beasts of the desert. The captives died, without a murmur, either by the sword, the axe, or the fire ; and the measures of retaliation were multiplied in a rapid proportion, which aggravated the horrors of rebellion, and excluded the hope of mutual forgiveness. In the beginning of the present century, the example of the Circumcellions has been renewed in the persecution, the boldness, the crimes, and the enthusiasm of the Camisards ; and if the fanatics of Languedoc surpassed those of Numidia, by their military achievements, the Africans maintained their fierce independence with more resolution and perseverance.[159]

Such disorders are the natural effects of religious tyranny , but the rage of the Donatists was inflamed by a frenzy of a very extraordinary kind ; and which, if it really prevailed among them in so extravagant a degree, cannot surely be

---

[159] The Histoire des Camisards, in 3 vols. 12mo. Villefranche, 1760, may be recommended as accurate and impartial. It requires some attention to discover the religion of the author.

paralleled in any country or in any age. Many of these
fanatics were possessed with the horror of life, and the desire
of ma   rdom ; and they deemed it of little moment by what
means, or by what hands, they perished, if their conduct was
sanctified by the intention of devoting themselves to the glory
of the true faith, and the hope of eternal happiness.[160] Sometimes they rudely disturbed the festivals, and profaned the
temples of Paganism, with the design of exciting the mos
zealous of the idolaters to revenge the insulted honor of thei
gods. They sometimes forced their way into the courts of
justice, and compelled the affrighted judge to give orders for
their immediate execution. They frequently stopped travellers
on the public highways, and obliged them to inflict the stroke
of martyrdom, by the promise of a reward, if they consented,
and by the threat of instant death, if they refused to grant so
very singular a favor. When they were disappointed of every
other resource, they announced the day on which, in the
presence of their friends and brethren, they should cast themselves headlong from some lofty rock ; and many precipices
were shown, which had acquired fame by the number of religious suicides. In the actions of these desperate enthusiasts,
who were admired by one party as the martyrs of God, and
abhorred by the other as the victims of Satan, an impartial
philosopher may discover the influence and the last abuse of
that inflexible spirit, which was originally derived from the
character and principles of the Jewish nation.

The simple narrative of the intestine divisions, which distracted the peace, and dishonored the triumph, of the church,
will confirm the remark of a Pagan historian, and justify the
complaint of a venerable bishop. The experience of Ammianus had convinced him, that the enmity of the Christians
towards each other, surpassed the fury of savage beasts
against man ;[161] and Gregory Nazianzen most pathetically
laments, that the kingdom of heaven was converted, by discord, into the image of chaos, of a nocturnal tempest, and
of hell itself.[162] The fierce and partial writers of the times,

---

[160] The Donatist suicides alleged in their justification the example
of Razias, which is related in the 14th chapter of the second book of
the Maccabees.

[161] Nullus infestas hominibus bestias, ut sunt sibi ferales plerique
Christianorum, expertus. Ammian. xxii. 5.

[162] Gregor. Nazianzen, Orat. i. p. 33. See Tillemont, tom. vi. p.
501, quarto edit.

ascribing *all* virtue to themselves, and imputing *all* guilt to their adversaries, have painted the battle of the angels and dæmons. Our calmer reason will reject such pure and perfect monsters of vice or sanctity, and will impute an equal, or at least an indiscriminate, measure of good and evil to the hostile sectaries, who assumed and bestowed the appellations of orthodox and heretics. They had been educated in the same religion, and the same civil society. Their hopes and fears in the present, or in a future life, were balanced in the same proportion. On either side, the error might be innocent the faith sincere, the practice meritorious or corrupt. Their passions were excited by similar objects; and they might alternately abuse the favor of the court, or of the people. The metaphysical opinions of the Athanasians and the Arians could not influence their moral character; and they were alike actuated by the intolerant spirit which has been extracted from the pure and simple maxims of the gospel.

A modern writer, who, with a just confidence, has prefixed to his own history the honorable epithets of political and philosophical,[163] accuses the timid prudence of Montesquieu for neglecting to enumerate, among the causes of the decline of the empire, a law of Constantine, by which the exercise of the Pagan worship was absolutely suppressed, and a considerable part of his subjects was left destitute of priests, of temples, and of any public religion. The zeal of the philosophic historian for the rights of mankind, has induced him to acquiesce in the ambiguous testimony of those ecclesiastics, who have too lightly ascribed to their favorite hero the *merit* of a general persecution.[164] Instead of alleging this imaginary law, which would have blazed in the front of the Imperial codes, we may safely appeal to the original epistle, which Constantine addressed to the followers of the ancient religion; at a time when he no longer disguised his conversion, nor

---

[163] Histoire Politique et Philosophique des Etablissemens des Européens dans les deux Indes, tom. i. p. 9.

[164] According to Eusebius, (in Vit. Constantin. l. ii. c. 45,) the emperor prohibited, both in cities and in the country, τα μυσαρα . . . . τῆς Εἰδωλολατρείας; the abominable acts or parts of idolatry. Socrates (l. i. c. 17) and Sozomen (l. ii. c. 4, 5) have represented the conduct of Constantine with a just regard to truth and history; which has been neglected by Theodoret (l. v. c. 21) and Orosius, (vii. 28.) Tum deinde (says the latter) primus Constantinus *justo* ordine et *pio* vicem vertit edicto; siquidem statuit citra ullam hominum cædem, paganorum templa claudi.

dreaded the rivals of his throne. He invites and exhorts, in the most pressing terms, the subjects of the Roman empire to imitate the example of their master; but he declares, that those who still refuse to open their eyes to the celestial light, may freely enjoy their temples and their fancied gods. A report, that the ceremonies of paganism were suppressed, is formally contradicted by the emperor himself, who wisely assigns, as the principle of his moderation, the invincible force of habit, of prejudice, and of superstition.[165] Without violating the sanctity of his promise, without alarming the fears of the Pagans, the artful monarch advanced, by slow and cautious steps, to undermine the irregular and decayed fabric of polytheism. The partial acts of severity which he occasionally exercised, though they were secretly prompted by a Christian zeal, were colored by the fairest pretences of justice and the public good; and while Constantine designed to ruin the foundations, he seemed to reform the abuses, of the ancient religion. After the example of the wisest of his predecessors, he condemned, under the most rigorous penalties, the occult and impious arts of divination; which excited the vain hopes, and sometimes the criminal attempts, of those who were discontented with their present condition. An ignominious silence was imposed on the oracles, which had been publicly convicted of fraud and falsehood; the effeminate priests of the Nile were abolished; and Constantine discharged the duties of a Roman censor, when he gave orders for the demolition of several temples of Phœnicia; in which every mode of prostitution was devoutly practised in the face of day, and to the honor of Venus.[166] The Imperial city of Constantinople was, in some measure, raised at the expense, and was adorned with the spoils, of the opulent temples of Greece and Asia; the sacred property was confiscated; the statues of gods and heroes were transported, with rude familiarity, among a people who considered them as

---

[165] See Eusebius in Vit. Constantin. l. ii. c. 56, 60. In the sermon to the assembly of saints, which the emperor pronounced when he was mature in years and piety, he declares to the idolaters (c. xii.) that they are permitted to offer sacrifices, and to exercise every part of their religious worship.

[166] See Eusebius, in Vit. Constantin. l. iii. c. 54—58, and l. iv. c. 23, 25. These acts of authority may be compared with the suppression of the Bacchanals, and the demolition of the temple of Isis, by the magistrates of Pagan Rome.

objects, not of adoration, but of curiosity ; the gold and silver were restored to circulation ; and the magistrates, the bishops, and the eunuchs, improved the fortunate occasion of gratify-ing, at once, their zeal, their avarice, and their resentment But these depredations were confined to a small part of the Roman world; and the provinces had been long since accus-tomed to endure the same sacrilegious rapine, from the tyranny of princes and proconsuls, who could not be suspected of any design to subvert the established religion.[167]

The sons of Constantine trod in the footsteps of their father, with more zeal, and with less discretion. The pretences of rapine and oppression were insensibly multiplied ; [168] every indulgence was shown to the illegal behavior of the Chris-tians ; every doubt was explained to the disadvantage of Pa-ganism ; and the demolition of the temples was celebrated as one of the auspicious events of the reign of Constans and Con-stantius.[169] The name of Constantius is prefixed to a concise law, which might have superseded the necessity of any future prohibitions. " It is our pleasure, that in all places, and in all cities, the temples be immediately shut, and carefully guarded, that none may have the power of offending. It is likewise our pleasure, that all our subjects should abstain from sacri-fices. If any one should be guilty of such an act, let him feel the sword of vengeance, and after his execution, let his property be confiscated to the public use. We denounce the same penalties against the governors of the provinces, if they neglect to punish the criminals." [170] But there is the strongest

---

[167] Eusebius (in Vit. Constan. l. iii. c. 54) and Libanius (Orat. pro Templis, p. 9, 10, edit. Gothofred) both mention the pious sacrilege of Constantine, which they viewed in very different lights. The lat-ter expressly declares, that " he made use of the sacred money, but made no alteration in the legal worship ; the temples indeed were impoverished, but the sacred rites were performed there." Lard-ner's Jewish and Heathen Testimonies, vol. iv. p. 140.

[168] Ammianus (xxii. 4) speaks of some court eunuchs who were spoliis templorum pasti. Libanius says (Orat. pro Temp l. p. 23) that the emperor often gave away a temple, like a dog, or a horse, or a slave, or a gold cup ; but the devout philosopher takes care to observe, that these sacrilegious favorites very seldom prospered.

[169] See Gothofred. Cod. Theodos. tom. vi. p. 262. Liban. Orat. Parental. c. x. in Fabric. Bibl. Græc. tom. vii. p. 235.

[170] Placuit omnibus locis atque urbibus universis claudi protinus templa, et accessu vetitis omnibus licentiam delinquendi perditis abnegari. Volumus etiam cunctos a sacrificiis abstinere. Qued siquis aliquid forte hujusmodi perpetraverit, gladio sternatur : facultates

reason to believe, that this formidable edict was either composed without being published, or was published without being executed. The evidence of facts, and the monuments which are still extant of brass and marble, continue to prove the public exercise of the Pagan worship during the whole reign of the sons of Constantine. In the East, as well as in the West, in cities, as well as in the country, a great number of temples were respected, or at least were spared; and the devout multitude still enjoyed the luxury of sacrifices, of festivals, and of processions, by the permission, or by the connivance, of the civil government. About four years after the supposed date of this bloody edict, Constantius visited the temples of Rome; and the decency of his behavior is recommended by a pagan orator as an example worthy of the imitation of succeeding princes. "That emperor," says Symmachus, " suffered the privileges of the vestal virgins to remain inviolate; he bestowed the sacerdotal dignities on the nobles of Rome, granted the customary allowance to defray the expenses of the public rites and sacrifices; and, though he had embraced a different religion, he never attempted to deprive the empire of the sacred worship of antiquity."[171] The senate still presumed to consecrate, by solemn decrees, the *divine* memory of their sovereigns; and Constantine himself was associated, after his death, to those gods whom he had renounced and insulted during his life. The title, the ensigns, he prerogatives, of SOVEREIGN PONTIFF, which had been instituted by Numa, and assumed by Augustus, were accepted, without hesitation, by seven Christian emperors; who were invested with a more absolute authority over the religion which they had deserted, than over that which they professed.[172]

---

etiam perempti fisco decernimus vindicari : et similiter adfligi rectores provinciarum si facinora vindicare neglexerint. Cod. Theodos. l. xvi. tit. x. leg. 4. Chronology has discovered some contradiction in the date of this extravagant law; the only one, perhaps, by which the negligence of magistrates is punished by death and confiscation. M. de la Bastie (Mém. de l'Academie, tom. xv. p. 98) conjectures, with a show of reason, that this was no more than the minutes of a law, the heads of an intended bill, which were found in Scriniis Memoriæ, among the papers of Constantius, and afterwards inserted, as a worthy model, in the Theodosian Code.

[171] Symmach. Epistol. x. 54.

[172] The fourth Dissertation of M. de la Bastie, sur le Souverain Pontificat des Empereurs Romains, (in the Mém. de l'Acad. tom. xv. p. 75—144,) is a very learned and judicious performance, which

The divisions of Christianity suspended the ruin of *Pagan ism* ;[173] and the holy war against the infidels was less vigorously prosecuted by princes and bishops, who were more immediately alarmed by the guilt and danger of domestic rebellion.   The extirpation of *idolatry*[174] might have been

---

explains the state, and proves the toleration, of Paganism from Constantine to Gratian. The assertion of Zosimus, that Gratian was the first who refused the pontifical robe, is confirmed beyond a doubt, and the murmurs of bigotry on that subject are almost silenced.

[173] As I have freely anticipated the use of *pagans* and *paganism*, I shall now trace the singular revolutions of those celebrated words. 1. Πάγη, in the Doric dialect, so familiar to the Italians, signifies a fountain; and the rural neighborhood, which frequented the same fountain, derived the common appellation of *pagus* and *pagans*. (Festus sub voce, and Servius ad Virgil. Georgic. ii. 382.) 2. By an easy extension of the word, *pagan* and rural became almost synonymous, (Plin. Hist. Natur. xxviii. 5 ;) and the meaner rustics acquired that name, which has been corrupted into *peasants* in the modern languages of Europe. 3. The amazing increase of the military order introduced the necessity of a correlative term, (Hume's Essays, vol. i, p. 555 ;) and all the *people* who were not enlisted in the service of the prince were branded with the contemptuous epithets of pagans. (Tacit. Hist. iii. 24, 43, 77. Juvenal. Satir. 16. Tertullian de Pallio, c. 4.) 4. The Christians were the soldiers of Christ; their adversaries, who refused his *sacrament*, or military oath of baptism, might deserve the metaphorical name of pagans ; and this popular reproach was introduced as early as the reign of Valentinian (A. D. 365) into Imperial laws (Cod. Theodos. l. xvi. tit. ii. leg. 18) and theological writings. 5. Christianity gradually filled the cities of the empire : the old religion, in the time of Prudentis (advers. Symmachum, l. i. ad fin.) and Orosius, (in Præfat. Hist.,) retired and languished in obscure villages ; and the word *pagans*, with its new signification, reverted to its primitive origin. 6. Since the worship of Jupiter and his family has expired, the vacant title of pagans has been successively applied to all the idolaters and polytheists of the old and new world.   7. The Latin Christians bestowed it, without scruple, on their mortal enemies, the Mahometans ; and the purest *Unitarians* were branded with the unjust reproach of idolatry and paganism. See Gerard Vossius, Etymologicon Linguæ Latinæ, in his works, tom. i. p. 420 ; Godefroy's Commentary on the Theodosian Code, tom. vi. p. 250 ; and Ducange, Mediæ et Infimæ Latinitat. Glossar.

[174] In the pure language of Ionia and Athens, Είδωλον and Λατρεία were ancient and familiar words. The former expressed a likeness, an apparition, (Homer. Odys. xi. 601,) a representation, an *image*, created either by fancy or art. The latter denoted any sort of *service* or slavery.   The Jews of Egypt, who translated the Hebrew Scriptures, restrained the use of these words (Exod. xx. 4, 5) to the religious worship of an image. The peculiar idiom of the Hellenists, or Grecian Jews, has been adopted by the sacred and ecclesiastical writers ; and the reproach of *idolatry* (Είδωλολατρεία) has stigmatized that visible

justified by the established principles of intolerance : but the hostile sects, which alternately reigned in the Imperial court, were mutually apprehensive of alienating, and perhaps exasperating, the minds of a powerful, though declining faction Every motive of authority and fashion, of interest and reason now militated on the side of Christianity ; but two or three generations elapsed, before their victorious influence was universally felt. The religion which had so long and so lately been established in the Roman empire was still revered by a numerous people, less attached indeed to speculative opinion than to ancient custom. The honors of the state and army were indifferently bestowed on all the subjects of Constantine and Constantius ; and a considerable portion of knowledge and wealth and valor was still engaged in the service of polytheism. The superstition of the senator and of the peasant, of the poet and the philosopher, was derived from very different causes, but they met with equal devotion in the temples of the gods. Their zeal was insensibly provoked by the insulting triumph of a proscribed sect; and their hopes were revived by the well-grounded confidence, that the presumptive heir of the empire, a young and valiant hero, who had delivered Gaul from the arms of the Barbarians, had secretly embraced the religion of his ancestors.

---

and abject mode of superstition, which some sects of Christianity should not hastily impute to the polytheists of Greece and Rome.

CHAPTER XXII.

JULIAN IS DECLARED EMPEROR BY THE LEGIONS OF GAUL. —
HIS MARCH AND SUCCESS. — THE DEATH OF CONSTANTIUS. —
CIVIL ADMINISTRATION OF JULIAN.

WHILE the Romans languished under the ignominious tyranny of eunuchs and bishops, the praises of Julian were repeated with transport in every part of the empire, except in
the palace of Constantius. The barbarians of Germany had
felt, and still dreaded, the arms of the young Cæsar; his
soldiers were the companions of his victory; the grateful
provincials enjoyed the blessings of his reign; but the favorites, who had opposed his elevation, were offended by his
virtues; and they justly considered the friend of the people as
the enemy of the court. As long as the fame of Julian was
doubtful, the buffoons of the palace, who were skilled in the
language of satire, tried the efficacy of those arts which they
had so often practised with success. They easily discovered
that his simplicity was not exempt from affectation: the ridiculous epithets of a hairy savage, of an ape invested with the
purple, were applied to the dress and person of the philosophic
warrior; and his modest despatches were stigmatized as the
vain and elaborate fictions of a loquacious Greek, a speculative soldier, who had studied the art of war amidst the groves
of the academy.[1] The voice of malicious folly was at length

---

[1] Omnes qui plus poterant in palatio, adulandi professores jam
docti, recte consulta, prospereque completa vertebant in deridiculum:
talia sine modo strepentes insulse; in odium venit cum victoriis
suis; capella, non homo; ut hirsutum Julianum carpentes, appellan-
tesque loquacem talpam, et purpuratam simiam, et litterionem Græ-
cum: et his congruentia plurima atque vernacula principi resonantes,
audire hæc taliaque gestienti, virtutes ejus obruere verbis impudenti-
bus conabantur, et segnem incessentes et timidum et umbratilem,
gestaque secus verbis comptioribus exornantem. Ammianus, s. xvii.
11.*

---

* The philosophers retaliated on the courtiers. Marius (says Eunapius
in a newly-discovered fragment) was wont to call his antagonist Sylla a
beast half lion and half fox. Constantius had nothing of the lion, but was
surrounded by a whole litter of foxes. Mai. Script. Byz Nov. Col. ii. 232.
Niebuhr, Byzant. Hist. 66. — M

silenced by the shouts of victory; the conqueror of the Franks and Alemanni could no longer be painted as an object of contempt; and the monarch himself was meanly ambitious of stealing from his lieutenant the honorable reward of his labors In the letters crowned with laurel, which, according to ancient custom, were addressed to the provinces, the name of Julian was omitted. "Constantius had made his dispositions in person; *he* had signalized his valor in the foremost ranks; *his* military conduct had secured the victory; and the captive king of the barbarians was presented to *him* on the field of battle," from which he was at that time distant about forty days' journey.[2] So extravagant a fable was incapable, however, of deceiving the public credulity, or even of satisfying the pride of the emperor himself. Secretly conscious that the applause and favor of the Romans accompanied the rising fortunes of Julian, his discontented mind was prepared to receive the subtle poison of those artful sycophants, who colored their mischievous designs with the fairest appearances of truth and candor.[3] Instead of depreciating the merits of Julian, they acknowledged, and even exaggerated, his popular fame, superior talents, and important services. But they darkly insinuated, that the virtues of the Cæsar might instantly be converted into the most dangerous crimes, if the inconstant multitude should prefer their inclinations to their duty; or if the general of a victorious army should be tempted from his allegiance by the hopes of revenge and independent greatness. The personal fears of Constantius were interpreted by his council as a laudable anxiety for the public safety; whilst in private, and perhaps in his own breast, he disguised, under the less odious appellation of fear, the sentiments of hatred and envy, which he had secretly conceived for the inimitable virtues of Julian.

---

[2] Ammian. xvi. 12. The orator Themistius (iv. p. 57, 57) believed whatever was contained in the Imperial letters, which were addressed to the senate of Constantinople. Aurelius Victor, who published his Abridgment in the last year of Constantius, ascribes the German victories to the *wisdom* of the emperor, and the *fortune* of the Cæsar. Yet the historian, soon afterwards, was indebted to the favor or esteem of Julian for the honor of a brass statue, and the important offices of consular of the second Pannonia, and præfect of the city. Ammian. xxi. 10.

[3] Callido nocendi artificio, accusatoriam diritatem laudum titulis peragebant. . . . Hæ voces fuerunt ad inflammanda odia probris omnibus potentiores. See Mamertin. in Actione Gratiarum in Vet. Panegyr. x' 5, 6.

The apparent tranquillity of Gaul, and the imminent danger of the eastern provinces, offered a specious pretence for the design which was artfully concerted by the Imperial ministers. They resolved to disarm the Cæsar ; to recall those faithful troops who guarded his person and dignity ; and to employ, in a distant war against the Persian monarch, the hardy veterans who had vanquished, on the banks of the Rhine, the fiercest nations of Germany. While Julian used the laborious hours of his winter quarters at Paris in the administration of power, which, in his hands, was the exercise of virtue, he was surprised by the hasty arrival of a tribune and a notary, with positive orders from the emperor, which *they* were directed to execute, and *he* was commanded not to oppose. Constantius signified his pleasure, that four entire legions, the Celtæ, and Petulants, the Heruli, and the Batavians, should be separated from the standard of Julian, under which they had acquired their fame and discipline ; that in each of the remaining bands three hundred of the bravest youths should be selected ; and that this numerous detachment, the strength of the Gallic army, should instantly begin their march, and exert their utmost diligence to arrive, before the opening of the campaign, on the frontiers of Persia.[4] The Cæsar foresaw and lamented the consequences of this fatal mandate. Most of the auxiliaries, who engaged their voluntary service, had stipulated, that they should never be obliged to pass the Alps. The public faith of Rome, and the personal honor of Julian, had been pledged for the observance of this condition. Such an act of treachery and oppression would destroy the confidence, and excite the

---

[4] The minute interval, which may be interposed, between the *hyeme adultâ* and the *primo vere* of Ammianus, (xx, 1, 4,) instead of allowing a sufficient space for a march of three thousand miles, would render the orders of Constantius as extravagant as they were unjust. The troops of Gaul could not have reached Syria till the end of autumn. The memory of Ammianus must have been inaccurate, and his language incorrect.*

---

* The late editor of Ammianus attempts to vindicate his author from the charge of inaccuracy. "It is clear, from the whole course of the narrative, that Constantius entertained this design of demanding his troops from Julian, immediately after the taking of Amida, in the autumn of the preceding year, and had transmitted his orders into Gaul, before it was known that Lupicinus had gone into Britain with the Herulians and Batavians.' Wagner, note to Amm. xx. 4. But it seems also clear that the troops were in winter quarters (hiemabant) when the orders arrived. Ammianus can scarcely be acquitted of incorrectness, in his language at least. — M.

resentment, of the independent warriors of Germany, who considered truth as the noblest of their virtues, and freedom as the most valuable of their possessions. The legionaries who enjoyed the title and privileges of Romans, were enlisted for the general defence of the republic ; but .hose mercenary troops hea:d with cold indifference the antiquated names of the republic and of Rome. Attached, either from birth or long habit, to the climate and manners of Gaul, they loved and admired Julian ; they despised, and perhaps hated, the emperor; they dreaded the laborious march, the Persian arrows, and the burning deserts of Asia. They claimed as their own the country which they had saved ; and excused their want of spirit, by pleading the sacred and more immediate duty of protecting their families and friends. The apprehensions of the Gauls were derived from the knowledge of the impending and inevitable danger. As soon as the provinces were exhausted of their military strength, the Germans would violate a treaty which had been imposed on their fears ; and notwithstanding the abilities and valor of Julian, the general of a nominal army, to whom the public calamities would be imputed, must find himself, after a vain resistance, either a prisoner in the camp of the barbarians, or a criminal in the palace of Constantius. If Julian complied with the orders which he had received, he subscribed his own destruction, and that of a people who deserved his affection. But a positive refusal was an act of rebellion, and a declaration of war. The inexorable jealousy of the emperor, the peremptory, and perhaps insidious, nature of his commands, left not any room for a fair apology, or candid interpretation ; and the dependent station of the Cæsar scarcely allowed him to pause or to deliberate. Solitude increased the perplexity of Julian ; he could no longer apply to the faithful counsels of Sallust, who had been removed from his office by the judicious malice of the eunuchs : he could not even enforce his representations by the concurrence of the ministers, who would have been afraid or ashamed to approve the ruin of Gaul. The moment had been chosen, when Lupicinus,[5] the general of the cavalry, was

---

[5] Ammianus, xx. 1. The valor of Lupicinus, and his military skill, are acknowledged by the historian, who, in his affected language, accuses the general of exalting the horns of his pride, bellowing in a tragic tone, and exciting a doubt whether he was more cruel or avaricious. The danger from the Scots and Picts was so serious, that Julian himself ha: some thoughts of passing over into the island

despatched into Britain, to repulse the inroads of the Scots and Picts; and Florentius was occupied at Vienna by the assessment of the tribute. The latter, a crafty and corrupt statesman, declining to assume a responsible part on this dangerous occasion, eluded the pressing and repeated invitations of Julian, who represented to him, that in every important measure, the presence of the præfect was indispensable in the counci l of the prince. In the mean while the Cæsar was oppressed by the rude and importunate solicitations of the Imperial messengers, who presumed to suggest, that if he expected the return of his ministers, he would charge himself with the guilt of the delay, and reserve for them the merit of the execution. Unable to resist, unwilling to comply, Julian expressed, in the most serious terms, his wish, and even his intention, of resigning the purple, which he could not preserve with honor, but which he could not abdicate with safety.

After a painful conflict, Julian was compelled to acknowledge, that obedience was the virtue of the most eminent subject, and that the sovereign alone was entitled to judge of the public welfare. He issued the necessary orders for carrying into execution the commands of Constantius; a part of the troops began their march for the Alps; and the detachments from the several garrisons moved towards their respective places of assembly. They advanced with difficulty through the trembling and affrighted crowds of provincials, who attempted to excite their pity by silent despair, or loud lamentations; while the wives of the soldiers, holding their infants in their arms, accused the desertion of their husbands, in the mixed language of grief, of tenderness, and of indignation. This scene of general distress afflicted the humanity of the Cæsar; he granted a sufficient number of post-wagons to transport the wives and families of the soldiers,[6] endeavored to alleviate the hardships which he was constrained to inflict, and increased, by the most laudable arts, his own popularity, and the discontent of the exiled troops. The grief of an armed multitude is soon converted into rage; their licentious murmurs, which every hour were communicated from tent to tent with more boldness and effect, prepared their minds for the

---

[6] He granted them the permission of the *cursus clavularis*, or *clabularis*. These post-wagons are often mentioned in the Code, and were supposed to carry fifteen hundred pounds weight. See Vales. ad Ammian. xx 4.

most daring acts of sedition; and by the connivance of their tribunes, a seasonable libel was secretly dispersed, which painted in lively colors the disgrace of the Cæsar, the oppression of the Gallic army, and the feeble vices of the tyrant of Asia. The servants of Constantius were astonished and alarmed by the progress of this dangerous spirit. They pressed the Cæsar to hasten the departure of the troops; but they imprudently rejected the honest and judicious advice of Julian; who proposed that they should not march through Paris, and suggested the danger and temptation of a last interview.

As soon as the approach of the troops was announced, the Cæsar went out to meet them, and ascended his tribunal, which had been erected in a plain before the gates of the city. After distinguishing the officers and soldiers, who by their rank or merit deserved a peculiar attention, Julian addressed himself in a studied oration to the surrounding multitude: he celebrated their exploits with grateful applause; encouraged them to accept, with alacrity, the honor of serving under the eye of a powerful and liberal monarch; and admonished them, that the commands of Augustus required an instant and cheerful obedience. The soldiers, who were apprehensive of offending their general by an indecent clamor, or of belying their sentiments by false and venal acclamations, maintained an obstinate silence; and after a short pause, were dismissed to their quarters. The principal officers were entertained by the Cæsar, who professed, in the warmest language of friendship, his desire and his inability to reward, according to their deserts, the brave companions of his victories. They retired from the feast, full of grief and perplexity; and lamented the hardship of their fate, which tore them from their beloved general and their native country. The only expedient which could prevent their separation was boldly agitated and approved; the popular resentment was insensibly moulded into a regular conspiracy; their just reasons of complaint were heightened by passion, and their passions were inflamed by wine; as, on the eve of their departure, the troops were indulged in licentious festivity. At the hour of midnight, the impetuous multitude, with swords, and bows, and torches in their hands, rushed into the suburbs; encompassed the palace;[7]

---

[7] Most probably the palace of the baths, (*Thermarum,*) of which a solid and lofty hall still subsists in the *Rue de la Harpe.* The buildings covered a considerable space of the modern quarter of the university, and the gardens, under the Merovingian kings, communicated

and, careless of future dangers, pronounced the fatal and irrevocable words, JULIAN AUGUSTUS! The prince, whose anxious suspense was interrupted by their disorderly acclamations, secured the doors against their intrusion; and as long as it was in his power, secluded his person and dignity from the accidents of a nocturnal tumult. At the dawn of day, the soldiers, whose zeal was irritated by opposition, forcibly entered the palace, seized, with respectful violence, the object of their choice, guarded Julian with drawn swords through the streets of Paris, placed him on the tribunal, and with repeated shouts saluted him as their emperor. Prudence, as well as loyalty, inculcated the propriety of resisting their treasonable designs; and of preparing, for his oppressed virtue, the excuse of violence. Addressing himself by turns to the multitude and to individuals, he sometimes implored their mercy, and sometimes expressed his indignation; conjured them not to sully the fame of their immortal victories; and ventured to promise, that if they would immediately return to their allegiance, he would undertake to obtain from the emperor not only a free and gracious pardon, but even the revocation of the orders which had excited their resentment. But the soldiers, who were conscious of their guilt, chose rather to depend on the gratitude of Julian, than on the clemency of the emperor. Their zeal was insensibly turned into impatience, and their impatience into rage. The inflexible Cæsar sustained, till the third hour of the day, their prayers, their reproaches, and their menaces; nor did he yield, till he had been repeatedly assured, that if he wished to live, he must consent to reign. He was exalted on a shield in the presence, and amidst the unanimous acclamations, of the troops; a rich military collar, which was

---

with the abbey of St. Germain des Prez. By the injuries of time and the Normans, this ancient palace was reduced, in the twelfth century, to a maze of ruins, whose dark recesses were the scene of licentious love.

> Explicat aula sinus montemque amplectitur alis;
> Multiplici latebrâ scelerum tersura ruborem.
> . . . . . pereuntis sæpe pudoris
> Cælatura nefas, Venerisque accommoda *furtis.*

(These lines are quoted from the Architrenius, l. iv. c. 8, a poetical work of John de Hauteville, or Hanville, a monk of St. Alban's, about the year 1190. See Warton's History of English Foetry, vol. i. dissert. ii.) Yet such *thefts* might be less pernicious to mankind than the theological disputes of the Sorbonne, which have been since agitated on the same ground. Bonamy, Mém. de l'Academie, tom. xv. p. 678—682.

offered by chance, supplied the want of a diadem;[8] the cere
mony was concluded by the promise of a moderate donative;[9]
and the new emperor, overwhelmed with real or affected grief,
retired into the most secret recesses of his apartment.[10]

The grief of Julian could proceed only from his innocence,
but his innocence must appear extremely doubtful[11] in the
eyes of those who have learned to suspect the motives and the
professions of princes. His lively and active mind was susceptible of the various impressions of hope and fear, of gratitude and revenge, of duty and of ambition, of the love of fame,
and of the fear of reproach. But it is impossible for us to
calculate the respective weight and operation of these sentiments; or to ascertain the principles of action which might
escape the observation, while they guided, or rather impelled,
the steps of Julian himself. The discontent of the troops was
produced by the malice of his enemies; their tumult was the
natural effect of interest and of passion; and if Julian had
tried to conceal a deep design under the appearances of chance,
he must have employed the most consummate artifice without
necessity, and probably without success. He solemnly declares,
in the presence of Jupiter, of the Sun, of Mars, of Minerva, and
of all the other deities, that till the close of the evening which
preceded his elevation, he was utterly ignorant of the designs
of the soldiers;[12] and it may seem ungenerous to distrust the

---

[8] Even in this tumultuous moment, Julian attended to the forms
of superstitious ceremony, and obstinately refused the inauspicious
use of a female necklace, or a horse collar, which the impatient
soldiers would have employed in the room of a diadem.

[9] An equal proportion of gold and silver, five pieces of the former,
one pound of the latter; the whole amounting to about five pounds
ten shillings of our money.

[10] For the whole narrative of this revolt, we may appeal to authentic and original materials; Julian himself, (ad S. P. Q. Atheniensem, p. 282, 283, 284,) Libanius, (Orat. Parental. c. 44—48, in Fabricius, Bibliot. Græc. tom. vii. p. 269—273,) Ammianus, (xx. 4,) and
Zosimus, (l. iii. p. 151, 152, 153,) who, in the reign of Julian, appears
to follow the more respectable authority of Eunapius. With such
guides we *might* neglect the abbreviators and ecclesiastical historians.

[11] Eutropius, a respectable witness, uses a doubtful expression,
"consensu militum," (x. 15.) Gregory Nazianzen, whose ignorance
might excuse his fanaticism, directly charges the apostate with presumption, madness, and impious rebellion, αυθάδεια, απόνοια, ασέβεια.
Orat. iii. p. 67.

[12] Julian. ad S. P. Q. Athen. p. 284. The *devout* Abbé de la Bleterie
Vie de Julien, p. 159) is almost inclined to respect the *devout* protestations of a Pagan.

honor of a hero and the truth of a philosopher. Yet the superstitious confidence that Constantius was the enemy, and that he himself was the favorite, of the gods, might prompt him to desire, to solicit, and even to hasten the auspicious moment of his reign, which was predestined to restore the ancient religion of mankind. When Julian had received the intelligence of the conspiracy, he resigned himself to a short slumber; and afterwards related to his friends that he had seen the genius of the empire waiting with some impatience at his door, pressing for admittance, and reproaching his want of spirit and ambition.[13] Astonished and perplexed, he addressed his prayers to the great Jupiter, who immediately signified, by a clear and manifest omen, that he should submit to the will of heaven and of the army. The conduct which disclaims the ordinary maxims of reason, excites our suspicion and eludes our inquiry. Whenever the spirit of fanaticism, at once so credulous and so crafty, has insinuated itself into a noble mind, it insensibly corrodes the vital principles of virtue and veracity.

To moderate the zeal of his party, to protect the persons of his enemies,[14] to defeat and to despise the secret enterprises which were formed against his life and dignity, were the cares which employed the first days of the reign of the new emperor. Although he was firmly resolved to maintain the station which he had assumed, he was still desirous of saving his country from the calamities of civil war, of declining a contest with the superior forces of Constantius, and of preserving his own character from the reproach of perfidy and ingratitude. Adorned with the ensigns of military and imperial pomp, Julian showed himself in the field of Mars to the soldiers, who glowed with ardent enthusiasm in the cause of their pupil, their leader, and their friend. He recapitulated their victories, lamented their sufferings, applauded their reso-

---

[13] Ammian. xx. 5, with the note of Lindenbrogius on the Genius of the empire. Julian himself, in a confidential letter to his friend and and physician, Oribasius, (Epist. xvii. p. 384,) mentions another dream, to which, before the event, he gave credit; of a stately tree thrown to the ground, of a small plant striking a deep root into the earth. Even in his sleep, the mind of the Cæsar must have been agitated by the hopes and fears of his fortune. Zosimus (l. iii. p. 155) relates a subsequent dream.

[14] The difficult situation of the prince of a rebellious army is finely described by Tacitus, (Hist. 1, 80—85.) But Otho had much more guilt, and much less abilities, than Julian.

lution, animated their hopes, and checked their impetuosity;
nor did he dismiss the assembly, till he had obtained a solemn
promise from the troops, that if the emperor of the East
would subscribe an equitable treaty, they would renounce any
views of conquest, and satisfy themselves with the tranquil
possession of the Gallic provinces. On this foundation he
composed, in his own name, and in that of the army, a specious
and moderate epistle,[15] which was delivered to Pentadius, his
master of the offices, and to his chamberlain Eutherius; two
ambassadors whom he appointed to receive the answer, and
observe the dispositions of Constantius. This epistle is inscribed with the modest appellation of Cæsar; but Julian
solicits in a peremptory, though respectful, manner, the confirmation of the title of Augustus. He acknowledges the
irregularity of his own election, while he justifies, in some
measure, the resentment and violence of the troops which
had extorted his reluctant consent. He allows the supremacy
of his brother Constantius; and engages to send him an
annual present of Spanish horses, to recruit his army with a
select number of barbarian youths, and to accept from his
choice a Prætorian præfect of approved discretion and fidelity.
But he reserves for himself the nomination of his other civil
and military officers, with the troops, the revenue, and the
sovereignty of the provinces beyond the Alps. He admon-
ishes the emperor to consult the dictates of justice; to distrust
the arts of those venal flatterers, who subsist only by the discord of princes; and to embrace the offer of a fair and honorable treaty, equally advantageous to the republic and to the
house of Constantine. In this negotiation Julian claimed no
more than he already possessed. The delegated authority
which he had long exercised over the provinces of Gaul,
Spain, and Britain, was still obeyed under a name more independent and august. The soldiers and the people rejoiced in
a revolution which was not stained even with the blood of the
guilty. Florentius was a fugitive; Lupicinus a prisoner.
The persons who were disaffected to the new government
were disarmed and secured; and the vacant offices were
distributed, according to the recommendation of merit, by a

---

[15] To this ostensible epistle he added, says Ammianus, private letters, objurgatorias et mordaces, which the historian had not seen, and
would not have published. Perhaps they never existed.

44*

prince who despised the intrigues of the palace, and the clamors of the soldiers.[16]

The negotiations of peace were accompanied and supported by the most vigorous preparations for war. The army, which Julian held in readiness for immediate action, was recruited and augmented by the disorders of the times. The cruel persecutions of the faction of Magnentius had filled Gaul with numerous bands of outlaws and robbers. They cheerfully accepted the offer of a general pardon from a prince whom they could trust, submitted to the restraints of military discipline, and retained only their implacable hatred to the person and government of Constantius.[17] As soon as the season of the year permitted Julian to take the field, he appeared at the head of his legions; threw a bridge over the Rhine in the neighborhood of Cleves; and prepared to chastise the perfidy of the Attuarii, a tribe of Franks, who presumed that they might ravage, with impunity, the frontiers of a divided empire The difficulty, as well as glory, of this enterprise, consisted in a laborious march; and Julian had conquered, as soon as he could penetrate into a country, which former princes had considered as inaccessible. After he had given peace to the Barbarians, the emperor carefully visited the fortifications along the Rhine from Cleves to Basil; surveyed, with peculiar attention, the territories which he had recovered from the hands of the Alemanni, passed through Besançon,[18] which had severely suffered from their fury, and fixed his headquarters at Vienna for the ensuing winter. The barrier of Gaul was improved and strengthened with additional fortifications; and Julian entertained some hopes that the Germans, whom he had so often vanquished, might, in his absence, be restrained by the terror of his name. Vadomair[19] was the

---

[16] See the first transactions of his reign, in Julian. ad S. P. Q. Athen. p. 285, 286. Ammianus, xx. 5, 8. Liban. Orat. Parent. c. 49, 50, p. 273—275.

[17] Liban. Orat. Parent. c. 50, p. 275, 276. A strange disorder, since it continued above seven years. In the factions of the Greek republics, the exiles amounted to 20,000 persons; and Isocrates assures Philip, that it would be easier to raise an army from the vagabonds than from the cities. See Hume's Essays, tom. i. p. 426, 427.

[18] Julian (Epist. xxxviii. p. 414) gives a short description of Vesontio, or Besançon; a rocky peninsula almost encircled by the River Doux: once a magnificent city, filled with temples, &c., now reduced to a small town, emerging, however, from its ruins.

[19] Vadomair entered into the Roman service, and was promoted

only prince of the Alemanni whom he esteemed or feared; and while the subtle Barbarian affected to observe the faith of treaties the progress of his arms threatened the state with an unseasonable and dangerous war. The policy of Julian condescended to surprise the prince of the Alemanni by his own arts: and Vadomair, who, in the character of a friend, had incautiously accepted an invitation from the Roman governors, was seized in the midst of the entertainment, and sent away prisoner into the heart of Spain. Before the Barbarians were recovered from their amazement, the emperor appeared in arms on the banks of the Rhine, and, once more crossing the river, renewed the deep impressions of terror and respect which had been already made by four preceding expeditions.[20]

The ambassadors of Julian had been instructed to execute, with the utmost diligence, their important commission. But, in their passage through Italy and Illyricum, they were detained by the tedious and affected delays of the provincial governors; they were conducted by slow journeys from Constantinople to Cæsarea in Cappadocia; and when at length they were admitted to the presence of Constantius, they found that he had already conceived, from the despatches of his own officers, the most unfavorable opinion of the conduct of Julian, and of the Gallic army. The letters were heard with impatience; the trembling messengers were dismissed with indignation and contempt; and the looks, the gestures, the furious language of the monarch, expressed the disorder of his soul. The domestic connection, which might have reconciled the brother and the husband of Helena, was recently dissolved by the death of that princess, whose pregnancy had been several times fruitless, and was at last fatal to herself.[21] The empress

---

from a barbarian kingdom to the military rank of duke of Phœnicia. He still retained the same artful character, (Ammian. xxi. 4;) but, under the reign of Valens, he signalized his valor in the Armenian war, (xxix. 1.)

[20] Ammian. xx. 10, xxi. 3, 4. Zosimus, l. iii. p. 155.

[21] Her remains were sent to Rome, and interred near those of her sister Constantina, in the suburb of the Via Nomentana. Ammian. xxi. 1. Libanius has composed a very weak apology, to justify his hero from a very absurd charge of poisoning his wife, and rewarding her physician with his mother's jewels. (See the seventh of seventeen new orations, published at Venice, 1754, from a MS. in St. Mark's library, p. 117—127. Elpidius, the Prætorian præfect of the East, to whose evidence the accuser of Julian appeals, is arraigned by

Eusebia had preserved, to the last moment of her life, the warm, and even jealous, affection which she had conceived for Julian; and her mild influence might have moderated the resentment of a prince, who, since her death, was abandoned to his own passions, and to the arts of his eunuchs. But the terror of a foreign invasion obliged him to suspend the punishment of a private enemy: he continued his march towards the confines of Persia, and thought it sufficient to signify the conditions which might entitle Julian and his guilty followers to the clemency of their offended sovereign. He required, that the presumptuous Cæsar should expressly renounce the appellation and rank of Augustus, which he had accepted from the rebels; that he should descend to his former station of a limited and dependent minister; that he should vest the powers of the state and army in the hands of those officers who were appointed by the Imperial court; and that he should trust his safety to the assurances of pardon, which were announced by Epictetus, a Gallic bishop, and one of the Arian favorites of Constantius. Several months were ineffectually consumed in a treaty which was negotiated at the distance of three thousand miles between Paris and Antioch; and, as soon as Julian perceived that his modest and respectful behavior served only to irritate the pride of an implacable adversary, he boldly resolved to commit his life and fortune to the chance of a civil war. He gave a public and military audience to the quæstor Leonas: the haughty epistle of Constantius was read to the attentive multitude; and Julian protested, with the most flattering deference, that he was ready to resign the title of Augustus, if he could obtain the consent of those whom he acknowledged as the authors of his elevation. The faint proposal was impetuously silenced; and the acclamations of "Julian Augustus, continue to reign, by the authority of the army, of the people, of the republic which you have saved," thundered at once from every part of the field, and terrified the pale ambassador of Constantius. A part of the letter was afterwards read, in which the emperor arraigned the ingratitude of Julian, whom he had invested with the honors of the purple; whom he had educated with so much care and tenderness; whom he had preserved in his infancy, when he was

---

Libanius, as *effeminate* and ungrateful; yet the religion of Elpidius is praised by Jerom, (tom. i. p. 243,) and his humanity by Ammianus (xxi. 6.)

eft a helpless orphan. "An orphan!" interrupted Julian,
who justified his cause by indulging his passions: "does the
assassin of my family reproach me that I was left an orphan?
He urges me to revenge those injuries which I have long studied to forget." The assembly was dismissed; and Leonas,
who, with some difficulty, had been protected from the popular
fury, was sent back to his master with an epistle, in which
Julian expressed, in a strain of the most vehement eloquence,
the sentiments of contempt, of hatred, and of resentment,
which had been suppressed and imbittered by the dissimulation of twenty years. After this message, which might be
considered as a signal of irreconcilable war, Julian, who, some
weeks before, had celebrated the Christian festival of the
Epiphany,[22] made a public declaration that he committed the
care of his safety to the IMMORTAL GODS; and thus publicly
renounced the religion as well as the friendship of Constantius.[23]

The situation of Julian required a vigorous and immediate
resolution. He had discovered, from intercepted letters, that
his adversary, sacrificing the interest of the state to that of the
monarch, had again excited the Barbarians to invade the provinces of the West. The position of two magazines, one of
them collected on the banks of the Lake of Constance, the
other formed at the foot of the Cottian Alps, seemed to
indicate the march of two armies; and the size of those
magazines, each of which consisted of six hundred thousand

----

[22] Feriarum die quem celebrantes mense Januario, Christiani *Epi-
phania* dictitant, progressus in eorum ecclesiam, solemniter numine
orato discessit. Ammian. xxi. 2. Zonaras observes, that it was on
Christmas day, and his assertion is not inconsistent; since the
churches of Egypt, Asia, and perhaps Gaul, celebrated on the same
day (the sixth of January) the nativity and the baptism of their
Savior. The Romans, as ignorant as their brethren of the real
date of his birth, fixed the solemn festival to the 25th of December,
the *Brumalia*, or winter solstice, when the Pagans annually celebrated
the birth of the sun. See Bingham's Antiquities of the Christian
Church, l. xx. c. 4, and Beausobre, Hist. Critique du Manicheisme,
tom. ii. p. 690—700.

[23] The public and secret negotiations between Constantius and
Julian must be extracted, with some caution, from Julian himself.
(Orat. ad S. P. Q. Athen. p. 286.) Libanius, (Orat. Parent. c. 51, p
276,) Ammianus, (xx. 9,) Zosimus, (l. iii. p. 154,) and even Zonaras,
(tom. ii. . xiii. p. 20, 21, 22,) who, on this occasion, appears to have
possessed and used some valuable materials.

quarters of wheat, or rather flour,[24] was a threatening evidence of the strength and numbers of the enemy who prepared to surround him. But the Imperial legions were still in their distant quarters of Asia; the Danube was feebly guarded; and if Julian could occupy, by a sudden incursion, the important provinces of Illyricum, he might expect that a people of soldiers would resort to his standard, and that the rich mines of gold and silver would contribute to the expenses of the civil war. He proposed this bold enterprise to the assembly of the soldiers; inspired them with a just confidence in their general, and in themselves; and exhorted them to maintain their reputation of being terrible to the enemy, moderate to their fellow-citizens, and obedient to their officers. His spirited discourse was received with the loudest acclamations, and the same troops which had taken up arms against Constantius, when he summoned them to leave Gaul, now declared with alacrity, that they would follow Julian to the farthest extremities of Europe or Asia. The oath of fidelity was administered; and the soldiers, clashing their shields, and pointing their drawn swords to their throats, devoted themselves, with horrid imprecations, to the service of a leader whom they celebrated as the deliverer of Gaul and the conqueror of the Germans.[25] This solemn engagement, which seemed to be dictated by affection rather than by duty, was singly opposed by Nebridius, who had been admitted to the office of Prætorian præfect. That faithful minister, alone and unassisted, asserted the rights of Constantius in the midst of an armed and angry multitude, to whose fury he had almost fallen an honorable, but useless sacrifice. After losing one of his hands by the stroke of a sword, he embraced the knees of the prince whom he had offended. Julian covered the præfect with his Imperial mantle, and, protecting him from the zeal of his followers, dismissed him to his own house, with less respect than was perhaps due to the virtue of an enemy.[26] The high office of

---

[24] Three hundred myriads, or three millions of *medimni*, a corn measure familiar to the Athenians, and which contained six Roman *modii*. Julian explains, like a soldier and a statesman, the danger of his situation, and the necessity and advantages of an offensive war. (ad S. P. Q. Athen. p. 286, 287.)

[25] See his oration, and the behavior of the troops, in Ammian. xxi. 5.

[26] He sternly refused his hand to the suppliant præfect, whom he sent into Tuscany. (Ammian. xxi. 5.) Libanius, with savage fury

Nebridius was bestowed on Sallust; and the provinces of Gaul, which were now delivered from the intolerable oppression of taxes, enjoyed the mild and equitable administration of the friend of Julian, who was permitted to practise those virtues which he had instilled into the mind of his pupil.[27]

The hopes of Julian depended much less on the number of his troops, than on the celerity of his motions. In the execution of a daring enterprise, he availed himself of every precaution, as far as prudence could suggest; and where prudence could no longer accompany his steps, he trusted the event to valor and to fortune. In the neighborhood of Basil he assembled and divided his army.[28] One body, which consisted of ten thousand men, was directed under the command of Nevitta, general of the cavalry, to advance through the midland parts of Rhætia and Noricum. A similar division of troops, under the orders of Jovius and Jovinus, prepared to follow the oblique course of the highways, through the Alps and the northern confines of Italy. The instructions to the generals were conceived with energy and precision: to hasten their march in close and compact columns, which, according to the disposition of the ground, might readily be changed into any order of battle; to secure themselves against the surprises of the night by strong posts and vigilant guards; to prevent resistance by their unexpected arrival; to elude examination by their sudden departure; to spread the opinion of their strength, and the terror of his name; and to join their sovereign under the walls of Sirmium. For himself Julian had reserved a more difficult and extraordinary part. He selected three thousand brave and active volunteers, resolved, like their leader, to cast behind them every hope of a retreat: at the head of this faithful band, he fearlessly plunged into the recesses of the Marcian, or Black Forest, which conceals the sources of the Danube;[29] and, for many days, the fate of

Insults Nebridius, applauds the soldiers, and almost censures the humanity of Julian. (Orat. Parent. c. 53, p. 278.)

[27] Ammian. xxi. 8. In this promotion, Julian obeyed the law which he publicly imposed on himself. Neque civilis quisquam judex nec militaris rector, alio quodam præter merita suffragante, ad potiorem veniat gradum. (Ammian. xx. 5.) Absence did not weaken his regard for Sallust, with whose name (A. D. 363) he honored the consulship.

[28] Ammianus (xxi. 8) ascribes the same practice, and the same motive, to Alexander the Great and other skilful generals.

[29] This wood was a part of the great Hercynian forest, which. in

Julian was unknown to the world. The secrecy of his march,
his diligence, and vigor, surmounted every obstacle ; he forced
his way over mountains and morasses, occupied the bridges
or swam the rivers, pursued his direct course,[30] without reflect-
ing whether he traversed the territory of the Romans or of
the Barbarians, and at length emerged, between Ratisbon and
Vienna, at the place where he designed to embark his troops
on the Danube. By a well-concerted stratagem, he seized a
fleet of light brigantines,[31] as it lay at anchor ; secured a
supply of coarse provisions sufficient to satisfy the indelicate,
but voracious, appetite of a Gallic army ; and boldly committed himself to the stream of the Danube. The labors of
his mariners, who plied their oars with incessant diligence, and
the steady continuance of a favorable wind, carried his fleet
above seven hundred miles in eleven days ;[32] and he had
already disembarked his troops at Bononia,* only nineteen
miles from Sirmium, before his enemies could receive any
certain intelligence that he had left the banks of the Rhine.
In the course of this long and rapid navigation, the mind of
Julian was fixed on the object of his enterprise ; and though
he accepted the deputations of some cities, which hastened to
claim the merit of an early submission, he passed before the
hostile stations, which were placed along the river, without
indulging the temptation of signalizing a useless and ill-timed

---

the time of Cæsar, stretched away from the country of the Rauraci
(Basil) into the boundless regions of the north. See Cluver, Ger-
mania Antiqua, l. iii. c. 47.

[30] Compare Libanius, Orat. Parent. c. 53, p. 278, 279, with Gregory
Nazianzen, Orat. iii. p. 68. Even the saint admires the speed and
secrecy of this march. A modern divine might apply to the progress
of Julian the lines which were originally designed for another
apostate : —

> ———————— So eagerly the fiend,
> O'er bog, or steep, through strait, rough, dense, or rare,
> With head, hands, wings, or feet, pursues his way,
> And swims, or sinks, or wades, or creeps, or flies

[31] In that interval the *Notitia* places two or three fleets, the Lauria
censis, (at Lauriacum, or Lorch,) the Arlapensis, the Maginensis ; and
mentions five legions, or cohorts, of Libernarii, who should be a sort
of marines. Sect. lviii. edit. Labb.

[32] Zosimus alone (l. iii. p. 156) has specified this interesting circumstance. Mamertinus, (in Panegyr. Vet. xi. 6, 7, 8,) who accompanied Julian, as count of the sacred largesses, describes this voyage in
a florid and picturesque manner, challenges Triptolemus and the
Argonauts of Greece, &c.

---

* Banostar. *Mannert.* — M.

valor. The banks of the Danube were crowded on either side with spectators, who gazed on the military pomp, anticipated the importance of the event, and diffused through the adjacent country the fame of a young hero, who advanced with more than mortal speed at the head of the innumerable forces of the West. Lucilian, who, with the rank of general of the cavalry, commanded the military powers of Illyricum was alarmed and perplexed by the doubtful reports, which he could neither reject nor believe. He had taken some slow and irresolute measures for the purpose of collecting his troops, when he was surprised by Dagalaiphus, an active officer, whom Julian, as soon as he landed at Bononia, had pushed forwards with some light infantry. The captive general, uncertain of his life or death, was hastily thrown upon a horse, and conducted to the presence of Julian; who kindly raised him from the ground, and dispelled the terror and amazement which seemed to stupefy his faculties. But Lucilian had no sooner recovered his spirits, than he betrayed his want of discretion, by presuming to admonish his conqueror that he had rashly ventured, with a handful of men, to expose his person in the midst of his enemies. "Reserve for your master Constantius these timid remonstrances," replied Julian, with a smile of contempt: "when I gave you my purple to kiss, I received you not as a counsellor, but as a suppliant." Conscious that success alone could justify his attempt, and that boldness only could command success, he instantly advanced, at the head of three thousand soldiers, to attack the strongest and most populous city of the Illyrian provinces. As he entered the long suburb of Sirmium, he was received by the joyful acclamations of the army and people; who, crowned with flowers, and holding lighted tapers in their hands, conducted their acknowledged sovereign to his Imperial residence. Two days were devoted to the public joy, which was celebrated by the games of the Circus; but, early on the morning of the third day, Julian marched to occupy the narrow pass of Succi, in the defiles of Mount Hæmus; which, almost in the midway between Sirmium and Constantinople, separates the provinces of Thrace and Dacia, by an abrupt descent towards the former, and a gentle declivity on the side of the latter.[33] The defence of this important post was intrusted to the brave Nevitta; who, as well as the

---

[33] The description of Ammianus, which might be supported by

generals of the Italian division, successfully executed the plan of the march and junction which their master had so ably conceived.[34]

The homage which Julian obtained, from the fears or the inclination of the people, extended far beyond the immediate effect of his arms.[35] The præfectures of Italy and Illyricum were administered by Taurus and Florentius, who united that important office with the vain honors of the consulship; and, as those magistrates had retired with precipitation to the court of Asia, Julian, who could not always restrain the levity of his temper, stigmatized their flight by adding, in all the Acts of the Year, the epithet of *fugitive* to the names of the two consuls. The provinces which had been deserted by their first magistrates acknowledged the authority of an emperor, who, conciliating the qualities of a soldier with those of a philosopher, was equally admired in the camps of the Danube and in the cities of Greece. From his palace, or, more properly, from his head-quarters of Sirmium and Naissus, he distributed, to the principal cities of the empire, a labored apology for his own conduct; published the secret despatches of Constantius; and solicited the judgment of mankind between two competitors, the one of whom had expelled, and the other had invited, the Barbarians.[36] Julian, whose mind was deeply wounded by the reproach of ingratitude, aspired to maintain, by argument as well as by arms, the superior merits of his cause; and to excel, not only in the arts of war, but in those of composition. His epistle to the senate and people of

collateral evidence, ascertains the precise situation of the *Angustiæ Succorum*, or passes of *Succi*. M. d'Anville, from the trifling resemblance of names, has placed them between Sardica and Naissus, For my own justification, I am obliged to mention the *only* error which I have discovered in the maps or writings of that admirabl: geographer.

[34] Whatever circumstances we may borrow elsewhere, Ammianus (xxi. 8, 9, 10) still supplies the series of the narrative.

[35] Ammian. xxi. 9, 10. Libanius, Orat. Parent. c. 54, p. 279, 280. Zosimus, l. iii. p. 156, 157.

[36] Julian (ad S. P. Q. Athen. p. 286) positively asserts, that he intercepted the letters of Constantius to the Barbarians; and Libanius as positively affirms, that he read them on his march to the troops and the cities. Yet Ammianus (xxi. 4) expresses himself with cool and candid hesitation, si *famæ solius* admittenda est fides. He specifies, however, an intercepted letter from Vadomair to Constantius, which supposes an intimate correspondence between them; "Cæsar tuus disciplinam non habet."

Athens [37] seems to have been dictated by an elegant enthusiasm; which prompted him to submit his actions and his motives to the degenerate Athenians of his own times, with the same humble deference as if he had been pleading, in the days of Aristides, before the tribunal of the Areopagus His application to the senate of Rome, which was still permitted to bestow the titles of Imperial power, was agreeable to the forms of the expiring republic. An assembly was summoned by Tertullus, præfect of the city; the epistle of Julian was read; and, as he appeared to be master of Italy, his claims were admitted without a dissenting voice. His oblique censure of the innovations of Constantine, and his passionate invective against the vices of Constantius, were heard with less satisfaction; and the senate, as if Julian had been present, unanimously exclaimed, " Respect, we beseech you, the author of your own fortune." [38] An artful expression, which, according to the chance of war, might be differently explained; as a manly reproof of the ingratitude of the usurper, or as a flattering confession, that a single act of such benefit to the state ought to atone for all the failings of Constantius.

The intelligence of the march and rapid progress of Julian was speedily transmitted to his rival, who, by the retreat of Sapor, had obtained some respite from the Persian war. Disguising the anguish of his soul under the semblance of contempt, Constantius professed his intention of returning into Europe, and of giving chase to Julian; for he never spoke of his military expedition in any other light than that of a hunting party. [39] In the camp of Hierapolis, in Syria, he communicated this design to his army; slightly mentioned the guilt and rashness of the Cæsar; and ventured to assure them, that if the mutineers of Gaul presumed to meet them

---

[37] Zosimus mentions his epistles to the Athenians, the Corinthians, and the Lacedæmonians. The substance was probably the same, though the address was properly varied. The epistle to the Athenians is still extant, (p. 268—287,) and has afforded much valuable information. It deserves the praises of the Abbé de la Bleterie, (Pref. à l'Histoire de Jovien, p. 24, 25,) and is one of the best manifestoes to be found in any language.

[38] *Auctori tuo reverentiam rogamus.* Ammian. xxi. 10. It is amusing enough to observe the secret conflicts of the senate between flattery and fear. See Tacit. Hist. i. 85.

[39] Tanquam venaticiam prædam caparet: hoc enim ad len' vadum suorum metum subinde prædicabat. Ammian. xxii. 7.

in the field, they would be unable to sustain the fire of their
eyes, and the irresistible weight of their shout of onset.
The speech of the emperor was received with military
applause, and Theodotus, the president of the council of
Hierapolis, requested, with tears of adulation, that *his* city
might be adorned with the head of the vanquished rebel.[40]
A chosen detachment was despatched away in post-wagons, to
secure, if it were yet possible, the pass of Succi; the recruits,
the horses, the arms, and the magazines, which had been prepared against Sapor, were appropriated to the service of the
civil war; and the domestic victories of Constantius inspired
his partisans with the most sanguine assurances of success.
The notary Gaudentius had occupied in his name the provinces of Africa; the subsistence of Rome was intercepted;
and the distress of Julian was increased by an unexpected
event, which might have been productive of fatal consequences. Julian had received the submission of two legions
and a cohort of archers, who were stationed at Sirmium; but
he suspected, with reason, the fidelity of those troops which
had been distinguished by the emperor; and it was thought
expedient, under the pretence of the exposed state of the
Gallic frontier, to dismiss them from the most important scene
of action. They advanced, with reluctance, as far as the
confines of Italy; but as they dreaded the length of the way,
and the savage fierceness of the Germans, they resolved, by
the instigation of one of their tribunes, to halt at Aquileia,
and to erect the banners of Constantius on the walls of that
impregnable city. The vigilance of Julian perceived at once
the extent of the mischief, and the necessity of applying an
immediate remedy. By his order, Jovinus led back a part of
the army into Italy; and the siege of Aquileia was formed
with diligence, and prosecuted with vigor. But the legionaries, who seemed to have rejected the yoke of discipline,
conducted the defence of the place with skill and perseverance; invited the rest of Italy to imitate the example of
their courage and loyalty; and threatened the retreat of
Julian, if he should be forced to yield to the superior numbers
of the armies of the East.[41]

---

[40] See the speech and preparations in Ammianus, xxi. 13. The
vile Theodotus afterwards implored and obtained his pardon from the
merciful conqueror, who signified his wish of diminishing his enemies
and increasing the numbers of his friends, (xxii. 14.)

[41] Ammian. xxi. 7, 11, 12. He seems to describe, with superfluous

But the humanity of Julian was preserved from the cruel alternative which he pathetically laments, of destroying or of being himself destroyed : and the seasonable death of Constantius delivered the Roman empire from the calamities of civil war. The approach of winter could not detain the monarch at Antioch ; and his favorites durst not oppose his impatient desire of revenge. A slight fever, which was perhaps occasioned by the agitation of his spirits, was increased by the fatigues of the journey ; and Constantius was obliged to halt at the little town of Mopsucrene, twelve miles beyond Tarsus, where he expired, after a short illness, in the forty-fifth year of his age, and the twenty-fourth of his reign.[42] His genuine character, which was composed of pride and weakness, of superstition and cruelty, has been fully displayed in the preceding narrative of civil and ecclesiastical events. The long abuse of power rendered him a considerable object in the eyes of his contemporaries ; but as personal merit can alone deserve the notice of posterity, the last of the sons of Constantine may be dismissed from the world, with the remark, that he inherited the defects, without the abilities of his father. Before Constantius expired, he is said to have named Julian for his successor ; nor does it seem improbable, that his anxious concern for the fate of a young and tender wife, whom he left with child, may have prevailed, in his last moments, over the harsher passions of hatred and revenge. Eusebius, and his guilty associates, made a faint attempt to prolong the reign of the eunuchs, by the election of another emperor ; but

---

labor, the operations of the siege of Aquileia, which, on this occasion, maintained its impregnable fame. Gregory Nazianzen (Orat. iii. p. 38) ascribes this accidental revolt to the wisdom of Constantius, whose assured victory he announces with some appearance of truth. Constantio quem credebat procul dubio fore victorem : nemo enim omnium tunc ab hac constanti sententia discrepebat. Ammian. xxi. 7.

[42] His death and character are faithfully delineated by Ammianus, (xxi. 14, 15, 16 ;) and we are authorized to despise and detest the foolish calumny of Gregory, (Orat. iii. p. 68,) who accuses Julian of contriving the death of his benefactor. The private repentance of the emperor, that he had spared and promoted Julian, (p. 69, and Orat. xxi. p. 389,) is not improbable in itself, nor incompatible with the public verbal testament which prudential considerations might dictate in the last moments of his life.*

---

* Wagner thinks this sudden change of sentiment altogether a fiction of the attendant courtiers and chiefs of the army, who up to this time had been hostile to Julian. Note in loco Ammian. — M.

their intrigues were rejected with disdain, by an army which now abhorred the thought of civil discord ; and two officers of rank were instantly despatched, to assure Julian, that every sword in the empire would be drawn for his service. The military designs of that prince, who had formed three different attacks against Thrace, were prevented by this fortunate event. Without shedding the blood of his fellow-citizens, he escaped the dangers of a doubtful conflict, and acquired the advantages of a complete victory. Impatient to visit the place of his birth, and the new capital of the empire, he advanced from Naissus through the mountains of Hæmus, and the cities of Thrace. When he reached Heraclea, at the distance of sixty miles, all Constantinople was poured forth to receive him, and he made his triumphal entry amidst the dutiful acclamations of the soldiers, the people, and the senate. An innumerable multitude pressed around him with eager respect, and were perhaps disappointed when they beheld the small stature and simple garb of a hero, whose unexperienced youth had vanquished the Barbarians of Germany, and who had now traversed, in a successful career, the whole continent of Europe, from the shores of the Atlantic to those of the Bos- phorus.[43] A few days afterwards, when the remains of the deceased emperor were landed in the harbor, the subjects of Julian applauded the real or affected humanity of their sove- reign. On foot, without his diadem, and clothed in a mourn- ing habit, he accompanied the funeral as far as the church of the Holy Apostles, where the body was deposited : and if these marks of respect may be interpreted as a selfish tribute to the birth and dignity of his Imperial kinsman, the tears of Julian professed to the world that he had forgot the injuries, and remembered only the obligations, which he had received from Constantius.[44] As soon as the legions of Aquileia were assured of the death of the emperor, they opened the gates of the city, and, by the sacrifice of their guilty leaders, obtained an easy pardon from the prudence or lenity of

---

[43] In describing the triumph of Julian, Ammianus (xxii. 1, 2) as- sumes the lofty tone of an orator or poet; while Libanius (Orat. Parent. c. 56, p. 281) sinks to the grave simplicity of an historian.
[44] The funeral of Constantius is described by Ammianus, (xxi. 16,) Gregory Nazianzen, (Orat. iv. p. 119,) Mamertinus, (in Panegyr. Vet. xi. 27,) Libanius, (Orat. Parent. c. lvi. p. 283,) and Philostorgius, (l. vi. c. 6, with Godefroy's Dissertations, p. 265.) These writers, and their followers, Pagans, Catholics, Arians, beheld with very different eyes both the dead and the living emperor.

Julian; who, in the thirty-second year of his age, acquired the undisputed possession of the Roman empire.[45]

Philosophy had instructed Julian to compare the advantages of action and retirement; but the elevation of his birth, and the accidents of his life, never allowed him the freedom of choice. He might perhaps sincerely have preferred the groves of the academy, and the society of Athens; but he was constrained, at first by the will, and afterwards by the injustice, of Constantius, to expose his person and fame to the dangers of Imperial greatness; and to make himself accountable to the world, and to posterity, for the happiness of millions.[46] Julian recollected with terror the observation of his master Plato,[47] that the government of our flocks and herds is always committed to beings of a superior species; and that the conduct of nations requires and deserves the celestial powers of the gods or of the genii. From this principle he justly concluded, that the man who presumes to reign, should aspire to the perfection of the divine nature; that he should purify his soul from her mortal and terrestrial part; that he should extinguish his appetites, enlighten his understanding, regulate his passions, and subdue the wild beast, which, according to the lively metaphor of Aristotle,[48] seldom fails to ascend the throne of a despot. The throne of Julian, which the death of Constantius fixed on an independent basis, was the seat of reason, of virtue, and perhaps of vanity. He despised the honors, renounced the pleasures, and discharged with incessant diligence the duties, of his exalted station; and there

---

[45] The day and year of the birth of Julian, are not perfectly ascertained. The day is probably the sixth of November, and the year must be either 331 or 332. Tillemont, Hist. des Empereurs, tom. iv. p. 693. Ducange, Fam. Byzantin. p. 50. I have preferred the earlier date.

[46] Julian himself (p. 253—267) has expressed these philosophical ideas with much eloquence and some affectation, in a very elaborate epistle to Themistius. The Abbé de la Bleterie, (tom. ii. p. 146—193,) who has given an elegant translation, is inclined to believe that it was the celebrated Themistius, whose orations are still extant.

[47] Julian. ad Themist. p. 258. Petavius (not. p. 95) observes that this passage is taken from the fourth book De Legibus; but either Julian quoted from memory, or his MSS. were different from ours. Xenophon opens the Cyropædia with a similar reflection.

[48] Ὁ δὲ ἄνθρωπον κελεύων ἄρχειν, προστίθησι καὶ θηρίον. Aristot. ap. Julian. p. 261. The MS. of Vossius, unsatisfied with the single beast, affords the stronger reading of θηρία, which the experience of despotism may warrant.

were few among his subjects who would have consented to
relieve him from the weight of the diadem, had they been
obliged to submit their time and their actions to the rigorous
laws which that philosophic emperor imposed on himself.
One of his most intimate friends,[49] who had often shared the
frugal simplicity of his table, has remarked, that his light and
sparing diet (which was usually of the vegetable kind) left
his mind and body always free and active, for the various and
important business of an author, a pontiff, a magistrate, a
general, and a prince. In one and the same day, he gave
audience to several ambassadors, and wrote, or dictated, a
great number of letters to his generals, his civil magistrates,
his private friends, and the different cities of his dominions.
He listened to the memorials which had been received, considered the subject of the petitions, and signified his intentions
more rapidly than they could be taken in short-hand by the
diligence of the secretaries. He possessed such flexibility of
thought and such firmness of attention, that he could employ
his hand to write, his ear to listen, and his voice to dictate;
and pursue at once three several trains of ideas without hesitation, and without error. While his ministers reposed, the
prince flew with agility from one labor to another, and, after a
hasty dinner, retired into his library, till the public business,
which he had appointed for the evening, summoned him to
interrupt the prosecution of his studies. The supper of the
emperor was still less substantial than the former meal; his
sleep was never clouded by the fumes of indigestion; and
except in the short interval of a marriage, which was the
effect of policy rather than love, the chaste Julian never
shared his bed with a female companion.[50] He was soon

[49] Libanius (Orat. Parentalis, c. lxxxiv. lxxxv. p. 310, 311, 312)
has given this interesting detail of the private life of Julian. He
himself (in Misopogon, p. 350) mentions his vegetable diet, and up-
braids the gross and sensual appetite of the people of Antioch.

[50] Lectulus . . . Vestalium toris purior, is the praise which Mamertinus (Panegyr. Vet. xi. 13) addresses to Julian himself. Libanius
affirms, in sober peremptory language, that Julian never knew a woman before his marriage, or after the death of his wife, (Orat. Parent.
c. lxxxviii. p. 313.) The chastity of Julian is confirmed by the impartial testimony of Ammianus, (xxv. 4,) and the partial silence of
the Christians. Yet Julian ironically urges the reproach of the people of Antioch, that he almost always (ὡς ἐπίπαν, in Misopogon, p.
345) lay alone. This suspicious expression is explained by the Abbé
de la Bleterie (Hist. de Jovien, tom. ii. p. 103—109) with candor and
ingenuity

awakened by the entrance of fresh secretaries, who had slept the preceding day; and his servants were obliged to wait alternately, while their indefatigable master allowed himself scarcely any other refreshment than the change of occupation. The predecessors of Julian, his uncle, his brother, and his cousin, indulged their puerile taste for the games of the Circus, under the specious pretence of complying with the inclinations of the people; and they frequently remained the greatest part of the day as idle spectators, and as a part of the splendid spectacle, till the ordinary round of twenty-four races [51] was completely finished. On solemn festivals, Julian, who felt and professed an unfashionable dislike to these frivolous amusements, condescended to appear in the Circus; and after bestowing a careless glance at five or six of the races, he hastily withdrew with the impatience of a philosopher, who considered every moment as lost that was not devoted to the advantage of the public or the improvement of his own mind.[52] By this avarice of time, he seemed to protract the short duration of his reign; and if the dates were less securely ascertained, we should refuse to believe, that only sixteen months elapsed between the death of Constantius and the departure of his successor for the Persian war. The actions of Julian can only be preserved by the care of the historian; but the portion of his voluminous writings, which is still extant, remains as a monument of the application, as well as of the genius, of the emperor. The Misopogon, the Cæsars, several of his orations, and his elaborate work against the Christian religion, were composed in the long nights of the two winters, the former of which he passed at Constantinople, and the latter at Antioch.

The reformation of the Imperial court was one of the first

---

[51] See Salmasius ad Sueton. in Claud. c. xxi. A twenty-fifth race, or *missus*, was added, to complete the number of one hundred chariots, four of which, the four colors, started each heat.

Centum quadrijugos agitabo ad fiumina currus.

It appears, that they ran five or seven times round the *Meta*, (Sueton. in Domitian. c. 4;) and (from the measure of the Circus Maximus at Rome, the Hippodrome at Constantinople, &c.) it might be about a four-mile course.

[52] Julian. in Misopogon, p. 340. Julius Cæsar had offended the Roman people by reading his despatches during the actual race. Augustus indulged their taste, or his own, by his constant attention to the important business of the Circus, for which he professed the warmest inclination. Sueton. in August. c. xlv.

and most necessary acts of the government of Julian.[53] Soon after his entrance into the palace of Constantinople, he had occasion for the service of a barber. An officer, magnificently dressed, immediately presented himself. "It is a barber," exclaimed the prince, with affected surprise, "that I want, and not a receiver-general of the finances."[54] He questioned the man concerning the profits of his employment; and was informed, that besides a large salary, and some valuable perquisites, he enjoyed a daily allowance for twenty servants, and as many horses. A thousand barbers, a thousand cup-bearers, a thousand cooks, were distributed in the several offices of luxury; and the number of eunuchs could be compared only with the insects of a summer's day.[55] The monarch who resigned to his subjects the superiority of merit and virtue, was distinguished by the oppressive magnificence of his dress, his table, his buildings, and his train. The stately palaces erected by Constantine and his sons, were decorated with many colored marbles, and ornaments of massy gold. The most exquisite dainties were procured, to gratify their pride, rather than their taste; birds of the most distant climates, fish from the most remote seas, fruits out of their natural season, winter roses, and summer snows.[56] The domestic crowd of the palace surpassed the expense of the legions; yet the smallest part of this costly multitude was subservient to the use, or even to the splendor, of the throne. The monarch was disgraced, and the people was injured, by the creation and sale of an infinite number of obscure, and even titular

---

[53] The reformation of the palace is described by Ammianus, (xxii. 4,) Libanius, Orat. (Parent. c. lxii. p. 288, &c.,) Mamertinus, (in Panegyr. Vet. xi. 11,) Socrates, (l. iii. c. 1,) and Zonaras, (tom. ii. l. xiii. p. 24.)

[54] Ego non *rationalem* jussi sed tonsorem acciri. Zonaras uses the less natural image of a *senator*. Yet an officer of the finances, who was satisfied with wealth, might desire and obtain the honors of the senate.

[55] Μαγείρους μὲν χιλίους, κουρέας δὲ οὐκ ἐλάττους, οἰνοχοους δὲ πλείους, σμήνη τραπεζοποιῶν, εὐνουχους ὑπὲρ τὰς μυίας παρὰ τοῖς ποιμέσιν ἐν ἦρι, are the original words of Libanius, which I have faithfully quoted, lest I should be suspected of magnifying the abuses of the royal household.

[56] The expressions of Mamertinus are lively and forcible. Quin etiam prandiorum et cænarum laboratas magnitudines Romanus populus sensit; cum quæsitissimæ dapes non gustu sed difficultatibus æstimarentur; miracula avium, longinqui maris pisces, alie i temporis poma, æstivæ nives, hybernæ rosæ.

employments; and the most worthless of mankind might purchase the privilege of being maintained, without the necessity of labor, from the public revenue. The waste of an enormous household, the increase of fees and perquisites, which were soon claimed as a lawful debt, and the bribes which they extorted from those who feared their enmity, or solicited their favor, suddenly enriched these haughty menials. They abused their fortune, without considering their past, or their future, condition; and their rapine and venality could be equalled only by the extravagance of their dissipations. Their silken robes were embroidered with gold, their tables were served with delicacy and profusion; the houses which they built for their own use, would have covered the farm of an ancient consul; and the most honorable citizens were obliged to dismount from their horses, and respectfully to salute a eunuch whom they met on the public highway. The luxury of the palace excited the contempt and indignation of Julian, who usually slept on the ground, who yielded with reluctance to the indispensable calls of nature; and who placed his vanity, not in emulating, but in despising, the pomp of royalty.

By the total extirpation of a mischief which was magnified even beyond its real extent, he was impatient to relieve the distress, and to appease the murmurs of the people; who support with less uneasiness the weight of taxes, if they are convinced that the fruits of their industry are appropriated to the service of the state. But in the execution of this salutary work, Julian is accused of proceeding with too much haste and inconsiderate severity. By a single edict, he reduced the palace of Constantinople to an immense desert, and dismissed with ignominy the whole train of slaves and dependants,[57] without providing any just, or at least benevolent, exceptions, for the age, the services, or the poverty, of the faithful domestics of the Imperial family. Such indeed was the temper of Julian, who seldom recollected the fundamental maxim of Aristotle, that true virtue is placed at an equal distance between the opposite vices. The splendid and effeminate dress of the Asiatics, the curls and paint, the collars and bracelets, which had appeared so ridiculous in the person of Constantine, were

---

[57] Yet Julian himself was accused of bestowing whole towns on the eunuchs, (Orat. vii. against Polyclet. p. 117—127.) Libanius contents himself with a cold but positive denial of the fact, which seems indeed to belong more properly to Constantius. This charge, however may allude to some unknown circumstance.

consistently rejected by his philosophic successor. But with the fopperies, Julian affected to renounce the decencies of dress; and seemed to value himself for his neglect of the laws of cleanliness. In a satirical performance, which was designed for the public eye, the emperor descants with pleasure, and even with pride, on the length of his nails, and the inky black ness of his hands; protests, that although the greatest part of his body was covered with hair, the use of the razor was confined to his head alone; and celebrates, with visible complacency, the shaggy and *populous*[58] beard, which he fondly cherished, after the example of the philosophers of Greece. Had Julian consulted the simple dictates of reason, the first magistrate of the Romans would have scorned the affectation of Diogenes, as well as that of Darius.

But the work of public reformation would have remained imperfect, if Julian had only corrected the abuses, without punishing the crimes, of his predecessor's reign. " We are now delivered," says he, in a familiar letter to one of his intimate friends, " we are now surprisingly delivered from the voracious jaws of the Hydra.[59] I do not mean to apply the epithet to my brother Constantius. He is no more; may the earth lie light on his head! But his artful and cruel favorites studied to deceive and exasperate a prince, whose natural mildness cannot be praised without some efforts of adulation. It is not, however, my intention, that even those men should be oppressed: they are accused, and they shall enjoy the benefit of a fair and impartial trial." To conduct this inquiry, Julian named six judges of the highest rank in the state and army; and as he wished to escape the reproach of condemning his personal enemies, he fixed this extraordinary tribunal at Chalcedon, on the Asiatic side of the Bosphorus; and transferred to the commissioners an absolute power to pronounce

[58] In the Misopogon (p. 338, 339) he draws a very singular picture of himself, and the following words are strangely characteristic : αὐτὸς προσέθηκα τὸν βαθύν τουτον, πώγωνα . . . . ταῦτά τοι διαθέοντων ἀνέχομαι τῶν φθειρῶν ὥσπερ ἐν λοχμῃ, τῶν θηρίων. The friends of the Abbé de la Bleterie adjured him, in the name of the French nation, not to translate this passage, so offensive to their delicacy, (Hist. de Jovien, tom. ii. p. 94.) Like him, I have contented myself with a transient allusion; but the little animal which Julian *names*, is a beast familiar to man, and signifies love.

[59] Julian, epist. xxiii. p. 389. He uses the words πολυκίφαλον ἴδραν in writing to his friend Hermogenes, who, like himself, was conversant with the Greek poets.

and execute their final sentence, without delay, and without appeal. The office of president was exercised by the venerable præfect of the East, a *second* Sallust,[60] whose virtues conciliated the esteem of Greek sophists, and of Christian bishops. He was assisted by the eloquent Mamertinus,[61] one of the consuls elect, whose merit is loudly celebrated by the doubtful evidence of his own applause. But the civil wisdom of two magistrates was overbalanced by the ferocious violence of four generals, Nevitta, Agilo, Jovinus, and Arbetio. Arbetio, whom the public would have seen with less surprise at the bar than on the bench, was supposed to possess the secret of the commission; the armed and angry leaders of the Jovian and Herculian bands encompassed the tribunal; and the judges were alternately swayed by the laws of justice, and by the clamors of faction.[62]

The chamberlain Eusebius, who had so long abused the favor of Constantius, expiated, by an ignominious death, the insolence, the corruption, and cruelty of his servile reign. The executions of Paul and Apodemius (the former of whom was burnt alive) were accepted as an inadequate atonement by the widows and orphans of so many hundred Romans, whom those legal tyrants had betrayed and murdered. But justice herself (if we may use the pathetic expression of Ammianus[63]) appeared to weep over the fate of Ursulus, the treasurer of the empire; and his blood accused the ingratitude of Julian, whose

---

[60] The two Sallusts, the præfect of Gaul, and the præfect of the East, must be carefully distinguished, (Hist. des Empereurs, tom. iv. p. 696.) I have used the surname of *Secundus*, as a convenient epithet. The second Sallust extorted the esteem of the Christians themselves; and Gregory Nazianzen, who condemned his religion, has celebrated his virtues, (Orat. iii. p. 90.) See a curious note of the Abbé de la Bleterie, Vie de Julien, p. 363.*

[61] Mamertinus praises the emperor (xi. l.) for bestowing the offices of Treasurer and Præfect on a man of wisdom, firmness, integrity, &c., like himself. Yet Ammianus ranks him (xxi. l.) among the ministers of Julian, quorum merita nôrat et fidem.

[62] The proceedings of this chamber of justice are related by Ammianus, (xxi. 3,) and praised by Libanius, (Orat. Parent. c. 74, p. 299, 300.)

[63] Ursuli vero necem ipsa mihi videtur flêsse justitia. Libanius, who imputes his death to the soldiers, attempts to criminate the court of the largesses.

---

* Gibbonus secundum habet pro numero, quod tamen est viri agnomen Wagner, notâ in loc. Amm. It is not a mistake; it is rather an error in taste. Wagner inclines to transfer the chief guilt to Arbetio. — M.

distress had been seasonably relieved by the intrepid liberality of that honest minister. The rage of the soldiers, whom he had provoked by his indiscretion, was the cause and the excuse of his death; and the emperor, deeply wounded by his own reproaches and those of the public, offered some consolation to the family of Ursulus, by the restitution of his confiscated fortunes. Before the end of the year in which they had been adorned with the ensigns of the prefecture and consulship,[64] Taurus and Florentius were reduced to implore the clemency of the inexorable tribunal of Chalcedon. The former was banished to Vercellæ in Italy, and a sentence of death was pronounced against the latter. A wise prince should have rewarded the crime of Taurus: the faithful minister, when he was no longer able to oppose the progress of a rebel, had taken refuge in the court of his benefactor and his lawful sovereign. But the guilt of Florentius justified the severity of the judges; and his escape served to display the magnanimity of Julian, who nobly checked the interested diligence of an informer, and refused to learn what place concealed the wretched fugitive from his just resentment.[65] Some months after the tribunal of Chalcedon had been dissolved, the prætorian vicegerent of Africa, the notary Gaudentius, and Artemius[66] duke of Egypt, were executed at Antioch. Artemius had reigned the cruel and corrupt tyrant of a great province; Gaudentius had long practised the arts of calumny against the innocent, the virtuous, and even the person of Julian himself. Yet the circumstances of their trial and condemnation were so unskilfully managed, that these wicked men obtained, in the public opinion, the glory of suffering for the obstinate loyalty with which they had supported the cause of Constantius. The rest of his servants were protected by a general act of oblivion; and they

---

[64] Such respect was still entertained for the venerable names of the commonwealth, that the public was surprised and scandalized to hear Taurus summoned as a criminal under the consulship of Taurus. The summons of his colleague Florentius was probably delayed till the commencement of the ensuing year.

[65] Ammian. xx. 7.

[66] For the guilt and punishment of Artemius, see Julian (Epist. x. p. 379) and Ammianus, (xxii. 6, and Vales, ad loc.) The merit of Artemius, who demolished temples, and was put to death by an apostate, has tempted the Greek and Latin churches to honor him as a martyr. But as ecclesiastical history attests that he was not only a tyrant, but an Arian, it is not altogether easy to justify this indiscreet promotion. Tillemont, Mém. Eccles. tom. vii. p. 1319.

were left to enjoy with impunity the bribes which they had accepted, either to defend the oppressed, or to oppress the friendless. This measure, which, on the soundest principles of policy, may deserve our approbation, was executed in a manner wh.ch seemed to degrade the majesty of the throne. Julian was tormented by the importunities of a multitude, particularly of Egyptians, who loudly redemanded the gifts which they had imprudently or illegally bestowed; he foresaw the endless prosecution of vexatious suits; and he engaged a promise, which ought always to have been sacred, that if they would repair to Chalcedon, he would meet them in person, to hear and determine their complaints. But as soon as they were landed, he issued an absolute order, which prohibited the watermen from transporting any Egyptian to Constantinople; and thus detained his disappointed clients on the Asiatic shore, till their patience and money being utterly exhausted, they were obliged to return with indignant murmurs to their native country.[67]

The numerous army of spies, of agents, and informers, enlisted by Constantius to secure the repose of one man, and to interrupt that of millions, was immediately disbanded by his generous successor. Julian was slow in his suspicions, and gentle in his punishments; and his contempt of treason was the result of judgment, of vanity, and of courage. Conscious of superior merit, he was persuaded that few among his subjects would dare to meet him in the field, to attempt his life, or even to seat themselves on his vacant throne. The philosopher could excuse the hasty sallies of discontent; and the hero could despise the ambitious projects which surpassed the fortune or the abilities of the rash conspirators. A citizen of Ancyra had prepared for his own use a purple garment; and this indiscreet action, which, under the reign of Constantius, would have been considered as a capital offence,[68] was reported to Julian by the officious importunity of a private enemy.

---

[67] See Ammian. xxii. 6, and Vales, ad locum; and the Codex Theodosianus, l. ii. tit. xxxix. leg. i.; and Godefroy's Commentary, tom. i. p. 218, ad locum.

[68] The president Montesquieu (Considerations sur la Grandeur, &c., des Romains, c. xiv. in his works, tom. iii. p. 448, 449) excuses this minute and absurd tyranny, by supposing that actions the most indifferent in our eyes might excite, in a Roman mind, the idea of guilt and danger. This strange apology is supported by a strange misapprehension of the English laws, "chez une nation .... où il est défendu le boire á la santé d'une certaine personne."

The monarch, after making some inquiry into the rank and character of his rival, despatched the informer with a present of a pair of purple slippers, to complete the magnificence of his Imperial habit. A more dangerous conspiracy was formed by ten of the domestic guards, who had resolved to assassinate Julian in the field of exercise near Antioch. Their intemperance revealed their guilt; and they were conducted in chains to the presence of their injured sovereign, who, after a lively representation of the wickedness and folly of their enterprise, instead of a death of torture, which they deserved and expected, pronounced a sentence of exile against the two principal offenders. The only instance in which Julian seemed to depart from his accustomed clemency, was the execution of a rash youth, who, with a feeble hand, had aspired to seize the reins of empire. But that youth was the son of Marcellus, the general of cavalry, who, in the first campaign of the Gallic war, had deserted the standard of the Cæsar and the republic. Without appearing to indulge his personal resentment, Julian might easily confound the crime of the son and of the father; but he was reconciled by the distress of Marcellus, and the liberanty of the emperor endeavored to heal the wound which had been inflicted by the hand of justice.[69]

Julian was not insensible of the advantages of freedom.[70] From his studies he had imbibed the spirit of ancient sages and heroes; his life and fortunes had depended on the caprice of a tyrant; and when he ascended the throne, his pride was sometimes mortified by the reflection, that the slaves who would not dare to censure his defects were not worthy to applaud his virtues.[71] He sincerely abhorred the system of Oriental despotism, which Diocletian, Constantine, and the patient habits of fourscore years, had established in the empire. A motive of superstition prevented the execution of the design, which Julian had frequently meditated, of relieving his head from the weight of a costly diadem;[72] but he absolutely refused the

---

[69] The clemency of Julian, and the conspiracy which was formed against his life at Antioch, are described by Ammianus (xxii. 9, 10, and Vales, ad loc.) and Libanius, (Orat. Parent. c. 99, p. 323.)

[70] According to some, says Aristotle, (as he is quoted by Julian ad Themist. p. 261,) the form of absolute government, the παμβασίλεια, is contrary to nature. Both the prince and the philosopher choose, however, to involve this eternal truth in artful and labored obscurity.

[71] That sentiment is expressed almost in the words of Julian himself. Ammian. xxii. 10.

[72] Libanius, (Orat. Parent. c. 95, p. 320.) who mentions the wish

title of *Dominus*, or *Lord*,[73] a word which was grown so familiar to the ears of the Romans, that they no longer remembered its servile and humiliating origin. The office, or rather the name, of consul, was cherished by a prince who contemplated with reverence the ruins of the republic; and the same behavior which had been assumed by the prudence of Augustus was adopted by Julian from choice and inclination. On the calends of January, at break of day, the new consuls, Mamertinus and Nevitta, hastened to the palace to salute the emperor. As soon as he was informed of their approach, he leaped from his throne, eagerly advanced to meet them, and compelled the blushing magistrates to receive the demonstrations of his affected humility. From the palace they proceeded to the senate. The emperor, on foot, marched before their litters; and the gazing multitude admired the image of ancient times, or secretly blamed a conduct, which, in their eyes, degraded the majesty of the purple.[74] But the behavior of Julian was uniformly supported. During the games of the Circus, he had, imprudently or designedly, performed the manumission of a slave in the presence of the consul. The moment he was reminded that he had trespassed on the jurisdiction of *another* magistrate, he condemned himself to pay a fine of ten pounds of gold; and embraced this public occasion of declaring to the world, that he was subject, like the rest of his fellow-citizens, to the laws,[75] and even to the forms, of the republic. The

---

and design of Julian, insinuates, in mysterious language, (θεῶν οὕτω γνόντων . . . . ἀλλ' ἤν ἀμείνων ὁ κωλύων,) that the emperor was restrained by some particular revelation.

[73] Julian in Misopogon, p. 343. As he never abolished, by any public law, the proud appellations of *Despot*, or *Dominus*, they are still extant on his medals, (Ducange, Fam. Byzantin. p. 38, 39;) and the private displeasure which he affected to express, only gave a different tone to the servility of the court. The Abbé de la Bleterie (Hist. de Jovien, tom. ii. p. 99—102) has curiously traced the origin and progress of the word *Dominus* under the Imperial government.

[74] Ammian. xxii. 7. The consul Mamertinus (in Panegyr. Vet. xi. 28, 29, 30) celebrates the auspicious day, like an eloquent slave, astonished and intoxicated by the condescension of his master.

[75] Personal satire was condemned by the laws of the twelve tables:

> Si male condiderit in quem quis carmina, jus est
> Judiciumque ———
>
> Horat. Sat. ii. 1. 82.

Julian (in Misopogon, p. 337) owns himself subject to the law; and the Abbé de la Bleterie (Hist. de Jovien, tom. ii. p. 92) has eagerly embraced a declaration so agreeable to his own system, and, indeed, to the true spirit of the Imperial constitution.

spirit of his administration, and his regard for the place of his nativity, induced Julian to confer on the senate of Constantinople the same honors, privileges, and authority, which were still enjoyed by the senate of ancient Rome.[76] A legal fiction was introduced, and gradually established, that cne half of the national council had migrated into the East; and the despotic successors of Julian, accepting the title of Senators, acknowledged themselves the members of a respectable body, which was permitted to represent the majesty of the Roman name. From Constantinople, the attention of the monarch was extended to the municipal senates of the provinces. He abolished, by repeated edicts, the unjust and pernicious exemptions which had withdrawn so many idle citizens from the service of their country; and by imposing an equal distribution of public duties, he restored the strength, the splendor, or, according to the glowing expression of Libanius,[77] the soul of the expiring cities of his empire. The venerable age of Greece excited the most tender compassion in the mind of Julian, which kindled into rapture when he recollected the gods, the heroes, and the men superior to heroes and to gods, who have bequeathed to the latest posterity the monuments of their genius, or the example of their virtues. He relieved the distress, and restored the beauty, of the cities of Epirus and Peloponnesus.[78] Athens acknowledged him for her benefactor; Argos, for her deliverer. The pride of Corinth, again rising from her ruins with the honors of a Roman colony, exacted a tribute from the adjacent republics, for the purpose of defraying the games of the Isthmus, which were celebrated in the amphitheatre with the hunting of bears and panthers. From this tribute the cities of Elis, of Delphi, and of Argos, which had inherited from their remote ancestors the sacred office of perpetuating

---

[76] Zosimus, l. iii. p. 158.

[77] Ἡ τῆς βουλῆς ἰσχὺς ψυχὴ πόλεως ἐστιν. See Libanius, (Orat. Parent. c. 71, p. 296,) Ammianus, (xxii. 9,) and the Theodosian Code, (l. xii. tit. i. leg. 50—55,) with Godefroy's Commentary, (tom. iv. p. 390—404.) Yet the whole subject of the *Curia*, notwithstanding very ample materials, still remains the most obscure in the legal history of the empire.

[78] Quæ paulo ante arida et siti anhelantia visebantur, ea nunc perlui, mundari, madere · Fora, Deambulacra, Gymnasia, lætis et gaudentibus populis frequentari; dies festos, et celebrari veteres, et novos in honorem principis consecrari, (Mamertin. xi. 9.) He particularly restored the city of Nicopolis and the Actiac games, which had been instituted by Augustus.

the Olympic, the Pythian, and the Nemean games, claimed a just exemption. The immunity of Elis and Delphi was respected by the Corinthians; but the poverty of Argos tempted the insolence of oppression; and the feeble complaints of its deputies were silenced by the decree of a provincial magistrate, who seems to have consulted only the interest of the capital in which he resided. Seven years after this sentence, Julian [79] allowed the cause to be referred to a superior tribunal; and his eloquence was interposed, most probably with success, in the defence of a city, which had been the royal seat of Agamemnon,[80] and had given to Macedonia a race of kings and conquerors.[81]

The laborious administration of military and civil affairs, which were multiplied in proportion to the extent of the empire, exercised the abilities of Julian; but he frequently assumed the two characters of Orator [82] and of Judge,[83] which are almost unknown to the modern sovereigns of

[79] Julian. Epist. xxxv. p. 407—411. This epistle, which illustrates the declining age of Greece, is omitted by the Abbé de la Bleterie; and, strangely disfigured by the Latin translator, who, by rendering ἀτέλεια, tributum, and ἰδιῶται, populus, directly contradicts the sense of the original.

[80] He reigned in Mycenæ at the distance of fifty stadia, or six miles, from Argos: but these cities, which alternately flourished, are confounded by the Greek poets. Strabo, l. viii. p. 579, edit. Amstel. 1707.

[81] Marsham, Canon. Chron. p. 421. This pedigree from Temenus and Hercules may be suspicious; yet it was allowed, after a strict inquiry by the judges of the Olympic games, (Herodot. l. v. c. 22,) at a time when the Macedonian kings were obscure and unpopular in Greece. When the Achæan league declared against Philip, it was thought decent that the deputies of Argos should retire, (T. Liv. xxxii. 22.)

[82] His eloquence is celebrated by Libanius, (Orat. Parent. c. 75, 76, p. 300, 301,) who distinctly mentions the orators of Homer. Socrates (l. iii. c. 1) has rashly asserted that Julian was the only prince, since Julius Cæsar, who harangued the senate. All the predecessors of Nero, (Tacit. Annal. xiii. 3,) and many of his successors, possessed the faculty of speaking in public; and it might be proved by various examples, that they frequently exercised it in the senate.

[83] Ammianus (xxi. 10) has impartially stated the merits and defects of his judicial proceedings. Libanius (Orat. Parent. c. 90, 91, p. 315, &c.) has seen only the fair side, and his picture, if it flatters the person, expresses at least the duties, of the judge. Gregory Nazianzen, (Orat. iv. p. 120,) who suppresses the virtues, and exaggerates even the venial faults, of the Apostate, triumphantly asks, whether

Europe. The arts of persuasion, so diligently cultivated by the first Cæsars, were neglected by the military ignorance and Asiatic pride of their successors; and if they condescended to harangue the soldiers, whom they feared, they treated with silent disdain the senators, whom they despised. The assemblies of the senate, which Constantius had avoided, were considered by Julian as the place where he could exhibit, with the most propriety, the maxims of a republican, and the talents of a rhetorician. He alternately practised, as in a school of declamation, the several modes of praise, of censure, of exhortation; and his friend Libanius has remarked, that the study of Homer taught him to imitate the simple, concise style of Menelaus, the copiousness of Nestor, whose words descended like the flakes of a winter's snow, or the pathetic and forcible eloquence of Ulysses. The functions of a judge, which are sometimes incompatible with those of a prince, were exercised by Julian, not only as a duty, but as an amusement; and although he might have trusted the integrity and discernment of his Prætorian præfects, he often placed himself by their side on the seat of judgment. The acute penetration of his mind was agreeably occupied in detecting and defeating the chicanery of the advocates, who labored to disguise the truths of facts, and to pervert the sense of the laws. He sometimes forgot the gravity of his station, asked indiscreet or unseasonable questions, and betrayed, by the loudness of his voice, and the agitation of his body, the earnest vehemence with which he maintained his opinion against the judges, the advocates, and their clients. But his knowledge of his own temper prompted him to encourage, and even to solicit, the reproof of his friends and ministers; and whenever they ventured to oppose the irregular sallies of his passions, the spectators could observe the shame, as well as the gratitude, of their monarch. The decrees of Julian were almost always founded on the principles of justice; and he had the firmness to resist the two most dangerous temptations, which assault the tribunal of a sovereign, under the specious forms of compassion and equity. He decided the merits of the cause without weighing the circumstances of the parties; and the poor, whom he wished to relieve, were condemned to

---

such a judge was fit to be seated between Minos and Rhadamanthus, in the Elysian fields.

satisfy the just demands of a noble and wealthy adversary. He carefully distinguished the judge from the legislator;[84] and though he meditated a necessary reformation of the Roman jurisprudence, he pronounced sentence according to the strict and literal interpretation of those laws, which the magistrates were bound to execute, and the subjects to obey.

The generality of princes, if they were stripped of their purple, and cast naked into the world, would immediately sink to the lowest rank of society, without a hope of emerging from their obscurity. But the personal merit of Julian was, in some measure, independent of his fortune. Whatever had been his choice of life, by the force of intrepid courage, lively wit, and intense application, he would have obtained, or at least he would have deserved, the highest honors of his profession ; and Julian might have raised himself to the rank of minister, or general, of the state in which he was born a private citizen. If the jealous caprice of power had disappointed his expectations, if he had prudently declined the paths of greatness, the employment of the same talents in studious solitude would have placed beyond the reach of kings his present happiness and his immortal fame. When we inspect, with minute, or perhaps malevolent attention, the portrait of Julian, something seems wanting to the grace and perfection of the whole figure. His genius was less powerful and sublime than that of Cæsar ; nor did he possess the consummate prudence of Augustus. The virtues of Trajan appear more steady and natural, and the philosophy of Marcus is more simple and consistent. Yet Julian sustained adversity with firmness, and prosperity with moderation. After an interval of one hundred and twenty years from the death of Alexander Severus, the Romans beheld an emperor who made no distinction between his duties and his pleasures ; who labored to relieve the distress, and to revive the spirit, of his subjects, and who endeavored always to connect authority with merit, and happiness with virtue. Even faction, and religious fac-

---

[84] Of the laws which Julian enacted in a reign of sixteen months, fifty-four have been admitted into the codes of Theodosius and Justinian. (Gothofred. Chron. Legum, p. 64—67.) The Abbé de la Bleterie (tom. ii. p. 329—336) has chosen one of these laws to give an idea of Julian's Latin style, which is forcible and elaborate, but less pure than his Greek.

tion, was constrained to acknowledge the superiority of his genius, in peace as well as in war, and to confess, with a sigh, that the apostate Julian was a lover of his country, and that he deserved the empire of the world.[85]

---

[85]

> . . . . Ductor fortissimus armis ;
> Conditor et legum celeberrimus ; ore manûque
> Consultor patriæ ; sed non consultor habendæ
> Religionis ; amans tercentum millia Divûm.
> Perfidus ille Deo, sed non et perfidus orbi.
>
> Prudent. Apotheosis, 450, &c.

The consciousness of a generous sentiment seems to have raised the Christian poet above his usual mediocrity.

CHAPTER XXIII.

THE character of Apostate has injured the reputation of
Julian; and the enthusiasm which clouded his virtues has
exaggerated the real and apparent magnitude of his faults.
Our partial ignorance may represent him as a philosophic
monarch, who studied to protect, with an equal hand, the
religious factions of the empire; and to allay the theological
fever which had inflamed the minds of the people, from the
edicts of Diocletian to the exile of Athanasius. A more accu
rate view of the character and conduct of Julian will remove
this favorable prepossession for a prince who did not escape
the general contagion of the times. We enjoy the singular
advantage of comparing the pictures which have been delineated by his fondest admirers and his implacable enemies.
The actions of Julian are faithfully related by a judicious and
candid historian, the impartial spectator of his life and death.
The unanimous evidence of his contemporaries is confirmed
by the public and private declarations of the emperor himself;
and his various writings express the uniform tenor of his
religious sentiments, which policy would have prompted him
to dissemble rather than to affect. A devout and sincere
attachment for the gods of Athens and Rome constituted the
ruling passion of Julian;[1] the powers of an enlightened understanding were betrayed and corrupted by the influence of

---

[1] I shall transcribe some of his own expressions from a short religious discourse which the Imperial pontiff composed to censure the
bold impiety of a Cynic. Ἀλλ' ὅμως οὕτω δή τι τοὺς θεοὺς πέφριχα,
καὶ φιλῶ, καὶ σέβω, καὶ ἄζομαι, καὶ πάνθ' ἁπλῶς τὰ τοιαῦτα πρὸς αὐτοὺς
πάσχω, ὅσαπερ ἄν τις καὶ οἷα πρὸς ἀγαθοὺς δεσπότας, πρὸς διδασκάλους,
πρὸς πατέρας, πρὸς κηδεμόνας. Orat. vii. p. 212. The variety and
copiousness of the Greek tongue seem inadequate to the fervor of
his devotion.

superstitious prejudice; and the phantoms which existed only in the mind of the emperor had a real and pernicious effect on the government of the empire. The vehement zeal of the Christians, who despised the worship, and overturned the altars, of those fabulous deities, engaged their votary in a state of irreconcilable hostility with a very numerous party of his subjects; and he was sometimes tempted by the desire of victory, or the shame of a repulse, to violate the laws of prudence, and even of justice. The triumph of the party, which he deserted and opposed, has fixed a stain of infamy on the name of Julian; and the unsuccessful apostate has been overwhelmed with a torrent of pious invectives, of which the signal was given by the sonorous trumpet[2] of Gregory Nazianzen.[3] The interesting nature of the events which were crowded into the short reign of this active emperor, deserve a just and circumstantial narrative. His motives, his counsels, and his actions, as far as they are connected with the history of religion, will be the subject of the present chapter.

The cause of his strange and fatal apostasy may be derived from the early period of his life, when he was left an orphan in the hands of the murderers of his family. The names of Christ and of Constantius, the ideas of slavery and of religion, were soon associated in a youthful imagination, which was susceptible of the most lively impressions. The care of his infancy was intrusted to Eusebius, bishop of Nicomedia,[4] who was related to him on the side of his mother; and till Julian

---

[2] The orator, with some eloquence, much enthusiasm, and more vanity, addresses his discourse to heaven and earth, to men and angels, to the living and the dead; and above all, to the great Constantius, (εἰ τις αἴσθησις, an odd Pagan expression.) He concludes with a bold assurance, that he has erected a monument not less durable, and much more portable, than the columns of Hercules. See Greg. Nazianzen, Orat. iii. p. 50, iv. p. 134.

[3] See this long invective, which has been injudiciously divided into two orations in Gregory's Works, tom. i. p. 49—134, Paris, 1630. It was published by Gregory and his friend Basil, (iv. p. 133,) about six months after the death of Julian, when his remains had been carried to Tarsus, (iv. p. 120;) but while Jovian was still on the throne, (iii. p. 54, iv. p. 117.) I have derived much assistance from a French version and remarks, printed at Lyons, 1735.

[4] Nicomediæ ab Eusebio educatus Episcopo, quem genere longius contingebat, (Ammian. xxii. 9.) Julian never expresses any gratitude towards that Arian prelate; but he celebrates his preceptor, the eunuch Mardonius, and describes his mode of education, which inspired his pupil with a passionate admiration for the genius, and perhaps the religion, of Homer. Misopogon, p. 351, 352.

reacned the twentieth year of his age, he received from his Christian preceptors the education, not of a hero, but of a saint. The emperor, less jealous of a heavenly than of an earthly crown, contented himself with the imperfect character of a catechumen, while he bestowed the advantages of baptism [5] on the nephews of Constantine.[6] They were even admitted to the inferior offices of the ecclesiastical order; and Julian publicly read the Holy Scriptures in the church of Nicomedia. The study of religion, which they assiduously cultivated, appeared to produce the fairest fruits of faith and devotion.[7] They prayed, they fasted, they distributed alms to the poor, gifts to the clergy, and oblations to the tombs of the martyrs; and the splendid monument of St. Mamas, at Cæsarea, was erected, or at least was undertaken, by the joint labor of Gallus and Julian.[8] They respectfully conversed with the bishops, who were eminent for superior sanctity, and solicited the benediction of the monks and hermits, who had introduced into Cappadocia the voluntary hardships of the ascetic life.[9] As the two princes advanced towards the years of manhood, they discovered, in their religious sentiments the difference of their characters. The dull and obstinate understanding of Gallus, embraced, with implicit zeal, the doctrines of Christianity; which never influenced his conduct, or moderated his passions. The mild disposition of the younger brother was less repugnant to the precepts of the gospel; and his active

---

[5] Greg. Naz. iii. p. 70. He labored to effect that holy mark in the blood, perhaps of a Taurobolium. Baron. Annal. Eccles. A. D. 361, No. 3, 4.

[6] Julian himself (Epist. li. p. 454) assures the Alexandrians that he had been a Christian (he must mean a sincere one) till the twentieth year of his age.

[7] See his Christian, and even ecclesiastical education, in Gregory, (iii. p. 58,) Socrates, (l. iii. c. 1,) and Sozomen, (l. v. c. 2.) He escaped very narrowly from being a bishop, and perhaps a saint.

[8] The share of the work which had been allotted to Gallus, was prosecuted with vigor and success; but the earth obstinately rejected and subverted the structures which were imposed by the sacrilegious hand of Julian. Greg. iii. p. 59, 60, 61. Such a partial earthquake, attested by many living spectators, would form one of the clearest miracles in ecclesiastical story.

[9] The *philosopher* (Fragment, p. 288,) ridicules the iron chains, &c., of these solitary fanatics, (see Tillemont, Mém. Eccles. tom. ix. p. 661, 662,) who had forgot that man is by nature a gentle and social animal, ἀνθρώπου φύσει πολιτικοῦ ζώου καὶ ἡμέρου. The *Pagan* supposes, that because they had renounced the gods, they were possessed and tormented by evil dæmons.

curiosity might have been gratified by a theological system which explains the mysterious essence of the Deity, and opens the boundless prospect of invisible and future worlds. But the independent spirit of Julian refused to yield the passive and unresisting obedience which was required, in the name of religion, by the haughty ministers of the church. Their speculative opinions were imposed as positive laws, and guarded by the terrors of eternal punishments ; but while they prescribed the rigid formulary of the thoughts, the words, and the actions of the young prince ; whilst they silenced his objections, and severely checked the freedom of his inquiries, they secretly provoked his impatient genius to disclaim the authority of his ecclesiastical guides. He was educated in the Lesser Asia, amidst the scandals of the Arian controversy.[10] The fierce contests of the Eastern bishops, the incessant alterations of their creeds, and the profane motives which appeared to actuate their conduct, insensibly strengthened the prejudice of Julian, that they neither understood nor believed the religion for which they so fiercely contended. Instead of listening to the proofs of Christianity with that favorable attention which adds weight to the most respectable evidence, he heard with suspicion, and disputed with obstinacy and acuteness, the doctrines for which he already entertained an invincible aversion. Whenever the young princes were directed to compose declamations on the subject of the prevailing controversies, Julian always declared himself the advocate of Paganism ; under the specious excuse that, in the defence of the weaker cause, his learning and ingenuity might be more advantageously exercised and displayed.

As soon as Gallus was invested with the honors of the purple, Julian was permitted to breathe the air of freedom, of literature, and of Paganism.[11] The crowd of sophists, who were attracted by the taste and liberality of their royal pupil, had formed a strict alliance between the learning and the religion of Greece ; and the poems of Homer, instead of being

---

[10] See Julian apud Cyril, l. vi. p. 206, l. viii. p. 253, 262. "You persecute," says he, "those heretics who do not mourn the dead man precisely in the way which you approve." He shows himself a tolerable theologian ; but he maintains that the Christian Trinity is not derived from the doctrine of Paul, of Jesus, or of Moses.

[11] Libanius, Orat. Parentalis, c. 9, 10. p. 232, &c. Greg. Nazianzen, Orat. iii. p. 61. Eunap. Vit. Sophist. in Maximo, p. 68, 69, 70, edit Commelin.